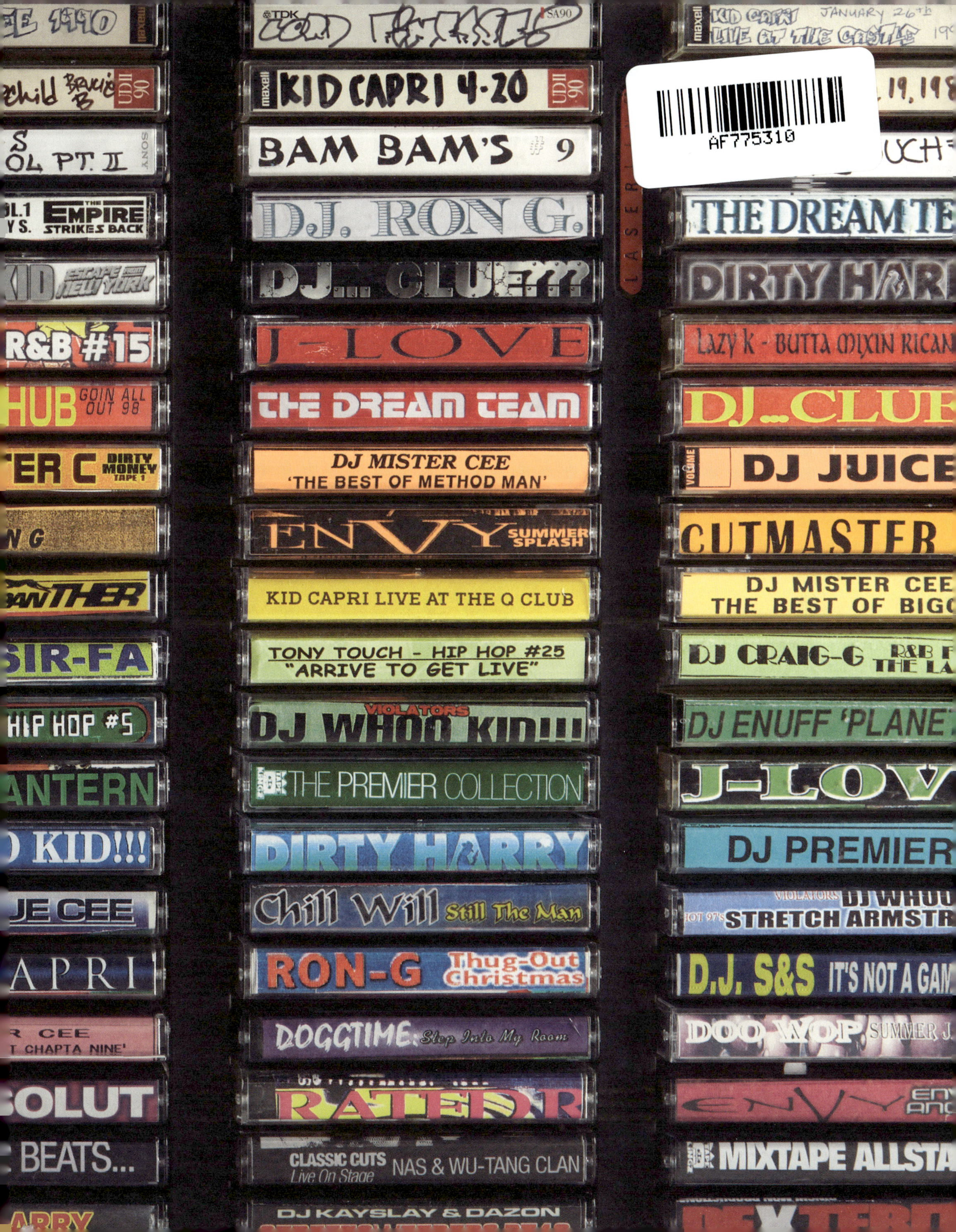
maxell
KID CAPRI 4-20
UD II 90
BAM BAM'S # 9
D.J. RON G.
DJ... CLUE???
J-LOVE
THE DREAM TEAM
DJ MISTER CEE
'THE BEST OF METHOD MAN'
ENVY SUMMER SPLASH
KID CAPRI LIVE AT THE Q CLUB
TONY TOUCH - HIP HOP #25
"ARRIVE TO GET LIVE"
VIOLATORS
DJ WHOO KID!!!
THE PREMIER COLLECTION
DIRTY HARRY
Chill Will Still The Man
RON-G Thug-Out Christmas
DOGGTIME Step Into My Room
RATED R
CLASSIC CUTS Live On Stage NAS & WU-TANG CLAN
DJ KAYSLAY & DAZON
KID CAPRI JANUARY 26th
LIVE AT THE CASTLE
THE DREAM TE
DIRTY HAR
Lazy K - Butta Mixin Rican
DJ JUICE
CUTMASTER
DJ MISTER CEE
THE BEST OF BIGG
DJ CRAIG-G
DJ ENUFF 'PLANE
J-LOV
DJ PREMIER
HOT 97's STRETCH ARMSTR
D.J. S&S IT'S NOT A GAM
DOO WOP SUMMER J
MIXTAPE ALLSTA
EMPIRE STRIKES BACK
ESCAPE FROM NEW YORK
R&B #15
HUB GOIN ALL OUT 98
ER C DIRTY MONEY TAPE 1
SIR-FA
HIP HOP #5
ANTERN
KID!!!
APRI
SOLUT
BEATS...

DO REMEMBER!

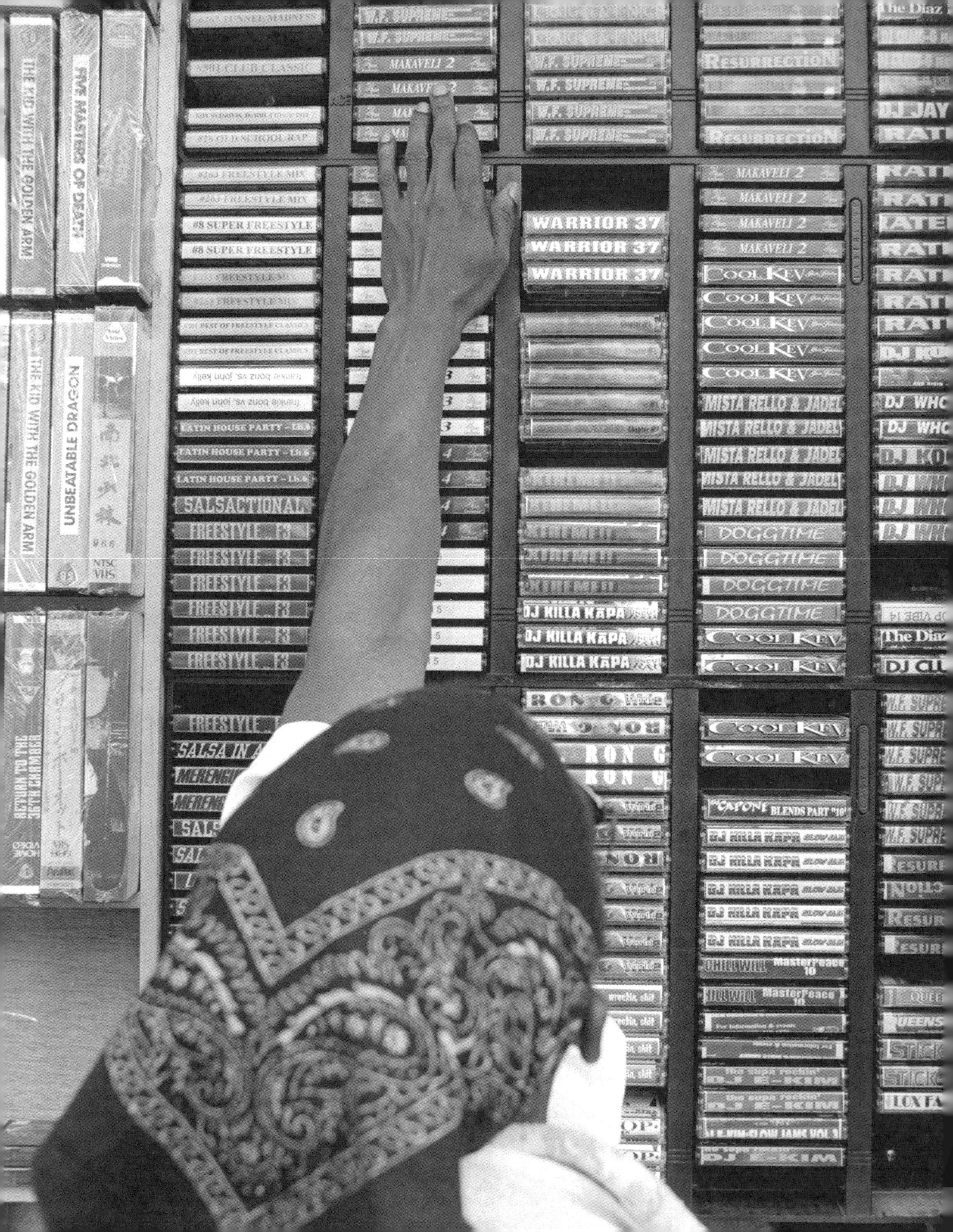
THE KID WITH THE GOLDEN ARM
FIVE MASTERS OF DEATH
UNBEATABLE DRAGON
NTSC
VHS
#263 TUNNEL MADNESS
#26 OLD SCHOOL RAP
#263 FREESTYLE MIX
#8 SUPER FREESTYLE
#201 BEST OF FREESTYLE CLASSICS
frankie bonz vs. john kelly
LATIN HOUSE PARTY - Lh.6
SALSACTIONAL
FREESTYLE .. F3
W.F. SUPREME
MAKAVELI 2
RESURRECTION
WARRIOR 37
COOL KEV
MISTA RELLO & JADEL
DOGGTIME
DJ KILLA KAPA
RON G
CAPONE BLENDS PART "10"
CHILLWILL MasterPeace 10
the supa rockin' DJ E-KIM
DJ JAY
The Diaz

DO REMEMBER!

THE GOLDEN ERA OF NYC HIP-HOP MIXTAPES

EVAN AUERBACH

DANIEL ISENBERG

RIZZOLI
NEW YORK

New York · Paris · London · Milan

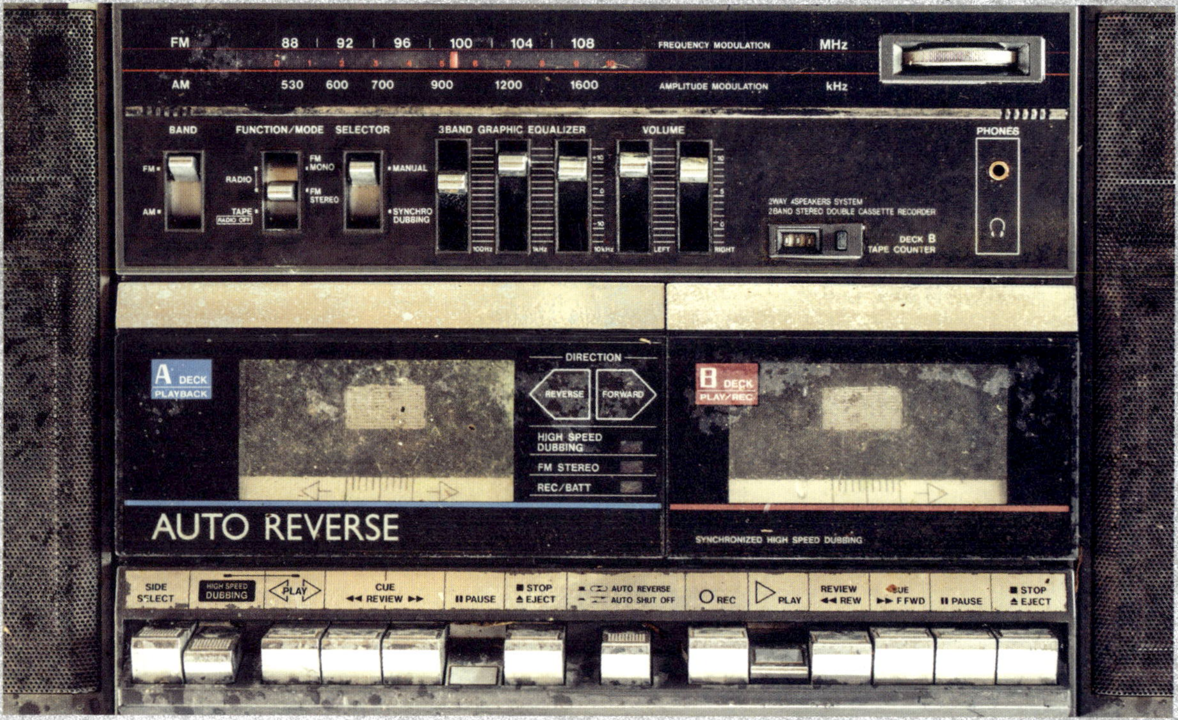
FM
88 92 96 100 104 108
FREQUENCY MODULATION
MHz
AM
530 600 700 900 1200 1600
AMPLITUDE MODULATION
kHz
BAND
FUNCTION/MODE SELECTOR
3BAND GRAPHIC EQUALIZER
VOLUME
PHONES
DECK B
TAPE COUNTER
DIRECTION
REVERSE
FORWARD
A DECK
PLAYBACK
B DECK
PLAY/REC
HIGH SPEED DUBBING
FM STEREO
REC/BATT
AUTO REVERSE
SYNCHRONIZED HIGH SPEED DUBBING
PLAY
CUE
REVIEW
PAUSE
STOP
EJECT
REC
PLAY
REVIEW
REW
PAUSE
STOP
EJECT

SIDE A

SIDE B

Fab 5 Freddy

I REMEMBER THE FIRST TIME I HEARD Grandmaster Flash and them. It was '79 and a graffiti writer named Caz from the Smith Projects in the Lower East Side blessed me with a tape. He told me they were hard to get your hands on, but he wanted me to hear this new sound going down.

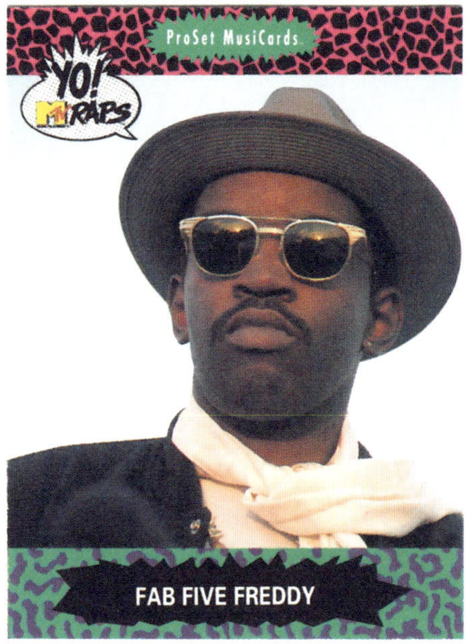

We popped the black tape into my large Sharp brand double-cassette boombox–and it was surely a copy of a copy of a copy. I couldn't clearly hear exactly what these syncopated voices were saying. The rhythm track, "Seven Minutes Of Funk," I'd never heard before. And the beat had my head nodding and my face screwed up into that "this is mean and funky" expression.

What I heard was beyond unique and very exciting. Flash was bringing parts of the song back perfectly, and then he cut in Harlem Underground Band's "Cheeba Cheeba" song. And the MCs, there weren't five of them yet so they were Grandmaster Flash and the Furious Four, rhyme rapping and smooth talking about how great a DJ he was and how no one was better on the microphone. That first listen was cool at a sub-zero level and I was frost-bitten, feeling it. I still have that tape in my stash.

It was all about those tapes. Cassette tapes were so crucial to the way hip hop spread from hood to hood in New York City in its infancy.

My whole life in hip-hop culture, I never owned turntables. I was always a boombox cat, so I could record–and listen. It was all about those tapes. Cassette tapes were so crucial to the way hip hop spread from hood to hood in New York City in its infancy. It wasn't on the radio all day everyday like now, or in record stores, or anywhere. Those tapes were cherished. They were prizes to me and the few who then knew.

The idea of the mixtape comes from the live recordings of early hip-hop parties using two turntables, a mixer and microphones for the masters of ceremony–the rapper. If you were blessed to have one of those, then that's how you knew there was something really special

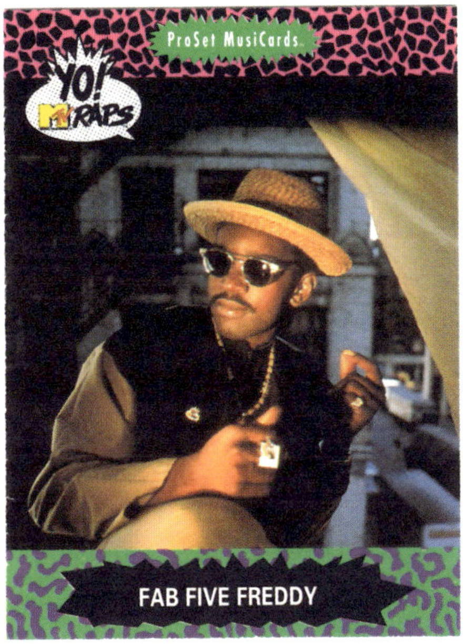

going on. You knew the names of the DJs, the rappers, the cool new slang, all these never-before-heard records, and you knew where that party was happening. The passion and the energy of how curious I was about all this when I heard the first inklings was indescribable. I was hooked and wanted to know more.

I'm from Bed-Stuy, Brooklyn. Because of my involvement in making the film *Wild Style* and a lot of the things I've done, many people assumed I was from the Bronx. No, I was just one of those really curious cats that caught a whiff of this in the early days and wanted to learn and understand, "What the hell was that? It sounds different. Where's it coming from?"

And how you got access was, typically, a cassette tape. That was the beginning of it all. DJs like Tony Tone, Charlie Chase and The Cold Crush Brothers, Grand Wizard Theodore and the Fantastic Romantic 5, The Treacherous Three, the Zulu Nation, Love Bug Starski, Doug E. Fresh, Johnny Wah and Rayvon–to name a few. DJs spinning and mixing, and MCs talking over the music, rhyming, and shouting people out. The call and response with the crowd screaming back, "Hoooo!" It was really going on just like that. I mean, it was incredible.

I can remember one club in particular, Harlem World, had great acoustics. And when Brooklyn started showing up, cats would have their boomboxes with them held up on their shoulders, recording. And the sound was so decent in the room you'd have a pretty good quality tape, along with the ambient sounds of the people in the crowd. You got a clear sounding tape of what cats were really doing and the vibes in the room. And that would be copied again and again, getting passed around all across town.

A lot of this became clear to me in the pre-production work leading up to making hip hop's first feature film, *Wild Style*, as that process gave me access. Me and Charlie Ahearn went to parties Uptown every other weekend at spots like T-Connection, Ecstasy Garage, Disco Fever, Celebrity Club and the Dixie. Anywhere and everywhere it was going down. Researching, listening, meeting people that we would eventually put in the movie–and getting decent quality tapes.

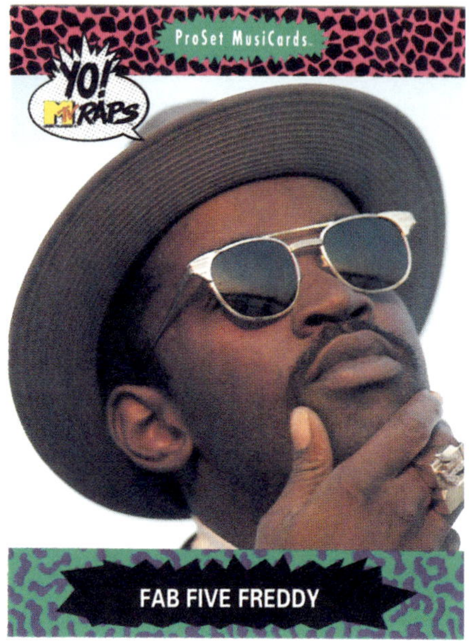

There was a whole series of cats that I followed as a kid in Brooklyn and got to see at summer block parties and park jams. Grandmaster Flowers, the original–the first Grandmaster, Pete "DJ" Jones, Plummer, Maboya, Frankie D and DJ Lance then known as Master D, my favorite. A lot of Bronx cats' original desire to be DJs was inspired by them. These were some of the guys that made DJing huge in New York City, and inspired Kool Herc and others to want to do this DJ thing–which led to the development of hip hop. Yes, there was a history before the history most know about today.

There were a couple people that sold early hip-hop party tapes with clean and clear audio, like Tape Kings. From those tapes, you could get the full fidelity effect of what Cold Crush Brothers and the rest were doing. Tape Master realized there was a market for these tapes, and he worked out a deal with the party promoters to let him plug a cassette deck into the house system. These were some of the best tapes that inspired everybody. So, in a way, they weren't consciously mixtapes. But then again, they were. That's the format. That's the original structure.

Later, in the early '90s, DJs like Kid Capri, Doo Wop, Ron G, and the Most Crew came along and quickly brought it to another level. They were emulating the vibe of those early Uptown beginning-of-hip-hop parties, all on tape. People forget that the whole idea of a mixtape, the foundation of this movement, was about DJs doing unique and special things. They were blending, bringing that break back on beat perfecto, making magnificent magic with that mixer and vinyl on the wheels of steel.

When Kid Capri's tapes blew up in New York, there were no slick graphics for the tape covers. Like white label records, all the info available was his name stamped on the tape and a date, like 10/9 or 3/5 written in ink. If you were plugged in and knew the deal, Kid Capri would post up slinging stacks of his latest tapes for twenty bucks a pop on corners in Harlem like 145th and 8th by Willie's Burgers, like he was selling drugs or some fire weed. The energy was strong and the demand was high, so he would sell out fast. I was hunting him down, missing him several times. It was such an incredible era, and seeing it all develop into this giant movement was like, "Wow."

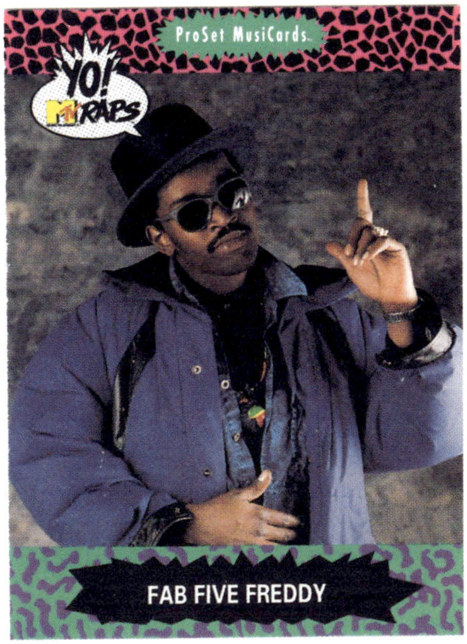

If you knew people–such a rare few, I'm talking among the most cutting edge peeps–these tapes circulated. People were copying the tapes and reselling them, spreading the word on the grapevine like, "Yo you gotta hear this!"

That was the idea behind me filming a *Yo! MTV Raps* episode at Rock 'N' Will's in Harlem. Here's this small record store where people could come and get these mixtapes. My idea was, "Let me show my national audience something new going on. We're going to see these DJs like Kid Capri and Ron G and The Hard Pack DJ crew explain this new thing, and give us all a demonstration." And it was like, "Bang!" That was one of many shows on the more interesting side of the culture for me, where we had something really special to share with people.

From there, the process in the scope of time was rapid. There was this transition in the mid-1990s from the idea of a mixtape being a platform for DJ personalities with flavor and skills to mix on the wheels of steel, to it becoming so hot that record companies flipped the script now saying, "Well, even though these DJs are bootlegging what we own, let's use these mixtapes as a free marketing tool and give the them a pass on the copyright issues. Let's let this happen because it's a great way to break our artists and records cheaply."

It became a whole new avenue for artists to connect with their audience, with artists eventually releasing their own mixtapes filled with original music and freestyles.

But it's important to remember the foundation for this entire hip-hop movement begins with a DJ playing some amazing music and creating a nice mix, comprised of the perfect sequence of songs to rock the house. It's just always been great for me to hear something so pure, raw, and special–just the right records and all of the subtle nuances that could easily be overlooked.

It was such an incredible era, and seeing it all develop into this giant movement was like, "Wow."

What was exciting for me was having that glimpse of the early history, and then hearing the evolution with Doo Wop, Kid Capri, Funkmaster Flex, Brucie B, and others where the vibe was like, "Oh wow, this feels like what those parties were like." Like you were at a dope spot–it felt like that. The DJ held it down.

Sometimes I still pop in that tape of Grandmaster Flash and them, and even over all the noise, snaps, crackles, hiss and pops, it takes me back. It makes me feel the vibe in those rooms, all these years later. That shit was incredible. That's the power of a mixtape.

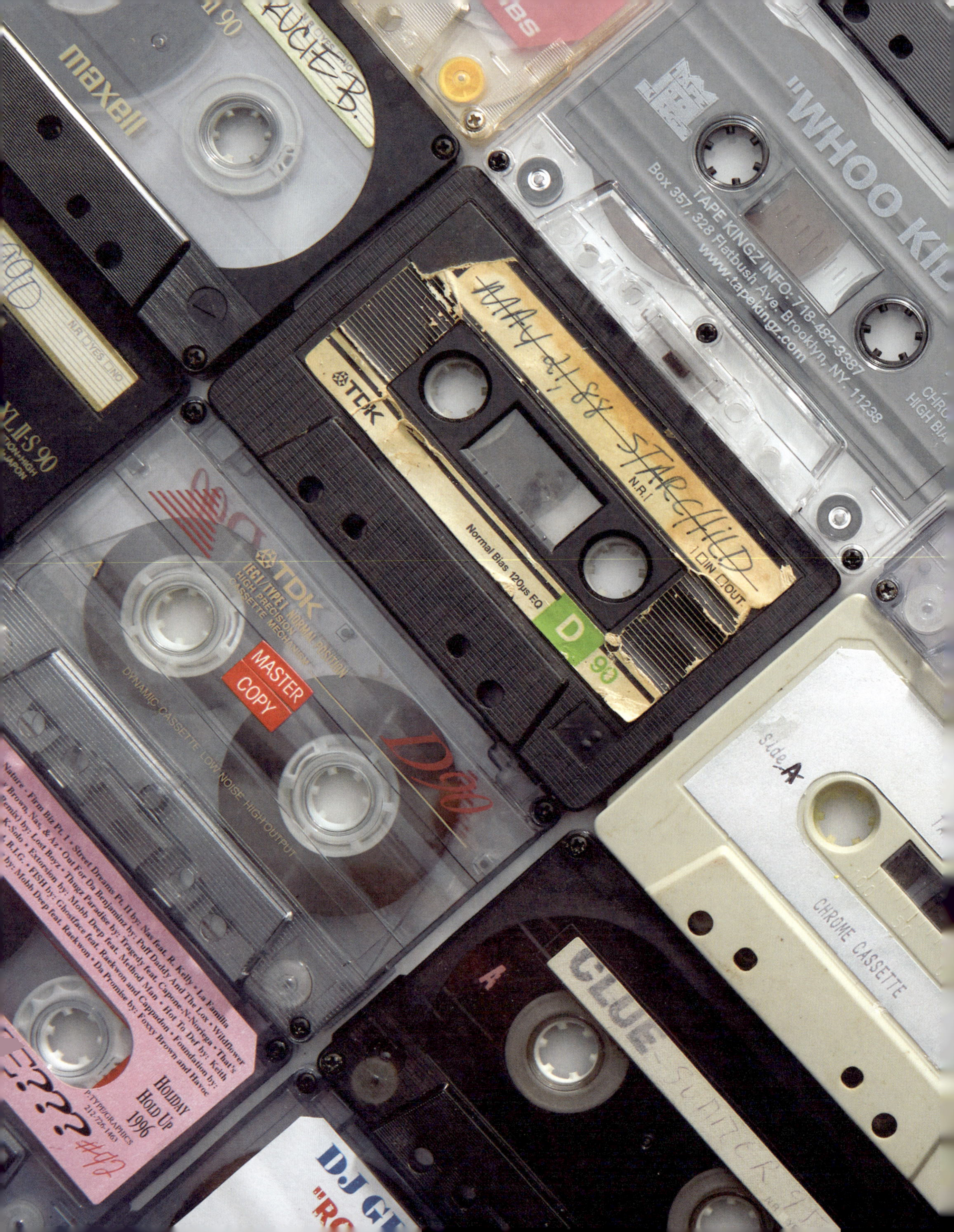

maxell
TDK
N.R.1
Normal Bias 120μs EQ
D
90
MASTER
COPY
TAPE KINGZ INFO: 718-482-3387
Box 357, 328 Flatbush Ave. Brooklyn, NY. 11238
www.tapekingz.com
"WHOO KID
CHROME CASSETTE
CLUE
HOLIDAY
HOLD UP
1996

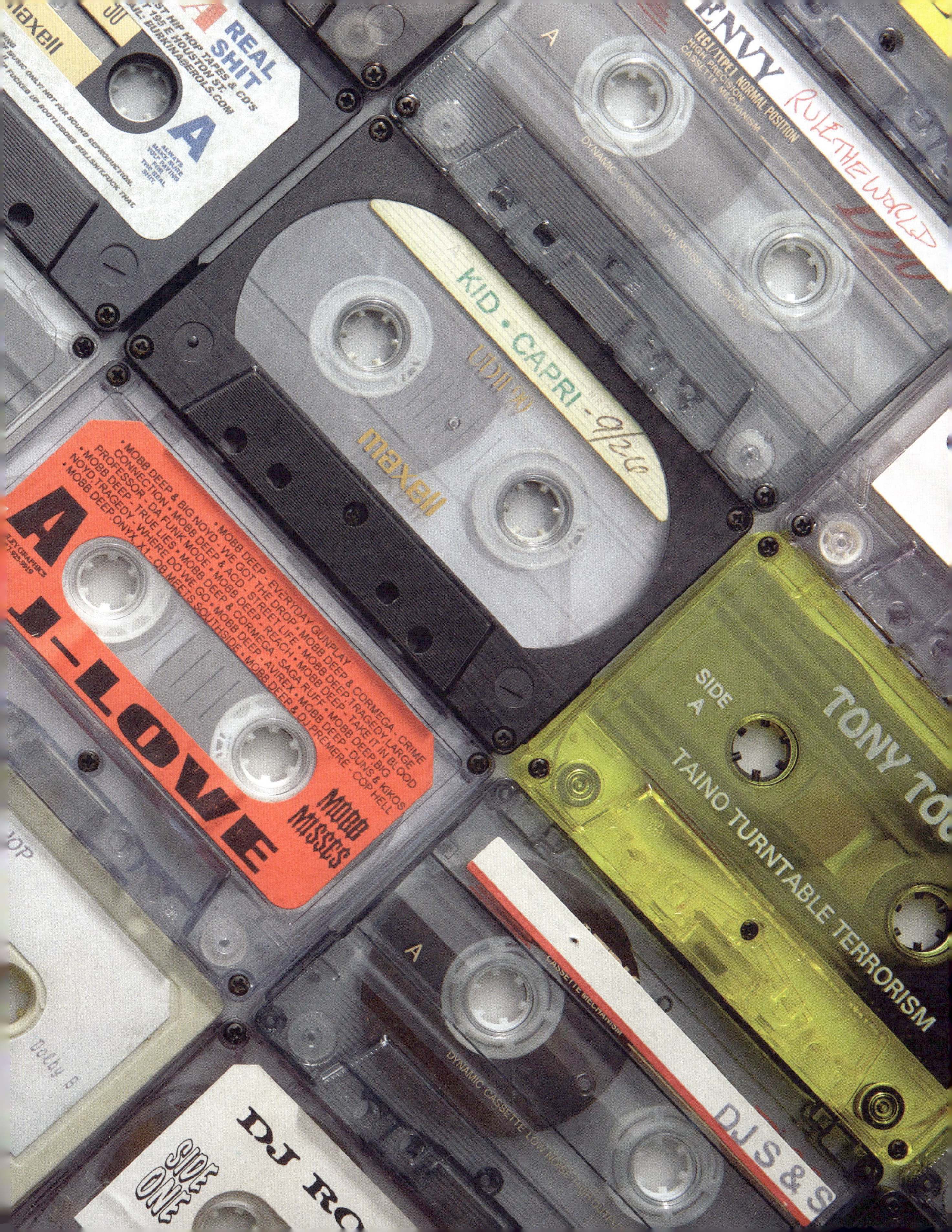
maxell
REAL SHIT
A
ENVY
IEC I/TYPE I NORMAL POSITION
HIGH PRECISION
CASSETTE MECHANISM
DYNAMIC CASSETTE LOW NOISE HIGH OUTPUT
KID • CAPRI
UDII 90
maxell
A
J-LOVE
MOBB DEEP - EVERYDAY GUNPLAY
SIDE A
TAINO TURNTABLE TERRORISM
CASSETTE MECHANISM
DYNAMIC CASSETTE LOW NOISE HIGH OUTPUT
Dolby B
SIDE ONE

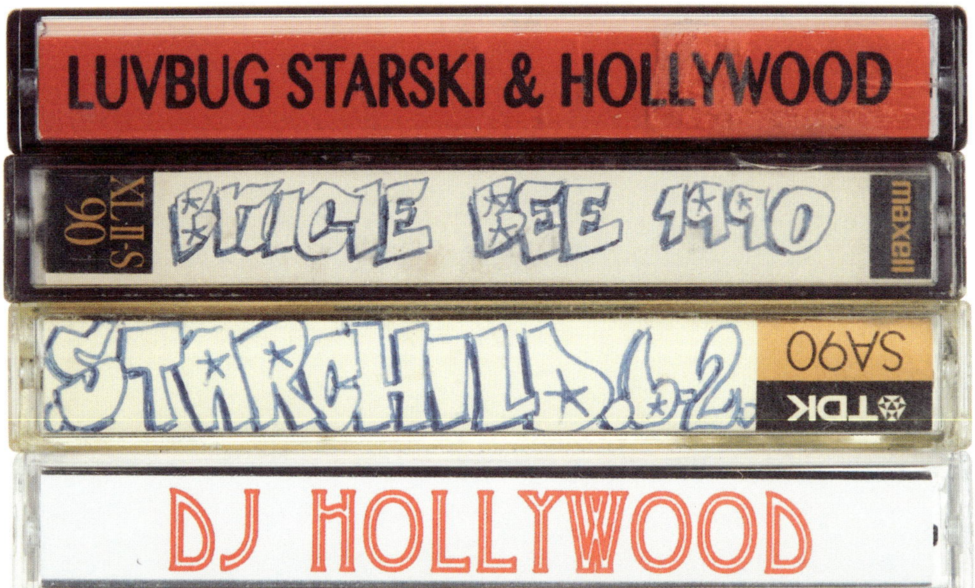
LUVBUG STARSKI & HOLLYWOOD
BRUCIE BEE 1990
maxell
XL-II-S 90
STARCHILD
TDK
SA90
DJ HOLLYWOOD
DJ STARCHILD NYC
LOVEBUG STARSKI
TDK
SA-X90
STARCHILD + BRUCIE B
DJ BRUCIE B

THE LIVE TAPES

In the early days of hip hop in New York City—dating back to the 1980s—a select group of DJs would record their live sets on cassettes and sell them in the streets. These tapes became both calling cards for DJs to promote themselves and spread their name, and keepsakes for fans who wanted to recreate the nightlife party vibes when they were hanging out around the way or driving through the city. The beginning of the golden era of hip-hop mixtapes in New York City starts with THE LIVE TAPES.

DJ HOLLYWOOD

All the Way Live: From 8-Tracks to Cassettes

Uptown legend DJ Hollywood is a mixtape pioneer in every sense of the term. From being one of the first DJs to record their set and sell it as a product to bringing his own voice into the live mix and establishing the DJ as a personality, DJ Hollywood's credit is due. And his story begins in the '70s, even before the cassette infiltrated the culture.

8-TRACK RECORDINGS

DJ Hollywood: At first, we had an 8-track recorder. I was just making tapes and selling them. I didn't have a multi-recorder where I could do a lot of pieces, so I did one at a time.

8-tracks were like $3.99 or something like that, I was selling them for $12. It was just a thing. At that time, a lot of hustlers were around and they could afford the $12 no problem, so they were like, "Let me get that." So every time I made one, I just had to come out and show that I had it, and it was sold.

A friend of mine had an 8-track recorder, an older dude. We also had a sound system. That was like one of the first coffins to come out. We had our two turntables, and I'm mixing and everything in a unit that we could carry–mobile. And we had some speakers that we could do weddings and small parties with, and that was the thing at the time.

That was it, for me. Record this stuff and I'll get an extra $12. It wasn't thought of as, "This is going to be the next trend!" But that goes throughout my career. Everything I've done, I've never thought of it as being the next tremendous thing.

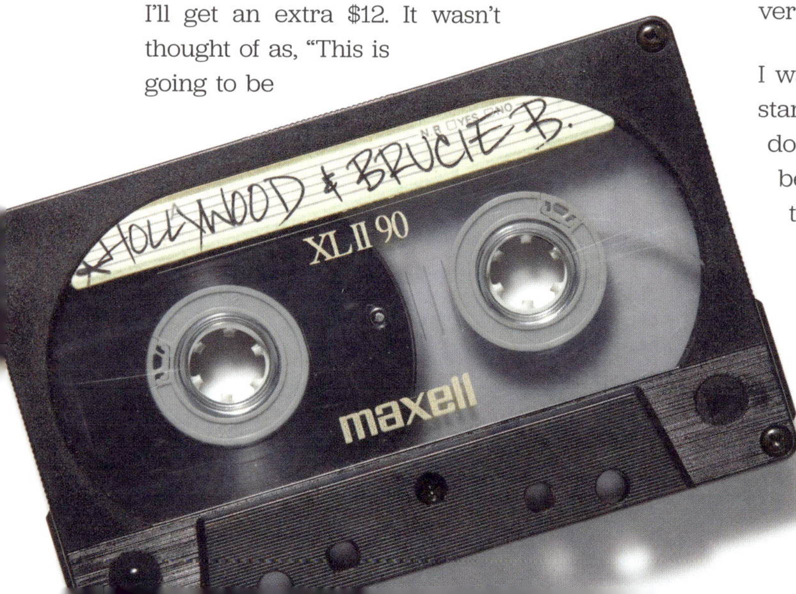

TWO TURNTABLES AND A MIC

When the turntable and the microphone came together, this changed the reception of music. And in that time period right there from the beginning, when I really started coming with it, there wasn't anybody, anywhere rapping to any records. And it wasn't because it was a rule, it's just that nobody was doing it.

I started doing it with two turntables and a microphone. I didn't have a band. So I'm picking and choosing spots in the record where I could talk, before the artist came in. Records back in the day were made with A sections, B sections, and a break. The A section would be when the record first came on and it'd give you the music. Then the B section would come when the artist would start performing. I could take that A section and break my conversation to that little bit of time in the flow of rap.

I was the first to start to cut the microphone and start kicking the flavor. There was nobody else doing that at that particular time. Cats got hip to it because the popularity of it started to travel with the tape.

TALKING ON THE MIC AT CLUBS

I was playing in Harlem at after-hours spots and in various little spots. You know, club life. There weren't a lot of places to do what you do, and they had rules in a lot of these clubs. Rules like–you can't talk. "Play the records, play the music, but keep your mouth shut. We don't want all of that talking." But I was already flying, so I got away with a lot of stuff. I came from a time period before they could set the rules.

INTRODUCTION OF THE CASSETTE

New York is a big spot. The one thing that New York had in common was that everybody had a car. A lot of the OJ cab drivers and guys with whips at that time had really big cars. And they all had this system in it where you could play music.

The cassette was invented, and this became the excitement of the street. Because now, the live parties you went to could be recorded on a tape–and you could ride around with that tape, and that could make you a famous person in your neighborhood. And everywhere the tape went, that sound went. People all over the city got used to that sound. That's what set the parties into crazy motion, because they're listening to the shit on the tape and they're saying, "Yo! That shit is hot, man. Where'd that come from?"

At this time, breaking records was something that DJs were doing because it only traveled on the tapes. "Before I Let Go," it never went to the radio–we broke that record on tape. When people got into that record, it was over.

THE SHIFT

The cassette shifted things because every Joe Blow could record. In the 8-track stages, only a few people could record because the 8-track recorder wasn't a big item. And it didn't pay much. The people who first started to venture into this, they didn't make money, they did it because they loved it. For a long time, love is a rough paycheck.

The cassette comes, and you can reproduce the cassette. You can make copies of that body of work. It could go in all different directions at the same time. Cab drivers and other people moving your advertisement out into the street changed the whole game. The cassette is what changed the reason you were making $30 to $40 to now you're making $150. You could sell more, so people knew who you were and your sound became wanted.

PARTY VIBES

Man, parties used to be wild! I was doing a lot of the major functions because I was headlining a lot of stuff. The Stardust Ballroom, Hotel Diplomat–the best of the best all landed in these spots. And those tapes were crazy. There were so many too. Every time you're playing now, you're recording.

THE MIXTAPE BOOM

When the popularity of the mixtape went up, so did the price. Once that happened, people were actually snooping around to find out where they could get a tape from. The pressure was: "I gotta have one, I gotta get a mixtape."

They had a few places where you could go and actually grab that tape. They had it labeled out, and they had the dates and times. You could get a collection of tapes. This is what the popularity of the tape game did for hip hop–period. This is the '80s. Welcome to the new era of what music is and how it's displayed.

IMPACT ON THE CULTURE

Everybody brought the party to life–but we began that history of a great party being written down step-by-step. That's what the mixtape made available. There were a lot of mixtapes out, but we had the more famous ones. The ones that lived for a long time.

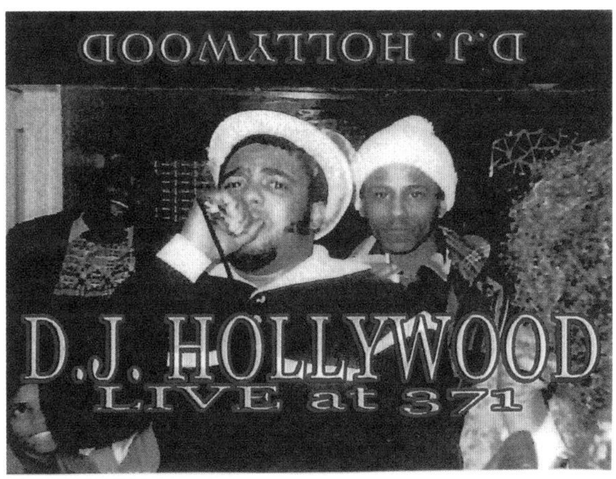

BRUCIE B

In the Club: Defining the Live Party Sound on Mixtapes

Along with the late greats Lovebug Starski and Starchild, Brucie B was one of Uptown's most popular DJs—and a direct descendant of DJ Hollywood. But not only did he record the parties he rocked through the late '80s at legendary spots like the Rooftop, he became one of the first DJs to truly monetize the mixtape.

EARLY DAYS

Brucie B: I started DJing when I was about 13 to 14, hanging out. At that time, Grandmaster Caz, who is a hip-hop legend, used to hang on my block. So we used to go to the old school jams at the park. 63 or Cedar Park, wherever there was a jam.

I had been DJing since '82–but I never had my own equipment, so I would always play on somebody else's. That's why everybody used to be like, "How are you so good at what you do?" I didn't get my equipment until '89, and at that time I was already playing in clubs.

Starchild was the one that introduced me to the clubs. The first club I played in was The Living Room on the East Side. From there, I would go to this after-hours spot called The Hilltop. I used to also go to Disco Fever, and that's where I met all the top notch DJs like Disco Bee, Lovebug Starski, Ronnie DJ, Junebug, and Sweet G.

But I was still unknown at the time, I was still coming up. My first gig, I got paid $20, because at that time Starchild was making $40 a night and he would split it with me.

THE ROOFTOP

I knew the owner of the Rooftop, Gus, who was my brother's best friend. He was a Harlem legend, getting money. He bought the building from Old Man Willie and came to me like, "Yo, B, you want to come to the Rooftop and we could do this thing together?" The Rooftop was a roller skating rink disco, so you could roller skate to about 3 or 4 in the morning. And then we'd dance for an hour. But this roller skating rink was different because the music that got played there was different.

I used to play hip-hop beats. I played reggae. I played jazz. I played anything that had a flow to it that you could roller skate to. I was just keeping that flow because no one wants to miss their step. So if anything had a flow to it, I'd play it.

ECHO CHAMBER

The DJs that I came up under–like Lovebug Starski, Starchild, and Hollywood–they would DJ and talk. I always remember Lovebug would tell me, "You gotta talk. You gotta say something. You gotta say your name. You can't just DJ because nobody will know you from your hands. People don't pay attention to that. They gotta hear you." So when I went to the Rooftop, it was different. I was with the architects of hip hop.

I had this mic that had an echo in it already. So when I used to talk, it would echo and that became my thing. It wasn't intentional. Everything that happened in my career that I did, it wasn't planned. It wasn't something that I dreamed about doing, it just happened.

LIVE TAPES

When it came to the tapes, everybody gave me credit for the mixtapes, like Red Alert. Before they were called mixtapes, they were just party tapes or live tapes. They started calling it a mixtape after the

Rooftop closed. Everybody was doing it, but the thing about mine was the people I was shouting out. At that time, if you had a nice car with a system in it, you came and got a Brucie B tape because you knew your name could be on that tape.

I used to give away tapes, I wasn't selling them at the time. Until Gus was like, "Man, you gotta start charging these cats for that." I used to sell tapes like I was selling drugs, and that's what cats thought I was selling in the beginning.

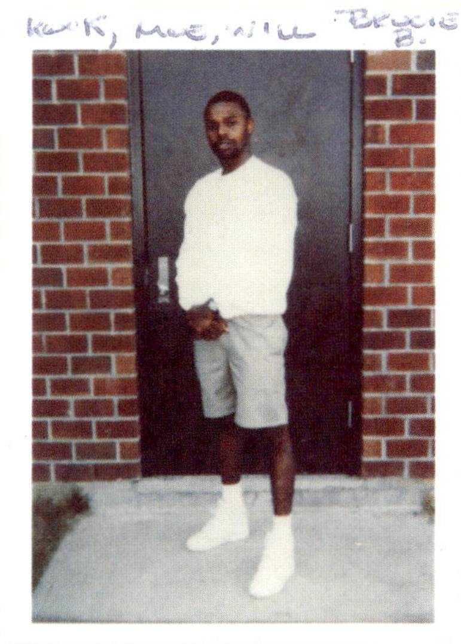

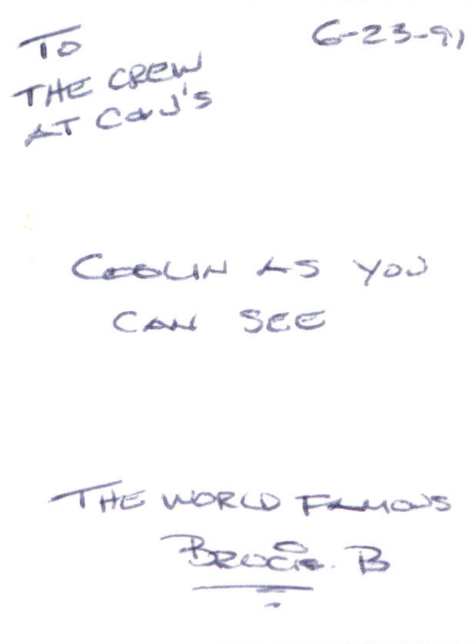

SELLING MIXTAPES IN THE STREET

Everything I did, as far as the tapes, was natural. How it became a business was like selling drugs. I knew it was in demand. At that time, I had a hook up at The Wiz on Third Avenue in the Bronx. I used to buy about 50 tapes and I had this high-speed dubber. So if I'm recording Friday, you wouldn't get that tape until next Friday. I was always selling the tape from last week because I'm making the new tape for next week.

Once the word got out, there was always a line for them. I used to get my tapes and go to all the drug blocks with all the dudes with money. I used to walk from 145th and St. Nick to Seventh Avenue, go through 144th because that was the money block, and I'd walk all the way down and hit 125th Street. That was definitely a money block because that's the Mecca of Harlem. And by the time I'd come back around, I'd be sold out.

I was getting $20 per tape. I never got no less than $20.

TAPES FOR HUSTLERS

You got the shout out if I saw you. A lot of these dudes with money, they knew how to skate. Back then, Rooftop or The Rink, roller skating was the thing.

My tapes got hotter when I did one for Alpo. I did this one little tape for him and he gave me like $300 or $400. I played like one record and shouted his name out through the whole tape, and he had the car with the crazy system. It was the Beastie Boys "Hold It Now, Hit It." I played the instrumental, the acapella, I cut the record–I did everything to it for 90 minutes.

Alpo used to ride down 8th Ave. and all around Harlem playing this tape with his name. So when a lot of other big time drug dealers heard it, that's when I got to the big boys. I was getting three or four hundred, all types of money. Alpo always gave me the most money. The most money I think I got from him was $700.

Alpo, Rich Porter, and Azie at that time, they were the main ones in Harlem with the name.

I did a tape for Rich Porter, but he only wanted James Brown. So I did a whole tape for him of James Brown and he asked me, "How much did he pay for his?" It was like a little competition between them, who could pay the most for a Brucie B tape.

TIME: 5:05pm

DATE: 7-31-91

WHAT UP FELLA'S? (ROCK, MOE, WILL) & CREW
HOW'S EVERYTHING GOING?
I HOPE YOUR ARE ALRIGHT. AS FOR ME
I'M COOLIN. I'M JUST WRITING ABOUT THE
TAPES I ASK FOR. I HOPE I WILL BE
RECEIVING THEM SOON. AND IF STARCHILD
SHOULD DROP BY GIVE HIM MY ADDRESS
AND TELL HIM TO DROP A COUPLE OF
LINES. OR LEAVE A PHONE NUMBER
WHERE I COULD GET INTOUCH WITH HIM.
I GOT TO GO BUT HERE'S A PICTURE OF
ME. I'M OUTTA SOOO.

LOVE & PEACE
BRUCE

(AKA) THE WORLD FAMOUS
BRUCE. B

P.S HERE'S THE DATES OF THE TAPES
I WANT. HOLLYWOOD, 2 COOL OUTS, 2 HIP HOP.
KOOL MOE D YO YO! ANITA BAKER GUY TONI TONY TONE

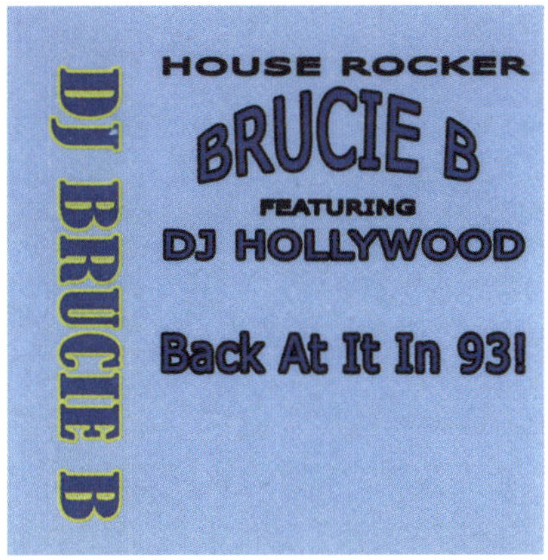

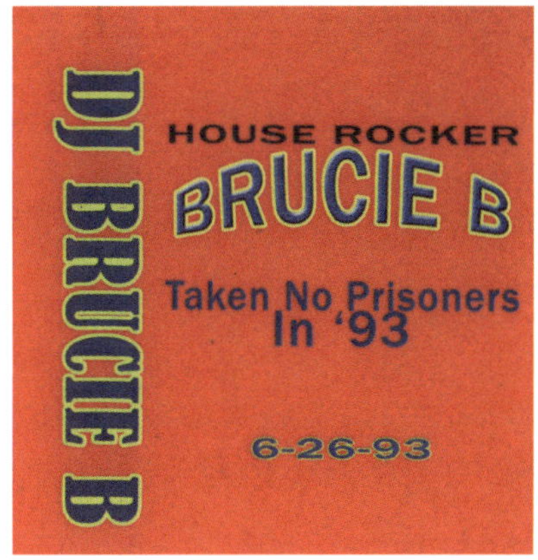

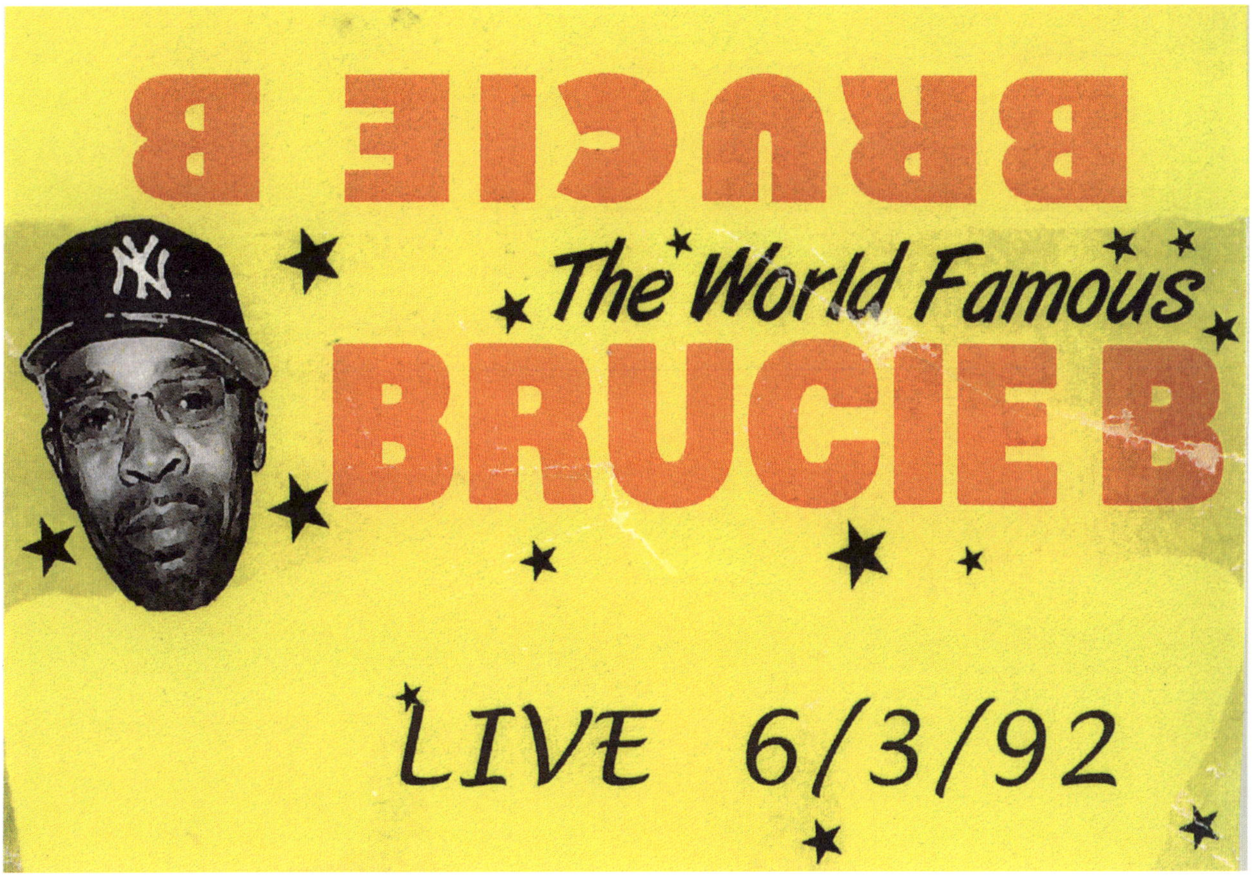

Brucie B: I didn't become "World Famous" until I went to London with Lovebug and we did a London Fresh Fest out there. We were on a tour with Grandmaster Flash, The Real Roxanne, it was a lot of the hot artists at the time—the '80s artists. When I came back from London, that's when it started. Starchild started calling me "The World Famous Brucie B."

BRUCIE B REMEMBERS THE LATE, GREAT UPTOWN DJS.

STARCHILD

Brucie B: Starchild was actually from Brooklyn. I met him through my man named Lance, and Starchild lived with me for like four or five years. The day I met him, he was getting evicted from his house, and he came and stayed with me.

Starchild put me on the path to the clubs because he was already in the clubs. He had this drive that was unbelievable. Once you made it to Disco Fever, you were outta there.

Hilltop was an after-hours spot. I was 16 years old, and I would get up at three o'clock in the morning and my mom would be like, "Where are you going?" And I would tell her, "I'm going to work to play some music."

This after-hours spot stayed packed Monday to Monday. Starchild would come up there at 4 and you would've thought it was a 1 o'clock prime time party. It's 12 in the afternoon, and we were in there jam-packed partying. I used to see people come from Disco Fever, because it was up the hill. When it closed at 4, everybody came up the hill. The '80s era was the cocaine era.

Starchild was unbelievable. He played at all the spots. Everybody knew Starchild.

LOVEBUG STARSKI

I met everybody through Starchild. Lovebug was one of the architects, he was a legend. When I met Lovebug, I never used to talk around him. I used to always listen and pay attention, but never talk.

Lovebug was a Taurus. He was a bull. He used to get in arguments at the drop of a dime. But I was always close to Lovebug. No matter how much he used to argue or get mad, I knew the trick to Lovebug. When he would get into his rage, I wouldn't say anything. I'm not arguing with a legend.

One day at Disco Fever, he got into an argument with Matty, the head guy over there. Starchild said, "Who's up there?" Lovebug said, "Bruce is." Starchild said, "Tell Bruce to get on and DJ." So I'm rocking and Lovebug said, "That's my protege." I was tearing them up. He knew I knew how to play, but he ain't know I knew how to play like that.

Lovebug was the one that took me overseas. I was Lovebug's DJ. That's why everyone says I'm your DJ's favorite DJ, because I used to DJ for him. I DJed most DJ's weddings.

Starchild and Lovebug, those were my brothers. They taught me a lot and I learned a lot from them. That's why I get annoyed with different DJs when they don't pay homage to them.

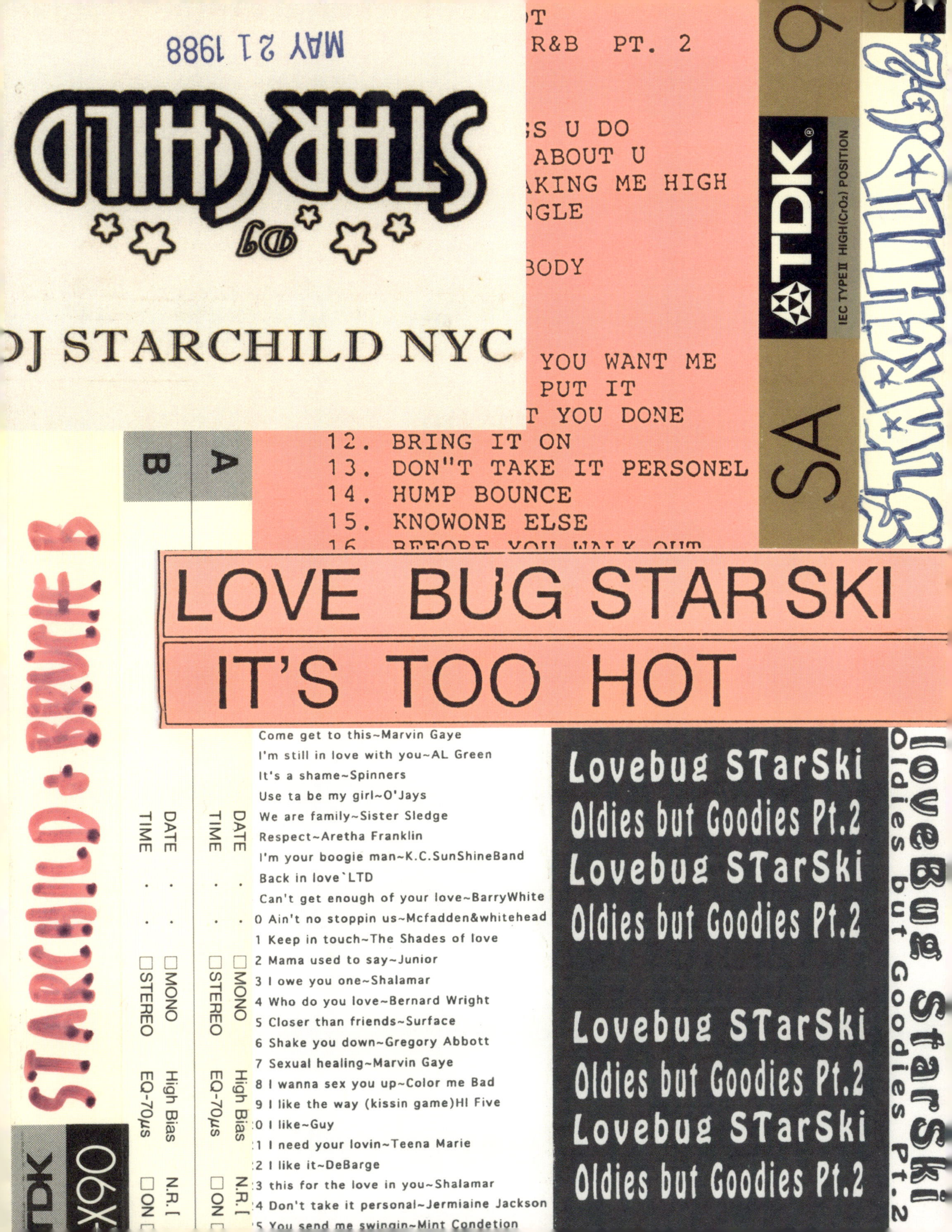
MAY 21 1988
STAR CHILD
DJ
DJ STARCHILD NYC
T
R&B PT. 2
GS U DO
ABOUT U
AKING ME HIGH
NGLE
BODY
YOU WANT ME
PUT IT
T YOU DONE
12. BRING IT ON
13. DON"T TAKE IT PERSONEL
14. HUMP BOUNCE
15. KNOWONE ELSE
TDK
IEC TYPE II HIGH(CrO2) POSITION
SA
A
B
DATE
TIME
MONO
STEREO
High Bias
EQ-70µs
N.R.
ON
STARCHILD + BRUCIE B
TDK
X90
LOVE BUG STARSKI
IT'S TOO HOT
Come get to this~Marvin Gaye
I'm still in love with you~AL Green
It's a shame~Spinners
Use ta be my girl~O'Jays
We are family~Sister Sledge
Respect~Aretha Franklin
I'm your boogie man~K.C.SunShineBand
Back in love`LTD
Can't get enough of your love~BarryWhite
0 Ain't no stoppin us~Mcfadden&whitehead
1 Keep in touch~The Shades of love
2 Mama used to say~Junior
3 I owe you one~Shalamar
4 Who do you love~Bernard Wright
5 Closer than friends~Surface
6 Shake you down~Gregory Abbott
7 Sexual healing~Marvin Gaye
8 I wanna sex you up~Color me Bad
9 I like the way (kissin game)HI Five
0 I like~Guy
1 I need your lovin~Teena Marie
2 I like it~DeBarge
3 this for the love in you~Shalamar
4 Don't take it personal~Jermiaine Jackson
5 You send me swingin~Mint Condetion
Lovebug STarSki
Oldies but Goodies Pt.2
Lovebug STarSki
Oldies but Goodies Pt.2
Lovebug STarSki
Oldies but Goodies Pt.2
Lovebug STarSki
Oldies but Goodies Pt.2
loveBug StarSki
Oldies but Goodies Pt.2

"~~RAP~~ CAR FLAVA"!

LOVEBUG STARSKI

1 Bounce — Doug E. Fresh
2 Come Clean — Jeru The Damaja
3 Lovely how i Let My Mind Flow — de La Soul
4 Method Man — Wu Tang Clan
5 Written On Ya Kitten — Naughty by Nature
6 Chief Rocka — Lord's of the Underground
7 Outa Here — KRS ONE
8 Break A Dawn — de La Soul
9 Check yo Self — Ice Cube
10 What Next — Leaders of the New Schoool
11 Brooklyn — M.C. Lyte
12 Somethin Special — Markie Dee
13 I Get Around — 2 PAC

SIDE B

1 I Got Aids's — Salt-N-Pepa
2 Flow Joe — Fat Joe
3 Street Nigga — (Do or Die) - "YBZ"
4 Boome This in your Vehicle — Alnteddd Experince
5 Duck ya Head — Dred Scott
6 Alright — "Doug E. Fresh" (Remix)
7 Alright — "Mecca Audio"
6 C'Mon Baby — FunkMaster Flex
8 69 — Parther M.C.
9 Shoop — Salt — N — Pepa
10 Flava — Triflin' Pac
11 Ruffneck — M.C. Lyte
12 Gangsta Lenn — DRS

LOVEBUG STARSKI

"Rap Car Flava"!

RAP 12-7 STARSKI RAP 12-7

1 Get Lifted — Frankie the Pacemaker
2 Who Am I — Snoop Dogg
3 Keep your head up — 2pac
4 Getto Jam — Domino
5 Dre Day — Dr. Dre
6 Shoop — Salt-N-Pepa
7 Freak it — Das EFX
8 Itz Da Joint — Joint Ventures
9 South Bronx — K.R.S.
10 Da Bounce Squad — Doo-Wop
11 U.N.I.T.Y — Queen Latifah
12 Put your Hand's up — Whooliganz
13 Method Man — Wu-Tang Clan
14 Bubbah Break — The Legion

-Side B-

1 Devil's Son — Big L
2 How About Some Hardcore — M.O.P.
3 Award Tour — T.C.Q
4 Come Clean — Jaru the Damaja
5 Bounce — Doug E. Fresh
6 Boom this in your Vehicle — Al-N-Tedd Exp.
7 Alright — Doug E. Fresh
8 Street's Of the Ghetto — Ed. O.G.
9 Alright — Mecca Audio
10 C'mon Baby — Funkmaster Flex
11 Street Niggez — YBZ
12 For All My Niggaz & Bitches — Snoop Dogg
13 Hey Hottie — 10° Below

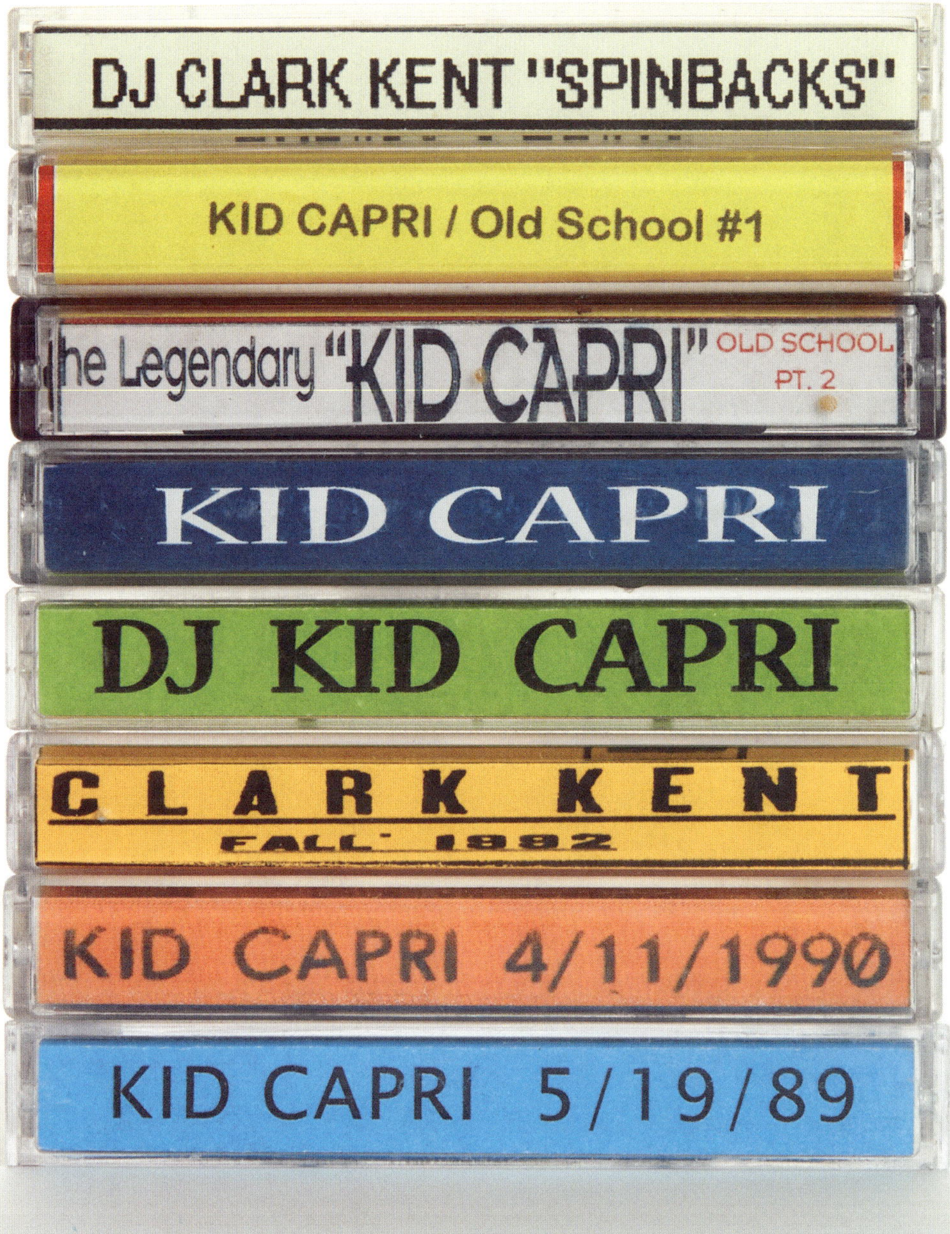
DJ CLARK KENT "SPINBACKS"
KID CAPRI / Old School #1
he Legendary "KID CAPRI" OLD SCHOOL PT. 2
KID CAPRI
DJ KID CAPRI
CLARK KENT
FALL 1992
KID CAPRI 4/11/1990
KID CAPRI 5/19/89

THE STREET TAPES

As live tape recordings grew in popularity Uptown and across New York City, the demand for DJ mixes grew with it. So DJs would start to emulate what was happening in the clubs at home, recording their sets directly to cassettes to be sold in their neighborhoods. With this came new opportunities to advance the overall production value and themes of their mixes, and the man at the forefront of it all was Kid Capri.

This is the story of THE STREET TAPES.

KID CAPRI

Take 'Em Uptown: Recreating the Club Experience on Mixtapes

Uptown's own Kid Capri is one of the most celebrated DJs in the history of New York hip hop. Not only did he help innovate in the world of mixtapes with conceptualized cassette releases like his *Old School* series and groundbreaking *52 Beats*, but his success creating and selling tapes led to him releasing two major label albums, becoming the in-house DJ on HBO's *Def Comedy Jam* and winning a GRAMMY for his production credit on Jay-Z's hit single "Hard Knock Life."

MIXTAPE LINEAGE

Kid Capri: We always had pause tapes we were doing back in the days when we were young, because we didn't have equipment. So we got along with that.

There was the Cold Crush tapes, The Fantastic Five tapes, the tapes that Tape Master put out with all the hip-hop groups at that time. We listened to those.

And then the other DJs–like Hollywood, Starchild, Lovebug Starski–when I came to the game, I was aware of them and I knew what they did. But I wanted to make sure I wasn't doing what they were doing. I didn't want to sound like them or talk like them. They were guys that I looked up to that I was watching.

MAKING A MARK

Starchild was the one that put me in S&S club. With us playing together, I was influenced by how he did things. But I just wanted to stay in my own lane. And my lane caught on because at the time, they were looking at DJs like if you weren't in an important group or on the radio, you were just somebody playing music.

I didn't want to be looked at like that. I took my mixtapes and did them a certain kind of way to where they were not only for the street, but they were also commercialized to reach anybody. And they ended up reaching all over the world.

So from that point, I was able to open the door to how a DJ should be seen and looked at, what kind of record selection to play, how to play the record, how you should talk on the microphone–just being a performer all the way around.

In terms of my reach, I didn't want to be stuck in New York. I was already hot in New York. I made my mark there, but I wanted to be other places. So in order for me to do that without them giving me a radio show or having a record, I decided to make my mixtapes. And they ended up going to different states that I hadn't been to. That's how I got popular. I was kind of marketing and distributing myself before I even knew I was doing it in that fashion and to that level.

RECORDING AT HOME

Most of the tapes that we heard were from live parties in clubs, like Brucie B live at the Rooftop or Starchild at the S&S Club. I would make my joints in my house and make it sound like it was in the club.

When I did the live tapes, that was like an extra. You could tell the difference. Studio version and then the live version of the album–I approached it like that. I was already in the clubs all over New

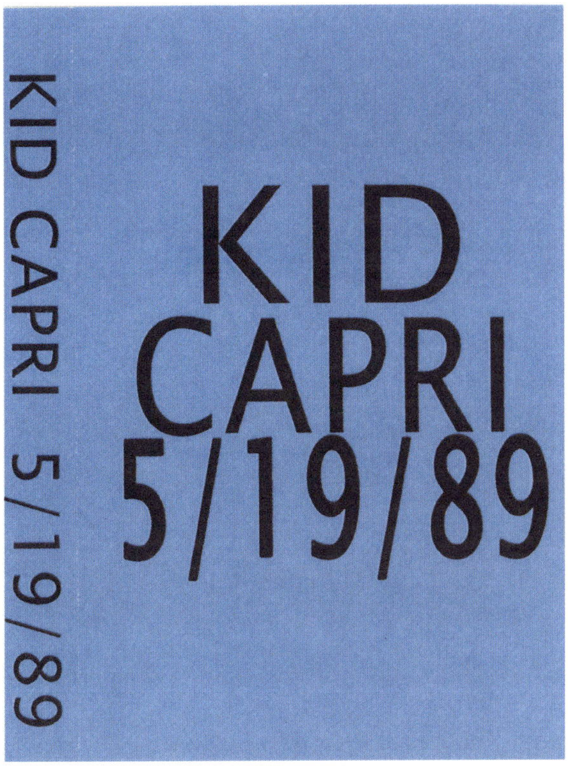
KID CAPRI 5/19/89
KID
CAPRI
5/19/89

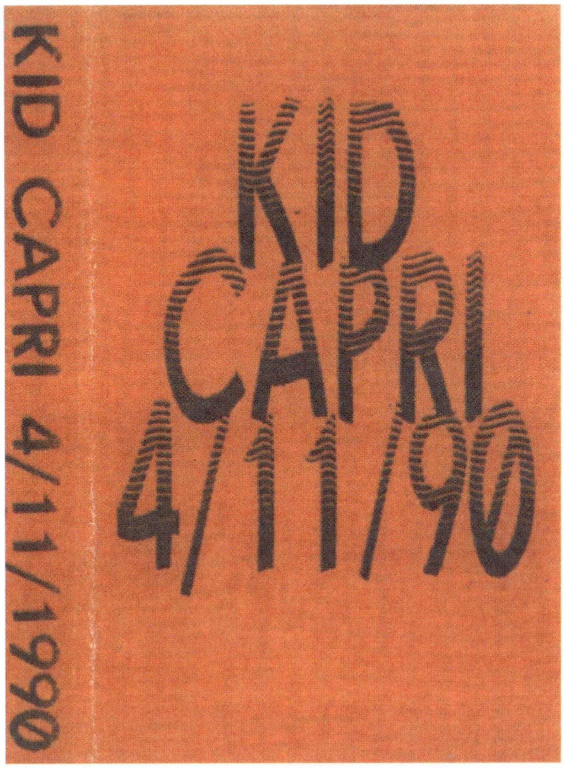
KID CAPRI 4/11/1990
KID
CAPRI
4/11/90

KID CAPRI LIVE AT THE Q CLUB
KID CAPRI
LIVE AT THE
Q
CLUB
3-1-1991

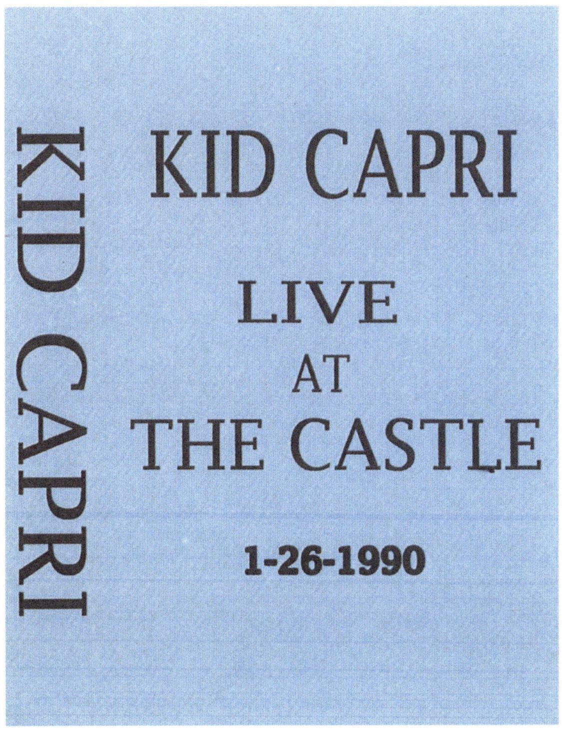
KID CAPRI
KID CAPRI
LIVE
AT
THE CASTLE
1-26-1990

York, but I was trying to get heard on a bigger scale. I went to a radio station and they wouldn't give me a job. So I said, "I gotta get heard some way." So I sat on the street corner and sold my mixtapes.

Being that I was able to make them in my house, I was able to set them up the way I wanted to instead of just pressing record at a party. I could make an intro. I could do certain things to make the tape have a build-up and capture people's attention. When I saw that it caught fire, I really went crazy with it.

THE DEFINITION OF A MIXTAPE

A mixtape is two turntables, put together with what music you're going to satisfy the world with. You have to make sure all these people are left happy at the same time. It's the same thing with when I get on the stage to go before a big ass crowd. No matter where in the world, it's me against them.

It wasn't me grabbing an artist, five or ten of his songs, slapping my words on there and that's a mixtape. No. I'm not dissing it, but that's not what my shit was. A mixtape is doing what I did, what Bruce did–that's a mixtape. Two turntables, music, microphone. You go and you be creative that way. That's a mixtape.

I'm not dissing but that's the truth of it, if you want to get down to basics. You're not mixing, playing one record behind each record in your editing studio. A mixtape is going in my studio with two turntables, no edits, no bullshit–going straight in.

You pressed play, recorded it, sat up all night and dubbed all the tapes until you had 100 tapes. Afterwards, you would go outside and sell them. That was it. That was my Internet. It was none of that new shit. Yes, I'm with all that now, but back then, it was the hustle.

A UNIQUE APPROACH

My tapes were a variety of different things. There were shout outs, there were different types of music that a lot of people weren't playing. It was playing records that, later on, became classic records. I did the Stephanie Mills and the "Impeach The President" mix, which changed the way R&B music had to be made. That mix was so big, R&B artists had to be on hip-hop beats. I was doing a lot of different things without even knowing I was molding it at the time.

SELLING TAPES ON THE STREET CORNER

I was sitting on the street corner, and I was selling tapes for $20. And people would come up to me and say, "Why would I buy a tape from you for $20? Who are you?" And I would say, "Just go play my tape. Put it in the car and listen. You'll be back tonight." And that's what they did.

And then, every car that drove by had my tape playing to the point where people from the Gulf War were coming back saying, "Your tape was the biggest thing on the ships." Police cars would be driving up and they'd be playing my tape. Mr. Softee–instead of playing the ice cream song, he'd be playing my mixtape in the truck.

I started seeing that it became something really big to where it opened the door for me to get on television, get my first tour, get my radio show. There were so many things that came after that just because I decided to swallow my pride and not care about how I looked on a street corner selling mixtapes.

SHOUT OUTS

You would shout people out just because you'd see them coming to a party, and they would offer you $500 or $1,000 for that tape so that they'd be the only one with it.

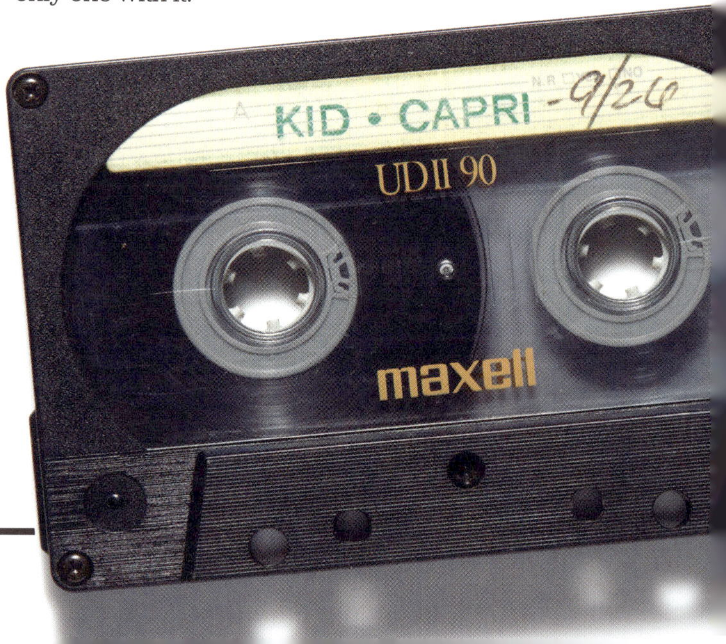

KID CAPRI'S TOP 5 BREAK BEATS

KID CAPRI: When we first started to play hip hop in the late '70s, these were the essential break beats that we used all the time--among a bunch of other ones.

1. The Honey Drippers - "Impeach the President"
2. Melvin Bliss - "Synthetic Substitution"
3. Freedom - "Get Up And Dance"
4. Rufus Thomas - "Do The Funky Penguin"
5. Bob James - "Take It To The Mardi Gras"

The more I refused to give it to them, the higher the price went. Especially the drug dealers–they had money coming out the ass. So it was nothing for them to give me whatever I wanted.

RELATIONSHIP WITH THE HUSTLERS

The drug dealers loved me more because I wasn't doing what they were doing. I wasn't a threat to them. I wasn't competition to them. I stayed in my lane, and with me being a hustler in my own way, it was respected.

I wasn't trying to be a street dude, but I was doing my shit around street niggas. I didn't give a fuck about that. I wanted to be on, that's the story right there. I did it by any means necessary.

I didn't agree with what they did, but I wouldn't knock what they did because without the drug dealers, I wouldn't have gotten known. They were the ones that would buy my mixtape. They were the ones playing my shit in their fly ass cars, driving up the street. So I would never say anything against them.

THE EMERGENCE OF TRACKLISTS

At first, there was no artwork. It would be me writing my name on a tape, bringing one of the masters to the store, and letting them get that master for a set price or whatever I charged. And then I sold mine on my own–hand-to-hand.

But what I did was, I put my name and the date on it. There was no tracklist. There was no picture. There was none of that. The moment that they came in with the pictures and the barcode, now you're dealing with something totally different. This was supposed to be underground.

That's the reason I stopped making the mixtape in the first place. Though it was with good intentions, their music being on my tapes was illegal. And that wasn't my idea of what I was doing when I got into it, but I recognized it. So it made me stop.

It made me say, "I'm not going to be responsible for people that took my tape, recorded it, sold it, made money, and bought mansions and cars." I was no longer gonna be responsible for that. In order to stop that, I decided to just stop making them all together. And fortunately, when I did that, my career went a whole different way and it just blew up.

Mixtapes were a stepping stone for me. It wasn't a career move. But the moment that those things happened, it made me say, "You know what? That's ain't going to be me. I'm out."

LEAVING ON TOP

'87 to '91 was my reign with the mixtapes. But I left the mixtape game as the Michael Jordan. I didn't fall off from the mixtape game. I left that at a very high place and decided to take my career a different way. Had I stayed with the mixtapes, it might have been a different game for the mixtape.

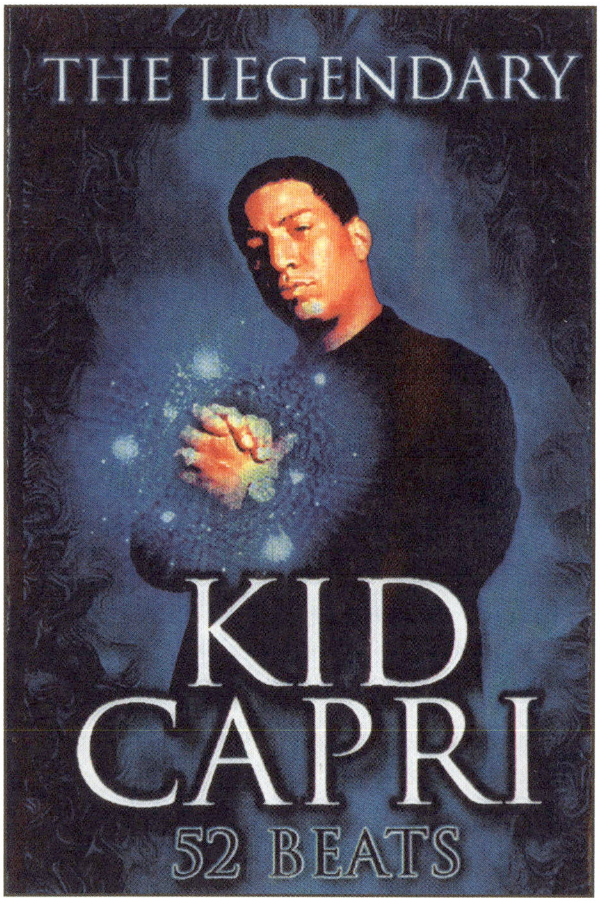

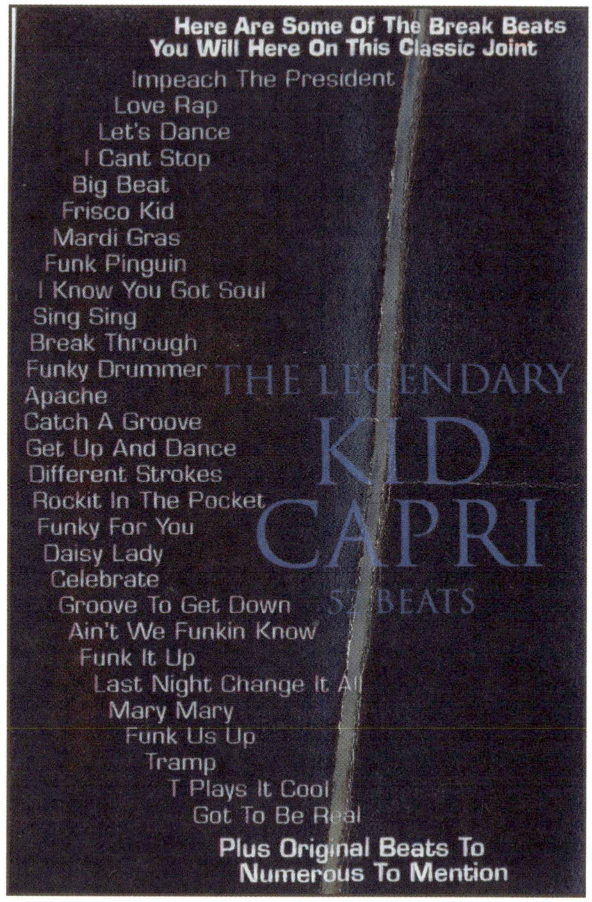

Kid Capri: The *52 Beats* tape wasn't even supposed to come out. That was a tape named for me, but I decided to put it out and it became one of my biggest hits.

KID CAPRI / Old School #1

1. RISING TO THE TOP
2. OUTSTANDING
3. DON'T LOOK ANY FURTH
4. HEART BEAT
5. MISDEMEANOR
6. COMPUTER
7. LETS GET IT ON
8. PLAYING YOUR GAME
9. BETWEEN THE SHEETS
10. I LIKE IT
11. I'LL TAKE YOU THERE
12. GROOVE ME
13. TALKING LOUD
14. TEDDY'S JAM
15. HIM OR ME
16. I LIKE
17. KUFF
18. TELEPHONE LOVE
19. JOY AND PAIN
20. BEFORE I LET GO
21. I FOUND LOVE

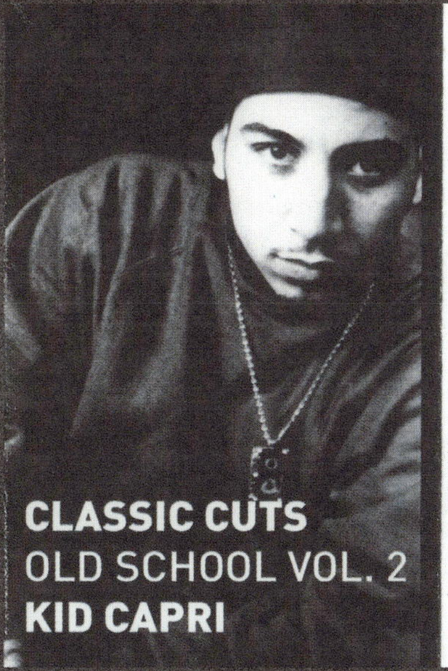

KID CAPRI // OLD SCHOOL VOL. 2

Side A:

Kid Capri - Intro
The Sylvers - Misdemeanor
Grace Jones - My Jamaican Guy
Gwen McCrae - Funky Sensation
Jocelyn Brown - Somebody Else's Guy
Cheryl Lynn - An Encore
Gwen McCrae - Seventh Heaven
Fonda Rae - Over Like A Fat Rat
Alicia Myers - I Want To Thank You
T.S. Monk - Can't Keep My Hands
Slave - Watchin' You

SIDE B:

The Jackson 5 - ABC
The Jackson 5 - Sugar Daddy
The Jackson 5 - I Want To Be Where You're At
King Floyd - Groove Me
The Staple Singers - I'll Take You There
Deniece Williams - Love Me Baby
Maze - Before I Let Go
The Fatback Band - I Found Lovin'
Keni Burke - Risin' To The Top
Mary Jane Girls - All Night Long
Midnight Star - I'm Curious
Prince - Pop Life
Grover Washington Jr. - Mister Magic
Marvin Gaye - I Play It Cool

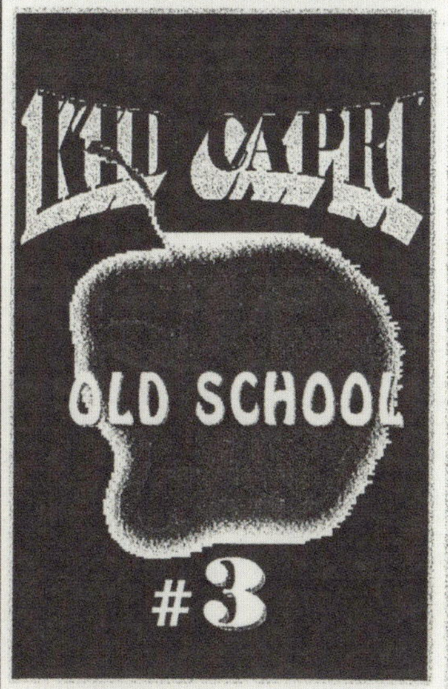

SIDE A

Pre-Intro
Jimmy Castor Bunch
Hey DJ Supreme Team Show
Rockin It Fearless Four
Spoonin's Rap - Spoonie Gee
Go See The Doctor - Kool Moe Dee
Latoya - Just Ice & DMX
Turn It Up Kool Moe Dee
Together Forever (Live at Hollis Park) - Run DMC
One Love - Whodini
Cracked Out
Girls - B Boys
Roxanne Roxanne - UTFO
Problems of the World Today - Fearless Four
F4000 - Fearless Four

SIDE B

The message Grand Master Melle Mel
rock box - Run DMC
The Breakdown - T. La Rock
The Entertainer - Doug E. Fresh
Cold Rock Stuff
Russell Simmons Feat - Jazzy J
Fresh Wild Fly & Bold - The cold Crush MC's
The Big Beat - Spoonie Gee
8th Wonder - Sugar Hill Gang
High Powered Rap - Disco Dave & The Crash Crew
Showdown Sugarhill Gang vs. Furious Five MC's
Hold It Now (Hit It) - Beastie Boys
Take It Off - Spoonie Gee

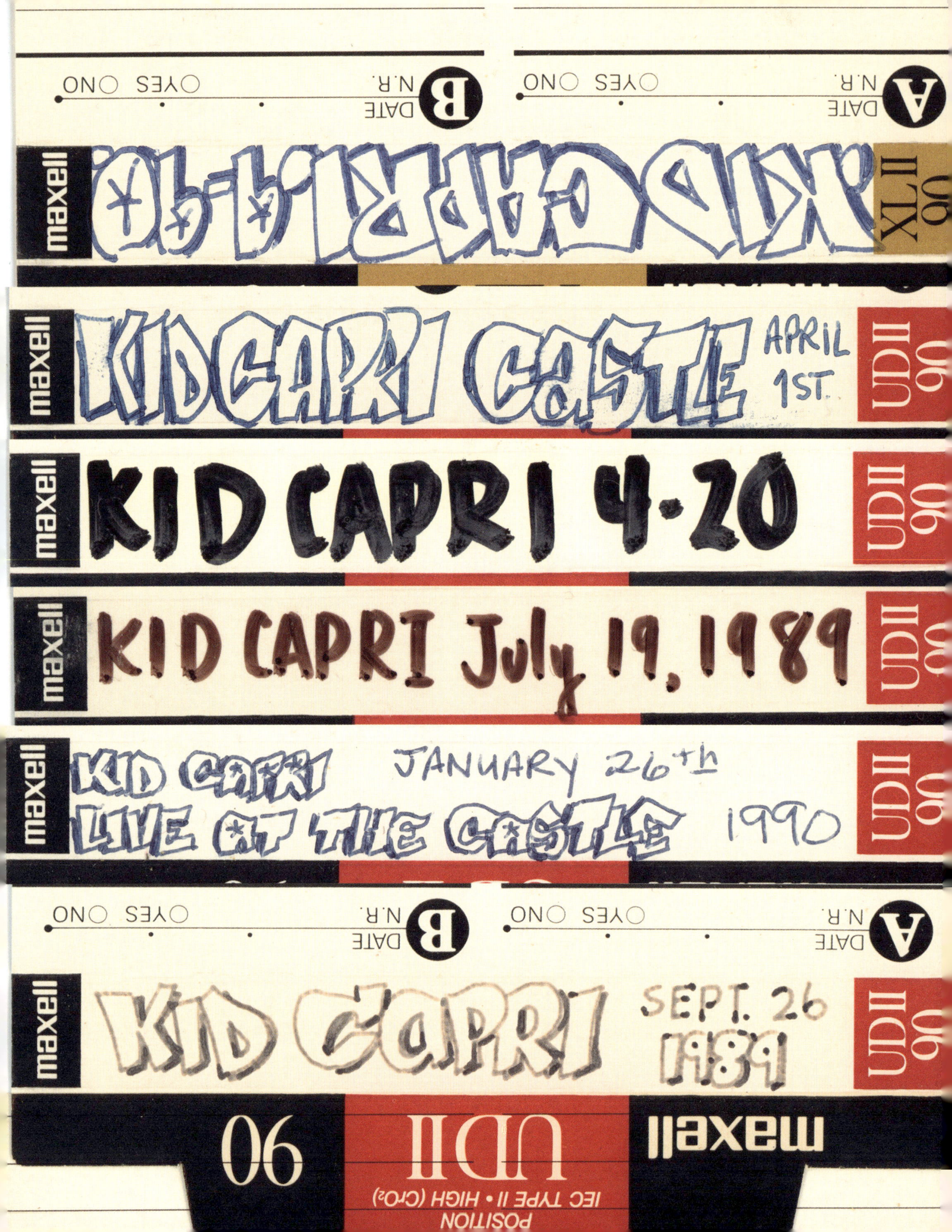

KID CAPRI CASTLE APRIL 1ST.
KID CAPRI 4-20
KID CAPRI July 19, 1989
KID CAPRI JANUARY 26th
LIVE AT THE CASTLE 1990
KID CAPRI SEPT. 26 1989
maxell
UDII 90

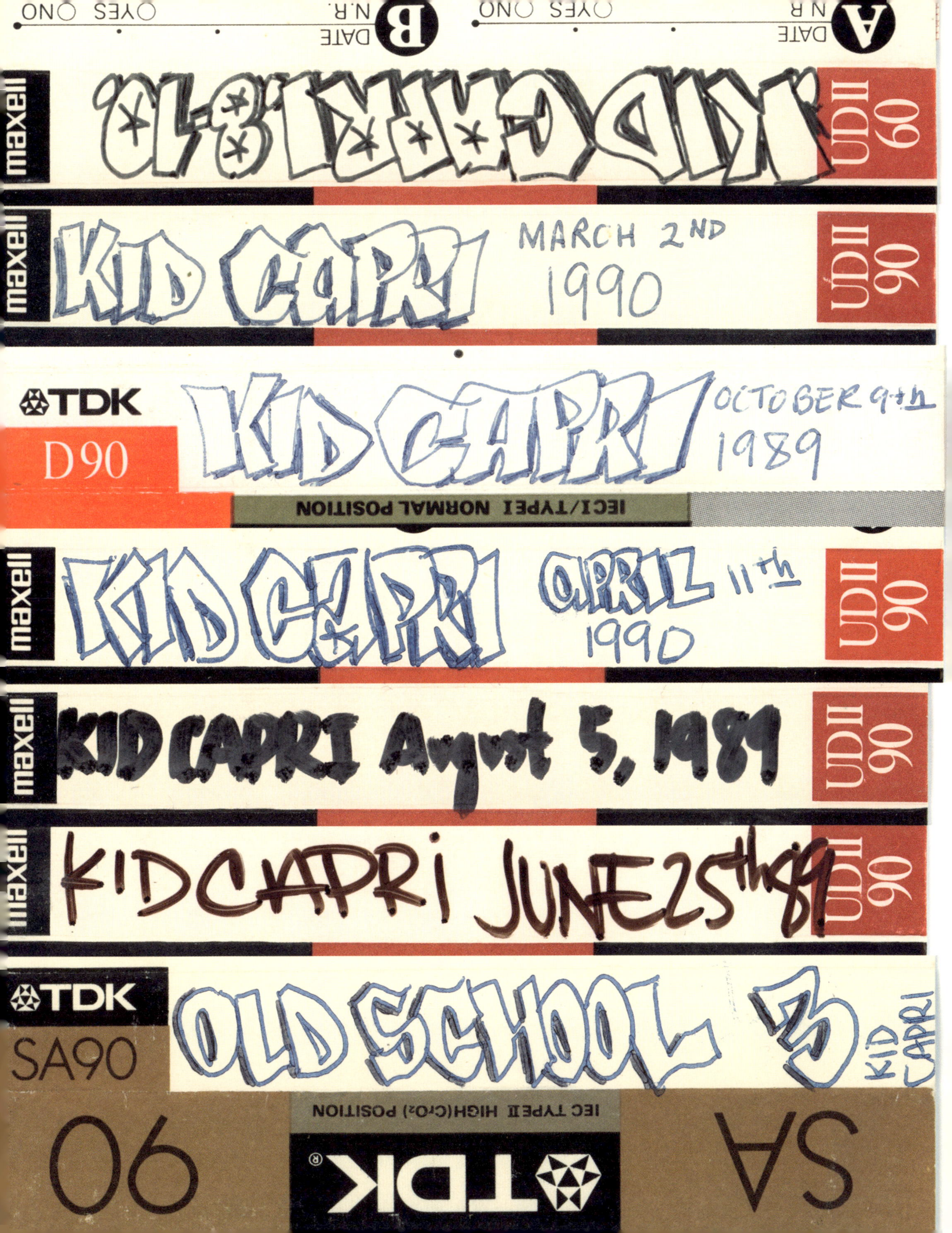

maxell
UDII 60
maxell
KID CAPRI
MARCH 2ND 1990
UDII 90
TDK
D90
KID CAPRI
OCTOBER 9th 1989
IEC I/TYPE I NORMAL POSITION
maxell
KID CAPRI
APRIL 11th 1990
UDII 90
maxell
KID CAPRI August 5, 1989
UDII 90
maxell
KID CAPRI JUNE 25th 89
UDII 90
TDK
SA90
OLD SCHOOL 3
KID CAPRI
IEC TYPE II HIGH (CrO2) POSITION
TDK
SA 90

DJ CLARK KENT

Real Recognize Real: Paying Homage to the Originators

Clark Kent has lived a storied life as a DJ, producer, and music executive. With roots in Brooklyn, Clark began DJing and recording his own tapes before he was old enough to drive a car. But ultimately, his career would take off in different ways, minimizing his involvement in the mixtape game. Still, his appreciation for the profound impact mixtape DJs made on the culture is abundant—especially Kid Capri and Brucie B.

MAKING TAPES

DJ Clark Kent: I started DJing when I was 9. And you know, as you keep DJing, at some point, if you're decent, somebody wants to hear you DJ outside of you DJing in your house. So you make a tape and you pass it on. I made my first tape when I was thirteen, I gave away my first tape when I was fourteen.

I never made the tapes for myself. I made the tapes for somebody who was asking, "Yo, make me a tape." "Okay, cool." Go in the crib, spend an hour and a half DJing, hand them a tape. What happens? That shit's in the neighborhood, in their car, blasting. "Who's that?" "Oh, that's Clark from over on Union Street." That damn near was one of the best promotional items around back then.

There was no revenue stream until later on in life, when I was like eighteen, nineteen, playing real clubs, and then recording what you do in a club. Usually somebody in the club was like, "I got $100 for the tape." If you played for four hours, you literally could make four tapes and then sell four tapes. It didn't even matter what was happening–it just mattered that they got the recording of the club. I recorded what I did in clubs so that any of the hustlers that were there could buy it. I didn't record it so that I could listen back.

KID CAPRI

When Kid Capri came in, that shit was a business for him. It was totally different. It wasn't just recording the club. He went home, sat down, and figured out, "I'm gonna do *52 Beats*, I'm gonna do R&B." That shit, I wasn't going to do. And I respect the shit out of Kid Capri for saying, "Okay, let me put this shit in order." He, to me, is the guy who really was the beginning of the mixtape game. It's almost like it set a precedent. Like, "Don't do this unless you have a plan."

Back then, a mixtape from Kid Capri was $20. When these other DJs started making mixtapes, they were $10. Why? Because they didn't have the focus. And the good part about Kid Capri is he kept it at $20. He didn't say, "I'm gonna bring mine down to meet yours."

145th and 8th Avenue, in front of Willie's Burgers. You damn near could have been a trash DJ, but if you had a tape, you could sell it there. But no one sold more on that corner than Kid Capri. Kid Capri sold tapes like rappers sell albums.

Once somebody got one of the original 100 or 200 copies that he sold himself, they were going down south and selling the shit in places like Virginia and North Carolina. Kid Capri became famous outside of New York City from his mixtapes being sold by someone who had a copy. He could travel all over the United States DJing based off the fame he got from mixtapes he did that he never traveled out of New York City for. It was ill.

Kid Capri is every mixtape DJ's father. I respect a lot of guys, but of all this mixtape shit, they literally can owe their careers to him. He's the first mixtape DJ to make an album. Everybody else wanted to do that shit is because of him.

BRUCIE B

DJ Clark Kent: Brucie B started by selling tapes out of the club. Then he was like, "Oh you want to buy the shit I just did here? Let me show you the shit I do out of my crib." The crazy part about it was, it didn't lose the feeling. The feeling was still there.

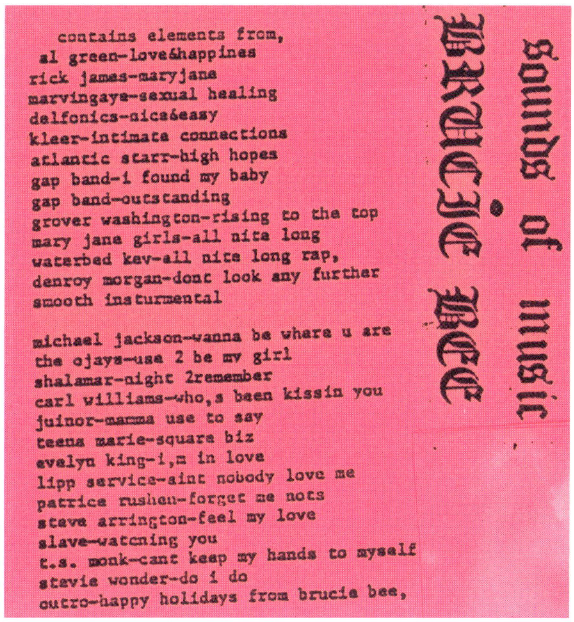

I used to be at the Rooftop every week. So the feeling, I live for that shit. His shit had a feeling and no one else's really did, except Kid Capri. But Kid Capri knows you have to look at Brucie B and go, "Yeah, he's the genesis."

Brucie B has the best mixtape voice ever. I would listen to a Brucie B mixtape over anybody's mixtape just because of his voice. When I heard that shit I was like, "Damn." It wasn't like he could cut or scratch better than anybody. He just sounded better than everybody. His voice floated on the microphone.

Kid Capri is every mixtape DJ's father.

BAHR BROWN

Coppin' Cassettes: A Life-Long Hip-Hop Fan Remembers The Uptown Mixtape Scene

When mixtapes exploded in New York City, Bahr Brown was there. One of New York City's foremost music, fashion, and sneaker culture connoisseurs, Bahr was just a kid from Brooklyn in the '80s making his way Uptown to Rice High School as a student, reveling in the wonders of the burgeoning Harlem hip-hop scene. He remembers it all too well, and he's got the mixtape collection to prove it.

ROOFTOP ERA

Bahr Brown: I was in high school from '84 to '88, and I went to Rice in Harlem. That put me into the mix with all of the kids that were going to the Rooftop. So Friday nights, me and my homeboys from Brooklyn would go Uptown, and we knew we weren't coming home until it would break day. We'd be coming out of the train and it'd be daylight out.

In the Rooftop, it had a Harlem vibe. We were Brooklyn dudes, so we stood out even from how we looked–dress-wise. We went up there more or less for the dancing, and not so much for the skating. At two o'clock, Brucie B would shut the music off, everybody would get off the skate floor, and then it would just be strictly dancing from two until like four in the morning. But I always remember an echo chamber and him saying, "If you got the car, then I got the tape. Come to the booth." And he would be selling tapes in the booth.

Back then I don't think it was called a mixtape. It was just, "Come back here and buy the tape." Some tapes were $20. But some were $100, because of the dudes who were getting money Uptown and all the shout outs. Those cats would be like, "Yo, I'll give you $100, $200–shout me out so when I get in my car and listen to it that night I can hear you shout me out." It was like a stamp. It showed you were getting money and you were there. That's what was circulating in high school.

When I was at Rice, I had a friend from Grant Projects, his name was Darryl Sweat. He was Keith Sweat's nephew. He moved around a lot because of who his cousin was, and he kept all of the Rooftop tapes. Maybe he would go through Keith sometimes, but for some reason, he would always have the newest one.

He was cool with me, like, "Yo, I'll let you dub this." And I'd take it home, dub it, and bring it back to him. That's how I started amassing my Rooftop collection.

DISCOVERING KID CAPRI

I went off to college in '88. So the next summer I came back was '89, and that's when I first heard Kid Capri.

I know the tape, it was *5/19/89*. It was the one where he had Ricky Ricardo from *I Love Lucy* singing and then "Keep On Movin'" dropped–Soul II Soul literally just came out that summer. So I heard that drop, and I forgot whose car it was in, but I was like, "What is that?!" He's like, "Yo, this dude Kid Capri, man." I was like, "Yo I need that tape!" So I got a dub of that.

I asked him, "Where did you get that?" He was like, "Uptown. You can go to different spots and sometimes he's up there and you can find him and get it." I found out where Rock and Will were, they were on 7th Avenue between 124th and 125th Street back then. Whenever I was Uptown, that would be my first stop.

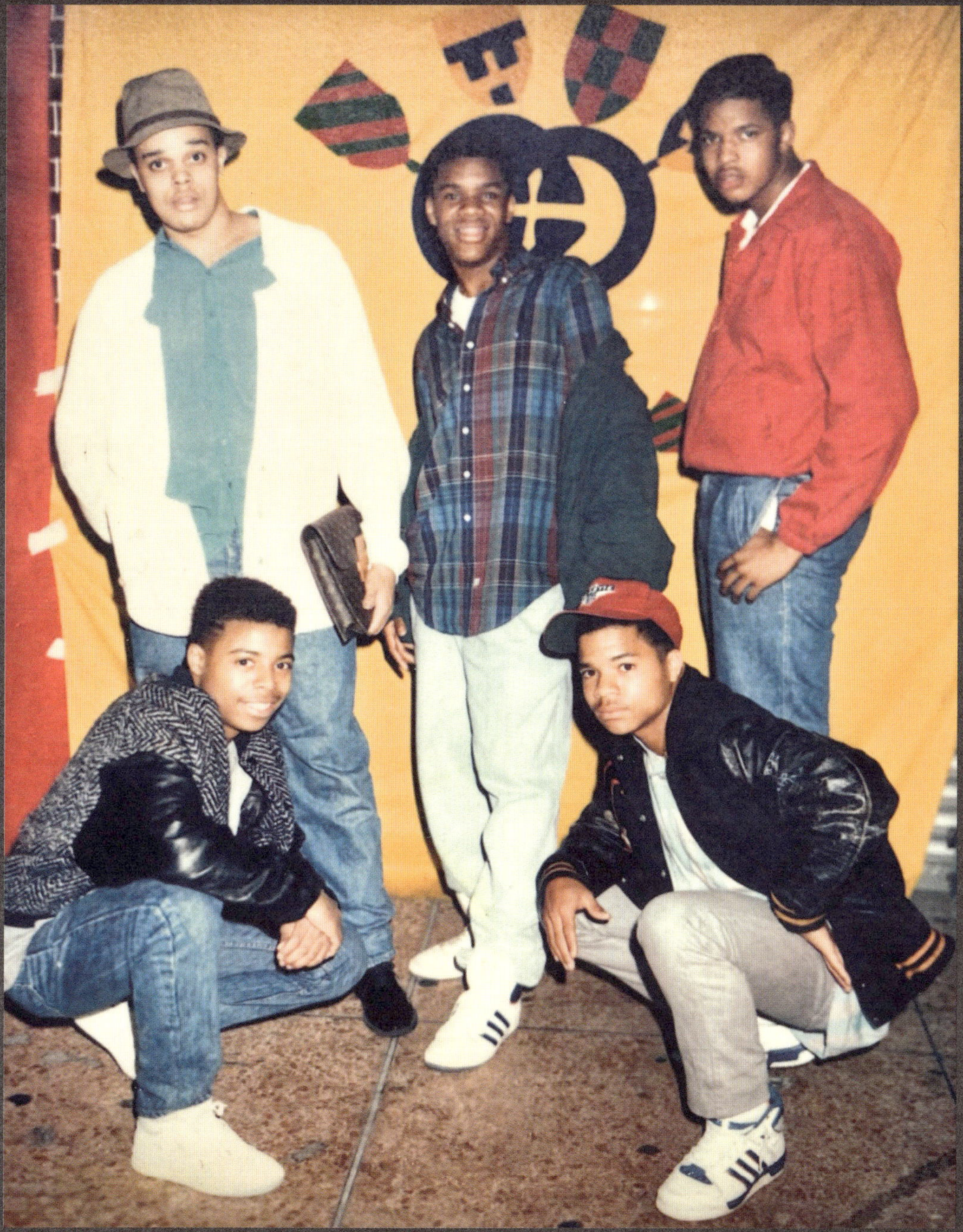

He'd have two tape cases and a cute girl with some tight jeans–like his homegirl–who would be like, "He got 'em, he got 'em." I would just cop straight from him.

My collection is all through '89: 5/19, 6/25, July 19th, August 5th, September '89. So I started literally every week. Capri would do some in the crib, but some would be live. I got one Kid Capri, January 26th, '90–Live at The Castle. His famous one in The Building in the Powerhouse, I have that too. But he didn't start doing that at first. He was doing mix-tapes from the crib and that got him buzzing. You had to have them.

COPPING TAPES DIRECTLY FROM KID CAPRI

We would come from The Rink in Jersey, which was that summer of '89, and come home to 145th to Willie's Burgers. You know how you would have school desks, like a seat with a desk connected? There was one of those right next to Willie's Burgers, and Kid Capri would be right there waiting for everybody to pull up. He'd have two tape cases and a cute girl with some tight jeans–like his homegirl–who would be like, "He got 'em, he got 'em." I would just cop straight from him.

They were $20, and those were masters. I copped a lot of joints from him. Right next to Willie's Burgers, he would post up and wait for The Rink crowd to come back into Manhattan. When you came back from Manhattan, it was mandatory that you come to 145th Street and 8th Avenue and get Willie's Burgers and just ride through slow, you know–frontin'. Just riding through with your peoples, you're with some chicks you met at The Rink, and you tell them to meet you at 145th. He would just be out there selling tapes.

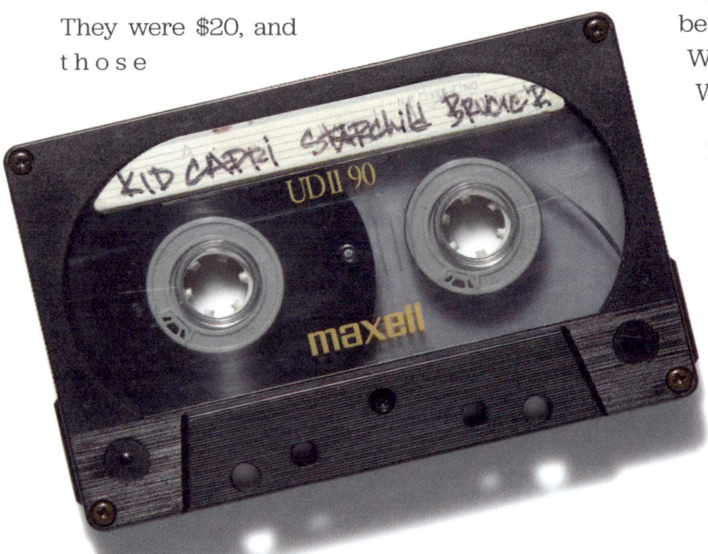

Kid was super-personable and humble. He would come out with a tape case with 30 tapes. So you figure, back in '89, if he sold all of these at $20, that's $600 right there. So you figure at $20 a pop, he was chillin'–he had no reason to have an attitude. He loved his customers. Some days, I'd buy like three from him. "This is the newest one, but do you have this one, that one, or this one?"

WILLIE'S LOUNGE

Across the street from Willie's Burgers was Willie's Lounge. That was an after-hours spot. I never went there, that was more for the older crowd or young hustlers in Harlem. If you were from Brooklyn, you had to be tapped into some Harlem hustlers to be up in there. There'd be gambling, and Starchild would be spinning. And he'd give those tapes to Rock and Will, and they'd be like, "Yo, I have Starchild in Willie's Lounge."

BREAKING RECORDS

Starchild and Brucie B's record selection, they're unmatched. They'd be breaking white records, like Phil Collins, Michael McDonald, playing shit like that in the hood. They're in the club and getting people to be like, "Oh, this is that shit." Even Frankie Beverly and Maze–our parents listened to it, but they turned those records into humongous records just playing them at after-hours spots and clubs.

Kid Capri would break whatever was out then, but then he would spin his own stuff. He broke Showbiz & A.G. "Party Groove," he broke the "Syndicate Posse" by Donald-D, he broke Soul II Soul records. He broke En Vogue "Hold On." Then his most famous blend–*10/9/89*–that was the one where he took the Stephanie Mills song "Something In The Way (You Make Me Feel)" and put it with "Impeach The President."

You know what it was with him? He was consistent. He would put tapes out every other week, but he would just switch it up. It would be some of the same things, but it would be stuff they wouldn't be playing on the radio. There wasn't Shazam back then, so he would scream out who it was.

Then he had the James Brown mix, he got that from Starchild. Starchild would do a whole James Brown mix that was like a thing, but he didn't have it on a mixtape. And Brucie too. It was known that Rich Porter would come into the Rooftop, Brucie would see him, and he knew Rich loved James Brown, and he would just spin a whole block of James Brown and shout out Rich Porter, "This for my man, RP." And it would be crazy.

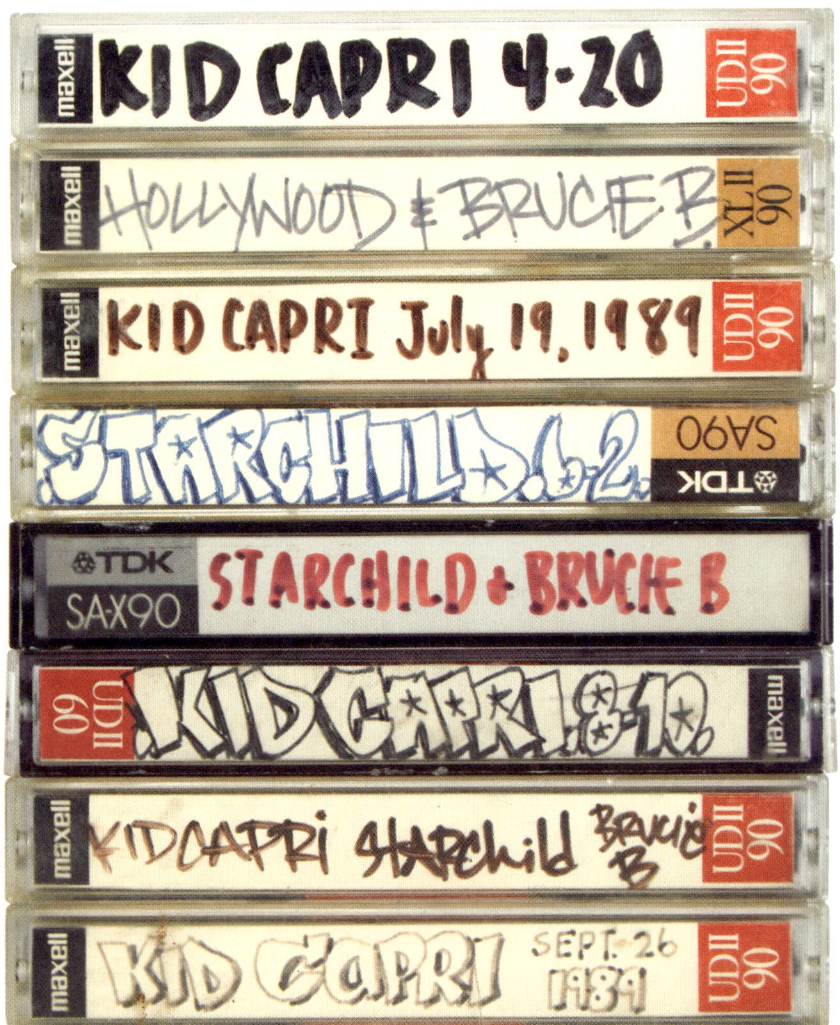

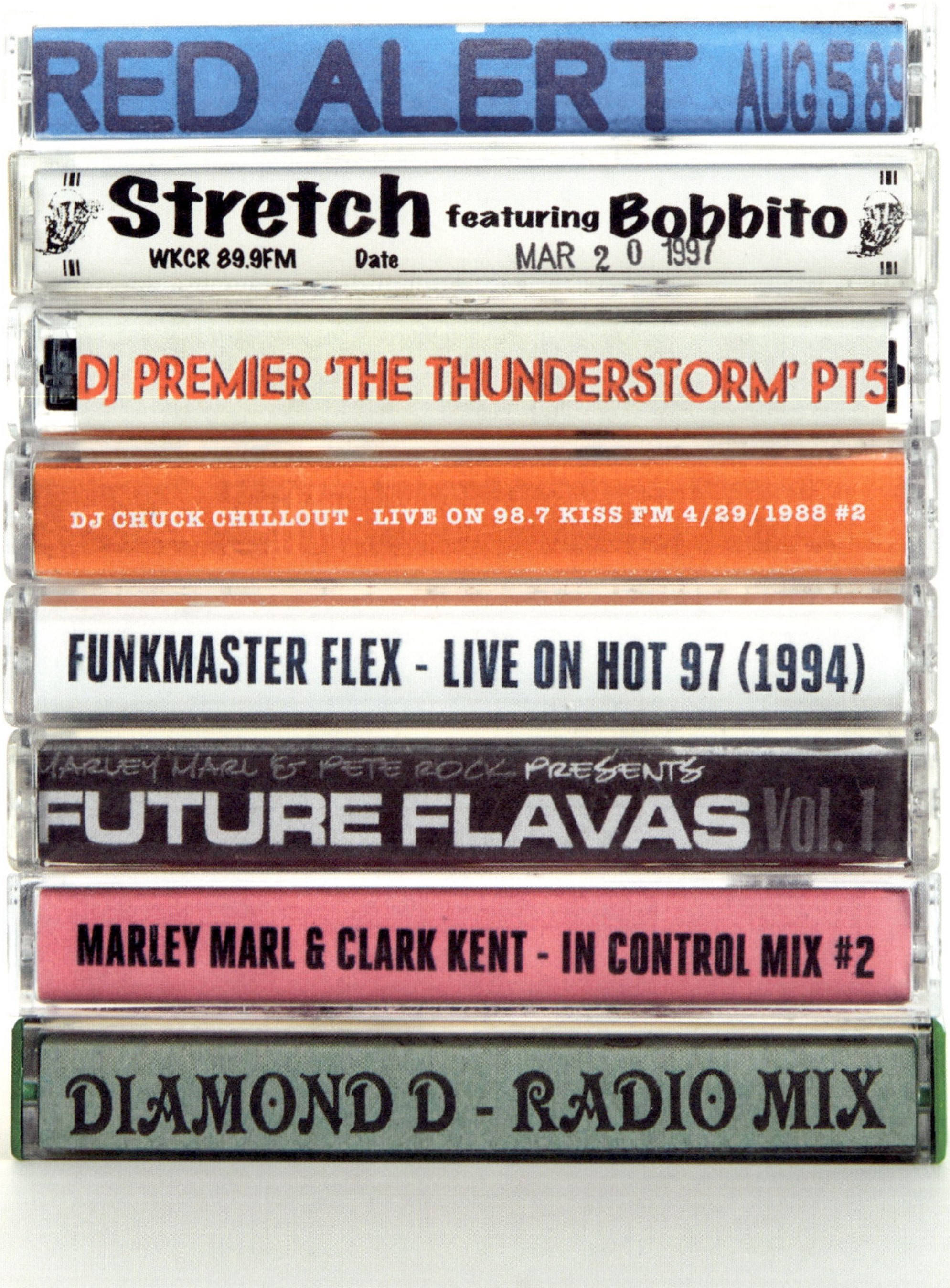
RED ALERT AUG 5 89
Stretch featuring Bobbito
WKCR 89.9FM Date MAR 2 0 1997
DJ PREMIER 'THE THUNDERSTORM' PT5
DJ CHUCK CHILLOUT - LIVE ON 98.7 KISS FM 4/29/1988 #2
FUNKMASTER FLEX - LIVE ON HOT 97 (1994)
MARLEY MARL & PETE ROCK PRESENTS
FUTURE FLAVAS Vol. 1
MARLEY MARL & CLARK KENT - IN CONTROL MIX #2
DIAMOND D - RADIO MIX

THE RADIO TAPES

Recording DJ sets off the radio and onto cassettes was one of the earliest forms of shareable mixtapes. Some hip-hop fans would sit tirelessly next to their tape deck radios, waiting to record their favorite DJs live on-air until the wee hours of the morning. And those tapes would make the rounds in schools and in the streets, and eventually would become actual products themselves. This is how THE RADIO TAPES took shape.

RADIO DAZE: *Making Tapes of Mix Show Recordings*

DJ Mister Cee: We used to record radio shows. The Supreme Team on WHBI, Zulu Beats with Afrika Islam on WHBI, Mr. Magic, Marley Marl. And, of course, Red Alert, Chuck Chillout. Even getting recordings of classic performances like the Cold Crush Brothers at Harlem World, and Brucie B and the famous Busy Bee versus Kool Moe Dee battle. The Force M.C.'s, before they were known as the Force M.D.s. We used to get those tapes, which came from copies of a copy of a copy.

It wasn't technically called a mixtape at that time, but those old performances, those old classic live radio shows when we used to sit up two, three, four o'clock in the morning listening to Jerry Bloodrock on the radio and recording his show—and then we would play it back at school the next day in the lunchroom—those were the early signs of what became a DJ creating a mixtape.

Rob "Reef" Tewlow: It all started with the radio, because there was only KISS, WBLS, 105.9, and some college stations. A lot of it was contingent on how strong of a signal you could get, whether it was WBAI in Long Island with Wildman Steve or the Awesome Two on 105.9. And before them, the Zulu Beats, but their signal wasn't as strong. So depending on what area of the city you were in, you may not have been able to get it or it was a shitty signal.

At first, you're taping with whatever bizarre sort of setup you had at your house. You had a boombox here and a home stereo here, and you're going back and forth between KISS and BLS for Mr. Magic or Red Alert or Chuck Chillout or Marley Marl, and you're trying to catch it. You're making these sort of lousy pause tapes, and you would trade them.

I remember it was a big deal when the first double cassette boombox came out where you could actually dub a tape. Then the next iteration of it was high speed dubbing. These are the little technological leaps and bounds that started to direct how things were going to go. The tech started to play a role in how things evolve and propagate and move around.

Dru Ha, Duck Down Records: It was recording on a boombox, waiting for certain songs to come on the radio, and then recording them so I could capture that song. Or, you know, tuning and getting different channels because you only had mix shows on certain nights of the week. It was either like BLS or KISS FM. And they didn't play hip hop five, six, seven days a week. They were only playing on Friday and Saturday nights.

Then you had underground radio, like Wildman Steve out in Long Island or Stretch and Bobbito on WKCR. I remember I didn't even know where, I would just try to tune it until I found it on certain nights like some E.T. shit. I'd zone in and all of a sudden, a Public Enemy song would come along and I'd be like "Oh I got it," and go back to my tape and record.

Obviously I wasn't selling those mixtapes, but I was definitely making my own version of a mixtape. I would record songs, stop, then go to a different station. And then if I was lucky, I could get it in some type of order. But that was a long shot.

DJ Eclipse: Recording a tape off the radio is the same thing as having a mixtape, because it's the same style. The only difference is that someone is kind of hosting it, which obviously mixtapes did as well. But some people didn't talk, some people did. But it was the same thing.

Just being on either Stretch and Bob's show or being on these mixtapes, it was how you got the word out. Because back then we were still limited in terms of how you would hear hip hop. It wasn't like you were hearing these types of artists during the day. They were still based on mix shows, so you would hear them on the weekends or at night or on college radio. Between that and the mixtapes, that was the whole medium of how we would hear the music that we liked.

DJ Mister Cee: I was a big fan of Mr. Magic and Marley Marl's The Rap Attack show, and I would record their show. And I remember specifically they would play exclusive Run-D.M.C. songs from that *Tougher Than Leather* album. Like they would play "Hit It Run" and songs like that, or "Perfection." And I would record them from the radio, then I would take my recording from the radio and play those songs in the club from a cassette before the album was out.

But of course, I would never play when Magic and Marley would have that "World premiere, world premiere" drop come in. I'm just playing it from when Run started rapping or when DMC started rapping, when the actual song kicked in. And then I would say something like, "I got something up my sleeve for y'all!"

The crowd was going crazy because they'd be like, "How do you have this?" They knew they heard it on Rap Attack but they'd wonder. At the time, I'm not the Mr. Cee that you know now. This is just me at local parties, basement parties, house parties that I'm doing in my projects in Bed-Stuy Brooklyn. And I would never reveal how I was able to play the record.

The mixtapes and the radio shows went hand-in-hand. –DJ ECLIPSE

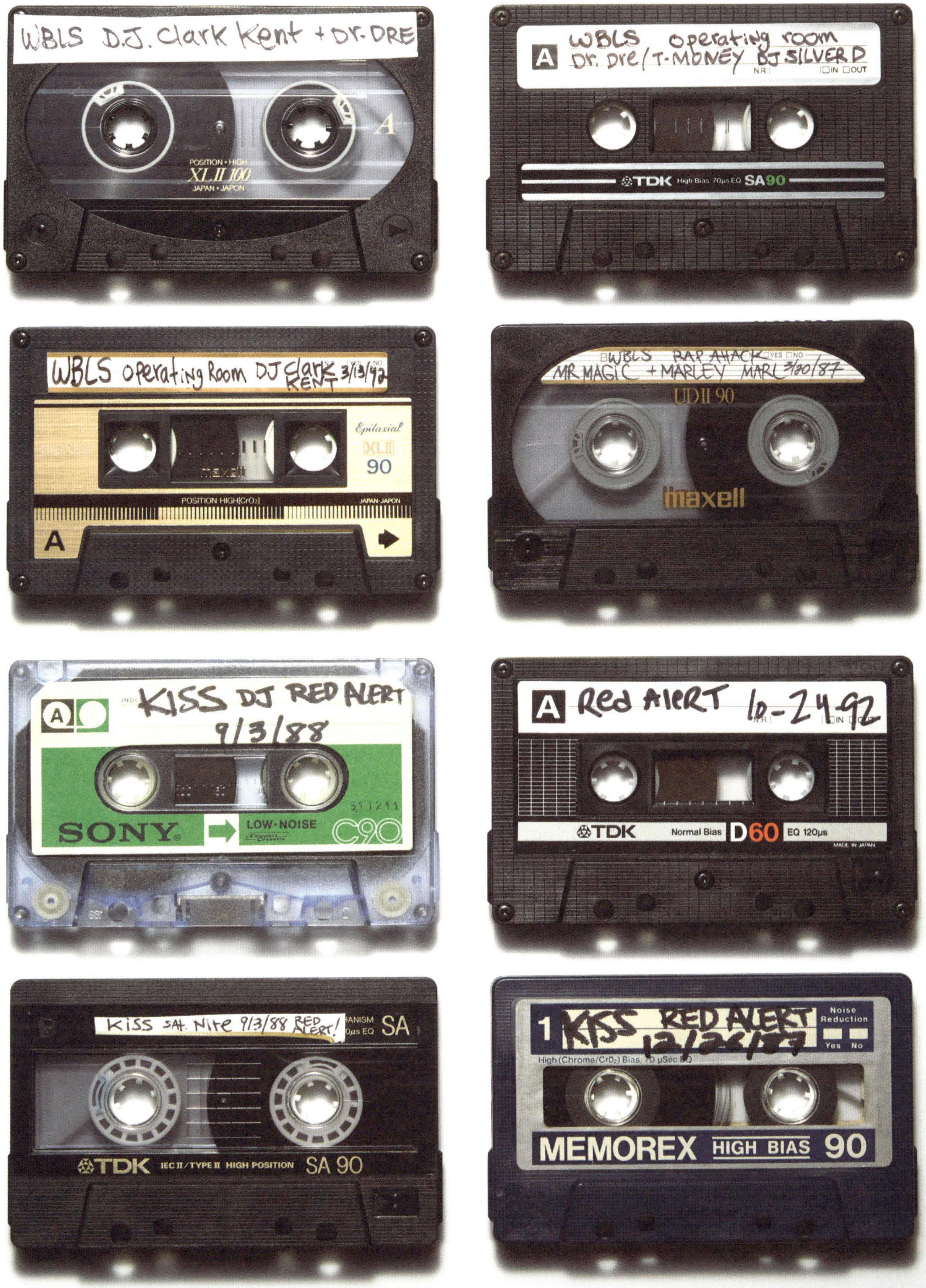
WBLS D.J. Clark Kent + Dr. DRE
POSITION • HIGH
XLII 100
JAPAN • JAPON
A
WBLS Operating room
Dr. Dre / T-MONEY DJ SILVER D
TDK High Bias 70μs EQ SA90
WBLS Operating Room DJ Clark KENT 3/13/92
Epitaxial
XLII
90
maxell
POSITION HIGH(CrO2)
JAPAN-JAPON
A
WBLS RAP AttACK
MR MAGIC + MARLEY MARL 3/20/87
UDII 90
maxell
KISS DJ RED ALERT
9/3/88
SONY
LOW-NOISE
C90
A Red AlerT 10-24-92
TDK Normal Bias D60 EQ 120μs
MADE IN JAPAN
KiSS SAt. Nite 9/3/88 RED ALERT!
SA
TDK IEC II/TYPE II HIGH POSITION SA 90
1 KISS RED ALERT 12/26/87
Noise Reduction
Yes No
High (Chrome/CrO2) Bias, 70 μSec EQ
MEMOREX HIGH BIAS 90

ZVI EDELMAN'S TOP 5 RADIO SHOW RECORDINGS

Record industry powerhouse Zvi Edelman breaks down his top five radio-recorded mix show tapes, all from his personal collection.

1. EVERY EPISODE OF RED ALERT ON 98.7 KISS FM. EVER.

ZVI: It's impossible to pick just one show, because I divide my life into pre- and post-discovery of Red Alert eras. When I was 8 or 9 years old--roughly '85, '86--my cousin put me on to a "show you can tape on the radio that has every rap song." Due to whatever divine intentions of the universe, I had just been gifted a radio with a tape deck and one Realistic brand cassette. And week after week, I stayed up listening to this funny, crazy guy who gave me entree to something totally radical and beyond my comprehension.

Just imagine one week you own six hip-hop albums and they're the entirety of your musical universe, and then a week later you're listening to drops from Mike Tyson and Kool Keith, unreleased songs by your favorite rappers and your future favorite rappers--Red Alert Productions birthed a whole style of rap, believe that--on-air talk about clubs you'll never go to, dozens of promos a night that never came out commercially, KRS getting busy over "Public Enemy #1." Fuck man, even the commercials were dope! Yeaaaaaaaaah!

2. THE OPERATING ROOM WITH SILVER D (1992)

It would probably be more fashionable to pick a night when Superman Clark Kent was DJing on this show, but Operating Room is the Clyde Drexler of mixshows--truly great but rarely spoken of--and Silver D perfectly fits that underdog mold. The hosts of this show were the Yo! MTV Raps crew, so it was funny as fuck. T Money should have become a household name. And this is a perfect capsule of '91/'92's tastes: "Uptown Anthem," "Scenario (Remix)," "Skinz," "Fakin' The Funk," "You Can't See What I Can See" and more, all sliced, diced, and doubled up with Glatt Kosher precision.

3. FUNKMASTER FLEX - "THE B.I.G. MACK NIGHT" / DIAMOND D PLAYS ORIGINALS (TIE)

These two nights of radio are perfect examples in very different ways of the greatness of Flex. It is hard to imagine now after being inundated with endless boring identikit breaks/originals tapes, but an actual genius producer--Diamond D--going on a big-time mix show to play sample sources was some revolutionary shit, and also probably the only time a David Axelrod song has ever been played on Hot 97.

The Biggie and Craig Mack freestyles are a monument to excitement. Flex is giddy--"It's like a flame of fire and I'm feeling the whole movement." "Code of the Streets" is pumping in the background, Biggie lets you know there's "nothing sweet about Fulton Street," and every single person who was tuned in did just like Flex says and "scrambled to pop their tape in," at which point Christopher Wallace proceeded to run Mad Lion, Melvin Bliss, and the Honeydrippers for their beats. And Craig blew Flex's mind by letting him know he was zoom zoom zooming when he was MC EZ in '88. History.

4. <u>STRETCH ARMSTRONG AND BOBBITO - WKCR 89.9 FM (DATE UNKNOWN, '94-ISH)</u>

Again, I could have picked a hundred Stretch and Bob shows, but this one has special resonance because I couldn't fathom how great this tape was the morning after it was recorded and I spent my entire "school day" savoring a Dutch Master filled with midtown's finest in the back of my cousin Mike's van. It has songs like Diamond D's smoked out remix of "Southernplayalisticadillacmuzik," Shorty Long's "Shortyz Doin His Own Thang," and Redman and Tame One's "Smoke A Blunt Too"--which I labeled "High As An Eagle" in purple paint marker on the tape itself--that may have been available on vinyl to cool people but certainly not to me.

When that "party people, you are about to witness something you've never witnessed before" drop hits, it's that feeling of being admitted to a secret club again. I knew other people wouldn't hear these songs for months, or ever. I also must state that DJ Stretch Armstrong never in his life blew a blend. A whole night of flawless mixes, every night.

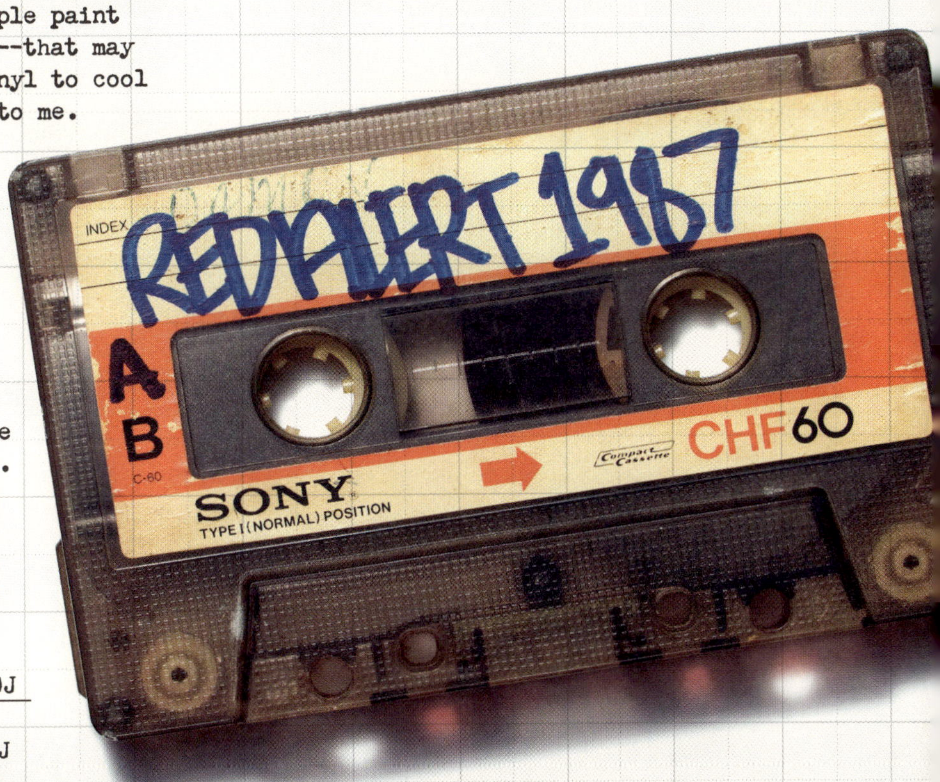

5. <u>WBLS THUNDERSTORM WITH DJ PREMIER - 2-18-94</u>

You know who's a better DJ than you? DJ Premier. The "you're 30 minutes away from another WBLS Thunderstorm" drop was a reason to be cheerful. Often, Preemo played dirty versions and cut the curses out live on the air like it was nothing. Big history bonus points on this night for the on-air presence of a young, just about to blow up Jeru, and the mentions of Gang Starr's Source magazine cover story. The way he shreds two copies of "C.R.E.A.M." and "It Ain't Hard To Tell" probably caused the retirement of a hundred bedroom DJs.

BOBBITO

Feeding the Streets: Radio Recordings Become Mixtape Must-Haves

Robert "Bobbito" Garcia is best known for being one-half of the legendary underground radio duo Stretch & Bobbito. In the '90s, Stretch Armstrong and Bobbito's WKCR 89.9 FM radio show recordings became so popular and in-demand with hip-hop fans that they were bootlegged worldwide in mixtape form, before eventually getting officially released through the renowned West Village record store Fat Beats.

PLAYING MIXTAPES ON-AIR

Bobbito: Interestingly enough, when Stretch and I started in 1990 on WKCR 89.9 FM, we felt a duty to play mixtapes or live recordings of concerts by Fantastic Romantic Five, Cold Crush Brothers, and Masterdon Committee from the early '80s on our show. So, we always had a respect for the cassette as it was.

FAN RECORDINGS

What we did during our four hour time slot on WKCR 89.9 FM for a lot of people was a mixtape. It was like, "They're doing a mixtape every single week." We weren't providing it to the listener–the audience was creating it themselves by virtue of taping.

Those cassettes were no different than me taping Red Alert, Special K and Teddy Ted, Awesome 2, The Dirty Dozen, and on and on. All those great radio shows that happened prior to us. Stretch was the same way–he would tape Marley Marl, Chuck Chillout, and Mr. Magic.

MIXTAPE-READY RADIO SETS

We weren't different from the audience. So our goal was to intentionally create a mixtape for ourselves, so we can listen to our Friday show and be like, "Yo! Look at all these crazy songs that we played!" So there was an undertone that we knew we could create a mixtape-esque experience for the audience, too.

We defied all regulations from the FCC, and even WKCR. We sometimes would play music for two hours without a mic break. That was unheard of in 1990, and moving forward. We were renegades.

BOOTLEGS

I wasn't aware until years later that individuals were selling our mixtapes in their respective communities and in schools. I directed the film *Stretch and Bobbito: Radio That Changed Lives*, and Busta Rhymes had that great line where he was like, "I used to sell your tapes in high school! Five dollars!" Which I was blown away by.

Eventually, I got wind that in the '90s, our tapes were being bootlegged en masse. And that came to my attention when me and Stretch went to Japan in 1995. We went to a record store, and right behind the cashier–literally prime real estate–I looked up and I saw like thirty of our cassettes for sale.

I was like, "Holy shit! The spine says Stretch and Bobbito, there's no hidden bootleg. It's deliberately being sold because of our names, our show, the music, and the artists that we feature."

At that point, our radio show did become part of the pantheon of great mixtapes of that era, although it wasn't a mixtape in the way you would think of a dude with a 4-track that's cleaning up the mixes, giving shout outs. It was a mixtape that went back to the original mixtapes of Brucie B and Kid Capri where they were just recording themselves live and selling that–that's the mixtape!

Eventually, Kid Capri wound up being more produced and polished in his mixtape presentations. But our radio show became a mixtape, in that it was duplicated and sold.

FAT BEATS DISTRIBUTION

My relationship with Fat Beats was so strong that I was able to get them to distribute our cassettes. I'd tape the show, give them the master, and then they would dupe it and we would get royalties–finally–because the tapes that were sold in Japan we couldn't account for.

I found out who was selling our tapes worldwide. It was a dude named Iain from Tape Kingz, who played a huge part in the exploitation and distribution of mixtapes. And to that end, he deserves a lot of praise. He did well for a lot of DJs. But I thought it was wrong for him to use our names to sell cassettes of ours and not share the profits with us. I told him that. He came up to WKCR with Finsta Bundy, he had put out a 12-inch. I forgot how I found out that he was the one bootlegging our tapes, but I was like, "Yo! How are you going to show up here and try to play it cool pushing this 12-inch when you owe us money?"

He came up like a week later and brought a check for me and Stretch. I have no idea if that check reflected how much money he made, but I was like, "Alright cool, we're good. Stop selling our tapes. We're going to do it with Fat Beats."

Listen, I was really never mad at him because people around the world know Stretch and Bobbito because some of them bought, heard from their friend, or duplicated a Tape Kingz illegal reproduction of our radio show. It's like he promoted and marketed us, and we didn't have to pay him for it. He did us a favor. I got DJ gigs for decades after due to the fact that me and Stretch's radio show blew up.

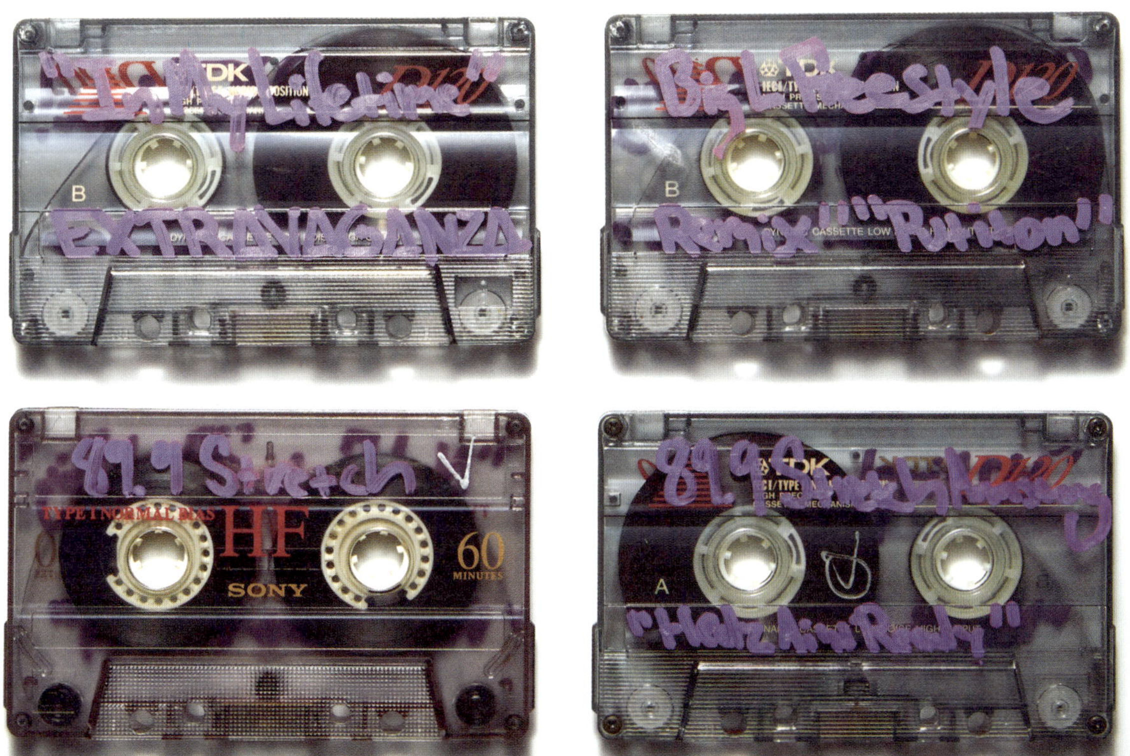

89 TECH 9 RADIO SHOW FREESTYLES

BOBBITO: It was our one year anniversary in October 1991, and I was like, "Yo, it's our first year. What should we do?" Stretch was like, "Why don't we play the freestyles from the past year in succession." I was like "Oh, that's dope!" I had already been compiling the freestyles so it was like, "Boom, let's just put it on a tape." Then that became one of our most popular show tapes--the freestyle compilations.

1. LARGE PROFESSOR, ORGANIZED KONFUSION, O.C. AND KOOL KEITH - Large Pro brought up his SP-1200 and himself, O.C., Pharoahe Monch and Kool Keith all rhymed. Prince Poetry as well--but there was a moment where it went from Large Pro to O.C. to Monch. I don't remember the order, it's in the film. That was a magical moment.

2. NAS - Nas came up and rhymed over Stretch's produced instrumental that never got released. It happened five months before *Illmatic* came out. The Nas and Large Pro nights happened two weeks from each other. It's the craziest shit. The crazier shit is that Gabe Toliver and Amir Lewis had come up to the show with cameras for two weeks in that same month. They came on the night that Das EFX came up and the night that Del came up. Instead of coming four weeks in a row--they didn't come up when Nas came up and they didn't come up the day that Large Pro and Kool Keith came up. We could've had all of that documented, we were this close. We weren't smart enough to know that all these people would become who they became.

3. THE NOTORIOUS B.I.G. - It's the one freestyle that became iconic that no one recorded. The *Freestyle Frenzy* tapes that we put out through Fat Beats didn't have it--no one had it. It happened at four in the morning. Very few listeners claim to even remember it. It was March 5th, 1992, so it was a year and change before he came out. Months from when he got signed. Luckily, we got it! Me and Stretch put out a remix of it and an officially licensed version of it on all digital platforms. It's over "Hand on the Pump" by Cypress Hill.

Me and Stretch always had a high level of respect for the mixtape DJ and the mixtape itself.

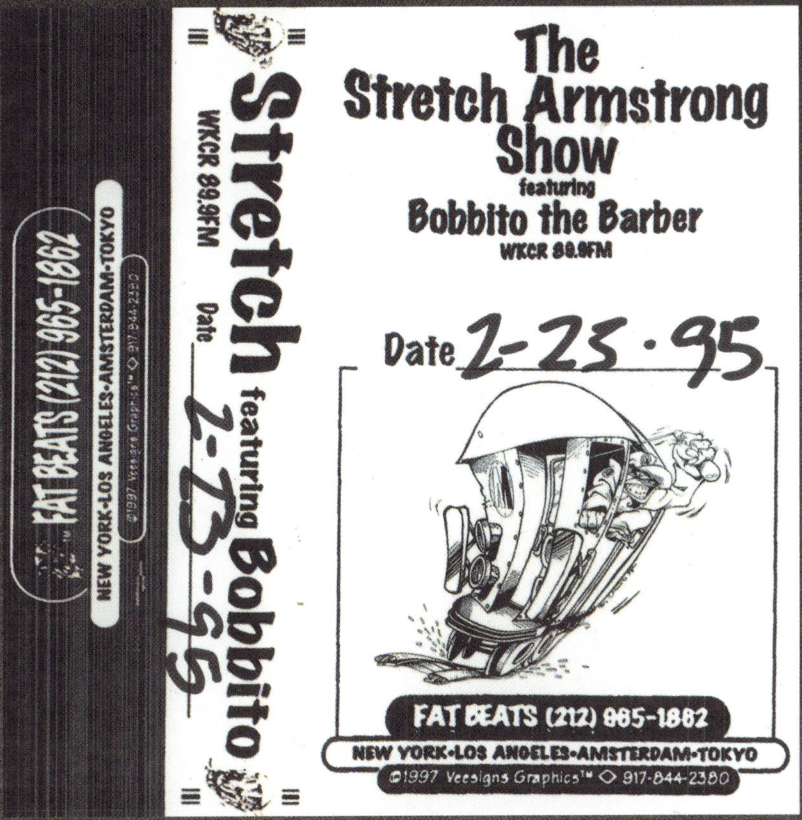
The Stretch Armstrong Show
featuring
Bobbito the Barber
WKCR 89.9FM
Date 2-23·95
FAT BEATS (212) 865-1862
NEW YORK·LOS ANGELES·AMSTERDAM·TOKYO
©1997 Veesigns Graphics™ ◇ 917-844-2380
Stretch featuring Bobbito
WKCR 89.9FM Date 2-23-95
FAT BEATS (212) 865-1862
NEW YORK·LOS ANGELES·AMSTERDAM·TOKYO

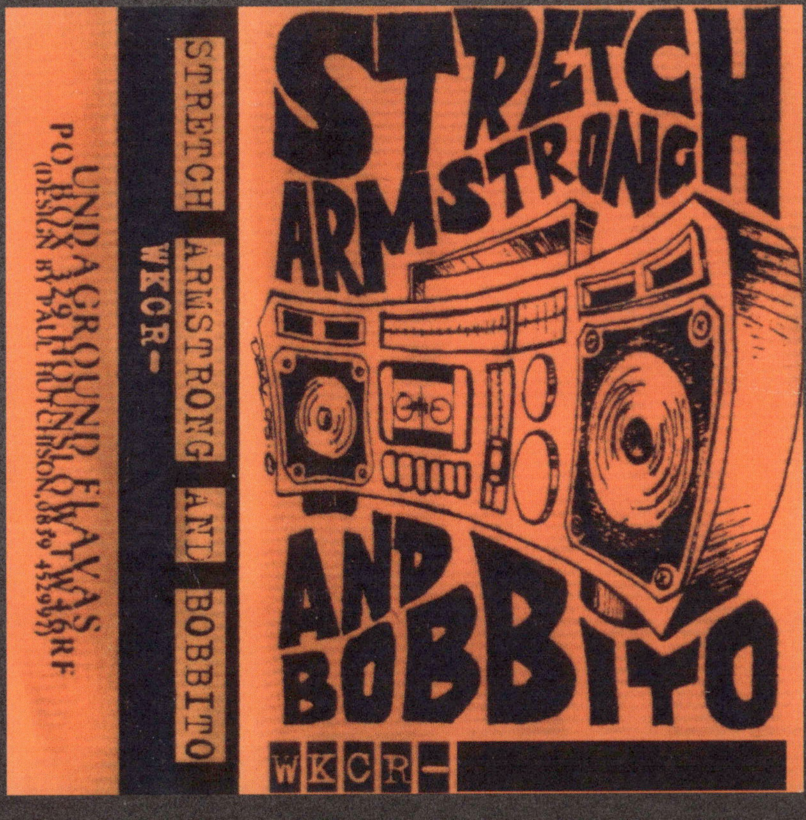
STRETCH ARMSTRONG
AND BOBBITO
WKCR-
STRETCH ARMSTRONG AND BOBBITO
WKCR-
UNDAGROUND FLAVAS

PETE ROCK

FM FLAVA: MAKING MIXTAPE MAGIC ON AIR

Hailing from just outside the five boroughs in Mount Vernon, Pete Rock has produced, rapped, and scratched on countless hip-hop classics, including Pete Rock and CL Smooth's "They Reminisce Over You" and Nas's "The World Is Yours." But he also has radio roots as a DJ, spinning alongside Queens legend Marley Marl on both WBLS and Hot 97. And those on-air moments became sought-after tape dubs and recordings that would circulate through the streets of the city.

IN CONTROL WITH MARLEY MARL

Pete Rock: I used to cut everything. I used to mix disco, cut breakbeats, hip-hop joints–I just didn't care. If I was in my room practicing, I pretended to be on the radio. That's the world I created.

Heavy D, my cousin, was like, "Yo, I'ma bring you around Marley man, he needs a DJ." That's when I met Marley. I was 14 years old and he was working with Heavy D. And at the time, an opportunity presented itself. I was in the right place at the right time, and Marley tried me out and liked me–and kept me on. The rest was history.

Before I came into the picture, it was him and Mr. Magic. It wasn't like they had a rotation of different DJs every week. It was just them. So to add me was a blessing. It really made me happy. It was one of the best feelings I've ever had.

It was my first time ever being on the radio. I was only 15 years old, and I'm on New York radio. That's fucking crazy. I'm not a known producer at this point, I'm just a DJ getting my name out there now that I'm on the radio in New York every weekend with Marley Marl. Straight out of high school.

FUTURE FLAVAS WITH MARLEY MARL

After *In Control,* I had my rap career. I wasn't on the radio at that time. I was on WBLS for like three years with Marley. And then we took a break and decided to do it again on underground radio, which was pirate radio. And then, we went from pirate radio to Hot 97 in New York.

Hot 97 had a show called *Future Flavas* that KRS-One was hosting, and we just took over the slot when the show wasn't going in the direction they planned. They hired us, and that's how it started.

There was no process. It was, "Let's just turn on the equipment and go for it." That's it. We do what comes out–and I think I can speak for Marley, too.

The show got better. I was playing dope joints, and we were inviting artists up there to do freestyles. Cormega, Wu-Tang. Everybody was coming to Marley's house, and we would do interviews with them, talk about the releases, and have them do freestyles.

RADIO RECORDINGS

I wasn't selling them, but I've heard that they were being sold. I mean, it is what it is. What are you going to do? We were dope on the radio. People wanted that vintage sound on tape. They wanted to hear that old way, the beginning, the origin of DJs and producers.

We were dope on the radio. People wanted to hear that vintage sound on tape.

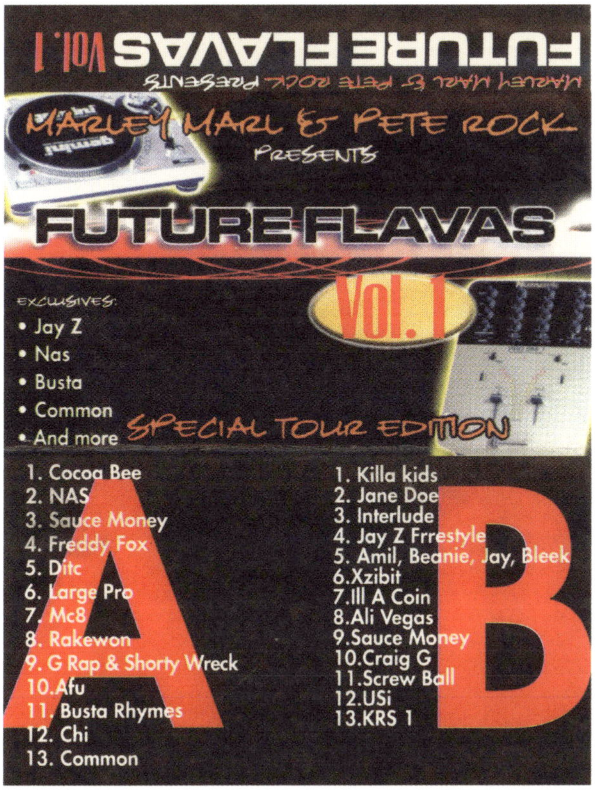
Marley Marl & Pete Rock
Presents
FUTURE FLAVAS
Vol. 1
Exclusives:
• Jay Z
• Nas
• Busta
• Common
• And more
SPECIAL TOUR EDITION
A
1. Cocoa Bee
2. NAS
3. Sauce Money
4. Freddy Fox
5. Ditc
6. Large Pro
7. Mc8
8. Rakewon
9. G Rap & Shorty Wreck
10.Afu
11. Busta Rhymes
12. Chi
13. Common
B
1. Killa kids
2. Jane Doe
3. Interlude
4. Jay Z Frrestyle
5. Amil, Beanie, Jay, Bleek
6.Xzibit
7.Ill A Coin
8.Ali Vegas
9.Sauce Money
10.Craig G
11.Screw Ball
12.USi
13.KRS 1

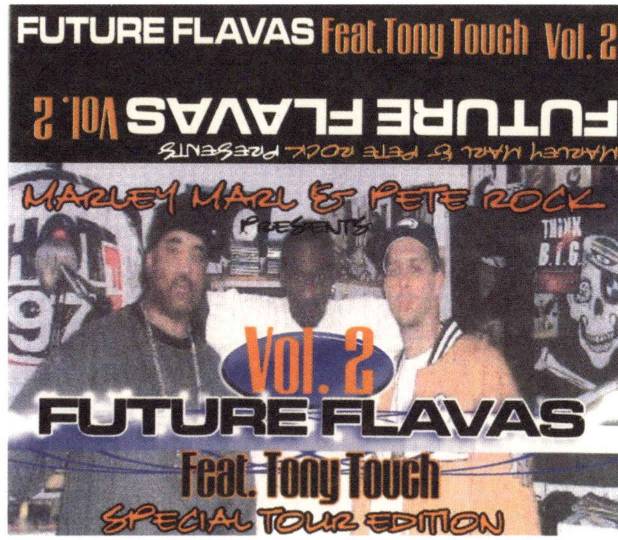
FUTURE FLAVAS Feat. Tony Touch Vol. 2
Marley Marl & Pete Rock
Presents
Vol. 2
FUTURE FLAVAS
Feat. Tony Touch
SPECIAL TOUR EDITION

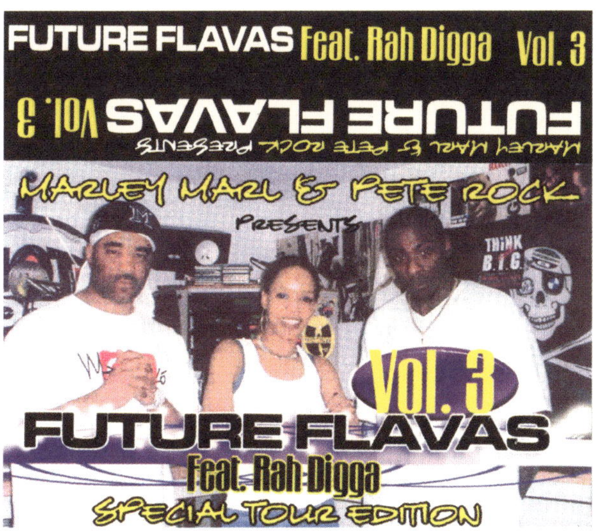
FUTURE FLAVAS Feat. Rah Digga Vol. 3
Marley Marl & Pete Rock
Presents
Vol. 3
FUTURE FLAVAS
Feat. Rah Digga
SPECIAL TOUR EDITION

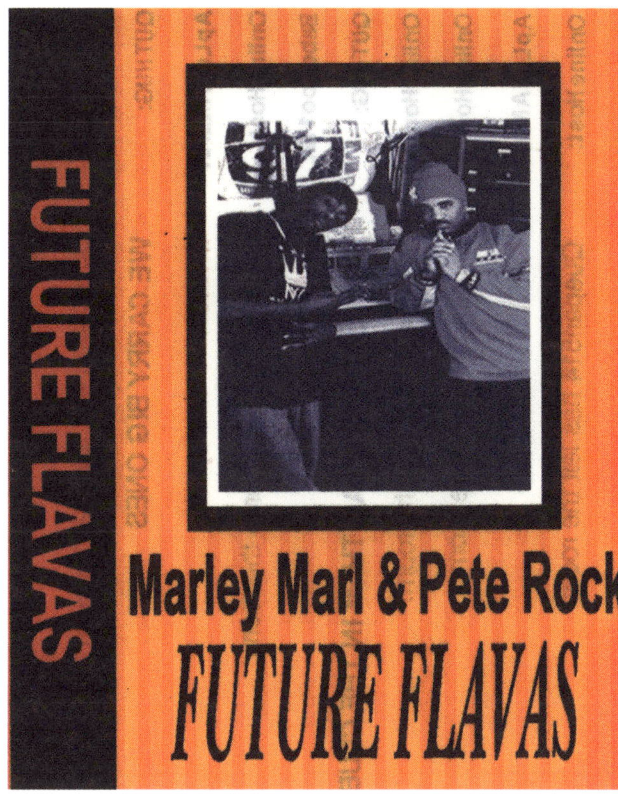
FUTURE FLAVAS
Marley Marl & Pete Rock
FUTURE FLAVAS

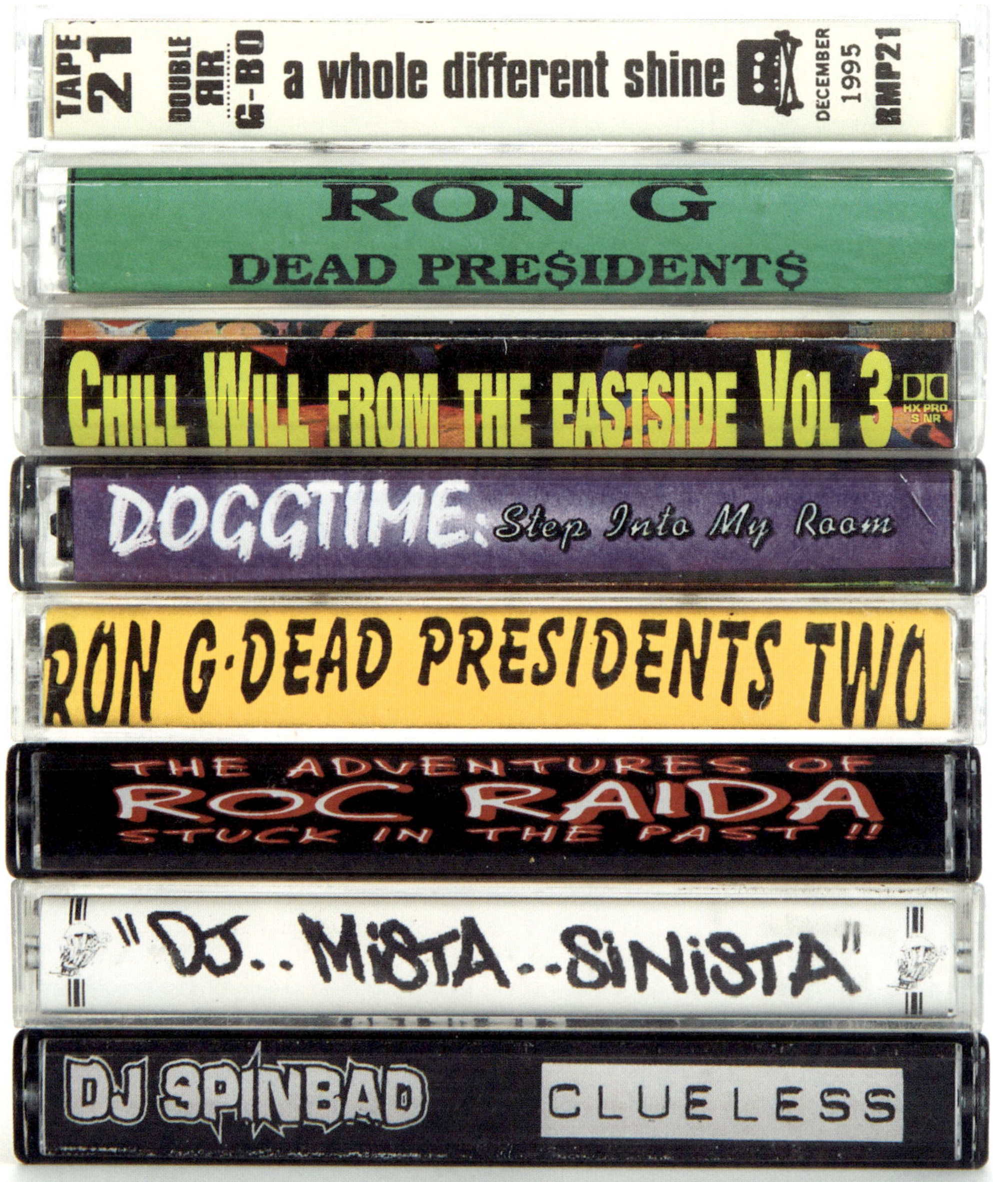
TAPE 21
DOUBLE AR
G-BO
a whole different shine
DECEMBER 1995
BMP21
RON G
DEAD PRE$IDENT$
CHILL WILL FROM THE EASTSIDE VOL 3
DOGGTIME: Step Into My Room
RON G-DEAD PRESIDENTS TWO
THE ADVENTURES OF
ROC RAIDA
STUCK IN THE PAST !!
"DJ..MISTA..SINISTA"
DJ SPINBAD
CLUELESS

THE SKILLS

As the popularity of hip-hop music in New York City continued to grow in the early '90s, so did the mixtape. And a new wave of DJs from across the boroughs was stepping up to flex their skills on cassettes and bring new ideas and energy to the mixtape game.

From the blends to the cuts, scratches, and overall recording quality and presentation of their mixtapes, this new crop of DJs was coming full force with THE SKILLS.

G-BO THE PRO

Behind the Boards: Bringing New Techniques to Mixtape Making

G-Bo The Pro and his partner Double R merged their Harlem hip hop and Latin influences to set a new standard for how mixtapes were produced and packaged. And though G-Bo himself chose to stay out of the spotlight, his impact with Double R on the New York mixtape scene was undeniable, and they would go on to become one of the greatest mixtape duos of all-time.

DJ SMILEY'S INFLUENCE

G-Bo The Pro: Locally, in East Harlem, we had a guy named DJ Smiley. DJ Smiley was making mixtapes, but not really in the hip-hop genre. He was making mostly freestyle tapes. He used to DJ at a place called El Morocco, he used to DJ at the Copa–so he was more on the Latin side of things.

Double R was trying to sort of improve upon Smiley. So before me and Double R got together, he was making freestyle, house tapes but was using sort of an overdub style.

So he would make a tape with a turntable, a tape deck, and another tape deck–I don't even think he had a set of turntables at the time. He was doing some crazy stuff. These overdub tapes sounded like they were three, four turntables at the same time–but he was doing it with one turntable and two tape decks.

He would open the back of the tape deck so that he could figure out what manipulated the speed of the motor on the tape. This dude was a cassette savant. Double R was a nut-ass when it came to precision and being able to manipulate tapes, and the pause. He was a maniac. If he made a mistake on the 44th minute, it was garbage. It was like, "Nah, we are gonna go back and redo that whole thing."

THE LATIN RASCALS

Double R had this dimension of making it sound like he had three or four turntables, and I think that came from the Latin Rascals.

The Latin Rascals were these two guys who would DJ on 98.7 KISS in New York. Again, they were more of the freestyle of the genre, but what they were doing DJ-wise was really innovative. They were playing keys on "Rock Box" and playing that on the radio, and we were just blown away. That is really who we drew our inspiration from, the Latin Rascals were crazy with it. But they weren't hip-hop guys, they weren't talking on tapes. They were super low.

When Double R and I got together, I had a little studio in the house and he asked me to do some scratches for him. The baby scratch is probably as complicated as I get, but it was better than what he could do. He came to the studio once and saw that I had this machine that I was making demos with.

I explained to him that it was a 4-track–"You can lay a beat, lay a vocal, lay a synth, and you can rewind." And it just struck him. Like, "Wait, I'm doing this the hard way. You have this thing that simplifies what I've been doing." Then I showed him a little intro that I did, based on what he was doing.

I was using intros to make songs. I was doing demos, I had rappers, I was making beats. So that's what I was using the 4-track for primarily. But because I knew Double R was coming over, I wanted to impress him.

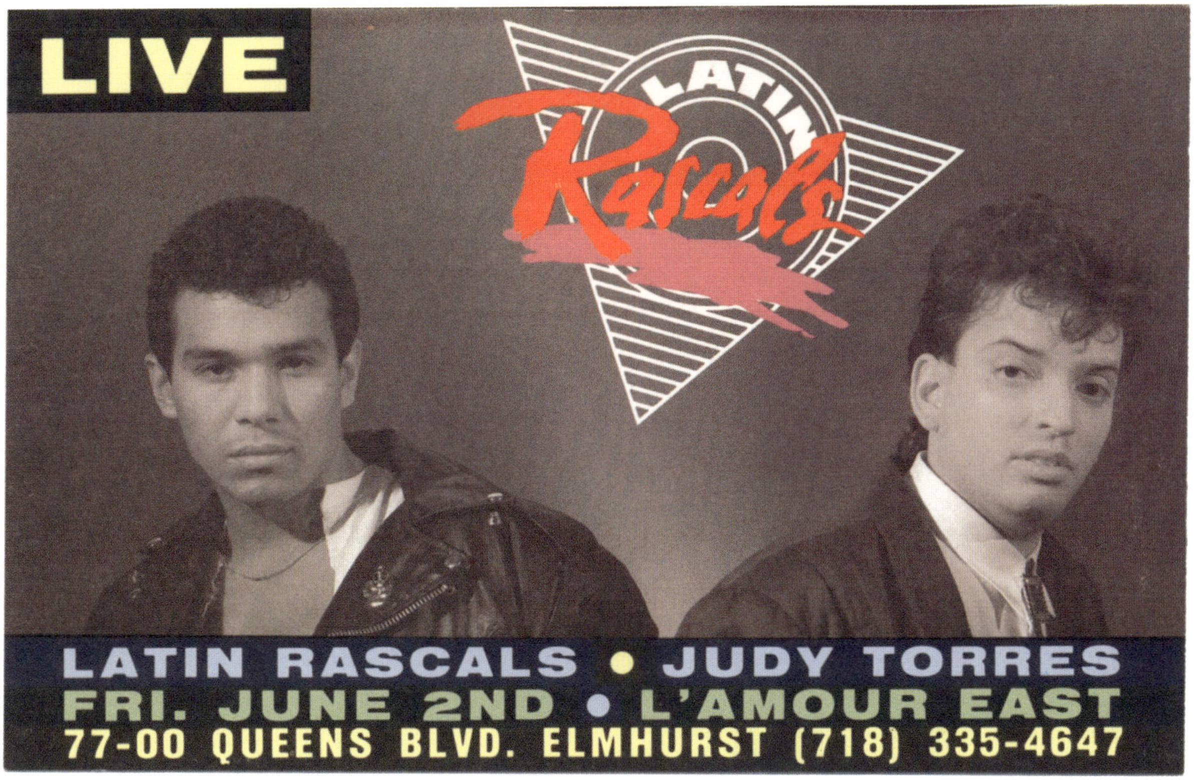

So I did a little Double R-esque intro and showed it to him. He was blown away, like, "We could do this, this, and this." And that was the beginning of him and I making hip-hop tapes together. 1991.

THE BIRTH OF DOUBLE R HIP-HOP TAPES

There was a store on the East Side of Harlem called Double Sounds, which was on 106th between 3rd and Lexington. If you wanted to put a system in your car, that's where you went. Double R used to sell his freestyle tapes outta there, and I guess somebody had a hip-hop tape and basically said to Double R, "Your tapes are dope, but you can't do this." So in a way, he kinda challenged Double R into making hip-hop tapes.

It was a confluence of things that happened simultaneously. Double R got challenged, he met with me and discovered the 4-track, and we did this thing together. When he went back with our first tape, the dude was just like, "Yo, my bad. I'm so sorry that I ever doubted your skills."

So to talk about what was happening at Harlem at the time–yes we heard of Bruice B, yes we heard of Starchild, yes we heard of Capri. *52 Beats* was out there. But I think we were more influenced by Smiley and the Latin Rascals. So we kinda put all that together. We had the Latin style of mixing and used hip hop to do it, and we layered things that didn't belong together. We added four things that had no business being together, and then DJs were like, "How the hell are they doing this?"

THE FIRST DOUBLE R AND G-BO THE PRO TAPE

We made our first tape. We put classics on there, then we put new records on there, and the reaction was just crazy. It was like, "What is this?" And there was no talking on the tape.

I like to call it the Class of '91–ourselves, Doo Wop, Ron G, S&S, Craig G and maybe a couple others. That's the Class of '91.

By '91, Capri stopped making tapes. But him, Brucie B, and Starchild loomed large in the culture. So, it

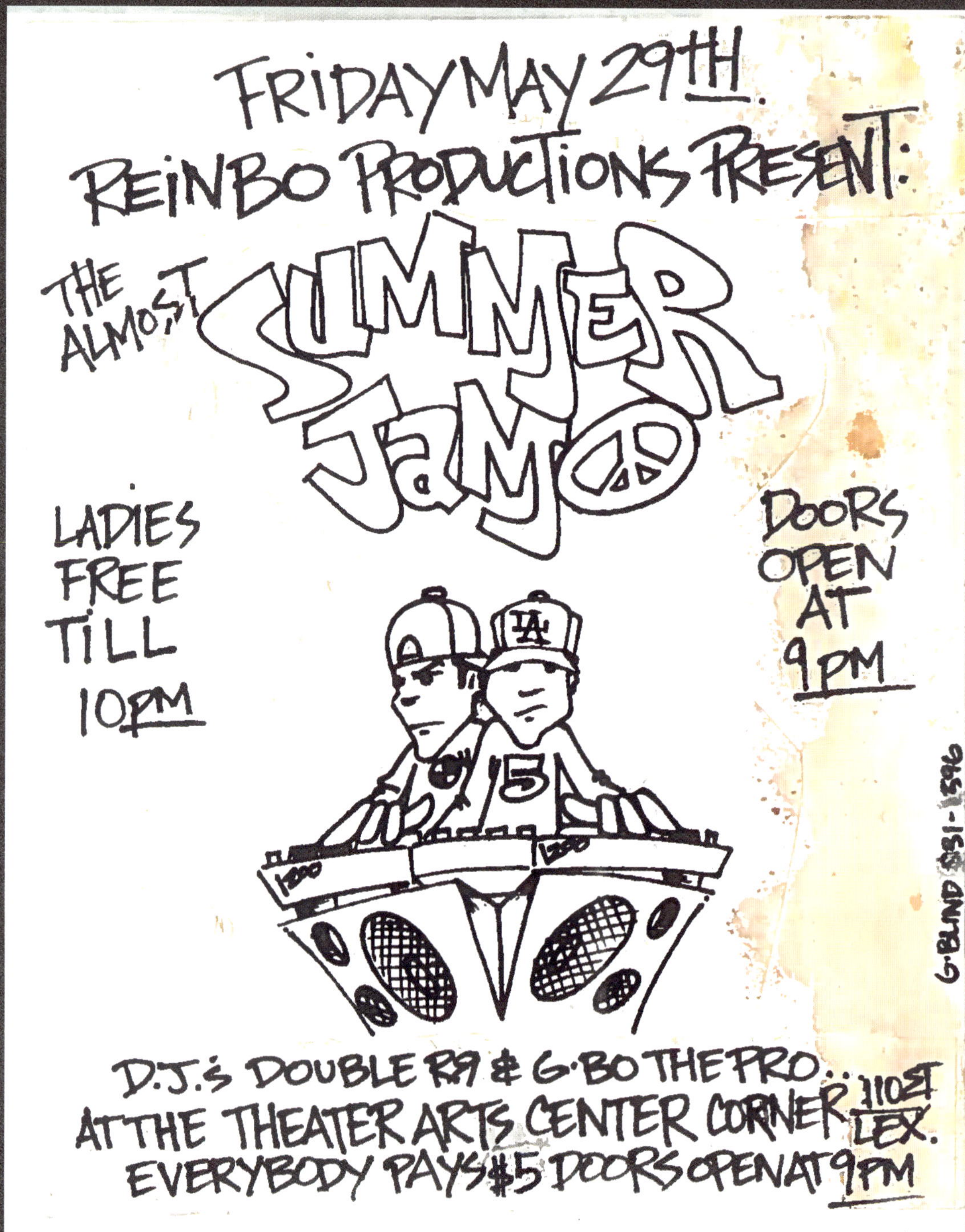
FRIDAY MAY 29TH.
REINBO PRODUCTIONS PRESENT:
THE ALMOST SUMMER JAM
LADIES FREE TILL 10PM
DOORS OPEN AT 9PM
D.J.'s DOUBLE R9 & G·BO THE PRO..
AT THE THEATER ARTS CENTER CORNER 110ST LEX.
EVERYBODY PAYS $5 DOORS OPEN AT 9PM
G·BLIND 831-1596

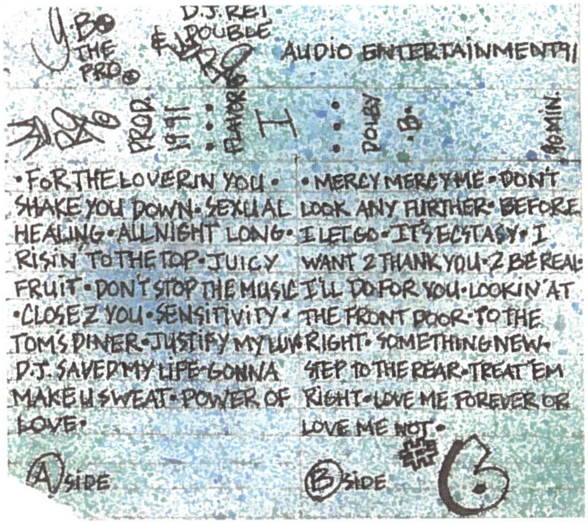
J.BO THE PRO ©
D.J. REI & DOUBLE RG
AUDIO ENTERTAINMENT 91
PROD. 1991
FLAVOR I
DOLBY B
90 MIN.
•FOR THE LOVER IN YOU• SHAKE YOU DOWN• SEXUAL HEALING• ALL NIGHT LONG• RISIN' TO THE TOP• JUICY FRUIT• DON'T STOP THE MUSIC •CLOSE 2 YOU• SENSITIVITY• TOM'S DINER• JUSTIFY MY LUV• D.J. SAVED MY LIFE• GONNA MAKE U SWEAT• POWER OF LOVE•
•MERCY MERCY ME• DON'T LOOK ANY FURTHER• BEFORE I LET GO• IT'S ECSTASY• I WANT 2 THANK YOU• 2 BE REAL• I'LL DO FOR YOU• LOOKIN' AT THE FRONT DOOR• TO THE RIGHT• SOMETHING NEW• STEP TO THE REAR• TREAT 'EM RIGHT• LOVE ME FOREVER OR LOVE ME NOT•
A SIDE
B SIDE #6

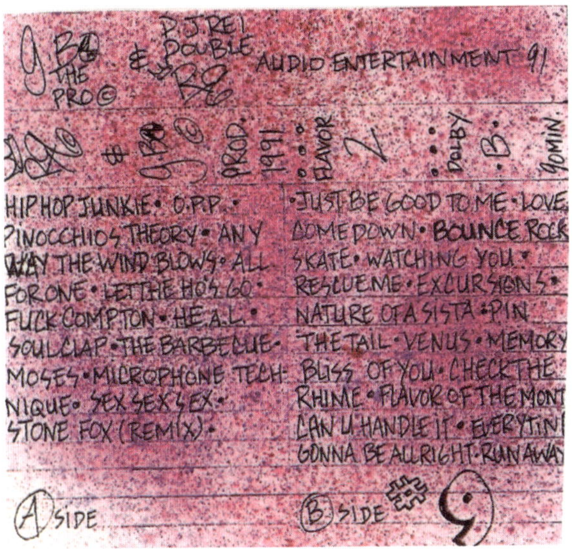
J.BO THE PRO ©
D.J. REI & DOUBLE RG
AUDIO ENTERTAINMENT 91
PROD. 1991
FLAVOR 2
DOLBY B
90 MIN.
HIP HOP JUNKIE• O.P.P.• PINOCCHIO'S THEORY• ANY WAY THE WIND BLOWS• ALL FOR ONE• LET THE HOS GO• FUCK COMPTON• H.E.A.L.• SOUL CLAP• THE BARBECUE• MOSES• MICROPHONE TECHNIQUE• SEX SEX SEX• STONE FOX (REMIX)•
•JUST BE GOOD TO ME• LOVE COME DOWN• BOUNCE ROCK SKATE• WATCHING YOU• RESCUE ME• EXCURSIONS• NATURE OF A SISTA• PIN THE TAIL• VENUS• MEMORY BLISS OF YOU• CHECK THE RHIME• FLAVOR OF THE MONT CAN U HANDLE IT• EVERYTIN GONNA BE ALLRIGHT• RUNAWAY
A SIDE
B SIDE #9

J.BO THE PRO ©
D.J. REI & DOUBLE RG
AUDIO ENTERTAINMENT 92
PROD. 1992
FLAVOR 3
THE FAT ONE
DOLBY B
90 MIN.
•HIP HOP JUNKIE• O.P.P. (LIVE)• HOW TO FLOW• MIND PLAYIN TRICKS• CHOURUSLINE• LOW DOWN NIGGA• NO VASELINE• A MINUTE TO PRAY, A SECOND 2 DIE• SOMETIMES I RHIME SLOW• ZONECOASTER• STROBE LIGHT HONEY• 718 KIT• RING THE ALARM• THE ADVENTURE• NIGHT SHIFT• BUGGIN' OUT• PEACEFUL JOURNEY...•
RUSH ON ME• MISTAKES OF A WOMAN• WHAT'S ON YOUR MIND• FAT RAT• PARTY GROOVE• I COULD JUST KILL A MAN• BORN KILLER• SCENARIO •I'LL WAX ANYBODY• MR. SCARFACE• PHUNKY FEEL ONE• THE CHOICE IS YOURS• CAKE AND EAT IT TOO• PRINCE OF DARKNESS•
A SIDE
B SIDE #10

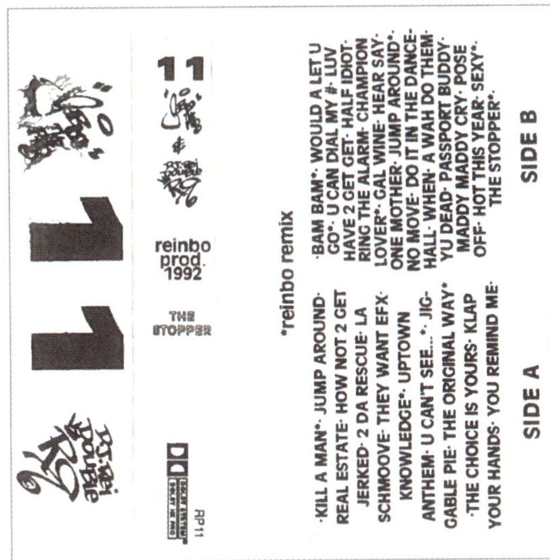
11
reinbo prod. 1992
THE STOPPER
RP11
*reinbo remix
·KILL A MAN*· JUMP AROUND· REAL ESTATE· HOW NOT 2 GET JERKED· 2 DA RESCUE· LA SCHMOOVE· THEY WANT EFX· KNOWLEDGE*· UPTOWN ANTHEM· U CAN'T SEE...*· JIGGABLE PIE· THE ORIGINAL WAY* ·THE CHOICE IS YOURS· KLAP YOUR HANDS· YOU REMIND ME·
SIDE A
·BAM BAM*· WOULD A LET U GO*· U CAN DIAL MY #· LUV HAVE 2 GET GET· HALF IDIOT· RING THE ALARM· CHAMPION LOVER*· GAL WINE· HEAR SAY· ONE MOTHER· JUMP AROUND*· NO MOVE· DO IT IN THE DANCEHALL· WHEN· A WAH DO THEM· YU DEAD· PASSPORT BUDDY· MADDY MADDY CRY· POSE OFF· HOT THIS YEAR· SEXY* THE STOPPER*·
SIDE B

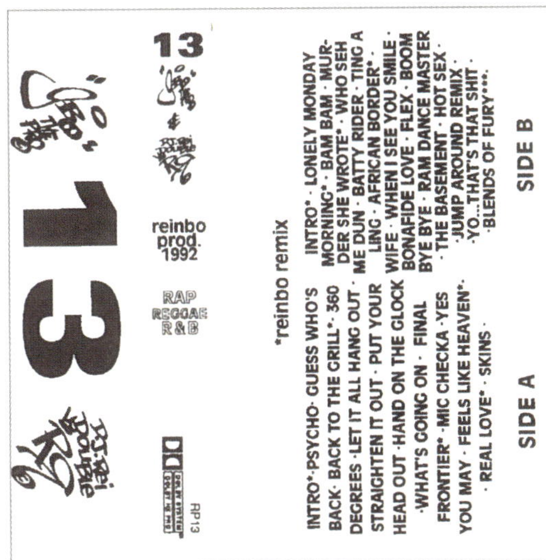
13
reinbo prod. 1992
RAP REGGAE R&B
RP13
*reinbo remix
INTRO*·PSYCHO· GUESS WHO'S BACK· BACK TO THE GRILL*· 360 DEGREES ·LET IT ALL HANG OUT · STRAIGHTEN IT OUT · PUT YOUR HEAD OUT ·HAND ON THE GLOCK ·WHAT'S GOING ON · FINAL FRONTIER* ·MIC CHECKA ·YES YOU MAY · FEELS LIKE HEAVEN*· ·REAL LOVE* · SKINS ·
SIDE A
INTRO* · LONELY MONDAY MORNING* · BAM BAM · MURDER SHE WROTE* · WHO SEH ME DUN · BATTY RIDER · TING A LING · AFRICAN BORDER* · WIFE · WHEN I SEE YOU SMILE · BONAFIDE LOVE · FLEX · BOOM BYE BYE · RAM DANCE MASTER · THE BASEMENT · HOT SEX · ·JUMP AROUND REMIX · ·YO... THAT'S THAT SHIT · ·BLENDS OF FURY**·
SIDE B

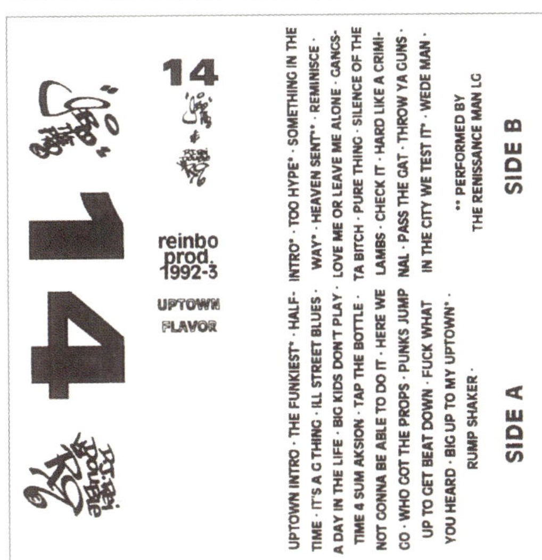
14
reinbo prod. 1992-3
UPTOWN FLAVOR
UPTOWN INTRO · THE FUNKIEST* · HALF-TIME · IT'S A G THING · ILL STREET BLUES · A DAY IN THE LIFE · BIG KIDS DON'T PLAY · TIME 4 SUM AKSION · TAP THE BOTTLE · NOT GONNA BE ABLE TO DO IT · HERE WE GO · WHO GOT THE PROPS · PUNKS JUMP UP TO GET BEAT DOWN · FUCK WHAT YOU HEARD · BIG UP TO MY UPTOWN* · RUMP SHAKER ·
SIDE A
INTRO* · TOO HYPE* · SOMETHING IN THE WAY* · HEAVEN SENT* · REMINISCE · LOVE ME OR LEAVE ME ALONE · GANGSTA BITCH · PURE THING · SILENCE OF THE LAMBS · CHECK IT · HARD LIKE A CRIMINAL · PASS THE GAT · THROW YA GUNS · IN THE CITY WE TEST IT* · WEDE MAN ·
** PERFORMED BY THE RENISSANCE MAN LG
SIDE B

was kind of a no-brainer that the DJs from the Class of '91 were gonna emulate these guys. They were gonna talk shit on the tape too, they were gonna give shoutouts too. They were gonna insert their personalities on the tape. But we were very anti-shoutout, anti-inserting ourselves as personalities on the tape. We wanted the music to speak for itself. That was one of the major tenets of our tapes–"Nah, we're gonna play the back and let the music be upfront."

So *Tape #9* was our first tape, and that just kind of set it off. That tape started to decimate, so we started to make copies and put it into stores. And it created anticipation.

I remember this guy that used to work at Downtown Records forever–Dante, black kid. His reaction to the tape initially was like, "You guys are trying to be like the Latin Rascals." But I guess as he started getting demand, he had to get on board, like, "You know what, this is dope. What you're doing here hasn't been done in hip hop. It's been done in freestyle and other ways, but this is new for hip hop." So it became accepted and then anticipated, and we just kept building on the anticipation.

TECHNOLOGY

Double R really in a sense was my mentor. I would not even fix my face to say that we were equals at the time. He's a little older than I am, and was already making tapes, so when he saw this machine he was just flabbergasted. It just opened up a whole world for him.

The machine that I had at the time was the Tascam 644. It looks like a mixing board with a cassette deck on the top right. It recorded four tracks and the tape speed was a little faster than a normal cassette. It recorded at a faster speed to improve the quality of the recording, I guess. So because that was the case, in order to record 45 minutes of tape, you needed two tapes and you had to fuse them together–it was insane. We had to use a special cassette deck with a good pause that you couldn't hear.

Most people at the time were doing their mixes live and if they made a mistake, it was what it was. They just glossed over it or talked over it or whatever. Our process was like production. It really was like taking the mindset of how you make a record and applying it to tape-making. It was a craft. Everything was meticulous.

Then we had to make a master of those 23 minutes, make another master of the other 23, and then dub that onto a tape deck where you couldn't hear the pause. We found a dope tape deck that when you released it, you wouldn't hear the little click sound. We were reinventing the wheel in a sense. With technology now, there's so much you can do. You can record on a computer, you don't have to splice. We were creating techniques that didn't exist.

The thing with hip hop that has always been sort of a constant is, we adapt technology to what we need it to do. So like the MPC, the SP-12, those things became famous because of how we adopted them. We tend to manipulate the technology to make it do what we need it to do. That's what we were doing with these crazy mixtapes.

Tascam would be appalled, like, "What? You're using our stuff to do that? That's not what it's meant for!" Like, "Yeah, we know."

AGREEING ON RECORDS

We put what we liked on the tape–there was nobody who could influence us in any way, shape, or form. Nobody could pay us to put a record on there, it was not gonna ever happen. We had to like it, we had to agree–Double R and I. Sometimes we would have fights about particular records, about putting records on or leaving them off.

I'm almost embarrassed to say this, but the first time I heard "You Remind Me" by Mary J. Blige, I didn't get why it was special. I was like, "We're gonna put that on? That's super regular." And he's like, "Bro, you are not seeing it! You're gonna be mad if we don't put this on!"

I didn't fight it too hard because he was my mentor and I trusted what he had to say about it. I say it's embarrassing now cause I'm like, "What! You didn't get Mary J. Blige?" When it dawned on me, finally, I felt like such an idiot.

INNOVATION

We would do custom lengths. They would be like 96 minutes so that if you tried to bootleg the tape, you'd miss an important part at the end, because we would do outros too in some cases. We were innovative in so many different ways–not just the way the tape sounded, but the physical, actual hardware of the tape.

TRACKLISTING

We were also one of the early innovators of how the tape looked. They used to laugh at us actually for putting a tracklist on the mixtape because it was supposed to be such a street thing. To list the names of the songs, that was almost like, "Who do you think you are? You think this is an album?" So we got laughed at a lot, until they realized "Okay, maybe we should do this too."

LOGO

That hand style was our guy, his name was G Blind. He flipped our names. If you look at the G-Bo The Pro, you see the little BMW symbol in the O. That's because I had a drop-top BMW at the time. So he flipped that–he bodied it. He did this technique where he would blow spit onto the marker, and the paper was here. It was almost like an airbrush effect. Bananas. He did this crazy-ass spitting-on-the-marker technique for three of our tapes.

CED THA DON "TRINIDADIAN GIRL"

When a remix of Ced Tha Don's "Trinidadian Girl" first appeared on a G-Bo The Pro and Double R tape, it was initially mistaken for a Slick Rick song due to the two MCs' vocal similarities. And though Ced never advanced beyond the song's success in the streets, "Trinidadian Girl" remains legendary due to its impact on mixtapes.

G-Bo The Pro: "Trinidadian Girl" was on *Tape #12*, and that was a song only we had—that was our boy that did that. It came out of not having enough records to put on a tape. It was an old demo that I had done with Ted Smooth, who is Double R's biological brother.

Me and Ted Smooth were partners before me and Ray aka Double R were partners. We were doing this "Trinidadian Girl" song, and Ted went his way doing mixtapes and clubs, and I got with his brother and we started making tapes. Those demos kind of fell by the wayside, they just didn't do anything. They were just sitting in my studio.

One day we needed a couple more records. When I let Double R hear "Trinidadian Girl," he hated the beat. He was like, "This beat is trash." So we used the acappella with the Das EFX beat and it sounded like, "Yo! Okay!" Everybody after that was like, "Yo, what's up with that Slick Rick record?" But that's not Slick Rick.

"Trinidadian Girl" took on a life of its own on the streets. I wish we could have parlayed it into a record deal and something else, but as it turned out, Ced didn't live here—he lived in South Carolina and it just was complicated. So it didn't work out. But that rang bells in the streets. I'm super proud of what it did.

When you heard "Trinidadian Girl" riding along the street and people were thinking it's Slick Rick, they were like, "Who? What?!" It was validation. It felt incredible to be able to have people appreciate and stand in line for your stuff.

RON G

Youngest in Charge: A New Blend King Reigns Supreme

"Yes indeed, New York City!" Harlem-bred DJ Ron G, also known affectionately as "The Mix King," came on the mixtape scene in the early '90s, picking up where guys like Kid Capri and Brucie B started. And one of his most notable contributions were his full-blown blend tapes, containing nothing but songs that took beats and vocals from two or more different records, start to finish. And the way these Ron G tapes would blend R&B vocals with hip-hop beats would go on to influence what would soon-after be known as "the remix."

INSPIRATION

Ron G: I grew up on 155th Street and 8th Avenue in Harlem. They used to have battle jams across the street in Rucker Park. I used to see DJ Smalls and Wiz Rob battle, one was on one side of the park, one was on the other side of the park. That was my first experience seeing DJs live. I think I was like 16 at that time.

When I heard Red Alert on 98.7 KISS, and Marley Marl on 107.5 FM, that blew me away. I was listening to Red Alert and how he used to scratch, and I said, "Damn, I wanna be a DJ." And Marley Marl was a DJ and a producer, and he used to always play Juice Crew and new music like that. And that inspired me and amped me up to want to be a DJ, and go out there and turn the turntables into an instrument.

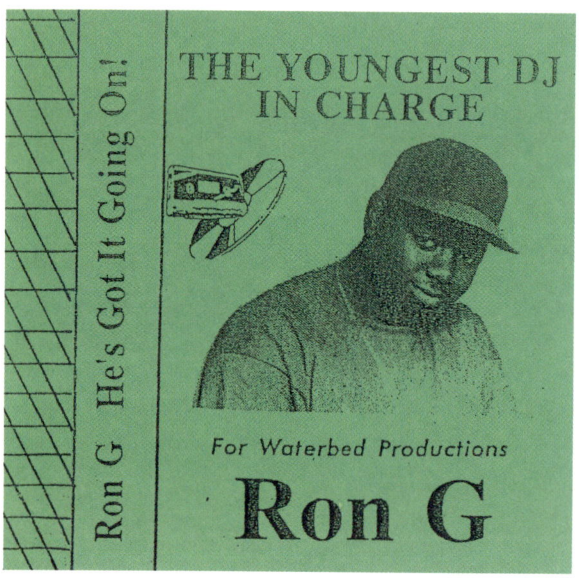

"Raw" by Big Daddy Kane, Eric B. and Rakim's "Eric B. Is President," "I Got it Made" by Special Ed, Chubb Rock's "Treat 'Em Right"–a lot of records at that time were inspirational, and made me wanna be playing the music in the clubs and on the tapes and all that.

FIRST DJ SET-UP

I got my first set-up when I started taking the DJ thing more seriously. My step-pops got me two turntables, and I got my mixer, and I would sit in the crib and practice every day until I felt like I could do the cuts that Red Alert was doing. Once I got them cuts, I said, "Okay, I'm a DJ. I'm ready."

FIRST MIXTAPE

My first tape that got around was *Mixes #1* aka *Blendz #1*. It had R&B on it like Michael Jackson, because I'm a huge Michael Jackson fan. RIP. Shout out to the family. And I would take loops of different Michael Jackson records and put a beat behind it. Then I'd take another acapella and put it in there. And that concept got me recognition on the mixtape circuit, as well as in the music industry. That helped people recognize me.

It had some songs on it that hadn't come out yet. A lot of times, we got test presses before the music came out. Tevin Campbell, Color Me Badd's "I Wanna Sex You Up," and different reggae songs and break beats that I would mess around with.

BLENDS

I heard various DJs doing blends at that time. I remember one time, I heard Kid Capri do a blend. I heard E. Bros do a blend. But I wanted to do something a little different. So I'd take the R&B songs that my mom had in her room–which would be Michael Jackson, Lou Rawls, Diana Ross, The Temptations–and I would take those on cassette, put them into my cassette player, play it, turn the bass all the way down, and then play a beat behind it. And people would be like, "Ohh!" That gave those songs a little more recognition for the hip-hop crowd. They might not have known Lou Rawls, but when they heard him on that hip-hop beat, that made them look into him, and also me as well.

In those days, you didn't have acapellas. So we had to use whatever creativity we could. We took the bass out, the mids out, and tried to keep the vocals in there somehow.

BREAK BEATS

When you go in the record stores and see the breakbeats, they'd have the listings on them, like "Bust A Break." And half of the time, you wouldn't know what they mean. But you knew it had beats on it.

I would buy the breakbeats, put a beat behind an R&B song, and next thing you know, people were going crazy, like, "Oh shit, this is hot!" Now, you'd probably recognize the breaks if you heard them because they've been used so much. Shout out to Mark the 45 King!

RECORDING

When I was still learning, I would use four cassette tape decks. I had one to play the cassettes that I had for the songs I didn't have on vinyl. I had two other cassette decks to make the copies, and I had another to record from one cassette deck to the other, with the mixer hooked up to the turntables.

That way, if I'm playing one song on a cassette deck, and two turntables, I could have the acapella playing, the beat on one turntable, then I could switch a second beat on the other turntable. And I could mess with the quality of the music because the cassette was coming from a whole different source than the mixer. At that time, we had little mixers that didn't have all that 25 different channel EQ and all shit on it. It was just Line 1 and Line 2, let's go.

SHOUT OUTS AND GETTING HEARD

I would duplicate the tapes myself, and then go to the nearest gas station. Some guys we would give it to, some for the girls, some we would try to get a dollar or two. But mainly, it was just about spreading your music and getting it out there before you even got a dollar out of it. Getting it played in the cars, that was my goal. If I can have ten cars drive by me while I'm outside between 3 and 6 p.m., then I'm accomplished. That will help me get a show.

A lot of the hustlers were supportive. They'd be like, "Yo, make me a tape, man!" So I'd make them a tape, and they'd show it to their crew and their girls. "Yo Ron said my name, check this out–'My man in the black BMW with the Porsche kit!'"

WBLS

When I first started on the radio, I was in high school. That came after I started making mixtapes. In those days, the cassettes were how you would create your fan base. And because I had created a huge fan base from doing the cassettes with the hip hop and R&B blends, I think after the whole blend collection, like *Mixes 6* or *7*, WBLS reached out and was like, "We want you on our station."

THE REMIX

Puff and Andre Harrell would call me down to Uptown Records, and ask me to bring my cassette tapes and stuff like that. I can't take nothing away from Puff though. He's brilliant, talented, smart. It's just that at a young age, I created a sound that was so popular amongst the urban markets, that anything coming out that was similar to that sound, you had to have already listened to the format I formed.

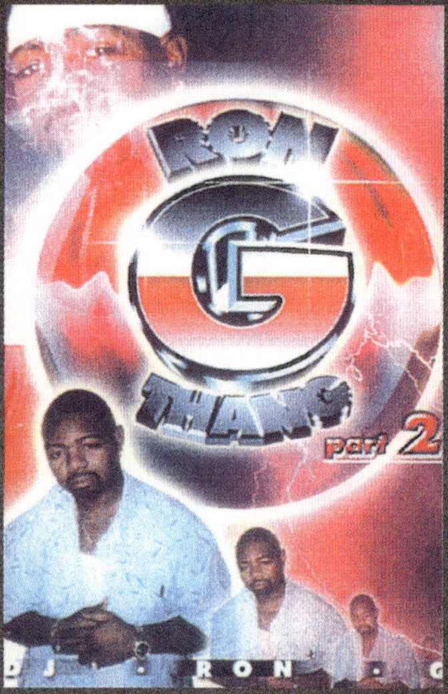
RON G THANG
part 2
DJ RON G

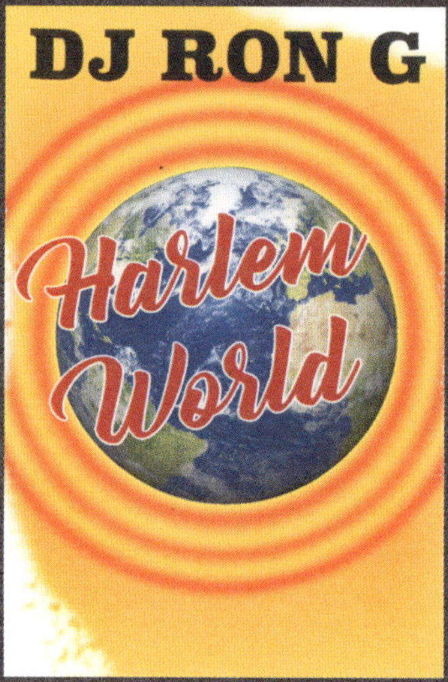
DJ RON G
Harlem World

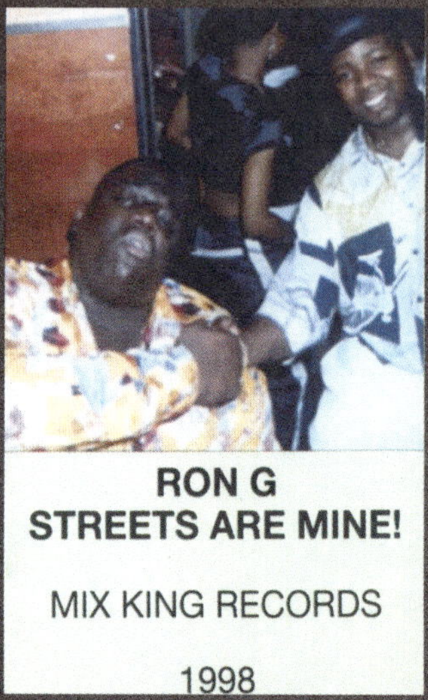
RON G
STREETS ARE MINE!
MIX KING RECORDS
1998

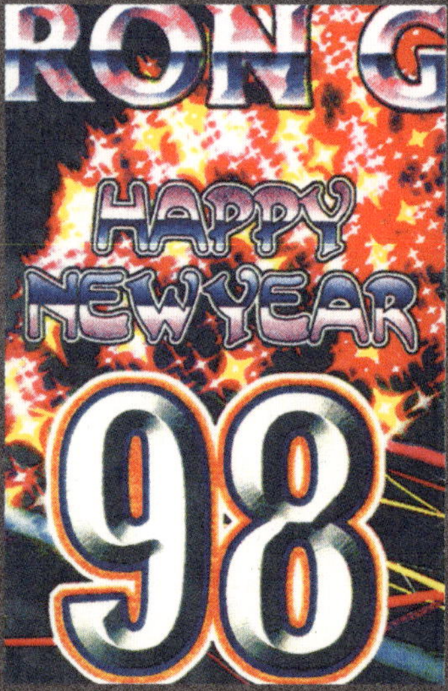
RON G
HAPPY NEW YEAR
98

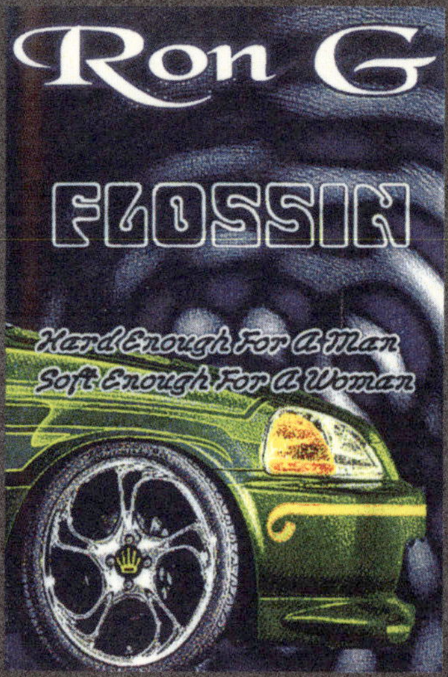
Ron G
FLOSSIN
Hard Enough For A Man
Soft Enough For A Woman

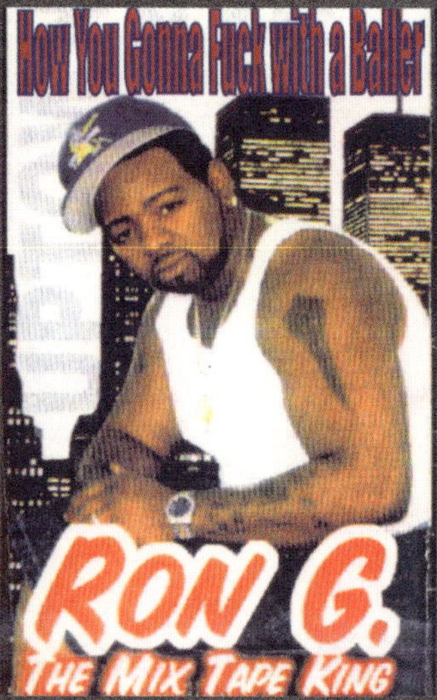
How You Gonna Fuck with a Baller
RON G.
THE MIX TAPE KING

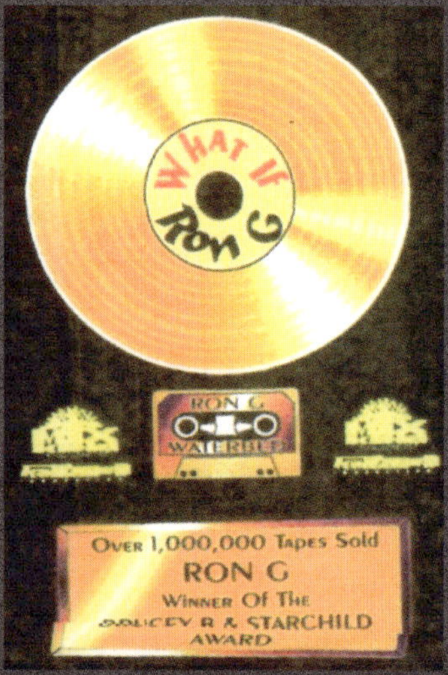
WHAT IF
Ron G
Over 1,000,000 Tapes Sold
RON G
Winner Of The
AWARD

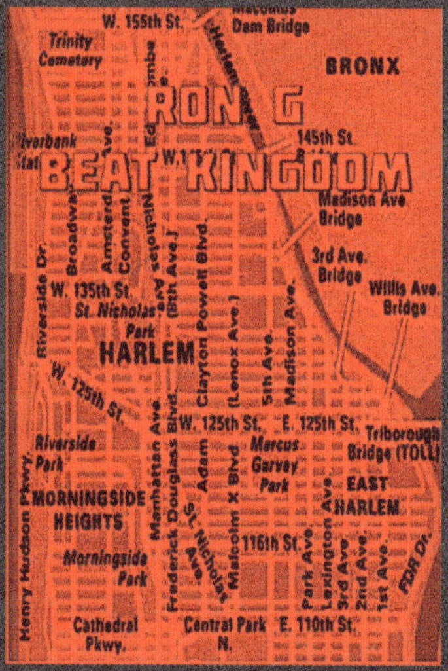
RON G
BEAT KINGDOM
W. 155th St.
BRONX
145th St.
Madison Ave. Bridge
3rd Ave. Bridge
Willis Ave. Bridge
W. 135th St.
HARLEM
W. 125th St.
E. 125th St.
Triborough Bridge (TOLL)
Marcus Garvey Park
EAST HARLEM
MORNINGSIDE HEIGHTS
Morningside Park
116th St.
Cathedral Pkwy.
Central Park N.
E. 110th St.
Henry Hudson Pkwy.
Riverside Dr.
Broadway
Amsterdam Ave.
Convent Ave.
St. Nicholas Ave.
Frederick Douglass Blvd.
Adam Clayton Powell Blvd.
Malcolm X Blvd.
Lenox Ave.
5th Ave.
Madison Ave.
Park Ave.
Lexington Ave.
3rd Ave.
2nd Ave.
1st Ave.
FDR Dr.

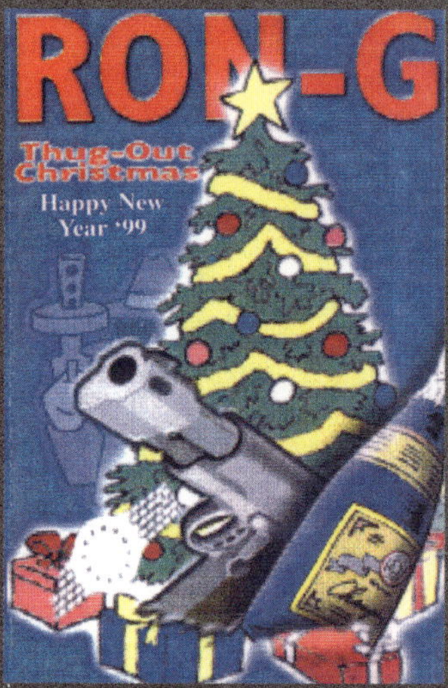
RON-G
Thug-Out Christmas
Happy New Year '99

"Peace to Ron G, Brucie B, Kid Capri, Funkmaster Flex, Lovebug Starski."

—THE NOTORIOUS B.I.G. "JUICY"

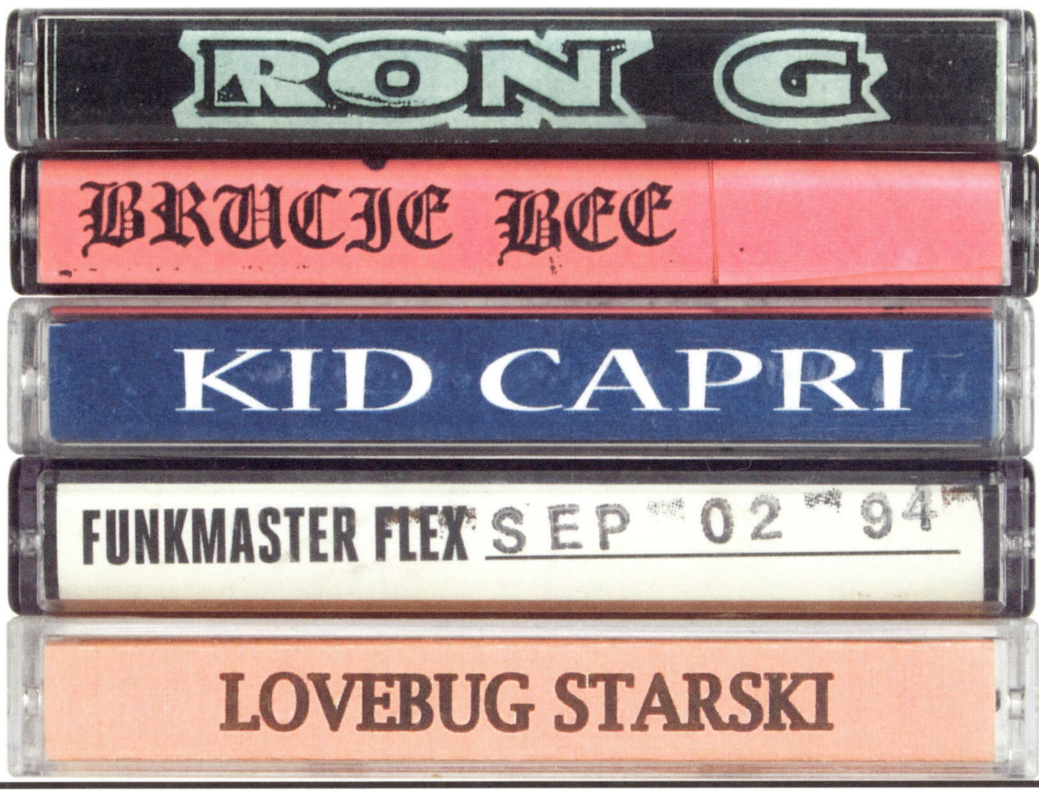

Whether they were laying down a verse for his tape or shouting out his name on their tape, the biggest MCs in the Big Apple during the '90s always showed the utmost respect to Ron G.

THE NOTORIOUS B.I.G.

Ron G: B.I.G. was my friend. He used to come to my crib all the time. He used to always tell me that me and Lil' Cease looked alike. So he already had a certain love for me, because I was like a chubbier Lil' Cease.

When B.I.G. said my name on "Juicy," it made me feel important. He could've mentioned so many other DJs. But for some reason, I was in his heart. It meant a lot to me. It showed not only that he was cool with me, but that he appreciated what I was doing in the hip-hop game. It showed me that I meant something to him.

B.I.G. was brilliant. He would always come to my house, and talk about how he wanted to be rich. Like, "Yo, the nigga Puff, he about to sign a nigga, G." And was like, "Yo, that's what's up!"

At first, you might not have known, because his lyrics were so dark! Like, "Damn, who the fuck you been talking to?! Where you living, in a cemetery twenty-four hours a day?" But that was his state of mind. Like, "Damn, who gonna keep a shotty in the shower while he's shitting?!"

But then, when he got around Puff, he cleaned him up, and he started to see the values of different kinds of music. So at that time, you might not have known what B.I.G. would become, but you knew that lyrically he was not a joke. His speech was dope. He had a twist of Jamaican in him, speaking that fly slang.

I had Biggie on my song "Stop The Break." First, I had KRS-One come up. Then I had Biggie. Then I had Raekwon and Killa Sin come up. Then I put O.C. on there, because he was a part of that whole Diamond D, D.I.T.C. era, and I liked that whole era, too. I was trying to showcase the top rappers at that time that were coming, and that were already hot.

I remember B.I.G. was asking me to play him some beats, for either his album or for Lil' Cease and the Junior M.A.F.I.A. album. And he said he liked two beats that I gave him, and he wanted to use them for himself. He was like, "I really want 'em. Hold 'em."

Then after a while, he said, "You know what? I'm gonna pay you out of my pocket because I don't think Puff is gonna purchase the tracks." So I said, "Okay cool." And that kind of helped me get the Trinity and the MPC60. And when I got those two machines, I did "We Thuggin'" for Fat Joe and took him platinum.

2PAC

B.I.G. was always coming to my house, and he would always tell me about this kid he liked named 2Pac. That was his homie. He was like, "Yo, Pac's letting me open up for him. Why don't y'all come support me?" And the club I think we went to was called The Country Club, on 86th Street between 2nd and 3rd. I really was down there to see B.I.G. perform, and I wound up meeting 2Pac. And I was like, "Man, 'Brenda's Got a Baby,' and 'Keep Ya Head Up,' this kid is dope." I was a fat dude wishing I had tattoos, like, "Damn, I gotta get skinny." Pac was the man. I was fascinated with his image.

Me and my mans ran up on him and were like, "Yo Pac, we're true fans. Is there any way we can get you on a Ron G tape?" And he was like, "Man, I heard of you through my nigga Biggie!" At that time, he was from New York, but he was still running in Baltimore and L.A. and all that shit. But he was a fan of what I was doing, and what I was doing for other rappers.

One day he called me, like, "Yo G." Then he called my manager like, "Yo, I'm in town. Where y'all niggas at?" He gave him the address like, "Come up." Ten minutes later, he knocked on my door. He had four dudes with him—Stretch, and three other dudes I didn't know. And he was like, "Make me a beat, man." After a while that was my thing.

And then he came on there like, "I'm trying to be strong, they

Ron G. – DEAD PRESIDENTS!!

Side A.

Ron G - Intro
It's A Struggle - feat WBC AllStars
Got My Mind Made Up - Tupac
Shadow Boxing - GZA feat Method Man
Dead President's - Jay Z
Lady (Remix) D'Angelo feat AZ
NoMore Games - Skindeep feat Lil Kim (Mix with Horace Brown)
Renee - Lost Boyz
Suspended in Time - Group Home
Funkorama - Redman
Live & Die for Hip Hop - Kriss Kross
Keep On Keep On - MC LYTE feat Escape

Side B

R Kelly - Intro + Who Can I Run To (Remix)
No More Pain - Tupac
Monifa - Come Home (Remix) feat AZ
Rafael Saadiq - "Ask of You" mix with N.Y. N.Y. N.Y.
Remmington Steele - Ron G H&K Funk Mix
Tasha - I Like it "Remix"
Motherless Child - Ghost Face Killer
Can't be Wasting My Time - Mona Lisa feat Lost Boyz
No One Else (Remix) - Total feat Da Brat etc.
Killing Me Softly - Fugees
Shout Out Mix
Still Shinin - Mobb Deep
Celebration - Truce feat It's Alive
Bambi - Lettin Niggaz Know. (Video Version)

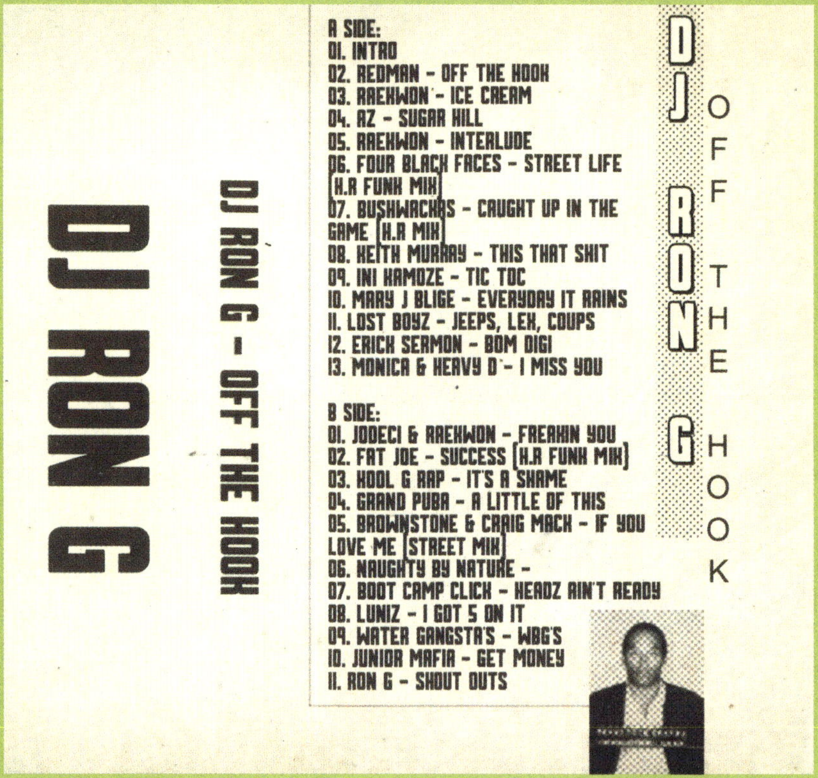

sending Armies out to bomb me/ Listen to Ron, the only DJ that can calm me." After that, I was like, "Whooo!" And that ended up being on the Big L joint "Deadly Combination."

After that, he was like, "Yo yo G, I'm out." And I was seeing him on the phone a little bit, but I wasn't really paying attention because I was trying to mix the beat real quick so he could take it. And at two o'clock in the morning, I was looking at the news, and I seen that he was shot at Quad Studios. And I was shaken by that, like, "Damn, I hope he knows I had nothing to do with that, because I love Pac and The Outlawz." It was a crazy time in my life.

Then two weeks later, I ran into The Outlawz in Jersey, and they were like, "Yo, 2Pac knows you ain't got nothing to do with it. Pac sends his love." So I was like, "Okay," and I felt free from that. I wouldn't hurt my nigga for nothing. I'm a true fan, and I'm as real as I can be, too. It's a blessing. It made me a part of history, though, in my own unique way. I had police knocking on my door for like three weeks straight, like, "Do you know anything?" I'm like, "Nah. I don't know. I'm just making beats."

I put a 2Pac song out maybe three weeks after, because I was still kind of shook behind that. I was like, "Damn, I don't want people feeling some type of way. Let me wait until I get a response." Then once The Outlawz said that, I was like, "Alright, cool." After that, I knew I was meant for more than just doing beats. I was meant to be a part of this hip-hop history. And that's when I started saying, "Let me do creative things, more than just mixtapes."

NAS

"Ron G's in the cassette deck, rockin' the shit G." Being a fan of Nas too, when I heard Nas say that, I was like, "Damn, Nas listens to my shit, too!?" It just felt good. Shout out to the homie Nas. But after a while, when so many people say your name in songs, you know you mean something to hip hop. I felt like this is where I belong, because everybody knows it now. It was always a blessing to me.

It's always challenging to keep the younger generation aware of what you're doing. But they do recognize me from that, like, "Yo, that's the kid Nas was talking about! Yo G been in the game, yo!" It helps.

JAY-Z

Dame Dash is from Harlem, so I knew him for a long time. They were just young brothers trying to come up in the business, create their sound, and get their label going. I remember them reaching out a couple times. For me, it was always fun. I would take the stuff and be like, "Aiight!"

I was working on a tape called *Dead Presidents*, because I had seen the movie. And that was slang for money. So when I made that cassette, I was saying, "This is money right here," not realizing that Jay-Z had come out with a song called "Dead Presidents" too.

That was my first time meeting Jay-Z and Dame Dash, because they actually brought me the record. They came to the radio station when I was on WBLS. I was inspired by that energy, and to help people be seen and heard. Any way I could help the culture, I was down for it.

Once I had the record, I was like, "Oh, this is perfect!" That's when I shouted on the song, "Niggas ain't fuckin' with this shit right here!" The song was hot, the tape was hot, and he was happy. Everything formatted together.

DMX

One time, Dee and Waah brought DMX to my studio, and he didn't have the deal with Irv Gotti at Def Jam yet. They were trying to get him the deal, but he needed to be heard. So they were like, "Ron, cook up a beat for us, and let X spit this 16, man." And that's what I would do for them. It was a beat you never heard, and it was like, "X, spit that." And boom, it's a Ron G exclusive. That's how I created my exclusives at that time. I had them come to the crib and do something that wasn't already out there.

REDMAN

Redman is a very unique hip-hop artist. Down to earth, cool as hell. I used to do parties in Jersey, and I remember when he first came in the game. He was so dope.

I did the beat for his *Off The Hook* freestyle. And he killed that. Smoked the whole crib out and did it. He heard the beat and was just like, "Yo press record."

He set the tone for the street rappers with that one, like, "Yo Redman is nice." Because it was freestyle, all off the head. He's nice at freestyling, so it was not a problem for him. He went in.

RON G'S 5 STEPS TO MAKING A PERFECT BLEND

The Mix King breaks it down.

1. YOU NEED A HOT BEAT - When I do a blend, most times I try to choose the beat first. And the beat gotta be hot. You want something that's outstanding, and nothing too noisy. Don't choose a beat with a whole bunch of horns and sounds.
2. YOU GOTTA USE A FAMILIAR ACAPELLA - Make sure it's clean, and also that it's a song people have heard before. Like if I scrolled through my acapella list, and I see Mya, a song that people don't remember, and Beyonce--I'm only gonna choose Beyonce or Mya.
3. MAKE SURE IT'S ON TIME - You can't have an acapella that's flying and not on speed with the beat. Now with Serato and the digital tools, it's a little easier. But you can't just go with the speed and just match 95 with 95. Sometimes that doesn't work, depending on the acapella. It might speed up and slow down in different parts. So I just try to be creative and match it up as best I can. But the timing has to match.
4. THE KEYS NEED TO MATCH - The key of the acapella and the beat have to match. It has to somewhat sound like it's in the same key range. I do it all by ear. Some people have the worst ear. I listen to some blends and I'm like, "What was he thinking?!" It just has to match. Sometimes it doesn't even have to be in the same key, it just gotta sound good. When I started producing, the A&Rs would tell me, "Yo G, this sounds good, but it's not in key." So I sat down and started learning. Because coming from the blend world, we go by what sounds good, but it's not necessarily in key. Some DJs got that ear, where they're like, "Yo, this is perfect."
5. BUILD UP THE EXCITEMENT - On the tape, you gotta build up the hype before the blend comes in, like I'd say in the first four or eight bars. You gotta talk, or scratch--do something that's gonna make people say, "Oh, I can't wait to hear what's coming." I usually start with the beat, but sometimes I might start with the acapella because I don't know what I'm gonna put with it yet. I'll be more experimental. But if you already know your set, you can start with either one.

DJ DOGGTIME

The Borough of Blends: Queens Got the Skills

Queens DJs contributed so much to the mixtape game during its formative years in the late '80s and '90s. And one of the borough's most prolific contributors was DJ Doggtime. A master of the blend who learned his chops studying Queens DJ legends like Grandmaster Vic, Doggtime put out dozens of mixtapes during his illustrious run. And at the heart of them all were his impeccable blends.

MIXTAPE BEGINNINGS

Doggtime: I always loved music, even starting back to church singing in the choirs. My father had his quartet groups, my brothers played instruments, so music has always been in the house.

My boy Verne let me hold his equipment. Me and my boy Sean went to Verne's house to battle him and his friend. I was trying to do blends. Everybody liked the idea of what I was trying to do, but I just couldn't do it. It wouldn't stay. This was like the summer of '87.

By the winter of '87–Christmas break–I asked Verne to borrow his equipment. I spent pretty much that whole recess just in the house and trying to learn how to DJ. Within about 4 to 6 weeks, I got the hang of it.

GRANDMASTER VIC AND DJ IRV

Grandmaster Vic is a Queens legend, but he's a worldwide legend. Any DJ from Queens comes from Grandmaster Vic, we all learned from him. He could do his tricks and stuff, but the blends, rocking the R&B, and knowing how to bring records in–everybody learned from Vic tapes.

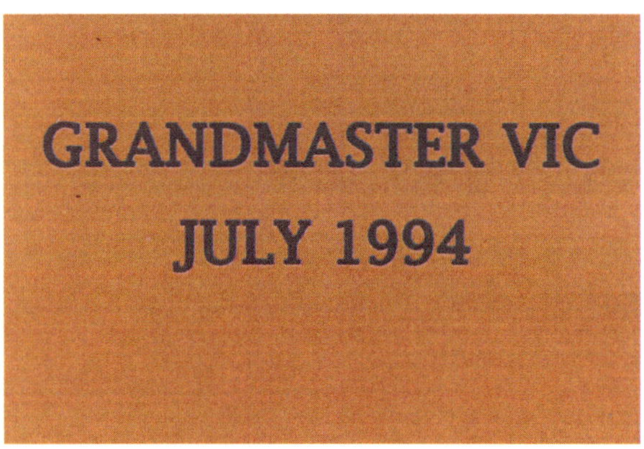

Also, what a lot of people don't realize is Irv Gotti was a DJ back then. So DJ Irv had his collection of tapes out as well. Going into high school, we had our Vic tapes and we had our Irv tapes. Everyone was listening to these tapes. So you would try to emulate what these guys were doing.

DEVELOPING A STYLE

I was in a sneaker store, and they were playing my tape. I'm listening and I'm like, "Yo, that's my tape!" The guy was trying to tell me that it's a Vic tape. I'm like, "No! That's my tape!"

I started listening and I said, "You know what, I sound too much like this guy because I've been listening to him for so long and studying him so much." I had to immediately stop getting tapes from him and really start working on my own thing. From that point, that's when I really started to grow as a DJ.

My main thing was always blends, I was never one for scratching. I was just never really that good at it. So many people were worried about the scratching. With blends, I found my niche. I took records and I'd see what matched. It's not only what sounds good together. For me, it was what felt good together.

FINDING ACAPELLAS

Back then, if the acapella wasn't available, you weren't getting it from the label. They did begin to press acapellas but they didn't sound that great. There would be bootleg acapellas and instrumentals, so you kind of get your hands on one or two of those to help you out.

RECORDING PROCESS

The biggest challenge, which I don't think people could do now, was making a whole side of a tape straight–no 4-track, no computer, no nothing. Just wax and turntables and you're doing blends. You have to make sure you bring the songs in and out at the right time, and if you mess up, you're doing the whole side over.

I'd lay the records out. I would have them stacked on the turntables, ready to go. Now, you gotta remember the pitches and stuff like that. Because even if you have the pitch written down, you still have to be on point. So if you write down the pitch as plus or minus one, it could be a hair different. Little things like that.

You also have to know the volume of it because now you're blending songs. I got Glenn Jones "At Last" and I got Biz Markie "Make The Music," but you have to know where to put those volume levels also. So you're doing a mixdown while you're blending. There was a whole lot going on back then.

Most of them I would nail. The thing that used to catch me was when the needle would skip. Other than that, I was pretty good.

SPREADING THE WORD

The barbershop Cutty's I was going to started selling my tapes. Freddy was the barber. I used to get my name in my head–Doggtime. That's it. Cutty's was the first one. Then Hot Watts on the Ave–it was Hot Watts before it was Hot Waxx. Paul was the guy. They were selling my tapes, and then it started getting out slowly, adding one store at a time.

Of course during the summer in Queens, you'd hear people driving by and playing music and things like that. I used to have my name on my license plates. I had to cut that out. I used to get stopped all the time. It was all love, but I had to take them off. "I can't get stopped by people like this." It was always love, though. Everyone always had a story about how the tape was cool.

DOGGTIME'S 5 RECORDS THAT ALWAYS HIT WITH A BLEND

1. The Gap Band - "We Can Make It Alright"
2. Stephanie Mills - "Something in the Way (You Make Me Feel)"
3. Alexander O'Neal - "You Were Meant to Be My Lady (Not My Girl)"
4. Channel 2 - "In Debt To You"
5. Mary J. Blige - "Be Happy"

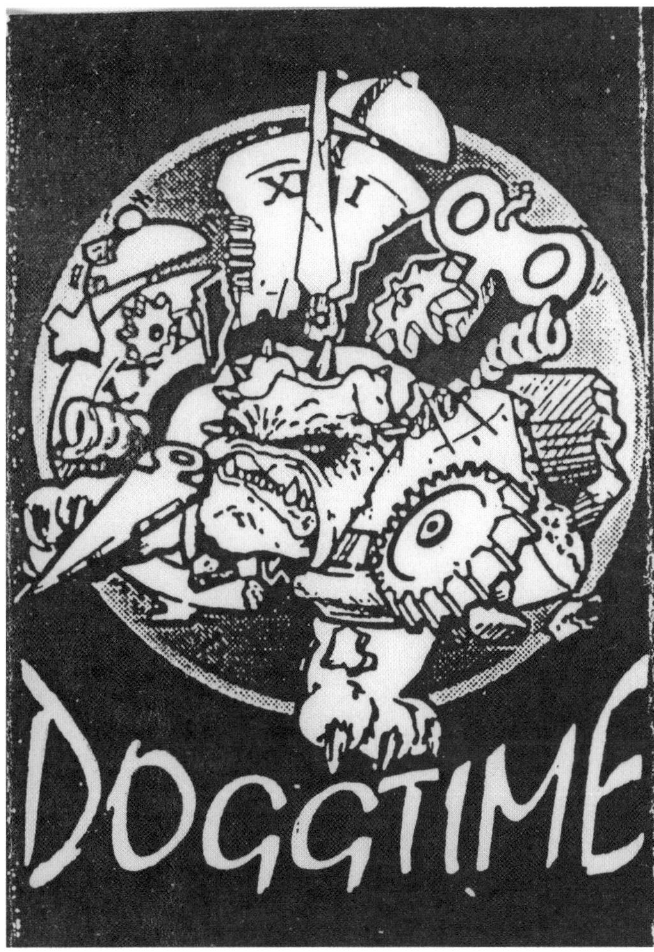

CHILL WILL FROM THE EASTSIDE

Flava in Ya Ear: Making "Masterpeaces" with the Fam

Chill Will From The East Side's name was well-respected across Harlem and throughout the boroughs for his consistency. He created a mixtape movement with his Fruit Flava fam, blending different styles of music with hip hop to create a unique listening experience for the tape-copping audience. And much of that innovation stemmed from his knowledge and early use of production equipment during the mixtape-making process.

DJ BACKGROUND

Chill Will: Jefferson Projects had a cul de sac next to a basketball court, and the older guys would DJ. That's when I was starting, like '89 or so. They used to have everything taped off.

Back in the day, I had to have my family help me. I had a little side gig, a job to get my equipment. I was one of the few DJs using the 6-track multi-tape. It was a Sansui dual cassette recorder where you could actually record into it and then the other side would master it.

I was doing production as well–I had artists. That's when I started creating my own mixtapes. I was actually an artist as well, I wrote and produced songs on the intros.

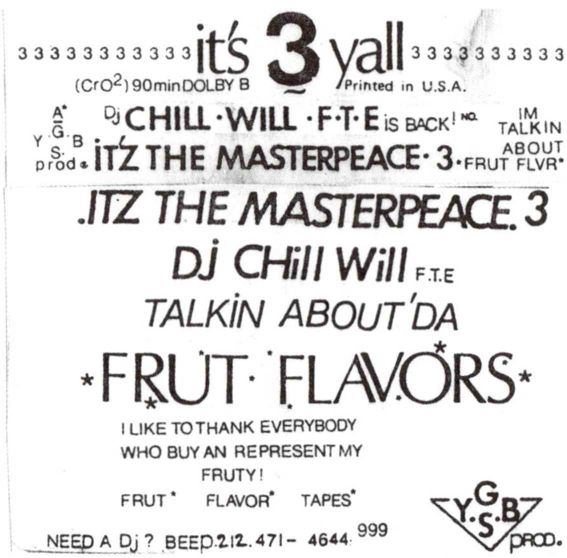

I was working with local talent at that time, recording and doing stuff with them. For instance, Black Rob, may he Rest In Peace, I still have the tracks from back then. Before he even got signed, he was doing his thing and I put something together for him. G. Dep, I had tracks with Loon–anybody from Harlem. Big L, may he Rest In Peace, he was on a track. I had the greats on there. I wouldn't say they started with me, but I was doing freestyles for people and I was also DJing.

If anybody knew me and they were involved, the story they always would tell back then was I was ahead of my time. They'd say, "That guy was futuristic." I just loved what I was doing and I was a creator.

STORY BEHIND THE NAME

In New York City, there's two DJ Chill Wills. I always give it up, too. Shout out Chill Will from the Get Fresh Crew and Doug E. Fresh. A lot of people get the two confused, so that's why I added "From The Eastside" at the end of DJ Chill Will. The other Chill Will was on the West Side.

It was funny, I went to one of his jams one time at the YMCA, and I had my entourage with me. I went there to support them and they were like, "This is the real Chill Will," going back and forth. It was all fun and games, but it was to the point where people didn't know who was who.

FRUT FLAVA FAM

I had my brother and sister actually on the cassettes. I had artists and people from the neighborhood, too. So I said, "You know what? Let's just call this 'The Frut Flava Fam.'" It's like a tongue twister, but it became popular. It stems from the different flavors of music I put on the cassette and the different freestyles and collaborations with artists.

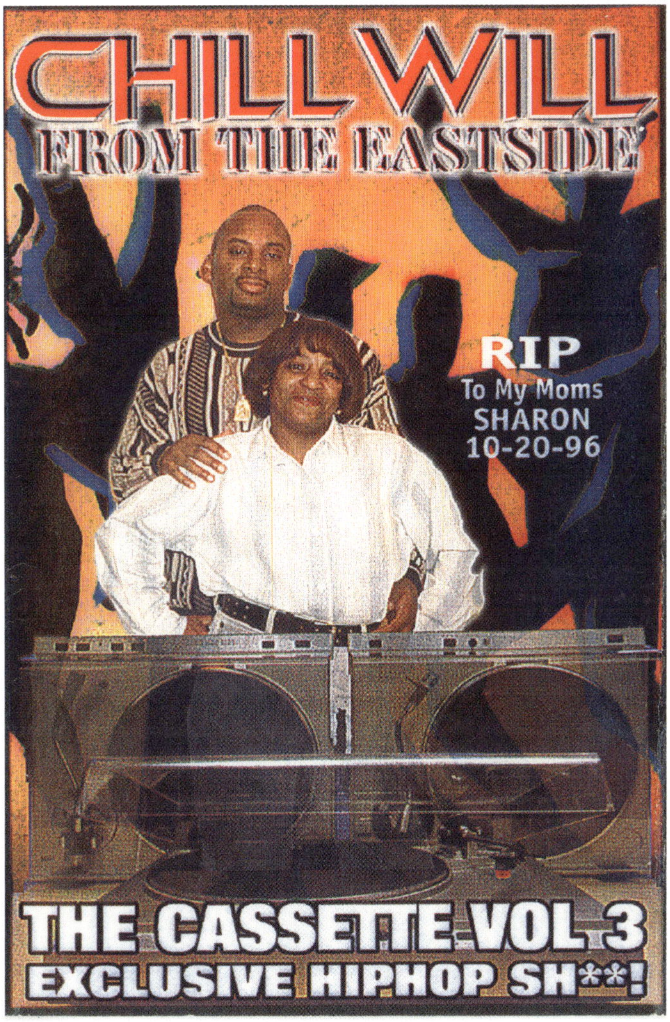

PROCESS OF CREATING BLENDS

There weren't too many 12-inch records that had the actual acapella on it. The trick to it was to EQ it. I had a good ear and a good way of blending the two together with the beats. I don't know, it's hard to explain. You had to have an ear. It's an art. It's like working at the mixing board–not everybody can't really mix, there's a certain ear you have to have.

The trick was to EQ it and then my thing that set me apart was my ad-libbing. People know Kid Capri–that's an MC, where he could control the crowd. I did that with the mixtapes with the ad-libs, "Aiiight!" and "here we go!" or "get fruity." I would captivate the people with the ad-libs.

My grandfather always used to listen to Coltrane, Dizzy Gillespie, different jazz. I grew up listening to jazz in the basement, he had a whole record collection. It stems from that I guess, just listening to different music. It helped me through mixing and blending.

PROMO

Back in the '80s and '90s, nobody really knew about promo. It was just my work ethic that made me become successful at it. I used to put my name on flyers–DJ Chill Will from the Eastside. I would go to the store and ask them, "Can I tape this on your window?"

At first, the main store I would go to was a beauty salon. I would ask if they'd mind playing my mixtape in the store. If people liked it, "Here goes ten tapes." Now, these are places that are not music stores, but these are places that people go to, like the supermarket.

I would also go into the buildings and slide flyers under people's doors. When I think about it now, that's insane. I went to every apartment sliding a flyer under everybody's door. I got popular from that.

A SPECIAL DEDICATION

My mom was my inspiration, and I would always let her hear stuff. She was always a fan of what I did. Everyone's mom would always complain, "Turn that down!" She stuck it out with me. When she passed, I wanted to put her on the cover. A lot of people knew her in the neighborhood as well. They called her Lil' Sharon.

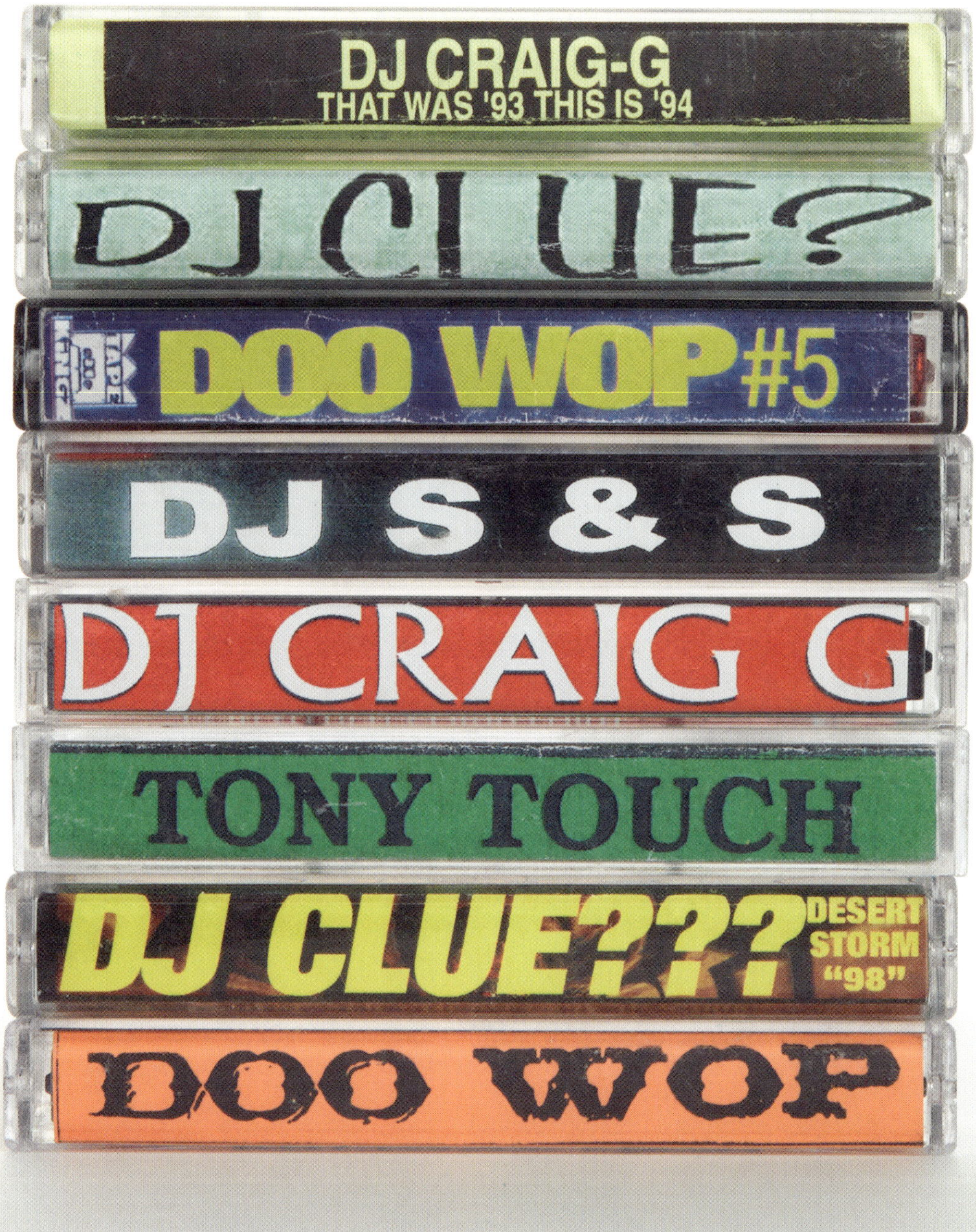
DJ CRAIG-G
THAT WAS '93 THIS IS '94
DJ CLUE?
DOO WOP #5
DJ S & S
DJ CRAIG G
TONY TOUCH
DJ CLUE???
DESERT STORM "98"
DOO WOP

THE EXCLUSIVES

At first, mixtape DJs earned recognition for the skills and techniques they displayed on their releases—from the cuts to the transitions to the blends. But in the early '90s, some mixtape DJs began to gain notoriety for the actual music they were playing, because it could only be found on their mixtape. Whether it was an early copy of a buzzworthy rapper's new single or B-side, or a freestyle that was recorded specifically for their tape, a crop of top DJs in NYC were changing the game with the full-fledged emergence of THE EXCLUSIVES.

DJ S&S

Put It On: Exclusives Infiltrate the Mixtape Game

Harlem's finest DJ S&S, aka DJ SNS, came up studying the greats that came before him like Brucie B and Kid Capri, before eventually becoming one of the greats himself. And beyond being one of the most energetic and exciting DJ voices and personalities in hip-hop history, his tapes were always in high demand because they continuously had the newest and hottest songs featured on them well before they were officially released.

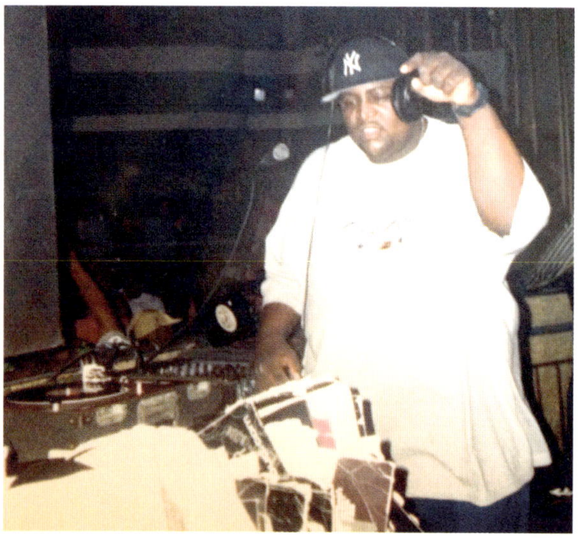

WORKING AT THE ROOFTOP

DJ S&S: I was only 15, listening to Brucie B Rooftop tapes. And then I got a job inside of Rooftop, putting on skates. I was interested in just watching the booth, I used to go through Brucie B's records. That's when I got introduced to "Computer Love," records like that, because I didn't know what those records were. That really put me on, being able to get into Rooftop at a young age, listening to Bruce DJing and watching him sell mixtapes.

"Droppin' Science," "Raw," "This Not for the Radio," "Small Time Hustler"–he played a lot of old school rap. But a lot of '80s R&B. Meli'sa Morgan "Fool's Paradise" was like Rooftop's anthem. He played another Meli'sa Morgan song called "Heartbreaking Decisions." He wasn't playing just the regular hits and singles, he was playing joints off the albums.

FIRST TAPES

I think in 1991, I started making tapes for my team on my block. My first one was called *218*. Nobody's tapes had names, it was all numbers. I was still working a regular job, doing my little tapes. Then the first tape I came out with in the store was *Old School #1*. It sounded just like Kid Capri's *Old School #1*. My first song was "Let's Get it On" by Marvin Gaye, that's how I started it off.

People started listening to me. I had a real hype voice, so that's what separated me. As Kid Capri's fame blew up, he became the icon he is. And Bruce was incarcerated, so it was Capri at that time. Then you had Triple C, Ron G, and them. I went to school with Ron. So I'm watching all these guys, and I'm trying to be different than everybody else.

TALKING ON TAPES

I used to study Kid Capri and Bruce. The rule of talking was, "Never talk during the verse." The reason people said that they hated when DJs talked is because niggas used to talk through the verse. Like, you're riding in the car vibing, and a motherfucker starts shouting out niggas during a verse? So I just made sure I stayed with the hook, and during the verse, I'll do like a "Yeah!" or "Come on!" to enhance your enjoyment. I'm hyping you.

Then I'll bring it back, like, "Oh, this record right here is crazy!! DJ S&S!! Come on!!" I'm treating it like it's a party, at all times. That's how I always wanted it to be. That's one thing I learned from Kid and Bruce. I want you to be groovin' like you're right there in front of me, and you're watching me.

Buckwild and EZ Elpee used to tell me, "You gotta start playing exclusives, stuff that no one's ever heard. You can't play the same records everybody else got."

EXCLUSIVES

I used to be in the Bronx a lot with Buckwild and EZ Elpee. I was really involved with the Diggin' In The Crates movement. Showbiz & A.G. and Party Arty–God bless the dead.

Buckwild and EZ Elpee used to tell me, "You gotta start playing exclusives, stuff that no one's ever heard. You can't play the same records everybody else got." They were doing it on their mixtapes, but they weren't as big as we were. So when I started, I took that shit to another level, because no one was really doing it.

Kid used to do it, but Kid was Kid. When he stopped doing mixtapes, he left that lane wide open. I was always at the labels, I had relationships with a lot of people, so niggas threw me records. Then shit just started going.

My hand-to-hand combat was so great in the streets, so niggas fucked with me. I used to be in the projects in Harlem, the Bronx. I'd go to Queens, I used to be in Yonkers, in White Plains. I used to be everywhere. I'd be dolo, or me and my man. And I played ball in a lot of places. And you know, when you play ball with a lot of cats, you form relationships. And I was killing parties. That really helped with the mixtapes a lot, too.

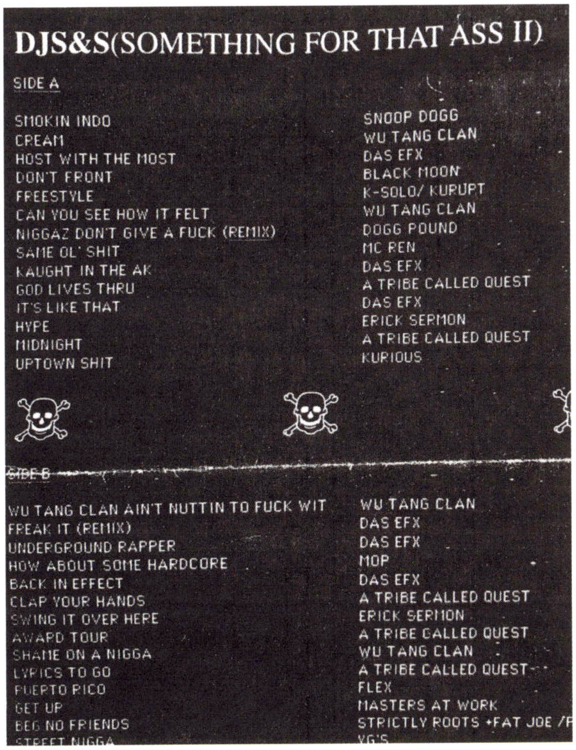

DJS&S(SOMETHING FOR THAT ASS II)

SIDE A

SMOKIN INDO	SNOOP DOGG
CREAM	WU TANG CLAN
HOST WITH THE MOST	DAS EFX
DON'T FRONT	BLACK MOON
FREESTYLE	K-SOLO/ KURUPT
CAN YOU SEE HOW IT FELT	WU TANG CLAN
NIGGAZ DON'T GIVE A FUCK (REMIX)	DOGG POUND
SAME OL' SHIT	MC REN
KAUGHT IN THE AK	DAS EFX
GOD LIVES THRU	A TRIBE CALLED QUEST
IT'S LIKE THAT	DAS EFX
HYPE	ERICK SERMON
MIDNIGHT	A TRIBE CALLED QUEST
UPTOWN SHIT	KURIOUS

SIDE B

WU TANG CLAN AIN'T NUTTIN TO FUCK WIT	WU TANG CLAN
FREAK IT (REMIX)	DAS EFX
UNDERGROUND RAPPER	DAS EFX
HOW ABOUT SOME HARDCORE	MOP
BACK IN EFFECT	DAS EFX
CLAP YOUR HANDS	A TRIBE CALLED QUEST
SWING IT OVER HERE	ERICK SERMON
AWARD TOUR	A TRIBE CALLED QUEST
SHAME ON A NIGGA	WU TANG CLAN
LYRICS TO GO	A TRIBE CALLED QUEST
PUERTO RICO	FLEX
GET UP	MASTERS AT WORK
BEG NO FRIENDS	STRICTLY ROOTS +FAT JOE /F
STREET NIGGA	YG'S

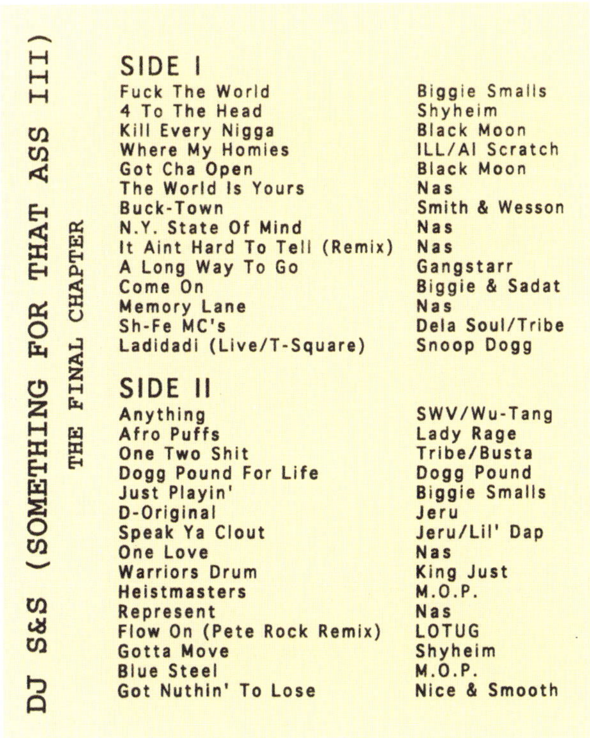

DJ S&S (SOMETHING FOR THAT ASS III)

THE FINAL CHAPTER

SIDE I

Fuck The World	Biggie Smalls
4 To The Head	Shyheim
Kill Every Nigga	Black Moon
Where My Homies	ILL/Al Scratch
Got Cha Open	Black Moon
The World Is Yours	Nas
Buck-Town	Smith & Wesson
N.Y. State Of Mind	Nas
It Aint Hard To Tell (Remix)	Nas
A Long Way To Go	Gangstarr
Come On	Biggie & Sadat
Memory Lane	Nas
Sh-Fe MC's	Dela Soul/Tribe
Ladidadi (Live/T-Square)	Snoop Dogg

SIDE II

Anything	SWV/Wu-Tang
Afro Puffs	Lady Rage
One Two Shit	Tribe/Busta
Dogg Pound For Life	Dogg Pound
Just Playin'	Biggie Smalls
D-Original	Jeru
Speak Ya Clout	Jeru/Lil' Dap
One Love	Nas
Warriors Drum	King Just
Heistmasters	M.O.P.
Represent	Nas
Flow On (Pete Rock Remix)	LOTUG
Gotta Move	Shyheim
Blue Steel	M.O.P.
Got Nuthin' To Lose	Nice & Smooth

S&S remembers obtaining and playing some of the most classic songs in hip-hop history on his mixtapes--early.

1. NAUGHTY BY NATURE "HIP HOP HOORAY"
I had "Hip Hop Hooray" a year before it came out. A nigga hit me off with a tape one day. I was chillin' at an industry party, and he was like, "Yo S&S, I got these Naughty songs. You want 'em?" I was like, "Oh shit, hell yeah!" So I played "Hip Hop Hooray." I forgot the tape number, it was in '92. That mixtape went everywhere. I was killin' 'em.

I had a beef with Treach after it came out. I got jumped at The Rink in Jersey. It was a learning experience. But I didn't understand the game back then. We squashed it the next day after, it almost got real crazy between us.

I was living in Jersey a while back, and we went to lunch one day and talked about it. He was like, "You gotta understand my nigga. What if somebody else would've done that record, taken that idea before the song officially came out?" And I understood, like, "Wow, you're right."

I kept going though. He was right about what he said, but at the time, I was young. What happened with the jumping is it enhanced me! Tommy Boy tried to take me off the shelves. But it was too late. They couldn't do a thing, because it wasn't in the stores. It wasn't legitimized. It was in tape spots, but by law, they couldn't do anything. You have a tape with one song on there with a whole bunch of other songs. There's no cover, there's no names, it's just a tape. You gotta sit there and find the song.

2. SNOOP DOGG "WHAT'S MY NAME?"
The first song had to be a song that no one was gonna have. And that's why I killed them that summer with *Something For Dat Ass*. "Deep Cover" had just dropped, and everybody was going crazy over Snoop Dogg. And I had "What's My Name?" two weeks after it came out, and no one had it. It wasn't clear at all. But the fucking streets did not care.

That summer, I was at a club in Harlem called Club 2000. And Dr. Dre and Snoop Dogg came to the club. I'm DJing, and I had the balls enough to give Snoop the mixtape. That's when the lists started. The nigga Snoop looked at the mixtape and saw Snoop Dogg "What's My Name?" He tapped Dr. Dre, and said, "He got 'What's My Name?'" Dre and them looked at me and said, "Who are you?!"

Real talk, I'll never forget this shit. The nigga Snoop looked at me and said, "Yo cuz, how'd you get this, cuz?" I said, "I'm in these streets." The nigga Snoop and Dre said, "Thank you. We appreciate you." They didn't care that the record leaked. It was the fact that a nigga from New York had a record that they were about to come out with in six months. This guy's first single. They shook my hand, bought me a drink, came in the booth for a minute, and broke out. There was no Instagram so I couldn't get any pictures or any shit like that, but it was a crazy moment. I can't front on that.

3. WU-TANG CLAN "PROTECT YA NECK"

I was walking on 134th Street and 8th Avenue at 7 o'clock at night. This nigga came running down, "Yo, you S&S right?" I'm like, "Yo, who are you?!" "I'm Ol' Dirty Bastard. Yo, niggas fuck with you! Here's this Wu-Tang shit. I need you to put this on your tape. I'm tellin' you, we about to blow!"

I'm like, "Wu-Tang?" He's like, "You don't know about us. Trust me, son." He gave me "Tearz," "Protect Ya Neck," and "M.E.T.H.O.D. Man." And I played all three of them shits.

Next thing you know, when "Protect Ya Neck" came out, it took the game by storm. They never forgot that. That's one thing I respect them for. RZA never forgets that. "Yo, you really showed us love."

4. CRAIG MACK "FLAVA IN YA EAR"

I remember I did a mixtape, I forgot the name of it, but I was about to put it out, end of '93. Puff Daddy rolls up on me with the 325 drop top, rims and everything. He goes, "Yo, you made your mixtape yet?" I was like, "Nah, I'm about to put it in the store right now." He's like, "I got this new Craig Mack, you gotta put it on your mixtape!" He played it in the car and said, "You got at least a week or two before I put this on the radio." I went back home, and did that whole shit over.

"Flava In Ya Ear." I had it before anyone even knew what it was. That shit hit the street, and was hot before Hot 97 had it.

5. THE NOTORIOUS B.I.G. FT. METHOD MAN "THE WHAT"

I was supposed to have B.I.G. on the tape. He was supposed to come to my house and give me a freestyle. We hung out the night before, we were in the club together. He said he had something to do, so he had to come to Midtown and he was gonna come to my house at about 9:30.

So I called him, and he was like, "Yo, I missed my appointment. After I left you I got more drunk. What you got over there?" I said, "I mean I got some records. I got the 'Fuck the World' and I got 'C'mon Motherfuckers.'" He's like, "Shit, what else you got?" I said, "Uh, that's about it, that's all I really have." He said, "Alright, play those. If Puff calls you, tell him I gave them to you."

I paid interns to steal for me. You were in that room and you hear something exclusive--they leave, "Here's $50 for you." That's how I got most of my exclusives back then. So when I had that, B.I.G. fucking laced me. He was making me hot in the streets.

That also was the mixtape I got in trouble for. I didn't know Nas' album had only ten songs, and I played "One Love," "Represent," "It Ain't Hard to Tell (Remix)," "Memory Lane," "The World is Yours," "N.Y. State of Mind." Shit, I was wildin'. I'm sorry.

DJ CRAIG G

Back To Back: Teaming Up to Smash The Streets with Exclusives

Whether solo or alongside frequent collaborator DJ S&S, DJ Craig G became known for coming strong with the crazy hip-hop exclusives on his mixtapes. And he was also revered for his slow jam and reggae series', making sure the streets were fed more than just the latest rap tracks. Before going on to become a beloved, out-of-state radio and club DJ, Craig G built his reputation in the mixtape game.

PARTNERSHIP WITH DJ S&S

Craig G: Myself and DJ S&S came from the same cloth, basically. He would record all his classic mixtapes in my house. We shared the same equipment in the mid-'90s. Whatever he didn't put out, that's when I would make a mixtape. We were getting the same songs. I would help him and he would help me. If it was my time to make a mixtape, I would take the songs that he didn't have on his tape and put them on mine.

We didn't clash heads. If he was making a hip-hop tape, then I would go and make an R&B tape, or a reggae or slow jam tape–which did well. Those were called *The Fuc Tapes*. That was so there wasn't competition. So when we went to the tape store, we didn't have the same songs on our tapes. S would get his sales on his hip-hop tapes, and I would get my sales on whatever I was doing, just to stay away from his lane. If I got a song and I wasn't making a hip-hop mixtape that week, I would give it to him. And vice versa.

We had our competition, but they were all our friends. It was a friendly competition to see who could put out tapes the fastest and get them on the streets first.

But me and S&S, we wanted to have a whole complete mixtape, and have our shit go from beginning to the end, all hotness. We know how the mixtape game was, so we wanted the hottest three, four, or five records right in the beginning. But you had to make the rest of the tape hot too, so you had to balance some of those songs.

People always wanted to know, "Why is S always shouting out Craig?" It's because I'm the first person he sees when he's making his tapes. So he always shouted me out first, and I was always that DJ that was right with him. It worked hand in hand. We had a friendship that turned into a business relationship, and we shined off of it. It got us to travel and see the world, just off the mixtapes. Out of apartment 5B.

RECORDING

It was always two 1200s. The mixer was probably a Gemini or an old school Rane mixer. And when we got those exclusives, everything was given to us on DAT or cassette. So we had to transfer the music that was on DAT to a cassette, because on the cassette decks you could press play and pause right on the spot. If you ever hear on the mixtapes, "Bass drop" or , "Drop that," it was like boom–you hit that pause button and the song was right there. And it sounds like you're playing it off of vinyl.

We always made sure our mixtape had a flow. You didn't want to go from the fastest record to a slow record then back to the fastest. So we tried to have a flow with it, like a party. Maybe that's because we're from Uptown, and Uptown DJs are about partying.

I thought every tape I was making was special. I felt I was up there with the Kid Capris, because he basically taught us how to put a hot tape together. Everything I did, I tried to put the best quality work out. It was just straight two turntables and a microphone. And everytime I put out a mixtape, I felt it was my best work. And I felt I was up there with the great ones.

EXCLUSIVES

In the mixtape game, it's all about relationships. You gotta have that relationship with a producer, or a fellow DJ, and of course an A&R or promotion director at the record label. Back then, DJs were at the record labels all the time. We were up there 24/7 looking for that exclusive. And they knew we were in the mixtape game, so they knew what we were gonna do with it.

Eventually I became the DJ for Ma$e, so I always had a great relationship with Bad Boy. Def Jam, Loud Records, all of them. So they knew I was coming with a tape, and they'd be like, "I'm gonna hold this for Craig." And they'd tell me, "You're the only one that got this," which I knew was a bunch of bullshit.

Funkmaster Flex had the Flip Squad at the time, and I had that relationship. I was in The Tunnel, and DJing at clubs downtown on the regular. So I always had nice industry relationships.

'90S IN NEW YORK CITY

That happened to be a good time for DJs. '92 to '96, definitely. Biggie–God rest his soul–he had New York in a frenzy. Anything Bad Boy had New York in a frenzy. Then we got introduced to Jay-Z, and the rest is history. I happened to come up in a great era. And I can still play these records to this day, and I can still call a lot of these guys my friends.

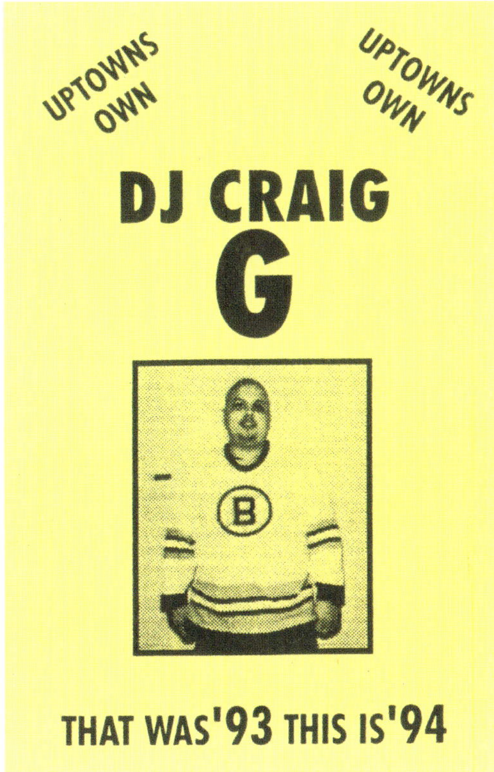

Fat Joe: I don't think Craig G ever liked me again in my life after that. What happened was Craig G used to look like me. And if I would talk to a girl in the Bronx, he would talk to her. People would think I was him, and people would think he was me. So I was bigging him up, but at the same time, making a joke out of it, because so many people would stop us. Craig G is dope.

Craig G: If you look at his early D.I.T.C. days, we look alike, straight up. When he had the Army fatigue suit on for "Flow Joe," we damn near had a resemblance. When I met Pun through him, Pun was like, "This the motherfucker that look like you!" It's just so crazy.

I got a shirt made that said, "I'm not Fat Joe, I'm not Big Pun, I'm DJ Craig G," and on the back it said, "Any questions?" I would wear that shirt faithfully because motherfuckers were getting me and Fat Joe and Big Pun mixed up. But Joe is a good dude. When my son passed away, Joe made a great donation to my family.

"Craig G, forever trying to look like me"

–FAT JOE "DEDICATION"

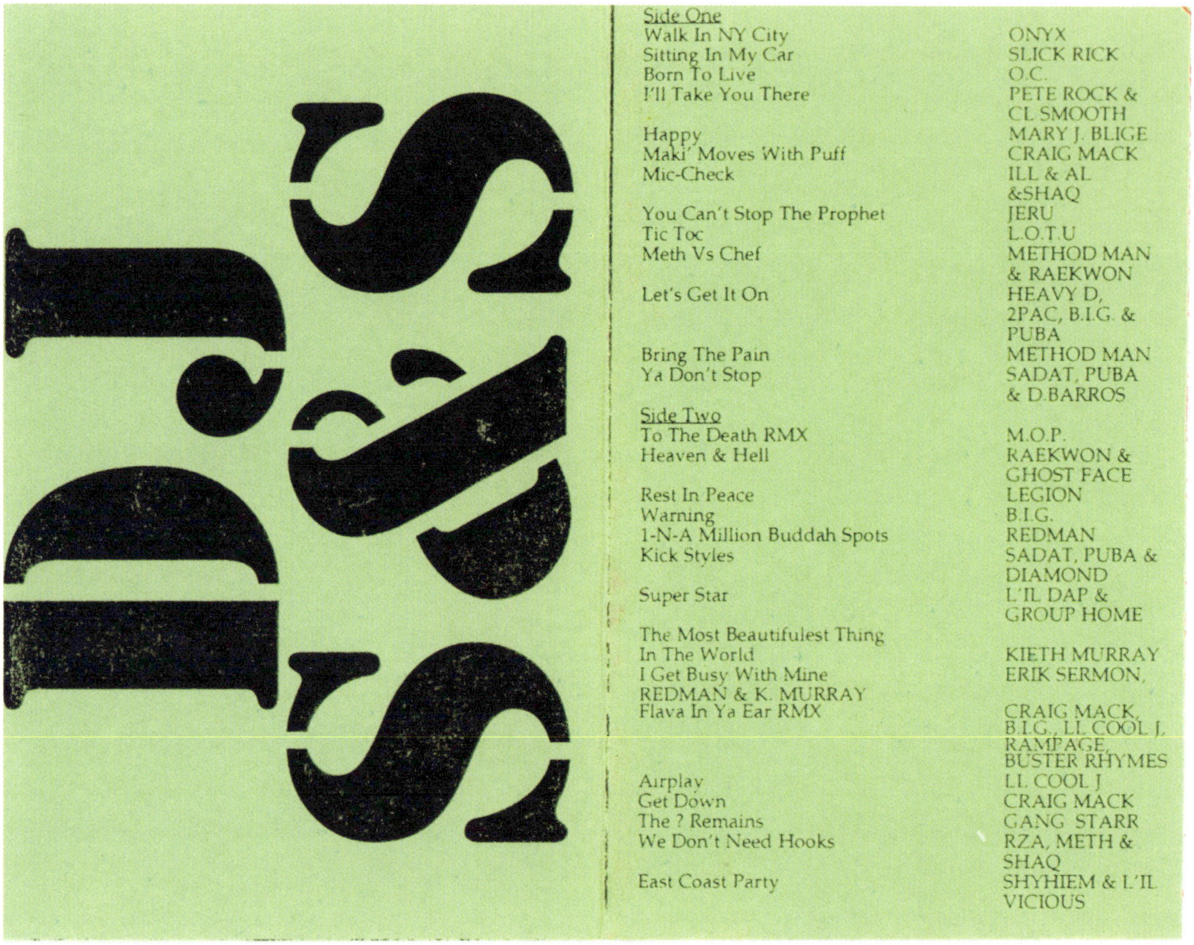

DJ S&S

Side One
Walk In NY City - ONYX
Sitting In My Car - SLICK RICK
Born To Live - O.C.
I'll Take You There - PETE ROCK & CL SMOOTH

Happy - MARY J. BLIGE
Maki' Moves With Puff - CRAIG MACK
Mic-Check - ILL & AL &SHAQ

You Can't Stop The Prophet - JERU
Tic Toc - L.O.T.U
Meth Vs Chef - METHOD MAN & RAEKWON

Let's Get It On - HEAVY D, 2PAC, B.I.G. & PUBA

Bring The Pain - METHOD MAN
Ya Don't Stop - SADAT, PUBA & D.BARROS

Side Two
To The Death RMX - M.O.P.
Heaven & Hell - RAEKWON & GHOST FACE

Rest In Peace - LEGION
Warning - B.I.G.
1-N-A Million Buddah Spots - REDMAN
Kick Styles - SADAT, PUBA & DIAMOND

Super Star - L'IL DAP & GROUP HOME

The Most Beautifulest Thing In The World - KIETH MURRAY
I Get Busy With Mine - ERIK SERMON, REDMAN & K. MURRAY
Flava In Ya Ear RMX - CRAIG MACK, B.I.G., LL COOL J, RAMPAGE, BUSTER RHYMES

Airplay - LL COOL J
Get Down - CRAIG MACK
The ? Remains - GANG STARR
We Don't Need Hooks - RZA, METH & SHAQ

East Coast Party - SHYHIEM & L'IL VICIOUS

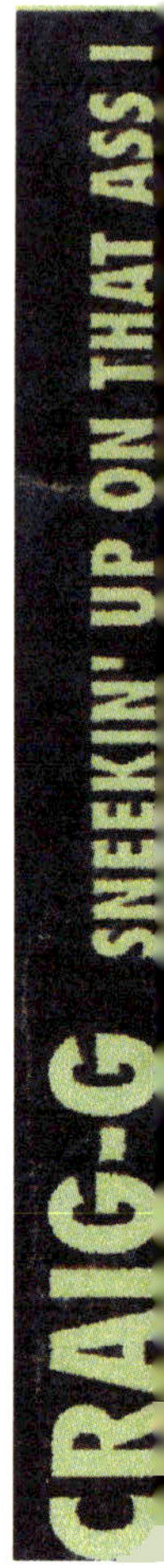

CRAIG-G SNEEKIN' UP ON THAT ASS I

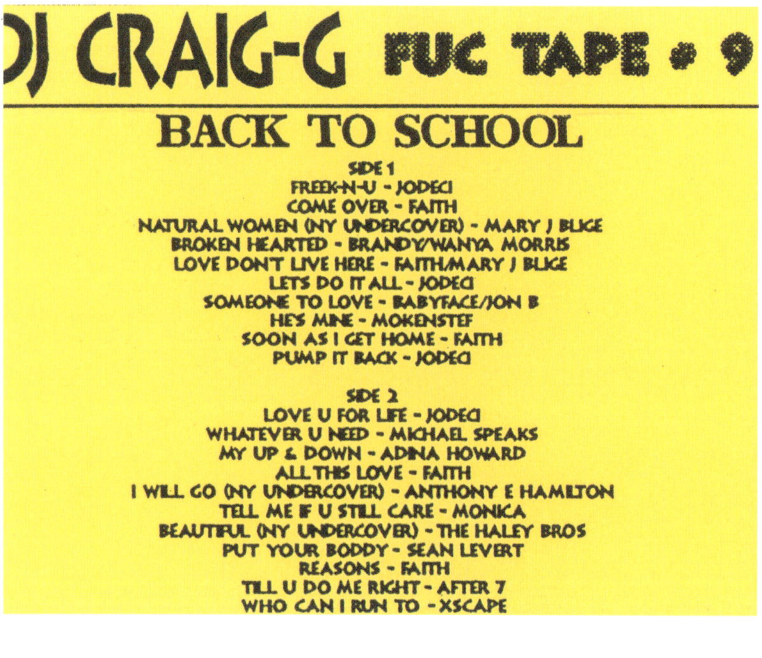

DJ CRAIG-G FUC TAPE # 9

BACK TO SCHOOL

SIDE 1
FREEK-N-U - JODECI
COME OVER - FAITH
NATURAL WOMEN (NY UNDERCOVER) - MARY J BLIGE
BROKEN HEARTED - BRANDY/WANYA MORRIS
LOVE DON'T LIVE HERE - FAITH/MARY J BLIGE
LETS DO IT ALL - JODECI
SOMEONE TO LOVE - BABYFACE/JON B
HE'S MINE - MOKENSTEF
SOON AS I GET HOME - FAITH
PUMP IT BACK - JODECI

SIDE 2
LOVE U FOR LIFE - JODECI
WHATEVER U NEED - MICHAEL SPEAKS
MY UP & DOWN - ADINA HOWARD
ALL THIS LOVE - FAITH
I WILL GO (NY UNDERCOVER) - ANTHONY E HAMILTON
TELL ME IF U STILL CARE - MONICA
BEAUTIFUL (NY UNDERCOVER) - THE HALEY BROS
PUT YOUR BODDY - SEAN LEVERT
REASONS - FAITH
TILL U DO ME RIGHT - AFTER 7
WHO CAN I RUN TO - XSCAPE

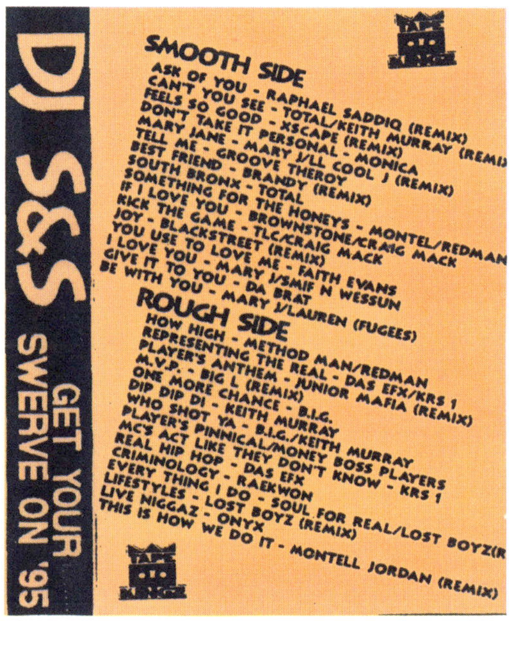

DJ S&S GET YOUR SWERVE ON '95

SMOOTH SIDE
ASK OF YOU - RAPHAEL SADDIQ (REMIX)
CAN'T YOU SEE - TOTAL/KEITH MURRAY (REMI
FEELS SO GOOD - XSCAPE (REMIX)
DON'T TAKE IT PERSONAL - MONICA
MARY JANE - MARY J/LL COOL J (REMIX)
TELL ME - GROOVE THEROY
BEST FRIEND - BRANDY (REMIX)
SOUTH BRONX - TOTAL
SOMETHING FOR THE HONEYS - MONTEL/REDMAN
IF I LOVE YOU - BROWNSTONE/CRAIG MACK
KICK THE GAME - TLC/CRAIG MACK
JOY - BLACKSTREET (REMIX)
YOU USE TO LOVE ME - FAITH EVANS
I LOVE YOU - MARY J/SMIF N WESSUN
GIVE IT TO YOU - DA BRAT
BE WITH YOU - MARY J/LAUREN (FUGEES)

ROUGH SIDE
HOW HIGH - METHOD MAN/REDMAN
REPRESENTING THE REAL - DAS EFX/KRS 1
PLAYER'S ANTHEM - JUNIOR MAFIA (REMIX)
M.V.P. - BIG L (REMIX)
ONE MORE CHANCE - B.I.G.
DIP DIP DI - KEITH MURRAY
WHO SHOT YA - B.I.G./KEITH MURRAY
PLAYER'S PINNICAL/MONEY BOSS PLAYERS
MC'S ACT LIKE THEY DON'T KNOW - KRS 1
REAL HIP HOP - DAS EFX
CRIMINOLOGY - RAEKWON
EVERY THING I DO - SOUL FOR REAL/LOST BOYZ(R
LIFESTYLES - LOST BOYZ (REMIX)
LIVE NIGGAZ - ONYX
THIS IS HOW WE DO IT - MONTELL JORDAN (REMIX)

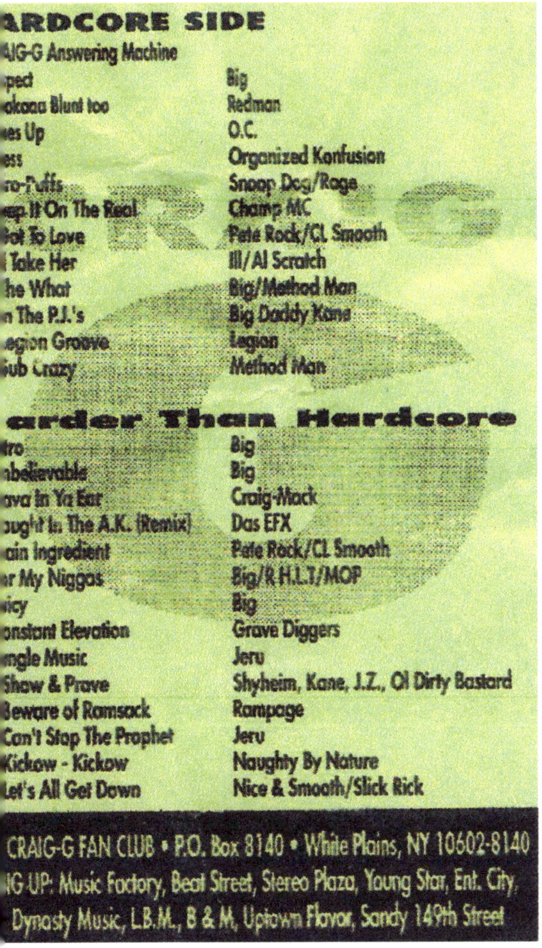
ARDCORE SIDE
AIG-G Answering Machine
ped - Big
okaaa Blunt too - Redman
es Up - O.C.
ess - Organized Konfusion
ro-Puffs - Snoop Dog/Rage
ep It On The Real - Champ MC
Got To Love - Pete Rock/CL Smooth
I Take Her - III/Al Scratch
he What - Big/Method Man
n The P.J.'s - Big Daddy Kane
egion Groove - Legion
ub Crazy - Method Man
arder Than Hardcore
tro - Big
nbelievable - Big
ava In Ya Ear - Craig-Mack
ought In The A.K. (Remix) - Das EFX
ain Ingredient - Pete Rock/CL Smooth
or My Niggas - Big/R.H.L.T/MOP
icy - Big
onstant Elevation - Grave Diggers
ungle Music - Jeru
Show & Prove - Shyheim, Kane, J.Z., Ol Dirty Bastard
Beware of Ramsack - Rampage
Can't Stop The Prophet - Jeru
Kickow - Kickow - Naughty By Nature
Let's All Get Down - Nice & Smooth/Slick Rick
CRAIG-G FAN CLUB • P.O. Box 8140 • White Plains, NY 10602-8140
IG UP: Music Factory, Beat Street, Stereo Plaza, Young Star, Ent. City,
Dynasty Music, L.B.M., B & M, Uptown Flavor, Sandy 149th Street

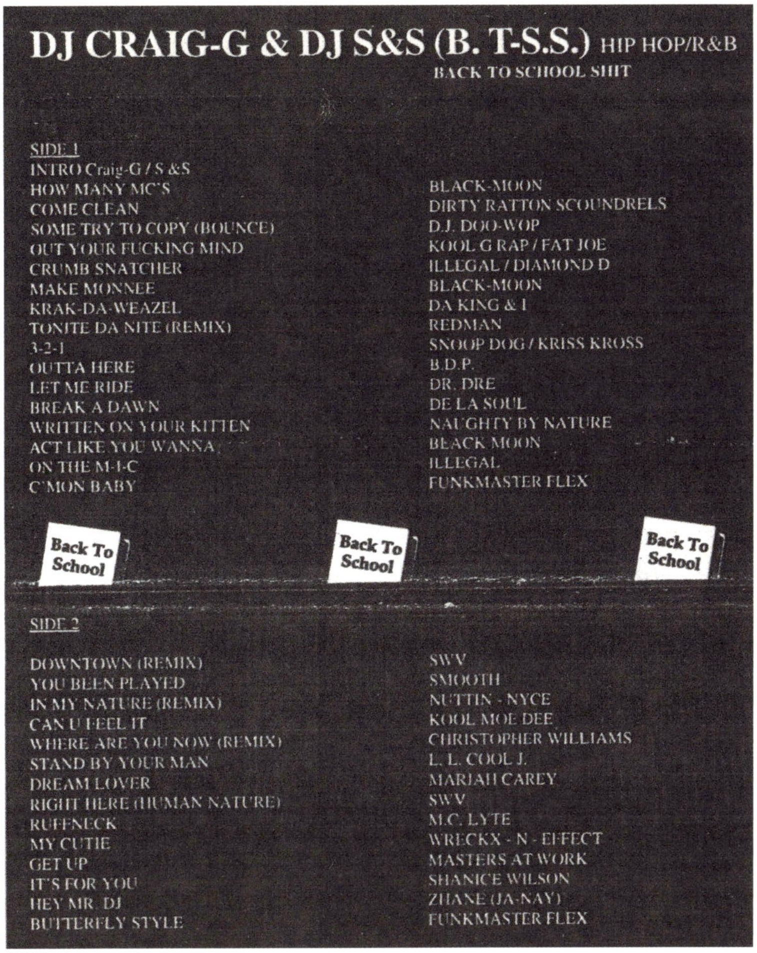
DJ CRAIG-G & DJ S&S (B. T-S.S.) HIP HOP/R&B
BACK TO SCHOOL SHIT
SIDE 1
INTRO Craig-G / S &S
HOW MANY MC'S - BLACK-MOON
COME CLEAN - DIRTY RATTON SCOUNDRELS
SOME TRY TO COPY (BOUNCE) - D.J. DOO-WOP
OUT YOUR FUCKING MIND - KOOL G RAP / FAT JOE
CRUMB SNATCHER - ILLEGAL / DIAMOND D
MAKE MONNEE - BLACK-MOON
KRAK-DA-WEAZEL - DA KING & I
TONITE DA NITE (REMIX) - REDMAN
3-2-1 - SNOOP DOG / KRISS KROSS
OUTTA HERE - B.D.P.
LET ME RIDE - DR. DRE
BREAK A DAWN - DE LA SOUL
WRITTEN ON YOUR KITTEN - NAUGHTY BY NATURE
ACT LIKE YOU WANNA - BLACK MOON
ON THE M-I-C - ILLEGAL
C'MON BABY - FUNKMASTER FLEX
Back To School
Back To School
Back To School
SIDE 2
DOWNTOWN (REMIX) - SWV
YOU BEEN PLAYED - SMOOTH
IN MY NATURE (REMIX) - NUTTIN - NYCE
CAN U FEEL IT - KOOL MOE DEE
WHERE ARE YOU NOW (REMIX) - CHRISTOPHER WILLIAMS
STAND BY YOUR MAN - L. L. COOL J.
DREAM LOVER - MARIAH CAREY
RIGHT HERE (HUMAN NATURE) - SWV
RUFFNECK - M.C. LYTE
MY CUTIE - WRECKX - N - EFFECT
GET UP - MASTERS AT WORK
IT'S FOR YOU - SHANICE WILSON
HEY MR. DJ - ZHANE (JA-NAY)
BUTTERFLY STYLE - FUNKMASTER FLEX

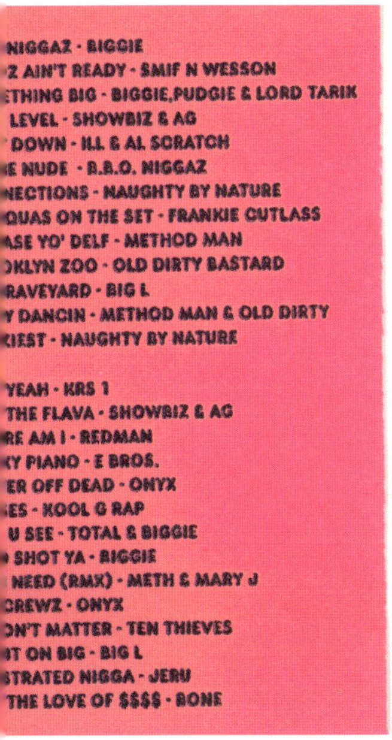
NIGGAZ - BIGGIE
Z AIN'T READY - SMIF N WESSON
ETHING BIG - BIGGIE,PUDGIE & LORD TARIK
LEVEL - SHOWBIZ & AG
DOWN - ILL & AL SCRATCH
E NUDE - B.B.O. NIGGAZ
NECTIONS - NAUGHTY BY NATURE
OUAS ON THE SET - FRANKIE CUTLASS
ASE YO' DELF - METHOD MAN
OKLYN ZOO - OLD DIRTY BASTARD
RAVEYARD - BIG L
Y DANCIN - METHOD MAN & OLD DIRTY
KIEST - NAUGHTY BY NATURE
YEAH - KRS 1
THE FLAVA - SHOWBIZ & AG
RE AM I - REDMAN
KY PIANO - E BROS.
ER OFF DEAD - ONYX
ES - KOOL G RAP
U SEE - TOTAL & BIGGIE
SHOT YA - BIGGIE
NEED (RMX) - METH & MARY J
CREWZ - ONYX
ON'T MATTER - TEN THIEVES
IT ON BIG - BIG L
STRATED NIGGA - JERU
THE LOVE OF $$$$ - BONE

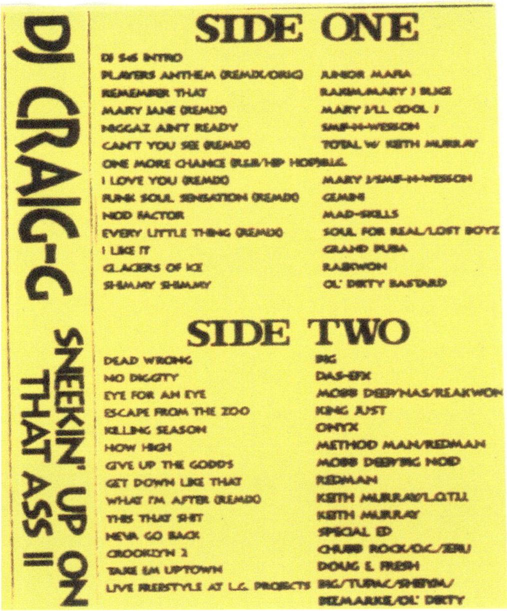
DJ CRAIG-G
SNEEKIN' UP ON THAT ASS II
SIDE ONE
DJ S&S INTRO
PLAYERS ANTHEM (REMIX/ORIG) - JUNIOR MAFIA
REMEMBER THAT - RAKIM/MARY J BLIGE
MARY JANE (REMIX) - MARY J/LL COOL J
NIGGAZ AINT READY - SMIF-N-WESSON
CAN'T YOU SEE (REMIX) - TOTAL W/ KEITH MURRAY
ONE MORE CHANCE (R&B/HIP HOP)BIG
I LOVE YOU (REMIX) - MARY J/SMIF-N-WESSON
FUNK SOUL SENSATION (REMIX) - GEMINI
NOD FACTOR - MAD-SKILLS
EVERY LITTLE THING (REMIX) - SOUL FOR REAL/LOST BOYZ
I LIKE IT - GRAND PUBA
GLACIERS OF ICE - RAEKWON
SHIMMY SHIMMY - OL' DIRTY BASTARD
SIDE TWO
DEAD WRONG - BIG
NO DIGGITY - DAS-EFX
EYE FOR AN EYE - MOBB DEEP/NAS/REAKWON
ESCAPE FROM THE ZOO - KING JUST
KILLING SEASON - ONYX
HOW HIGH - METHOD MAN/REDMAN
GIVE UP THE GOODS - MOBB DEEP/BIG NOD
GET DOWN LIKE THAT - REDMAN
WHAT I'M AFTER (REMIX) - KEITH MURRAY/L.O.T.U.
THIS THAT SHIT - KEITH MURRAY
NEVA GO BACK - SPECIAL ED
CROOKLYN 2 - CHUBB ROCK/O.C./JERU
TAKE EM UPTOWN - DOUG E. FRESH
LIVE FREESTYLE AT L.G. PROJECTS - BIG/TUPAC/SHEYON/BIZMARKIE/OL' DIRTY

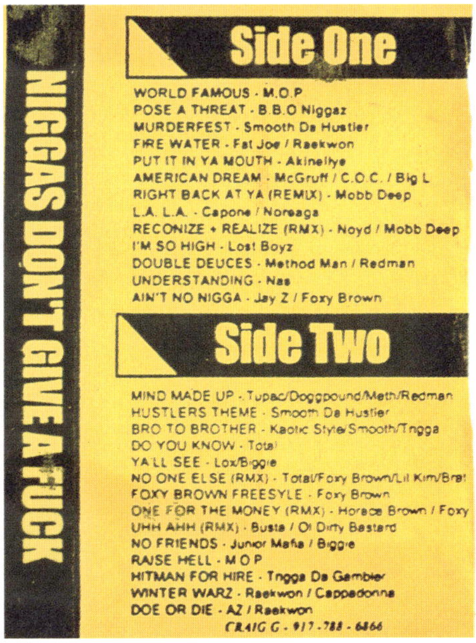
NIGGAS DON'T GIVE A FUCK
Side One
WORLD FAMOUS - M.O.P
POSE A THREAT - B.B.O Niggaz
MURDERFEST - Smooth Da Hustler
FIRE WATER - Fat Joe / Raekwon
PUT IT IN YA MOUTH - Akinelye
AMERICAN DREAM - McGruff / C.O.C. / Big L
RIGHT BACK AT YA (REMIX) - Mobb Deep
L.A. L.A. - Capone / Noreaga
RECONIZE + REALIZE (RMX) - Noyd / Mobb Deep
I'M SO HIGH - Lost Boyz
DOUBLE DEUCES - Method Man / Redman
UNDERSTANDING - Nas
AIN'T NO NIGGA - Jay Z / Foxy Brown
Side Two
MIND MADE UP - Tupac/Doggpound/Meth/Redman
HUSTLERS THEME - Smooth Da Hustler
BRO TO BROTHER - Kaotic Style/Smooth/Trigga
DO YOU KNOW - Total
YA'LL SEE - Lox/Biggie
NO ONE ELSE (RMX) - Total/Foxy Brown/Lil Kim/Brat
FOXY BROWN FREESYLE - Foxy Brown
ONE FOR THE MONEY (RMX) - Horace Brown / Foxy
UHH AHH (RMX) - Busta / Ol Dirty Bastard
NO FRIENDS - Junior Mafia / Biggie
RAISE HELL - M O P
HITMAN FOR HIRE - Trigga Da Gambler
WINTER WARZ - Raekwon / Cappadonna
DOE OR DIE - AZ / Raekwon
CRAIG G - 917 - 788 - 6866

DJ DOO WOP

Bounce on 'Em: The Explosion of the Mixtape Freestyle

Bronx legend DJ Doo Wop not only brought the live party vibes to his tapes, but he took the idea of exclusives to another level by creating intros that featured never-heard-before, custom-made freestyles by the most popular and up-and-coming MCs in the game, including himself and his collective The Bounce Squad. And with his *95 Live* series, he took those intros to even higher levels by including an extended lineup of freestyles featuring MCs from across all the boroughs, which was something that had never been done before.

INSPIRATION

Doo Wop: The first time I heard a mixtape was definitely a Kid Capri tape. It was the beginning of when mixtapes were really starting to be in everybody's radio and car or whatever. It was around the time when Kid Capri was doing The Castle. We would go by The Castle, but we would never really go in. Me and my crew, we didn't really like to be all up in the club, we just liked to go when the club let out, to fuck with the girls and all that. We were that type.

But we would hear the music coming out of all the cars with the talking over it. And I was already a DJ–I'd been a DJ since I was 9. So I was DJing nine to ten years before I heard a mixtape. But, I never talked on the mic. I never rapped. All I did was DJ. House parties, jams outside, parties in the projects, community centers, that type of thing. But I never looked at it like this was what I was gonna do for the rest of my life.

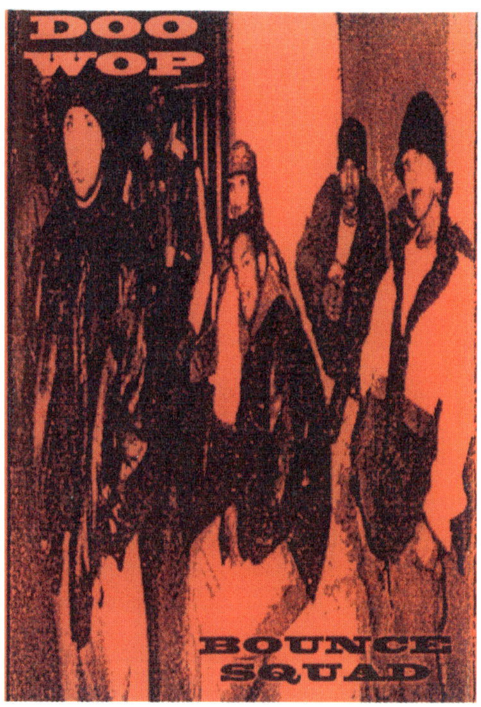

Then, when the mixtapes came out, it kind of drew me in, because it brought the DJ to the forefront. He had his own personality, and his own name that he could brand. It wasn't just that the MC was the star like, "Oh, by the way, this is my DJ." It was more of, "Nah, this is me. I'm taking over. I'm gonna talk, I'm gonna spit, I'm gonna handle the crowd, I'm gonna do whatever." And I liked that. So I took a shot at it.

FIRST TAPE

My first tape was probably something I did for my hood, I couldn't even tell you. Back then, we just named them the date that we made them. It would be like Doo Wop *1/12/89* or something like that. It had Grand Daddy I.U., Lakim Shabazz, those type of joints. U.M.C.'s from Staten Island. Hip-hop shit.

Around that time, even though I wasn't known yet from the mixtape shit, I was connected through Ed Lover, who was a friend of a friend. He kind of liked my style, so he hooked me up with these dudes, and they would just send me mad records. So even back then, I would get records first, just like the radio DJs would get them. I would get advanced copies, and that helped me out too, because a lot of other cats weren't getting that.

DUPLICATING AND SELLING TAPES

I was mostly known in the beginning Uptown–Bronx and Harlem. I wasn't really too known in Queens. I didn't care about that shit. I just wanted people to know me in the Bronx and Harlem. I figured I could just blow up there, and I'd be good. But I drove around and saw what stores sold mixtapes, and kept a note–125th, 137th, whatever. The night we'd make them, we'd copy them and label them. But there was no track list back then, so it was easier. You didn't have to make a fly ass cover and do all the graphics. We had a Telex machine that dubbed three, four tapes at a time. And they had some you could snap into another one and it would make eight. My man would sit there all night, I'd give him $20 or $40 and he'd do it. And the next day, we'd come out, and we'd go sell the tape.

It was hard in the beginning, because they'd be like, "We only know Kid Capri, Brucie B, and Starchild. Who are you?" Stereo Palace was the Mecca of mixtapes. It was these two white cats from Brooklyn, and they had a store on 125th directly across the street from the Apollo Theater, and they kept a speaker outside playing mixtapes all day. It was an electronics store, but the mixtapes is where they got all their bread. You'd go all the way in the back, and they'd have all the tapes in a glass case. And I'd be like, "Damn, I'd love to see my shit up there."

So I went in there one time when I first started and tried to sell them a tape. They were like, "We've never heard of you." I was like, "Aiight, cool. Whatever." So I left, it was a Friday. Saturday afternoon, I went there with a boombox and a case of tapes, and I sat in front of their store and played my tapes in front of there. It sounds like a cliche story, but it's the truth. People actually walked up and bought tapes from me, $20 a pop. I was like, "Wow," because in there, those shits were like $10, $15. And after that, obviously, they started selling my tapes.

RAPPING ON TAPES

I rapped a little here and there before, but I always wanted to fuck with it. It was cool, because when you make a tape, you're in the comfort of your own crib. It was like, "Let me try it." If I listen back to the old shit now, I'd probably laugh at it. But it helped

DOO WOP'S 3 KEYS TO MAKING A DOPE MIXTAPE INTRO

I would do a mix of everything on my tapes, but the main thing was always the intro. People tell me to this day, "Your tapes were bangin', but I strictly bought them for the intro. I got my money's worth with the intro alone."

1. THINK OF A CONCEPT - Something current that's going on, something that will keep people's attention. The intro can tell a story and dictate the whole feel of the tape.
2. FIND AN ILL SKIT - For the beginning, to grab their attention. Something short and right to the point, but still deep enough so it's not like, "Oh I'm gonna grab a clip from *Scarface*." Do your work and search for some other shit that nobody really knows, but it might spark something in their brains. Like, "Oh, I remember that."
3. GET A DOPE BEAT AND RAPPER - Get somebody rapping, spitting some fire, and an ill beat for them to come in on and rhyme to. With The Bounce Squad, we always left them wanting more so they're like, "Oh, there's gonna be a part two to this? This is gonna be crazy."

me, because I got much, much better as time passed.

THE BOUNCE SQUAD

My crew was always called The Bounce Squad. But they were not rappers. When I'd go put a tape out, or go pick up my money, I'd be with like twenty dudes. And I would say their names on every tape.

Then, I had a talent contest in the hood, trying to find some rappers that I could pair up and bunch together. This is before Wu-Tang. I took one dude, Snagglepuss, who was like our Method Man. He was the charismatic dude, the good looking guy, who had the punchlines and the voice.

Then I had the girl Uneek who I had met before because she was down with the Ghetto Girlz, who did the "My Mind is Playing Tricks on Me," the girl version, called "My Man's Playing Tricks on Me." I always like her style. Then I got two dudes from Edenwald, Aulthat and Rev Gotti. And I called us The Bounce Squad.

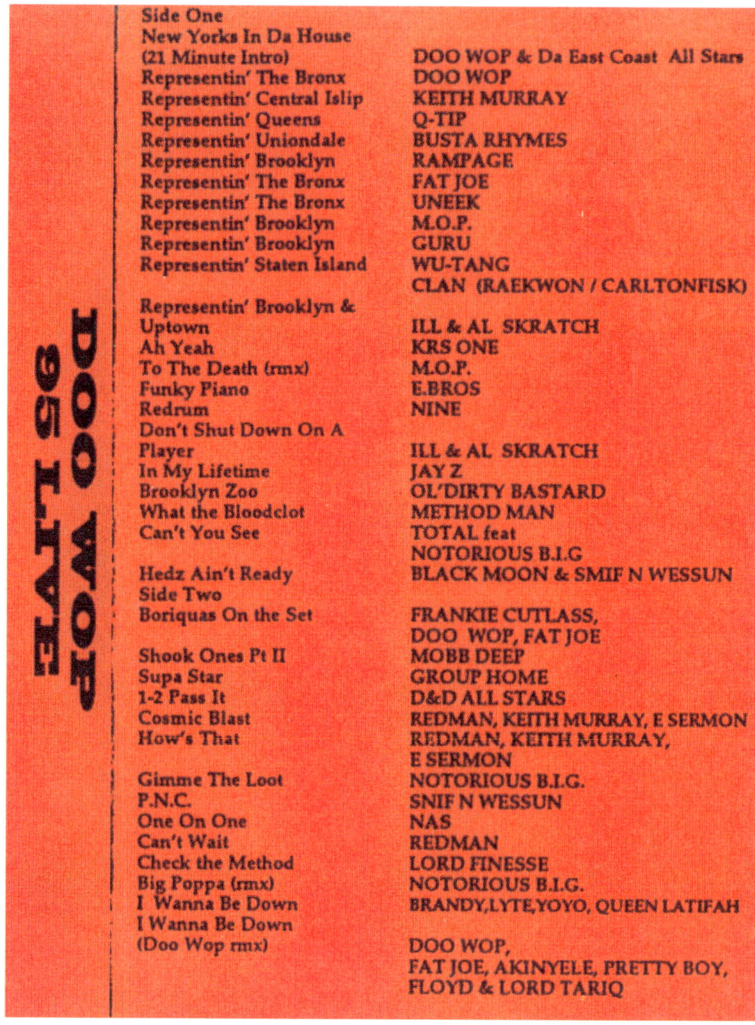

Lord Tariq, he was a Bronx legend since forever, and he was on somebody else's tape, but it wasn't really flourishing much. So when I put him on mine, everybody automatically thought, "Oh, that's another Bounce Squad nigga." So we all rhymed on the beginning of the tapes. *Summer Jam '93* is when I introduced them, and that took it to another level. So now on every tape, it was like, "Not only are we gonna hear Wop rhyming, we're gonna hear that whole crew."

95 LIVE

It was all the rappers on the radio. Keith Murray had "The Most Beautifullest Thing," Raekwon's album had just dropped. It wasn't easy to initiate it, but then it got so easy, because even though we were poppin' in the streets, I didn't know these rap cats knew me like that.

I got a phone call from Fatman Scoop, who was the street rep guy for Tommy Boy at the time. He was the one that calls you like, "Hey, you got that record?" He called all the DJs, that was his job. So he called me one day, and it was just one of those generic calls, "Hey, what's up Doo Wop? Did you get the *New Jersey Drive* record?" And I was like, "I got it, Scoop. Everything's good." And I was about to hang up, and he was like, "Hold up. Busta wants to say what's up." And I didn't even know Busta knew who I was. And I'm not being humble, I'm serious. He got on the phone and was like, "Dude, anytime you need me,

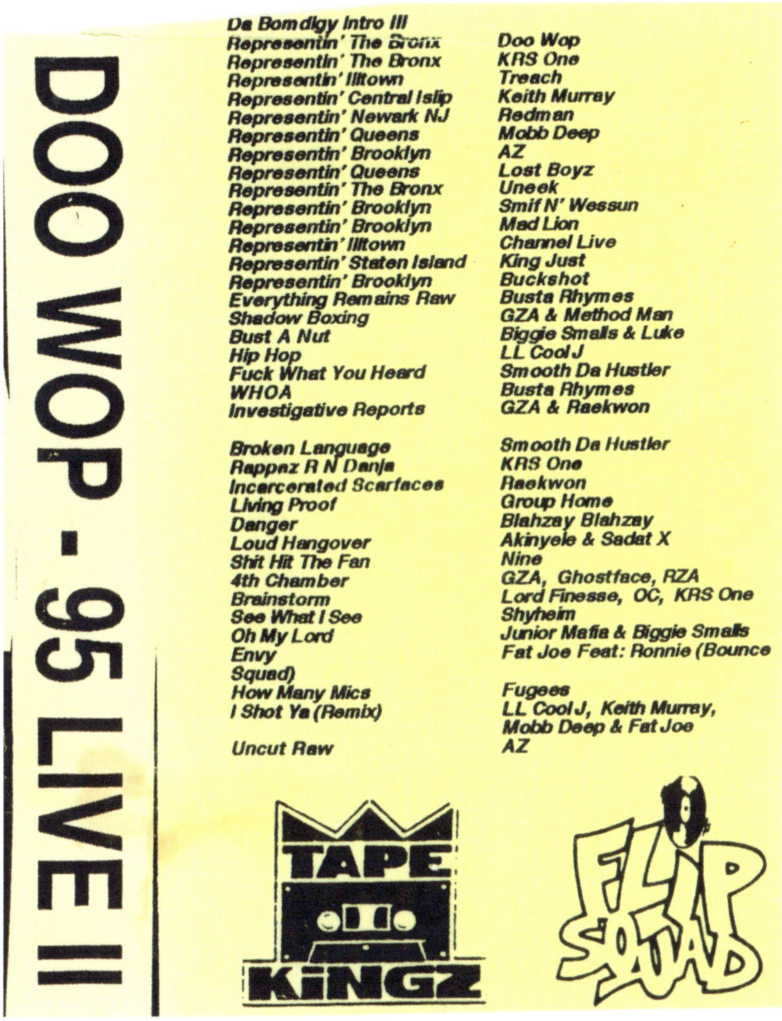

DOO WOP - 95 LIVE II

Da Bomdigy Intro III	
Representin' The Bronx	Doo Wop
Representin' The Bronx	KRS One
Representin' Uptown	Treach
Representin' Central Islip	Keith Murray
Representin' Newark NJ	Redman
Representin' Queens	Mobb Deep
Representin' Brooklyn	AZ
Representin' Queens	Lost Boyz
Representin' The Bronx	Uneek
Representin' Brooklyn	Smif N' Wessun
Representin' Brooklyn	Mad Lion
Representin' Uptown	Channel Live
Representin' Staten Island	King Just
Representin' Brooklyn	Buckshot
Everything Remains Raw	Busta Rhymes
Shadow Boxing	GZA & Method Man
Bust A Nut	Biggie Smalls & Luke
Hip Hop	LL Cool J
Fuck What You Heard	Smooth Da Hustler
WHOA	Busta Rhymes
Investigative Reports	GZA & Raekwon
Broken Language	Smooth Da Hustler
Rappaz R N Danja	KRS One
Incercerated Scarfaces	Raekwon
Living Proof	Group Home
Danger	Blahzay Blahzay
Loud Hangover	Akinyele & Sadat X
Shit Hit The Fan	Nine
4th Chamber	GZA, Ghostface, RZA
Brainstorm	Lord Finesse, OC, KRS One
See What I See	Shyheim
Oh My Lord	Junior Mafia & Biggie Smalls
Envy	Fat Joe Feat: Ronnie (Bounce
Squad)	
How Many Mics	Fugees
I Shot Ya (Remix)	LL Cool J, Keith Murray, Mobb Deep & Fat Joe
Uncut Raw	AZ

Havoc of Mobb Deep: Doo Wop was a major, major player in the mixtape game. So I could imagine us being like, "Oh shit, like we're fucking with Doo Wop right now." His tape was like the number one tape in Queensbridge. People were stealing those tapes. So for us to even be working with him, it was crazy. Doo Wop was from Uptown, so most of the time when you heard Doo Wop tapes, it would be artists from Uptown. For us to even be circulating on a Doo Wop tape, that showed us how big we had become in New York.

I'm here. I love y'all, I love The Bounce Squad." And he gave me his number.

That kind of made it easy from there. I was like, "Wow. If Busta knows me, these other dudes must know me as well." And I was already friends with Fat Joe, so he got me Raekwon's number. Rae was like, "Doo Wop? From Uptown?" Because there was a Doo Wop from Staten Island. "Hell yeah, I'm there."

These niggas all came to the studio. I had them in a little studio where only four people fit comfortably–Q-Tip, M.O.P., Raekwon, Busta Rhymes, and Fat Joe. All in there at one time. And not a dime was exchanged. They never talked money or nothing. They wanted to be on my tape. They wanted to have that street outlet to say what they want and not worry about the labels.

95 LIVE PART TWO

You see what I did on *Part Two*, right–all R&B, old school type mellow beats. I had AZ rhyming off of "Curious." I had Mr. Cheeks rhyming off "Keep Rising to the Top." That's the kind of music I love. You won't catch me in the car listening to too much hip hop. I like old school R&B a lot. That's one reason I like that tape a lot. And, to me, I already had knowledge of how to put it together a little better since I already made *95 Live*.

WOP REMEMBERS A FEW OF HIS FAVORITES.

1. Q-TIP - I gotta say Q-Tip because of the process of him laying that verse down. He came in the studio to do *95 Live*. The first time I met him was probably that day in the studio. He goes, "So what's this about?" And I was like, "It's pro-New York. I'm gonna split the boroughs up, I'm having rappers from every borough, and of course you're gonna rep Queens. Here's the beat." He was like, "Okay, alright."

   He rapped to the original "Shook Ones." He said, "Loop the beat for me and record me." He goes in the booth and he freestyles off his head for probably about nine minutes. Straight off the head. And I'm like, "I don't need anything that long, what is he doing?" Some parts were like eh, but some parts were real dope.

   It was his whole process. I'm just sitting there buggin'. He comes out and he's like, "You got a pen and a pad? Aight, play that back for me." And he then starts taking parts of the freestyle and making it into one verse.

2. BIG PUN - That was on *Bronx Tale*. He came to D&D and he said, "What beat do you want me to rap to?" And I said, "Can you please rap to this?" And I gave him the cover of Lord Tariq and Peter Gunz "Deja Vu." Even though that's his people, Big Pun is just a funny dude. He was like, "Oh I hate this shit," and he threw the record. But then he was like, "Let's do it. C'mon, let's go."

   He went in the booth and he fucking murdered that beat. Big Pun would run out of breath, so he would do, "No doubt I'm from the X and I've seen it all, shorty with dreams of playing ball, turnin' fiends or playin' Seton Hall," and then he would stop. And he'd be like, "Alright, next bar, next bar, next bar." He built it up--two bars, two bars, two bars until it was done. When motherfuckers heard it, they had no idea. It's nothing bad, there's a lot of rappers that do that just to perfect the sound of the breath control and stuff.

3. BIG L - He came and killed that Jay-Z and Sauce Money "Pre-Game" beat for me. This dude did his verse and said, "How's that, Wop?" And I said, "Oh my God it's fucking crazy." Then he said, "But let me do one more in case you don't like that one later." I'm dying to find that because they were on ½ inch reels, and the owner of that studio moved to Florida somewhere. I have yet to find him. I'm trying to track him down because he's got all those reels of *95 Live*. And Big L did that extra verse. I would just give that extra verse to his family, it's only right. But I still would love to hear it because I don't remember what he did.

4. PRODIGY - Not necessarily because of the wordplay, but what it sparked. He rapped to "Hail Mary" on *Gangsta's Paradise*. E Moneybags, Rest In Peace, he brought him through. I already knew Prodigy, but I didn't have a direct contact to him. E-Money Bags told me, "Yo, he gotta get on that tape, he gotta get some shit off." I'm like, "Shit, Prodigy? Hell yeah."

So he's like, "Yo, give me the 'Hail Mary' beat." We had to go get it from Rock and Soul I think. And he was going at Jay, like directly--he said "Hova." So everybody knew what it was, it wasn't a subliminal. I'm like, "Ugh, how are they gonna look at me now? Every time I drop a tape I go to Roc-A-Fella Records." I'd go to the labels and drop a few off. So I didn't go to Roc-A-Fella when that tape came out, that was the one label I skipped.

Two days after it came out, Lenny called me from Roc-A-Fella and said, "Yo, why didn't you drop the new tape off?" And he starts laughing like he obviously heard it. And he's like, "Yo, come on man, come drop that shit off, man. We don't care. We wanna hear that shit." And then Bleek gets on the phone like, "Yo, bring that shit through. Bring that shit tonight." Back then, you couldn't just be like, "Let me just Google it real quick and listen to it."

I went and dropped some shit off with them, and then during that same timeframe, Jay did Summer Jam and debuted "Takeover" live. So he was answering them. I know he was answering them because of what they said in *The Source* in an interview, that the "Hail Mary" freestyle really put him in fifth gear. That was a crazy battle. It segued into him and Nas and into "Takeover."

5. BUSTA RHYMES - For *95 Live*, he rapped off the Q-Tip remix of "The World Is Yours." He wanted that beat, and he was the first one we heard talking about the Illuminati and "there's only five years left."

We're in this tiny little studio called Noise in the Attic on 38th Street on 8th Avenue, two blocks from D&D. Raekwon was in there, Fat Joe was in there. They were looking at Busta through the glass like little kids. They were boys and shit, they're all friends, but they were just buggin'. When you listen to it again, he's rhyming one way with his cadence, and then it goes another way. Those were not two tracks, he did that straight. He was jumping in and out of character in one take. It was fucking amazing.

BONUS: BOUNCE SQUAD - The Bounce Squad freestyles for *Summer Jam '94*--everything good happened when that freestyle came out. And then after that, shit just exploded in the wrong direction because of business shit.

We blew up so fast off of that freestyle and got so much attention that some of us mentally weren't ready, and we flipped on each other and there was no more Bounce Squad after that. I think that was the last tape where it was the full Bounce Squad.

But it was a dope ass session. Everybody was on their A game. I had Sadat, Fat Joe, and Lord Tariq in between us because they were like extended family to The Bounce Squad. They were always around us, they loved rapping with us.

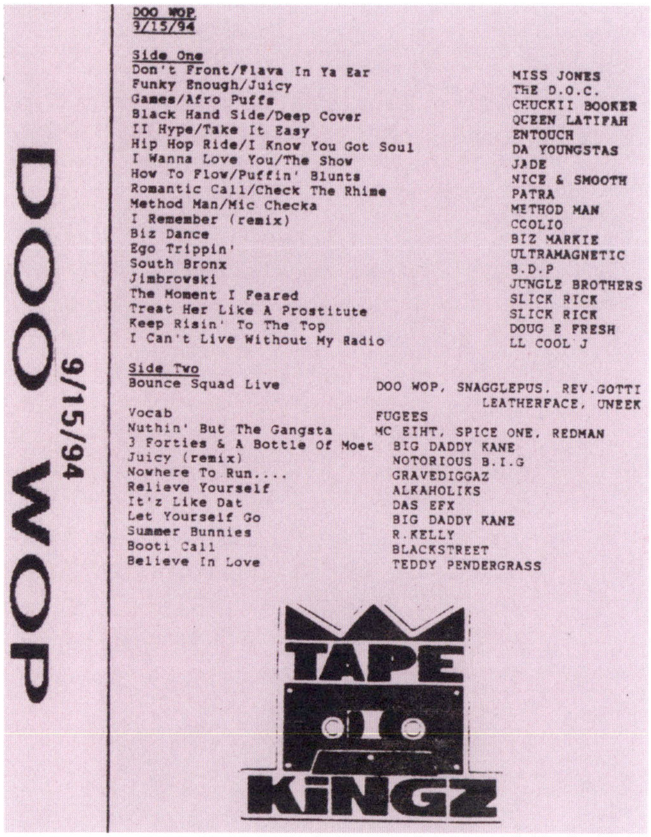
DOO WOP
9/15/94
Side One
Don't Front/Flava In Ya Ear — MISS JONES
Funky Enough/Juicy — THE D.O.C.
Games/Afro Puffs — CHUCKII BOOKER
Black Hand Side/Deep Cover — QCEEN LATIFAH
II Hype/Take It Easy — ENTOUCH
Hip Hop Ride/I Know You Got Soul — DA YOUNGSTAS
I Wanna Love You/The Show — JADE
How To Flow/Puffin' Blunts — NICE & SMOOTH
Romantic Call/Check The Rhime — PATRA
Method Man/Mic Checka — METHOD MAN
I Remember (remix) — CCOLIO
Biz Dance — BIZ MARKIE
Ego Trippin' — ULTRAMAGNETIC
South Bronx — B.D.P
Jimbrowski — JUNGLE BROTHERS
The Moment I Feared — SLICK RICK
Treat Her Like A Prostitute — SLICK RICK
Keep Risin' To The Top — DOUG E FRESH
I Can't Live Without My Radio — LL COOL J
Side Two
Bounce Squad Live — DOO WOP, SNAGGLEPUS, REV.GOTTI LEATHERFACE, UNEEK
Vocab — FUGEES
Nuthin' But The Gangsta — MC EIHT, SPICE ONE, REDMAN
3 Forties & A Bottle Of Moet — BIG DADDY KANE
Juicy (remix) — NOTORIOUS B.I.G
Nowhere To Run.... — GRAVEDIGGAZ
Relieve Yourself — ALKAHOLIKS
It'z Like Dat — DAS EFX
Let Yourself Go — BIG DADDY KANE
Summer Bunnies — R.KELLY
Booti Call — BLACKSTREET
Believe In Love — TEDDY PENDERGRASS
TAPE KiNGZ
DOO WOP 9/15/94

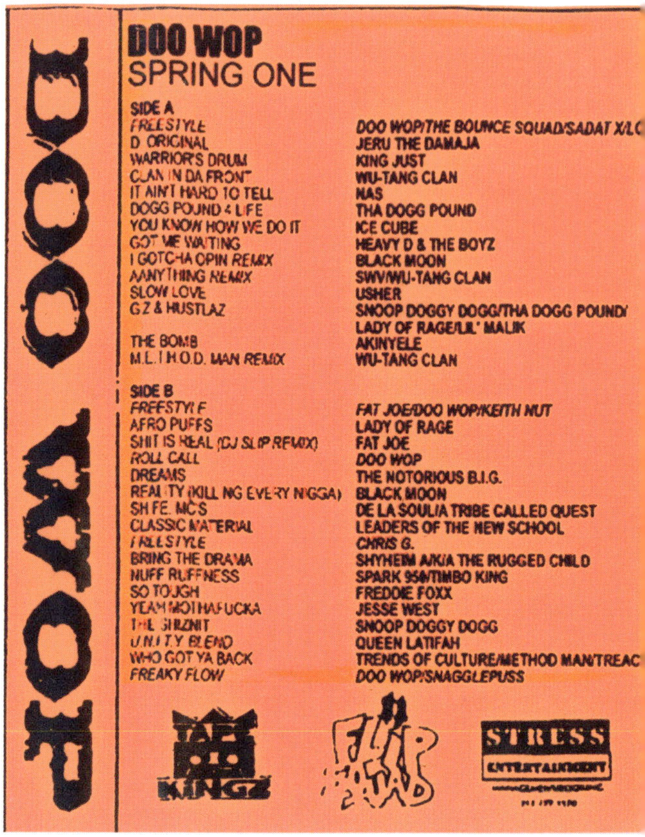
DOO WOP
DOO WOP
SPRING ONE
SIDE A
FREESTYLE — DOO WOP/THE BOUNCE SQUAD/SADAT X/L
D ORIGINAL — JERU THE DAMAJA
WARRIOR'S DRUM — KING JUST
CLAN IN DA FRONT — WU-TANG CLAN
IT AIN'T HARD TO TELL — NAS
DOGG POUND 4 LIFE — THA DOGG POUND
YOU KNOW HOW WE DO IT — ICE CUBE
GOT ME WAITING — HEAVY D & THE BOYZ
I GOTCHA OPIN REMIX — BLACK MOON
ANYTHING REMIX — SWV/WU-TANG CLAN
SLOW LOVE — USHER
GZ & HUSTLAZ — SNOOP DOGGY DOGG/THA DOGG POUND/
LADY OF RAGE/LIL' MALIK
THE BOMB — AKINYELE
M.E.T.H.O.D. MAN REMIX — WU-TANG CLAN
SIDE B
FREESTYLE — FAT JOE/DOO WOP/KEITH NUT
AFRO PUFFS — LADY OF RAGE
SHIT IS REAL (DJ SLIP REMIX) — FAT JOE
ROLL CALL — DOO WOP
DREAMS — THE NOTORIOUS B.I.G.
REALITY (KILLING EVERY NIGGA) — BLACK MOON
SH FE MCS — DE LA SOUL/A TRIBE CALLED QUEST
CLASSIC MATERIAL — LEADERS OF THE NEW SCHOOL
FREESTYLE — CHRIS G.
BRING THE DRAMA — SHYHEIM A/K/A THE RUGGED CHILD
NUFF RUFFNESS — SPARK 950/TIMBO KING
SO TOUGH — FREDDIE FOXX
YEAH MOTHAFUCKA — JESSE WEST
THE SHIZNIT — SNOOP DOGGY DOGG
U.N.I.T.Y. BLEND — QUEEN LATIFAH
WHO GOT YA BACK — TRENDS OF CULTURE/METHOD MAN/TREAC
FREAKY FLOW — DOO WOP/SNAGGLEPUSS
TAPE KINGZ
FLIP SQUAD
STRESS ENTERTAINMENT

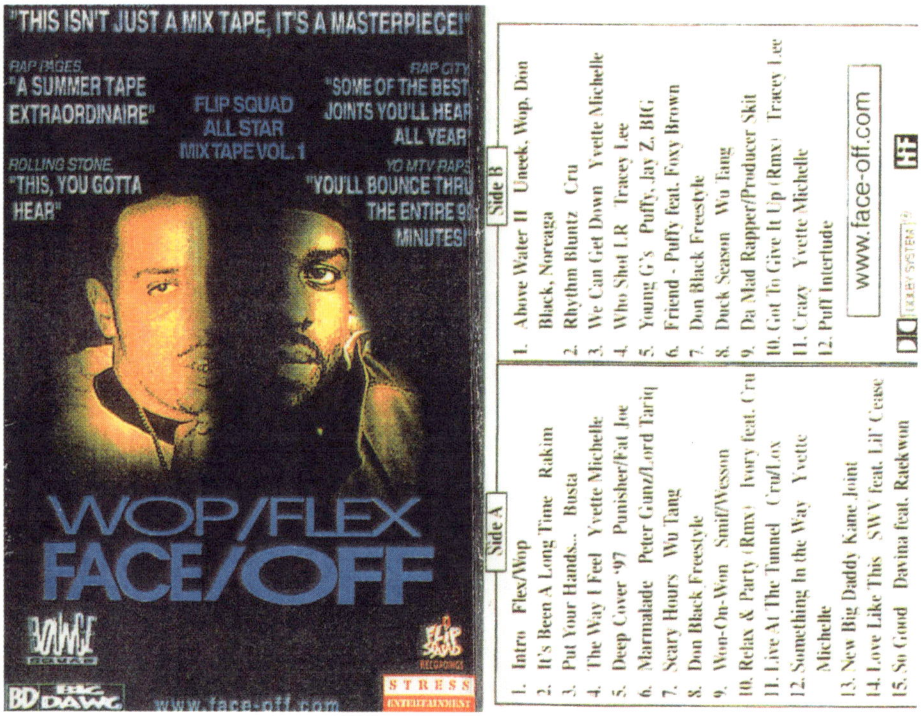
"THIS ISN'T JUST A MIX TAPE, IT'S A MASTERPIECE!"
RAP PAGES
"A SUMMER TAPE EXTRAORDINAIRE"
FLIP SQUAD ALL STAR MIXTAPE VOL. 1
RAP CITY
"SOME OF THE BEST JOINTS YOU'LL HEAR ALL YEAR"
ROLLING STONE
"THIS, YOU GOTTA HEAR"
YO MTV RAPS
"YOU'LL BOUNCE THRU THE ENTIRE 9 MINUTES!"
WOP/FLEX
FACE/OFF
BIG DAWG
FLIP SQUAD RECORDINGS
STRESS ENTERTAINMENT
www.face-off.com
Side A
1. Intro Flex/Wop
2. It's Been A Long Time Rakim
3. Put Your Hands... Busta
4. The Way I Feel Yvette Michelle
5. Deep Cover '97 Punisher/Fat Joe
6. Marmalade Peter Gunz/Lord Tariq
7. Scary Hours Wu Tang
8. Don Black Freestyle
9. Won-On-Won Smif/Wesson
10. Relax & Party (Rmx) Ivory feat. Cru
11. Live At The Tunnel Cru/Lox
12. Something In the Way Yvette Michelle
13. New Big Daddy Kane Joint
14. Love Like This SWV feat. Lil' Cease
15. So Good Davina feat. Raekwon
Side B
1. Above Water II Uneek, Wop, Don Black, Noreaga
2. Rhythm Bluntz Cru
3. We Can Get Down Yvette Michelle
4. Who Shot I.R. Tracey Lee
5. Young G's Puffy, Jay Z, BIG
6. Friend - Puffy feat. Foxy Brown
7. Don Black Freestyle
8. Duck Season Wu Tang
9. Da Mad Rapper/Producer Skit
10. Got To Give It Up (Rmx) Tracey Lee
11. Crazy Yvette Michelle
12. Puff Interlude
www.face-off.com

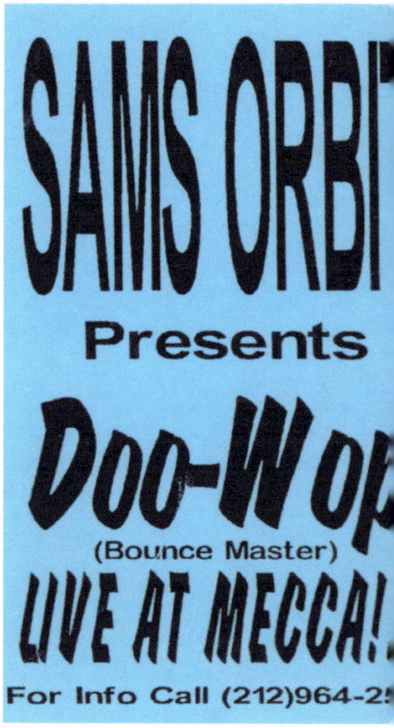
SAMS ORBI
Presents
Doo-Wop
(Bounce Master)
LIVE AT MECCA!
For Info Call (212)964-2

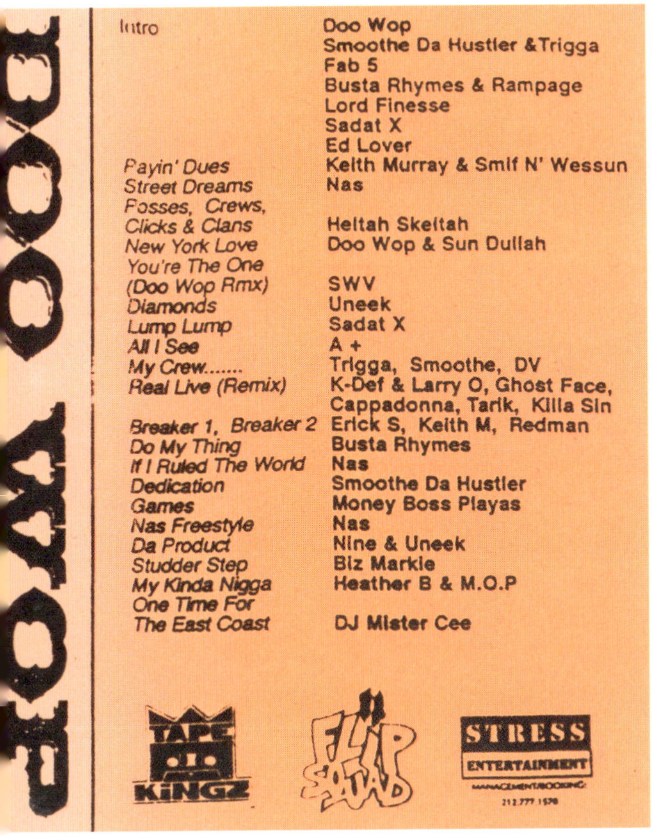
DOO WOP
Intro Doo Wop
Smoothe Da Hustler &Trigga
Fab 5
Busta Rhymes & Rampage
Lord Finesse
Sadat X
Ed Lover
Payin' Dues Keith Murray & Smif N' Wessun
Street Dreams Nas
Posses, Crews, Clicks & Clans Heltah Skeltah
New York Love Doo Wop & Sun Dullah
You're The One (Doo Wop Rmx) SWV
Diamonds Uneek
Lump Lump Sadat X
All I See A +
My Crew....... Trigga, Smoothe, DV
Real Live (Remix) K-Def & Larry O, Ghost Face, Cappadonna, Tarik, Killa Sin
Breaker 1, Breaker 2 Erick S, Keith M, Redman
Do My Thing Busta Rhymes
If I Ruled The World Nas
Dedication Smoothe Da Hustler
Games Money Boss Playas
Nas Freestyle Nas
Da Product Nine & Uneek
Studder Step Biz Markie
My Kinda Nigga Heather B & M.O.P
One Time For The East Coast DJ Mister Cee
TAPE KiNGZ
FLIP SQUAD
STRESS ENTERTAINMENT
MANAGEMENT/BOOKING
212.777.1570

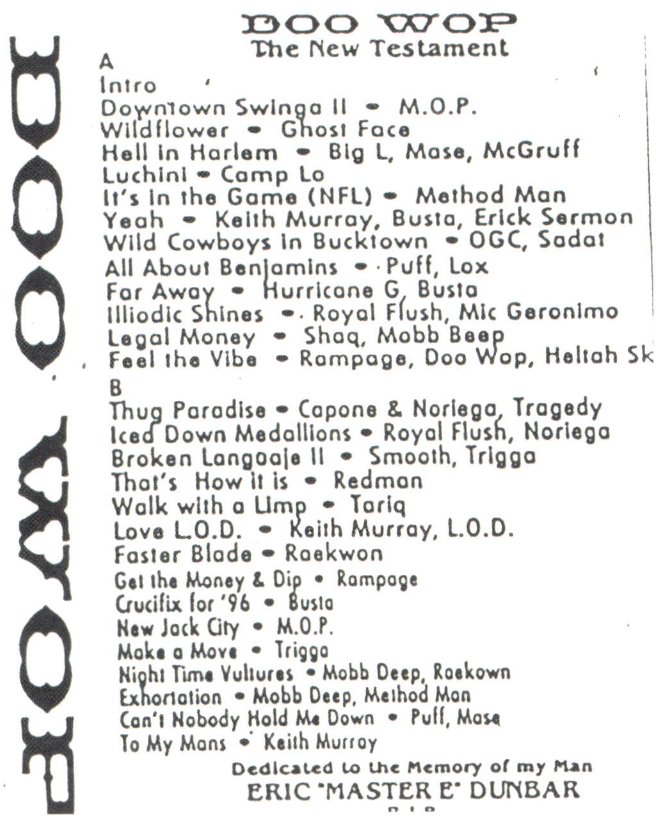
DOO WOP
DOO WOP
The New Testament
A
Intro
Downtown Swinga II • M.O.P.
Wildflower • Ghost Face
Hell in Harlem • Big L, Mase, McGruff
Luchini • Camp Lo
It's in the Game (NFL) • Method Man
Yeah • Keith Murray, Busta, Erick Sermon
Wild Cowboys in Bucktown • OGC, Sadat
All About Benjamins • Puff, Lox
Far Away • Hurricane G, Busta
Illiodic Shines • Royal Flush, Mic Geronimo
Legal Money • Shaq, Mobb Beep
Feel the Vibe • Rampage, Doo Wop, Heltah Sk
B
Thug Paradise • Capone & Noriega, Tragedy
Iced Down Medallions • Royal Flush, Noriega
Broken Langoaje II • Smooth, Trigga
That's How it is • Redman
Walk with a Limp • Tariq
Love L.O.D. • Keith Murray, L.O.D.
Faster Blade • Raekwon
Get the Money & Dip • Rampage
Crucifix for '96 • Busta
New Jack City • M.O.P.
Make a Move • Trigga
Night Time Vultures • Mobb Deep, Raekown
Exhortation • Mobb Deep, Method Man
Can't Nobody Hold Me Down • Puff, Mase
To My Mans • Keith Murray
Dedicated to the Memory of my Man
ERIC "MASTER E" DUNBAR

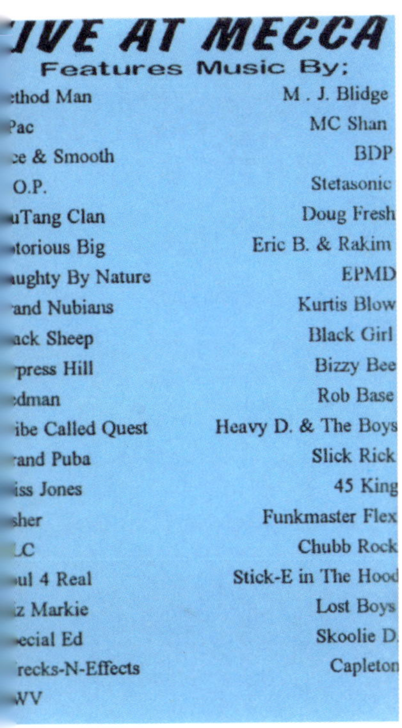
IVE AT MECCA
Features Music By:
thod Man M . J. Blidge
Pac MC Shan
e & Smooth BDP
O.P. Stetasonic
uTang Clan Doug Fresh
torious Big Eric B. & Rakim
aughty By Nature EPMD
and Nubians Kurtis Blow
ack Sheep Black Girl
press Hill Bizzy Bee
dman Rob Base
ibe Called Quest Heavy D. & The Boys
and Puba Slick Rick
iss Jones 45 King
sher Funkmaster Flex
LC Chubb Rock
ul 4 Real Stick-E in The Hood
z Markie Lost Boys
ecial Ed Skoolie D.
recks-N-Effects Capleton
WV

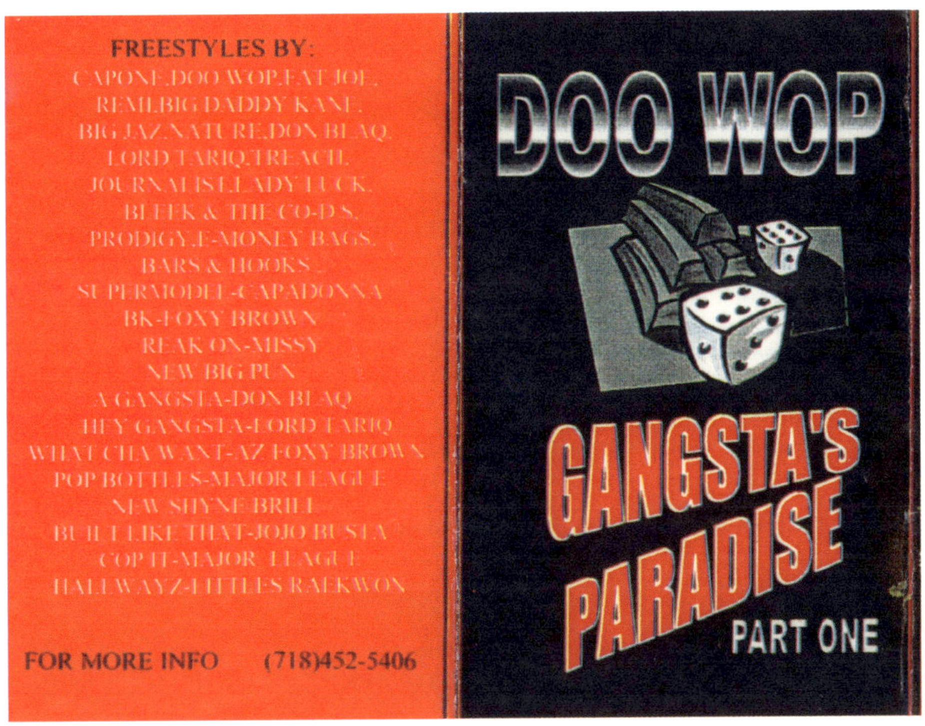
FREESTYLES BY:
CAPONE,DOO WOP,FAT JOE,
REMI,BIG DADDY KANE,
BIG JAZ,NATURE,DON BLAQ,
LORD TARIQ,TREACH,
JOURNALIST,LADY LUCK,
BLEEK & THE CO-D.S,
PRODIGY,E-MONEY BAGS,
BARS & HOOKS
SUPERMODEL-CAPADONNA
BK-FOXY BROWN
REAK ON-MISSY
NEW BIG PUN
A GANGSTA-DON BLAQ
HEY GANGSTA-LORD TARIQ
WHAT CHA WANT-AZ FOXY BROWN
POP BOTTLES-MAJOR LEAGUE
NEW SHYNE BRILL
BUILT LIKE THAT-JOJO BUSTA
COP IT-MAJOR LEAGUE
HALLWAYZ-LITTLES RAEKWON
FOR MORE INFO (718)452-5406
DOO WOP
GANGSTA'S PARADISE
PART ONE

DJ TONY TOUCH

Power Cypha: Taking Mixtape Freestyles Even Further

Tony Touch had already been dropping dope mixtapes one-by-one since the start of the '90s, flexing his top-notch DJ skills while lacing listeners with the newest, hottest songs. But it was his *Power Cypha 50 MCs* series that truly buried his competition.

Where Doo Wop started with the freestyles, Tony Touch continued by creating a three-volume series of mixtapes that each featured 50 MCs rhyming over 50 beats—and the concept was perfectly executed each time. Eventually, the two DJs would team up to form an unstoppable duo, the Diaz Brothers.

FIRST TAPES

Tony Touch: I started my shit in '91. I kept it simple by just numbering my tapes. *Hip-Hop* #1, or *Reggae* #1. *R&B Blends* #1. And to this day, I stuck with that formula, so people are able to go back through their collection if they're missing something. It's easy to track.

Hip-Hop #1 was my first tape. Plain and simple. To this day, I do it all live in one take. Sometimes there will be mistakes. But for the most part, the recordings have always been live. Straight to cassette.

I organize my playlist before I make the tape, and put the records in sequence. And I'll have a couple of practice sessions to see if one record works well going into the other. They're planned out, but they're all recorded live. I would pre-record my intros though, and add some special effects. But I would go straight through on the cassette live.

INSPIRATION

52 Beats is the one tape that really stands out for me. That set it off for a lot of New York DJs. And there was another DJ in Brooklyn named Johnny T. He was the one that kind of inspired me to record and put everything in different genres. He would do hip hop, or Latin, or club music. He was the first guy I saw doing it like that. He was making tapes before a lot of the Brooklyn heads.

EXCLUSIVES

That definitely changed the game a little bit. It was a great marketing tool for the guys that were doing it and getting the early records. The only thing for me is that sometimes just because it was an exclusive didn't mean it was a dope record. I kind of stuck to my guns and made sure everything I put out was quality hip hop, whether it was new or even if it was out for a month. I just wanted to make sure I put those bangers on every cassette so they would stand the test of time. Sometimes you may get a record, and the quality may not even sound that great. I would have just preferred to have an official recording of it and do the record justice.

It's always been about skills. There's no denying that people were into hearing the newest, newest songs first. It got to a point where there were a few people fighting for those first records. I didn't even want to compete with that. I stood in my own lane, and made sure my fan base was catered to. My fan base wanted to hear clean mixes. Good quality cassettes. They wanted the cassettes to sound good in their car. They didn't want to hear all highs. Part of the whole skill process was the recording process and having good engineering skills. Making sure your shit was EQ'd right. That's something I took pride in.

POWER CYPHA 50 MCS SERIES

I had done intros a few times with live rappers before, like Buckshot, Smif-N-Wessun, and O.C.

before I got to *#50*. Doo Wop was the first one to have multiple MCs on a cassette. He did *95 Live*. It was groundbreaking, and every DJ was on the shit when he put that out. He raised the stakes, and took the game to another level.

A year later, when I got up to my 50th mixtape, I wanted to try to take what he did to another level, and try to do what he did with *50 MCs*. I think he had like 15 or something like that. It was an anniversary cassette, and I wanted to make it special. And I also knew that with what Doo Wop did, I had to step it up.

50 MCS VOLUME 1

90 percent of it was recorded at D&D Studios. There were other studios, too. Chung King, and a couple of independent studios I had to go into to work with other rappers. But most of it was done at D&D. It was all through relationships I had built through the years. I was DJing in so many clubs, so people knew me from that. I was on Hot 97 for a little bit, we had *The Mic Check Show* up there. So it was that, and also a big chunk of it was just being at D&D Studios, casually dropping in for other sessions. I would get artists like that, too.

The most standout session from the first volume had to be the Boot Camp session. That's the one where Funkmaster Flex played the whole thing on the radio. It was like 12 minutes long. That shit got a lot of love. That was one of the things that put me on the map.

50 MCS VOLUME 2 & 3

Out of all three of them, Volume 2 was probably my favorite one. The momentum was really strong off of the first one. I had a little more clout, so I was able to get a couple more big dogs on there. Another reason it's my favorite is because it has the Big Pun session and the Big L on the same tape. That was some timeless shit. And we had Redman, and also the whole Diggin' In The Crates crew on that. That shit was definitely official.

For *Volume 3*, Eminem was doing work with Game Recordings. I had a relationship over there with Jonathan Shecter. So they were able to hook that up for me. Plus, I had a relationship with Paul Rosenberg when they had first dropped *The Slim Shady EP*. I was really early on that record. I didn't really know him, but I was in the loop early with people he was involved with. That shit turned out to be crazy. That was like late '98, early '99.

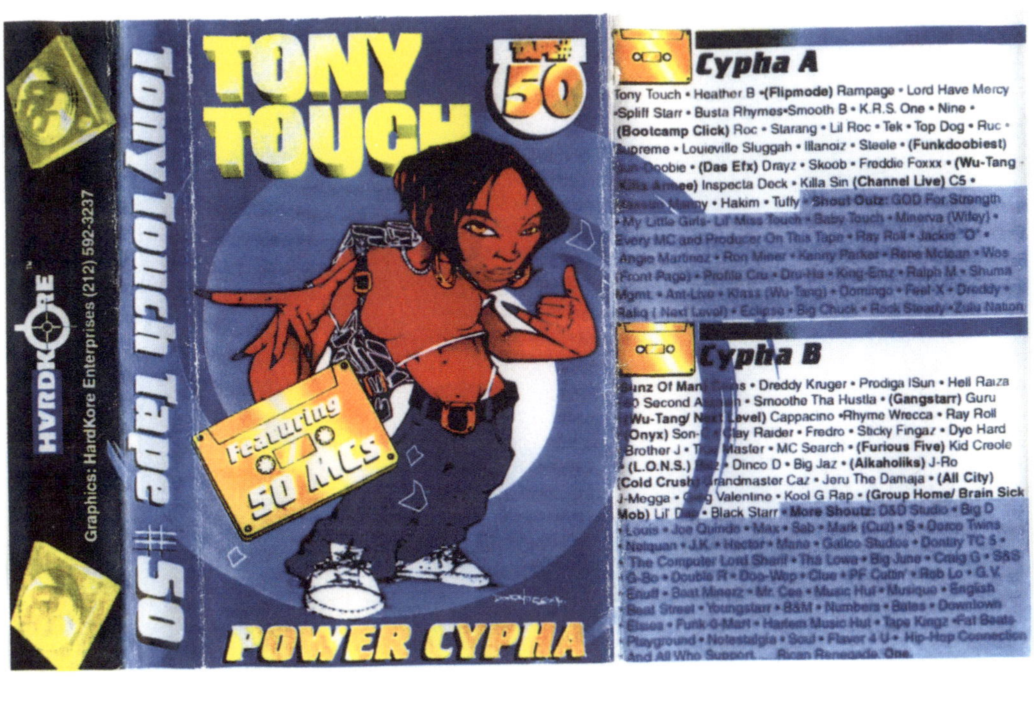

HIP HOP #15*

******** RAP 15 ********
** A NEW BEGINNING **

A) DWYCK - GANGSTARR (WIT NICE-N-SMOOTH)
GHETTO RED HOT - SUPER CAT
TRUE FU-SHNICK - FU-SHNICKENS
SHE SED IT WAZ GRATE - ED O.G.-N- DA BULLDOGS
LET DA HOES GO - NAUGHTY BY NATURE
JUMP AROUND - HOUSE OF PAIN
JUMP - KRISKROSS (TOUCH MIX!)
CAN'T STOP DA BUMRUSH - KRISKROSS
YA BROTHER DOES - ROXANNE (THE REAL)
FAKIN DA FUNK - MAIN SOURCE
JACKIN 4 BEATS - ICE CUBE
EYE KNOW - DE LA SOUL
****
DEEP COVER-- DR. DRE WIT SNOOP DOG
EYE EXAMINATION - DEL (FUNKY HOMOSAPIEN)
GEAR - ROXANNE WIT CHUBB ROCK
STONED IS DA WAY OF DA WALK - CYPRESS HILL
13 -N- GOOD - KRS-1
ILLEST BROTHER - GANG STARR
DON'T CURSE - (HEAVY D-KOOL G.RAP-GRAND PUBA-
C.L.SMOOTH-BIG DADDY KANE-PETE ROCK-Q-TIP.)
STROBELITE HONEY - BLACK SHEEP
ALL SOULED OUT - PETE ROCK -N-C.L.SMOOTH
HOW DO I LUV THEE - QUEEN LATIFAH
NUFF RESPECT - BIG DADDY KANE
MR. LOVER MAN - SHABBA RANKS

SPECIAL SHOUT OUT TO THE "REAL ROXANNE" WE BORN
BLOW UP THIS YEAR GIRL.......BORIQUAS IN EFFIZ
TONY TOUCH PRODUCTIONS

RAP 16

RAP 16
BUSHWICK BAD BOY MIX

A) TONY TOUCH N D STROY
TWO FOR THE TIME-----NUBIAN CRACKERS
EAST COAST----DAS EFX
THE BIG MAN----CHUBB ROCK
ROAD RUNNER (REMIX)---CHI ALI
SOUL BROTHER # 1-----PETE ROCK N C.L.
SO WHAT YOU WANT---BEASTIE BOYS FEAT.
CYPRESS HILL
RAINING REVOLUTION---ARRESTED DEVELOPMENT
HEADCRACKER-----DOUBLE XX POSSE
PASS THE VIBES----POWERULE (WASSUPP!!)
COSMIC ARK----X CLAN
FUNKY TECHNICIAN----LORD FINESSE/MIKE SMOOTH
BIZ MARKIE MEGAMIX----TONY TOUCH IN EFFEZNECT

B) ORIGINAL WAY----KRS ONE W/ FREDDIE FOXX
TOP BILLIN---AUDIO 2 (CLARK KENT 92 MIX)
PLACE WHERE WE DWELL (BROOKLYN)--GANG STARR
UNSOLVED MYSTERIES----ALL CITY PRODUCTIONS
IF IT AINT ROUGH,IT AINT RIGHT---PETE ROCK
C.L. SMOOTH
CANT HOLD IT BACK---K SOLO
NUFF OF THE RUFF STUFF---QUEEN LATIFAH
DONT SWEAT THE TECHNIQUE----ERIC B-N-RAKIM
BIG MAMA----SHANTE
JUMP AROUND----HOUSE OF PAIN
MIC CHECKA-----DAS EFX

PEACE TO ALL HARDCORE RAP CREWS...MI GENTE UP
IN BUSHWICK....AND L.E.S. IN EFFECT!!!!!
ALSO STUPID BIG SHOUT OUT TO THE POWERULE POSSE!

HIP HOP 17 * TONY TOUCH

RAP 17
for the HARDCORE

A) WISHING ON A STAR---COVER GIRLS (TOUCHED)
GO BROOKLYN----HOUSE RATED
FINAL FRONTIER-----MC REN
SKINZ----PETE ROCK,CL SMOOTH,GRAND PUBA
HES GONNA CATCH IT----RSO
YES YOU MAY----LORD FINESSE (BIG L)
HOMEGIRL DONT PLAY THAT---YO YO
SHAKER-----COOLY LIVE
HAND ON THE GLOCK----CYPRESS HILL
TENNESSEE---(A PIECE) REMIX A. DEVELOPMENT
TAKE IT PERSONAL----GANG STARR
JUSSUMEN-----DAS EFX (PETE ROCK REMIX)
360° WHAT GOES AROUND----GRAND PUBA
CROSSOVER------EPMD
BABALU BAD BOY-----MELLOW MAN ACE

B) RELAX WIT PEP-----ERIC B & RAKIM
EX GIRL TO THE NEXT GIRL---GANG STARR
MIC CHECKA REMIX----DAS EFX
VERTICAL JOYRIDE----ZA.M.G.(WASSUP)
XODUS------X CLAN
FOR PETES SAKE----PETE ROCK ,C.L. SMOOTH
PASS THE MIC----THE YOUNGSTERS
LET IT ALL HANG OUT---A.D.O.R
BITCH GET A JOB----LIL BASTARDS
LOVE AINT LIKE THIS----COMPREDATOR
PARTY OVER HERE----LORD FINESSE (REMIX)
TOSS IT UP---ZHIGGE
HOW NOT TO GET JERKED----KRS 1 (B.D.P)
PUNISHER---ERIC B AND RAKIM
CORRUPTION----ROXANNE (WORLD PREMIERE) X
D.J. TONY TOUCH KICKING THE NEW HIP HOP FL

18 TOUCH of HIP HOP

HIP HOP #18
TONY TOUCH ON THE SCENE

A) HERE IT COMES----M.C. SERCH
BEATS AINT LIKE THIS----COMPREDATOR
TOSS IS UP -----ZHIGGE
PARTY OVER HERE---INST.--LORD FINESSE
THE BOP STEP-----THE FUTURE SOUND
SCRATCH BRING IT BACK----EPMD
LONELY MONDAY MORNING-----SNOW
PUT YOUR HEAD OUT---HOUSE OF PAIN,CYPRESS HILL
CATCHIN WRECK----SHOWBIZ & A.G.
BEHIND THE SCENES----M.C. REN
PEOPLE EVERYDAY----ARRESTED DEVELOPMENT
CHANGES IVE BEEN GOING THROUGH---MARY BLIGE
ONE NIGHT STAND-----FATHER M.C.

B) SILOQUY OF CHAOS----GANG STARR
CUMIN AT CHA----EPMD W/DAS EFX
A.D.A.M.-----X CLAN
*BRAND NEW HEAVIES RAP SESSION (TOUCHED) *
A TASTE OF MAIN SOURCE,KOOL G RAP,GRAND PUBA
*& GANG STARR *
BASEMENT--------PETE ROCK C.L. SMOOTH
DOWN THE LINE----NICE N SMOOTH W/ BASS BLASTER
MILOT,PREACHER EARL,GANG STARR
IF ONLY----DAS EFX
KEEP THE BEAT----ERIC B AND RAKIN
SEX IS ALL THAT-----RED HOT LOVER LOVER TONE
YA WISH YOU COULD----SPECIAL ED (LOOK BACK)
REAL LOVE-----MARY BLIGE
BACK IN THE DAYZ------DOUG E FRESH (GET FRESH)
BACK TO THE GRILL-----SERCH,RED HOT LOVER LOVER
CHUBB ROCK, NASTY NAS

DEDICATED TO THE MEMORY OF ALBERT GONZALEZ...MAY
YOUR SOUL REST IN EVERLASTING PEACE.....YOUR BOY
TONY TOUCH......

TONY TOUCH 19 WIP HOP

RAP ATTACK # 19
D. J. TONY TOUCH GETTIN
--BUCK--

A) JUMP-----KENNY DOPE (TOUCHED)
JUMP AROUND REMIX----HOUSE OF PAIN W/
PETE ROCK
DWYCK-----GANG STARR/NICE N SMOOTH(TOUCHED)
REAL LOVE ---MARY BLIGE (ACCAPELLA)(TOUCHED)
NOBODY'S SAFE CHUMP----EPMD
SHAMROCKS AND SHENANIGANS---HOUSE OF PAIN
STRAIGHT FROM THE SEWER---DAS EFX
FREESTYLE (YO THATS THAT SHIT)---DIAMOND
AND PSYCHOTIC NEUROTICS
TRUE FU-SHNICK--REMIX AND(TOUCHED)-FU SHCNICKINS
PICK IT UP-----KENNY DOPE
360° WHAT GOES AROUND----GRAND PUBA
BEATS TO RHYMES----RUN DMC (TOUCHED)
JACK OF SPADES----K.R.S. ONE (TOUCHED)

B) NO SHAME IN MY GAME----GANG STARR
GOODBYE----RICHIE MELODY
HAND UP-----KENNY DOPE (THUMBS UP DUDE)
CANT FRONT ON ME---PETE ROCK C.L.SMOOTH
FOOTPRINTS-----TRIBE CALLED QUEST
GOOD THANG----GLENN JONES(SUPERMEN REMIX)
ONE FOR THE TIME-----NUBIAN CRACKERS
HEADBANGER---EPMD,K-SOLO,REDMAN***PUMPIN***
HOLY RUM SWIG-----X CLAN
PSYCHO-----LORDS OF THE UNDERGROUND
RUMP SHAKER------WRECKS N EFFECT
BACK TO BACK RHYMING---LORD FINESSE/ANDRE THE GIANT
TOP O THE MORNING TO YA---HOUSE OF PAIN
WHERE THERES A WILL THERES A WAY---ROXANNE(SUP)

D.J. TONY TOUCH CATCHIN IT, BUSHWICK ON THE MAP
BELLEEEEE DAT!!!!!!!!! TOUCH N D STROY, WATCH OUT
FOR IT!!!!!!PEACE AND KEEP IN FOCUS!!!!!

TONY TOUCH RAP 20

D.J. TONY TOUCH PRESENTS
RAP 20
FOR THE HEAD

A) BLUNT MIX---EAST SIDE HOODS (TOUCHED)
STILL DIGGIN----SHOWBIZ & A.G.
FEEL THE VIBE,FEEL THE BEAT----K.R.S ONE
SOCIAL NARCOTICS----MC SERCH FEAT. FATAL
BEST KEPT SECRET----DIAMOND D
HERE WE GO-----THE CRAZY BUNCH
3 MEN AT CHUNG KING---RED HOT LOVER TONE,
GRAND PUBA, CHUBB ROCK
GOOD COP, BAD COP BEATS
HOT SEX-----TRIBE CALLED QUEST (WHERE YA AT)
HAUL AND PULL----DADDY FREDDY (UNDERSTAND ME!!)
NOT GOING TO BE ABLE TO DO IT---DOUBLE X POSSE
GUESS WHOS BACK----HOUSE OF PAIN
REST ASSURED----ERIC B AND RAKIM
MOMMA CAN I GET SOME---ROXANNE WITH THE LITTLE
BASTARDS
HOW FREAKY ARE YOU---2nd DEGREE (WHAT UP D)

B) STONED IN THE WAY OF THE WALK (REMIX)--CYPRESS
HILL
THATS HOW YOU ROLL A BLUNT---REDMAN
TAKE TWO AND PASS----GANG STARR
RUFF NECK-----DOUBLE X POSSE
CROSSOVER (SLAMMIN REMIX)-------EPMD
HOUSE AND THE RISING SUN---HOUSE OF PAIN FEAT.
SON OF FUNK DOOBIEST
STRAIGHTEN IT OUT----PETE ROCK AND CL SMOOTH
DO WHAT I GOTTA DO----PUBLIC ENEMY
DANCE TO THIS-----SHANTE
SOUL BY THE POUND----COMMON SENSE
WHATS GOING ON-----ERIC B AND RAKIM
REPRESENT-----SHOWBIZ,A.G. LORD FINESSE, BIG L
DESHAWN
LOST IN THE STORM--(MARLEY MARL REMIX)-CHUBB ROCK
F--K RODNEY KING-----WILLIE 9
D.J. TONY TOUCH (LIVE) PUMP THIS!!!!!!!!!
BUSHWICK IN DA HOUSE

B-BOY HIP HOP 21

A) WHO GOT THE PROPS---BLACK MOON(BUSHWICK!!)
PUNKS JUMP UP TO GET BEAT DOWN---BRAND NUBIAN
BOUNCE TO THIS----SHOWBIZ,A.G.,BLACKSHEEP
THE PURE THANG------DOUBLE X POSSE
RATED R---------REDMAN
ROUGH HOUSE-----ROUGH HOUSE SURVIVORS
DEM NO WORRY ME-----SUPERCAT,HEAVY D (HIP HOP)
BOGLE-----BUJO BANTON(HIP HOP MIX)
CLAP YA HANDS--------NUBIAN CRACKERS
YO THATS THAT SHIT-----DIAMOND D
SILLY RABBIT-----MELLOW MAN ACE

B) TONIGHTS THE NIGHT-----REDMAN
YABADABADOO-----CHUBB ROCK & GUESTS
COMIN AT CHA------EPMD, DAS EFX
HITS THE HEAD------MC SERCH
GIVE IT UP-----RED HOT LOVER TONE
SILENCE THE LAMBS------SHOWBIZ, A.G.
CAUGHT UP IN THE SYSTEM---UNDERGROUND MAFIA
EVERYTHING IS FAIR-----TRIBE CALLED QUEST
TAKE IT EZ------COMMON SENSE
DEADLY RHYMES------SHANTE, KOOL G RAP
LETTERMAN------K SOLO
I GOT A MAN-----POSITIVE K

D.J. TONY TOUCH CATCHING WRECK, BUSHWICK GOT
IT GOING ON..... PUMP THIS......

DJ TONY TOUCH RAP 23

RAP 23
D.J.TONY TOUCH

A) INTRO
THROW YA GUNZ--------ONYX
4 BETTER OR 4 WORSE----PHARCYDE
YOU KNOW WHAT IM ABOUT----LORD FINESSE
FLIP DA SCRIPT-----THE KING AND I
WATCH YO NUGGETS-----REDMAN,ERICK SERMON
OFF THE WALL-----BLACK SHEEP
CHECK IT OUT (REMIX)---GRAND PUBA/MARY BLIGE
WHOS THE MAN------HEAVY D (***)
PUNKS JUMP UP TO GET BEAT DOWN---REMIX
BRAND NUBIANS/DIAMOND D
FAT POCKETS----SHOWBIZ AND A.C.
KOOL LIKE DAT-----DIGABLE PLANETS
THE FUNKIEST----FUNK DOOBIEST
DAYS OF OLD------PARIS (A PIECE)

B) CASULTIES OF WAR---REMIX----ERIC B AND RAKIM
FREEDOM GOT AN A.K.-------LENCH MOB
TAP THE BOTTLE-----YOUNG BLACK TEENAGERS
WE CAME TO GET WRECK-----ROUGH HOUSE SURVIVORS
w/ SADDAT X
OFFICER-----PHARCYDE
FUNKY LEMONADE--------CHI ALI (REMIX)
PSYCHO-----LORDS OF THE UNDERGROUND (TOUCHED)
BRAIN 2 YOU-------THE KING AND I
DONT BE A 304---------AMG
WHAT--------TRIBE CALLED QUEST
GANGSTA BITCH-------APACHE
FOR THE NON-BELIEVES-------MOBB DEEP
STRAIT OUT THE JUNGLE----JUNGLE BROTHERS
I GOT IT MADE-------SPECIAL ED

PEACE TO ALL THE BROTHERS IN BUSHWICK, L.E.S.
EAST NEW YORK,UPTOWN,QUEENS,JERSEY!!!!!! KEEP
PUMPIN THIS......D.J. TONY TOUCH PRODUCTIONS

TONY TOUCH HIP HOP 24

RAP WAR
- HIP HOP 24!!!!!!!!

A) I GOT IT BAD YALL----KING TEE (ALKOHOLIKS)
NUTHIN BUT A G THANG----DR. DRE, SNOOP DOGG
HERE WE GO-----FUNKMASTER FLEX PROJECT
FUNKY JEEP MUSIC
GUNSHOT------KENNY DOPE FEATURING SHAGGY
TIME 4 SOME ACTION-------REDMAN
CHECK IT OUT YALL----FRANKIES BEATS
CHECK IT----------REMIX---LORDS OF THE UNDER
GOOD TIME-----KOOL MOE DEE
HOODY MIX-----CUTLASS
RAKIN IN THE DOUGH-----ZHIGGE
LOUDER THAN A BOMB---PUBLIC ENEMY REMIX
WHO GOT THE PROPS-----BLACK MOON

B) BRING IT ON -----ALI DEE w/ KOOL G RAP
FRIGGA you-----YANKEE B, TUNDA MUZIK
WALK LIKE A DUCK-----KURIOUS GEORGE
SIX MILLION WAYS----FLEX PROJECT
PUFF THE HEAD-----MC SERCH
RAP PRIME MINISTER----PETE NICE,DADDY RICH
WRECK SHOP---WRECKX IN EFFECT (DUB)
SILENCE OF THE LAMBS----SHOWBIZ,AG (REMIX)
TONY TOUCH CUTS
OH SUZANNA----MR. FREEZE,HOMEWRECKERS w/GRAN
PUBA

DA WHOLE KIT AND KABOODLE----MAD KAP
I WANNA ROCK (DOO DOO BROWN)---LUKE
DJ TONY TOUCH FLEXIN----EVIL D IN THE HOUSE

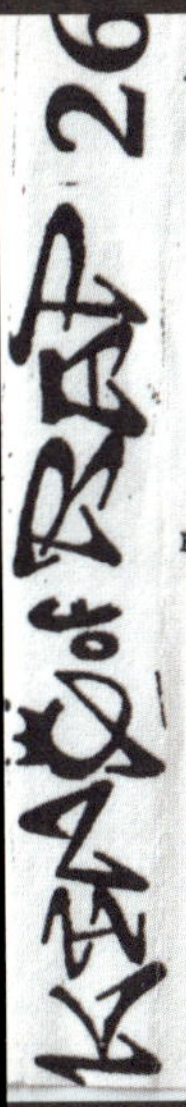

A) INTRO-----TOUCH N D STROY
UNRATIONAL----ARTZ OF ORIGIN
SNEAKIN UP ON YA-----FU SCHNICKENS
MAKE SOME NOISE------TONY T
BUSS DAT ASS-----KING TEE / ALCOHOLICS
ROLL WITH THE FLAFOR---NAUGHTY BY NATURE, CH
FU,FREDDIE FOXX LATIFAH
HEAVY D,D NICE, DRESS
HOODS COME FIRST----NAUGHTY BY NATURE
DIPPITY----EAST SIDE HOODS
IGPAY ATINLAY-----BLACK MADNESS
BOW WOW WOW-----FUNK DOOBIEST
I GET WRECKED---TIM DOGG AND KRS ONE
WHO YA GONNA SHOOT WIT THAT----LENCH MOBB

B) PUBLIC ENEMY SERVICE ANOUNCEMENT (CB-4)
HOW IM COMIN-----LL COOL J
OFF AND ON----TRENDS OF CULTURE
DOWN WITH THE KING----RUN DMC
BLUE FUNK------HEAVY D
ITS NOT A GAME----PETE ROCK CL SMOOTH
A DAY IN THE LIFE---DIAMOND W/ BRAND NUBIANS
THROW YOUR GUNS-----ONYX
SHITTIN ON EM-----FUNK DOOBIEST
PUM PUM DUB----EAST SIDE HOODS
GET YOUR WEIGHT UP-----APACHE
BOUNCE TO THIS------SHOWBIZ AND AG W/DRES (R
BLACK COP-----B.D. P
LET ME RIDE-----DR. DRE
DOLLY MY BABY----SUPERCAT W/ MARY BLIGE

THAT BUSHWICK BANDELERO DID IT AGAIN!!!!!!PO
BIG UP THE M.C. D STROY .TOUCH N D TROY COMIN

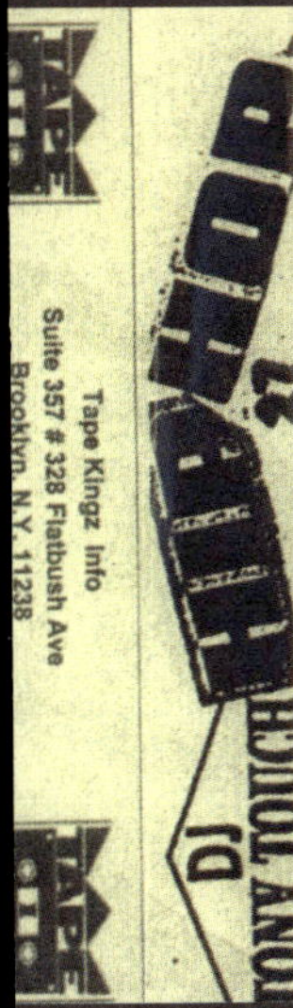

RAP 27

A) HIP HOP HEAVEN

TOO SMOOTH-----MASTERS AT WORK(INTRO)
PUERTO RICO-----LIL MS' BIG MUSIC
ARGS THE MAN-----HOUSE OF PAIN
FRUCK WHAT YOU HEARD-----DIAMOND
TEST THE ROCKET LAUNCHER-----CHOCLATE BAM BOO
MADD SKILLZ-----LORDS OF THE UNDERGROUND
ROLL WITH THE FLAVOR-----KAFKI BOUNCE TRACK
FLAVOR UNIT MC.S
SLAM -----ONYX (LET THE BOYZ BE BOYZ)
N.F.A.-----NO FRONTIN ALLOWED-----LL COOL J W/
THE LORDS OF THE UNDER.
ZULU WAR CHANT REMIX---AFRIKA BAMBATTA(TIME ZONE)
ITS ON-----NAUGHTY BY NATURE
THE MIX LORDS-----TONY T
FLIP DA SCRIPT-----(DJ PREMIER REMIX) KING AND I
DADDY-----A.D.I.
LOVE ME OR LEAVE ME ALONE-----BRAND NUBIANS
FUNKY SMILE-----EAST SIDE HOODS (A PIECE)

B) CRUZ POP-----THE YOUNGSTAS
HIT EM FROM THE BACK-----MOBB DEEP
LORD JAZZ HIT ME ONE TIME-----LORDS OF THE UNDER..
DA BEE HIGUZ-----ONYX
BLOODY VIBE 93-----MASTERS AT WORK (PIECE)
LET ME BE THE ONE-----INTRO
THE EM-----D.J.ENUFF AND THE TEK HOODS
DIPPITY-----EAST SIDE HOODS (A PIECE)
FUNKADELIC RELIC-----LL COOL J
HEY GIRL-----APACHE
LIVIN IN A ZOO-----P.E.
WELCOME TO THE TERRORDOME-----P.E.
COME ON LETS MOVE IT-----SPECIAL ED
WARM IT UP KANE-----BIG DADDY KANE
CAN I KICK IT-----TRIBE CALLED QUEST
OODLES OF O's-----DE LA SOUL
NO DELAYIN-----NICE N SMOOTH
ROAD TO THE RICHES-----KOOL G RAP
THE BIG PAYBACK-----EPMD

D.J. TONY TOUCH ON S**E NEW SHIT,....HAD ENOUGH!!
BIG UP,D-STROY,RAYROLL,OVEX,GEE,ENUFF,CUTLASS
AND ALL BROOKLYN,UPTOWN CREWS.....

HIP HOP 28
GET IT STRAIGHT

A) ON THE RUN----KOOL G RAP & POLO
FROM DA BRICKS----LORDS OF THE UNDER..
IBWin WIT MY CREWin----------YO YO
THREE LITTLE INDIANS----RUN DMC
WRECK BREAKBEAT
NO EQUAL-------THE BEATNUTS
WHERES IT AT------FUNKD OO BIEST
HOLD DOWN THE FORT-----MOBB DEEP
STRANDED ON DEATH ROW---DR. DRE & CREW
TONIGHTS THE NIGHT TOUCH MIX**************
TONIGHTS THE NIGHT---REDMAN
GRAB YOUR GAT!!!----TIM TOG,PREACHER EARL,ME

B) CONT......
PASSIN ME BY------PHARCYDE
INNER CITY BOUNDARIES-----FREESTYLE FELLOWSHIP
WHATS NEXT ON THE MENU---PETE ROCK CL SMOOTH
HERE COMES THE BREAK---MAD KAP
WRECK BREAKBEAT
HITTIN SWITCHES-------ERICK SERMON
REIGN OF THE TECH-----BEATNUTS
COME ON EVERYBODY-----P.F. CUTTIN
DONT WALK AWAY---JADE (TOUCH MIX)
GET OPEN-----RUN DMC
THATS WHEN YA LOST----SOULS OF MISCHIEF
GO BANG------(O' DOUBLE M
THE BUDDA CHANT----MASTERS AT WORK
HOW YOU GET A RECORD DEAL----BIG DADDY KANE
PARTY AND BULLSHIT-------BIG

D.J. TONY TOUCH ON THE CONTROL!!!!!!PEACE

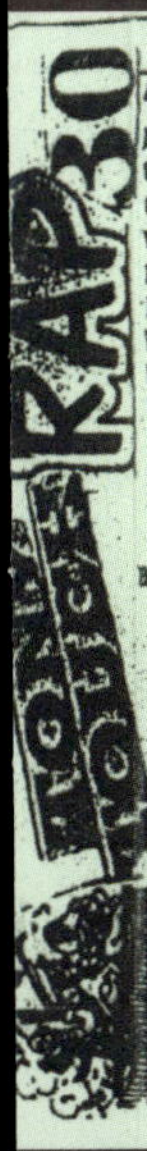

DOWN AND DIRTY!!!

A) ILL INTRO------TOUCH AND D STROY
MADE IN AMERICA-----DEL
WILD BROOKLYN BANDITS------BLACK MADNESS
CRAZY DRUNKEN STYLE-----MASTA ACE INC.
VALLEY OF THE SKINZ------TRENDS OF CULTURE
DEAR DIARY----------AKINYELE
FLOW JOE-------FAT JOE(THE GANGSTA)
WHOS AT THE DOOR-----SHAM & THE PROFESSOR
WHEN THE SHIT GOES DOWN-----CYPRESS HILL
REAL NIGGAZ--------TEK HOODS
IZIT NATURAL--------- THE YOUNGSTAS
DO YOU WANNA HEAR IT----NUBIAN CRACKERS(TOUCHED)
BOOMIN IN YA JEEP------SCREECHY DAN (KENNY DOPE)
GET UP--------MASTERS AT WORK

B) BOOM WITH THIS--------BUJRO BANTON
IZ U WIT ME---------THE YOUNGSTAS
COME ON EVERYBODY-----RUN DMC
ALL I THINK ABOUT IS YOU-----JUNGLE BROS.
IM THE BIZ MARKIE----BIZ MARK
ROLLIN WITH UM DADDA------MASTA ACE INC.
INSANE IN THE MEMBRANE----CYPRESS HILL
FREAK MODE----INSTRUMENTAL REMIX--FUNK DOOBY.
MIND YOUR BUSINESS-----GRAND PUBA
TRANSIT RIDE--------GURU
CLOSE THE CRACKHOUSE------X' CEAN;PRT.BIG DADDY KA
ATTITUDE------------RUMPLESTILSKINZ
I PUT IT ON-----JAMALSKI
WHATS UP DOC----FU SCHNICKENS/SHAQUILLE O NEAL

ANOTHER HYPE TONY TOUCH PRODUCT!!! THANX FOR ALL
SUPPORT!!!!!PUMP PUMP PUMP....PUMP IT UP!!!!!

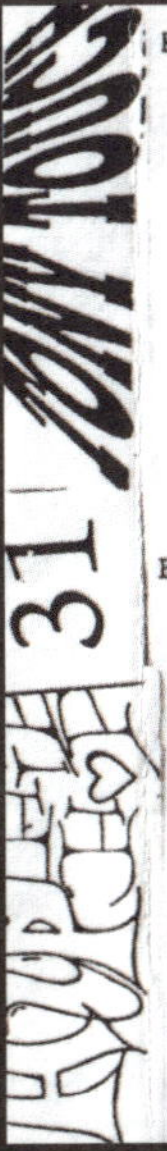

WELL DONE

R.I.P.----ED ROCK & PLEX !!!!!WELL MISS YOU
BREAK A DAWN------DE LA SOUL
SHIFTEE(TOUCH MIX)--ONYX
LIVE AND DIRECT BREAK---FRANKIE & PEACEMAKER
WATCH THE SOUND-----FAT JOE,PUBA,DIAMOND D
WHATS NEXT-------LEADERS OF THE NEW SCHOOL
CASH IN MY HANDS------NICE AND SMOOTH
AINT GOING OUT LIKE THAT---CYPRESS HILL
STOP SHAMMIN'--------BIG DADDY KANE
LIVE AND DIRECT BREAK---FRANKIE F. (WRECK)
FREAK OUT--------NIKKI D
COME ON BABY-----FUNKMASTER FLEX (FLIP SQUAD)
ONLY WHEN IM DRUNK-----THE ALKAHOLIKS
MAKE MY DAY----------BUJO BANTON (TROOPA MIX)

B) ASHLEY ROACHCLIP INTERVIEW---CHEECH AND CHONG
I WANNA GET HIGH----CYPRESS HILL
ONE IN A MILLION----PETE ROCK, CL SMOOTH
LAST CALL-----THE ALKAHOLIKS
RETURN OF THE CRAZY ONE----DIGITAL UNDERGROUN
STAY REAL--------ERICK SERMON
WE GETZ BUZY------------ILLEGAL FEAT. ERICK SER
BOOTLEGGA (REMIX)------HOODRATZ
FINE TUNE THE MIC---MAESTRO FRESH WES, SHOWBI
EN FOCUS---------DE LA SOUL
TONIGHTS THE NIGHT (REMIX)----REDMAN
GRAND GROOVE----INTELLIGENT HOODLUM
MR. SCARFACE:PART 3 THE FINAL CHAPTER

TONY TOUCH ON SOME ILL SHIT...FREAKIN THE FUN
CHECK ME OUT(WEPA WEDNESDAYS) AT CLUB 440

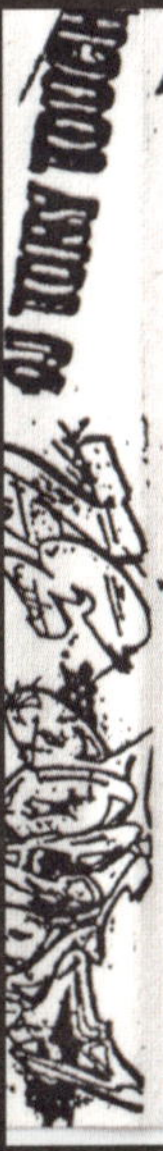

HIP HOP 32
TONY TOUCH MIX!

A) TOUCH INTRO---------D.J. TONY TOUCH
LOVELY HOW I LET MY MIND FLOAT------DE LA SOUL
BIZ MARKIE
HOW MANY EMCEES-------BLACK MOON
YOU MUST BE OUT YOUR FUCKIN MIND-----APACHE
KOOL G RAP, FAT JOE
THATS HOW IT IS---DISSESHOWEDO MIX------CASUAL
SLAUGHTAHOUSE------DEATH MIX------MASTA ACE INC.
TURN THA PARTY OUT-----ALKAHOLIKS (feat. LOOT
PACK)
OUTTA HERE-----KRS ONE (TOUCHED)
WHERES IT AT (MUGGS REMIX)---FUNKDOOBIEST
AAAAYY YOOOOOM ALRIGHT------DOUG E FRESH
FREAKS-----DOUG E FRESH
SHOOT TO KILL------------MAD LION

B) THREE LIL PUTOS-----CYPRESS HILL
LET THE BIG BOYZ PLAY----TRENDS OF CULTURE
IN THE WOODS------DE LA SOUL
NUBIAN CRACKER BREAK
DEATH BECOMES YOU-----PETE ROCK,CL SMOOTH
HERE WE GO AGAIN--------POOR RIGHTEOUS TEACHERS
SPONTANEOUS----(13 MC'S DEEP)-LEADERS OF THE N
OH MY GOSH (OH-OW)-----EAST SIDE HOODS
SHIT IZ REAL------BLACK MOON (BIG UP)
93 TILL INFINITY---SOULS OF MISCHIEF
SKINNY DIP--------ED O.G. BULLDOGS
RETURN OF THE BOOM BAP----KRS ONE
FEEL THE FLAVOR------MAD FLAVOR
ON THE M.I.C.----ILLEGAL--LORD FINESSE, A.G.

TONY TOUCH IN EFFIZNECT. SHOUT OUTS TO D STROY,
HELQUAN,TWINS,CREAM O LO,DE LA SOUL,BLACK MOON
DOUG E FRESH,FINESSE,AND ANYONE WHO BUMPS THIS

Wop and Toca remember how they united to become one of the dopest mixtape DJ duos in NYC hip-hop history.

Doo Wop: I was on the ultimate high off of *95 Live*, and a lot of people were doing stuff like that after my tape. Honestly, I don't know if I was referring to Tony or not when I did that rhyme on *Summer Jam 96*, I was just throwing that out there to all the DJs. I don't know if I had even heard *50 MCs* yet, or if that even bothered me. Because that to me was different. The whole tape was rapping. It was dope. So I didn't even include that in my shit, probably, I don't know. But I was just like, "To all y'all niggas biting my style..." on the intro to *Summer Jam 96*, when I rhymed to "The Bizness" with De La Soul and Common. So that's the one that Tony took a little offense too, and said something on his next one.

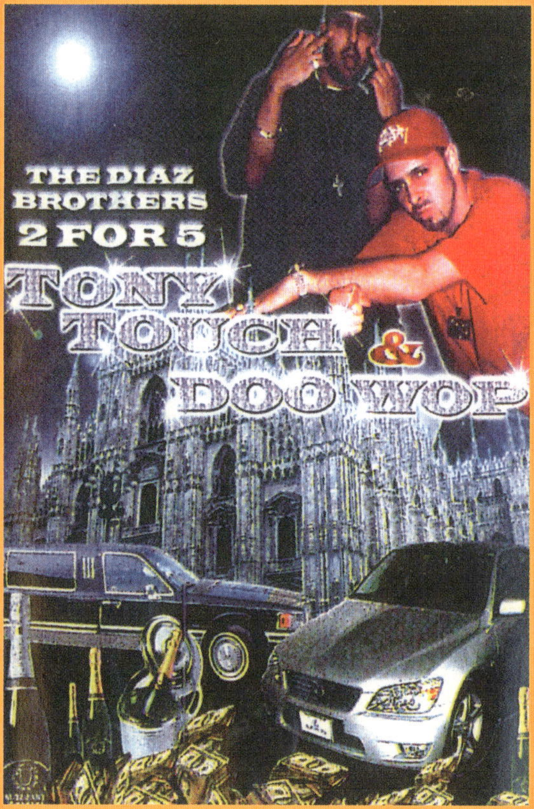

Then, someone told me to come meet up with him, and I went to D&D one night, and we came up with the Diaz Brothers right on the spot and did the intro. We laid down the "Phone Tap" beat, I went up to Harlem and got some weed, and came back and did that shit. And we've been the best of friends ever since. It almost seemed like it was meant to be.

Tony Touch: In the beginning, there was a little, not tension, but it was competitive. I know that after he dropped *95 Live*, there were a few people that did intros on their tapes. I took it to a whole other level. But he called a few people out, and I might have responded. Not really calling him out, but defending my shit, and kind of throwing back. Little darts thrown at each other on cassette. So it was really intense competition in the beginning.

That didn't last too long, though. We had some mutual friends that brought us together. It was all love, and the energy was right. He's one of the most creative guys I've ever worked with, as far as DJs. He's just a real creative cat. I think he's a dope MC. Since we both rhyme, and we're both Spanish, and both from the mixtape movement, the stars just lined up for us. When we did the first Diaz Brothers tape, that was one of the hottest cassettes on the street.

Doo Wop: *2 For 5* was our second tape, I believe. Everything with Tony was bugged out, because rapping style-wise were both different. He's more animated and I'm more laid back. But every time we'd do something and listen to it, we'd get so hype because it gels.

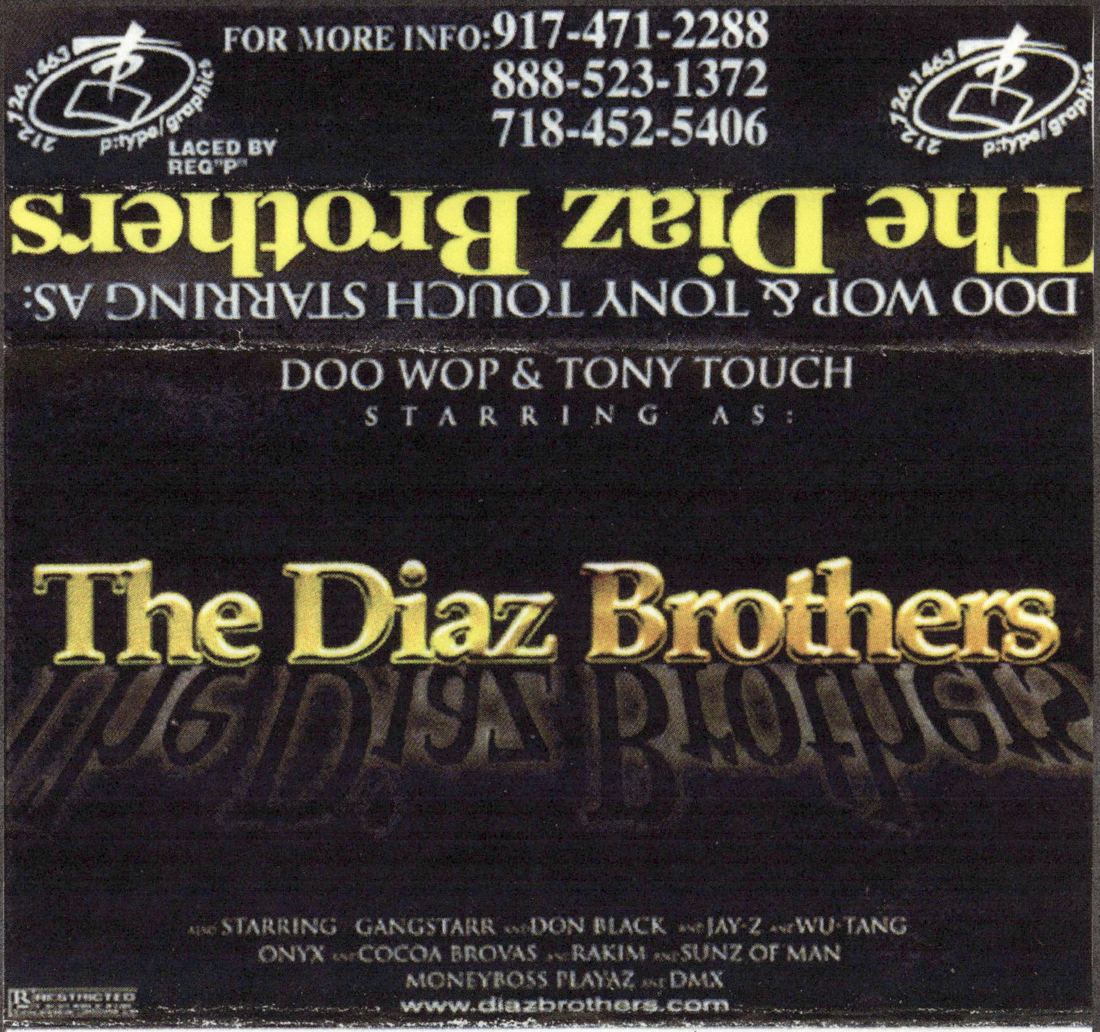

NOW PLAYING AT MIX TAPE SPOTS EVERYWHERE!!

Side 1

1. Phone Tap Intro Tony Touch, Doo Wop, Don Black
2. Blackstreet Blend
3. Doo Wop Freestyle
4. Forbidden Don Black
5. Area Code 212 Moneyboss Playaz w/Lord Tariq
6. Friend or Foe 98 Jay-Z
7. Pull It Cam/DMX
8. KRS/Common Live on Hot 97
9. DMX Blend
10. Dollar Bill Moneyboss Playaz
11. 357 CAM
12. The Birth AZ/RZA
13. Weekend Dave Hollister, Redman, E-Double
14. Can't Get You Off My Mind Mary J. feat. The Lox

Side 2

1. 4, 3, 2, 1 Intro Doo Wop & Tony Touch
2. I Put In Work Gangstarr
3. New York Rakim
4. Spanish Harlem Cocoa Brovas, Tony Touch, Hurricaine G
5. Avirex Mobb Deep
6. The Worst Wu-Tang/Onyx
7. Open Mic Nite High & Mighty
8. Puerto Rock Warriors Nas & Yankee
9. Slang Editorial Cappadonna
10. Wishful Thinking Punisher, Cypress, Fat Joe, Kool G Rap
11. Rhyme No More Jay-Z
12. Mad Love Nice & Smooth
13. High Drama Mike Zoot, Mos Def Shawn J Period
14. Life is Reality Sunz Of Man
15. 24 Hours To Live Mase & Co.
16. Call Of The Drum Tony Touch

DJ CLUE

The Question Mark Man: A Queens DJ Becomes the King of Exclusives

DJ Clue came through in the mid-'90s and completely upended the mixtape exclusives game, to the point where he was getting new records by the biggest and most buzzworthy artists before anyone, including artists like The Notorious B.I.G., Nas, Jay-Z, Mobb Deep, Wu-Tang Clan, The LOX, and more.

Following in the footsteps of guys like DJ S&S and Doo Wop, Clue would drop exclusives on his mixtapes sometimes months before they were set to be released as singles or album cuts. Countless '90s hip-hop classics were heard for the first time on Clue tapes, and how he did it was often a mystery, hence the question mark attached to the end of his name. He also gave himself "The Question Mark Man" nickname because at the time, no one in the game knew what he looked like.

Fittingly, Clue had been called out early in his mixtape-making career by The Notorious B.I.G. on Hot 97 for playing unreleased music from *Ready To Die* on his tapes. During a Funkmaster Flex on-air interview, B.I.G.'s warning was simple–"Clue, I'm looking for you. If you're listening, watch your back." Clue, looking to raise his mysterious profile and status in the streets even more, took the audio from the interview and flipped it into an intro for his next tape, *Scarecrow's Birthday*.

Thanks to his relentless consistency, Clue would eventually become the industry go-to for hip-hop exclusives, and his tapes became a staple for breaking new records and artists in a way that other mixtape and radio DJs couldn't keep up with. And yes, thanks to a peacemaking phone call he made to Puff, Clue got into B.I.G. and Bad Boy's good graces, and would be the first to play–with permission–some of the most beloved Biggie records of his career.

DJ S&S: Clue was making 60 minute mixtapes. Some Queens niggas was fucking with him, but he wasn't really on the radar, radar. Clue got big off all that Nas shit. His manager was Scarecrow, who was Steve Stoute's brother. And Steve Stoute managed Nas at the time. So it was like, "Queens looks out for Queens." And he was getting B.I.G. joints illegally, and B.I.G. wanted to beat the shit out of him. That blew him up, too. You got Biggie shouting you out on the radio talking about, "I'm gonna kill you." So the streets are like, "Who is this Clue nigga?" That's all she wrote from there. Then Puff Daddy gave him "Hypnotize" and all that.

DJ Drama: I remember the first time I heard "Who Shot Ya" on a Clue tape. I remember the first time hearing the Eddie F record with Biggie, Pac, Grand Puba, and Heavy D. That was on Clue's *Back to School* tape.

DJ Whoo Kid: People hated Clue because he probably was in the right place at the right time, but he knew how to maneuver to get the exclusives. Stealing exclusives was big. The day I really knew I wanted to be a DJ is when Biggie was on Hot 97 talking about, "I want to kill DJ Clue for leaking 'One More Chance.' It's unfinished. It's one verse." But to a DJ, one verse is enough. You're gonna buy the CD, but we got the record early. This is the record. So it was the adrenaline rush of an artist looking for you, and you know you ain't supposed to put this out. And the fans, they went crazy, like, "Oh shit, a new Clue tape's coming out with more exclusives."

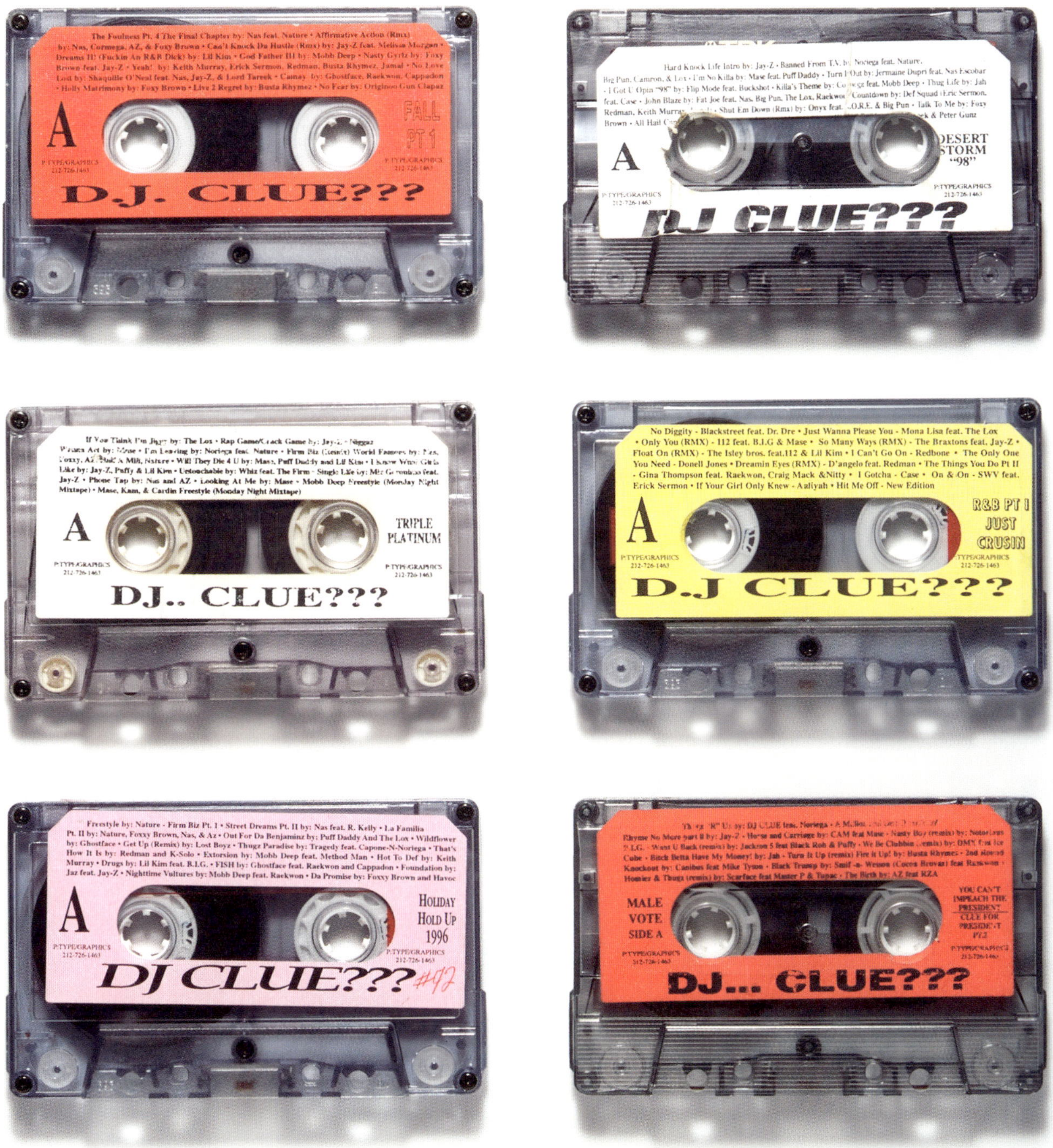
The Foulness Pt. 4 The Final Chapter by: Nas feat. Nature • Affirmative Action (Rmx) by: Nas, Cormega, AZ, & Foxy Brown • Can't Knock Da Hustle (Rmx) by: Jay-Z feat. Melissa Morgan • Dreams II! (Fuckin An R&B Dick) by: Lil Kim • God Father III by: Mobb Deep • Nasty Gyrlz by: Foxy Brown feat. Jay-Z • Yeah! by: Keith Murray, Erick Sermon, Redman, Busta Rhymez, Jamal • No Love Lost by: Shaquille O'Neal feat. Nas, Jay-Z, & Lord Tareek • Camay by: Ghostface, Raekwon, Cappadon • Holly Matrimony by: Foxy Brown • Live 2 Regret by: Busta Rhymez • No Fear by: Originoo Gun Clapaz
A
FALL PT 1
P:TYPE/GRAPHICS 212-726-1463
D.J. CLUE???
Hard Knock Life Intro by: Jay-Z • Banned From T.V. by: Noriega feat. Nature, Big Pun, Camron, & Lox • I'm No Killa by: Mase feat. Puff Daddy • I Got U Opin "98" by: Flip Mode feat. Buckshot • Killa's Theme by: Mobb Deep • Thug Life by: Jah feat. Case • John Blaze by: Fat Joe feat. Nas, Big Pun, The Lox, Raekwon • Countdown by: Def Squad (Eric Sermon, Redman, Keith Murray • Shut Em Down (Rmx) by: Onyx feat. & Big Pun • Talk To Me by: Foxy Brown • All Hail
A
DESERT STORM "98"
P:TYPE/GRAPHICS 212-726-1463
DJ CLUE???
If You Think I'm Jiggy by: The Lox • Rap Game/Crack Game by: Jay-Z • Niggaz Wanna Act by: Mase • I'm Leaving by: Noriega feat. Nature • Firm Biz (Remix) World Famous by: Nas, Foxxy, AZ • Will They Die 4 U by: Mase, Puff Daddy and Lil Kim • Like by: Jay-Z, Puffy & Lil Kim • Untouchable by: Whiz feat. The Firm • Jay-Z • Phone Tap by: Nas and AZ • Looking At Me by: Mase • Mobb Deep Freestyle (Monday Night Mixtape) • Mase, Kam, & Cardin Freestyle (Monday Night Mixtape)
A
TRIPLE PLATINUM
P:TYPE/GRAPHICS
DJ.. CLUE???
No Diggity - Blackstreet feat. Dr. Dre • Just Wanna Please You - Mona Lisa feat. The Lox • Only You (RMX) - 112 feat. B.I.G & Mase • So Many Ways (RMX) - The Braxtons feat. Jay-Z • Float On (RMX) - The Isley bros. feat.112 & Lil Kim • I Can't Go On - Redbone • The Only One You Need - Donell Jones • Dreamin Eyes (RMX) - D'angelo feat. Redman • The Things You Do Pt II - Gina Thompson feat. Raekwon, Craig Mack &Nitty • I Gotcha - Case • On & On - SWV feat. Erick Sermon • If Your Girl Only Knew - Aaliyah • Hit Me Off - New Edition
A
R&B PT I JUST CRUSIN
P:TYPE/GRAPHICS 212-726-1463
D.J CLUE???
Freestyle by: Nature - Firm Biz Pt. 1 • Street Dreams Pt. II by: Nas feat. R. Kelly • La Familia Pt. II by: Nature, Foxxy Brown, Nas, & Az • Out For Da Benjaminz by: Puff Daddy And The Lox • Wildflower by: Ghostface • Get Up (Remix) by: Lost Boyz • Thugz Paradise by: Tragedy feat. Capone-N-Noriega • That's How It Is by: Redman and K-Solo • Extorsion by: Mobb Deep feat. Method Man • Hot To Def by: Keith Murray • Drugs by: Lil Kim feat. B.I.G. • FISH by: Ghostface feat. Raekwon and Cappadon • Foundation by: Jaz feat. Jay-Z • Nighttime Vultures by: Mobb Deep feat. Raekwon • Da Promise by: Foxxy Brown and Havoc
A
HOLIDAY HOLD UP 1996
P:TYPE/GRAPHICS 212-726-1463
DJ CLUE???
MALE VOTE SIDE A
YOU CAN'T IMPEACH THE PRESIDENT
P:TYPE/GRAPHICS
DJ... CLUE???

5 CLASSIC DJ CLUE DROPS

Though he was far from the originator of talking on tapes, DJ Clue's echo-enhanced style of vocal drops influenced many of his peers. Whether he was shouting out artists, tape sellers, or music industry connects, letting listeners know that they were about to hear an exclusive song, or just hyping up his mix, Clue always came correct with the microphone enhancements. Here are a few of his most quotables, including the one that inspired the title of this book.

1. "DO REMEMBER!"
2. "CLUEMANATTI!"
3. "FAT SHOUT!"
4. "NEW SHIT!"
5. "THAT'S RIGHT!"

Havoc of Mobb Deep: Clue was really big around our way. Back in the days in Queensbridge, everybody used to be fiending to get his tapes. So early on, when me and P started popping, we were looking for Clue to give him songs to put on his mixtape. That gained us notoriety among the hip-hop community, in general and on the New York scene.

Those moments of hearing yourself for the first time on a mixtape were big. The radio was one thing, but with the mixtape, all of your homies had that. The homies used to steal each other's tapes, so for you to be in circulation on things that were sought after? That was like, "Damn, rewind that back real quick!"

Mixtapes helped you build your foundation. Before radio would even grasp onto what was going on, the hood had the mixtapes. The mixtape DJs were the ones that were really actually breaking artists back then. Because a lot of times, for the radio, you would have to pay the radio people to be on. Whereas the mixtape, it can be somebody around your way just making mixtapes and you could slide them a song.

Buckwild, Producer: I've heard my mixtapes in the streets and I've also heard my production on mixtapes. But the biggest record on a mixtape I heard the most was the "Fast Life" record. Because by then, Clue was the biggest mixtape DJ ever, Nas was a huge artist and G Rap was the G.O.A.T. That was the record everyone was talking about. If you were on a Clue tape, no matter who you were, you made it.

Genovese, MC: I remember Clue came by to see us, because we were really the hottest dudes coming up. Genovese, Mo Money, Kasino, and The LOX are really all one. He heard "Love Or Lust," and he was like, "I need this for an exclusive, you can't give this to nobody." I didn't know he was going to put that at the start of the tape with Biggie. Your first song on a mixtape goes after Biggie's freestyle? It was humbling at that point. At that time, Clue was on top. For a young artist, if you had a freestyle on Clue, you made it.

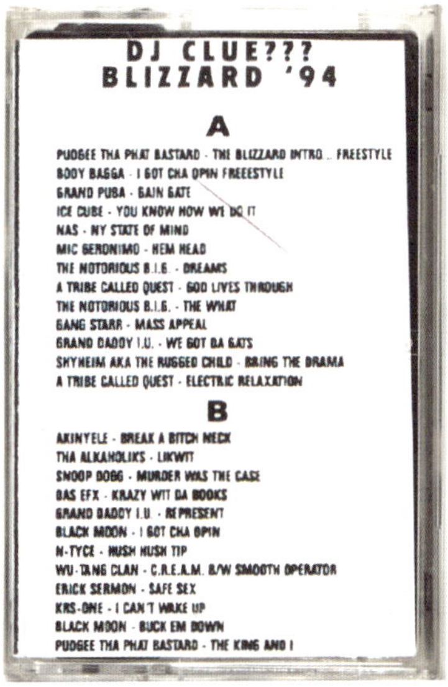
DJ CLUE???
BLIZZARD '94
A
PUDGEE THA PHAT BASTARD - THE BLIZZARD INTRO... FREESTYLE
BODY BAGGA - I GOT CHA OPIN FREEESTYLE
GRAND PUBA - 6AIN 6ATE
ICE CUBE - YOU KNOW HOW WE DO IT
NAS - NY STATE OF MIND
MIC GERONIMO - HEM HEAD
THE NOTORIOUS B.I.G. - DREAMS
A TRIBE CALLED QUEST - 600 LIVES THROUGH
THE NOTORIOUS B.I.G. - THE WHAT
GANG STARR - MASS APPEAL
GRAND DADDY I.U. - WE GOT DA GATS
SHYHEIM AKA THE RUGGED CHILD - BRING THE DRAMA
A TRIBE CALLED QUEST - ELECTRIC RELAXATION
B
AKINYELE - BREAK A BITCH NECK
THA ALKAHOLIKS - LIKWIT
SNOOP DOGG - MURDER WAS THE CASE
DAS EFX - KRAZY WIT DA BOOKS
GRAND DADDY I.U. - REPRESENT
BLACK MOON - I GOT CHA OPIN
N-TYCE - HUSH HUSH TIP
WU-TANG CLAN - C.R.E.A.M. B/W SMOOTH OPERATOR
ERICK SERMON - SAFE SEX
KRS-ONE - I CAN'T WAKE UP
BLACK MOON - BUCK EM DOWN
PUDGEE THA PHAT BASTARD - THE KING AND I

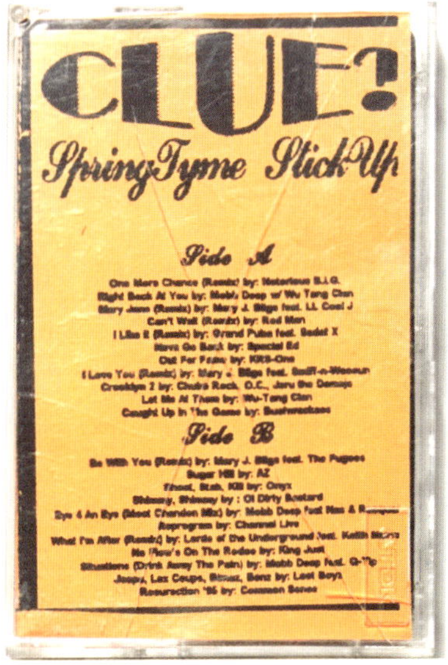
CLUE?
SpringTyme StickUp
Side A
Side B

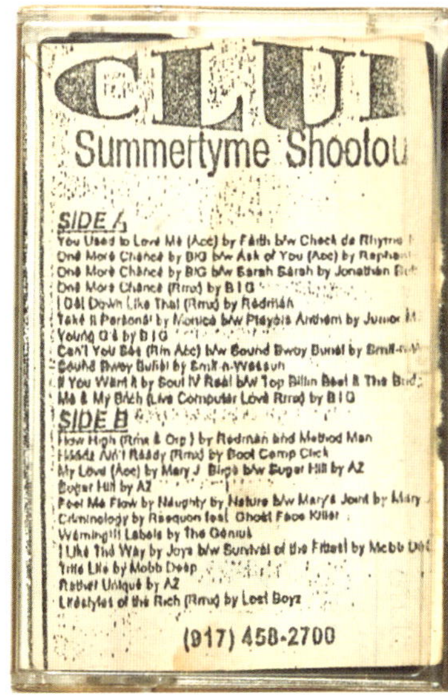
CLUE
Summertyme Shootou
SIDE A
SIDE B
(917) 458-2700

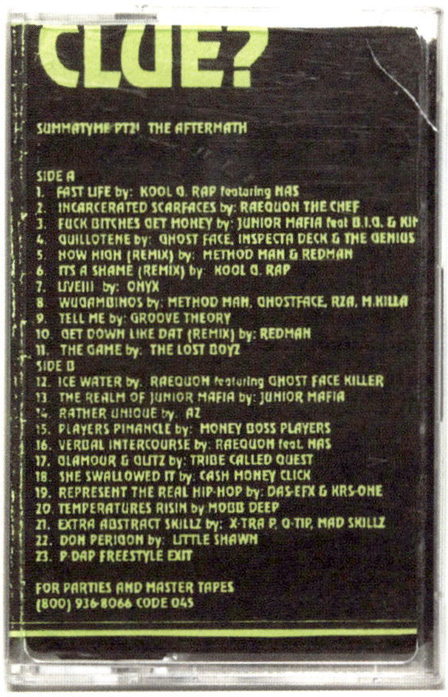
CLUE?
SUMMATYME PT2! THE AFTERMATH
SIDE A
1. FAST LIFE by: KOOL G. RAP featuring NAS
2. INCARCERATED SCARFACES by: RAEQUON THE CHEF
3. FUCK BITCHES GET MONEY by: JUNIOR MAFIA feat B.I.G. & KIM
4. GUILLOTENE by: GHOST FACE, INSPECTA DECK & THE GENIUS
5. HOW HIGH (REMIX) by: METHOD MAN & REDMAN
6. ITS A SHAME (REMIX) by: KOOL G. RAP
7. LIVEIII by: ONYX
8. WUGAMBINOS by: METHOD MAN, GHOSTFACE, RZA, M.KILLA
9. TELL ME by: GROOVE THEORY
10. GET DOWN LIKE DAT (REMIX) by: REDMAN
11. THE GAME by: THE LOST BOYZ
SIDE B
12. ICE WATER by: RAEQUON featuring GHOST FACE KILLER
13. THE REALM OF JUNIOR MAFIA by: JUNIOR MAFIA
14. RATHER UNIQUE by: AZ
15. PLAYERS PINANCLE by: MONEY BOSS PLAYERS
16. VERBAL INTERCOURSE by: RAEQUON feat. NAS
17. GLAMOUR & GLITZ by: TRIBE CALLED QUEST
18. SHE SWALLOWED IT by: CASH MONEY CLICK
19. REPRESENT THE REAL HIP-HOP by: DAS-EFX & KRS-ONE
20. TEMPERATURES RISIN by MOBB DEEP
21. EXTRA ABSTRACT SKILLZ by: X-TRA P, Q-TIP, MAD SKILLZ
22. DON PERIGON by: LITTLE SHAWN
23. P DAP FREESTYLE EXIT
FOR PARTIES AND MASTER TAPES
(800) 936-8066 CODE 045

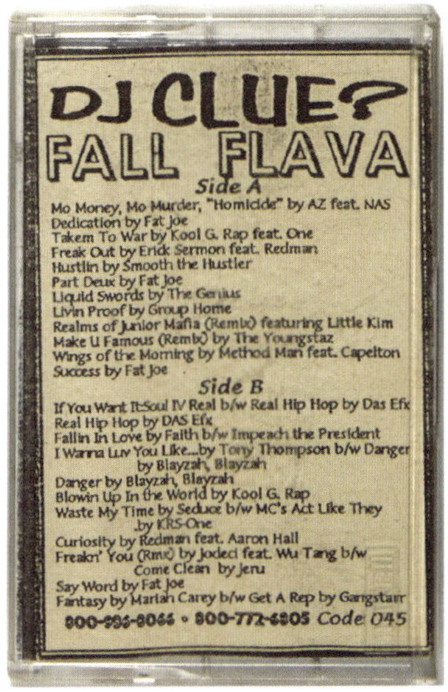
DJ CLUE?
FALL FLAVA
Side A
Mo Money, Mo Murder, "Homicide" by AZ feat. NAS
Dedication by Fat Joe
Takem To War by Kool G. Rap feat. One
Freak Out by Erick Sermon feat. Redman
Hustlin by Smooth the Hustler
Part Deux by Fat Joe
Liquid Swords by The Genius
Livin Proof by Group Home
Realms of Junior Mafia (Remix) featuring Little Kim
Make U Famous (Remix) by The Youngstaz
Wings of the Morning by Method Man feat. Capelton
Success by Fat Joe
Side B
If You Want It:Soul IV Real b/w Real Hip Hop by Das Efx
Real Hip Hop by DAS Efx
Fallin In Love by Faith b/w Impeach the President
I Wanna Luv You Like...by Tony Thompson b/w Danger by Blayzah, Blayzah
Danger by Blayzah, Blayzah
Blowin Up In the World by Kool G. Rap
Waste My Time by Seduce b/w MC's Act Like They by KRS-One
Curiosity by Redman feat. Aaron Hall
Freakin' You (Rmx) by Jodeci feat. Wu Tang b/w Come Clean by Jeru
Say Word by Fat Joe
Fantasy by Mariah Carey b/w Get A Rep by Gangstarr
Code 045

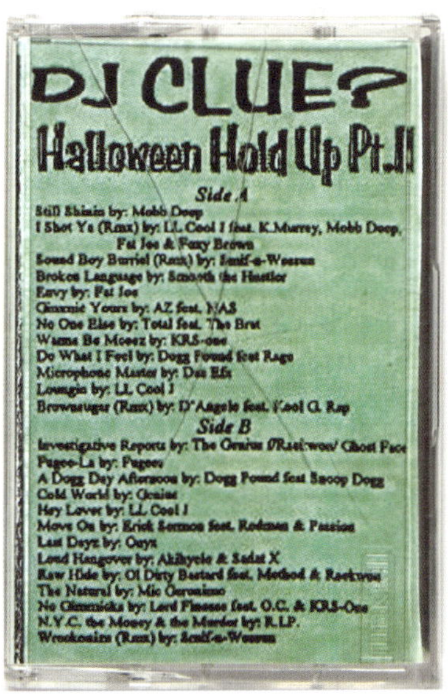
DJ CLUE?
Halloween Hold Up Pt.II
Side A
Side B

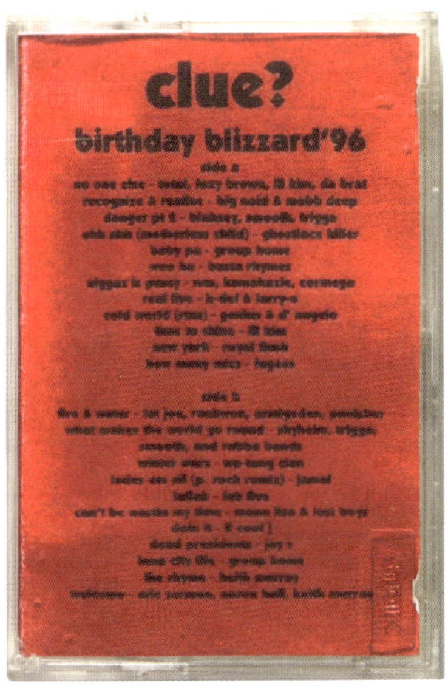
clue?
birthday blizzard'96

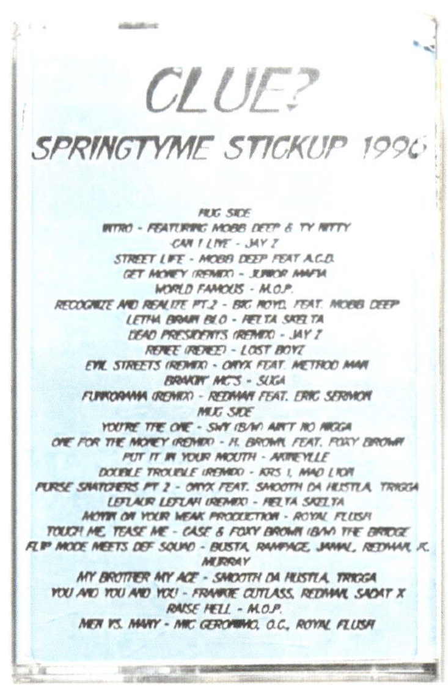
CLUE?
SPRINGTYME STICKUP 1996

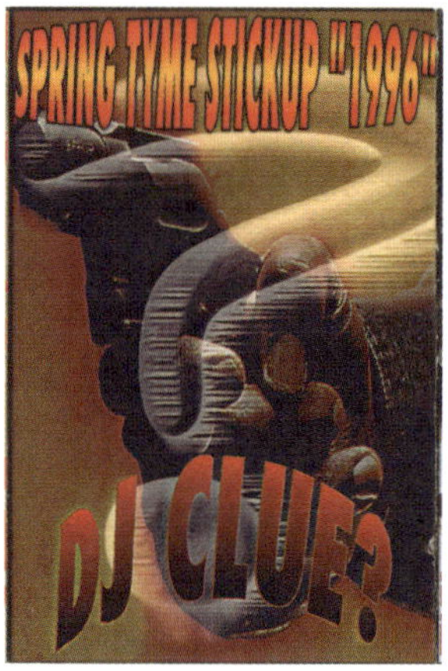
SPRING TYME STICKUP "1996"
DJ CLUE?

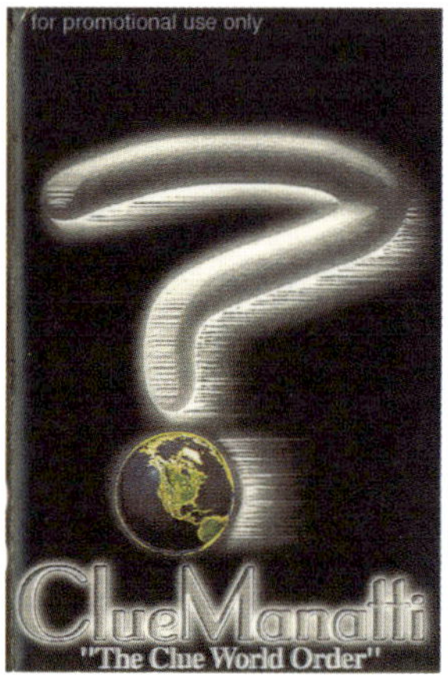
for promotional use only
ClueManatti
"The Clue World Order"

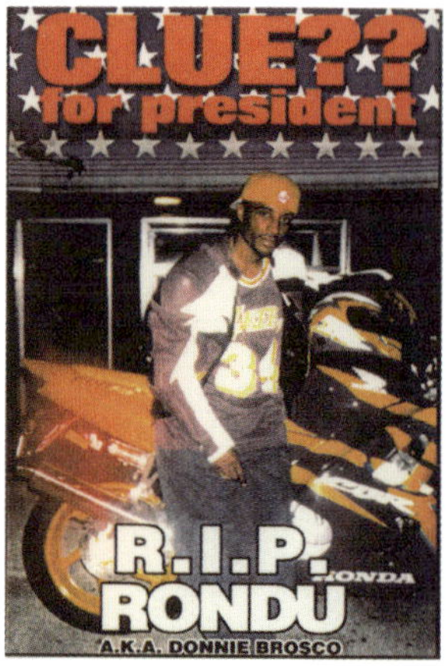
CLUE?? for president
R.I.P.
RONDU
A.K.A. DONNIE BROSCO

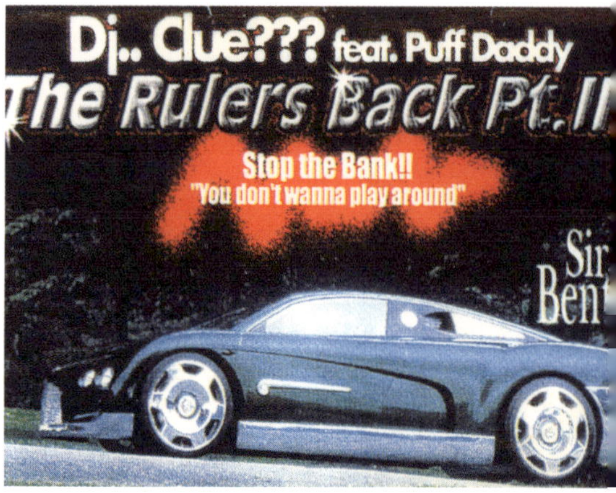
Dj.. Clue??? feat. Puff Daddy
The Rulers Back Pt.II
Stop the Bank!!
"You don't wanna play around"
Sir
Ben

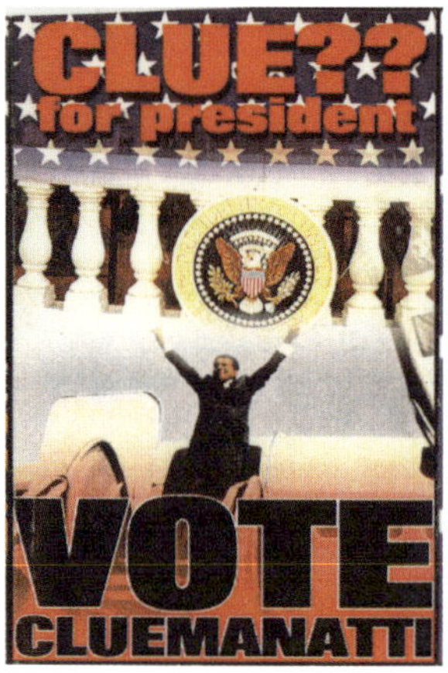
CLUE?? for president
VOTE
CLUEMANATTI

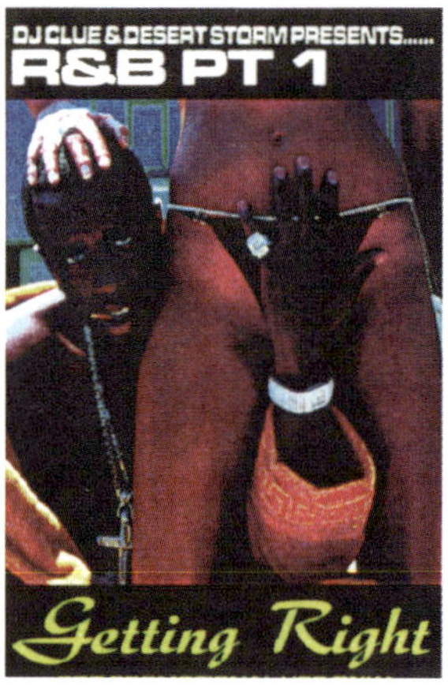
DJ CLUE & DESERT STORM PRESENTS......
R&B PT 1
Getting Right

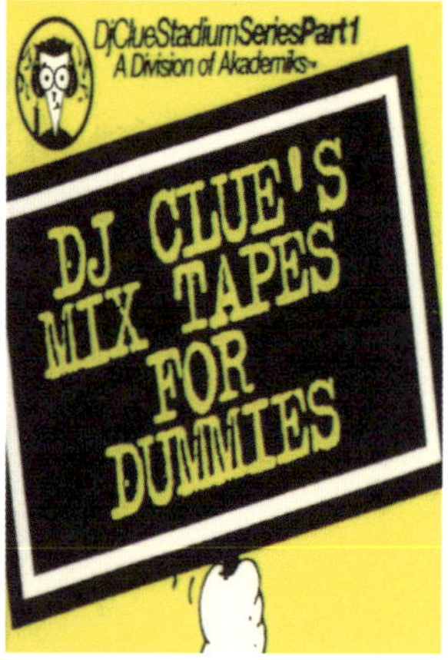
DjClueStadiumSeriesPart1
A Division of Akademiks
DJ CLUE'S
MIX TAPES
FOR
DUMMIES

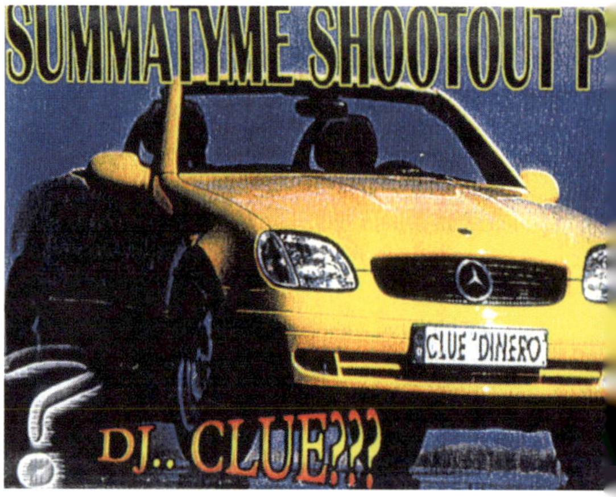
SUMMATYME SHOOTOUT P
CLUE 'DINERO'
DJ.. CLUE???

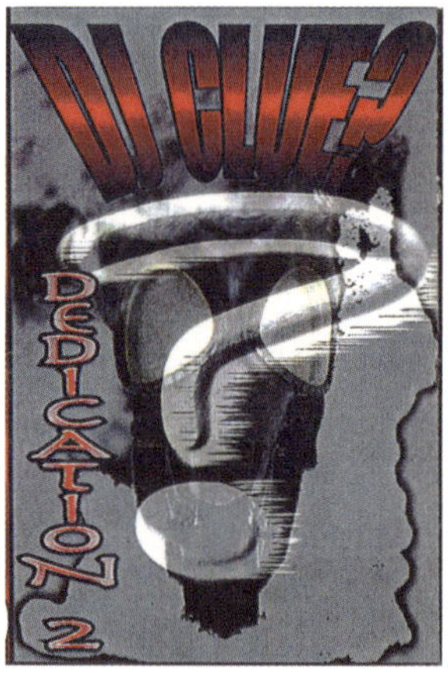
DJ CLUE?
DEDICATION 2

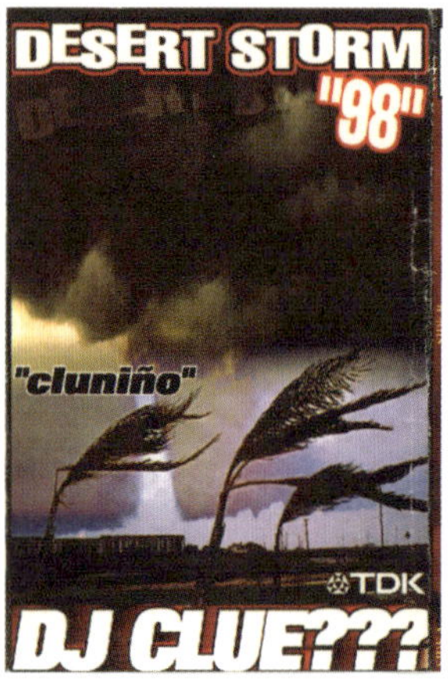
DESERT STORM
"98"
"cluniño"
TDK
DJ CLUE???

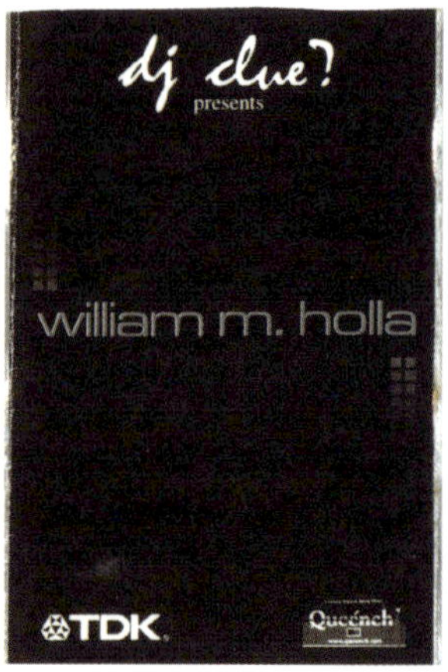
dj clue?
presents
william m. holla
TDK

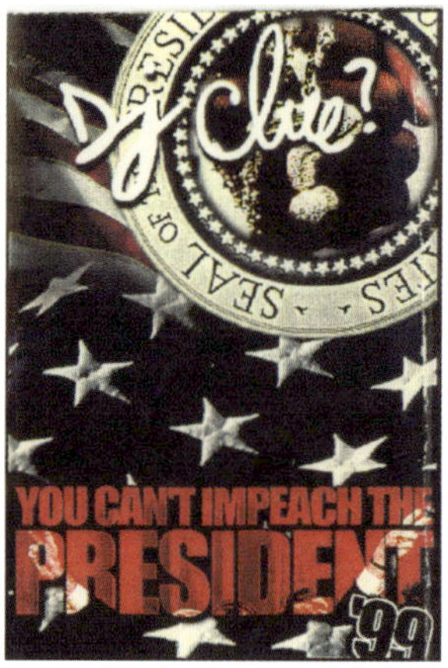
Dj Clue?
SEAL OF
YOU CAN'T IMPEACH THE
PRESIDENT
'99

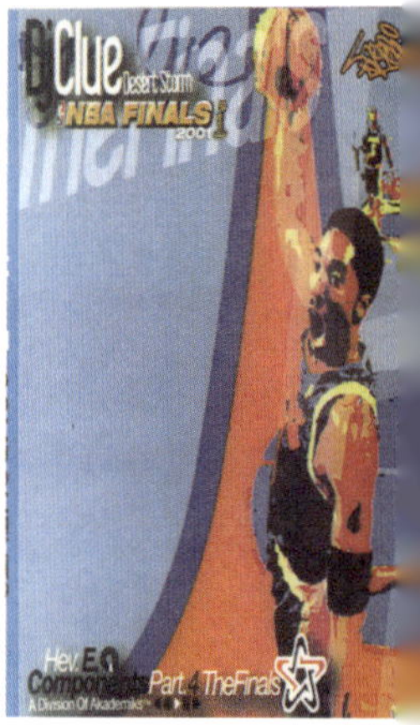
DjClue
Desert Storm
NBA FINALS

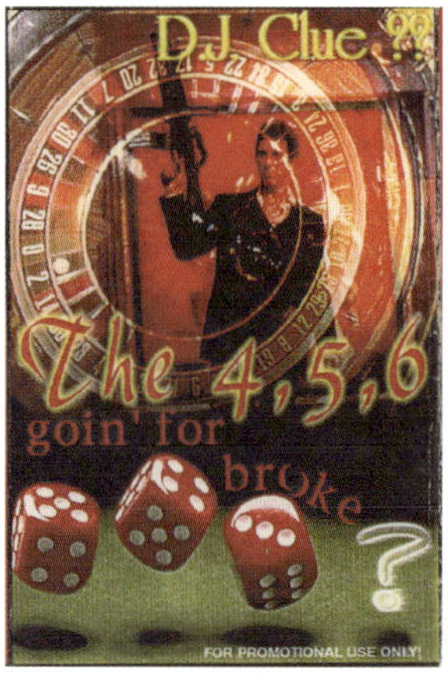
DJ Clue?
The 4,5,6
goin' for broke
FOR PROMOTIONAL USE ONLY!

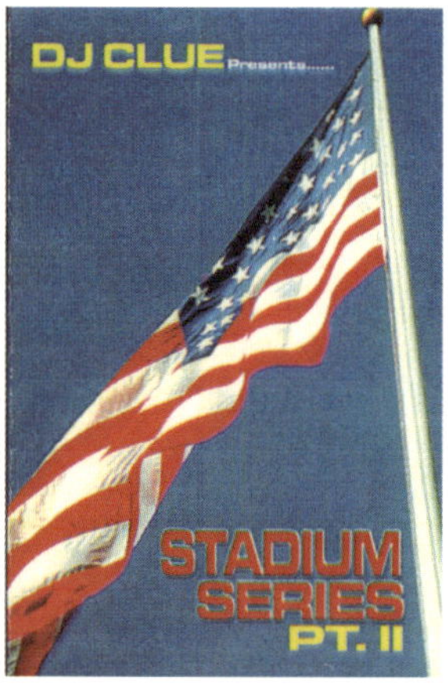
DJ CLUE Presents......
STADIUM
SERIES
PT. II

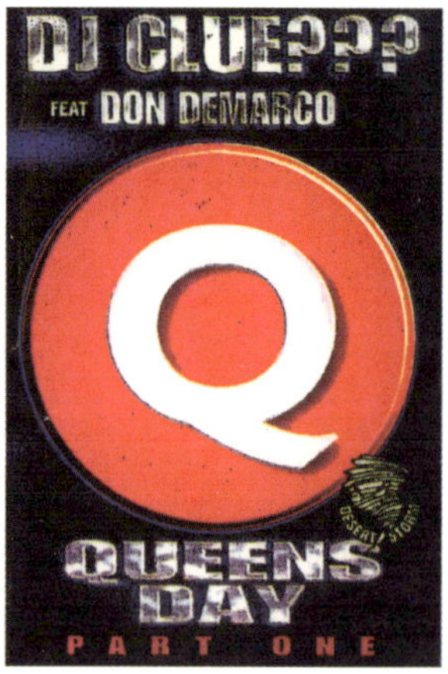
DJ CLUE???
FEAT DON DEMARCO
QUEENS
DAY
PART ONE

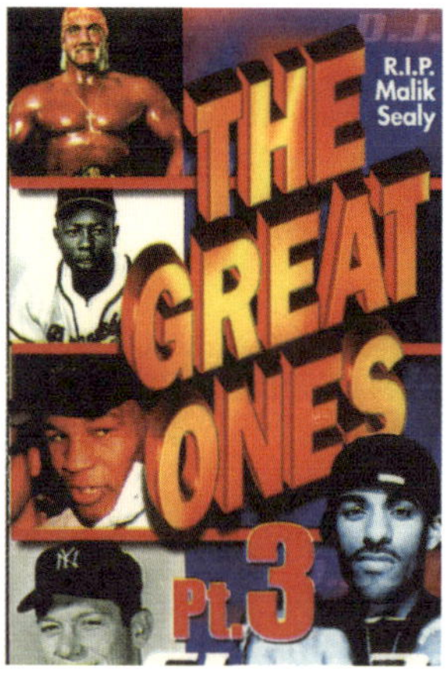
R.I.P.
Malik
Sealy
THE
GREAT
ONES
Pt.3

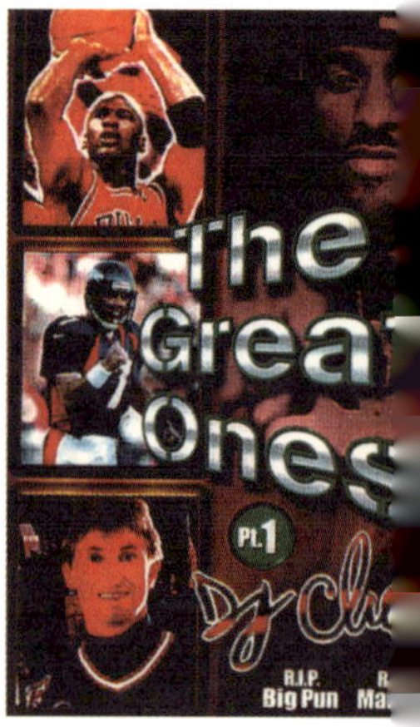
The
Great
Ones
Pt.1
R.I.P.
Big Pun

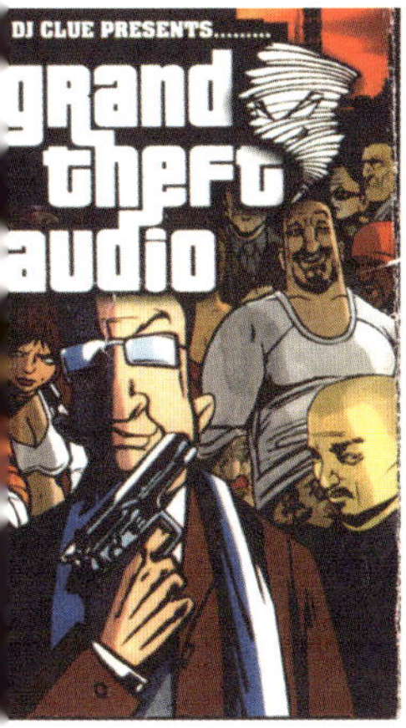
DJ CLUE PRESENTS.........
grand theft audio

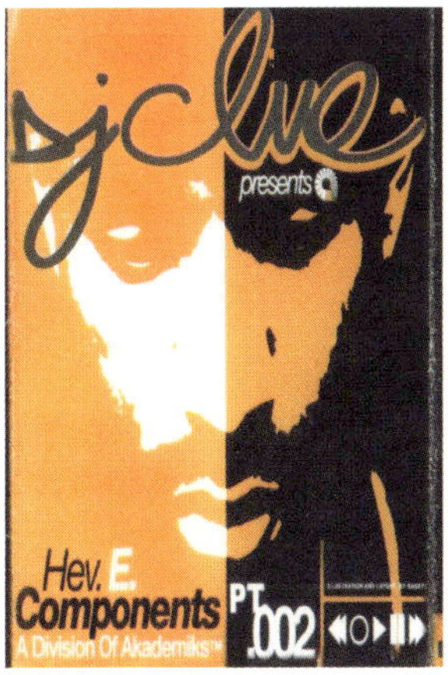
dj clue
presents
Hev. E. Components
A Division Of Akademiks
PT .002

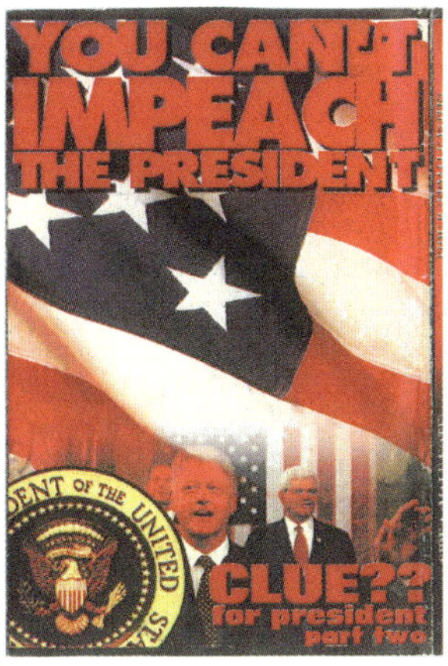
YOU CAN'T IMPEACH THE PRESIDENT
CLUE??
for president
part two

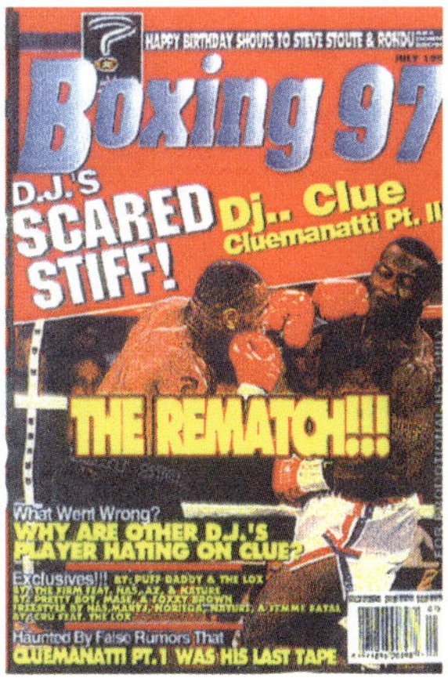
HAPPY BIRTHDAY SHOUTS TO STEVE STOUTE & RONDU
Boxing 97
D.J.'S SCARED STIFF!
Dj.. Clue
Cluemanatti Pt. II
THE REMATCH!!!
What Went Wrong?
WHY ARE OTHER D.J.'S PLAYER HATING ON CLUE?
Haunted By False Rumors That
CLUEMANATTI PT.1 WAS HIS LAST TAPE

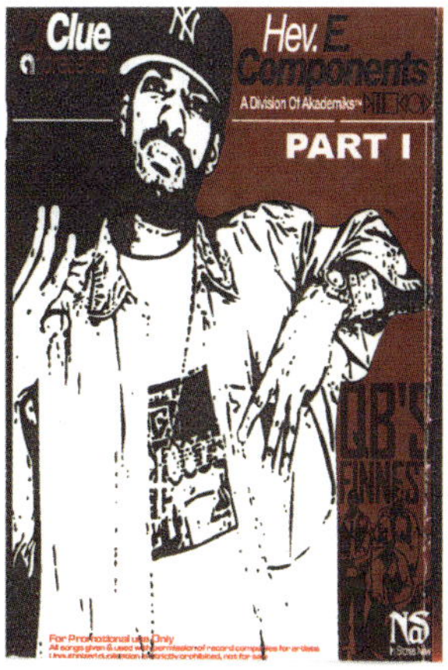
Clue
Hev. E. Components
A Division Of Akademiks
PART I

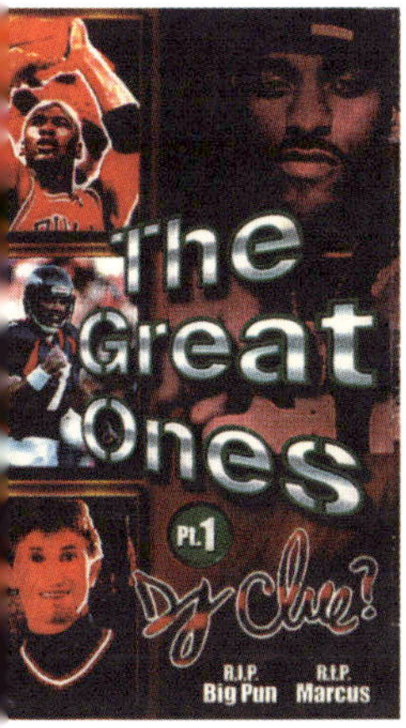
The Great Ones
Pt.1
Dj Clue?
R.I.P. Big Pun
R.I.P. Marcus

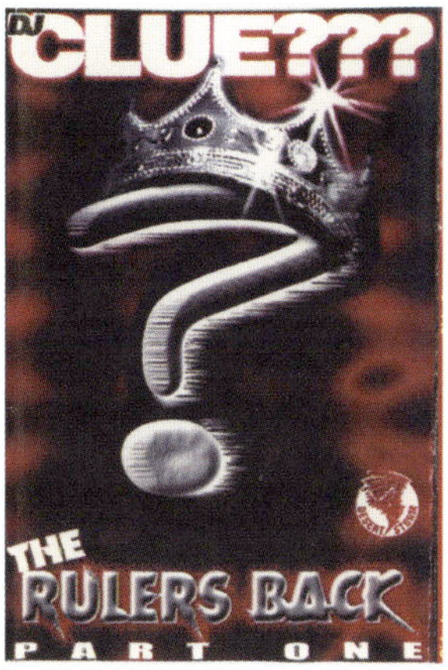
DJ CLUE???
THE RULERS BACK
PART ONE

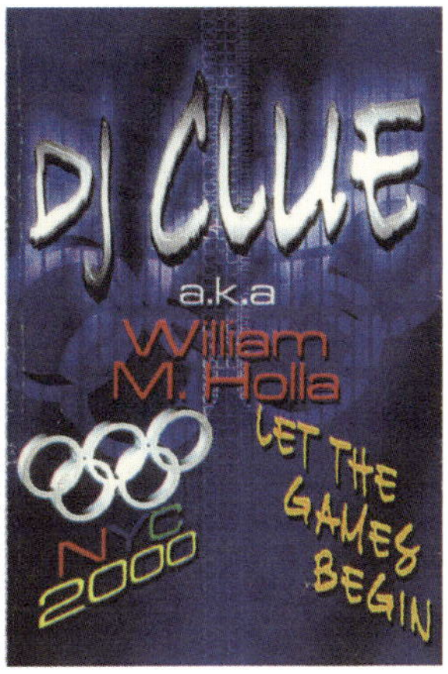
DJ CLUE
a.k.a
William M. Holla
NYC 2000
LET THE GAMES BEGIN

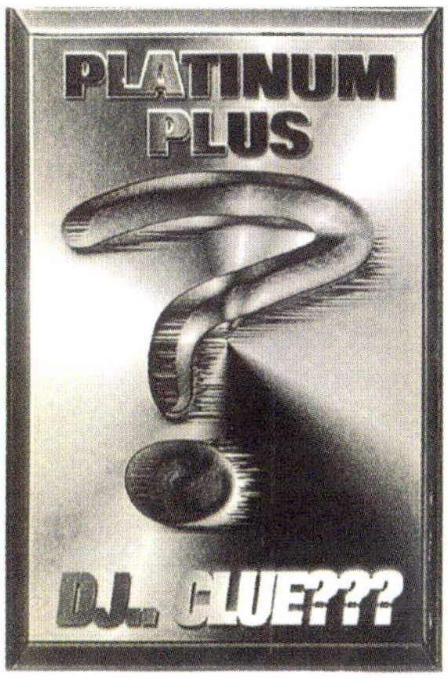
PLATINUM PLUS
DJ.. CLUE???

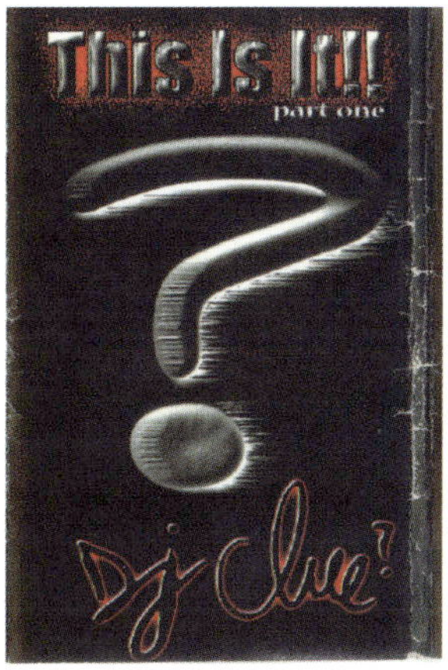
This Is It!!
part one
Dj Clue?

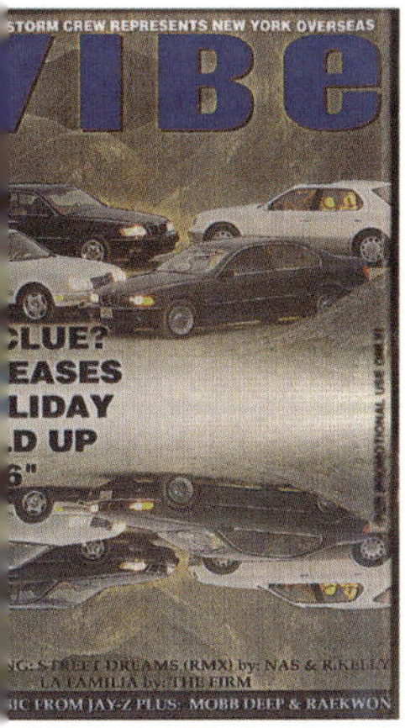
STORM CREW REPRESENTS NEW YORK OVERSEAS
VIBE
FOR PROMOTIONAL USE ONLY

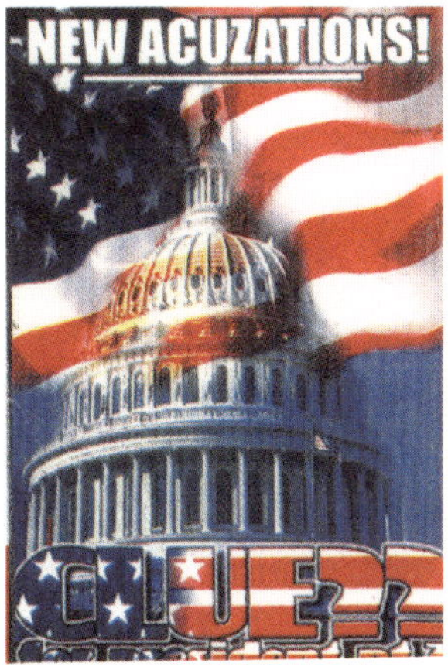
NEW ACUZATIONS!

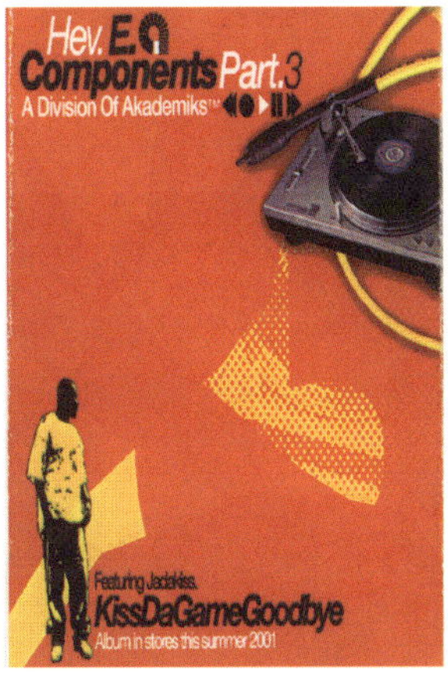
Hev. E. Components Part.3
A Division Of Akademiks
Featuring Jadakiss
KissDaGameGoodbye
Album in stores this summer 2001

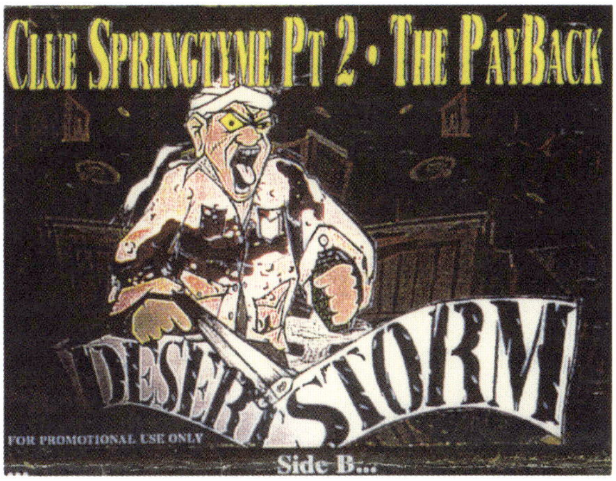
CLUE SPRINGTYME PT 2 • THE PAYBACK
DESERT STORM
FOR PROMOTIONAL USE ONLY
Side B...

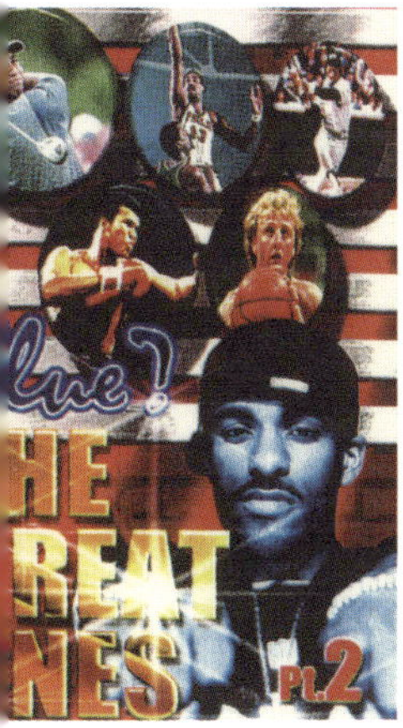
Pt.2

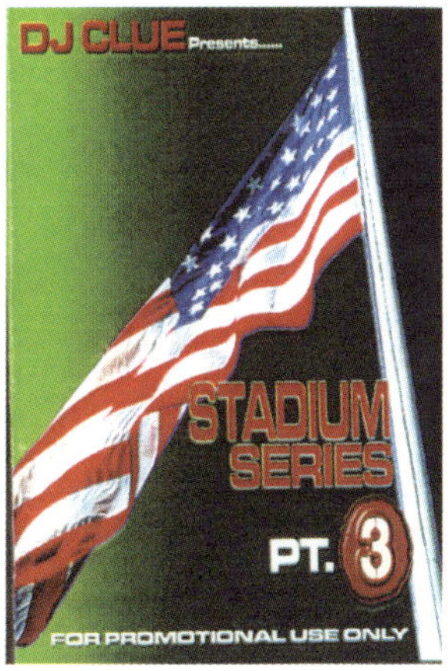
DJ CLUE Presents......
STADIUM SERIES
PT. 3
FOR PROMOTIONAL USE ONLY

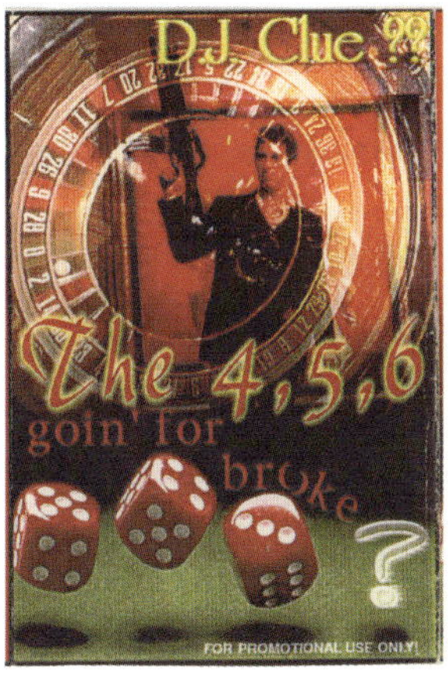
D.J. Clue
The 4,5,6
goin for broke
FOR PROMOTIONAL USE ONLY

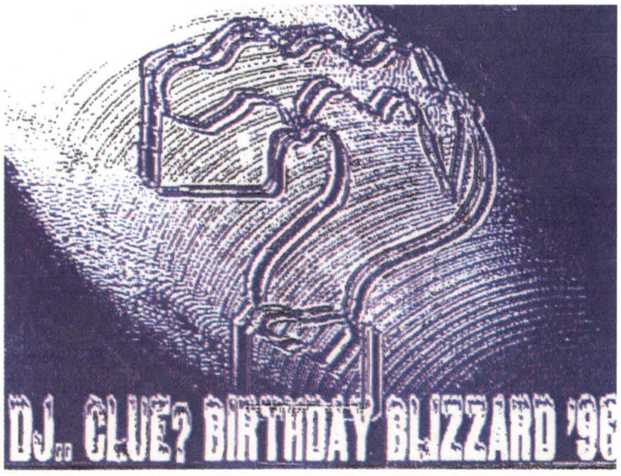
DJ.. CLUE? BIRTHDAY BLIZZARD '96

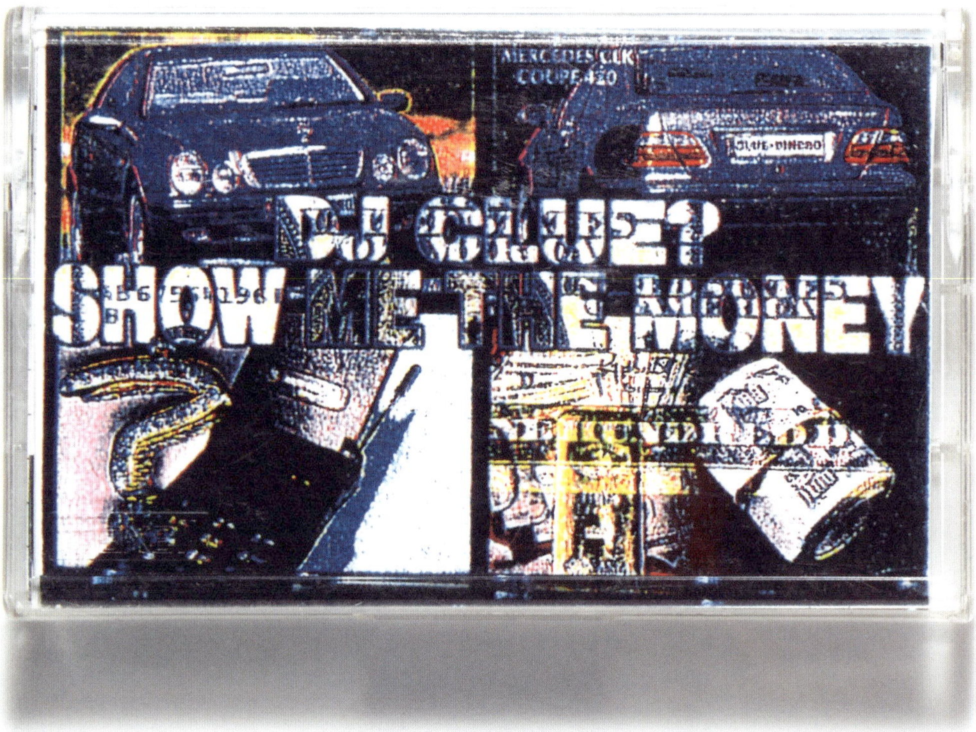
MERCEDES CLK
COUPE 420
CLUE DINERO
DJ CLUE?
SHOW ME THE MONEY

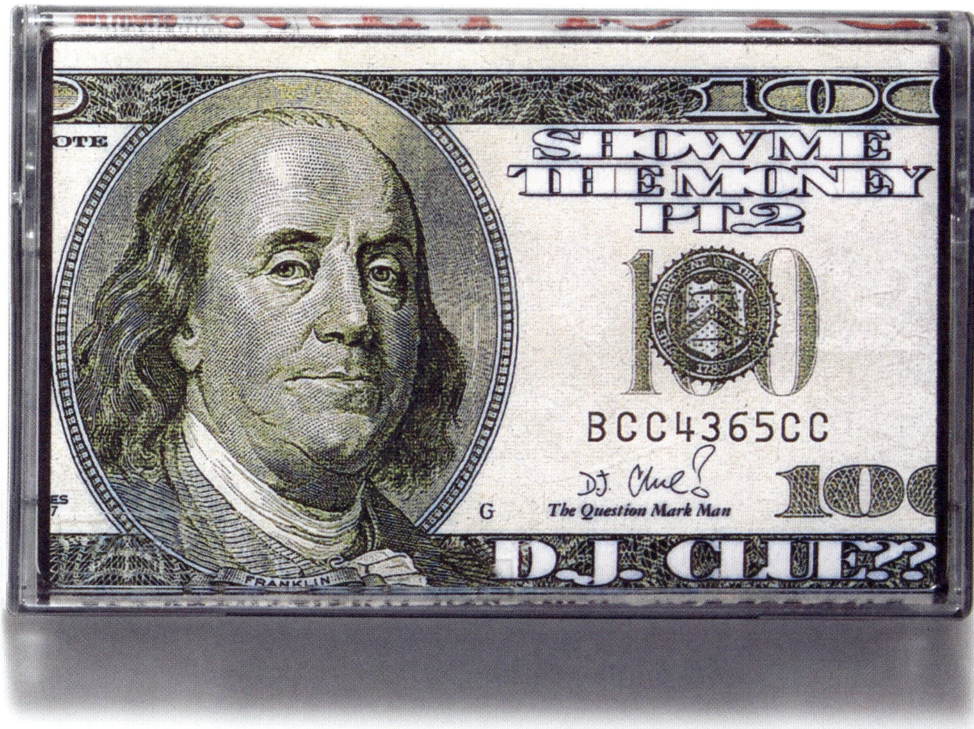
SHOW ME
THE MONEY
PT 2
BCC4365CC
The Question Mark Man
D.J. CLUE?

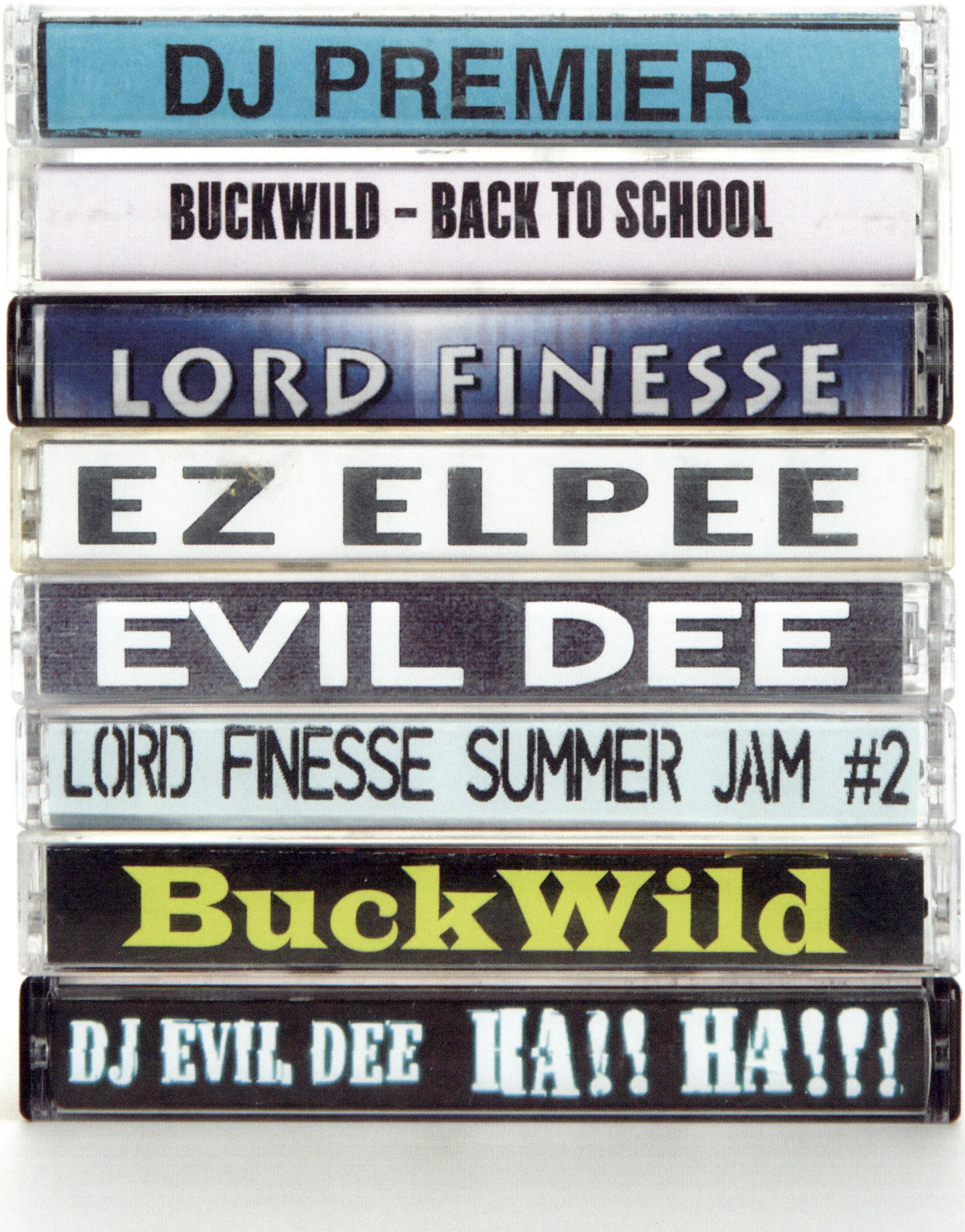
DJ PREMIER
BUCKWILD - BACK TO SCHOOL
LORD FINESSE
EZ ELPEE
EVIL DEE
LORD FINESSE SUMMER JAM #2
BuckWild
DJ EVIL DEE HA!! HA!!!

THE PRODUCERS

New York City is home to some of the most legendary hip-hop producers of all-time. Producers who made sampling an art form, who shifted the sound of the genre, who crafted timeless classics that helped define a generation. Interestingly enough, a handful of these producers also got their start as mixtape DJs, and in some cases, continued to make tapes well into their production careers. And these tapes became canvases for them to display their DJ skills, plus showcase their work behind the boards and beat machines. Nuff props to THE PRODUCERS.

DJ EVIL DEE

Buck 'Em Down: Killing Every Beat and Mixtape In Sight

DJ Evil Dee has worn different hats throughout his career. Best known for being Black Moon's DJ and one-half of production duo Da Beatminerz with his brother Mr. Walt, he's also a legendary Brooklyn-based mixtape DJ who's been celebrated across the world for always coming correct with the dope mixes. Yes, the master craftsman behind Boot Camp classics like *Enta Da Stage, Dah Shinin'* and *Nocturnal* was simultaneously putting in crazy work with the cassettes.

IMPORTANCE OF HAVING YOUR MUSIC ON MIXTAPES

Evil Dee: Having your stuff on a mixtape back then was just like having it on the radio. Mixtapes were getting pumped in the cars more than the radio at the time, because the mixtapes had more of what people wanted to hear. They weren't playing a lot of hip hop on New York radio. New York radio only played hip hop on the weekends. So having your record on a mixtape back then was very, very important.

When we first did "How Many MC's...," I remember New York radio was not trying to play the record. We had a beef with Chuck Chillout, who used to manage us. We fired Chuck Chillout, and his retaliation was, "I will make sure no one plays this record." All of his homeboys were on New York radio and he told them not to play the Black Moon record. So no New York radio DJ was playing it.

What we did was give the record to all the mixtape DJs, and all of them played it. That was only in New York. And then outside of New York, we sent it to the regular DJs and they rocked it. So "How Many MC's..." blew up in New York from mixtape play. Then, we got added to *Yo! MTV Raps*, and we got in the rotation.

Red Alert was the first one to be like, "Yo, fuck this, this record is hot." I don't even think the cats at KISS spoke to him about it. I think he just said on his own, "Let me just play this record." Then after he played it, everybody started playing it. But mixtapes in New York and the underground is what blew that record up.

WORKING RETAIL AND EXPANDING MIXTAPE BUSINESS

I started working at Knickerbocker Records. When my boss sold the place, the next owners that bought it hired Tony Touch, so that's how we met. He worked after me. You know how cats in the neighborhood would be like, "Yo son, there's some dude in the store trying to be you, son." I went to the store and met Tony and we were cool. We've been friends to this day. Tony Touch is my dude.

I also worked retail at Beat Street. Then when I left Beat Street, I went two blocks down to the Brooklyn Bargain Bazaar. I used to buy sneakers and stuff there. So I go in the back and I see this record store. I started to go through the records they have and the owner was DJ Johnny T. He was like, "Yo, I know you. Don't you work at Beat Street?" And I was like, "Used to work at Beat Street." He was like, "Why don't you work with me?" And I was like, "Aiight, cool."

At the time, I was making a nice amount of money selling tapes around my way in Bushwick. He knew about my tapes. He was like, "Yo, I know you make mixtapes, I make mixtapes too. Why don't you make a mixtape for me so I can sell it?"

I made the mixtape live in the record store, one shot each side. He took the tape and he was like, "Yo, I want to show you something." I went to his spot and it was the first time I ever saw a Telex machine. He had the 1 to 24 Telex machine and he was running them off. 24 copies of a tape in 3 minutes. I was like, "I need one of those machines."

He also showed me how to sell tapes via UPS. He sent them through COD and he had a list of clients and was selling them like that. I was sitting there seeing how he was doing that and I was like, "That's kinda hot." So I made a couple of tapes for him and that blew me up through his system. I just made sure on my tapes that I shouted out my pager number. Customers started hitting me up and I started getting customers like that, too.

MAKING MOVES

When I started selling tapes, I was like, "I want my tapes to be heard." So I was dating this girl at the time whose mother was a dispatcher for Quick Cabs. I walked over to Quick Cabs and I asked my girlfriend's mom, "Yo, how many cab drivers do you have?" And she said, "Oh, we got about 30." I said, "Alright, cool."

I just started making my clientele like that, and it got to the point where I knew that my boss wasn't in the record store on Saturdays. So Saturdays were like, "If you want mixtapes, then come on a Saturday–do not come any other day." Cats would come on Saturday and I would sell mixtapes out of the record store. I would always sell out. I would go there with about 100 tapes and by the end of the day I would have none.

BLACK MOON

First and foremost I'm a DJ, and I love music. So I was making tapes. We were recording the first album and I was still dropping mixtapes. I'd use the mixtapes as a vehicle for promo–"Working on that new Black Moon album, what up!" Just to shout shit out.

Then when we went on tour, I would bring 100 mixtapes per show and I would just throw tapes in the audience–the same way I was giving out samples for free at first at home. I would give tapes to people and I would get rid of 100 tapes per show.

I made a mixtape that had hip hop, R&B, reggae, some boogie and a little bit of house on it. I shouted out all the cab drivers and the cab company and gave it to the cab company. So the cab drivers were driving all around Bushwick playing my tape.

And then, being that I was working at Knickerbocker Records, all the drug dealers were coming in buying cassettes for their systems, so I'd give them all a free Evil Dee tape. Then they'd hit me up, "I need another tape." Then they'd be $20.

A couple of dudes would drive up and you'd hear the system bumping, those are the dudes I would sell the tapes to. If somebody came in and bought a bunch of hip-hop tapes, then I would throw in an Evil Dee mixtape.

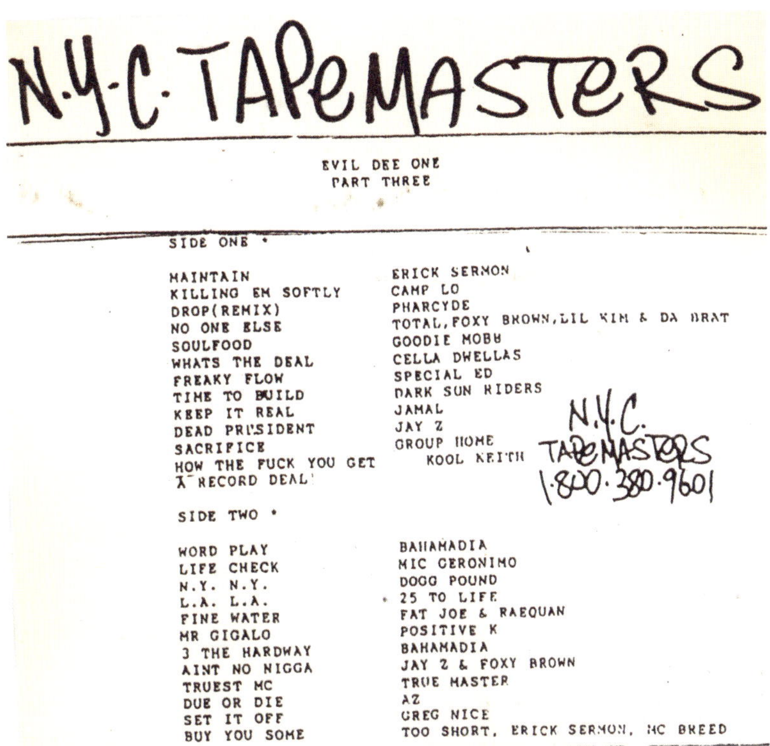
N.Y.C. TAPEMASTERS

EVIL DEE ONE
PART THREE

SIDE ONE •

MAINTAIN	ERICK SERMON
KILLING EM SOFTLY	CAMP LO
DROP(REMIX)	PHARCYDE
NO ONE ELSE	TOTAL, FOXY BROWN, LIL KIM & DA BRAT
SOULFOOD	GOODIE MOBB
WHATS THE DEAL	CELLA DWELLAS
FREAKY FLOW	SPECIAL ED
TIME TO BUILD	DARK SUN RIDERS
KEEP IT REAL	JAMAL
DEAD PRESIDENT	JAY Z
SACRIFICE	GROUP HOME
HOW THE FUCK YOU GET A RECORD DEAL	KOOL KEITH

N.Y.C. TAPEMASTERS 1·800·380·9601

SIDE TWO •

WORD PLAY	BAHAMADIA
LIFE CHECK	MIC GERONIMO
N.Y. N.Y.	DOGG POUND
L.A. L.A.	25 TO LIFE
FINE WATER	FAT JOE & RAEQUAN
MR GIGALO	POSITIVE K
3 THE HARDWAY	BAHAMADIA
AINT NO NIGGA	JAY Z & FOXY BROWN
TRUEST MC	TRUE MASTER
DUE OR DIE	AZ
SET IT OFF	GREG NICE
BUY YOU SOME	TOO SHORT, ERICK SERMON, MC BREED

I remember my group being like, "Yo, you're bananas. Why are you giving that away? You should be selling them." But when I gave them those, these are all the people that are hitting me back for more. We were using UPS and we were shipping mad tapes. I was going crazy for a minute. It got to the point where we couldn't handle the sales. Instead of running the tapes, we hooked up with different people in the area and just sold masters.

TAPES IN JAPAN

One of the illest things that ever happened was the first time I went to Japan to do some Black Moon stuff. I walked into this store, Manhattan Records, and looked at the tape wall. I was like, "Oh shit, you got Clue, you got Tony, you got Doo Wop." I was like, "Yo, this is dope." Still, I was kind of like, "But where are my tapes at?"

I turned to the next wall and it was nothing but Evil Dee tapes. I had that many tapes. And they had all of my radio shows. Not only the radio shows from New York, but the radio shows from D.C. that I was doing with Steph Lova, I think that was 95.5. I was doing Saturdays at noon with her. The mixtape shit was crazy. When I saw that wall in Japan, I was like, "Yo! It makes sense now."

SOUNDBOMBING VOL. 1

We had the Black Moon shit and I still had the mixtapes rocking. I had a meeting with Rawkus, they were just starting. The cats at Rawkus, Brian and Jarret the owners, they were like, "Yo, you still do tapes?" I'm like, "Hell yeah I still do tapes." They were like, "We're about to go to this convention, can you make us a tape for it?" And I was like, "Sure, no doubt." So I made this tape for them and it was called *Soundbombing*. It was supposed to be given away for free at the convention.

I raided their records. Mos Def and them, I was like, "What records y'all got? Let me see." And I had everybody come to D&D to do their freestyles. After they did their freestyles, I took everything home and made a mixtape. Simple as that. I didn't make the whole thing in a studio or anything like that. I made it how I usually make my mixtapes.

I turned in the master to Rawkus, and they liked it so much they called me back later on that day and said, "We understand you made this for the convention, but we want to put it out." I'm like, "Don't put that shit out, c'mon that's corny." They're like, "Nah, people need to hear this, we need to put this out as a record." I'm like, "Nah, nah, chill." They're like, "No, fuck that, we'll give you X amount of dollars." I think they gave me ten grand up front.

I was like, "If y'all want to put it out, fuck it, I'll let y'all do whatever." And that tape right there is a classic. Everybody and their mother was like, "Oh my God." And that was the first time Rawkus ever made a profit off of an album.

That also led to us to getting a Beatminerz deal at Rawkus. They hit me up and they were like, "Yo, you should do another *Soundbombing* mixtape." I was like, "Nah, I'm not doing that. They were like, "Well, can we do one?" And I was like, "Sure, do one." On the second *Soundbombing*, all I did was produce the Eminem record, "Any Man." That's a Beatminerz record.

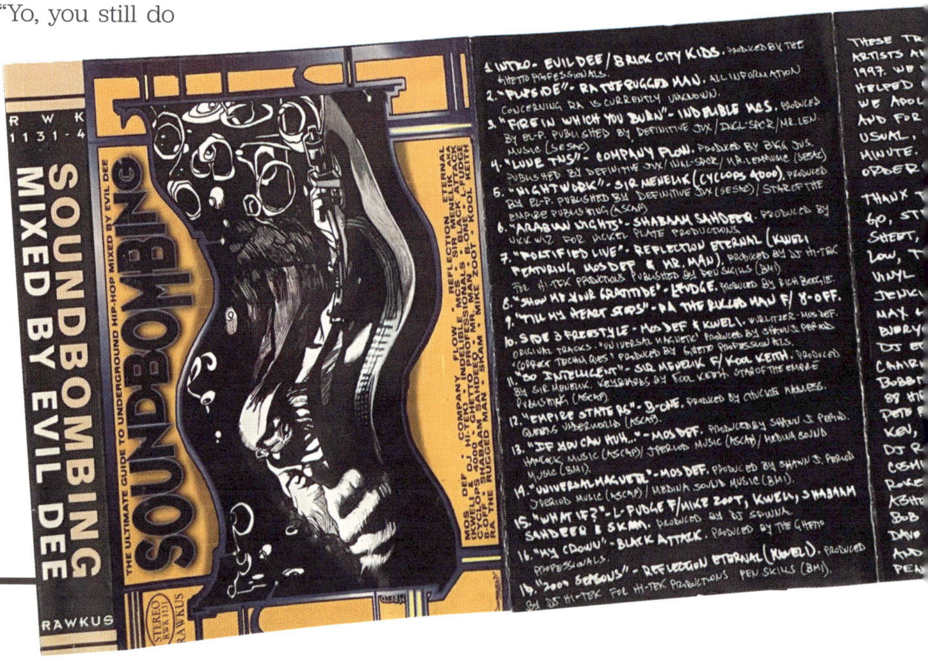

Evil Dee: When I first started making mixtapes, I didn't even talk on my tapes. The first Evil Dee tape doesn't have any talking on it. What made me start talking on the tapes was this—I sold a couple tapes and I was on the corner of my block trying to talk to this girl. This dude drives up with my tape, and I knew it was my tape because I heard my blends. And me, trying to stroke my ego, I said, "Yo, my man who made that tape?" The dude looked at me and said, "Me, mothafucker!" And he drove off. The girl laughed at me and she walked away. I was mad as hell.

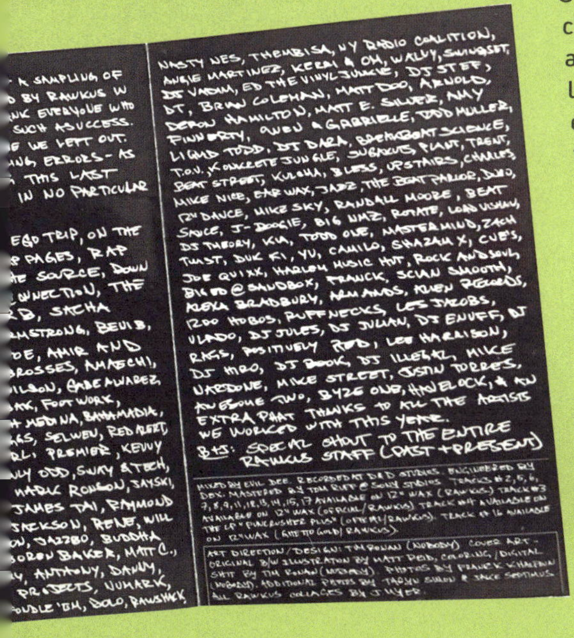

A couple weeks before, I was in Harlem and I bought a Kid Capri tape from Kid Capri. When I listened to the tape before, I was like, "Yo, this dude's talking, he's bugging. I don't want to hear all this talk, talk, talk." Because that's not how we did it in Brooklyn. It was silent. So when I was sitting on that stoop I was like, "We gotta think of something. I don't want to talk like Kid Capri does, but I got to think of something to say on my tapes so people know it's me." Me and my boys sat there for about an hour or so doing different sayings. "It's Evil Dee!" "Nah, this ain't gonna work."

So my boy Butta L was sitting there with us. Butta L's mom comes up the block and she speaks Spanish. She was like, "Luis, Luis, eat chicken." So we start laughing and clowning on Butta L. "Butta L eatin' chicken! Butta L eatin' chicken!"

Somehow "Butta L eating chicken" got flipped around and my boy Dominique was like, "Evil Dee is on the mix, eating chicken!" We flipped it from that to "Evil Dee is on the mix, c'mon and kick it!" When we did that, I was like, "Yo, that's kinda hard right there."

I was making my mixtape and I was like, "How am I gonna apply it?" So I started the tape off and you just heard, "Evil Dee is on the mix, c'mon kick it," and I dropped the first record. I was like, "Okay this might work at the beginning of the tape." But it was like, "Nah, just say it right before the verse comes in on each record." And that's how I started doing it.

When I made tapes with that, some cats were like, "Nah man, that rolling skating call, get that shit on outta here." I was like, "You know what, if you don't want the tape with that on it, you're not going to get the tape, B." Cats were like, "Fuck it." People got used to it, and eventually people started saying it.

The first time I went to Paris, our plane was late and we landed and went straight from the airport to the venue. So I get to the venue, and I'm thinking we're doing maybe 500 people. We walk on stage, I look in the crowd, and they're going crazy. I go, "Okay, that's about 1,000, maybe 2,000 people." Then I look up and there's 2,000 more. I was like, "Yo!"

I'm setting up the turntables, talking to the crowd and I was like, "We're ready! Evil Dee is on the mix!" And the crowd yelled, "C'mon kick it!" And that was the first time that ever happened to me. I said, "Yo, that's ill." I said it again, and they said it louder. I just dropped whatever song, I think "Powaful Impact" was the first song we were performing that night. And the place erupted. In the back of my mind, I was like, "Yo, we made it."

BUCKWILD

Before the Beats: Using Mixtapes as a Production Platform

D.I.T.C. producer Buckwild created countless classics with the who's who of New York City rap legends—O.C. "Time's Up," Big L "Put It On," Kool G Rap featuring Nas "Fast Life," The Notorious B.I.G. "I Got A Story To Tell," Black Rob "Whoa," and the list goes on and on. But before he became a beast behind the boards, he made a name for himself in Harlem and the Bronx as a mixtape DJ. And without even realizing the impact it would make on the future, he was breaking ground as one of the first DJs to feature their own original production on tapes in the form of artist freestyles and exclusive remixes.

INSPIRATION

Buckwild: When I first started, I was going to J&J Variety to cop tapes. I frequently bought Rooftop tapes and, of course, Kid Capri tapes on the regular. I think I had every Kid Capri tape that came out. Everything that was new and flavorful was Kid Capri.

All of us who came after Kid Capri were his kids. Every DJ that catches the record and has his thing to say when he brings the record in or when the record is playing, even if you are young and you don't know, you got it from Kid Capri. Pay homage to the greatest DJ ever.

EXCLUSIVES

When I started doing tapes, Will from Rock 'N' Will's introduced me to 12-inches, because they were a record store too. So with the promo records, he'd be like, "Yo, you need this to put on your record." I remember he gave me Ed O.G. "I Got To Have It" and no one had it. No one knew who it was.

The dope thing about that was it taught us–me, S&S, Most Crew, Showtime, EZ Elpee–the art of digging for records that weren't out or no one ever heard. I always wanted to introduce something that you probably would never hear and didn't even think of hearing. I would throw in a couple of blends and acapellas that you could never get, and since I had equipment, I would make instrumentals of some of the songs that were out that you couldn't get either. Those were the things where everybody had their niche.

Capri wasn't DJing anymore, and he was playing exclusives that nobody had. Once he slowed down, I was like, "Yo let me just put some records on the tape that I like." One of my boys from my hood, Joe Sacks, was like, "Yo man, you should sell your tapes. You should take them to Rock 'N' Will's where you buy your shit."

So I made a tape and took it to Will and Rock, and it was like a test. And it did alright. Then I kept going from there. "Just keep going with the exclusive shit.

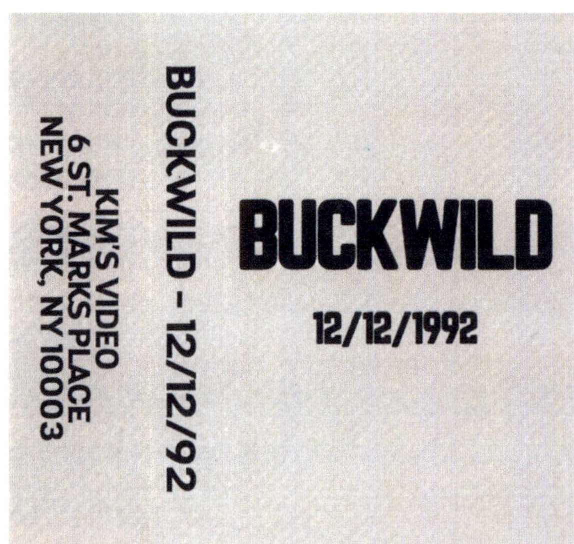

When you got shit that nobody has, that's what they want. They'll pay for that." And that was that.

ORIGINAL PRODUCTION ON MIXTAPES

I was the first to make a beat and have an artist rhyme on that beat on a mixtape, which was Lord Finesse, Lord Tariq, and a couple other cats. 'Nesse had a little beef with the Lords of the Underground. It's dead now, we're all cool. I guess it was just an ego thing as kids. He's Lord Finesse, they're Lords of the Underground. Both are "Lords."

But it was a very popular tape. And everybody was like, "Oh, you got that tape with Finesse and Lords of the Underground?" I made the beat, put it on the 4-track, and that was that. It wasn't a record, it was just something we did for the tape. It was my introduction to production.

When I did that, I was like, "I can really make beats." People were like, "Yo, where'd this beat come from? This beat is hot." I was like, "I just put it on the 4-track." But we didn't know it would be the pathway for the people now.

I always believed in the progression, so I was like, "I graduated. I've arrived." I was making so many songs that I didn't really have time to make mixtapes.

GRADUATING TO PRODUCER

I was like, "Okay, I'm making beats now so I don't need to make mixtapes." So I would give them to my friends and they would play them and that was that. I always believed in the progression, so I was like, "I graduated. I've arrived." I was making so many songs that I didn't really have time to make mixtapes.

All of my early production was probably all on mixtapes. The first record that came out was "Shit is Real" with Diamond and Lord Finesse. Then it was O.C. "Time's Up." Then Organized Konfusion "Stress," which is another record that sounded like nothing else that was ever out.

REMIXES

I was really busy as a producer. When I came in the game, it was like a storm. Pete Rock is someone I've always looked up to. He used to DJ with Chuck Chillout and them on the radio, and he had the most incredible remixes. So when people were like, "Hey, can you do a remix for this?" I was like, "Why not? I used to do this shit on the mixtapes, so let's see if I can do it."

We made beats and put acapellas to them. You had Pete Rock doing remixes, Puffy doing remixes. But even in the underground, guys like Premier and EZ Elpee, we took the 1200, the 950, and we made our own beat. Two-tracked it or hit play, put acapellas to records that people knew, and put our own beat to it. And people would be like, "This is crazy. This is an Elpee remix. This is hot. You can only get this on this tape."

Everything that was going on with music and with making beats, we were doing and putting on mixtapes. It was like we had a radio show. We were like, "You know what? Instead of having this dude come and bring his record, we're going to have him come in and freestyle." Mixtapes were as important in the '90s as the records were.

LORD FINESSE

Triple Threat: Rocking Mixtapes as a Producer, DJ, and MC

Not only is Lord Finesse one of the most witty, punchline-packing MCs of all-time, he's also one of the illest producers to ever come out of the Big Apple. But that's not all. Yes, the D.I.T.C. legend gets busy on the 1s and 2s too, making him a true triple threat—MC/Producer/DJ. With roots as a mixtape DJ, Lord Finesse was able to leverage his talents early on in multiple ways, featuring new tracks he produced as his own mixtape exclusives, and flexing his skills on his peers' classic tapes like Doo Wop's *95 Live* and Tony Touch's *50 MCs Part Two*.

FIRST TAPES

Lord Finesse: I think I went to my brother Showbiz's crib and did one or two tapes there, because he had the microphone, the echo-he had everything. "Yo 'Nesse, here's the keys, go make the tape." So I would go to his house, and I would go to the Music Factory on 42nd Street and all of these places and just buy all the latest records.

I was talking, but I don't know if I would call it a personality. I just wanted you to hear my voice on my tape. I was rapping, but when I was doing mixtapes, my rap career was off. I was the Funky Technician at that point. I already started my rap career, but I think in my downtime, I would make tapes.

TAPE SPOTS

There were a couple of spots in the Bronx, but Rock 'N' Will's was top of the class. If you were going to do a mixtape, you wanted your mixtape to be in the prime locations. They were on 125th Street, and they had people from out of town and all over just pull up and snatch a ton of different tapes.

I had a nice assortment of stores that I dropped off the masters to. It was a hustle for me. If I could do a mixtape once a month and charge $100 to $150 a master and have 8 to 10 stores, I wasn't mad at that. We're talking about '91, '92.

MEETING BIG L AT ROCK 'N' WILL'S

I was doing an autograph signing at Rock 'N' Will's for *Funky Technician*. In comes this dude with his man, and he comes through and he sends his boy over. He didn't approach me. His boy was like, "Yo, my man over here wants to rhyme for you. He's nice."

At that time, everybody was approaching me and I didn't hear anything prolific that ever caught my ear. So I said I'd get my manager, they can chop it up, and if he's dope, then we could take it from there. I guess that wasn't good enough for L. He sent his boy back over and his boy was like, "Look man, he'll rhyme for you. If he's not nice, then he won't ever bother you again."

At that time at Rock 'N' Will's, there was a DJ booth set up in the back. I don't know who was cutting, but he was rhyming for me off of Otis Redding's "Hard to Handle." When he was finished, I asked for his number. I've never run across a kid at that age that sounded like him. For him to be that nice at that age, the upside was undeniable.

ORIGINAL PRODUCTION ON MIXTAPES

That was the producer side of me. Doing certain things that you knew would be deemed different, that other DJs couldn't do or didn't have access to do.

I was producing at that point, so I was actually trying to slip in production I did on those mixtapes. When I did "Come On" for B.I.G., that was one of the joints I had before anybody. That might have been around '93.

It made a nice impact, but the way I did it–I kind of put it out there, but I didn't want to put it too far out there because the song wasn't out yet. Those who knew, knew.

"Suicidal Thoughts" and "Come On" were made at the same time. There's footage of that in Hit Factory. The only thing I'm missing is a cassette with Jesse West and Puffy on the ad-libs when we were rhyming off of "Suicidal Thoughts."

MIXTAPE FREESTYLES

With the freestyles, the value was different because I wasn't rhyming on everybody's mixtapes. I rhymed on Buck's, Doo Wop's once or twice, I did Tony Touch's *50 MCs*, and maybe one or two other people. But that was it.

I wasn't on Clue's tapes, and Clue asked me before. I remember I was with Akinyele in Queens when he asked me. I just had more of a rapport with people like Doo Wop because they were playing my music. It was a favor-for-favor type of thing.

Doo Wop's *95 Live*, the freestyle on that was crazy. I remember that because the shit I was saying

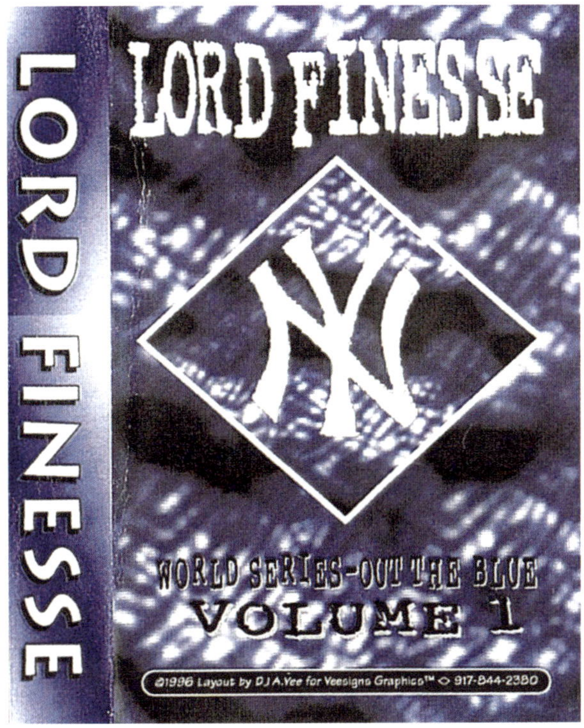

was some other shit at the time. I remember doing Buckwild's infamous Lords of the Underground diss. The mixtape version was more classic because it was me, Lord Tariq, and so many other underground up-and-coming artists.

50 MCs Volume 2, I think I recorded at D&D in the A room. I went into it from a certain stand point that it's going to be out there and everybody's talking about the first *50*, so when I'm on this one, I want everyone to talk about the verse I'm going to drop. It was a hell of a verse. "Benjamins" was the hottest beat out at the time, and I knew I was going to kill that.

My goal was to not drop anything wack. Even to this day, if I'm doing music or records, if I can't top what I've already done or if I can't come within range, why do it? I don't want to be known for dropping 40 points and now I'm somewhere where I'm dropping 8 points and I'm comfortable with that.

EZ ELPEE

Tapes Open Doors: Turning Mixtape Greatness into Production Success

Multi-Platinum Producer EZ Elpee got his start as a mixtape DJ, earning his stripes in the Bronx and Harlem for dope mixes that were known to feature exclusive music, including one of Big L's earliest freestyles. Thanks to his relationships with fellow mixtape DJ/producers Buckwild and Lord Finesse, he was able to turn his mixtape success into a career behind the boards. And ironically, his first big hit, the Junior M.A.F.I.A. duet "Get Money" featuring The Notorious B.I.G. and Lil' Kim, was first heard on a DJ Clue mixtape.

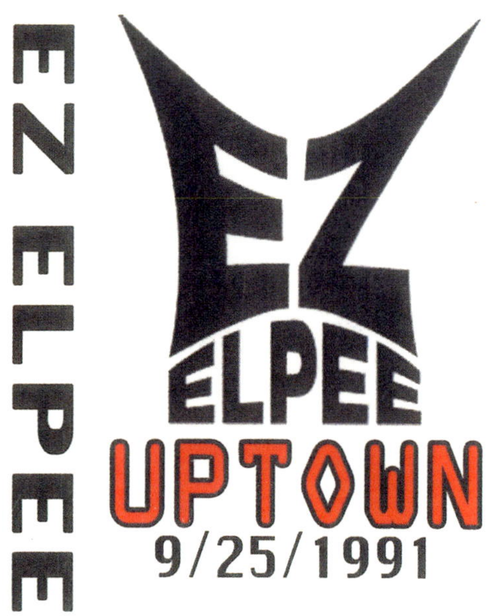

EARLY INFLUENCES AND GETTING STARTED

EZ Elpee: I was a DJ from the age 8 or 9, going until I started doing production–that's when I sat the DJing all the way down. Prior to that, I was always a DJ.

Around my area, the biggest DJ was Triple C. A couple of my friends lived just outside of Soundview, right across the street from the projects, and they were like, "Yo! Triple C has this mixtape, it's fire!" I was like, "Triple C? Who the hell is this?"

They were like, "Yo, the next thing is mixtapes." So I got a Triple C mixtape on Southern Boulevard, and I was like, "Okay, he sounds good on the mic with it. I can do this." I had the 1200s already, and I went and got this reverb for like $50 or $60. And I said, "I'm going to make mixtapes, watch me." It was a competition for me.

And as time went on, I had a following. I didn't know that I was getting the notoriety until I bumped into Guru one day, and he was like, "Yo man, I fuck with your mixtapes. Your shit right." I was like, "Oh wow!" Then I ended up meeting Buck after that.

EXCLUSIVES

When I first started making mixtapes, it wasn't about what was hot in the streets. It was about what needed to be heard that everybody wasn't up on. It wasn't only about the best records.

One day, a couple of things fell in my hand. One of the things was an early release of Rakim's *Follow the Leader* album. Another thing was some Snoop shit with Daz, Kurupt, and them. It was like an album of demos. I was like, "Oh, I'm going to put this on my tape." That's how it started with the exclusives.

SWITCH TO PRODUCTION

The mixtape game ran until about '93. Once I started getting into the beats, things changed. It was like my new toy, and I had to take it seriously. I was going through changes as far as my parents getting a divorce–my mother stayed in the city in Manhattan and my father stayed at an apartment in the Bronx. He was like, "Hey, yo, you gotta pay half the rent." I'm like, "Bro, I'm 18."

Watching and being around Finesse and Buckwild was definitely an inspiration, especially watching the records they did in the early stages come to fruition and turn into actual records. When Finesse took a hold of Buck, it turned into some other kind of shit. I'm around Buck every day, so it was like, "Come on, you're coming too."

Lord Finesse is one of the keys to New York City. He was the conduit to everything. And he was never selfish. If you didn't have him, this game would be ugly. There are so many people that came from him.

PRODUCING "GET MONEY" FOR BIGGIE

The beat was made, and we went right to B.I.G.'s apartment and played it for him in his bedroom. It was me, O.Gee, Lord Finesse, and Buck. Finesse drove us. The four of us were in the car and we went right to St. James Place. We used to be on the phone when Finesse and B.I.G. would be snapping on each other, so we were familiar with him already. He was just like, "Come to the crib. I got the Junior M.A.F.I.A. shit, I need some beats."

Then, that shit was three 12-hour studio sessions. There was a whole party in there. I walk in the first session, Faith is there, Mary J. Blige is there, and I'm just like, "What the fuck we got going on here?" You would not even know you were at a session, you would think you were at a fucking party. His sessions had a lot of people in there–20, 30, 40 people easily.

The beats that everybody else wouldn't pick or didn't understand, B.I.G. would understand. His craft was already mastered. He was like, "If you give me the right beat, man, this shit gonna go." I don't think he knew about "Get Money" though. He was like, "This is just going to be a street joint." I said, "Yo, you gonna clean that up?" He was like, "Nah, I ain't cleaning that up." He ended up having to clean it up.

DJ CLUE PREMIERING "GET MONEY"

When DJ Clue was breaking "Get Money," you didn't even know I did it. There weren't any tags on it or anything. "Who did the beat?" "EZ Elpee." "Oh man, this guy here is going." From there, I totally shut down from making mixtapes and I went in and made records.

APPRECIATION FOR THE MIXTAPE GAME

Mixtapes in general helped everybody in some way, shape, size, or form. It's just what you did with it after. They didn't give you an instruction manual in our era. You had to make it yourself. Me doing music was just like a kid from New York saying, "I'm going to Hollywood and I'm going to be an actor." It was the same thing.

When DJ Clue was breaking "Get Money," you didn't even know I did it. There weren't any tags on it or anything. "Who did the beat?" "EZ Elpee." "Oh man, this guy here is going." From there, I totally shut down from making mixtapes and I went in and made records.

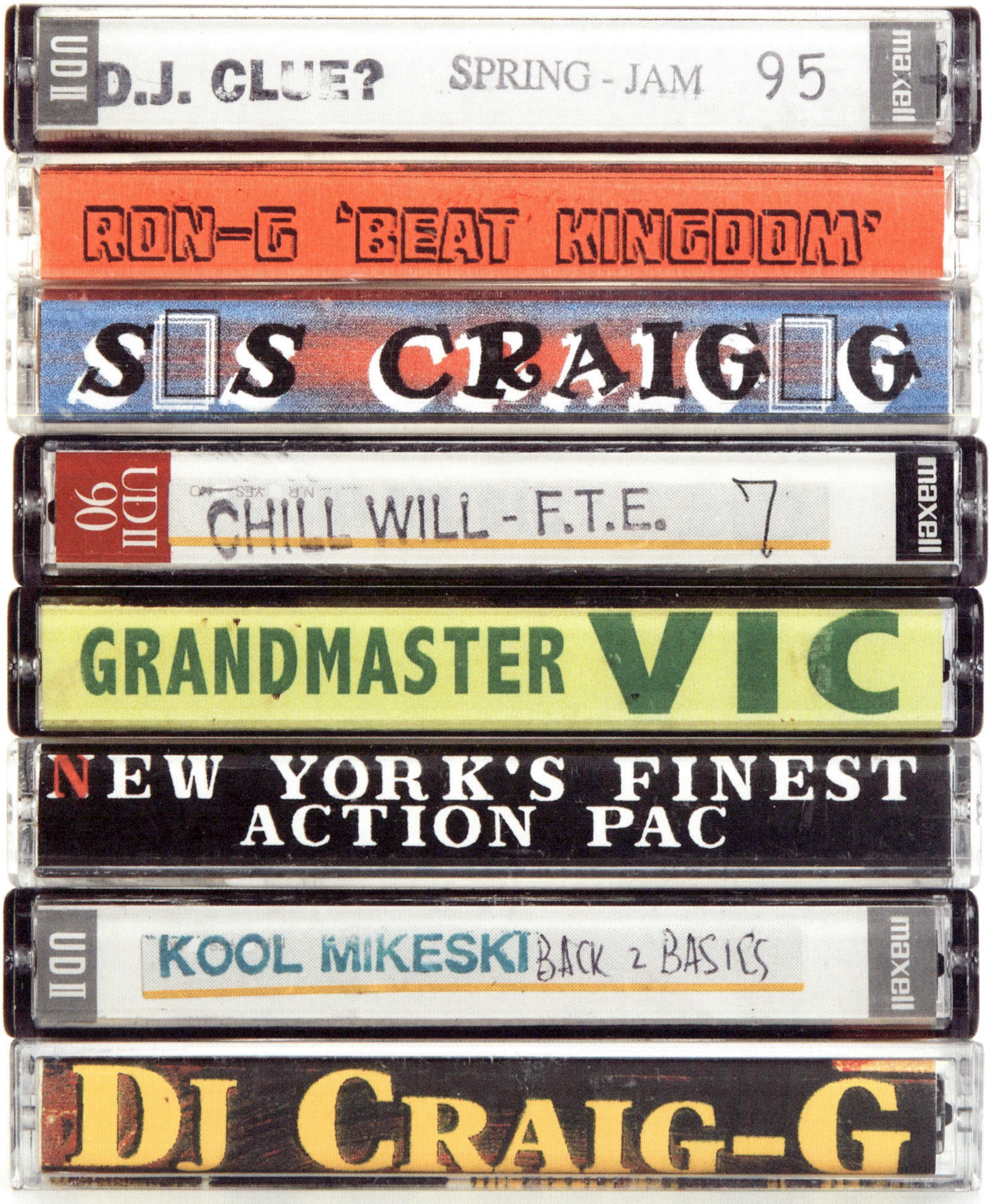
UD II
D.J. CLUE? SPRING - JAM 95
maxell
RON-G 'BEAT KINGDOM'
S S CRAIG G
UD II 90
CHILL WILL - F.T.E. 7
maxell
GRANDMASTER VIC
NEW YORK'S FINEST
ACTION PAC
UD II
KOOL MIKESKI BACK 2 BASICS
maxell
DJ CRAIG-G

THE STORES

Selling mixtapes started out as a hand-to-hand business, with DJs pushing their own products inside the clubs at gigs or outside on the street corners. But as demand grew, local mom-and-pop shops started popping up across the five boroughs and became places where fans could go to cop the latest mixtape releases. And larger record stores that sold official albums and singles releases started stocking street mixtapes on their shelves, too.

Though it wasn't exactly legal, selling mixtapes became a lucrative business for many store owners, and a direct outlet for DJs to get their music to hip-hop fans beyond their neighborhoods. The power of the mixtape in the '90s was most definitely strengthened by THE STORES.

ROCK: ROCK 'N' WILL'S

Pushin' Tapes: Opening Up Shop in Harlem

In the early days of mixtape popularity in NYC, Rock 'N' Will's on 125th Street in Harlem was one of the first places fans could go to find the hottest new tapes. And it became such an important hub for the mixtape game and the Uptown hip-hop movement that Fab 5 Freddy filmed an episode of *Yo! MTV Raps* at the store, with appearances by Kid Capri, Ron G, and more. But even before Rock 'N' Will's opened its doors, Rock's family history in the music and mixtape game had even deeper roots.

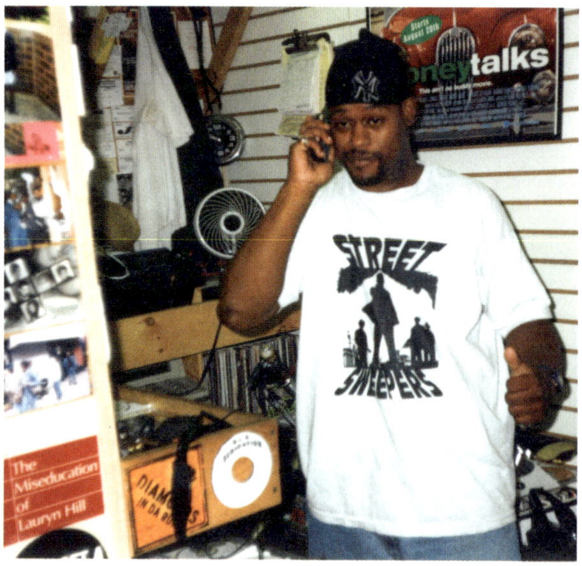

125TH STREET

Rock: We were vendors on 125th Street, right across the street from the Apollo. There was a store called the Record Hole, we used to set up in front. The guy would have a speaker outside, and we took it from there. After vending, we got the first store. And after that, we had two or three more stores all on 125th Street. Record shops, variety shops–but the main shop was records.

On the street, we sold everything from skully hats, gabardine pants, wigs, whatever. If you look at the movie *Black Caesar* with Fred Williamson, there's a clip in there when he comes down 125th Street with me and my brothers in there at the stand. So I got the proof if you need it.

We had a big family. I had nine brothers and sisters. So it was a family business on the street along with all the other merchants and peddlers. Everybody knows a big family.

J&J VARIETY AND MEETING WILL

My father was a hustler extraordinaire, and it rubbed off on me. We had ice stands, everything. At the store we had on 124th and 7th–J&J Variety–he would hire a lot of people from the community or different young people. So he hired Will. And there was a guy from Brooklyn named Murph, he came from the streets with us. A real good guy.

J&J Variety, that was my father's store. My brother had a store that was called CJ's Music City. My brother became a bus driver and he turned the store over to me. Will came up with the idea to put up a sign: Rock 'N' Will's. He was really instrumental in everything.

We moved over to 125th Street in like '90, '91, that was Rock 'N' Will's. Anything before that was J&J's. Being that it was my father's store, we'd go back and forth. It was no big deal. When we moved on, Murph took over the mixtape store on 7th Avenue.

PERSONAL TAPES

Being that we had the record shop, people used to

come in before Brucie B and Kid Capri to get mixtapes. They would go down a song list and check off what they wanted on the tape, and we would make the tape like that. No talking, just records.

They were called mixtapes. A hustler or whatever, he's got three or four cars, we'd make a tape for each car. He'd give me a list of the Top 20 songs that he'd want and I'd go home and make it. Guy Fisher, I've dealt with them all. The clientele was immaculate.

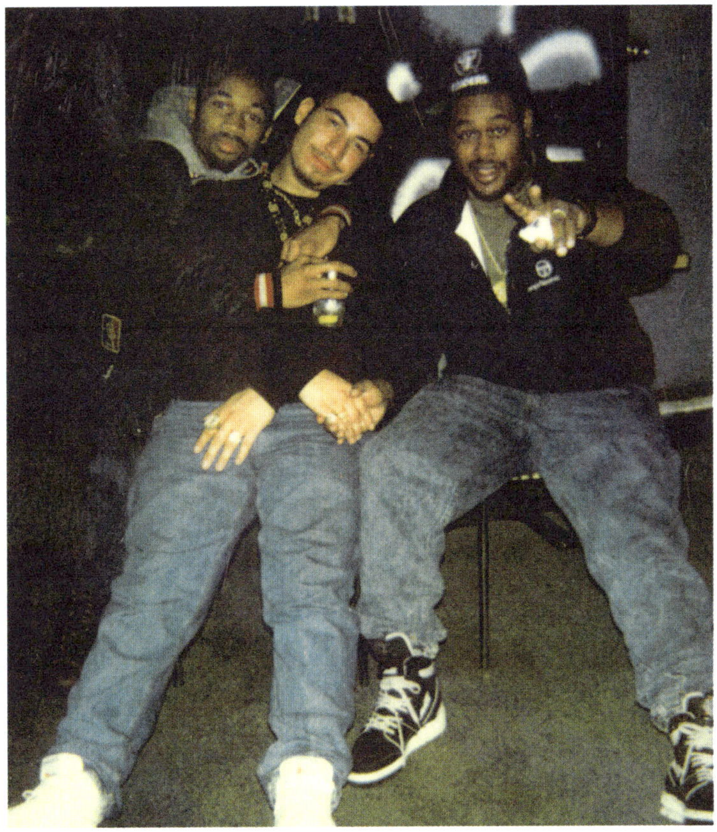

MASTERS
One of the first ones was Brucie B *Rooftop*. Brucie B, he would bring me tapes and we would pay for the masters. Someone like maybe Kid Capri charged $200 for a master–he was top of the line. Once Kid blew up, everybody came.

Kid Capri was a really nice guy. Him and Will were more on a good page. He was alright with me because I'm straight business when you come to me, you're getting your money. We didn't have any problems like that. Lord Finesse was under Will. Buckwild started right here, too. He used to always want to trade tapes. He was a customer first, he used to buy everything. He soaked it all up.

HARD PACK
We would have a session maybe every two weeks where we would invite all the DJs and all the rappers down. That was The Hard Pack. Everybody would slide through from the Most Crew, Starski, Starchild, Kid Capri, whoever. Every two weeks or whatever, we had a home DJ like the incredible D-Wiz. But Will had his own DJs and I had my own DJs, my top DJs, because we used to pay for the mixtapes. We had my starting five and his starting five.

IN-STORE EPISODE OF *YO! MTV RAPS*
That was in '92. When you saw me on *Yo! MTV Raps*–that was worldwide. We definitely got more foot traffic after that. I was selling vinyl, too. I remember selling to Japanese guys, one record for maybe $1,500. Stuff like that.

COMPETITION
Everyone was jumping on the bandwagon. Believe me. Harlem Music Hut, Stereo Palace, those are the two that I can remember off hand. Stereo Palace would offer DJs $200, $300 for their master. Then you had the Africans, they really messed the game up. They had 1,000 brothers. So they would buy the master, and it would be straight from here to California overnight.

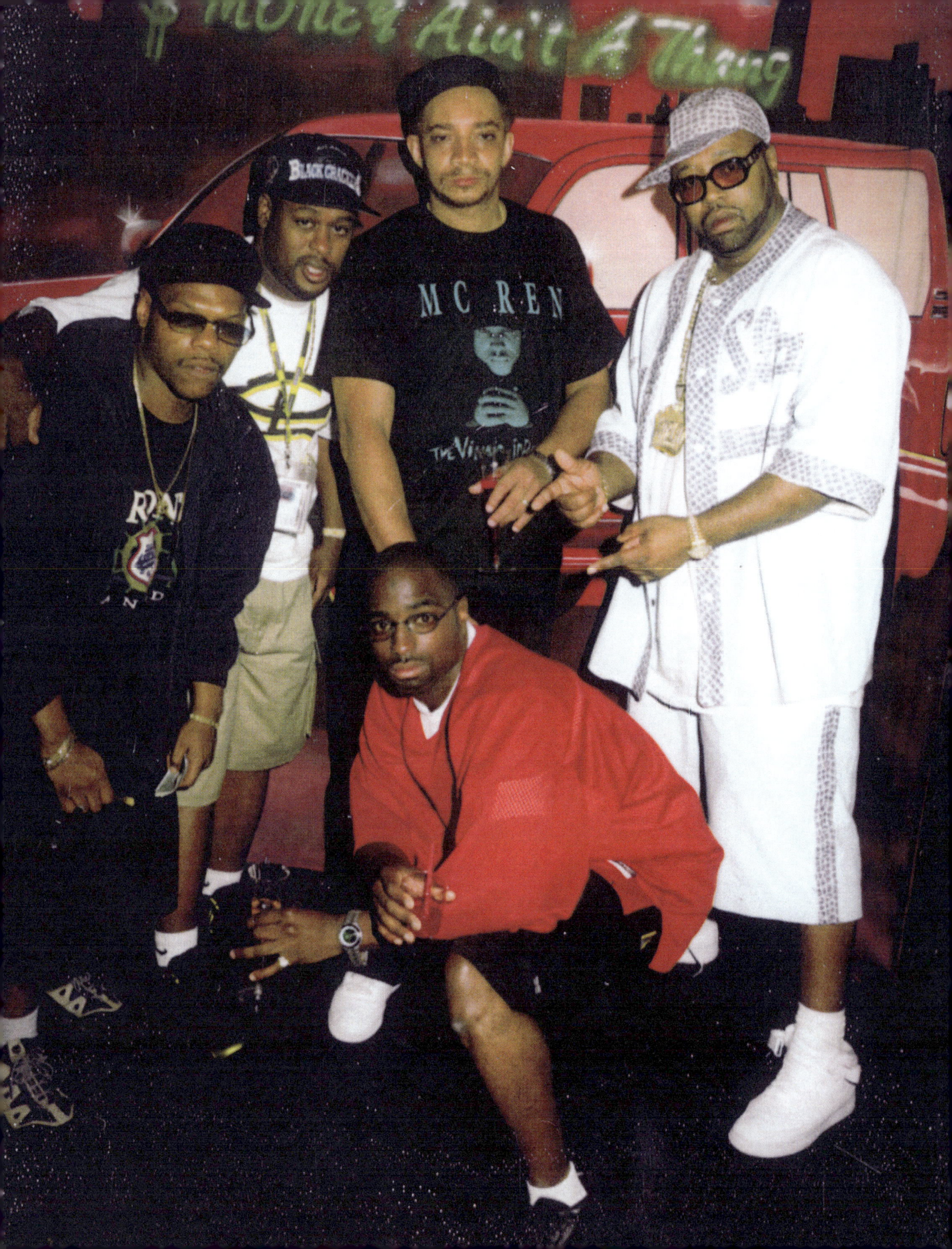

Money Ain't A Thang
MC REN

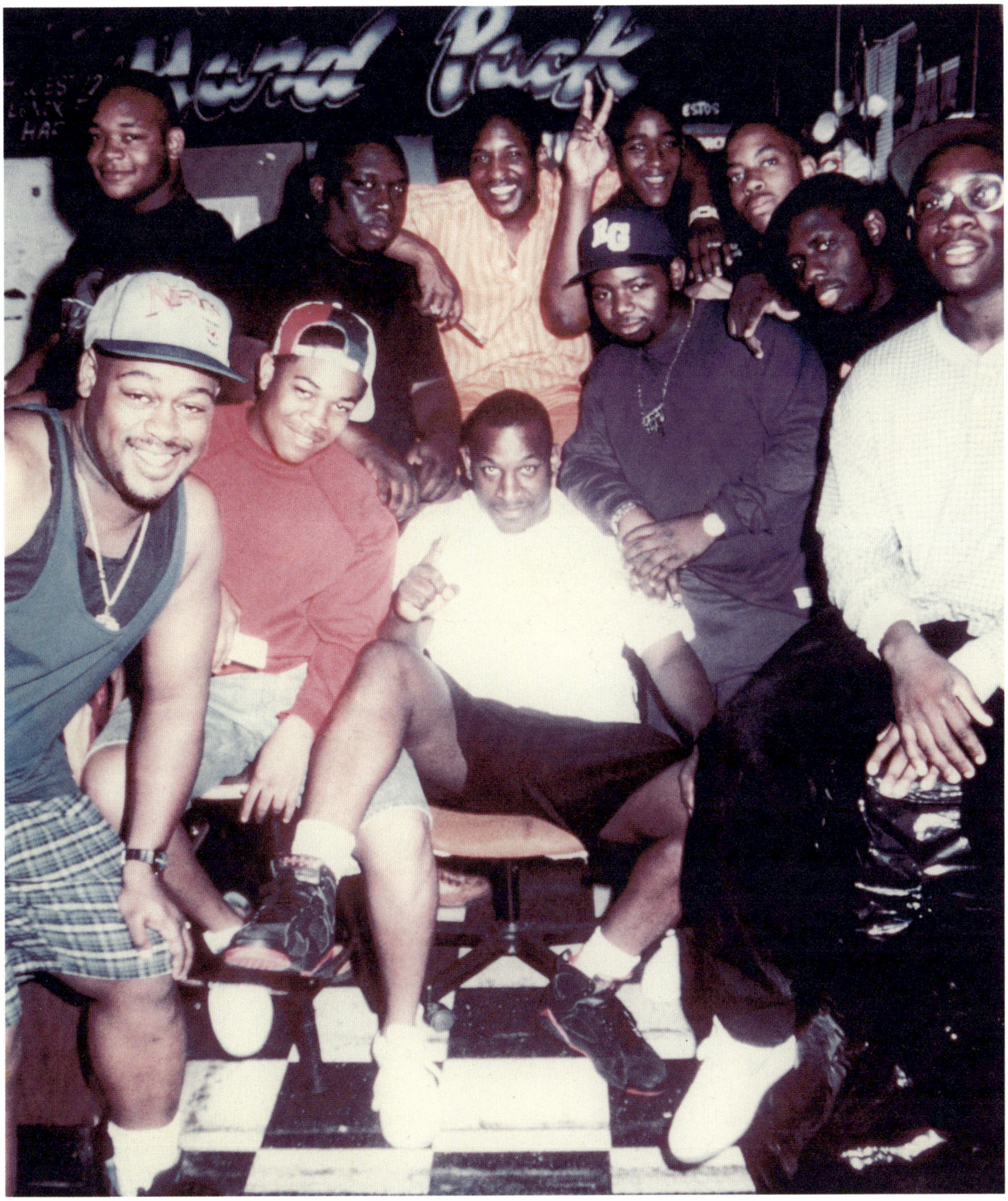

Mobstyle
1,2,3 + Remix Vol 9

(1)(A) Gangs Wise
Calvary Club
Mike Slice (1)(2)

NGK
Joe Vibes 7/7
6/18 Blends

Carton TNT - Castle
Tony Touch Gods
Rooftop 85
Fly Guy

D-Demo
9-26
Flava for Days
Beats
Old School
No Date v
DDemo 3,7

Double R Ted
1-29-91 - Smooth Raps #4
RR-14
1991 - Freestyle House
Ed Smooth Raggae #2
10,15,18,19
10-93

Triple C
12/27
5/21 Pt 1,2
OS 4
10-20
1/8
Circle Club
Block Party

Ron G
Ron G Starski
Cotton Club
4-1-92
R+B-4 EPMD
It's on 94
Starski Ron G
Bruce B BSS
Ladies Nite 9/3
Real Real BTSS
VA - 1 082
Party - 1

Juice
18, 19, 21, 23
25, 27, 28
29, 31, 33
34, 36, 37
Old to New

Ron G
4-22-93
2-20
Summer Jam
BTSS Pt 2
Miss Jones / Fat Beats
RIP Moins Nasty Nas 2
No Date Hold you tight (Blend)
Ron G (Slow)
(Re-EMPD)
Ron G Party
New / Eric B Rap Generation
Dead Presidents "2"
Off the hook
Ron G + Triple C
It's on 2/11
Diamonds forever
3/26 10/13
6/17 5/16
6/3 Slow

Lord Finesse
7-1
Back To School 93
2/1
12/10
1/17
11-5
No Date 91
J. Live
Enemy Therapist done
10-17
10-2
7-22

(1)(B)

Bruce B.
Freaky Friday
2.5, 10-16 1-4
BB Hollywood
Bruce B the Savoy
10-11, 10-25
10-17-96, 7/27
3-9-96
Final Four Anniversary
8-1-89 Live
Bruce Bee Live 1,2
2009 New Years
April Fool 94
2/28

Buckwild
7.26
~~5-23~~
~~10-6~~
~~Slow 10.9~~
S+S
Bad boy / Stop ya
6-5 - 11-4
8.9 2.10
BTSS
Fuck Everbody
S+S Greg G
ND & F
Something for that Ass II
It's not A game
nigger Ain't nice
Old School 1, 2, 3, 4

Starski
4/6
8/1
Fever (1993 Live)
Big Daddy Kane
Cold Crush
Lord Finesse
Water Bed Kev.
Slow Jams
8/10 R+B
Puff Daddy
B Day Tunnel 1,2

Carton TNT
11-26 Castle

K Capri
4/12
Bruce B (BSK)
K Capri
Starchild
8-1-89
10-18
10-26
KCVA Pt 2
11/14/88
11/8, 523
12/10 10,6
6/6/89
Clark Kent
5/5 Castle
Carton TNT
9/10/89
4/1, 10.9 Slow
12/21
My Static Noise
Make-Loud School
5/25
4/6/89
5/9/89
6.23
4.19 Big Apple
6.22
9 Clubs Live 1, 2, 3
Kid Capri
MC Lite Capaco
7/3 8/6
8/22 5/17
12/28
3/9/89
4/20 Live VA.
2/20/91
R+B KC
8-11 Castle
2/3
9/4
10-18 Castle Live
3-10 Castle

Bruce Bee
1-10 Slow
Old School Beats
Roof Top
Hollywood Bruce B #3
12-4-89 R+B
11-4-88
10-31
87 Roof Top
Bruce Dan Club Rock
Hollywood Bruce #2
11-18
4-5
No Date Starchild
BB Return
Kane KG Rap
1.5
Cool Out
10/99 - 12/3/89
Special Disco Mix
The Savoy 2/97
+ Love Bus
Starski
Lenny the 1,2
Barber Live
Queens Live 1,2, 3/6
1/20/90
1/5
Freaky Friday
10-8
Black Silk 2/97
feat Capone
Two Plus Plus one Ent
OSR+P
2-10-89
Roof Top
5.23
1-11-89
2-14-88
7-19-85
3-1-89
9-19-87

Starchild
Live
~~Zestress~~
2-27-2
6-2
Mobstyle
11-10
10-20-9
4-8
7/19/90
SSC
Busy Bee
B Day
Kil Cap
Ron Allen
Rink KK
Bubba
Castle
9-8 90
Slow
12-22
6-6
3/13
9/10
7/1
Fever Red Alert 19
Live P.J.
6/15/96
7/28/9
5/13/9
SC Live XMAS
Roof Top
SC 3/5
Chill Place

TNT Reggae (3) Ted Smooth – Reggae – 6-25-91 Stan Strong – Prop Jack

Double J – Party Slammer Live Ron G Slow Jam II, It's A R+B Thing

Town – Freak man R+B DJ – Priest – Harlem River Drive Pt.2 Lord F. 10-20

Mike Nice	Starchill	Doo Wop	Hardpack	Kid Capri	Bruce B
iggaLove + Big Budda	11-16	the New festivities ent	Buster Club	11-26	5/16/99
	6-19-96	Woopisim Pt.2	HP-1	RIP Jissy G	Live Booms
22, No DATE	Old School	Kool Kirk +	004 8,10,92	the Party 3.1	7.6
hinild Blnd 8	3-28-94	Doo Woop Doo Wop Cookout 94	HP-11	52 Beats	1987 Old School Classics
nickMan Tapes Blnds 1993	1-10 Starchild Slow	Live 93	0000-1 WFF4	James Brown	Brucee II + 8/12
lue #33	10-10	Live 95 Pt2	Goodie/Plenty	OS 1,2,3	7-29-89
Hle Wrek-93	OldSchool 1	Spring Pt1	HP-NoDate	11-16 3-9-89	9-18-89
game spring 1	Live at Willie Lounge	Dow Woop -1-1	12/14 HP-3 HP 8	6-25 5-17	10-31-89
mage-3	0023	Summer Jam	0011	KC Party	Kid capri – Master
mpage 4-11-93	STARCHILD DISCO Fever 1980	Summer Jam 93	Harlem Week 4, 1	9-12 ~~Disco Blues~~	4.24, 11-1 7-6 Cool out
g Time Blend 1,2		11/18	~~Street Funk~~		
School of Oldies NGK 1989	STARCHILD 053	Fall Flava 1	G4G	Old Disco Music	4-1
.C. Perry B		Fall Flava-2		10-9 Slow	BB052
-23-89		Tunnel		10-19	Old Time Music BB89
		Digs Brothers		7-3 1-21	
nny Rock 4-4-91		Bad Boy Vol.2		7.13 6-10	Bruce B Kid capri live 8.20

Jazzy Joyce	Starski LB	Doo Wop	S+S – B. Wild	Kid Capri	Bruce B (31)
		Winter-Cool #5 Out		5-13 8-6	BB 8/15
5/12	3/27	Winter Jams	Blends	Doggin Shit 8/5 – 822	Cool out 8.12 W-C
ck To School 13	III - LoveBus	Birthday	OldSchool 94	2-22-89	~~Cool out~~ 5-23 Rooftop
le P. 2/9	~~Old School~~ Boat Ride	~~FlashBack~~ Spring Pt.2	BuckWild 1/17	6-3 2-7	B. Bee Rooftop 60 mins
Nice – 9/26	Starski Flash	Spring Pt2	12-10 R+B Pt.2 Pt.3	10-30 12-21	Hollywood Slow/Jams
ried Carton TNT Winter Place	Eddie Cheba	Spring-Pt.2 94 Vol. Face off Doo Wop	Butthh Tape	12-10 4-1 10-9-Slow	
Nice 11-20		Doo Wop #5 Wop Flex		Castle #5	
Nice DDEMO ple C		Xmas Jam		12-7 4-1	
-MN. Blends 11/1		Cool Out 93		5-2 Slow	
nice Tape mp Tape 3.26		DooWop #4		Reggae Stuff 8/12/89	
		DooWop/K Slay		Slow Stuff	

~~wTime~~ ShowTime	ShowTime				
0-9, Live	Jam O Ice Pt 5	Bronx Tales		Kid Capri Castle 9/9	
2 Blends #2	R+B 5			8/31 Pt1,2	
e Earl ool of Oldies 1989	OG OS:4			11/30	DJ DR. DUSS + JAZZY G ~~Reet To Reel #1+2~~,
1.20				12/23 Slow	EBros
ag 12/7				No Date 6.23	
lpack 004					
- Sticks T.S. B.D 3/13					
-Nice Red handed					
Springfield					

COPPIN' TAPES AT ROCK 'N' WILL'S

Bahr Brown: You'd be like, "What mixtapes do you have?" And Rock would pull out a list for you. It wasn't like they were out on display.

Then he'd pull out a zip case and it'd just be a bunch of new shit. He'd be like, "I got this, I got this." And then he'd play it for you. And that was an experience in itself. He'd put in a joint and you're just waiting for him to push fast forward a little bit and be like, "Alright."

The intro would grab you. You'd be like, "Okay, I've never heard that." It was just an experience, and Rock was a hustler. He would try to get you to buy as many as possible. That's what it was.

Rock and Will were the best. I gave them a lot of bread. I know I fed their families—for real.

TRIPS TO BURKINA IN MANHATTAN

Havoc of Mobb Deep: That was the one I used to travel to a lot just to go get my mixtapes. I didn't travel up to Harlem too much, but Burkina was right in the city. I mean, damn, they had like a million mixtapes in there. And, you know, we would have to go back frequently because sometimes those tapes used to pop.

BX MIXTAPE SPOTS

KamTV, Podcast Host: We would drive down to the Bronx from White Plains and search for mixtapes and places that looked like they sold music. It became a religious kind of thing where each week we would take the trip. Eventually, we had multiple mixtape spots and contacts. Black at Sammy's Fashion on Fordham, Uptown Flava on Grand Concourse and the one on Southern Boulevard—and eventually down to Ali at Scheme on 125th Street in Harlem.

At that time, the deals were like 5 for $20. And if they really messed with you, they would give you an exclusive. Someone gave me a copy of Jay-Z's *Vol. 3* album a couple weeks before it came out.

ACTION PAC REMEMBERS THE HARD PACK

Action Pac: That was Rock's idea. He had a little DJ booth set up in the back of the store, and he'd have people come through. He'd call us up, "Yo, I have Ron coming through, I got so and so coming through. Let's do something together."

There were no real big name rappers. I think A.G. came through from D.I.T.C. and did a freestyle. Showtime was really the one that would do a lot of talking on the mic. My man Ty Wiz would freestyle. We'd just be in the back having fun, smoking blunts and drinking, chilling for an extended period of time, and recording a mixtape live. Those were kind of his exclusives back then.

WORKING AT MUSIC FACTORY

Mr. Walt of Da Beatminerz (Queens Location):
I used to work at Music Factory on Jamaica Avenue. You had people like Grandmaster Vic and DJ Irv, who later became Irv Gotti. These guys were buying records from me and putting them on their tapes. Then people like DJ Doggtime, Ike Love, and all these other DJs from Queens were getting their stuff up. This was all before Clue, he came years later.

What killed Music Factory was the bootleg tape, but also the mixtapes. Everybody was making and selling them, so people would rather buy the mixtape than buy the albums. I wasn't mad because mixtapes were a part of the culture. We used to sell our own mixtapes in there. When my brother Evil Dee started making tapes, he came in at the right time. His mixtapes were going like water.

Craig G (Brooklyn Location):
When it came to mixtapes, I'd be at the counter selling stuff. And they'd be like, "Yo Craig, what's the hot shit?" And I'd show them all the tapes, but they'd be like, "Fuck that, I want yours." So here I am grabbing my shit, which is sort of a conflict of interest. But hey, the customer said they wanted the Craig G shit.

Biggie came into the store a couple times and dropped off something real nice to me. But he also went and dropped it to Flex and Enuff and the other DJs in the city. So I wasn't so exclusive with it. Now B.I.G.'s at that legendary status, one of the greatest to ever do it. So it's like, "Oh shit, B.I.G. brought me something hand-to-hand."

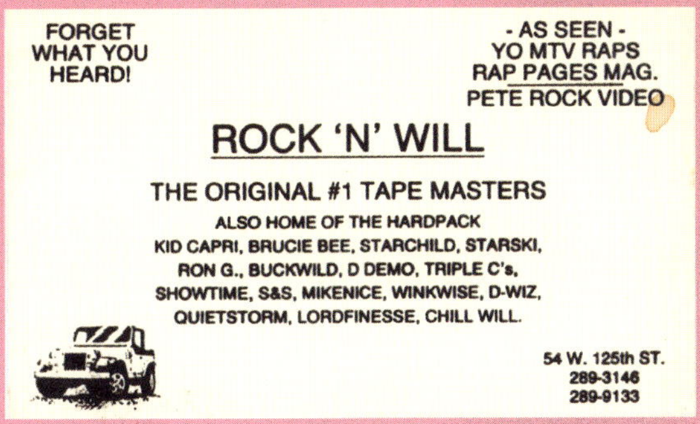

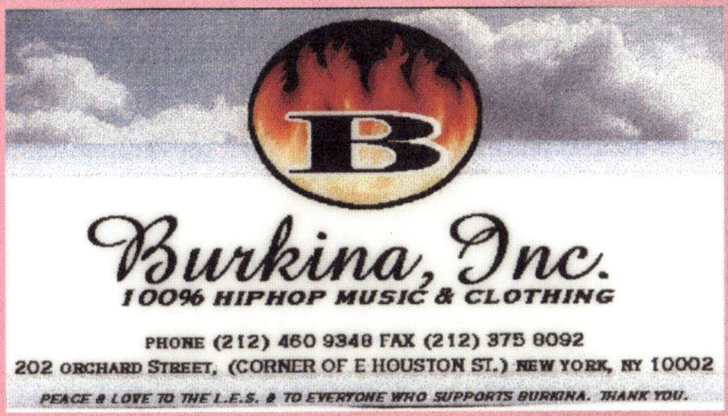

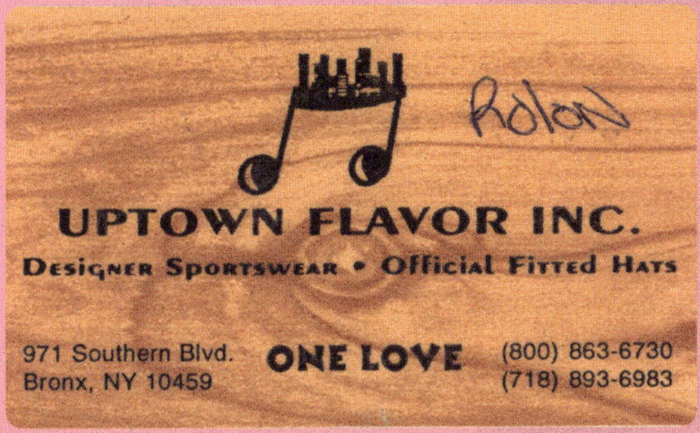

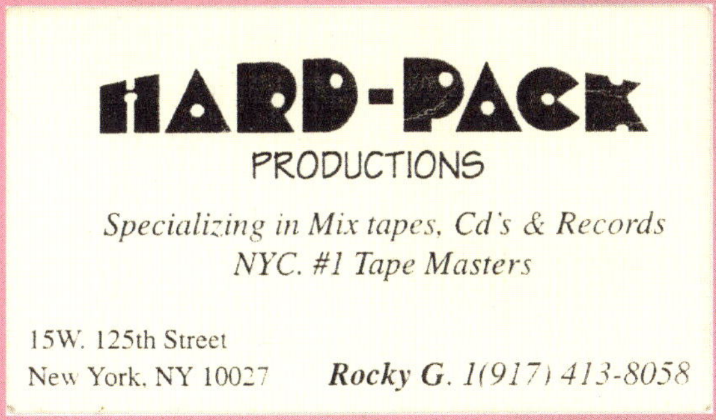

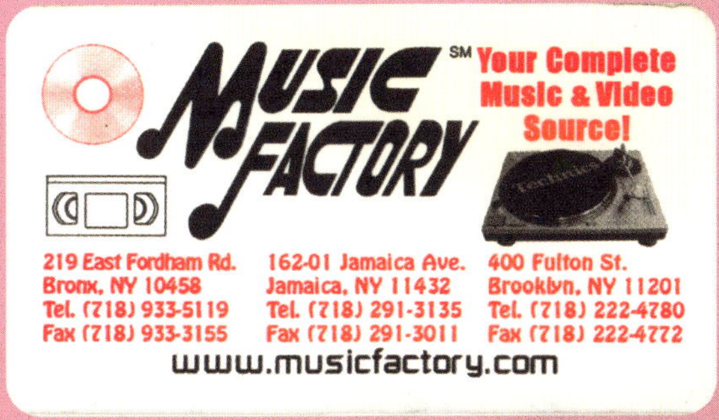

MR. WALT'S
TOP 5 QUEENS DJS

1. GRANDMASTER VIC - You've got to give it to the King. He's the pioneer. He's the guy. When you're talking about Queens DJ culture, you cannot not say Grandmaster Vic.

2. DJ FLAMBOYANT - Flamboyant used to DJ, and he used to work with us at the Music Factory. But he used to be really heavy in the DMC championship. And he's from Southside, and he used to go heavy with the blend. And after the DMC, he went to DJ for Onyx.

3. DJ DEWITT - He's Freddie Foxxx/ Bumpy Knuckles' original DJ. And he's another one who pioneered the game in Queens, I think he's from Southside too. He was the OG. He was one of the respected DJs. He was quiet but when he got on those turntables, you knew what it was.

4. DJ IRV - Y'all know him as Irv Gotti, the loudmouth asshole who was behind Murder, Inc. This is why I respect him so much, because he was an asshole back in the '80s. Like, the person that y'all see now is the same person when he was DJing in Hollis. But he was incredible on those turntables.

5. DJ DOGGTIME - I saw him come up on some humble beginnings. He was so eager to do stuff and he was a really nice guy. And then he just became a monster in Queens with the mixtapes. I was proud of him, because he was one of the humble guys.

DARRYL MCCRAY: HOUSE OF NUBIAN

Nubian Love: Mixtapes Create a Cultural Hub

Nestled on 8th Street in the West Village, House of Nubian was a go-to spot for music and mixtape fans downtown, including some of the era's most notable celebrities. And Darryl McCray, who started as a street vendor, was the one keeping its doors open through all the challenges of running a business.

SELLING TAPES IN THE WEST VILLAGE

Darryl McCray: I started selling mixtapes back in October of 1989 when it was in full swing. I had a corner of the market because I was out on West 4th Street in Manhattan. I had a whole three or four blocks locked down.

Back in the day, everybody was trying to sell stuff out in the streets. This was in the '80s, and in those days it seemed that you needed to be a licensed vendor to sell mixtapes. It was really hard to get a license back in those days. I'm a U.S. Marine, so I had just come home and I was able to get a license pretty quickly. There was no hold-back for the military getting licenses.

FROM HOUSE TO HIP HOP

We were doing really good with house tapes. And then there was a lot of hip hop out there. I remember right around the time EPMD started popping, it was like everything was hip hop overnight. House music was always moving, but then all of the sudden it was hip hop. It blasted through.

DIFFERENT LOCATIONS

Right after Dinkins changed the law that said you could no longer have vendors out there, I tried to move like everybody else. And I went from making $2,000 a day to making 50 cents a day. I said, "This ain't gonna work." Fortunately for me, I had gobs of cash stashed and I opened up my first store.

23 West 8th Street was my first store. I split it off with another guy–he had one side and I had the other side. I started to make money, slowly but surely. I outgrew his store pretty quickly because he was selling leather and handbags and stuff like that. He was one of those knuckleheads that wouldn't let me play music in the store because it was his store. I split that with him until I couldn't be there anymore. It wasn't working for either one of us.

NEXT STORES

I opened up a store to myself at 1 West 8th Street right next to 5th Avenue. It was a small little box, but it was nice. That's when it started thriving. And still in those days, I wasn't taking credit cards, everything was cash. I think I was there for about a year and that's when it really blew up, because I put a big sound system in there.

Jimi Hendrix's studio Electric Lady was right across the street. All of the sudden, out of nowhere, I got on the map. Bobby Brown started hanging out in the store. Lil' Kim came through.

Erykah Badu would come in and sing in the store after being at the studio. People would lose their minds, like, "Oh my gosh, it's a concert." I started to be the place to be.

But I was outgrowing the location because you could only get 20 people in there, tops. There were so many people outside trying to get in. Jada Pinkett, Queen Latifah, Harold Miner–they used to call him Baby Jordan, Duane Martin, Omar Epps. Everybody started coming in and I outgrew that quickly.

Then I moved to 35 West 8th Street, which was a huge store. Right in front of MacDougal Street. By the time I opened that store, I was already big time. I started making crazy loot, branching off of music into stuff like hip-hop fashion. I was rolling, man.

EMPLOYEES AND VIBE

I hired the hottest dime piece chicks you could ever see. All of the girls that worked in my store were always the flyest of the fly. So my priority–you had to be some eye candy. I even hired some gay dudes and gay girls just because of the area. So everybody came into my store just to be around the vibe. We'd have music playing and incense burning. People were meeting people there. It was a really cool place and environment. I was the only black-owned business owner on the block. We were blasting music all the time.

Malcolm-Jamal Warner, he actually came in and played a trick and pretended like he was an employee. I let him get behind the cash register and ring up customers. People were like, "Don't I know you?" and he'd be like, "What do you mean?" Shock G–same thing, he came in and acted like an employee.

RELATIONSHIPS WITH MIXTAPE DJS

Tony Touch was cool. He would come in and drop off tapes every now and then. Evil Dee would come in on the regular. Clue came in like every other day. Mister Cee, even Wendy Williams would come in there because she was doing mixtapes.

FAMOUS CUSTOMERS

Jimmy Iovine came in and bought like one mixtape of everything I had in the store, $10 a piece. I didn't know who he was. Somebody told me he was a record producer. Later on I realized, "Oh shit, he's the man."

Beyonce's mom came in with Solange and bought a whole bunch from me one time. I talked to her like a regular customer because I didn't know who she was. She came back when Beyonce started dating Jay-Z and she bought *Streets Is Watching* from me. She said, "Who is this Jay-Z character? I don't know anything about him. What do you know about him?" I said, "Oh, here's his joints." She said, "Let me get that." She came into the store quite a few times.

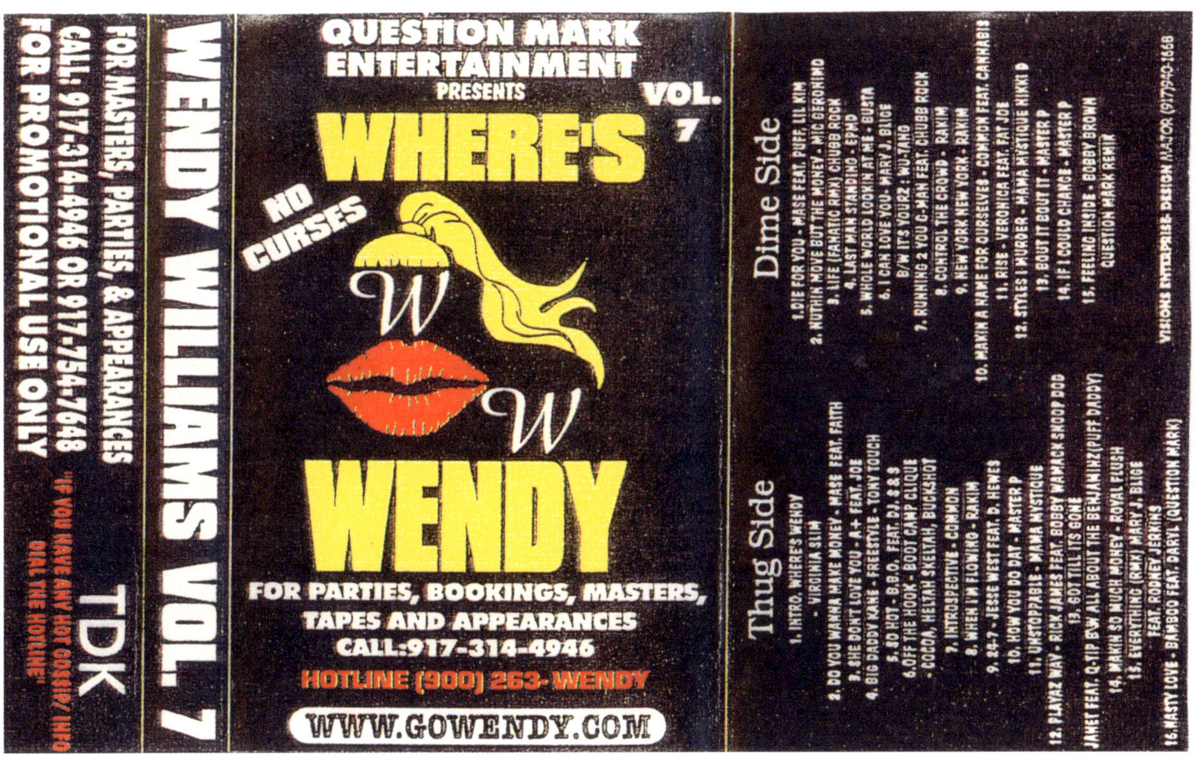

PHIL ORAMA: HARLEM MUSIC HUT

He's a Business, Man: The Face of Harlem's Premiere Mixtape Spot

Phil Orama is the founder of Harlem Music Hut, one of the most well-known mixtape spots in New York City that thrived during the '90s and early 2000s. And it all started from his days of selling mixtapes as a vendor on 125th Street. Not only did Phil run a successful business that became a staple in the culture, he was instrumental in shaping how business was done between DJs and store owners, and played a huge role in popularizing the tracklist on mixtapes.

SELLING TAPES ON THE STREET

Phil Orama: I used to sell mixtapes on the street. I was working at the hospital, and I got into a fight with some guy and lost my job. One of my friends was selling tapes and said, "Phil, man, you can make money doing this. This is a thing to do." I took my last paycheck, which was $167, and I bought a couple boxes of blanks, a boombox, some batteries, and that was it. That's all I could afford.

I went out, and we broke the night making copies of the stuff he had. He had some old classics like The Stylistics, The Delfonics, some salsa classics, and a couple of hip-hop tapes. I didn't know until like a year later, but he took a Double R tape and edited out the Double R names and the shoutouts. He was like, "Oh, I made this tape."

I set up on 125th Street right between Broadway and Old Broadway, on the south side of the street, in front of this restaurant we used to call Stinkin' Lincoln–it was a Lincoln Fried Chicken. There was a dude that used to sell bootleg tapes, so I started selling mixtapes on the other side of him. I got one of those TV dinner tables and just went out there.

The first day I sold 13 tapes at $10 a pop, so that was $130. The second day I only sold one tape. I was depressed. I said, "Oh shit, this is effed up, man. This is embarrassing." But I said, "Let me try one more day." The third day I sold 18 tapes–$180. By the end of the week I was like, "I can make money doing this shit." And that's what I started doing.

EXPANDING THE BUSINESS

Right away, a light bulb lit up on top of my head. I said, "I can leave somebody here and go to another spot and set up." I hired my cousin and I would set her up downstairs, and she would man the table for me while I was upstairs dubbing tapes. One thing led to another, and she wanted a spot of her own. Then I started setting up and sending my other cousin or a friend of mine to work. And before you knew it, I had about 10 to 12 people working for me.

It was all over. Down Canal Street, Uptown. One of my cousins would get people to work for me, and I used to do the 60-40 split. So you sell 10 tapes, you make $40 and I make $60. But I would set you up with a radio, with the batteries, the whole shebang. The gig with that was you would play one or two records, and people would stop if you played the hit record and always want to know what was on the rest of the tape.

TRACKLISTS

In the early days when mixtapes were out, only a few of the DJs would put down what records were on their tapes. There were no tracklists. So I hired my cousin, and I said, "I want you to listen to this and write down all of the songs."

I went down to Kinko's and I started to create playlists. I put these little designs on there with different fonts, and I created my own brand. It was called DJ PROfessional Mixtapes. PRO in highlights because that's my name–Philip Raymond Orama.

CONNECTING WITH DOUBLE R

At this time, I wasn't buying masters from anybody. This was my boy giving me the tapes, and some of the tapes were ones that he made. But we needed newer stuff. So the dude was like, "Yeah, I'll get you another tape." I think it was another Double R tape with the shoutouts edited out.

I'm out there selling tapes one day and this dude comes up to me and it happens to be Double R. He's like, "Yo! Why are you selling my tape?!" This was the first time I got confronted about selling a tape without permission. I'm like, "Yo dude, I didn't know that was you guys." We arranged a deal, and I started buying tapes directly from him. That was my first professional relationship to legitimize this business. They were one of the biggest in the mixtape scene.

TELEX MACHINE

Before long, the DJs started finding out about me. Because I was consistent, I would always be out on the block. I was there every day, and we were making money. And I started getting more spots.

Every time a DJ would find out about us, they would come to us and try to get paid. That was part of the game. You had to pay these guys for their mixtapes.

Buying masters was my business model. Some would want some crazy amount, like, "I want $300 for my master." But I wasn't selling mixtapes like that at first, so it started out at $50, $80 for a master.

I was a student at the city university, and I applied for an American Express credit card and bought a Telex machine. That was a big investment, I think it was $2,300.

Prior to that, I had about 15 double decker tape decks. I would have people set them up in the morning for 100 tapes, and I would continue to make tapes all

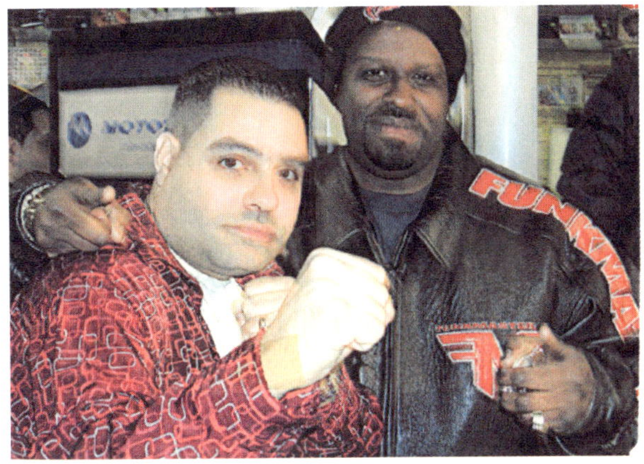

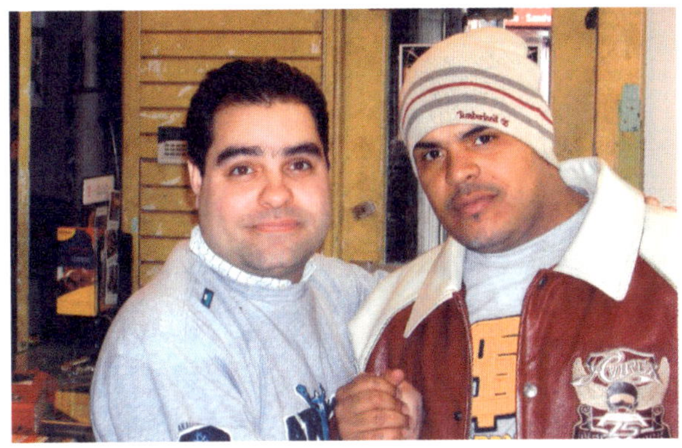

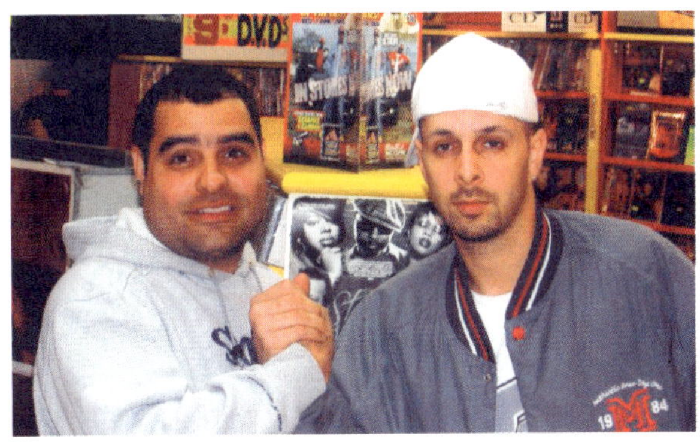

day because I couldn't keep up with the demand. So when we got the Telex machine, it became a whole other monster. That's when everything changed.

OPENING A STORE

When Giuliani became mayor, he started cracking down on street vendors. So I would send somebody out with a tape kit, and they would come back like, "Oh man, they took the mixtapes." I started running up a lot of Ls. I was like, "Damn, I can't continue like this. This is not good."

I was at the table across from where I lived. There was a Chinese restaurant that was there. One day my boy Sammy Sam came to visit me, who would eventually open up Sam's Orbit. I'm standing there and I said, "Sam, you see that restaurant across the street? That's going to be my store." He looked at me and said, "You can't open up a store and start selling mixtapes." I said, "Yeah, watch me. I'm gonna open up the Harlem Music Hut right there."

Lo and behold, I contacted the landlord, and he was in financial straits and needed some money. He gave me a super-sweet ten year deal on the lease, with a ten year option. I took every last penny that I had to open up the store. I literally didn't have money to build out the store or convert it to anything.

HARLEM MUSIC HUT BEGINNINGS

As I got money, I built up the store. The street vending thing lost its beauty because it was over when the cops were harassing people on the street. It became like the Wild Wild West on 125th Street. You couldn't even walk on the sidewalk because there were so many people selling in the street. You had the businesses paying rent and taxes, and they would just take over and harass everybody. It was a problem.

RELATIONSHIPS WITH DJS

The DJs used to come to me, "Hey Phil, I'm gonna drop this tape and I want you to do the artwork for me." So that became a side business. Then I opened up a copy shop with color machines. I tried to industrialize everything and make everything bigger than it was. I always had big ambitions. It just led from one thing to another.

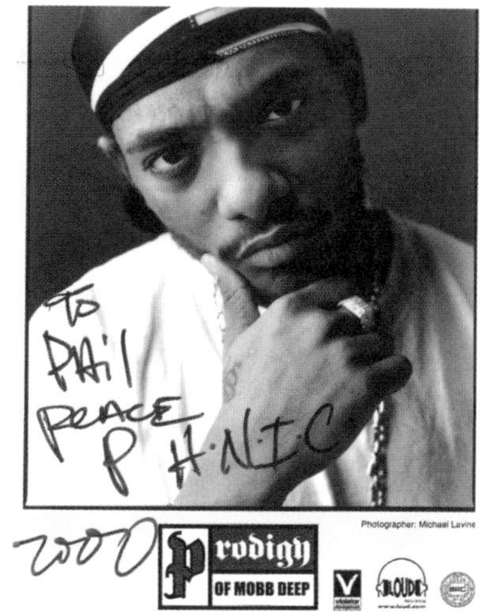

As far as DJs coming to the store, everybody was different. I never had any problems with any DJs. Maybe little misunderstandings here and there, but it was pretty straight forward. The more you wanted for your master, you had to sell. You had to be able to prove yourself.

SELLING TAPES

The trick with selling the mixtapes was that you could play a portion of the mixtape that people loved, and just press repeat and play those same records all day long. They'd say, "Oh what's that playing? I want that." They had those intros, and those parts of the tape that people would gravitate to.

Everybody had good tapes. Double R tapes were the number one sellers all the time. Doggtime, Doo Wop, Tony Touch, Clue. Everybody had their run. There were certain DJs that I didn't appreciate what they were doing. They didn't have respect for the game.

The trick with selling the mixtapes was that you could play a portion of the mixtape that people loved, and just press repeat and play those same records all day long. They'd say, "Oh what's that playing? I want that."

KERBY KERB'S TOP 5 HARLEM MUSIC HUT ARTIST IN-STORE APPEARANCES

Former Harlem Music Hut employee Kerby Kerb remembers some of their best.

1. THE LOX - The first crazy in-store was The LOX with their first album. The whole Ruff Ryders was there. Before they even pulled up, we promoted it and had flyers and shit. And before they came up, they were on Hot 97 and said where they were going to be at--and that shit was crazy.

People were outside wanting to get in. The LOX were in the store, they had champagne and were just chilling, signing autographs. It looked like a listening party. The whole hood came out. That was one of the dopest in-stores I was a part of.

2. TERROR SQUAD - That was at the Bronx location. They came to Harlem too, but the one in the Bronx, that shit was crazy. We had everybody up there. Fat Joe came first with Armageddon, then Tony Sunshine, Cuban, and Prospect. This was like four months before Pun passed away.

People were already lined up. It was so crazy that our neighbors right next to us were mad because there were so many people on the sidewalk. They were like, "What's going on?" The cops came and they were like, "You can't be doing this, you gotta let us know." We were like, "We didn't get a chance, we didn't have time."

The cops came with the barriers. And then Pun pulled up in the Benz, pulled his chain out of the sunroof, and everybody went crazy. They just walked in the store. We had the whole block, it was like a two-way street and it was packed.

3. FABOLOUS AND CASSIDY - They were just shopping. Fab came in first--he was chillin' and we were talking. Then Cassidy walked in. That's the first time I had seen two artists bump into each other at the store. The owner Phil was talking to them, chopping it up. Then they bought some mixtapes and music and probably some DVDs or something. I think Fabolous had already dropped his first album and Cassidy was on the come up. They dapped each other up. It was a cool moment.

4. FLIPMODE SQUAD - That was like '98, before the album came out. That's when Busta was skinny with dreads. They were mad cool. Spliff Star, he was mad funny. There were always lines when there was an in-store.

5. LIL' KIM - She pulled up in a limo and had her team with her. She came in and had a chinchilla on. She was mad humble, mad cool. She took pictures with us and some fans. She signed some autographs.

Everybody that I ever came across, they were all mad cool. I never met anyone that was full of shit or whatever. They were all humble. Celebrities would come and cop, whether it was a DVD or a regular CD or a mixtape, and it was always love.

BONUS MIKE TYSON - Mike Tyson pulled up with his chauffeur in a blue Rolls-Royce Phantom. He came in and he was like, "Yo, what's the hottest mixtape?" It was crazy because he did his time already, so he had the tat on his face. He looked intimidating.

Phil was like, "Yo man, I wanna take a picture with you." And he was serious, like, "You wanna take a picture with me?" He stood up like he was ready to fight, then he was like, "Aight, let's take a picture." That was a dope moment. We used to have it on the wall, every time we would take pictures with celebrities.

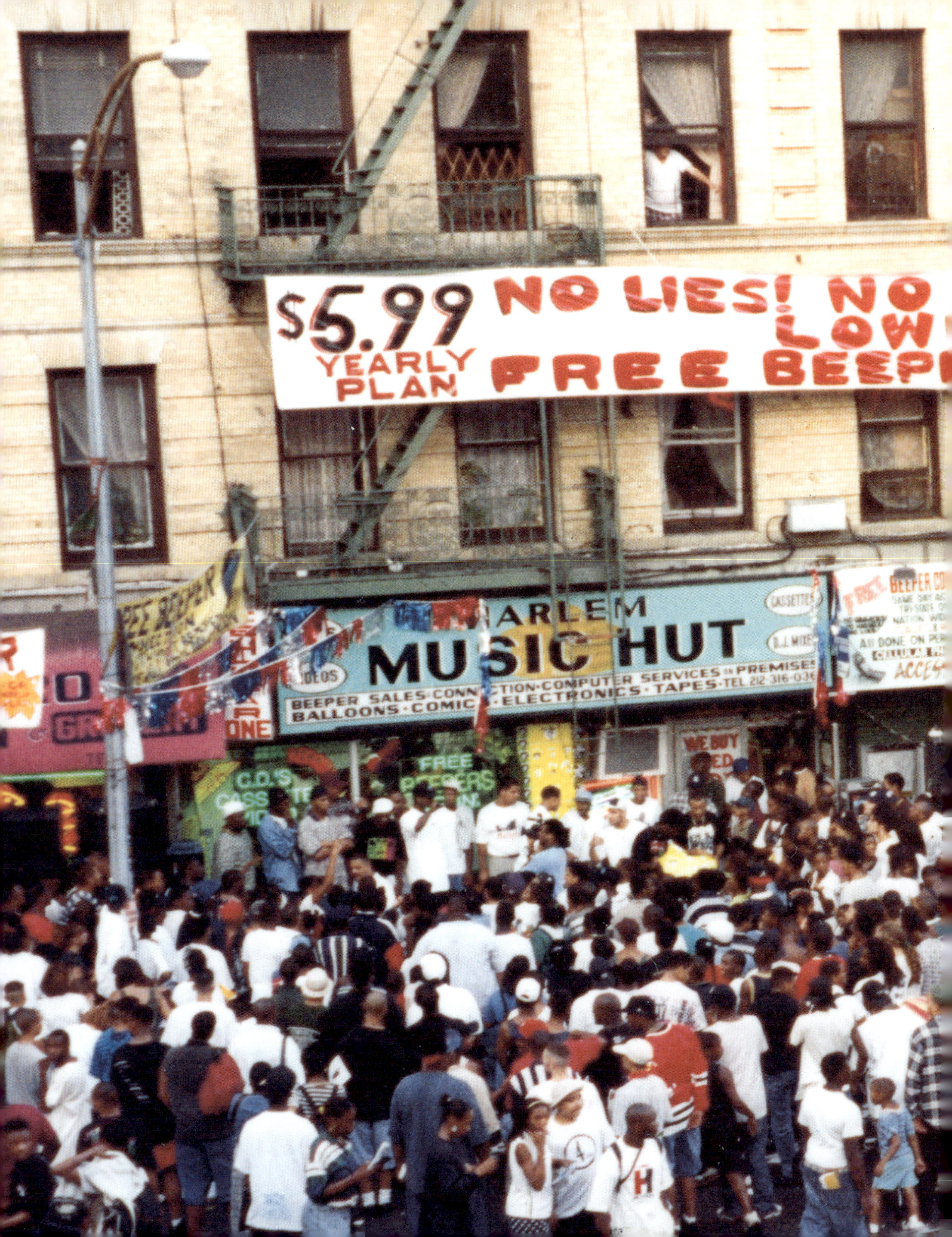

$5.99
YEARLY PLAN
NO LIES! NO
LOW
FREE BEEP
HARLEM
MUSIC HUT
CASSETTES
D.J. MIXES
VIDEOS
BEEPER SALES·CONNECTION·COMPUTER SERVICES ON PREMISES·TEL 212-316-036
BALLOONS·COMICS·ELECTRONICS·TAPES
FREE BEEPERS
WE BUY

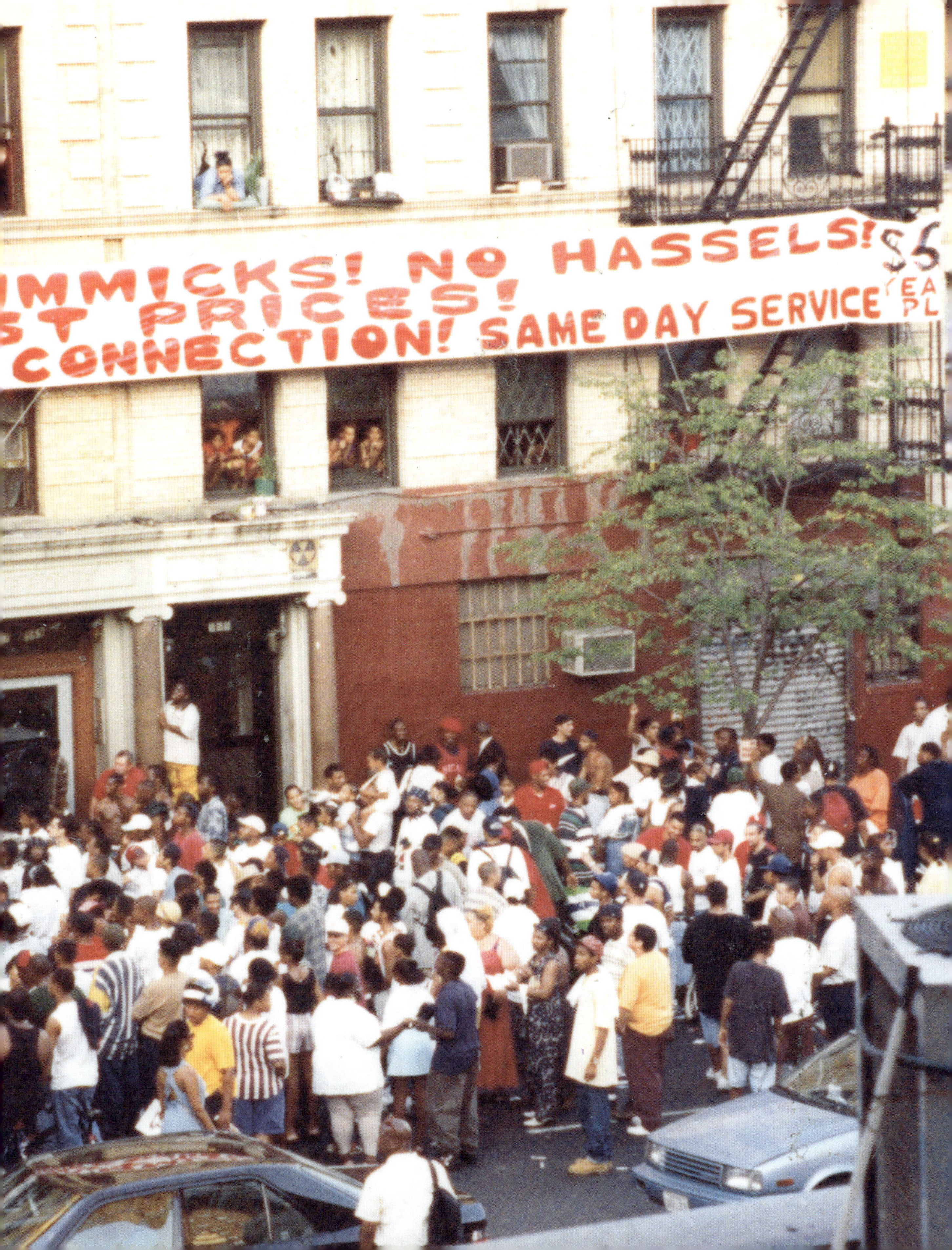
IMMICKS! NO HASSELS! $5
ST PRICES!
CONNECTION! SAME DAY SERVICE

PHAT HITZ

RECORDS
TAPES CD,s
------&------
MORE

TEL: 292-2079
FAX: (516)292-2106

81 MAIN ST.
HEMPSTEAD, NY 11550

C.J.'S MUSIC CITY
ROCK / WILL / MOE

Tapemakers - We Have Kid Capri
Brucie B - Starchild - Starski -
Demo - Showtime - Buckwild -
MIKE NICE - RON G.

BE SAFE
HOMMIE!

54 West 125th St.
Bet. Lenox - 5th Aves.
New York, N.Y. 10027
212-348-7472

THE DREAM TEAM
MUSIC STORE
HOT DAY AND JAE SUPREME

CD'S, VIDEOS, CASSETTES AND VINYL FOR D.J.'S
WHOLESALE AVAILABLE
741 ST. NICHOLAS AVENUE
(BETWEEN 147TH ST. & 148TH ST.)
NEW YORK NY 10031

TEL: 212-234-1379 TEL:212-234-1353

TOP-FLOOR ENTERTAINMENT
PROFESSIONAL D.J.s
D.J. CRAIG—G
BEEPER 212-871-0472
D.J. S&S
BEEPER 917-897-0199
WE DO: RAP • R&B • REGGAE • OLD SCHOOL • HOUSE

CORNERSTONE
promotion
WWW.THEFADER.COM
COREY CL LLEWELLYN
tel.212.741.7100 fax.212.741.4747 pager. 888.924.9485
CL@CORNERSTONE.COM
Eddie – 1917 – 712 – 4294
71 west 23rd street, suite 903, new york, ny 10010

HARLEM MUSIC HUT
DJ MIXED TAPES
CD'S
BEEPER SALES & CONNECTION
VIDEO
ELECTRONICS AIR BRUSHING COMICS
567 W. 125 St. NY 10027 (212) 316-0361

CEO
RON

Basement Mix Records

Super DJ/Prez
Eddie

Home of
The D.J.'s

Mixing The Best Jams For You!
171 Sheridan Avenue
Brooklyn, NY 11208
(718) 277-8146
Fax (718) 348-5874

FAT JAMS
Mixed Tapes, Mixed C.D.'s Production
Talent Agent
472 Fulton St.
Brooklyn, New York 11201
(718)625-4907
We Represent the Nations Top DJ's

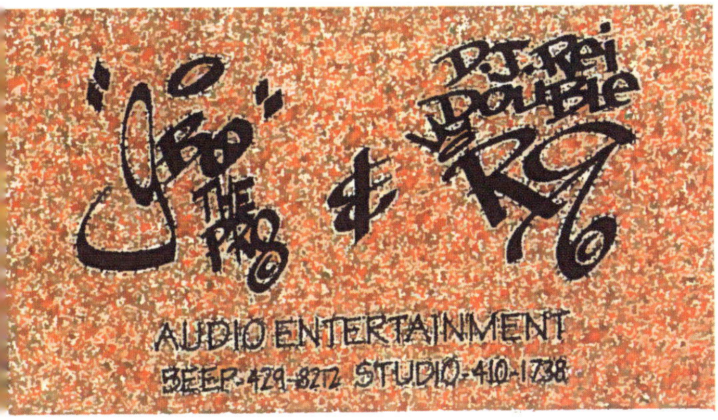
"Bo" The Pro
&
D.J. Rei Double R
AUDIO ENTERTAINMENT
BEEP-429-8212 STUDIO-410-1738

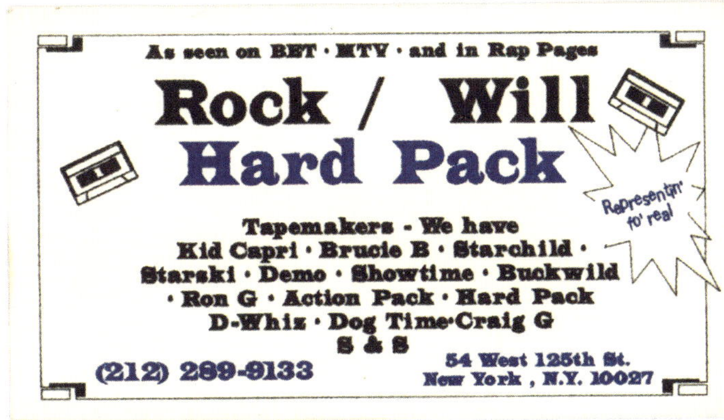
As seen on BET · MTV · and in Rap Pages
Rock / Will
Hard Pack
Representin' fo' real
Tapemakers - We have
Kid Capri · Brucie B · Starchild ·
Starski · Demo · Showtime · Buckwild
· Ron G · Action Pack · Hard Pack
D-Whiz · Dog Time·Craig G
S & S
(212) 289-9133
54 West 125th St.
New York , N.Y. 10027

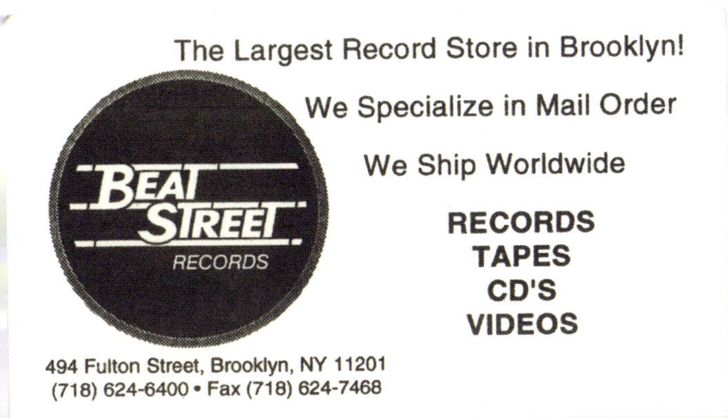
The Largest Record Store in Brooklyn!
We Specialize in Mail Order
We Ship Worldwide
BEAT STREET RECORDS
RECORDS
TAPES
CD'S
VIDEOS
494 Fulton Street, Brooklyn, NY 11201
(718) 624-6400 • Fax (718) 624-7468

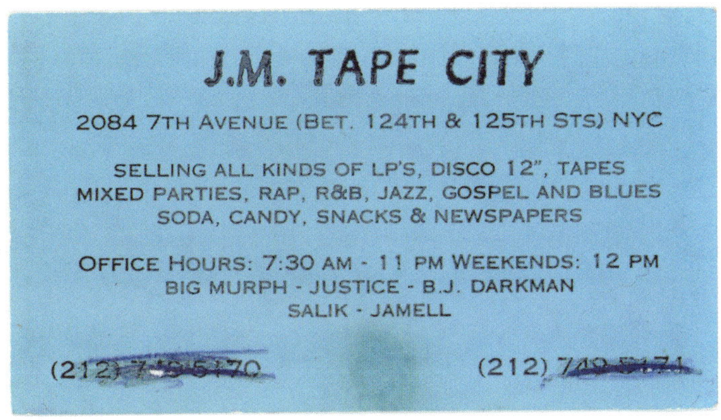
J.M. TAPE CITY
2084 7TH AVENUE (BET. 124TH & 125TH STS) NYC
SELLING ALL KINDS OF LP'S, DISCO 12", TAPES
MIXED PARTIES, RAP, R&B, JAZZ, GOSPEL AND BLUES
SODA, CANDY, SNACKS & NEWSPAPERS
OFFICE HOURS: 7:30 AM - 11 PM WEEKENDS: 12 PM
BIG MURPH - JUSTICE - B.J. DARKMAN
SALIK - JAMELL
(212)
(212)

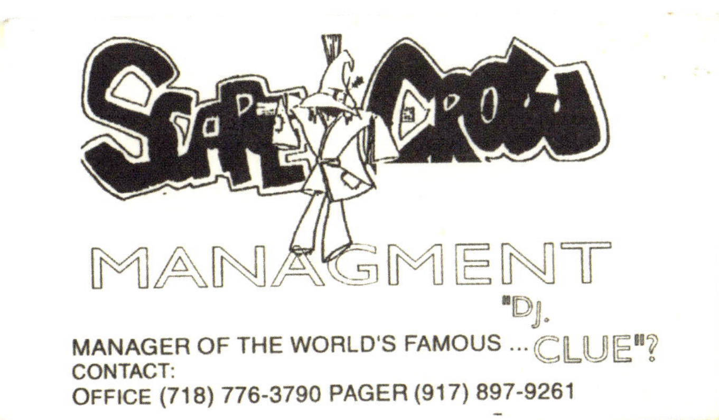
MANAGMENT
MANAGER OF THE WORLD'S FAMOUS ... "DJ. CLUE"?
CONTACT:
OFFICE (718) 776-3790 PAGER (917) 897-9261

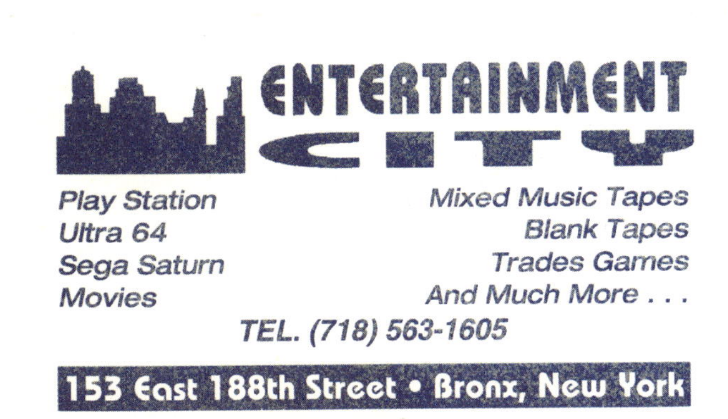
ENTERTAINMENT
CITY
Play Station
Ultra 64
Sega Saturn
Movies
Mixed Music Tapes
Blank Tapes
Trades Games
And Much More . . .
TEL. (718) 563-1605
153 East 188th Street • Bronx, New York

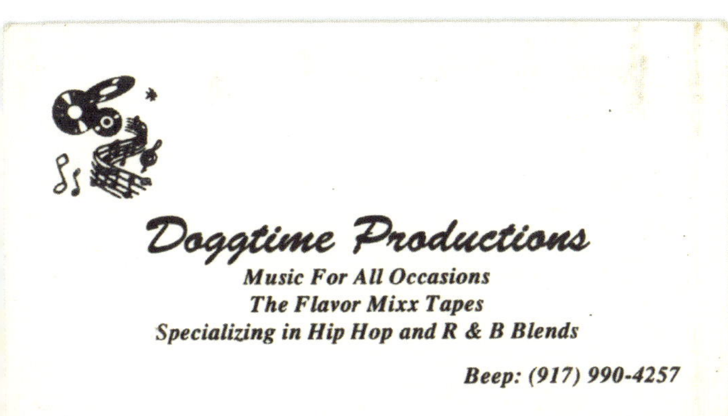
Doggtime Productions
Music For All Occasions
The Flavor Mixx Tapes
Specializing in Hip Hop and R & B Blends
Beep: (917) 990-4257

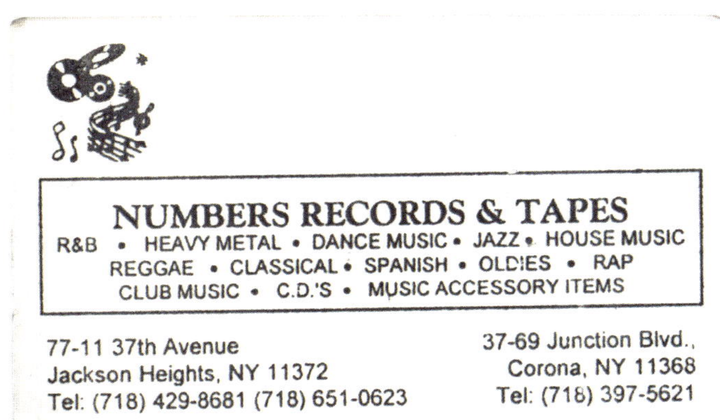
NUMBERS RECORDS & TAPES
R&B • HEAVY METAL • DANCE MUSIC • JAZZ • HOUSE MUSIC
REGGAE • CLASSICAL • SPANISH • OLDIES • RAP
CLUB MUSIC • C.D.'S • MUSIC ACCESSORY ITEMS
77-11 37th Avenue
Jackson Heights, NY 11372
Tel: (718) 429-8681 (718) 651-0623
37-69 Junction Blvd.,
Corona, NY 11368
Tel: (718) 397-5621

MOUSTAPHA'S FLAVOR
FOR THE BEST IN MIXED TAPES AND CD'S
CLUE, DJ WHOO KID, DJ RC, DJ BOODA - BARBA
CUTMASTER "C", DJ ENVY, DJ K BLACK, BIG DOG
ACTION PAC - FAN DJ RELLO - JADEL - DREAM TEAM
89-31 165th Street
Jamaica, NY 11432
Cell: (917) 495-3908
Phone: (718) 658-0095

---

165 FLAVA
FATTEST "BLEND" TAPES
ALL THE BEST D.J.'S IN THE WORLD
INCLUDING FIDEL MUZIK
REGGAE R&B HIP-HOP CALYPSO AFRICAN
plus: costume jewelry, electronics & african art & craft
92-01 165 STREET, JAMAICA, N.Y. 11432
RAHIM GUEYE TEL: .... MAKTAR
9173561932

P.A. RENTED
D.J. BEE
AND
COMPANY
BOOMING SYSTEM
JOSE B. 1-917-872-7962
HOME: 1-718-320-0538
A.J. 1-917-458-3458
HOME: 1-718-379-5565
DAVID W. 1-917-458-5733
JOHNNY JAY 1-917-851-6379

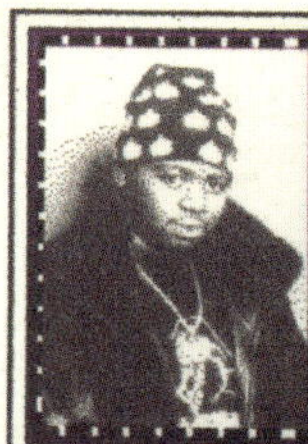
D.J.Ron G
Production
Remixes
Tapes
MIX KING RECORDS
H.R.Funk
Colonial Pk.Sta.
P.O.Box 180 N.Y. 10039-0116
page (917)469-0868
office(212)862-3158

LOVEBUG STARSKI
Wit All the Flava!
BEEP [redacted] ANYTIME
1-888-727-9641

---

165 FLAVA - ABRAHAM
All new release tapes & CD's
R&B HIP HOP REGGAE CALYPSO
All the Best DJ Mix in TOWN
Plus: Costume Jewelry electronic & African Art & Craft
Plus: Shades and much more
Tel: 718-297-4779
92-01 165 Street Jamaica, NY, 11432

THE WORLD Famous BRUCIE B
917/874-2533

Youngstar
2395 GRANDCONCOURSE, BRONX, NY 10468 • TEL.718-933-2117

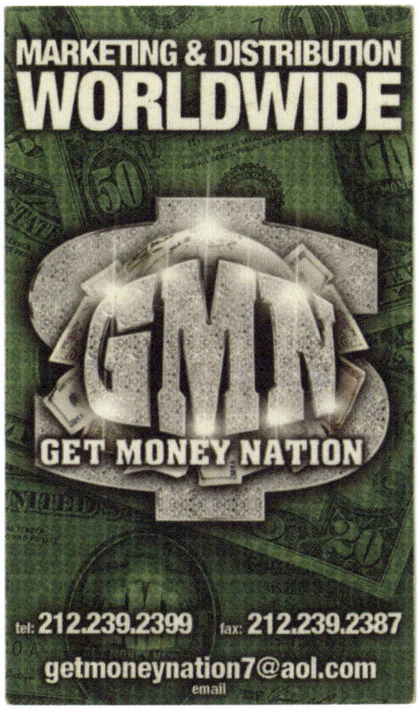
MARKETING & DISTRIBUTION
WORLDWIDE
GMN
GET MONEY NATION
tel: 212.239.2399 fax: 212.239.2387
getmoneynation7@aol.com
email

PARTY
PATROL
BRUCIE B
D.J.
A.K.A
BRUCE ROBINSON
917 • 739 • 8971
175 5th Ave.
Suite 2347
New York, N.Y. 10010

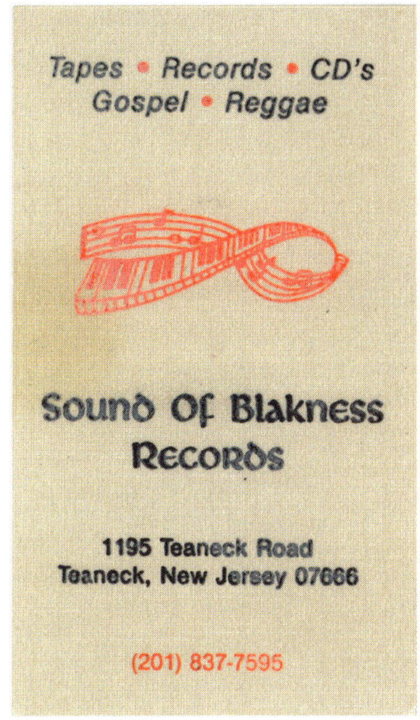
Tapes • Records • CD's
Gospel • Reggae
Sound Of Blakness
Records
1195 Teaneck Road
Teaneck, New Jersey 07666
(201) 837-7595

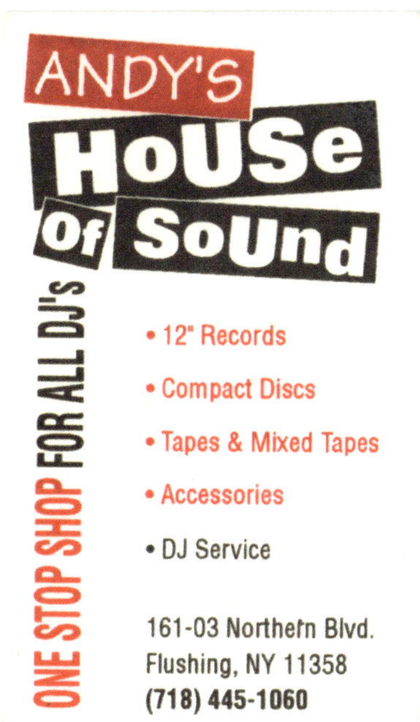
ANDY'S
HoUSe
Of SoUnd
ONE STOP SHOP FOR ALL DJ's
• 12" Records
• Compact Discs
• Tapes & Mixed Tapes
• Accessories
• DJ Service
161-03 Northern Blvd.
Flushing, NY 11358
(718) 445-1060

the official internet source for mixtape culture
TAPE KINGZ
steve
tel: 718 422 7690 • fax: 718 422 7686
cell: 917 689 0390
e.mail: steve@tapekingz.com
www.tapekingz.com

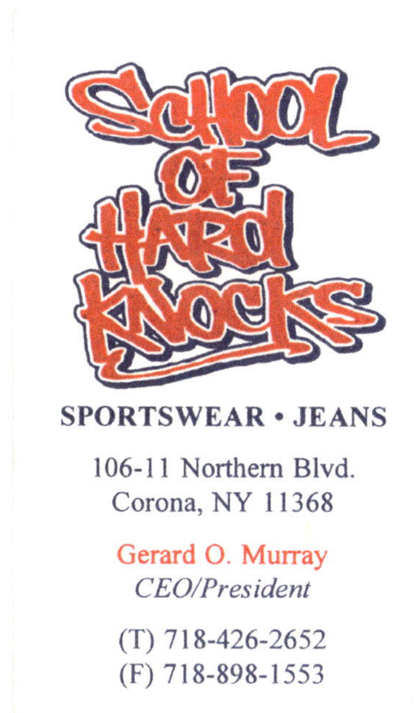
SCHOOL OF HARD KNOCKS
SPORTSWEAR • JEANS
106-11 Northern Blvd.
Corona, NY 11368
Gerard O. Murray
CEO/President
(T) 718-426-2652
(F) 718-898-1553

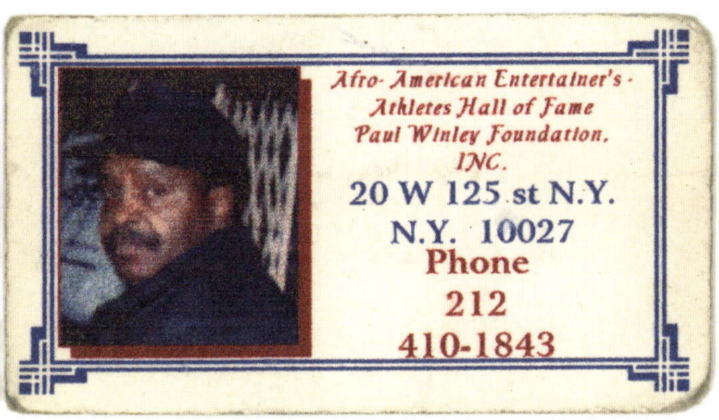
Afro-American Entertainer's -
Athletes Hall of Fame
Paul Winley Foundation,
INC.
20 W 125 st N.Y.
N.Y. 10027
Phone
212
410-1843

TEL: 695-3953-4
FAX: 564-5358
Rock and Soul Electronics, Inc.
AUDIO • VIDEO • TV • CAMERAS • WATCHES
RECORDS • TAPES • CD'S
D.J. EQUIPMENTS
462 SEVENTH AVENUE
NEW YORK, N.Y. 10018
Bet. 35th & 36th St.

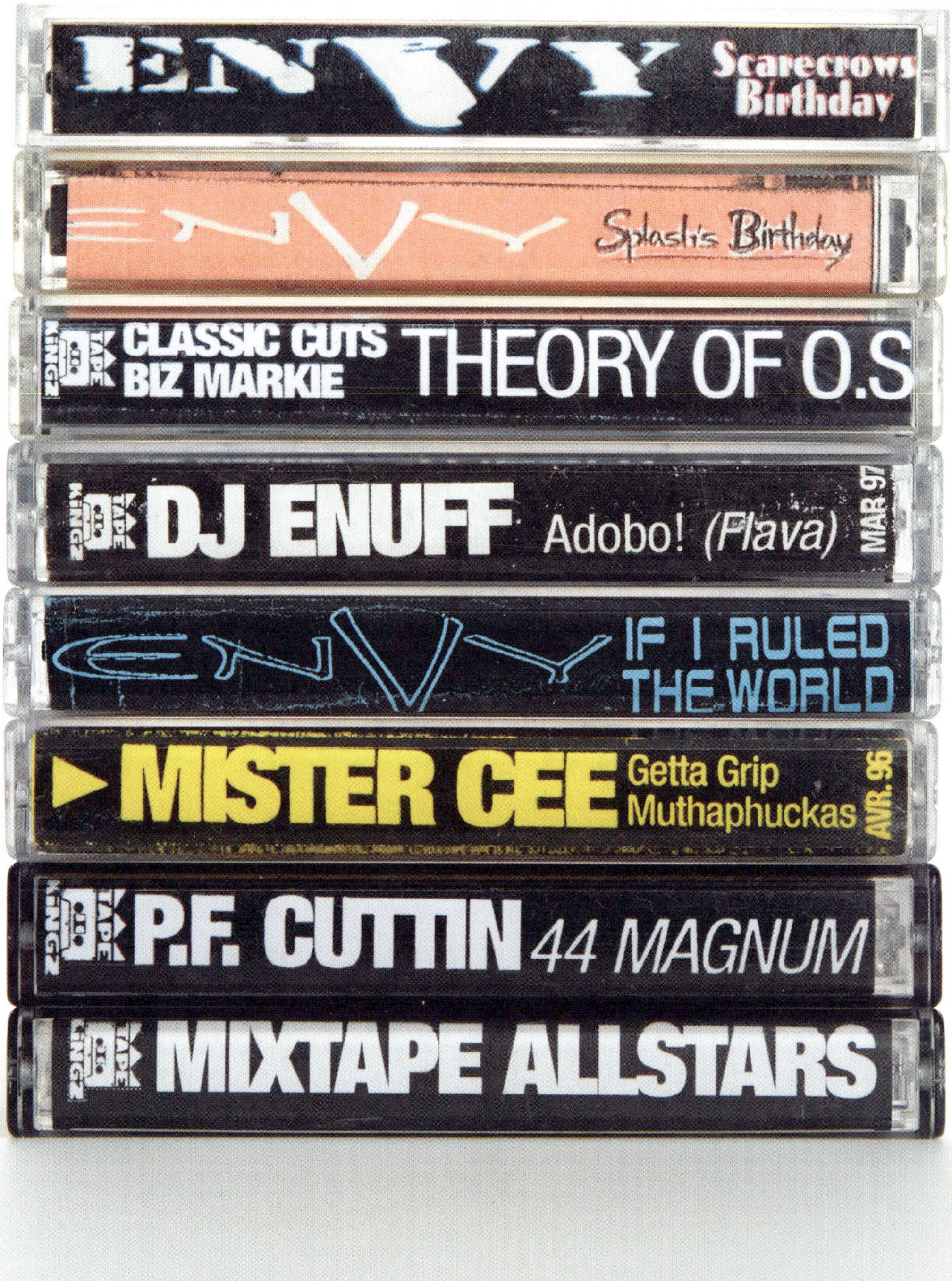
ENVY
Scarecrows Birthday
ENVY
Splash's Birthday
TAPE KINGZ
CLASSIC CUTS
BIZ MARKIE
THEORY OF O.S
TAPE KINGZ
DJ ENUFF
Adobo! (Flava)
MAR 97
ENVY
IF I RULED THE WORLD
MISTER CEE
Getta Grip
Muthaphuckas
AVR. 96
TAPE KINGZ
P.F. CUTTIN
44 MAGNUM
TAPE KINGZ
MIXTAPE ALLSTARS

THE HUSTLE

Don't get it twisted—just like any other street business, selling mixtapes is a grind. Sure, in the early cassette days, there was a bit more of a gray area when it came to dealing with the law, but it was still risky. And with competition on corners across the city, it required a savvy business mind and a go-getter attitude to be successful. Like Jay-Z said, you can't knock THE HUSTLE.

IAIN MCNEE: TAPE KINGZ

Mixtape Royalty: The Brand That Ruled the Streets

Tape Kingz just might be the most recognizable brand name and logo in the history of New York City mixtapes. Founded by partners Steve and Iain, both originally from the UK, Tape Kingz became the biggest mixtape distributor in New York and across the country, and eventually expanded their business overseas. They were also the first mixtape outlet to advertise and sell mixtapes in *The Source* magazine via mail order. And their success can be attributed not only to how hard they worked, but to their passion for the music itself and their strong relationships with the top mixtape DJs in NYC.

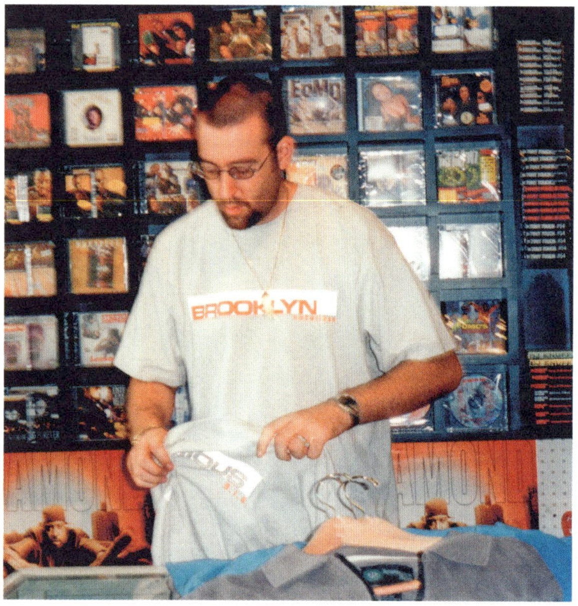

STARTING OUT

Iain McNee: I started selling tapes with my friend Carl. Carl lived in Bed-Stuy, and I met him through another friend who I met working with the Coalition for the Homeless, and he lived in Marcy. My friend in Marcy was trying to be a rapper, and Carl was his DJ. We used to go to Carl's house, play around on the turntables, microphones, things like that.

At that point, I was living in Harlem. So I saw these tapes in J&J Variety on 124th and 7th. I was living on 115th and 7th, so just a few blocks up. Carl had also seen them, because he used to travel to 125th all the time. These were, like, Kid Capri tapes, and they used to sell them for like $20 a pop.

At this point, we got a collection of them together, and we started like, "Let's make copies for each other and try to sell what's happening Uptown in Brooklyn." Because $20 was a lot of money at the time.

The first place we ever sold to was called the Car Studio on Fulton Street in Bed-Stuy. They kitted-out all the cars. Their customers wanted something different in the tape decks, so we used to sell them in there.

Carl was a security guard at Madison Square Garden, so he only had limited time off. So every other Saturday or on certain Sundays, we'd go post up on Canal Street. We had a step right by Pearl Paint, and we'd be making dubs of the tapes during the week. We used to stand there and sell the tapes for $10 a pop.

I was making more on a Sunday than I was as a delivery driver in Manhattan. I was off the books, because I was illegal in New York at that time. I was very eager to keep it going, so it was frustrating for me if Carl was like, "Oh no, the Knicks are home I can't do it." That was obviously a good job for him–it was a regular income. For me, it was very different.

At some point, Carl just wanted to do his thing and continue working. The risk was far greater for him, but I really didn't care. I had nothing to lose. What's the worst that can happen to me? "You gotta leave the country?" For him it's gonna be way worse. Like, I didn't have a social security number, I'm outside the system.

So he chose to go with his job, and I think by that time I'd been fired from my job, so I wanted to put as much time into selling the tapes as I could. That's where Tape Kingz was born from. Tape Kingz was the name, that was my idea.

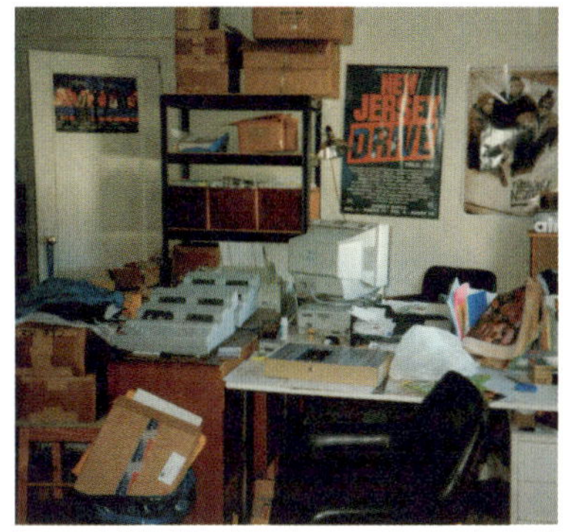

BROOKLYN BOUND

I moved to Brooklyn and started pursuing the DJs in Brooklyn. Mister Cee might have been the first DJ we got tapes from.

We tried working with the Uptown DJs by then, where we were paying for the masters. Ron G, Doo Wop, S&S, Craig G. Then, when we started to get the Brooklyn tapes, we went to Enuff, Evil Dee, Tony Touch, PF Cuttin, Mister Cee, all of them, to buy master tapes. So it just started from there really.

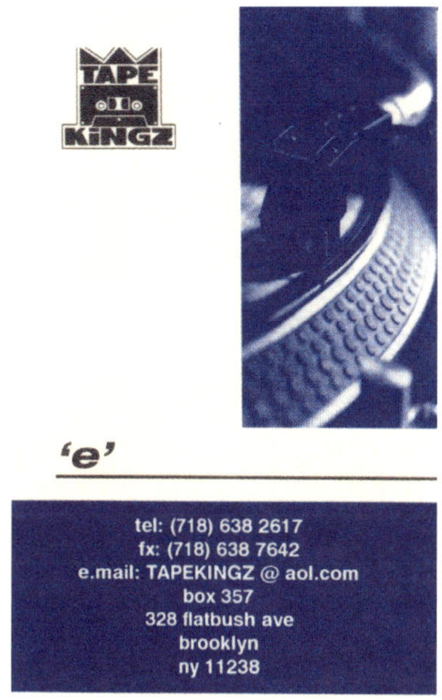

GETTING ESTABLISHED

I like to think throughout Tape Kingz's existence, we always tried to do things the right way. If we were ever approached with anything, we always sought out a solution.

With all the Brooklyn DJs, everything would go through them. Pay for the masters, do the duplications. But by this time, the DJs were also seeing that we got the tapes everywhere. They were in all the stores, and people were talking about them.

We had a lot of exclusives, especially with the Brooklyn DJs. None of the Uptown DJs were exclusive to us, we would just buy a master. They were also doing their thing in the Bronx and Uptown and everything. They had all the little mom-and-pop stores there, the barbershops, the independent record stores.

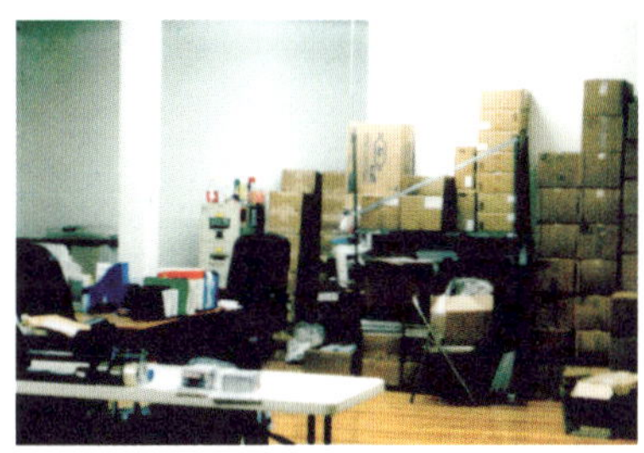

Tape Kingz didn't have that, but we did have everything in Brooklyn. But more importantly, we had everything overseas and the rest of the U.S. All my time was devoted to making contacts with DJs, and trying to build the mail order business–that's how I wanted to do it. I got the Tape Kingz logo, and was buying the equipment, building up. I went from having a room in a shared house to eventually making enough money with the tapes to get a one-bedroom rent stabilized apartment on Flatbush Avenue and Sterling Place. And that became the first Tape Kingz office. 200 Sterling Place, Apartment 3D.

I actually just wanted to get the tapes to hear the new music. There wasn't a business model other than I knew I needed to pay rent to continue living in New York City. I needed to sell tapes. I tried all the methods, they weren't particularly enjoyable–working in sneaker stores, working in warehouses, delivering flowers, working at a bagel store, working on construction sites. So, to do this, it was like a dream. I can actually make money and focus my entire day on working on what could potentially be a good business. And that's what it turned into.

DAILY OPERATION

By that time, there were Telexes. Telexes were twice the speed as the Tascam. We probably had 4 or 6. But that allows you to do more. If you have 4–that's like 12 tapes every 3 minutes. I got girls in the neighborhood, they'd come work, dubbing the tapes. I'd have to show them what to do, but eventually it made sense to get people to do that. And I'd go make the deliveries by cab or by train depending on where the store was.

COVERS

The first tapes–the tracklisting tapes–I used to type them out on a computer or something, print them out, and shrink them. There was a copy place on the corner of 7th Avenue and Flatbush, I used to go there. I got to know the guy because we were there every 5 minutes. We didn't have a photocopier at that time. So all the copies would go through him–shrink them down and get them printed on different colored paper. That must be like '93-'94.

TAPE KINGZ LOGO

I went to BMT Lines, it was a graffiti shop all the way in Bay Ridge. It was the guys behind Lordz of Brooklyn. It was the only graf shop that I knew of in Brooklyn. For the Tape Kingz logo, I wanted it to be somebody who knew about hip hop who could get the feeling of what I was trying to do.

I think the guy's name was Dino. They were quite famous within graffiti circles. It was the first and last version of the logo–that's it. A lot of people were definitely drawn to the logo. It created a perception, so they'd go, "It's Tape Kingz, the quality is gonna be good."

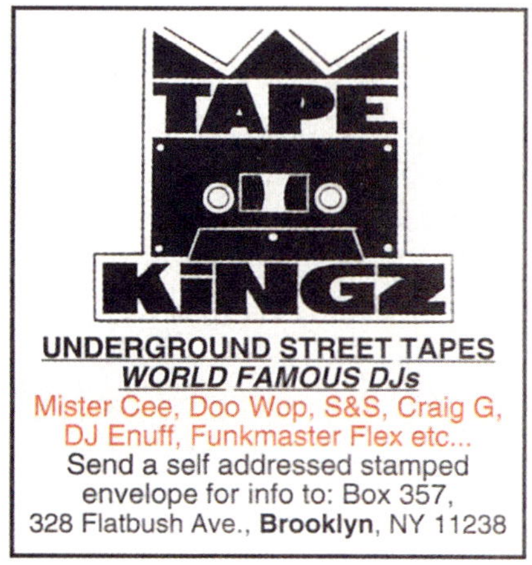

RECORD STORES

The first one we got into in Brooklyn was Jackpot. It was like a record store chain. And McCrory's, they were in Newark, the Bronx, Jamaica, Queens, and downtown Brooklyn on Fulton Street. In the basement of these stores, depending on which store you're in, they would sell records and tapes, CDs, everything.

So behind the counter, this guy took the chance and said, "Give me a few, we'll see how they go." Next thing you know I'm down there every other day with tapes.

And getting in Beat Street was huge because that was the king of Fulton Street.

The more money that came in, the more DJs I wanted to make tapes. Obviously a lot of DJs wanted to make tapes for Tape Kingz as well, so a lot of people used to send in tapes for us to check out.

SACK OF GOLD

We also set up in a jewelry store in downtown Brooklyn called Sack of Gold. We had a showcase in the back and we sold all the tapes there. The guy next door was doing gold fronts.

We couldn't do the Sack of Gold thing everyday. It became a problem, it didn't look good for the owners there because Carl had to work, and I couldn't commit either for that length of time. You're in one place too much. It's much better to be out and about, meeting people–trying different things, finding different places to sell to. You're spending all that time at the back of the jewelry store, but the guy in the record store who you're wholesaling to, he's selling more. It just didn't work out.

It was much better to make the tapes and put them into the people's hands to sell them. So I tried to cut down. After that, I didn't do any hand-to-hand selling. No more tapes being sold on stoops or anything like that.

THE SOURCE MAGAZINE

We were the first company to advertise in *The Source* magazine. It took me 2 years to get into *The Source*. They didn't want to put adverts for the newer mixtapes because it would mess with the advertisements for the record labels.

Eventually, mixtapes became a thing *The Source* couldn't ignore anymore. There were a few other companies who tried to do it, but Tape Kingz won because we were the first–we always got prominence.

All the calls and letters came in from everywhere else in the U.S. That's when it went nuts. We would do COD packages, we'd do all the stores, and a lot of money was coming in. Lots of mail-order stuff as well from people all over the U.S.

FOR THE PROMO

Most DJs looked at mixtapes as promotional tools. I don't think they looked at mixtapes like, "That's the plan." Their plan was for them to do what DJs are still doing to this day, and that's playing music out. Maybe some of them were getting their own record deal or whatever–the mixtapes were to raise their profile.

There's nothing worse for a record store manager than a guy who brings you 50 tapes and they sell out within a few days, and you call him for some more and you don't see him for three weeks. Well, that moment was over now.

I think if you ask a lot of the DJs, they'll say, "Tape Kingz raised our profile." We got very good at filling orders fast, which was easy to do because you just buy more Telexes as you see the demand rise, or get more staff if you need more tapes done faster.

WORKING WITH DJS

Usually, the DJs would be pretty perceptive about how well their tape would sell. A lot of times the DJs would actually come to my apartment to bring the master tape. Mister Cee, DJ Enuff, Evil Dee–they'd always come to the apartment.

The apartment was the warehouse. The shelves had all the tapes we made in advance, so when we'd get orders we wouldn't have to change the Telexes all the time. And the DJs would see what the competition was. They'd say, "Oh, he's got the same songs as me." So many times the DJs would pick up everyone else's tape and be like, "Oh, he's still playing this? Oh, what!" It was a real mixtape, DJ, social club type thing. It was good times.

The deals were different. Someone would come in and go, "Oh, can you hit me off with a little more you think?" I'm like, "I got zero problem paying more if I sold more of the last one or if the new one you're about to give me is ridiculous." I can't remember anyone complaining about what they got. And I never told Enuff, Evil Dee, or Mister Cee, "Oh, that's for me. No one else can have it."

STRESS ENTERTAINMENT

I got a lot of stuff through Stress Entertainment and Jessica Rosenblum, like Biz Markie tapes, Funkmaster Flex live tapes–The Tunnel Live from Mecca. Getting stuff from her got us a lot of exclusives–we were selling things like, "No one's got these."

COMPETITION

There was no competition. The only competition was if a DJ wanted to do it independently. Craig G would go to a store and go, "I got S&S tapes, and I got P-Nice as well." Whereas when Tape Kingz came, "I got 20 to 25 tapes. I got everybody."

Like any of the Brooklyn DJs–Cee, Enuff, Evil Dee–those tapes were coming to Tape Kingz first. If Ron G is getting the Ron G tape, he's getting all these masters to all the stores Uptown the same day he's doing the tape. The difference is, I'm gonna have that duplicated as soon as I get back home. And I've got a network of stores.

BIG FAX

The fax machine was king. We had a big list of all the stores–"This is what's new." Certain stores would be enough business where it would be worthwhile faxing them. Every Monday morning, people would call from all over the country, "What's new from over the weekend?" Everyone was eager to hear the new stuff all the time.

PRICING

$5. That was steady. It was a steady $5 a tape for the longest time.

Masters, it depends. We'd pay anywhere from $100 to $1,000, depending on who it was, what the tape was, what was on it. DJ Premier. *50 MCs*. Because there were gonna be that many tapes we were gonna sell.

It was only fair to give something big in the beginning. There were tapes where we would go back–I know with Mister Cee we would be like, "This tape is doing good, here's another $100." I can't remember anyone saying, "I think you sold way too many. You need to give me more." Most people would cost you on their next tape.

STAYING OUT OF TROUBLE

We paid taxes. We had $1,000 in an account that could show, "This is what we are doing to get money." We took DJ bookings as well–that was the cover up.

When we were online, we spent a lot of money getting the website to sell the tapes online as well. I wouldn't say it was crazy, but we sold maybe 150 a day, at its best. So it's still a good amount of money, maybe more I can't remember exactly.

I can remember a guy in Miami–Hip-Hop Connection–he got busted. He had like the whole SWAT team and all he was doing was mixtapes, not counterfeiting other people's albums. He was quite brazen as far as thinking everything was sweet, like, "Hey everyone, give me money I'm selling mixtapes!"

I never did that. It was always a very understated advertisement in *The Source*. And the other way you heard about Tape Kingz is if you were in the know. I was never gonna talk to someone who I think is outside that particular groove. "Yeah, I'm the guy who sells mixtapes! You should listen to some of my mixtapes!" Never ever.

You had to know what I was talking about if I was talking to you about what I do, which I chose not to do. Why would I want to bring attention to myself? I'm selling illegal mixtapes, there's a lot of money coming in. It would be stupid to do that.

We used to send tapes to the jails. We'd get written a lot of letters, mail-orders sending money in, we had more and more stores, independent stores that would place orders. So there were all these different areas. Then, we would wholesale into Japan, France, and Germany as well. So it was quite a large volume of tapes that all added up to a lot.

There were no different charges, no special deals for anybody. Because as soon as that happens, it doesn't take long for people to find out. I don't remember anybody getting any special prices or anything like that.

TAPE KINGZ EUROPE

Tape Kingz Europe was a guy from England who worked for me in New York, but he had a kid and came back. So, you know, "Why don't you do in England what the guys in France and Germany are doing and just get the masters from us and try to sell in the U.K.?" Basically it was the same branding, but I'm not making the tapes–I didn't want to ship the tapes. I just wanted to ship a master tape to save me from doing the duplicating in New York. That happened in Paris, Hanover, and England.

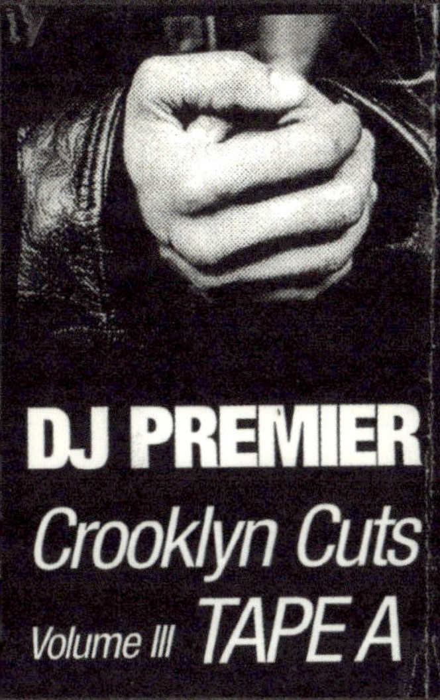

DJ PREMIER Crooklyn Cuts (Tape A)

A Side	
Intro	**DJ Premier**
Anticipation	**M.O.P.**
Worldwide	**Royal Flush**
Live To Regret	**Busta Rhymes**
Too Many Suckas	**Hilfiguez**
Camay	**Ghostface / Cappadonna / Raekwon**
Tried By 12	**East Flatbush Project / Des**
Who Dat	**All City**
Leave Your Style Cramped	**PMD**
Bum Deal	**Natural Resource**
Shine	**Mr. Voodoo**
B Side	
Every Man 4 Himself	**Nine**
Cranium	**Gauge**
Think Not	**Al Tariq**
The Interview	**Sadat X**
Stakes Is High (Rmx)	**De La Soul / Mos Def / Enoli**
Walk With A Limp	**Money Boss Players**
Hell On Earth	**Mobb Deep**
Freestyle	**Nas**
People Time	**Nonchalant / Krs One**

This Is a Tape A of a Four tape Collection, so don't miss Tapes B•C•D• Coming Soon Only On Tape Kingz ! So Dont Be Fooled By Any Bootleggers..

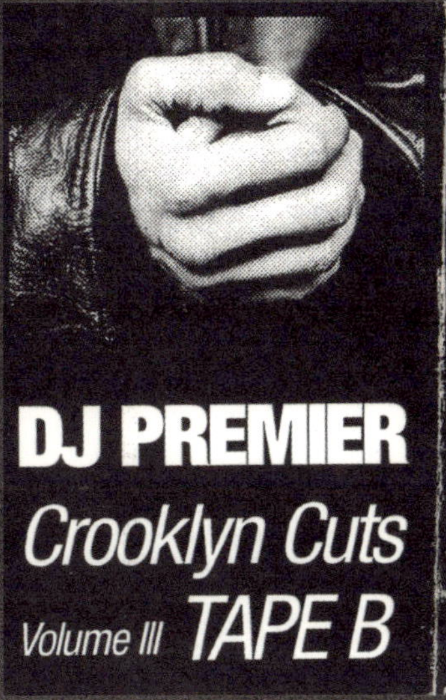

DJ PREMIER Crooklyn Cuts (Tape B)

A Side	
What Is Hip Hop ?	**Greg Tate**
Head Over Wheels	**G-Depp**
Regrets	**Jay-Z**
American Dream	**Children Of The Corn**
Money To Make	**Trybal Men**
The Obvious Joint	**Adagio**
For All Those	**J-Force**
I Want It All	**La The Darkman**
? V's Scratch	**Roots**
B Side	
The Bitch In Yoo	**Common**
Elevators	**Outkast**
Check The Method	**Lord Finesse**
How I'm Livin	**Jeru The Damaja**
Lick A Shot	**Dead Poets Society**
Therapy	**Heltah Skeltah**
Get Ya Swerve On	**Dutchmin**
My Kinda Nigga	**Heather B / M.O.P.**
Get A Grip Mutha......	**Paula Perry / Que 45**
New Jack City	**M.O.P**

This Is a Tape B of a Four tape Collection, so don't miss Tapes A•C•D• Coming Soon Only On Tape Kingz ! So Dont Be Fooled By Any Bootleggers..

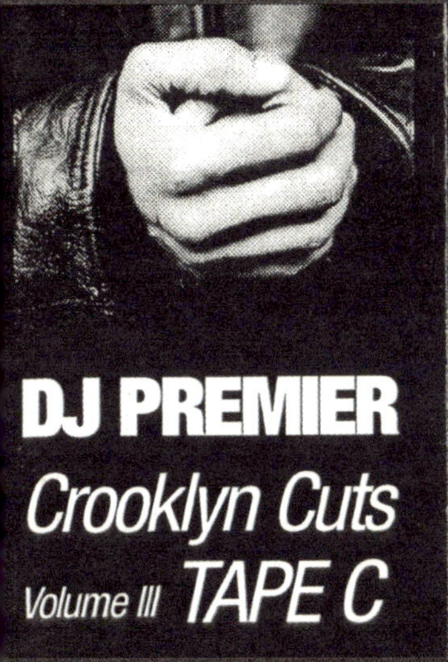

DJ PREMIER Crooklyn Cuts (Tape C)

A Side	
Intro	**DJ Premier**
Screwed Up	**Screwball**
Kool Kat	**PMD**
Just Maintain	**Xzibit / Hurricane G**
More Trife Life	**Mobb Deep**
All About The Benjamins	**Puff Daddy / Mase**
Tremendous	**Mama Mystique**
No Fear	**O.G.C**
Fish	**Ghostface / Cappadonna / Raekwon**
What Eva Man	**Redman**
We Dat Nice	**Poor Righteous Teachers**
B Side	
Intro	**DJ Premier**
Luchini	**Camp Lo**
Marintin	**Rass Kass**
Babylon	**Outkast**
One Live To Live	**Voodoo**
Animal Instinct	**Mobb Deep / Ty Nitty**
Games Sober	**Sadat X / Money Boss Players**
Boogie Down's Got That Flava	**Foundation & Rezidue**
Gunn Clapp	**O.G.C**
Better Dayz	**Sharpshooters**
Against The Grain	**Sauce Money**

This Is a Tape C of a Four tape Collection, so don't miss Tapes A•B•D• Coming Soon Only On Tape Kingz ! So Dont Be Fooled By Any Bootleggers..

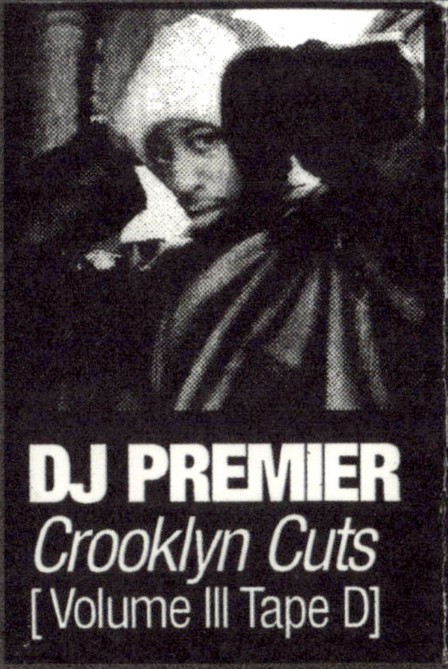

DJ PREMIER *Crooklyn Cuts* (Tape D)

A Side	
Intro	**DJ Premier**
Downtown Swinga "96"	**M.O.P**
Divine Styles	**Mixed Elements**
Wildflower	**Ghostface**
Rock Da Spot	**Redman**
Unstoppable	**Mic Geronimo**
Eyes May Shine (Rmx)	**Xzibit / Mobb Deep**
Foundation	**Big Jaz / Jay-Z / Sauce Money**
Gods, Earths, 85ers	**Poor Righteous Teachers**
International Rules	**M.F Grimm / Fatman Scoop**
All Hands	**Frankenstein**
B Side	
Intro	**DJ Premier**
Wordplay	**A.T.C.Q**
Street Dreams (Rmx)	**Nas / R.Kelly**
Love L.O.D	**Keith Murray / Kel Vicious / So Grand**
Nightime Vultures	**Mobb Deep / Raekwon**
Panic	**Roots**
Push Up Ya Lighter	**Roots / Bahamadia**
Do What Ya Feel	**Redman / Method Man**
Don't Get It Twisted	**Foundation & Rezidue**
Broken Language II	**Smothe / Trigger**
Drugs	**Lil Kim**
Up On Prospect	**Hilfiguz**

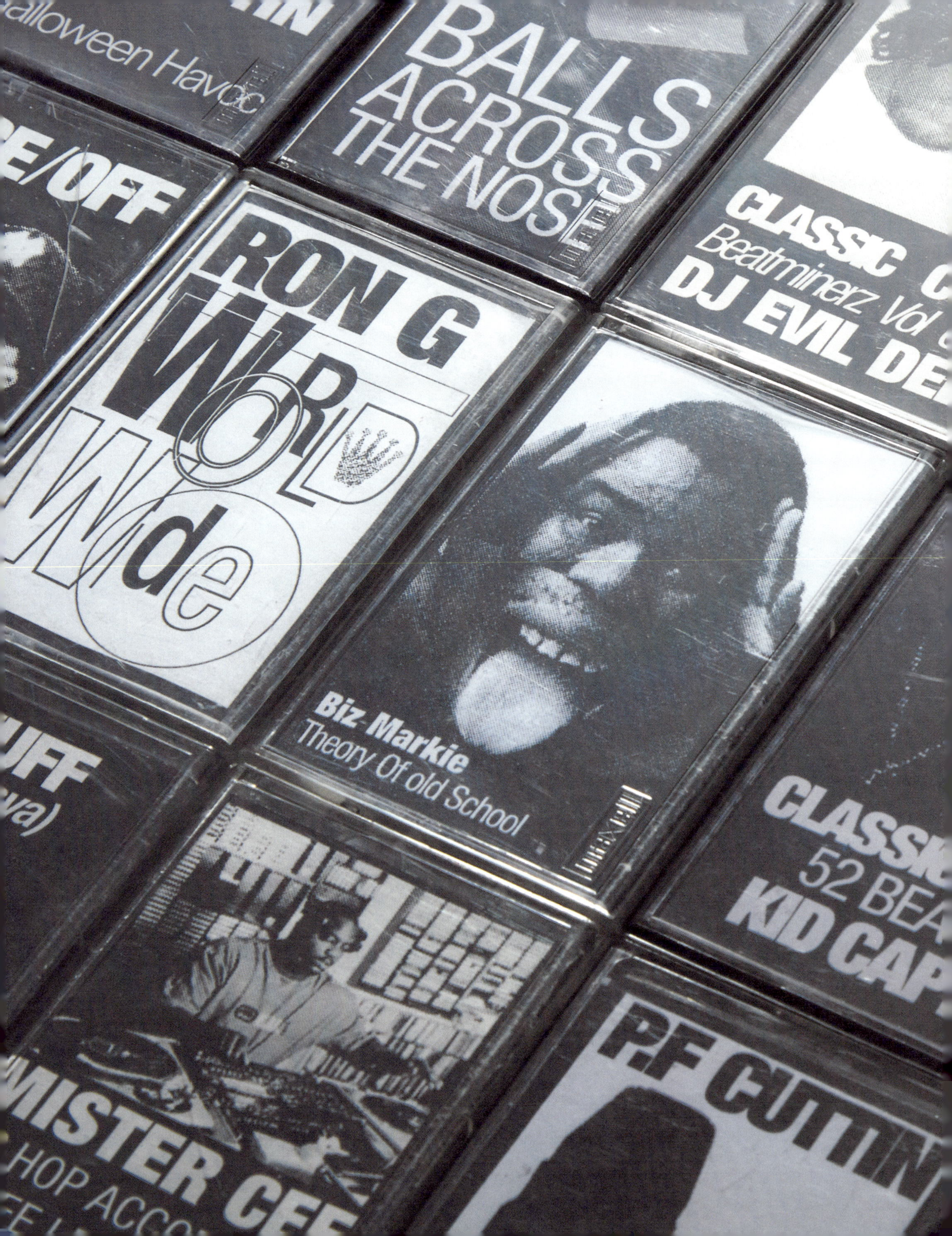
Halloween Havoc
BALLS ACROSS THE NOS
CLASSIC
Beatminerz Vol
DJ EVIL DE
RON G
Biz Markie
Theory Of old School
CLASSIC
52 BEA
KID CAP
P.F CUTTIN
MISTER CEE
HOP ACCO

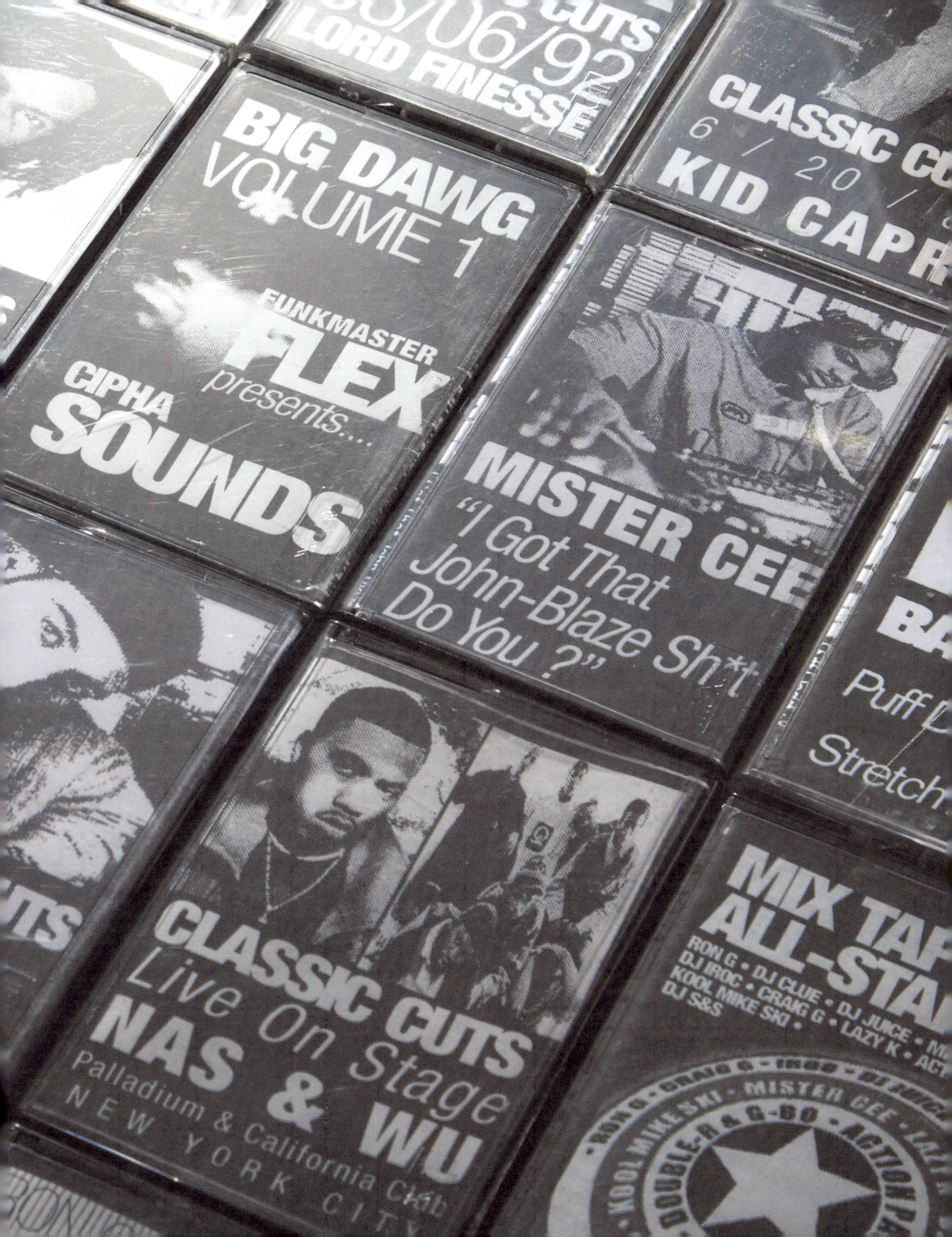
LORD FINESSE
CLASSIC CUTS
KID CAPRI
BIG DAWG
VOLUME 1
FUNKMASTER
FLEX
presents...
CIPHA
SOUNDS
MISTER CEE
"I Got That
John-Blaze Sh*t
Do You ?"
Puff D
Stretch
CLASSIC CUTS
Live On Stage
NAS & WU
Palladium & California Club
NEW YORK CITY
RON G • DJ CLUE • DJ JUICE
DJ IROC • CRAIG G • LAZY K
KOOL MIKE SKI
DJ S&S
MISTER CEE
DOUBLE-R & G-BO
KOOL MIKE SKI

RAP MAGS: ORDERING MIXTAPES OUT OF *THE SOURCE*

Mixtape collector and hip-hop enthusiast Tim Burton remembers how he discovered and purchased mixtapes from the ads in the back of *The Source* magazine during his teenage years growing up in Canada.

Tim Burton: *The Source* is where I first saw the idea of mixtapes, which I think was the same for a lot of people outside of New York because you saw the little ads. Whether it was Tape Kingz or Tape Connections, that was the gateway. I'd put something in the mail and usually in Canada it would take two weeks to get there and two weeks to get back. I'd send in the information and get a catalog back a month later. So already right there I'm behind from the new tape coming out compared to someone in New York. But once I got on that mailing list, they just kept sending the catalogs. Getting the catalog in itself was an experience.

The thing about mixtapes too was I'd see a song listed in like the Fat Tape section of *The Source*, and a lot of times I'd be like, "I don't have Stretch and Bob in Canada—I have no mix shows that actually play these songs." So mixtapes were the way to get to hear those songs you read about in *The Source* that weren't on albums.

I was always looking at which tape would give me the best bang for my buck in regard to the songs I hadn't heard or the ones I read about. As I got the catalogs, it became research, just like reading *The Source*.

OVERSEAS STEEZ: DISCOVERING MIXTAPES IN THE UK

UK-based DJ and writer Step One is the man behind *Only Built 4 zShare Links*, a carefully curated hip-hop blog featuring, among other gems, digitized versions of classic mixtapes. And he fondly remembers his first exposure to rap mixtapes, and how they played a role in his life as a DJ.

COPPING TAPES IN LONDON

DJ Step One: I grew up in a small town with no hip-hop scene, so my initial exposure to mixtapes was through record store adverts in *Hip Hop Connection* magazine and excerpts of tapes that Tim Westwood would play on his radio show.

Eventually, I was old enough to start traveling into London to buy music. And on one of my first trips on New Year's Eve '94, I picked up a couple of Doo Wop tapes—*Xmas Jams '93* and *Fall Flava*. Both remain two of my favorite tapes to this day.

One of them was playing in the store while I was browsing, and the hyped-up Bounce Squad freestyles on the intro really caught my attention. Hearing rappers over other artists' beats wasn't nearly as common as it would be a few years later. Wop was definitely a pioneer in that respect as those Bounce Squad sessions really made his tapes stand out and became his trademark.

Back to the tape, once the freestyle is done, he drops Snoop's "Gz & Hustlaz" and gets on the mic, "Right about now, back on that shit, it's the Doo Wop, straight from Uptown baby pa!"

It sounded great, bringing some extra energy to a song I already loved. As a 16-year-old white kid living in the English suburbs, it also seemed to add a layer of authenticity to the listening experience—"This is what they're listening to in NYC."

From then on, I'd try and pick up a tape on each trip. I was mainly buying vinyl as I wanted to DJ, but the tapes would provide me with a guide on what to look out for and shape my future "wants" list of joints to pick up next time. A big chunk of my record collection can be traced back to having heard the artist or a particular song on a mixtape first.

CATALOG #18

TAPE KiNGZ

HOW TO GET MY ORDER

ALL TAPES $10

To Order :
Make a Money Order payable to TAPE KINGZ and mail to the following address with the names of the tapes you would like to purchase. Add the Shipping And Handling charges to receive your order. Be sure to write your name and address clearly when ordering and include a phone number if possible.

SHIPPING & HANDLING CHARGES :

One Tape..	$1.60
Two Tapes...	$2.00
Three Tapes.......................................	$3.00
International orders ..One Tape	$3.75
2 Tapes or More (Europe,Canada,Japan etc)	$6.95

MAIL TO :
Box 357
328 Flatbush Ave
Brooklyn
NY 11238

TAPE KiNGZ

THE TAPES :
Recorded on Maxell XL II High Bias Chrome Tapes. All Tapes are recorded from masters obtained from the DJ's down with Tape Kingz and are the highest quality mix tapes you'll find anywhere ! (for real, go ahead and try everyone else's shit)

WHEN DO I GET MY ORDER :
Tapes are mailed out the same day or next day after the order is received. You can call Tape Kingz at 718-638-2617 to check on your order. Best time to call is between 12 and 3 weekdays, you'll be speaking to 'E', STEVE, RICKI or ROB

WE ALSO WHOLESALE, PRICES ARE : $5 PER TAPE FOR THE INITIAL ORDER, 50 TAPES AND NO LESS THAN 5 TAPES PER TITLE.

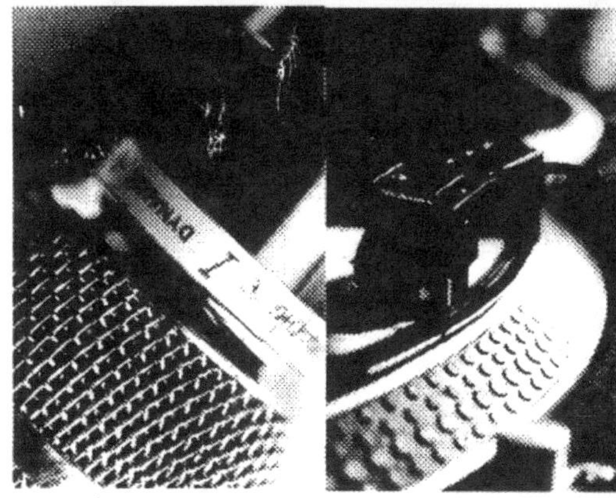

MISTER CEE "I Got John Blaze Shit, Do You?"

L Side	
Victory	**Puffy / B.I.G / Busta**
The Ten Tape Commandments	**Doo Wop**
Hoodium	**Mobb Deep / Rakim / Big Noyd**
Dangerous	**O.C. / Big L**
1,2 Many	**Common**
Never Seen Before (Rmx)	**EPMD**
How Ya Livin'	**Positive K / M.O.P.**
Building	**Khrist / Havoc**
Soul In The Hole	**Wu All Stars**
Sosa	**AZ**
The Projects (Rmx)	**Wu-Tang**
Down Wit Us	**Redman**
Smith Bros.	**Smith Bros.**
Talk Of The Town	**Rampage**
Young G's	**Puffy / Biggie Smalls / Jay-Z**
Baby, Baby	**Pretty Boy / Foxxy / Mase**
Off The Books	**Beatnuts / Big Pun**
Live At THe Tunnel	**Cru / The Lox**
G Side	
RNF Takin' Over	**RNF / Tracey Lee**
Put Your Hands Where...	**Busta Rhymes**
Been Around The World	**Puffy / B.I.G / Mase**
Likwidation	**Alkaholiks**
Bubblin'	**Cru**
Iced Down Medallions	**Royal Flush / Noreaga**
Young Cassanovas	**Junior Mafia / Mase**
Reminding Me (Of Sef)	**Common / Chantay Savage**
It's Been A Long Time	**Rakim**
True Confessions	**Iman Thug / Tragedy**
I'm Not A Player	**Big Punisher**
Against The Grain	**Sauce Money**
Unstoppable	**Mama Mystique**
Get The Money And Dip	**Rampage / Busta**
Niggas We Roll Wit	**Canibus / McGruff**
Rare Species	**Mobb Deep**
It's On You Tonight	**Pretty Boy / Foxxy**
Stayin' Alive (Rmx)	**Wyclef / Kam / Pras / Forte**

MISTER CEE R&B Buttas #7

L Side	
Lovely	**Raw Breed ***
We Can Get Down	**Myron ***
If I Had You (Rmx)	**Frankie / Jadakiss (Lox)**
Summer Love	**Yvette Michelle**
Love Somebody Else	**Miss Jones / Lox**
Need Your Love	**Big Bub / Queen Latifah / Heavy D**
Love Like This	**SWV / Lil Ceaser**
High Velocity	**Leschea**
Fix *(Soulfood Rmx)*	**Blackstreet / Jay-Z**
Dont Stop What You Doing	**Puffy / Lil Kim**
Bounce	**Tanya Von / Cru**
Distant Lover (Rmx)	**Taral / Grand Puba**
Guantanamera	**Wyclef / Celia Cruz**
No Doubt (Rmx)	**702 / Canibus**
Up Jumps Da Boogie	**Timbaland & Magoo / Missy**
Do You Know	**Puff Daddy**
So Good (Rmx)	**Davina / Raekwon**
G Side	
Kick In The Door	**Biggie Smalls ***
Someone	**SWV / Puffy ***
When I'm With You	**Mary J Blige**
Hot Like Fire (Rmx)	**Aaliyah / Missy**
What About Us	**Total / Missy**
You Make Me Wanna....	**Usher**
Give It Up	**SWV / Lil Kim**
I Love You Baby	**Puffy / Black Rob**
You Should Be Mine	**Brian McKnight /Mase**
U Know Da Place	**Leschea / Masta Ace**
Honey	**Maria Carey / Lox / Mase**
It's Alright	**Queen Latifah**
When Doves Cry	**Genuwine**
Big Bad Mamma	**Foxxy / Dru Hill**
Crazy	**Yvette Michelle**
Feel So Good	**Mase**
Friend	**Puffy / Foxxy Brown**
Gotham City (Rmx)	**R.Kelly / Strings**
Can You Feel It *(Ron G Rmx)*	**Uncle Sam**

*** Special Mister Cee Mix**

TONY TOUCH Power Cypha #2

Freestyle	***Tony Touch***
Freestyle	***Hurricane G***
Freestyle	**25 To Life *(Iman Thug / Tragedy / Khadafi)***
Freestyle	***Noreaga***
Freestyle	**Lost Boyz Crew *(Cannibus / Mr.Cheeks)***
Freestyle	***Big Daddy Kane***
Freestyle	**D.I.T.C *(O.C / Fat Joe / Lord Finesse / Big L / A.G / Diamond D)***
Freestyle	**Powerule *(Mike Miller / Prince)***
Freestyle	**Artifacts *(Tame 1 / El The Sensei)***
Freestyle	**Sonz Of Man *(Killa Priest)***
Freestyle	**Wu-Tang *(Masta Killa)***
Freestyle	**Royal Fam *(Timbo King)***
Freestyle	**Terror Squad *(Shorty Prospect / Big Punisher)***
Freestyle	***Mad Lion***
Freestyle	***Guatauba (Yankee)***
Freestyle	***Rey Pirin***
Freestyle	**Bounce Squad *(Doo Wop / Don Black / Uneek)***
Freestyle	**Hot 97 *(Angie Martinez / Ed Lover)***
Freestyle	**Hit Squad *(Pmd / Blast / Poogie / L The Pro / Nocturnal)***
Freestyle	***S.R.***
Freestyle	***Shorty No Mas***
Freestyle	***Shyheim***
Freestyle	***Ski***
Freestyle	***Sadat X***
Freestyle	***Pete Rock***
Freestyle	**Def Squad (Redman / Keith Murray)**
Freestyle	**Dutchmin *(Kenny Rugged / Tony Ruffin)***
Freestyle	**Next Level *(D,V. Alias Christ / Trigga)***
Freestyle	**Dread Shaka**
Freestyle	**Afu Rasta**
Freestyle	**Terror Squad *Cuban Link / Triple Sies***
Freestyle	**The Roots *Black Thought / Rahzel***
Freestyle	**Bahamadia**
Freestyle	**Charlie Brown**
Freestyle	**Shadez Of Brooklyn *(Tee Black / Choclate Tye / Steven King)***
Freestyle	***Krumbsnatcher***
Freestyle	***EZ. D***
Freestyle	**A Is A Crew *(Taino)***
Freestyle	***Nitty Gritty***
Freestyle	**Cru *(Yogi / Chaddio)***
Freestyle	**Bootcamp Clique *(Budda Junkie / Buckshot)***

RON G Just Like Candy

SIDE A	
After 12 Before 6	**Sam Salter ****
Pimp This Love	**Christion**
You Make Me Wanna	**Usher**
Other Side Of The Game	**Erykah Badu**
Oh La La *(Exclusive)*	**Demond / Storm 6**
Someone	**Puffy / SWV**
What About Us	**Total ****
Kiss & Tell	**Brownstone ****
Just Like Candy	**Eightball & MJG**
Love The Dough	**Biggie / Jay-Z**
SIDE B	
Cant Let Go	**Laurnea**
When You Cry	**SWV**
We Can Get Down	**My Ron / Spinderella**
So Good	**Davina / Raekwon**
Sock It To Me	**Missy / Da Brat**
Hot Like Fire (Rmx)	**Aaliyah**
Going Nowhere	**Changing Faces / Tracey Lee**
Sanctified Girl	**Joe**
Hoodium	**Mobb Deep / Big Noyd / Rakim**
The Way You Talk	**Jagged Edge / Da Brat / JD**
Guantanamera	**Wyclef**
Dont Stop The Music	**Playa**

HOT NEW RELEASES

DOO WOP / FUNK FLEX
FACE / OFF (RAP)

D-DEMO
THE HEIST PT 3 (RAP)

MISTER CEE
JOHN BLAZE, DO YOU? (RAP)
R&B BUTTAS #7
ALSO AVAILABLE ON CD $12.99 EACH

EVIL DEE
OLD SCHOOL HIP HOP (VOLUMES 1 THRU 4)
SUMMER SCHOOL (VOLUMES 1 THRU 3) (RAP)

CRAIG G
SUMMER JAMZ (RAP)
FUC #12 (SLOW JAMZ)

NICK BONDZ
STOCKS & BONDZ #10 (RAP & REGGAE)

LS ONE
MAKE EM BOUNCE

LAZY K Never Ending Saga

SIDE A	
Intro	**Lazy K**
Freestyle (Exclusive)	**Sunz Of Man**
Freestyle (Exclusive)	**Shaolin Stample Town P.J.**
Die Hard *(Exclusive)*	**Genevesse**
Man Behind The Mic	**Queen Pen**
I Am Not A Player *(Exclusive)*	**Big Punisher**
Relax And Party	**Ivory / Cru**
Freestyle @ The Tunnel	**Lox / Cru**
I Got Next	**Krs One**
Of The Books	**Beatnuts**
Danger *(Exclusive)*	**G.P Wu Chamber**
Calm Down	**Capone/Noreaga Nas**
Review	**Wu-Tang**
As High As Wu-Tang Get	**Method Man**
It's Yourz	**Wu-Tang Clan**
Freestyle (Exclusive)	**Sunz Of Man**
Tore Down *(Exclusive)*	**Alkaholiks**
Killin It *(Exclusive)*	**Alkaholiks**
Channel 10	**Capone-n-Noreaga**
Hoodlum	**Mobb Deep / Big Noyd / Rakim**
SIDE B	
Pick It Up *(Lazy K Mix)*	**Redmen**
I Always Love That Money	**Mo Money**
MCA Sampler (Exclusive)	
Illa Noyz	**Boot Camp Clique**
Freestyle (Exclusive)	**Heltah Skeltah**
Thug Paradise	**Tragedy / Capone**
Somebody Else *(Exclusive)*	**Hurricane G**
Black Gangstas	**Capone-n-Noreaga**
So Good	**Davina / Raekwon**
To All DJ's *(Exclusive)*	**Warren G**
Year Of The Dragon	**Refugee Allstars**
Escobar 97	**Nas**
Intro	**Krs One**
Blowe	**Krs One**
Big Bad Mamma	**Foxxy Brown / Dru Hill**
Freestyle (Exclusive)	**Mass Appeal**

SPLASH

Hustle Hard: Taking Over New York City One Tape at a Time

There aren't many people who can say they had their hand in the early success of two of the biggest hip-hop mixtape and radio DJs of all-time. But Splash can. A host and personality on mixtapes himself, Splash helped jump-start the careers of both DJ Clue and DJ Envy, establishing relationships with different stores and helping them both to make their names known through the streets of Queens and across NYC.

COMING UP IN QUEENS

Splash: I grew up in Queens, three blocks away from Clue and Envy. Me and Clue were best friends since he used to be a paper boy. Sleepovers, basketball in the backyard, lining up Michael Jordan cards with a white piece of paper on the back of it and making up our own stats of wins and losses and 3-pointers–all stuff that kids did.

As we got older, we got jobs together, hustled together working in the flea markets–all that. Then he got his parent's car, it was a silver Nissan Sentra. We started driving around listening to cassette tapes. Our favorite one was probably Naughty by Nature's "O.P.P."

We used to do all of our music shopping at Dynasty Records in Queens on the Colosseum block. Then it turned into mixtapes. We heard of DJ Ike Love and all his blends that he was doing. We were buying Ike Love and Ron G mixtapes.

MC DRAMA AND DJ XTREME

DJ Clue, his name was MC Drama because he liked to freestyle. Clue met up with this kid named DJ Xtreme who showed him how to DJ. DJ Xtreme was heavy into reggae, but he had a little hip-hop sense. He decided to show Clue how to DJ, and they made their first mixtape.

Me and Clue used to drive around–we had a route that we would do every day to find chicks, and all the music that we used to play was early '90s hip hop. Anytime we would drive past and see a chick dancing, we would make a u-turn and get their number.

It got easier to get chicks' numbers once we were doing our mixtapes, because we would be like, "Here's my mixtape! We'll give you a shout out. What's your number?" Most of the time–smash. Sometimes we didn't get to.

By the first or second mixtape, MC Drama and X came up with the name Clue. On their first mixtape, the logo that they were using was like the video game guy with the magnifying glass. That was the first Clue. It was a high number–I think it was Clue *#24*. The reason they didn't want to start at *#1* was that they didn't want anybody to think that they were first starting out. The second tape ended up being Clue *#24B*.

As Clue was going out, they separated and went to the stores to try and cover the market as much as they could. So while MC Drama was going toward the stores, his name was getting bigger because of the type of music he was playing. This was before exclusives–these were just blends of regular songs. The Africans and the bootleggers kept calling him Clue, so he took the name on himself and kind of pushed DJ Xtreme to the side.

I don't remember exactly what happened, but at the beginning it was him and Xtreme doing it. They both were talking at times and they both were DJing. Clue didn't have the experience Xtreme had. But he took it in his own way and started blending, got turntables, got speakers, got everything, and that was it.

HOSTING TAPES

I got locked up. I was selling drugs and sold to an undercover and had to go away to juvie. I got sentenced to 18 months. I did 10 months, and by the time I came back, Clue was making a name for himself because he was selling these mixtapes. And where I was, I was getting popular because I was getting all the tapes early.

When it was time for me to come out, he was like, "How about you host and I DJ?" I was like, "Hell yeah! I'm down for that."

Clue's name was ringing off, and when I came home he started being managed by this kid he was friends with named Kendell–Steve Stoute's brother aka Scarecrow. Clue and Kendell went to Kingsborough Community College and they became friends there. So, when I came home, I knew nothing of him other than that when I got off the bus, there were three people waiting there for me–Clue, Kendell, and our friend Melinda. By that time, Clue already started getting exclusives. It wasn't just blends anymore.

WORKING WITH DJ CLUE

When Clue took over the game and started selling his tapes, Jamaica Ave. opened up at 5 o'clock. Me and Clue were there almost every single day, at least 5 times a week. We'd drive the Colosseum block in that Nissan Sentra blasting his mixtape. We used to park in front of the Colosseum from 5 to 7.

We still didn't have cover art yet. I remember going to Kinko's and making the copies. In the beginning it was just tape decks 1-to-1 and that took forever. Then there were multiple tape decks, before the

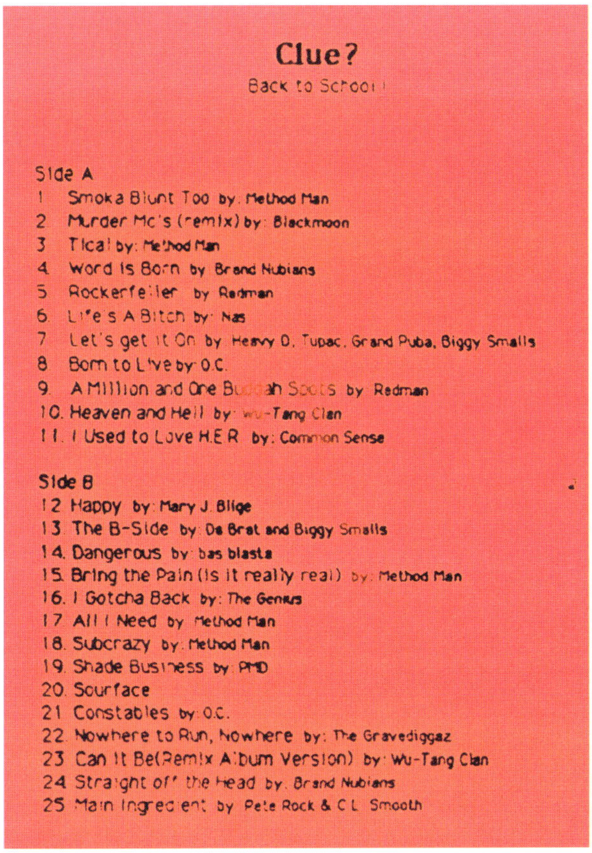
Clue?
Back to School

Side A
1 Smoka Blunt Too by: Method Man
2 Murder Mc's (remix) by: Blackmoon
3 Tical by: Method Man
4 Word is Born by Brand Nubians
5 Rockerfeller by Redman
6 Life's A Bitch by: Nas
7 Let's get it On by Heavy D, Tupac, Grand Puba, Biggy Smalls
8 Born to Live by O.C.
9 A Million and One Buddah Spots by Redman
10. Heaven and Hell by: Wu-Tang Clan
11. I Used to Love H.E.R by: Common Sense

Side B
12 Happy by Mary J. Blige
13 The B-Side by Da Brat and Biggy Smalls
14. Dangerous by bas blasta
15. Bring the Pain (Is it really real) by Method Man
16. I Gotcha Back by: The Genius
17 All I Need by Method Man
18. Subcrazy by Method Man
19. Shade Business by PMD
20. Sourface
21 Constables by O.C.
22. Nowhere to Run, Nowhere by: The Gravediggaz
23 Can It Be(Remix Album Version) by: Wu-Tang Clan
24 Straight off the Head by. Brand Nubians
25 Main Ingredient by Pete Rock & C L Smooth

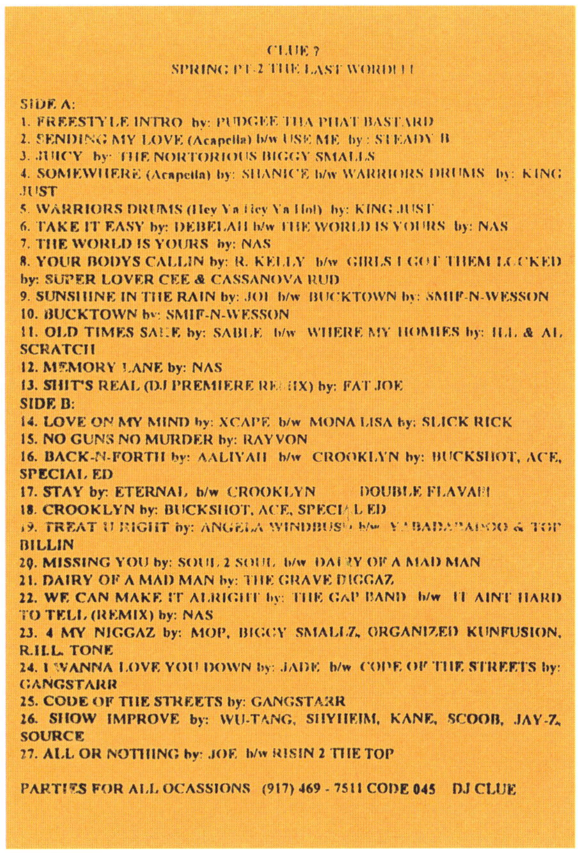
CLUE ?
SPRING PT-2 THE LAST WORD!!!

SIDE A:
1. FREESTYLE INTRO by: PUDGEE THA PHAT BASTARD
2. SENDING MY LOVE (Acapella) b/w USE ME by : STEADY B
3. JUICY by: THE NORTORIOUS BIGGY SMALLS
4. SOMEWHERE (Acapella) by: SHANICE b/w WARRIORS DRUMS by: KING JUST
5. WARRIORS DRUMS (Hey Ya Hey Ya Ho!) by: KING JUST
6. TAKE IT EASY by: DEBELAH b/w THE WORLD IS YOURS by: NAS
7. THE WORLD IS YOURS by: NAS
8. YOUR BODYS CALLIN by: R. KELLY b/w GIRLS I GOT THEM LOCKED by: SUPER LOVER CEE & CASSANOVA RUD
9. SUNSHINE IN THE RAIN by: JOI b/w BUCKTOWN by: SMIF-N-WESSON
10. BUCKTOWN by: SMIF-N-WESSON
11. OLD TIMES SAKE by: SABLE b/w WHERE MY HOMIES by: ILL & AL SCRATCH
12. MEMORY LANE by: NAS
13. SHIT'S REAL (DJ PREMIERE REMIX) by: FAT JOE
SIDE B:
14. LOVE ON MY MIND by: XCAPE b/w MONA LISA by: SLICK RICK
15. NO GUNS NO MURDER by: RAYVON
16. BACK-N-FORTH by: AALIYAH b/w CROOKLYN by: BUCKSHOT, ACE, SPECIAL ED
17. STAY by: ETERNAL b/w CROOKLYN DOUBLE FLAVA!!
18. CROOKLYN by: BUCKSHOT, ACE, SPECIAL ED
19. TREAT U RIGHT by: ANGELA WINDBUSH b/w YABADABADOO & TOP BILLIN
20. MISSING YOU by: SOUL 2 SOUL b/w DAIRY OF A MAD MAN
21. DAIRY OF A MAD MAN by: THE GRAVE DIGGAZ
22. WE CAN MAKE IT ALRIGHT by: THE GAP BAND b/w IT AINT HARD TO TELL (REMIX) by: NAS
23. 4 MY NIGGAZ by: MOP, BIGGY SMALLZ, ORGANIZED KUNFUSION, R.ILL. TONE
24. I WANNA LOVE YOU DOWN by: JADE b/w CODE OF THE STREETS by: GANGSTARR
25. CODE OF THE STREETS by: GANGSTARR
26. SHOW IMPROVE by: WU-TANG, SHYHEIM, KANE, SCOOB, JAY-Z, SOURCE
27. ALL OR NOTHING by: JOE b/w RISIN 2 THE TOP

PARTIES FOR ALL OCASSIONS (917) 469 - 7511 CODE 045 DJ CLUE

Telex machines. Clue's mother was very important in the process also because when he went to sleep, she took over the duplication.

LINKING WITH DJ ENVY

I didn't really know Envy. I used to see Envy all the time as the guy who used to come across the street to Clue's house and ring the doorbell and be like, "Yo, is Clue here?" He would always come ask for records. I thought he was just trying to get into it as a hobby. I didn't know the Envy story of him selling mixtapes pretending he was Clue.

I was working at Kmart. I see Scarecrow and he's telling me that he's not fucking with Clue anymore, and he's fucking with a kid named Envy. He was like, "I want to start managing him and I need a host on his tape." I said, "Sure, no problem."

Envy's name was DJ Shrimp and his man was DJ Mono. Mono showed Envy how to DJ, but when Envy started taking their mixtapes around, all of the bootleggers started calling him Envy. So Envy took the name and started doing mixtapes.

DUPLICATION

After a cassette was done, we'd go to the Telex machine. First, we'd make a master copy, and then make two more after that, so we could run it on three Telex machines at the same time and make multiple copies.

Then we'd write out the list of songs and go to our cover designer NOJO's house. As soon as he was finished, we would be on our way to Kinko's or Village Copier on 13th Street–they were open 24 hours. We'd get no sleep and make as many copies as we could of the recording.

Once things started getting better, I would be home copying and Envy would make those runs because we both couldn't afford to be at the same place at the same time.

GETTING TAPES IN STORES

In the beginning it was both of us, but after that I took on the responsibility of calling every mixtape store possible and getting it out there. If they didn't know about us–"Can I send you a copy?" Back in those days, you had to print out a big sheet so they could hang it on a wall or put it in their mixtape book so people could just flip through the pages and see your whole playlist.

Stores were always $10 a tape and masters went anywhere from $100 to $500. Depending on who it was, we had to charge a certain amount because we knew they moved units. We used to sell like 400 copies a week at Beat Street. Their money was great.

CUSTOMERS OUTSIDE NYC

I started establishing relationships with the record labels. They felt that they needed to get us records once we got on their radar. I asked some of these people to get their store list.

We had lists from Universal, Chris Green at Epic–so we knew where they were servicing records to and we took advantage of every store possible. We couldn't just stay in NYC. We took it to Oneonta, Syracuse, Albany, and Binghamton.

As time went on, people started calling for Envy to DJ, and we entered different markets. Someone wants him to come to Maryland? "Y'all got mixtape stores out there? Cool, I want that list." One store is good enough, because it could grow to two or three stores. That's why $20,000 off of mixtapes became a thing.

We had over 100 stores within New York, and then out of town. When I say out of town, that includes Jersey, Connecticut, Massachusetts, and then further away like Maryland, Virginia, Florida, Indiana. Later on we had that, but when we first started we were excited to have 10 out of town stores. We had Syracuse and Albany on lock also for a while. We had probably 5 or 6 spots in Syracuse at one point.

SPREADING THE NAME

It was word of mouth. I remember we also made sure to have the number on the cassette cover. I don't know if anyone did it first before Clue, but we would put the whole tracklist on a sticker that went on the cassette tape itself. So we had the number on there in case people lost the tape cover, and now you have the actual tracklist as a sticker on there and that also had the number on the bottom. So we left it to where anybody can find you. For a party, to get mixtapes, if it was the RIAA complaining–somebody could always find you.

My number was on there because Envy didn't want to be bothered. For Clue's, if it wasn't mine in the beginning, then it was Clue's by himself.

SCHEDULING AND EXCLUSIVES

Every DJ is going to be beaten to the punch at some point. We scheduled our tapes to where if we did it on August 1st and released it by August 2nd or 3rd, we are not looking for songs for the next tape until about August 15th. Now you start the reprogramming of, "Alright, now we gotta spend a week and a half finding songs and putting it together and making sure it's great enough to put out."

Of course, if we get a hold of a Jay-Z song and maybe four other songs and we didn't have enough songs to fill out a playlist, someone's going to put out a mixtape before us. There's nothing you can do about it.

There were also some songs where I went to the label and there was some sucker shit. I hated that shit. "Yo, listen to this," and they'll pull out the CD or the ADAT or the reel and they'll be like, "I can't give it to you yet. I already promised Clue I'd give it to him," or, "I promised Flex he could premiere it first." What the fuck? You can't do that.

Because Clue was Roc-A-Fella, I remember him having certain songs before us. I heard "People's Court" like five months before Clue had it on the *Backstage* soundtrack, but I couldn't get it because it was for that.

IF I RULED THE WORLD

We were doing a few mixtapes with Envy and it was fine. Then we went to Scarecrow's house, and he got the call for a song–2Pac "Hit 'Em Up." Also,

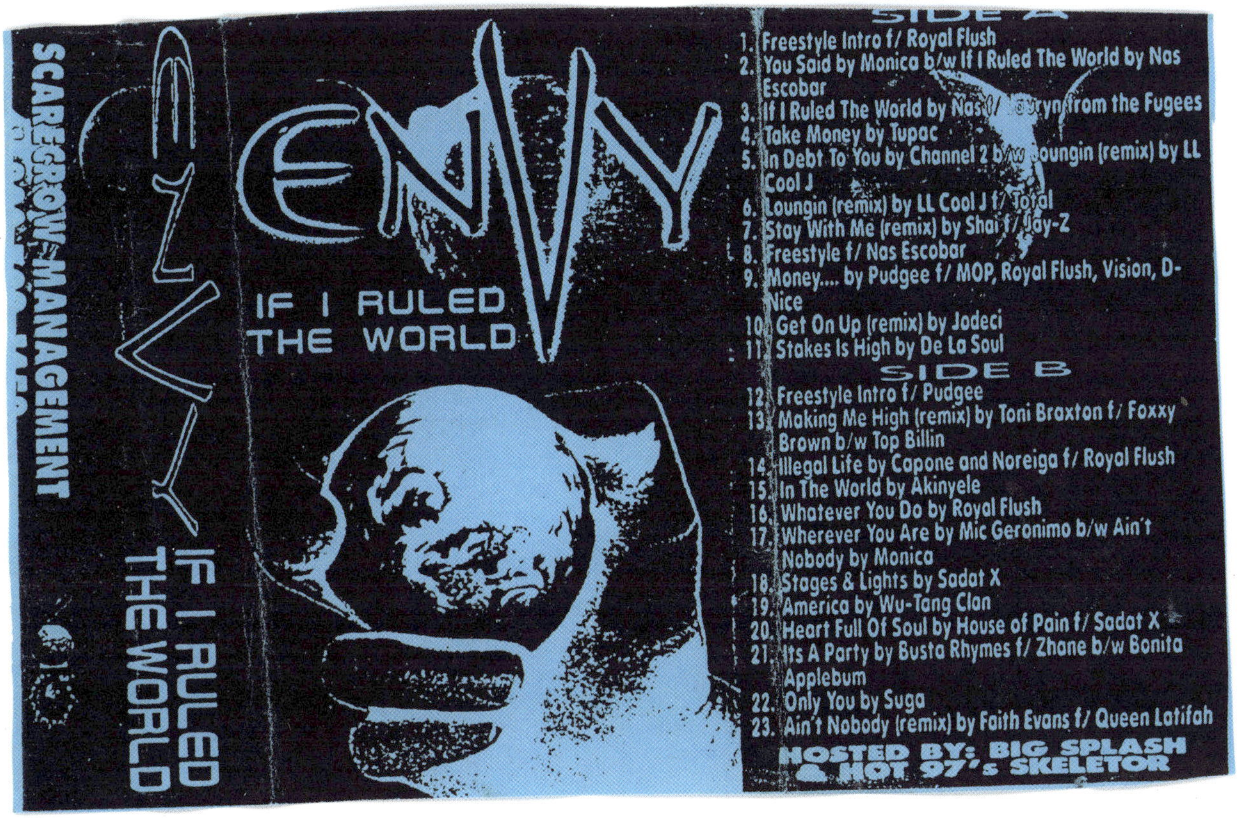

Nas and Lauryn Hill "If I Ruled The World." The tape had a globe on it. This is where Splash starts to make money with Envy.

The Nas record being first makes sense–it was new, we were the first ones with it, the connection with Scarecrow and Steve Stoute being brothers, and the fact that Nas came to the house. Envy had met Nas recently. Envy reached into his pocket to pull out a mixtape and Nas pulled a gun on him in the middle of getting a haircut. I'm guessing that's the reason for the name of the mixtape and the song.

I was at Dynasty Records playing the tape, and you would've thought I was 2Pac. I'm asking the store owner to send everybody who comes in to the back. I'm playing "Hit 'Em Up" and at the beginning, middle, and end of the song people are going up to the counter and buying it. They start telling other people about it, so more people start coming into the store. So now it looks like a mini-concert instead of everybody just listening to the song. As soon as it was over, I would rewind it and tell everybody to give me like 30 seconds and then I played it again and again. No exaggeration, we probably sold like 70 mixtapes in about an hour and a half.

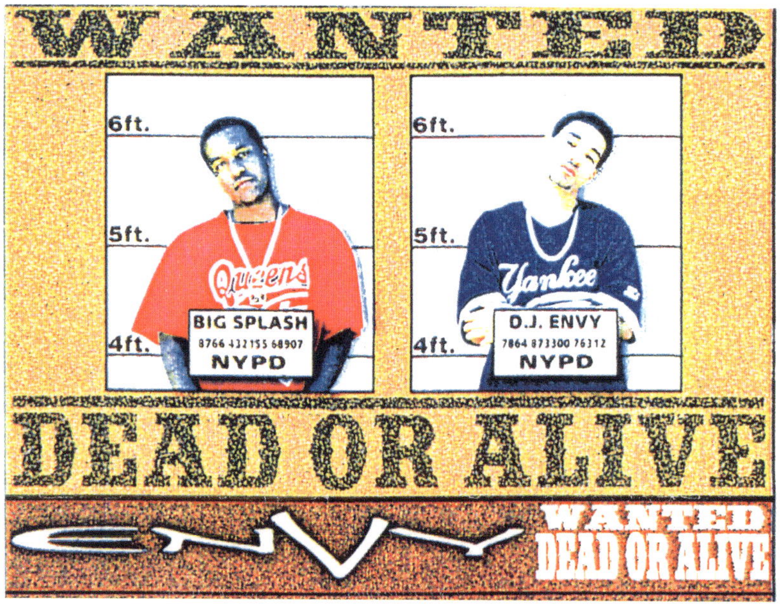

I feel like this mixtape gave Envy a name, and it was the first mixtape that I made major money on. I used to get a few dollars before, but that one blew it up. We made tons of money on that mixtape. It was an eye-opener for me.

APPEARING ON TAPE COVERS

Wanted Dead or Alive was the first cover with our faces on there. I remember Envy saying, "Are we sure we want to put our pictures on this? Are we sure we want to let people know what we look like outside of the mixtape stores?" I was like, "Fuck it, let's go for it."

SHOUTING OUT GIRLFRIENDS

The funny thing about mixtapes is that shit used to get me in trouble. If I had just finished a relationship, all they had to do was listen to Envy's mixtape because if I shouted out Envy's wife, I'd always shout out the girl I was messing with right after. I never realized I was telling on myself. My exes would be like, "You're messing with so and so." I would be like, "How do you know?" And they would say, "From the mixtapes." I would shout out girl after girl and give it away.

FOR PROMOTIONAL USE ONLY

Clue got two or three letters from the RIAA telling him to stop putting out a mixtape. I think that was early, and that's when he decided to put "For Promotional Use Only." And then, that started going on everybody's tape cover, or "Not For Sale."

SPLASH'S 5 ESSENTIAL QUEENS MIXTAPE SPOTS

1. DYNASTY RECORDS - There was a Dynasty Records on the Colosseum block and in the Colosseum Mall. Two different stores--same owner, same name. Dynasty Records in the Colosseum had a little booth with their own little table where they had a DJ stand, and then they had the cashier right next to it. They sold everything from vinyl to cassette tapes to mixtapes. But they didn't sell equipment.

   When you went to Dynasty Records on the Colosseum block itself, that was a true record store. There was like a mini-me inside the mall, and if you needed turntables, needles, coffins, t-shirts, posters, and all that stuff, they just directed you to the bigger store.

2. HOT WAX - Hot Wax was across the street from the Gertz Mall in the back of an appliance store. And there wasn't any promotion for Hot Wax at all out front. It looked similar to the music store in *Juice* where the vinyl was on the wall in those little black holders and everything--that was on one side. The desk was on the other side with mixtapes behind it. The turntables were there, and that was it.

3. ABRAHAM AND MUSTAFA - Abraham had a little walkthrough, it was very tight in his spot. He'd open a little sliding door and have nothing but mixtape covers on there. You couldn't even open up your arms, it looked like an alleyway and it was very dark. It was the definition of a hole in the wall. He had one of those electrician's flashlights in there to light it up so you could see. He kept money on him and the mixtapes were all just on the wall.

   Mustafa had a sliding case in front of the jewelry store, and then he finally was able to have a little table inside the jewelry store. That was it. He never moved from there. I'm sure the owners of the jewelry store were pissed off, but they were happy they were getting rent from him. Any time I went in there, they'd be like, "I got new jewelry. I got new 14 karat, 18 karat, 24 karat." "Nah, nah, I'm here for Mustafa." Mustafa always got the first shout out on the mixtape, before Abraham.

4. NUMBERS - Numbers was in Corona on Junction Boulevard, and in Jackson Heights. The one in Jackson Heights was much smaller. I found Numbers coming out of a sneaker store. I was like, "What's that?" I went over there and gave them about 20 tapes, and then we were good after that. We made good money with them.

5. ANDY'S HOUSE OF SOUND - Andy's House of Sound was in Flushing on Northern Boulevard. He had very few hip-hop records in there, but he had a lot of pop and rock, like Metallica stuff. He had a few mixtapes, but they were names of DJs that I never heard of before with just writing on them, no playlist or nothing. I had to tell him, "Look, this is the sheet that we give. You can put it up on this wall, but you're going to need a binder." Sure enough, he got a binder.

   Andy's House of Sound was very low in the cut. I was happy no one else found out about it.

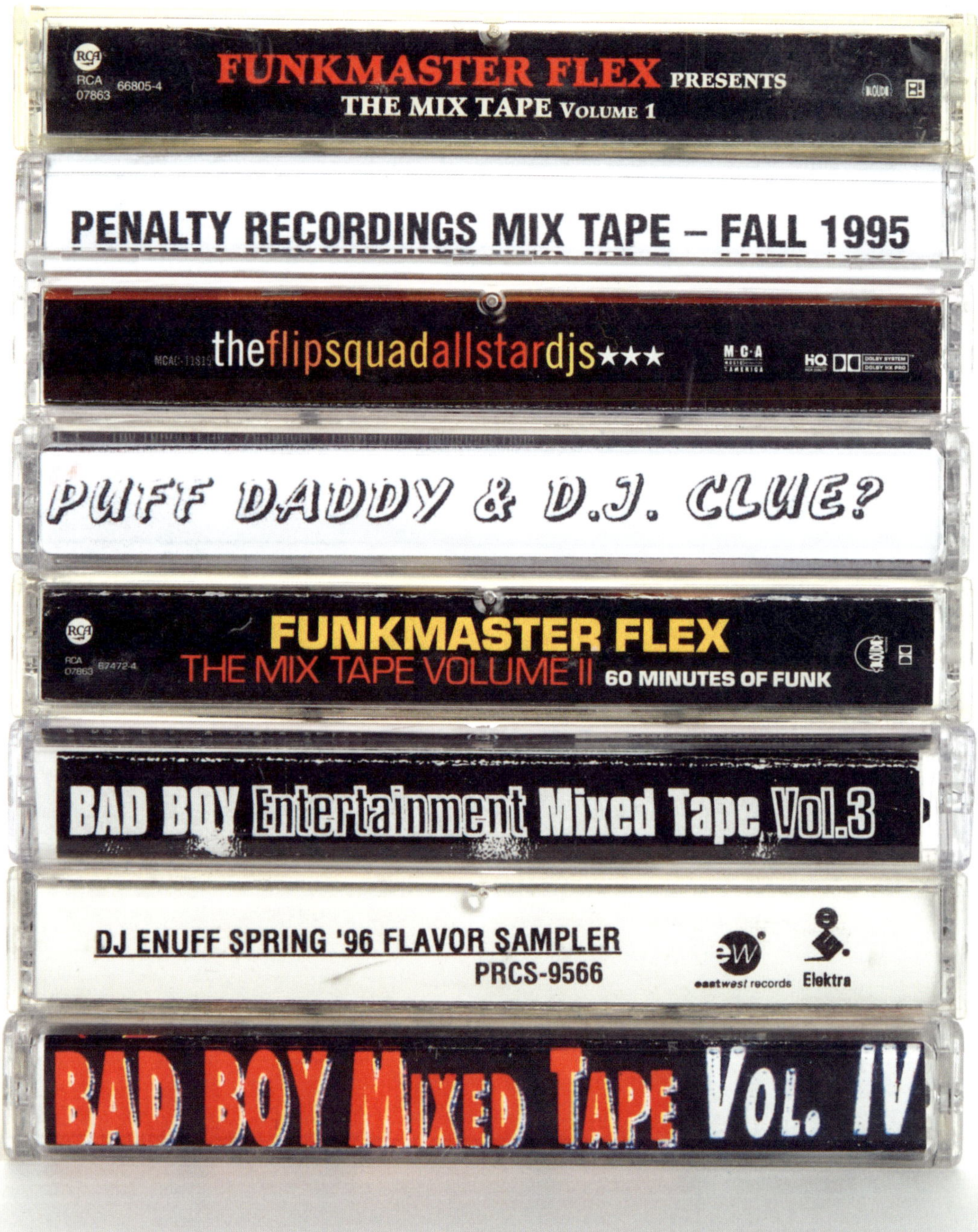
FUNKMASTER FLEX PRESENTS
THE MIX TAPE VOLUME 1
RCA
07863 66805-4
PENALTY RECORDINGS MIX TAPE – FALL 1995
theflipsquadallstardjs★★★
PUFF DADDY & D.J. CLUE?
FUNKMASTER FLEX
THE MIX TAPE VOLUME II 60 MINUTES OF FUNK
RCA
07863 67472-4
BAD BOY Entertainment Mixed Tape Vol.3
DJ ENUFF SPRING '96 FLAVOR SAMPLER
PRCS-9566
eastwest records
Elektra
BAD BOY MIXED TAPE VOL. IV

THE INDUSTRY

With the popularity of mixtapes growing rapidly through the boroughs, it was only a matter of time before the record labels took notice—and took advantage. Mixtapes were a direct outlet to hip-hop customers' ears, and with the right DJ playing an artist's music, they were also a priceless co-sign. Eventually, record labels started releasing their own mixtapes with the biggest names in the game, and sampler tapes to support upcoming releases. Yes, mixtapes definitely made a big impact on THE INDUSTRY.

DRU HA

The Promo: Using Mixtapes as a Music Marketing Tool

Originally from White Plains, New York, Duck Down label co-founder Dru Ha was the man behind the scenes helping groups like Black Moon, Smif-N-Wessun, Heltah Skeltah, and O.G.C. make noise. And one of the keys to their success was the relationships Dru and the rest of the Boot Camp Clik formed with mixtape DJs, hitting them off with new music and exclusive freestyles.

GETTING ARTISTS ON MIXTAPES

Dru Ha: It was crucial for me in that era when I really got started with the groups Black Moon and Smif-N-Wessun. Right off the bat, part of our promotion strategy was that we had to reach out to these guys. It was like, "I've got to get to Tony Touch. I've got to get to Doo Wop and ask them if they would want a freestyle from Buckshot or would they feature O.G.C. on a mixtape." That's my overall encompassing memory of just how critical and important the mixtape was to the startup and promotion of an artist, coming from the record label side of it.

At that point, I was so early in the business that I didn't really know what I was doing. It was just more that I felt like I had to be everywhere. And that was one of the lanes that you needed to be on–the right mixtapes.

BUILDING RELATIONSHIPS WITH MIXTAPE DJS

You use every available outlet. Sometimes it was from the group. Evil Dee knew Tony Touch, they were both from Bushwick. So you had common ground there.

DJ Clue would come by because Nervous had a lot of house records and breakbeats. Nervous was kind of known for that, so some of the guys would come up to get those pieces of vinyl. That's where I first met Clue–he would come by once a month and we'd get his tape, give him vinyl, and start to form those relationships.

Tony was just family through E, so like right away, there was natural synergy there. We met Doo Wop through Tony, then Kid Capri as we got a little bit bigger just through mutual respect, working the circuit. That's how it would develop. If you were out there and going up to radio stations or visiting clubs or going to certain spots in the city, you eventually would probably run into these guys.

Now, if they cared was another story. You've got to give them a reason. You can't negotiate with yourself. You might think something's important, but the other person on the other side may not. So all you can do is try to build your case.

But we were fortunate, having those groups so early–Black Moon, Smif-N-Wessun, and eventually Heltah Skeltah. That opened a lot of doors for us, because these guys all wanted them on their tapes and it made the job a lot easier. We did run into some problems with Nervous at that time though, because we were using exclusives and different music from those albums, and they objected to it.

IMPORTANCE OF DOO WOP'S *SUMMER JAM '96* FAB 5 FREESTYLE

The Fab 5 Doo Wop one was a standout to me because I felt like for them it was almost like a coming out party. They were no longer being held down by Buck and Smif-n-Wessun. They went at it and they destroyed that one. To me, it was like, "Alright, that was a great moment for them as individual groups."

50 MCs BOOT CAMP FREESTYLE GETTING RADIO PLAY

I remember Flex used to play that freestyle from the top to the end and we'd have like a nine minute block on Hot 97. Even then, I was amazed that we'd have a nine minute block of radio, but the instrumental on the freestyle kept changing so it made his job a little easier to play it. But it was also amazing as a label to get that type of promo, with a mixtape freestyle that had all these different artists on it.

BUCKSHOT SINGLE ON _60 MINUTES OF FUNK VOL. 2_

We were a huge part of Flex's mixtapes because Buck was on the lead single with the "I Ain't No Joke" sample–"Follow My Lead." So that was a big deal, with Flex having his mixtapes on Loud. We actually made a video with them. We were very calculated with how we made that record and how it was done with Flex in the studio. And the record that Buck picked kept it in mixtape style format, rhyming over someone else's beat.

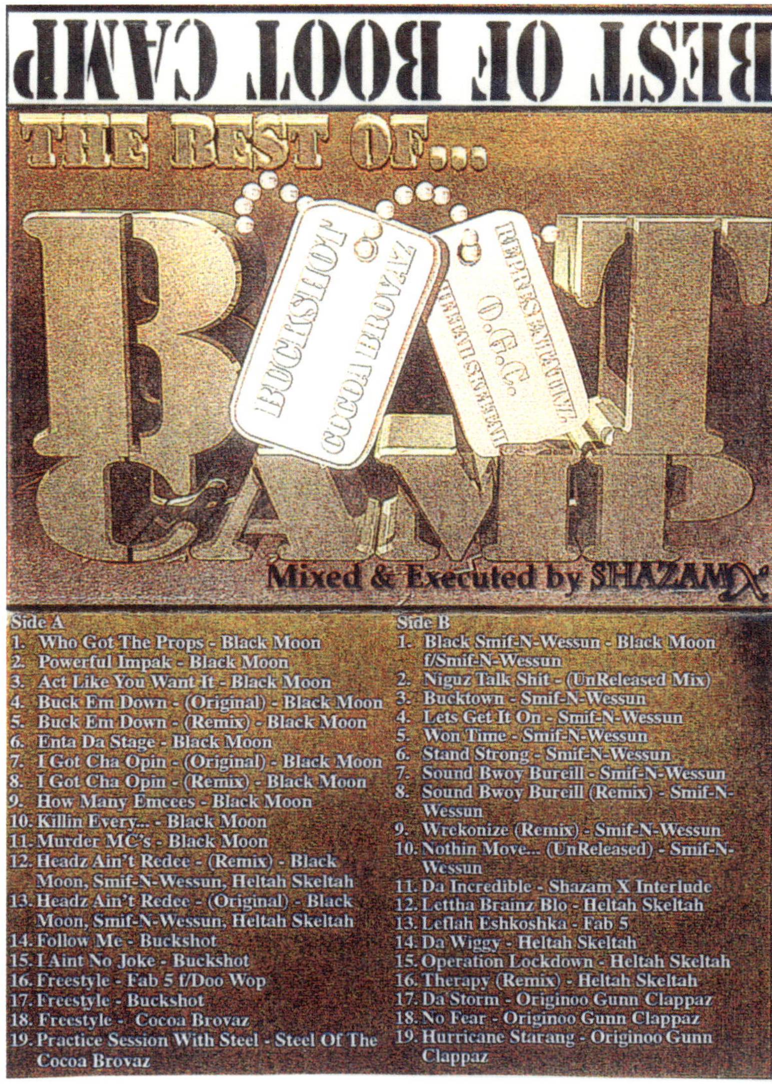

THE VALUE OF MIXTAPES

We started to figure out that there was a lot of value to the freestyles and mixtapes. I think that's why we started to make our own, which speaks to some of the strategy too.

These guys were selling who knows how many copies of these things, and they didn't have to pay anybody. So you had the record label ripping the artists off back then–the game hadn't evolved yet to where artists had figured it out. And then you had the mixtape DJs out on the streets selling it as an unofficial project, and the artist wasn't really seeing or getting anything from it other than obviously the promotion.

But once you reached a certain point, then you could just balance the scales saying, "Well, the promotion is nice, but I'm also hoping to sell this." And that's what kind of drove some of our strategy. We had to make our own and find a way to exploit it, too. Because, at the end of the day, this is all business.

IT WAS WRITTEN:

MIXTAPES INSPIRE *THE SOURCE* MAGAZINE'S CONTENT

Jonathan Shecter aka Shecky Green was instrumental in helping to make *The Source* magazine the unofficial "Hip-Hop Bible." With a 5-mic album rating system and features on the brightest stars and biggest trends in hip hop, the magazine helped spawn debates and discussions about both the music and the culture. And after moving from Boston to NYC during *The Source*'s relative infancy, he was there to witness how mixtapes directly inspired the evolution of the music itself, as well as the magazine with the addition of the must-read, mixtape-inspired monthly column "Fat Tape."

CANAL STREET

Shecky Green: We moved to New York in 1990. We had an office on 594 Broadway. That was when I got very immersed in the cassette culture of New York. I also didn't live far from Canal Street, where the African merchants set up table stands. I remember that very well. There were just a few at first, but then by '92, '93 there were a bunch. Mixtape stands, literally the size of a closet. There would be a guy who would fill up all the wall space with hundreds of these tapes.

Matty C, who is a friend and one of the first people that we hired at *The Source*, or myself would go to Canal Street. Houston to Canal is a great cross section of downtown culture. When you got to Canal, it was a little dirtier, nastier, crowded, and old.

I was in the middle of it from the labels and all of that, so I didn't feel the need to always go. I knew that existed, but I didn't follow it too closely because I was trying to get the music before them. Our job was to get the advanced cassette from the label before they did.

FAT TAPE

Matty C had the idea to mimic a mixtape and pick songs that were buzzing. This is the stuff that's brand new, hot, and that you would put on a mixtape. It was the songs we would put on a mixtape if we were making one, in a column.

I remember King Sun came out with a song called "Fat Tape." I believe that might have inspired it. Matty was the man on the scene for that and Unsigned Hype. Sometimes I would throw some things in there, but it was mainly Matty's thing.

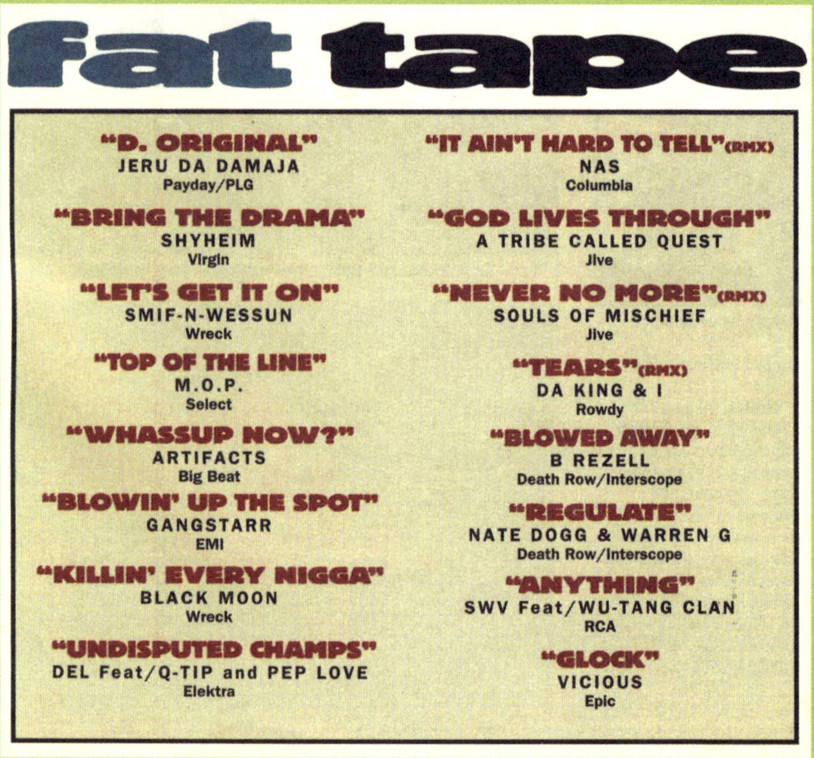
fat tape

"D. ORIGINAL"
JERU DA DAMAJA
Payday/PLG

"BRING THE DRAMA"
SHYHEIM
Virgin

"LET'S GET IT ON"
SMIF-N-WESSUN
Wreck

"TOP OF THE LINE"
M.O.P.
Select

"WHASSUP NOW?"
ARTIFACTS
Big Beat

"BLOWIN' UP THE SPOT"
GANGSTARR
EMI

"KILLIN' EVERY NIGGA"
BLACK MOON
Wreck

"UNDISPUTED CHAMPS"
DEL Feat/Q-TIP and PEP LOVE
Elektra

"IT AIN'T HARD TO TELL"(RMX)
NAS
Columbia

"GOD LIVES THROUGH"
A TRIBE CALLED QUEST
Jive

"NEVER NO MORE"(RMX)
SOULS OF MISCHIEF
Jive

"TEARS"(RMX)
DA KING & I
Rowdy

"BLOWED AWAY"
B REZELL
Death Row/Interscope

"REGULATE"
NATE DOGG & WARREN G
Death Row/Interscope

"ANYTHING"
SWV Feat/WU-TANG CLAN
RCA

"GLOCK"
VICIOUS
Epic

TALENT ON TAPE:
USING MIXTAPES TO FIND WHO'S NEXT

Now one of the leading executives in the music business, Rigo "Riggs" Morales got his start in the industry as a music journalist for *The Source*. In addition to Fat Tape and the coveted Quotable of the Month, one of the columns Riggs was regularly responsible for was Unsigned Hype, where the magazine would shine a light on a buzzworthy, breakthrough artist. And quite often, he used mixtapes to mine for MCs to cover in the column—which ultimately would lead to labels showing interest in Unsigned Hype artists.

Riggs Morales: I used to do Quotable of the Month, Unsigned Hype and the Fat Tape—that was one page. With Fat Tape, I was already trained to come in and just pluck album cuts from albums that were released during that month. So, the bangers to put in that column, which is basically a mixtape.

We got everything early. We got exclusive previews of albums, we had every mixtape DJ under the stars dropping off joints. With that, you relied on mixtapes for an excellent, curated list of what people were thinking about. For me, it was looking for artists on the Unsigned Hype level.

It had an effect all over the magazine, because for me it was a sense of music discovery, artist discovery, and it allowed me to stay ahead. Look, it got competitive after a while. You had *VIBE*, you had *Rap Pages*. It's just like, "Guys, we have to pay attention."

So we were early on Lord Tariq—before "Uptown Baby." He was already on our radar. Then, when him and Peter Gunz came into the mix, we caught it early and gave them their flowers before it became this big thing.

The mixtapes were the starting point for a lot of future classic shit. Like for example, I heard "Niggaz Done Started Something," a lot of the early LOX stuff, and a lot of early Ma$e on mixtapes, years before they became big. If you were nice and you were on a mixtape, it stood out for me. Genovese, he was an "Unsigned Hype" of mine, and I remember he was on a mixtape with The LOX. That was the hub. Like, "I'm gonna use these mixtapes to see who's out there and deserves a shot."

During year one and two at *The Source,* we started seeing record labels sign mixtape artists. Even Funk Flex was taking the mixtape approach with his album. The mixtape culture was now seeping into the business side.

If you were nice and you were on a mixtape, it stood out for me.

CIPHA SOUNDS

In the Mix: Making Multiple Mixtape Moves

"Cipha Sounds don't get gassed!" Those are the famous words of Funkmaster Flex, Ciph's big homie at Hot 97 who gave him one of his first big looks—the chance to do a mixtape promoting N.O.R.E.'s debut album for Penalty Records. And being someone who, in addition to making his own street mixtapes and helping Flex with his Loud Records mixtape releases, also worked as an A&R at Rawkus Records, an employee at Fat Beats, and a DJ at New York's hottest hip-hop nightclub The Tunnel, Cipha Sounds witnessed multiple ways mixtapes infiltrated the industry.

USING MIXTAPES FOR PERSONAL PROMO

Cipha Sounds: I was a big, big fan and consumer of mixtapes, and I always wanted to make them. I would make them for friends, but not like big ones that were sold on the street. My career took me the radio route.

I was Flex's intern for many years, but I wasn't on the air. Even though I say I was with Hot 97 for 17 years, probably 4 to 6 of those were just straight up being an intern. Even though I was at the radio station every single day, it wasn't like I was known or getting exposure. So I looked at mixtapes as promotional material to get my name out there. The mixtapes were little commercials for DJs so we could get gigs.

The beauty of being at the radio station was all the artists were coming through. The hardest part of the mixtape game is getting an artist to host it, or do a freestyle, or a feature. So I was lucky to be in a place where the artists used to come all the time. Me and Flex talked about getting my name and the Big Dawg Pitbulls name out there more, so we were like, "Alright, let's do some mixtapes."

YA HEARD! PENALTY MIXTAPE

"Ya heard" is what N.O.R.E. used to say. N.O.R.E. was my first rapper friend. I met a lot of rappers, but N.O.R.E. was like one year younger or older than me, and I remember calling to ask him if I could DJ his 21st birthday party or something like that. He had just got home from jail. I was a big Capone-N-Noreaga fan.

To take it back even further, Mayhem and Martin Moor had a show on WNYU 89.1. You know the Wu-Tang skit before "Protect Ya Neck," that's from that show. "Play it again and again." So I was friends with DJ Riz, and I basically became Riz's intern. Riz used to always go to NYU to hang out with those guys. Mayhem and Martin Moor ended up being A&Rs at Penalty Records, while I'm on my journey at Hot 97 with Flex. We were all really cool and we all became the college radio guys that were now getting into the industry and trying to produce records and make a mark.

CNN blew up, and then N.O.R.E. was gonna do a solo album. And they wanted Flex to do the mixtape. They were like, "Yo, you think Flex would do it?" And I was like, "I don't know, I'll ask him." He was like, "I don't want to do it. You do it and I'll host it."

I wanted to do it so badly, and he goes, "Tell them we'll do it for ten grand." And in my mind, ten grand was the most money I ever heard in my life. I go, "They're not gonna give us ten grand, that's impossible." He goes, "Ciph, if my name's on it, they're gonna give us ten grand."

I was so fucking scared, like, "He said he wants to do it for ten grand." They went and had a talk and said,

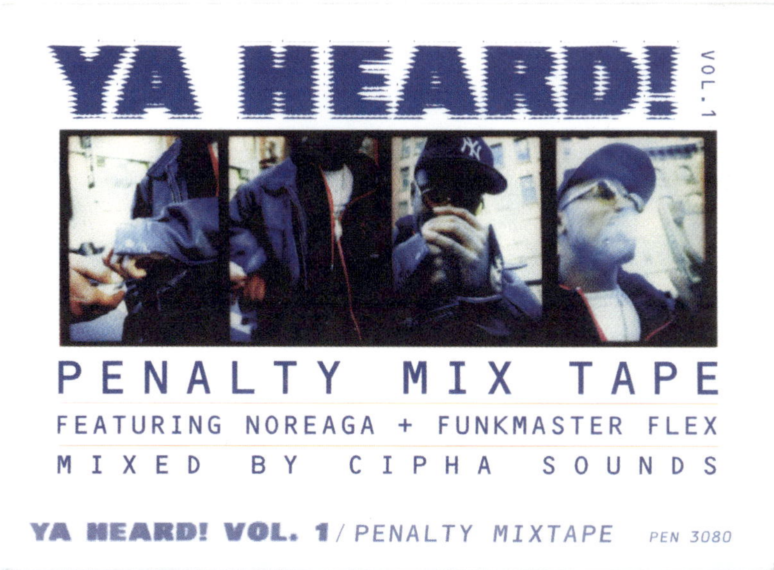

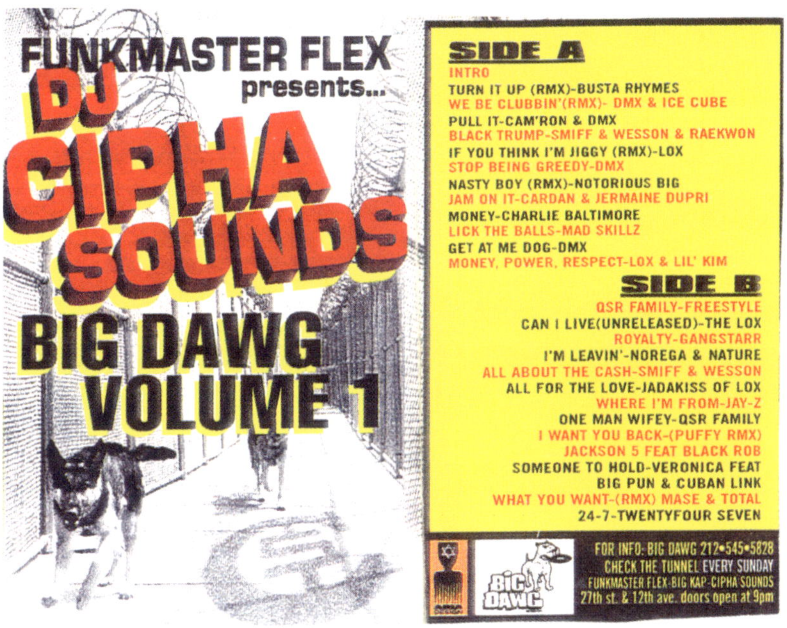

"Okay cool." That's when I learned, "Oh, I don't know what money is or how to make money." I think Flex gave me $1,500 and I was ecstatic. I was super-excited to make it. I wanted to make it like an actual mixtape and play all the new N.O.R.E. songs, and also play all the banging Capone-N-Noreaga songs. They're like, "Yeah we love that idea, let's do it."

They gave me this exclusive N.O.R.E. Christmas vinyl, it was green and red and promotional, but it had some unreleased songs. Like the song, "Married to Marijuana," which didn't make the album or the CNN album. This is before CDJs, before Serato, so they gave me all of the new N.O.R.E. songs on DAT. I had to mix the records of the old CNN songs, and then I would have to pause it and play the DAT and go back to mixing. But I tried to make it seamless.

To this day, that tape got me the biggest response of anything I've ever done or put out. N.O.R.E. was super happy, N.O.R.E. and Flex became super cool, and all of this came from me knowing Mayhem and Martin Moor from the radio.

SAMPLERS VS. MIXTAPES

Samplers before, to me, were just boring. You get like 30 seconds or one minute of a song that's coming out. I guess back then we didn't know any better and they just gave them out and a lot of stuff blew up from those. But, why not make it to where you never want to eject it until the album comes out. Then you're excited for the album. It wasn't done before, but the answer was right there. "Let's just make this entertaining."

I guess the difference was it had a little cost to it, where the label had to use some of the marketing budget. As opposed to just making a sampler and there's no cost, just whatever the material is. So that was maybe the only downside to a label–trying to save money. Penalty was a new label trying to shine, so they went for it. Same with Rawkus, they were more in touch with the culture.

TUNNEL TAPES

The Tunnel was the biggest hip-hop party in New York. It was on Sunday nights. The party was actually called Mecca, and eventually they started calling it the name of the club, the Tunnel. If you watch the movie *Kids*, it's in that movie. It was a famous techno, house club on Fridays and Saturdays, but on Sundays they did hip hop.

If you watch the video of DMX's "Get At Me Dog," that's the best depiction of how it was in the Tunnel. It was the grimiest, ghettoest shit. People getting robbed, people getting beat up. The greatest performances with 2,500 people. And we were *breaking* records. Records you never heard before anywhere else were being broke in the Tunnel.

One of my biggest regrets is not getting my hands on those Tunnel tapes. There was a guy that worked for Funkmaster Flex named Frankie Juga, he carried Flex's crates. Frankie Juga would record every night at the Tunnel. There were so many legendary nights there. A couple of them we put out, the ones with covers. And Tape Kingz put them out, but I'm sure they got them from Frankie Juga.

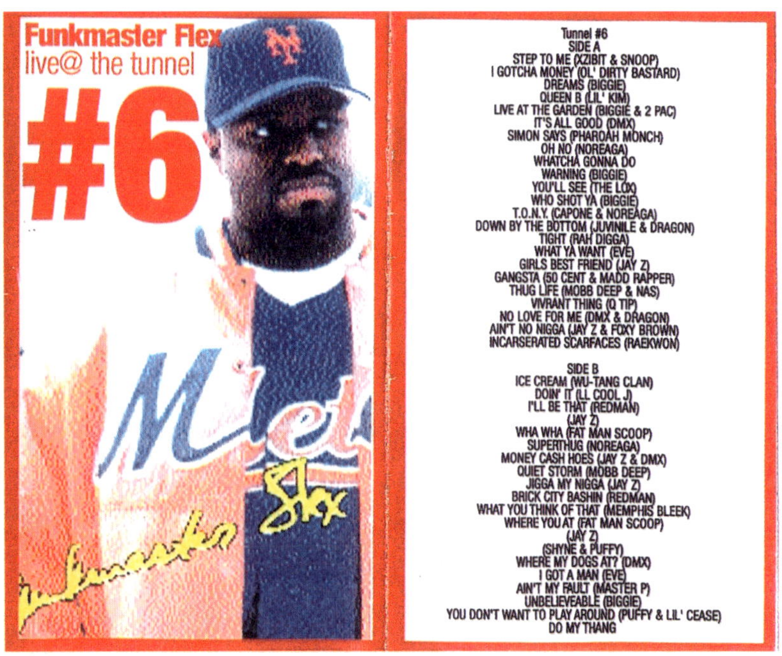

UNSPOKEN RULES OF BEING AN OPENER

You can't play all the hot hit records. DJing now is a fucking mess. Every DJ is playing all the hot records over and over. That's why I hate going to clubs now. Back then, you had to keep the crowd entertained, but not play all the newest hot records. You had to save those for Flex.

But that's where the mixtapes come into play. I learned a lot of dope R&B and soul shit from listening to Ron G and Kid Capri tapes. I'd bring my walkman with the tape to Rock and Soul and be like, "What's this song?" "Oh that's Gap Band." Or Frankie Beverly, or whatever. And I would buy the records because of the mixtapes. They were like the promo to the old school.

FAT BEATS JOB

Working at Fat Beats in my underground days was the greatest. I met all of my favorite DJs. Everyone wanted to do album releases at Fat Beats. I met Premier, Gang Starr, Outkast, Big L, Lord Finesse, Diamond D, Showbiz–all of those guys.

The best thing about Fat Beats was that it was all vinyl except for a couple of mixtapes. They didn't respect Clue, S&S, or Doo Wop in Fat Beats. They were too commercial. There were Tony Touch tapes and some really underground, indie stuff, and Stretch and Bob tapes from the show. That's another thing I regret not getting is every one of those Stretch and Bob tapes. Stretch and Bob mixtapes would sell like fire in Fat Beats.

Once in a while some hood dude would come in and be like, "Yo, you got Clue tapes?" They got treated like dogshit. Ill Bill would be like, "Nah, we don't sell fucking Clue tapes." We used to have the Beat Junkies, Qbert, and those guys. Roc Raida. Rob

Swift's *Soulful Fruit* had to be like platinum in the underground world. It was like jazz hip hop. They were mixtapes, but they were like art.

60 MINUTES OF FUNK

Flex got a deal with Loud Records, which was one of the hottest labels at the time. Loud Records had the Alkaholiks, Mobb Deep, Wu-Tang, the Cella Dwellas. Flex got a deal and was like, "I want to put out mixtapes on an actual label." And they were like, "Well, that's not really going to work. It's going to be too expensive."

On a mixtape, you could take any beat and people would rhyme over it and you would put it out. Like Doo Wop *95 Live*, Tony Touch *50 MCs*. So the label was like, "We're not going to be able to clear any of those records." Flex was like, "We'll just use all Loud records, and all Loud instrumentals."

So I would go to the studio with an MPC60 or MPC2000 and take Loud records, any Wu-Tang, any Mobb Deep, any Xzibit–he was on Loud, too–and I would take their songs and loop them and add a 4 count DJ intro. And people would rhyme over them. They would press up the vinyl of those freestyles, and Flex would mix them to make the DJ album. This was the attempt at getting as close to that street mixtape feel in a legal aspect.

I would be in D&D Studios every night. I would go in the daytime and chop up the beats, I'd bring them to Flex, and he'd be like, "Yeah, use this one and this one." Then Big Pun, Fat Joe, Jay-Z, everybody would come to D&D and record these songs for the album.

60 MINUTES OF FUNK RECORDING SESSIONS

Jay-Z and Flex have always had this contentious relationship. They both help each other and hate each other. I'm in the studio and I'm chopping up beats. Jay-Z comes with Dame Dash and somebody else and I'm like, "What's up Jay?" And they're like, "Where's Flex?" I'm like, "Oh, he's not here yet." "He's not here?" I'm like, "No, but I got the beat loaded up and all ready to go." He's like, "Nah I don't record for–" I forget what he called me, but it was like "bitch boys" or "peons" or something. I was like, "Wow!" And he just left. You know that Jay-Z *Reasonable Doubt* arrogance. I had to call Flex and tell him he left. He's like, "This motherfucker–why do I have to be there? The beat is there. The studio is there." Jay-Z said he wasn't recording without Flex. Just some Brooklyn shit. Pun–he was still new, but he was heating up in the streets. Joe was like to Flex, "I'll do a song on your album, but Pun's gotta be on it." And Pun came through to D&D.

Pun was a prankster. He had a plate of food. He looks at me and puts the plate up and says, "Hey, can you hold this plate up for a second while I get up?" So he puts his arm on the arm of the couch like he's going to get up. I hold the plate for him. He's getting up, and then he sits back down and starts laughing. Like, "Oh, you want me to throw out your plate!?" He would do shit like that all the time.

It was just cool to watch all of these artists 100% be down to do this for Flex because they knew this was going to get them on the air. These were all underground artists that didn't necessarily get a lot of airplay in the daytime. They were late night guys.

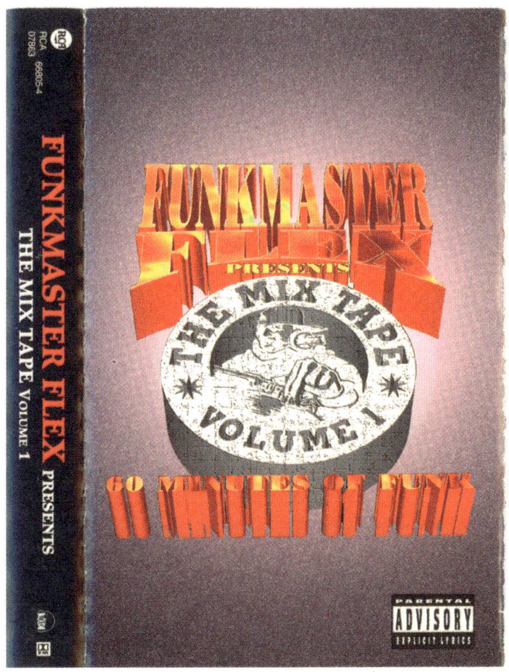

BAD BOY MIXTAPES:
Puff Daddy Teams Up with the Hottest DJs in NYC

"I wanna make a tape that's gonna have motherfuckers partying. I don't wanna make no shit where we just play all our Bad Boy shit and niggas is just listening and shit. I wanna make a joint that's gonna have niggas in they Jeeps rockin', honeys in the beauty parlors rockin', all them niggas on they corners gettin' they money rockin'. I wanna do a Bad Boy mixtape, word up."

Puff Daddy has always been a smart businessman who's in touch with his audience. So of course, he knew the importance of the mixtape game early on, as it was one of the platforms that helped the two pillars to Bad Boy's foundation, Craig Mack and The Notorious B.I.G., become larger than life in the streets.

But rather than just feed mixtape DJs exclusive songs, he decided to take over the mixtape game in a way that no record label had done before by creating his own Bad Boy mixtape series, featuring four of the biggest and most beloved DJs in New York City—DJ Clue, Doo Wop, Stretch Armstrong, and DJ S&S.

BAD BOY MIXTAPE VOL.1

After DJ Clue moved past his previous issues with Bad Boy, where he was called out live on Hot 97 by Biggie for leaking new music on his tape without permission, Puff tapped the leading exclusives kingpin of the moment to set the Bad Boy Mixtape series off. On *Volume 1*, Clue took a backseat on the mic as Puff played the role of host, talking all over the intro and throughout the tape. It was a chance for Puff to directly bring his infectious energy to the streets as 1995 was an exciting time for Bad Boy Records, coming off the success of *Ready To Die* and Craig Mack's *Project: Funk Da World.*

And though Puff encouraged Clue to play joints by other flourishing New York artists like Mobb Deep, Smif-N-Wessun, Grand Puba, Ol' Dirty Bastard, and Onyx, he made sure the tape was littered with Bad Boy hits and exclusives like The Notorious B.I.G.'s new "One More Chance (Remix)," Total's B.I.G.-featured, funk-driven single "Can't You See," and an unreleased, early solo version of B.I.G.'s "Young G's." And with that, it looked like Clue's issues with Biggie were officially behind him, and the Bad Boy Mixtape series was off to the races.

BAD BOY MIXTAPE VOL. 2

Doo Wop: I was real cool with Bad Boy at the time, I was getting mad shit. Like, whoever gave me that "Bust a Nut" shit with Biggie for *95 Live Part Two* was like, "Here, this shit ain't never coming out."

And I had a manager at the time who was big, Jessica Rosenblum, who ran the Tunnel. She had the biggest DJ crew, The Flip Squad, which I was a part of at the time with Funk Flex, Big Kap, Mister Cee, Biz Mark, Mark Ronson, Cipha Sounds, all these people. So Puff called her because he was starting to do all those tapes, and he definitely wanted me, so we did that.

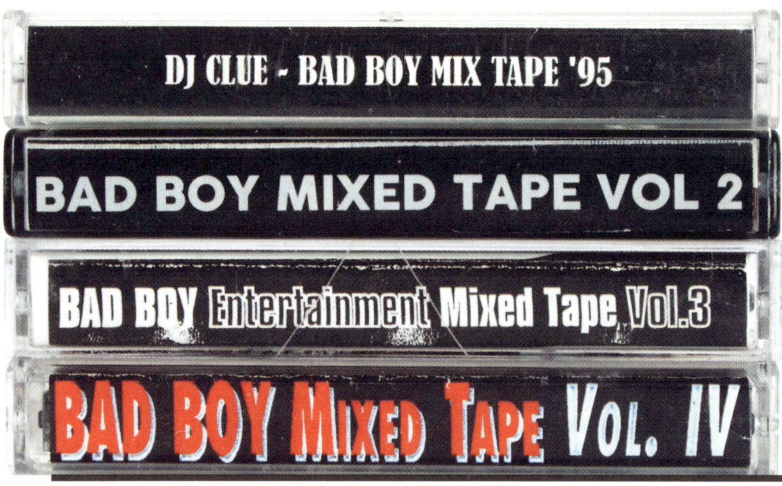

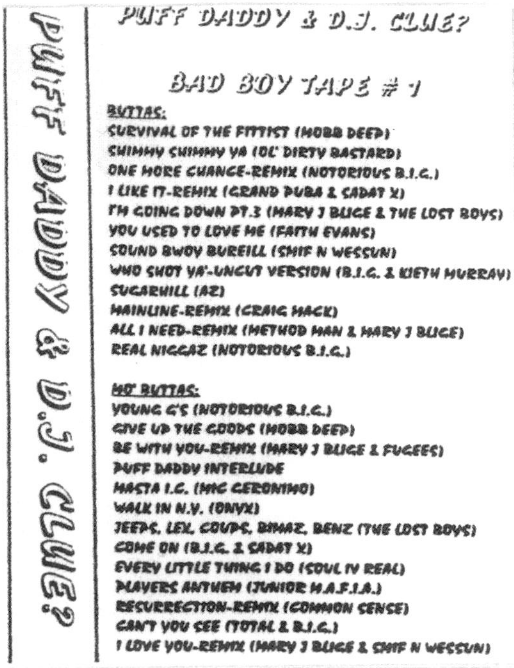

PUFF DADDY & D.J. CLUE?

PUFF DADDY & D.J. CLUE?

BAD BOY TAPE # 1

BUTTAS:
SURVIVAL OF THE FITTIST (MOBB DEEP)
SHIMMY SHIMMY YA (OL' DIRTY BASTARD)
ONE MORE CHANCE-REMIX (NOTORIOUS B.I.G.)
I LIKE IT-REMIX (GRAND PUBA & SADAT X)
I'M GOING DOWN PT.3 (MARY J BLIGE & THE LOST BOYS)
YOU USED TO LOVE ME (FAITH EVANS)
SOUND BWOY BUREILL (SMIF N WESSUN)
WHO SHOT YA'-UNCUT VERSION (B.I.G. & KIETH MURRAY)
SUGARHILL (AZ)
MAINLINE-REMIX (CRAIG MACK)
ALL I NEED-REMIX (METHOD MAN & MARY J BLIGE)
REAL NIGGAZ (NOTORIOUS B.I.G.)

MO' BUTTAS:
YOUNG G'S (NOTORIOUS B.I.G.)
GIVE UP THE GOODS (MOBB DEEP)
BE WITH YOU-REMIX (MARY J BLIGE & FUGEES)
PUFF DADDY INTERLUDE
MASTA I.C. (MIC GERONIMO)
WALK IN N.Y. (ONYX)
JEEPS, LEX, COUPS, BIMAZ, BENZ (THE LOST BOYS)
COME ON (B.I.G. & SADAT X)
EVERY LITTLE THING I DO (SOUL IV REAL)
PLAYERS ANTHEM (JUNIOR M.A.F.I.A.)
RESURRECTION-REMIX (COMMON SENSE)
CAN'T YOU SEE (TOTAL & B.I.G.)
I LOVE YOU-REMIX (MARY J BLIGE & SMIF N WESSUN)

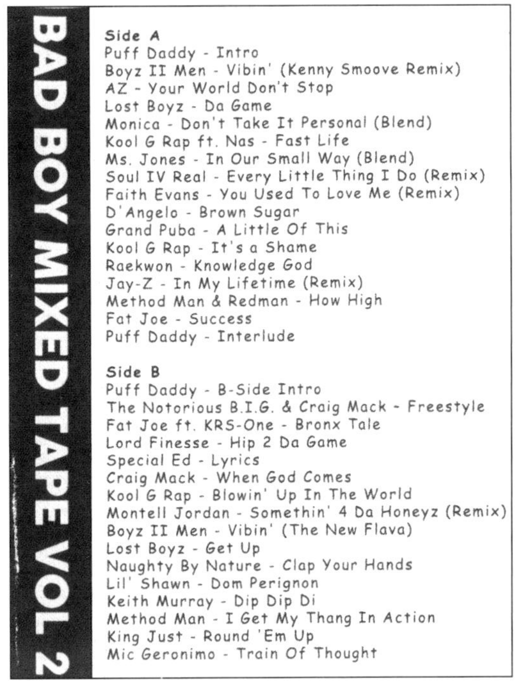

BAD BOY MIXED TAPE VOL 2

Side A
Puff Daddy - Intro
Boyz II Men - Vibin' (Kenny Smoove Remix)
AZ - Your World Don't Stop
Lost Boyz - Da Game
Monica - Don't Take It Personal (Blend)
Kool G Rap ft. Nas - Fast Life
Ms. Jones - In Our Small Way (Blend)
Soul IV Real - Every Little Thing I Do (Remix)
Faith Evans - You Used To Love Me (Remix)
D'Angelo - Brown Sugar
Grand Puba - A Little Of This
Kool G Rap - It's a Shame
Raekwon - Knowledge God
Jay-Z - In My Lifetime (Remix)
Method Man & Redman - How High
Fat Joe - Success
Puff Daddy - Interlude

Side B
Puff Daddy - B-Side Intro
The Notorious B.I.G. & Craig Mack - Freestyle
Fat Joe ft. KRS-One - Bronx Tale
Lord Finesse - Hip 2 Da Game
Special Ed - Lyrics
Craig Mack - When God Comes
Kool G Rap - Blowin' Up In The World
Montell Jordan - Somethin' 4 Da Honeyz (Remix)
Boyz II Men - Vibin' (The New Flava)
Lost Boyz - Get Up
Naughty By Nature - Clap Your Hands
Lil' Shawn - Dom Perignon
Keith Murray - Dip Dip Di
Method Man - I Get My Thang In Action
King Just - Round 'Em Up
Mic Geronimo - Train Of Thought

It was easy to do, because I had it organized, where I'd be like, "Harve Pierre is in the house," and then he'd go in and do the same thing after me. I had it orchestrated. And then he gave me the freestyle with B.I.G. and Craig Mack overseas rhyming off the "Rockafella (Remix)" beat that nobody had ever heard before that tape. And it had the original version of AZ's "Your World Don't Stop." I love that record.

When I brought it to Puff he wanted to chill in the studio and have me give him a little direction for his part. From the beginning until the end—the whole 90 minutes of the tape—he stayed in the booth and talked whenever I would signal him, or whenever he felt it. He got in that zone. There was a part where I was like, *"Uptown in the motherfuckin' house, New York in the..."* whatever, whatever. And he'd continue because I left it open for him. So he knew how to play that.

BAD BOY MIXTAPE VOL. 3

The LOX's first introduction to the world as part of the Bad Boy family was on "You'll See," which featured a flip of EPMD's "You're A Customer" instrumental and a guest verse by labelmate The Notorious B.I.G. "You'll See" premiered as the first song on Side A of *Bad Boy Mixtape Volume 3*, and was never officially released to the public on a LOX single or album.

But rather than just feed mixtape DJs exclusive songs, he decided to take over the mixtape game in a way that no record label had done before . . .

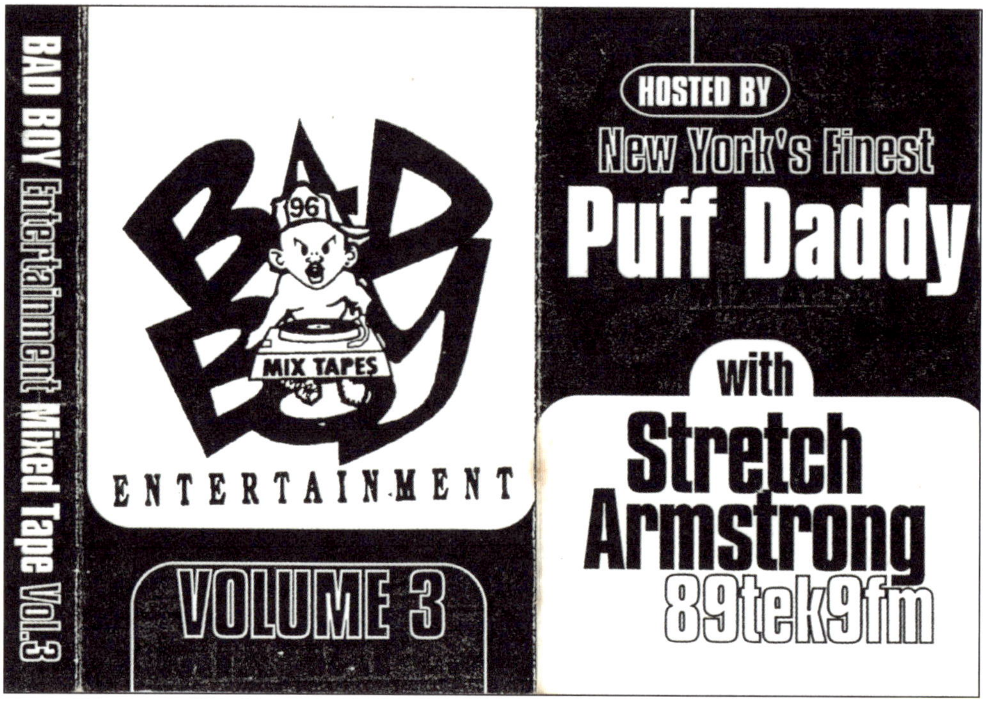

Also on Side A was "On The Real," an exclusive Marley Marl-produced street banger featuring Nas, Cormega, and Kamakazee. It was only fitting that Cormega's first feature after his release from jail was alongside Nas, his Queensbridge brethren who famously dropped his name on the *Illmatic* single "One Love." And though a solo remake of "On The Real" was released years later on an anniversary pressing of *Illmatic*, the original version with Cormega that appeared early on *Bad Boy Mixtape Volume 3* remains a mixtape classic.

Jadakiss: That was the glory years. Puff had us on a trial like, "I wanna sign y'all but I don't really know." He was really gonna sign us, but that was just back then how the CEOs and all of them were on it. So he was like, "I'ma throw y'all on this joint to see," like it was a tester. But just for him to submit us a beat like, "We want y'all to write to this," we were like, "Hell yeah."

Ruff Ryders were our managers back then. Dee brought us down to the studio, so that was like an experience for us, going to Puff's studio, because we were only used to being in our studios. We'd never really been in the big joints. So we came there, we chillin', and he gave us the beat like, "Take this beat and come back in a day or two and when you come back we're gonna lay it with you."

I guess he went to B.I.G. like, "I got these new kids, they're crazy," and he gave it to B.I.G. And you know B.I.G. was already with just getting on anything hot. But it was like, "Yo, our first joint is with B.I.G." But we didn't get to actually meet B.I.G. We didn't know him, he just did it off Puff's word. But it came out right.

We were walking around with copies of that in all pockets, like, "Yo pop this in, we got that 'You'll See.'" It was crazy. We had New York and Yonkers on smash when "You'll See" came out. We were on top of the world. Because it was all talk, "Yo we're going to have a meeting with Puff Daddy, we might be signing to Bad Boy." Yeah right. But then when you heard that, it was like "Yo!" So that was like a good introduction to the world.

Cormega: "On The Real" was the first song I did when I came home from jail. I came home and went to Marley's house, Marley scooped me up. Marley had a record deal for me before I went to jail, and a production deal. It was up to me. So as soon as I came home from jail, Marley was ready to go. I just came home at the time. I wasn't used to being in the studio. I wasn't comfortable. It took me a while to get acclimated to being in the studio again. But I was definitely anxious to get on a song. I thought it was a cool record, and people ended up enjoying it, and I was happy for that. That was my first real song that was out since I came home.

BAD BOY MIXTAPE VOL. 4

DJ S&S: Puff had Clue, Doo Wop, Stretch Armstrong, and then me for *Volume 4*. It was supposed to be called *And the Winner Is....* He had a whole plan for what he wanted to do, with the Farrakhan intro and the 2Pac diss. Being around Puff, you get to see what type of talent he really is. When it's time for him to execute, he executes.

Puff had that Biggie freestyle, and he gave it to me for the mixtape. He had that to make it hot. Puff ain't gonna put nothing out if it ain't hot.

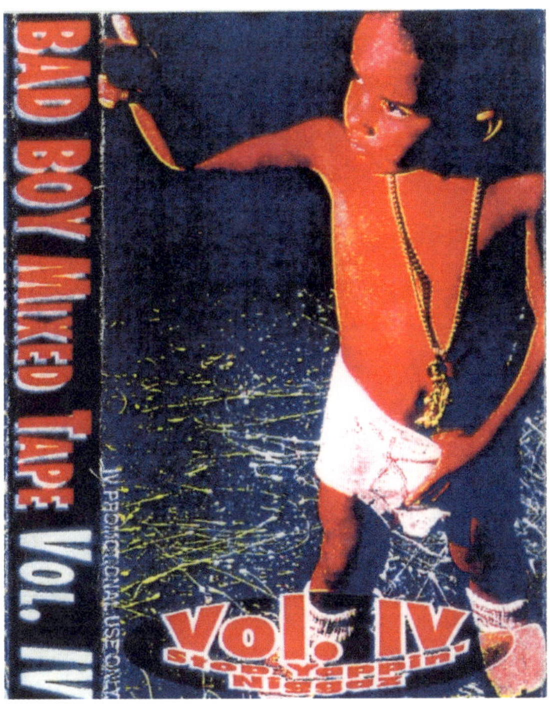

"We got some complaints that we talk too much on the mixtapes. We're not gonna talk too much on this one y'all."

–PUFF DADDY, *BAD BOY MIXTAPE VOL. 4*

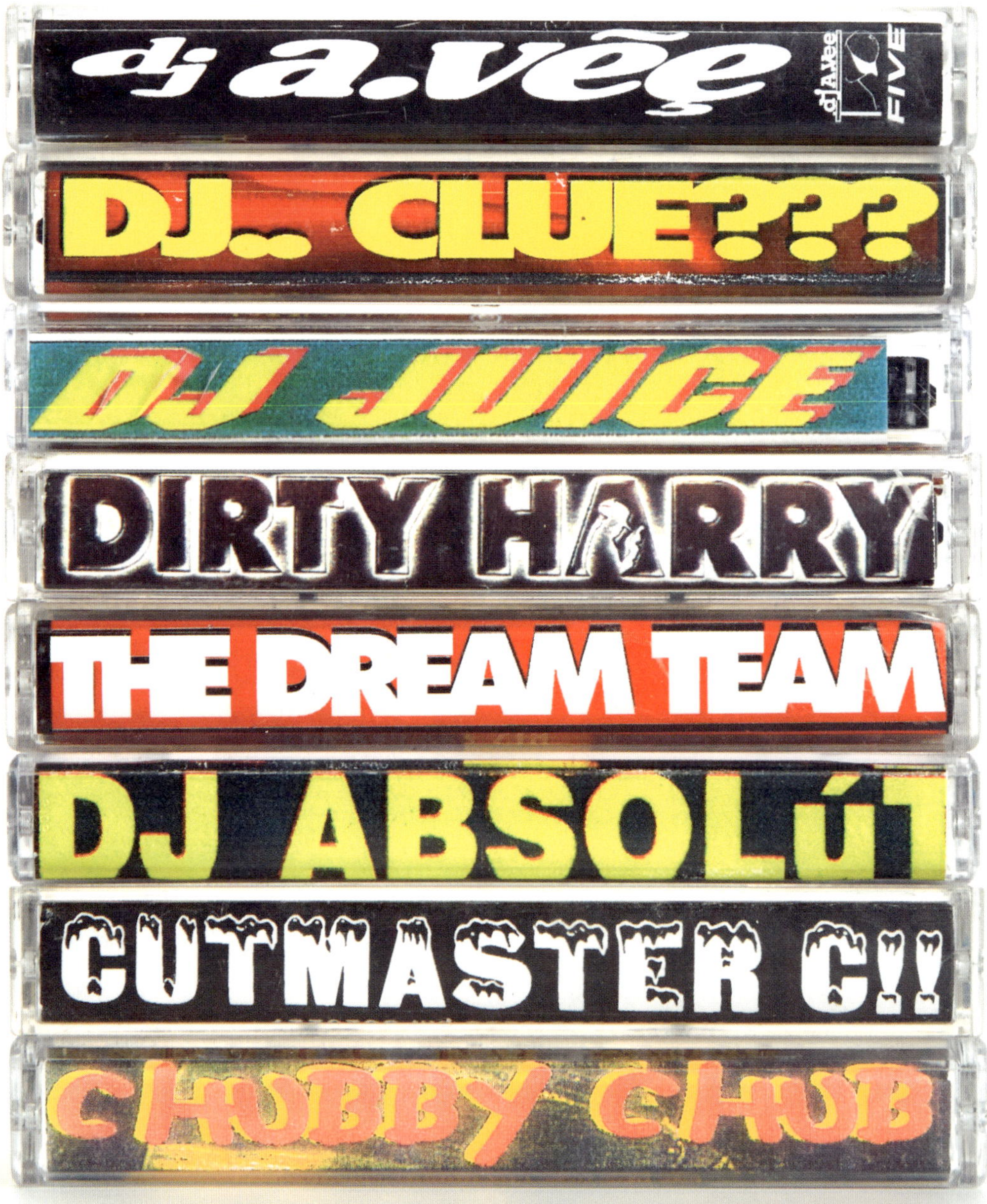
dj a.vēē
FIVE
DJ.. CLUE???
DJ JUICE
DIRTY HARRY
THE DREAM TEAM
DJ ABSOLúT
CUTMASTER C!!
CHUBBY CHUB

THE ARTWORK

In the beginning, mixtapes circulated with no cover art or tracklists. In many cases, the tapes didn't even have titles. There was just a date or a number on it, or the name of the club the DJ's set was recorded at.

Eventually, as mixtapes were sold in stores, that would evolve into stamps on the cassettes themselves with the DJ's name on it. And from there, hand-written lists or printouts of what songs were on the tape. And if the DJ wanted to get fancy, maybe there was a logo of some sort.

Then, in the mid-'90s, DJs started to step their marketing games up by teaming with graphic artists and illustrators to create covers for their mixtape releases. And once cover art became popularized and damn near essential in the mixtape world, to truly make an impact with a release, mixtape DJs needed THE ARTWORK.

NOJO

Pixels Poppin': Designing Mixtape Art for the Streets

There were only a couple graphic designers in New York that the elite mixtape DJs would seek out for cover art, and NOJO was one of them. Working with DJs like Envy, Dirty Harry, and Whoo Kid, NOJO would draw inspiration from pop culture to make eye-catching and clever mixtape covers, often working off nothing but the title of the tape given to him by the DJ.

GETTING STARTED

NOJO: My uncle opened up a clothing store, he was a professional graphic designer. I got into designing through him, and seeing the wonder of him being able to create something from nothing. So I had been playing around on the computer.

A friend of mine that used to come to the store said, "Hey, I got a DJ, you think you could do a cover for me?" I said, "Okay, why not?" It wasn't anything like I was planning to get into the industry. I was just doing a favor for a friend. I think I charged him a 40–a beer–to do the cover too.

After I did that cover, he came to me a couple weeks later and said, "Yo! Everybody's going crazy over this!" And I'm like, "Over what?" He said, "The cover! I got these people lined up. They want this and that." He was really excited about everything. It was uphill from there.

DJ Boogie Black was the first. I don't even remember the cover. I did a couple of them for him. Right after that, I started dealing with Whoo Kid and Envy.

GRAPHIC DESIGN TOOLS

In '93, '94, we were using Photoshop and QuarkXPress. There wasn't any Illustrator. They had Adobe freehand and Aldis paint, I believe that's what it was called. Back then, those were $1,500 to $2,000 programs. So if you weren't getting them on the black market, you were basically using whatever you could get your hands on.

A lot of these new designers don't know what Photoshop 1 was. You didn't have layers, you had to work in alpha channels. It was completely different. If you didn't know what you were doing, you couldn't do it.

I was self-taught. I never went to school for it. I watched my uncle's creative process, and that gave me the roadmap on how to create myself.

NETWORKING

It was a small community in Queens, everybody knew each other. I think Whoo Kid, Envy, and Clue all lived in the same two, three block areas. They said, "Who did this for you? Give me his contact info." That's where the networking started. I was working from home out of my bedroom with a little tiny computer, and they would come to my house.

Whoo Kid was like, "Put your number on the tape. You need your number on it." Because Whoo Kid from the very beginning was, other than Clue, the most business-minded DJ I had ever come across. This man had a vision.

THE BRIEF AND THE PROCESS

They'd come with a word. "This is the name of it, make it hot." That's been my career–"make it hot." No concept, no nothing. There were very few times a DJ would ever come with a concept. I would say 99% of the time I did it all on my own. They would just give me the name of the tape and I'd take it from there.

Two days later, they'd come to the house, look at it, and we'd make changes on the fly. Then I'd go to Kinko's. I'd print out a crisp master from their copy machine, then I'd go to the copy machine and start running off duplication. Then after the duplications, I'd take it to the cutter and cut out each tape, package them, wrap them up and deliver that to the DJ–and they'd pay me.

I really didn't make any money. I would make maybe $25, $50 at the most. They'd buy a $100 package, and $75 of that went into Kinko's pocket.

After that, some would want to do 200, 300, 500. But most DJs of the time didn't have that audience, they didn't have that reach. They weren't popular. Everybody was still hungry, they were hustling just to get a name. Even if they had a name, it didn't mean they were actually selling that amount of product.

At the very beginning, DJs weren't putting out high volume. Plus, if my memory serves me correct, DJs would print out 100 masters and then sell that to the stores to duplicate. So it was masters based. Then from there, I think Clue was actually the first one to make it a lucrative business by selling volume himself. I could be wrong on that, but that's what I recall hearing back at the time.

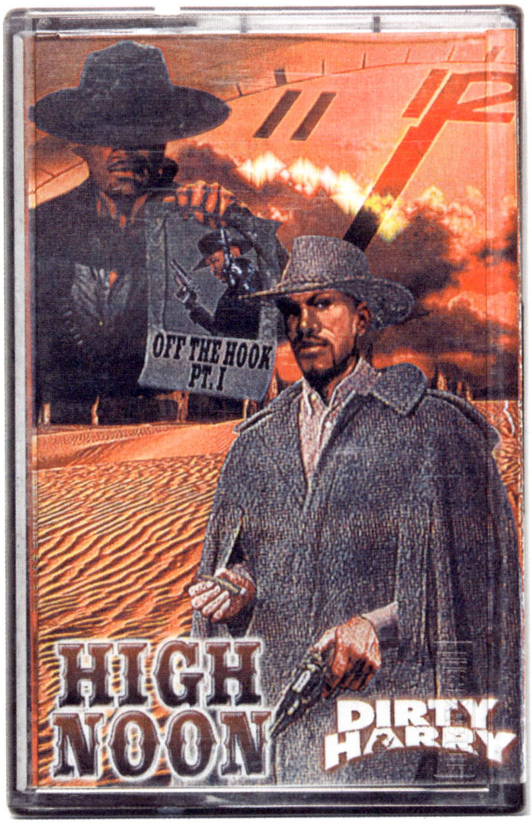

HIGH NOON

The face on the *High Noon* tape, that's my uncle. I think I scanned Clint Eastwood's body off a VHS cover. Then my uncle airbrushed his face on it. Then I just put it in the background and made that happen.

Dirty Harry is a cop, he's not a cowboy. The whole idea of Clint Eastwood translates from cowboys into him being a cop. It just worked and it fit.

STORE VISITS

Every time I'd go to work or to school, I'd pull up to see what DJs were dropping, just to research what's going on out there and who's doing what. You had to improve and redefine your skillset.

FREQUENCY

The frequency of drops was one tape a month or one tape every three weeks, and I didn't have a lot of clients back then. Then it got to the point where I might be doing two or three a day. If I did ten a week, that was my limit. It takes too much of a toll on you.

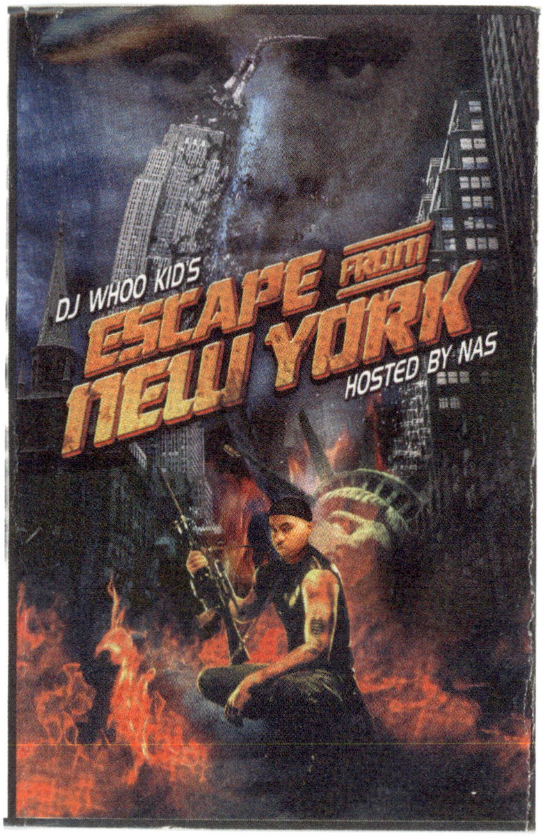

After ten, it starts to become a blur. I don't remember half of them anymore. Because you're just churning out a product, you're not doing the creative process to where you're putting out something that's even worth remembering.

COPYRIGHT ISSUES

The whole industry was bootleg. You stole, you did anything you possibly could to get the cover to look right. At the time, the labels didn't care about us. No professional company cared about us. So it didn't really matter what we did. We were street art.

Street art, at the time, even though it was making money for the DJs, companies didn't even look our way. They never looked down from their perches to care about what we were doing, so we could get away with doing anything–and we did.

IMPORTANCE OF DETAIL

I never wanted to be a street level designer. From the very beginning, I wanted to design billboards and movie posters. Have my work in Hollywood lights. That's always been my dream.

The attention to detail if you pull up an *Esquire* magazine, that's what I've always admired. I wanted to work for *Esquire* at one point. So pushing myself to think along the lines of that detail is what drove me to do a lot of the work I've done.

INSPIRATION

Every week, I would go and buy every magazine I possibly could. *VIBE* and *The Source* only dropped once a month, so I'm picking up *GQ*, obscure fashion magazines from Italy, this art magazine from over here, *Architectural Digest*. Just looking through magazines trying to come up with different ways of thinking, different ideas, because you never know what the client is going to ask you for.

ESCAPE FROM NEW YORK

Everybody was like, "You switched the head out." That's Nas's head on the body. Whoo Kid said, "It's called *Escape From New York*," and I didn't know what to do. I just took the movie poster, and I remember he was so mad at me for switching out the head. He said, "I don't like heads on bodies." He didn't appreciate that at all. That was the first time and the last time I did that.

NOJO: P-Type was three guys—Reg P, Mr. H, and Conrad. Reg P was the forefront designer. I believe he was the best of the three. He was one that I used to have personal conversations with.

At the time, Kinko's was ground zero for the industry. They worked at Kinko's, so they didn't pay—it was all profit for them. They would go to work and actually do the covers. I'd see them designing. I was watching Reg P do the DJ Clue cover with *The Source* magazine right there on the spot, trying to get the little dots out of the scan of Clue's picture like, "I can't get this. I gotta try this filter. I gotta try that filter." It was very interesting.

I have a profound respect for what P-Type did and who they were. They were always cool, never disrespectful. Even though, at the time, it was either P-Type or NOJO. We were the only two that people were pursuing. I never really felt it was a competition, personally. Every time I saw them it was, "Hey what's going on, how you doing? Oh, this looks good." Reg actually helped me, like, "If you change to green it might print a little better." And he wouldn't charge me for it.

Without P-Type, I wouldn't have done it. If they didn't start it, then nobody would have ever come to me and said, "Hey, could you do a cover as well?"

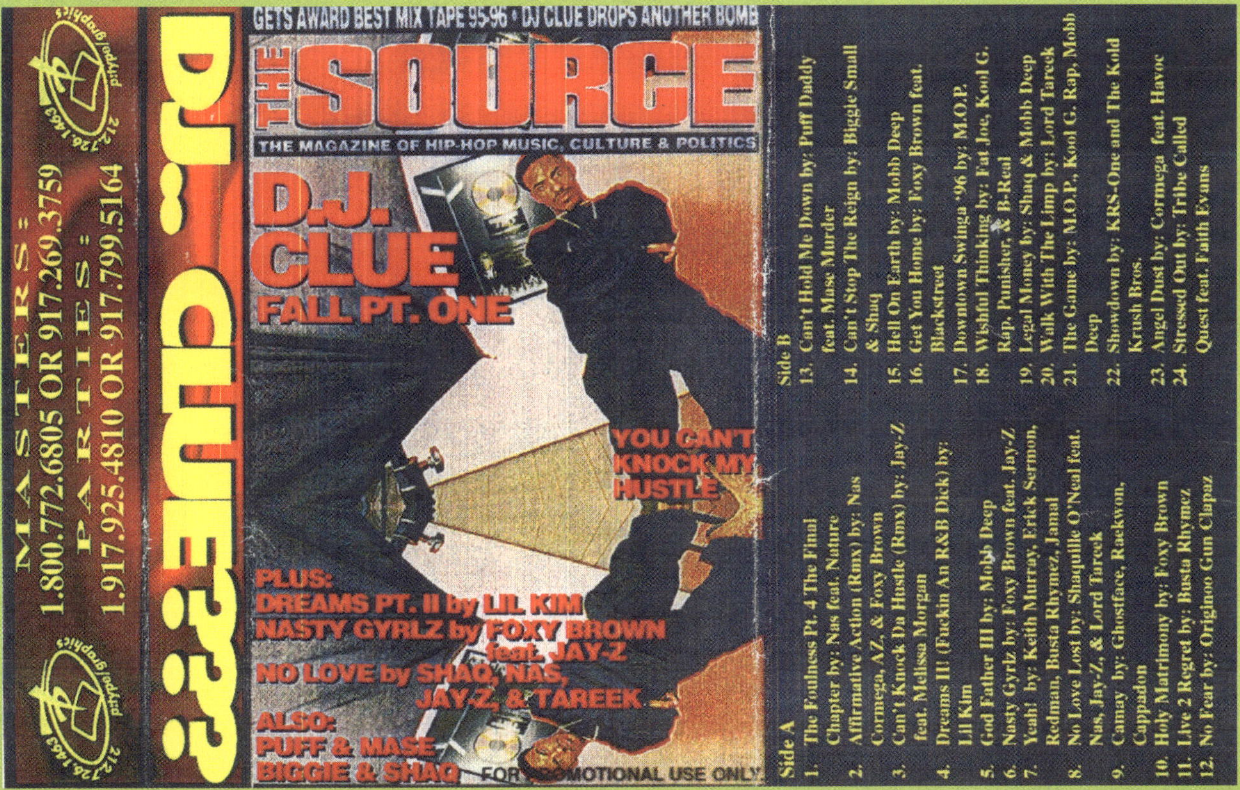

DONTAY TC5

Gift of Graf: Bringing Street Art to Mixtape Covers

Street artist and graffiti guru Dontay TC5 is the man responsible for drawing and designing covers for some of the most memorable Tony Touch mixtapes ever. Using original hand styles and characters inspired by what was happening in hip hop and street culture at the time, Dontay TC5 designed covers for the three-volume *Power Cypha 50 MCs* series, the infamous *5 Deadly Venoms of Brooklyn* tape, and so many more.

GETTING STARTED

Dontay TC5: I had an article in *VIBE* magazine–I was doing characters with Bonz Malone. I think that stuff trickled over to Tony Touch because he was part of the Rock Steady crew, and Rock Steady was close with TC5. Everybody used to hang out at Rock Steady Park Uptown.

Tony Touch reached out to do characters for his mixtape. One of the first mixtapes was *50 MCs* and I think it was a hit. He was just like, "Yo, I need you to do *all* the covers." I must have done maybe 20, 30 covers for him.

PROCESS

He'd hit me on a Thursday, and I'd have it by that Sunday. Like two days. Because sometimes when you're an artist, certain things have to inspire you to be motivated. You could sit down and just draw, but I'm a weirdo. I like to sit down and let it go in my head for a while and then I'll be like, "Okay, now I'll draw it." Visualize it in the mind, and then I put it on paper.

OTHER ILLUSTRATION WORK

I was doing *VIBE* when I was doing this. I did a few issues of *The Source*. I did a couple of Funkadelic covers for Polygram Records. Numerous cartoons for hospitals. A lot of stuff. This is kind of what launched my career.

TONY TOUCH *BUBBLIN'* COVER

This is where I started switching up my style a little bit, because I was a huge fan of Gen 13 comic books. So I was reflecting on my shading and drawing skills, that was the inspiration. This shit crazy right here. This was all hand drawn except for the tiles in the back.

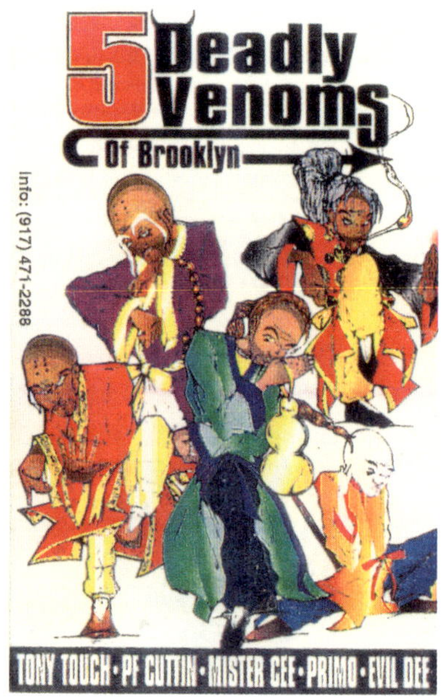

Dontay TC5: This blew up crazy right here. This was inspired from a Triple Five Soul shirt. I'm a kung fu fanatic. That's the end all be all for me. When he said that he was going to do the *Five Deadly Venoms*, I said, "Don't even say any more." Because that was one of my favorite movies at the time.

These characters were all drawn on separate papers. Me and my main hardcore Shareef, we went through it. I was just like, "Yo, I need the snake, the lizard, and all of that." I was just thinking about the characters, I wasn't even thinking about the DJs. There's some similarities—Evil Dee had dreads, so I did him with the long hair. Premier was always bald-headed.

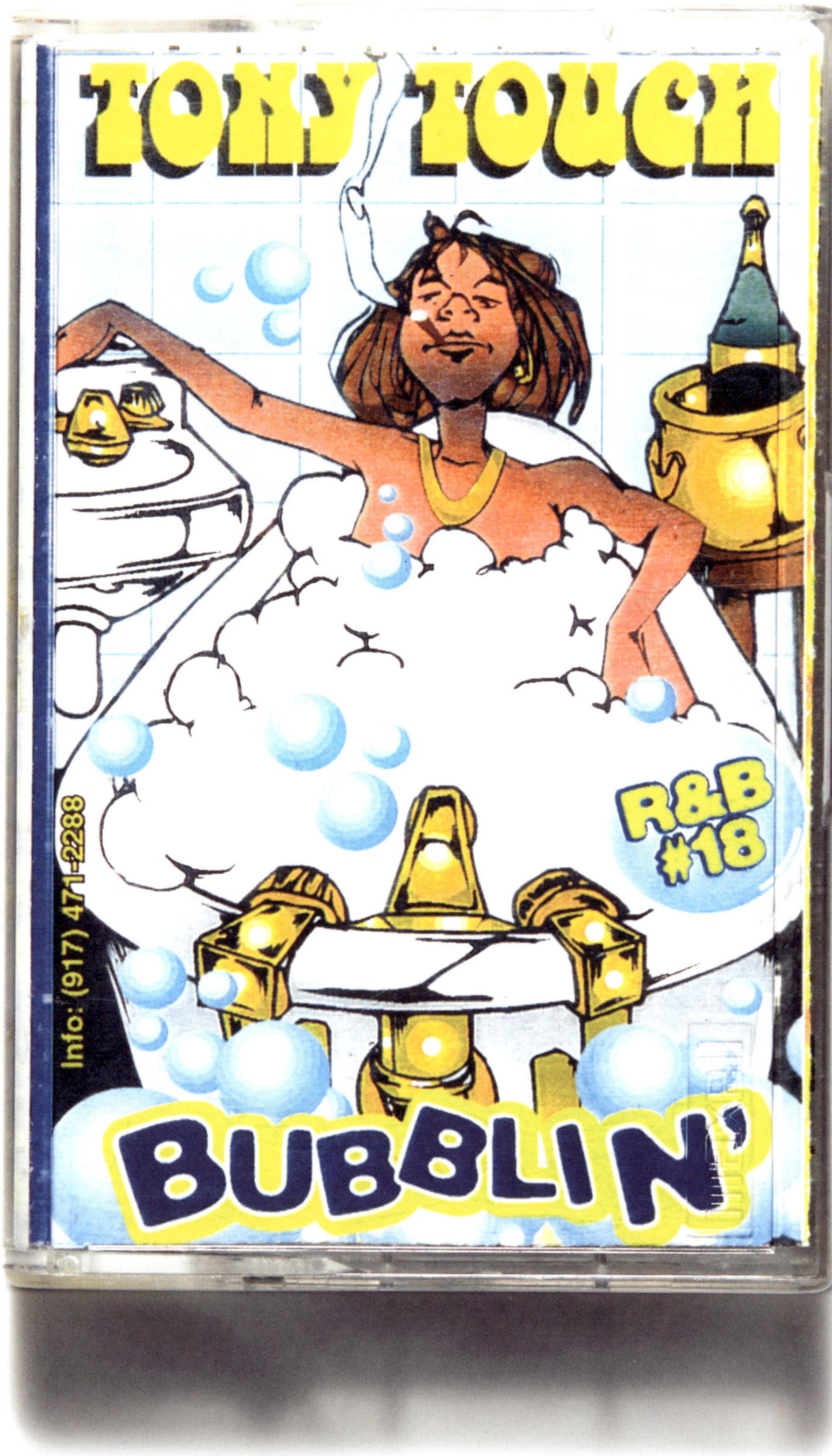
TONY TOUCH
Info: (917) 471-2288
R&B
#18
BUBBLIN'

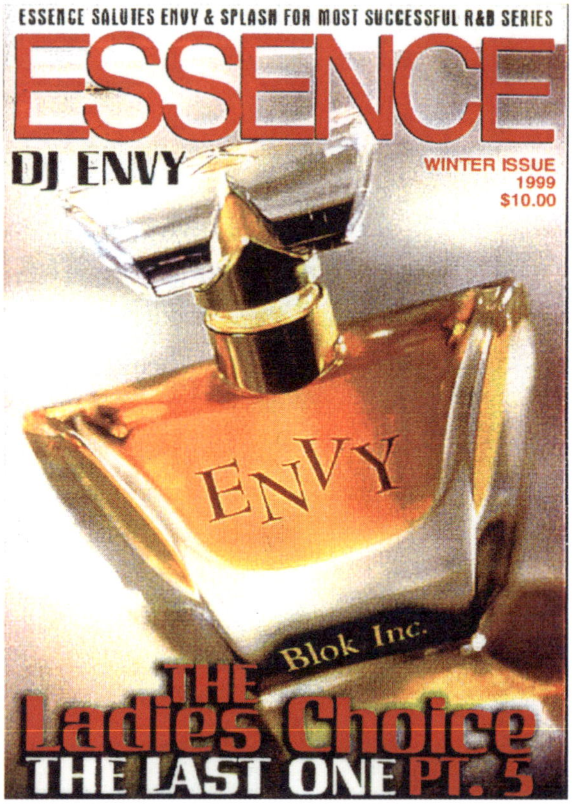
ESSENCE SALUTES ENVY & SPLASH FOR MOST SUCCESSFUL R&B SERIES
ESSENCE
DJ ENVY
WINTER ISSUE
1999
$10.00
ENVY
Blok Inc.
THE
Ladies Choice
THE LAST ONE PT. 5

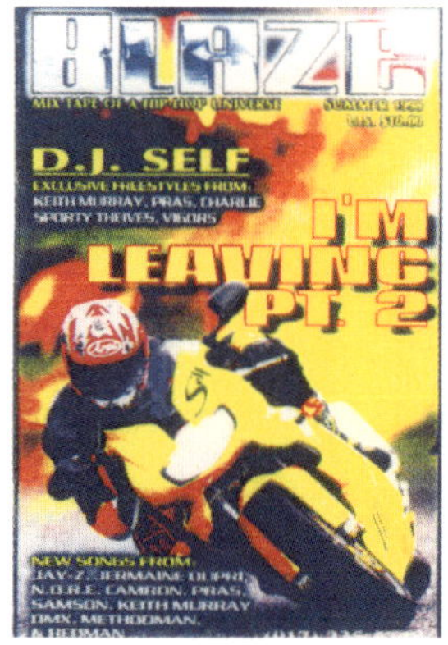
D.J. SELF
I'M
LEAVING
PT. 2

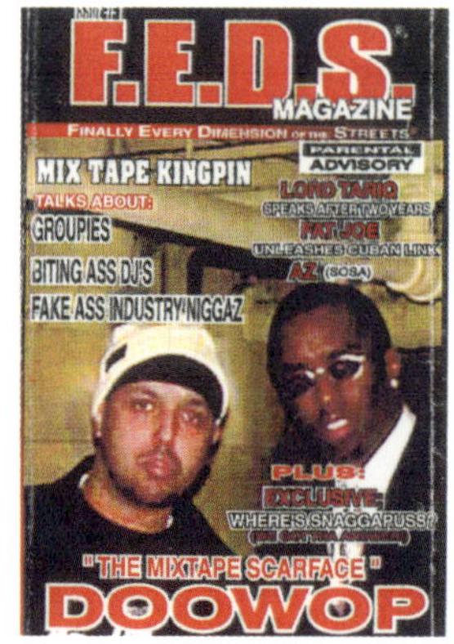
F.E.D.S.
MAGAZINE
MIX TAPE KINGPIN
TALKS ABOUT:
GROUPIES
BITING ASS DJ'S
FAKE ASS INDUSTRY NIGGAZ
"THE MIXTAPE SCARFACE"
DOOWOP

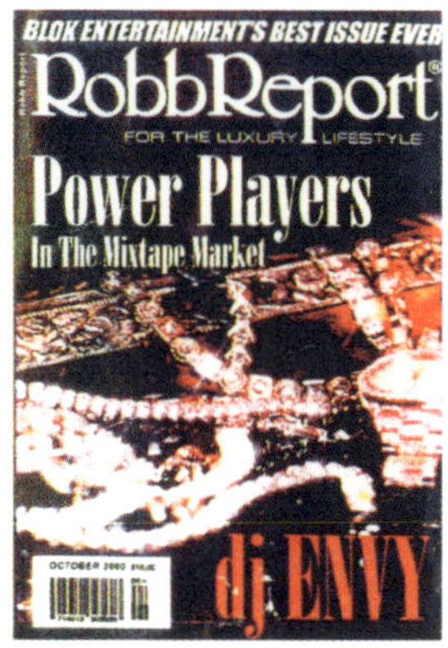
BLOK ENTERTAINMENT'S BEST ISSUE EVER
RobbReport
FOR THE LUXURY LIFESTYLE
Power Players
In The Mixtape Market
dj ENVY

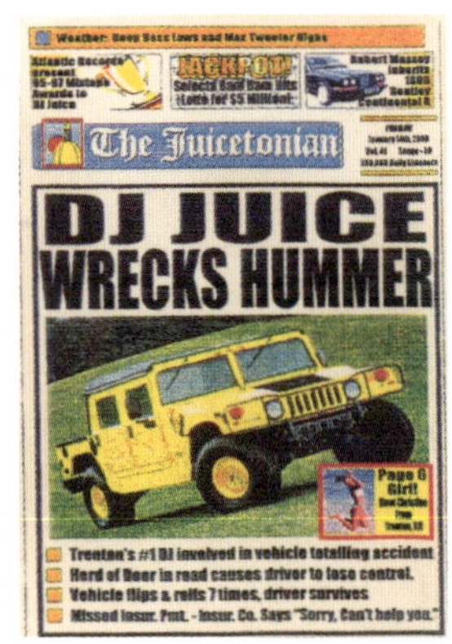
The Juicetonian
DJ JUICE
WRECKS HUMMER

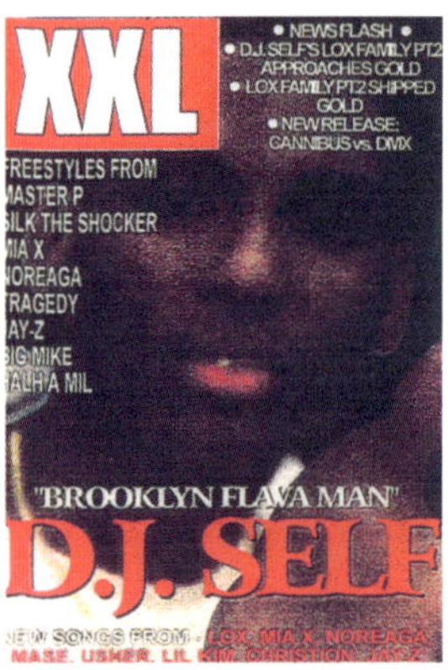
XXL
• NEWS FLASH •
FREESTYLES FROM
"BROOKLYN FLAVA MAN"
D.J. SELF

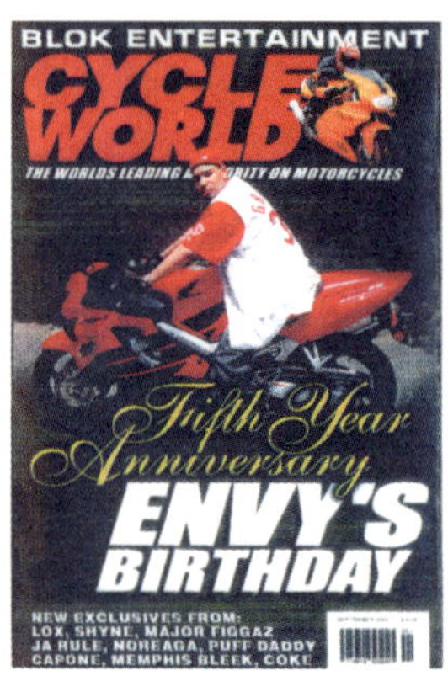
BLOK ENTERTAINMENT
CYCLE WORLD
Fifth Year
Anniversary
ENVY'S
BIRTHDAY
NEW EXCLUSIVES FROM:
LOX, SHYNE, MAJOR FIGGAZ
JA RULE, NOREAGA, PUFF DADDY
CAPONE, MEMPHIS BLEEK, COKE

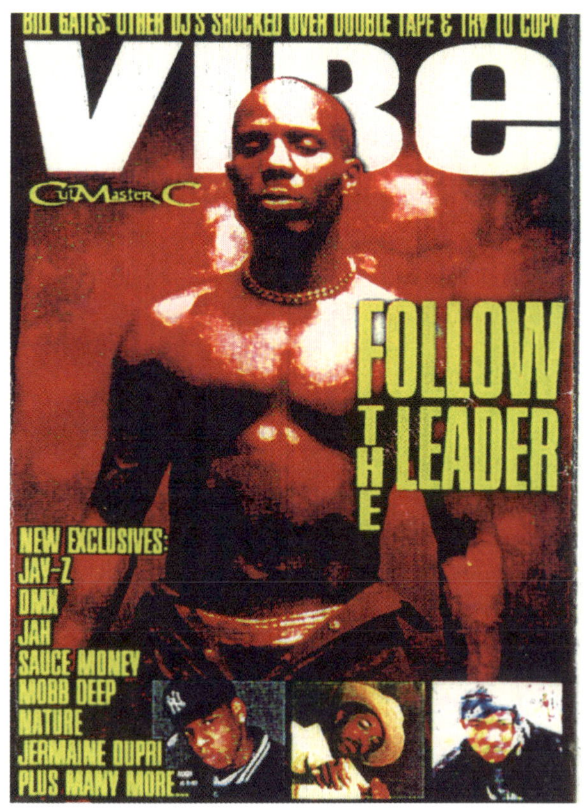
VIBE
CutMaster C
FOLLOW
THE
LEADER
NEW EXCLUSIVES:
JAY-Z
DMX
JAH
SAUCE MONEY
MOBB DEEP
NATURE
JERMAINE DUPRI
PLUS MANY MORE...

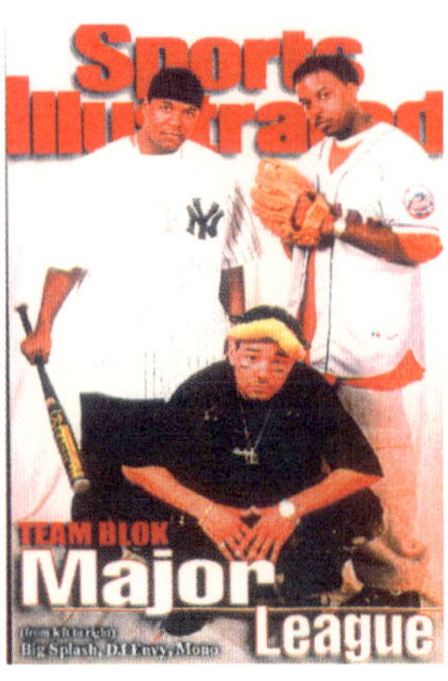
TEAM BLOK
Major
League

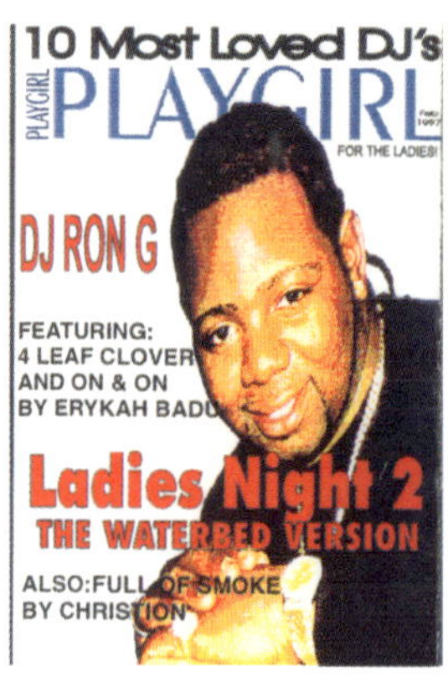
10 Most Loved DJ's
PLAYGIRL
FOR THE LADIES!
DJ RON G
FEATURING:
4 LEAF CLOVER
AND ON & ON
Ladies Night 2
THE WATERBED VERSION

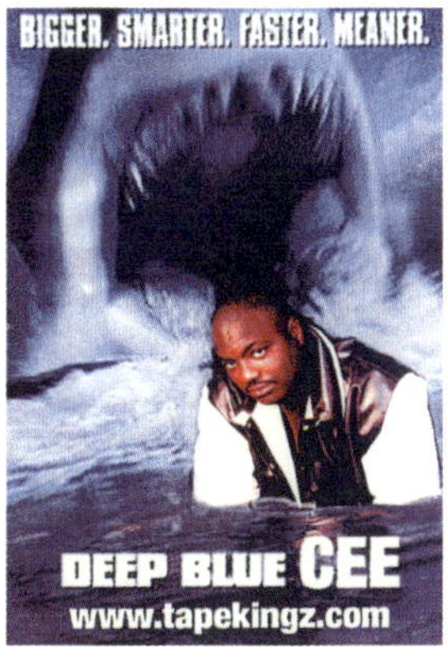
BIGGER, SMARTER, FASTER, MEANER.
DEEP BLUE CEE
www.tapekingz.com

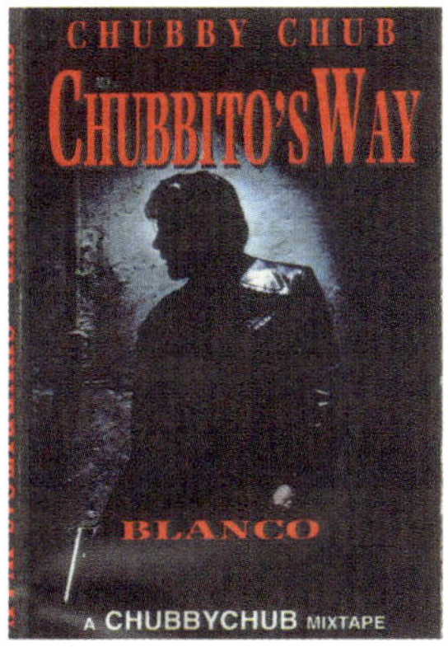
CHUBBY CHUB
CHUBBITO'S WAY
BLANCO
A CHUBBYCHUB MIXTAPE

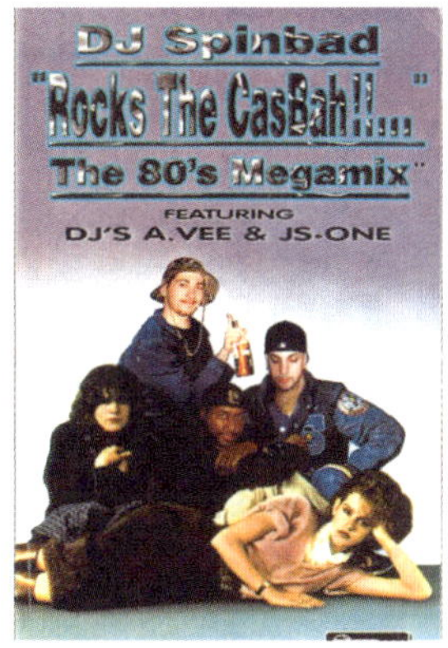
DJ Spinbad
"Rocks The CasBah!!..."
The 80's Megamix"
FEATURING
DJ'S A.VEE & JS-ONE

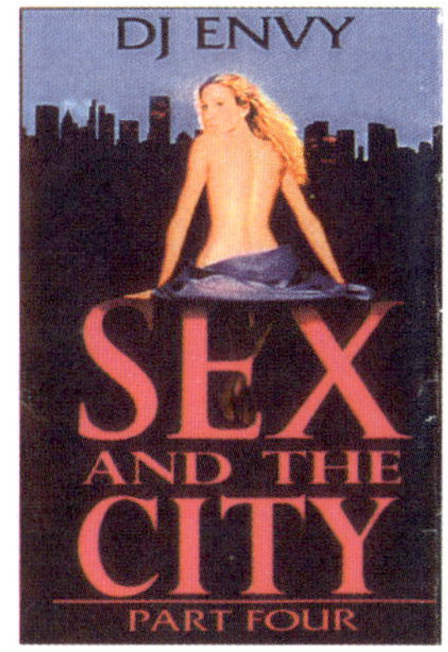
DJ ENVY
SEX
AND THE
CITY
PART FOUR

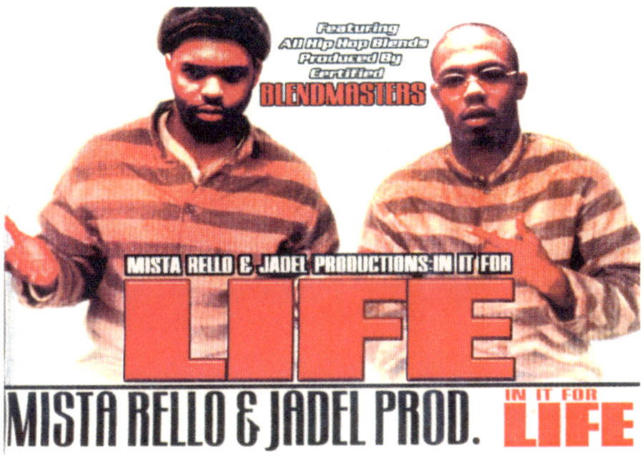
Featuring
All Hip Hop Blends
Produced By
Certified
BLENDMASTERS
MISTA RELLO & JADEL PRODUCTIONS: IN IT FOR
LIFE
MISTA RELLO & JADEL PROD.
IN IT FOR
LIFE

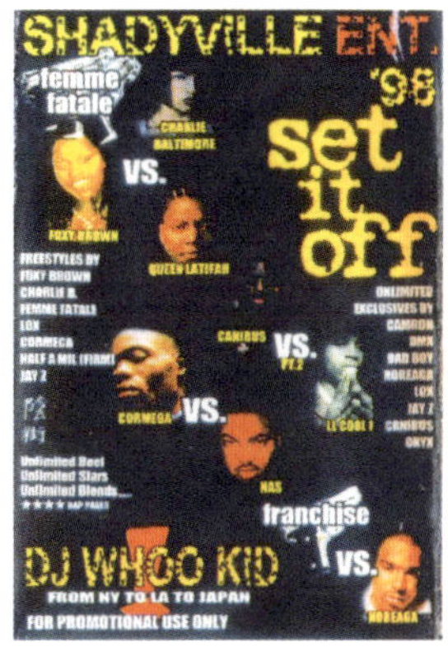
SHADYVILLE ENT.
femme fatale
'98
set it off
vs.
vs.
vs.
franchise
vs.
DJ WHOO KID
FROM NY TO LA TO JAPAN
FOR PROMOTIONAL USE ONLY

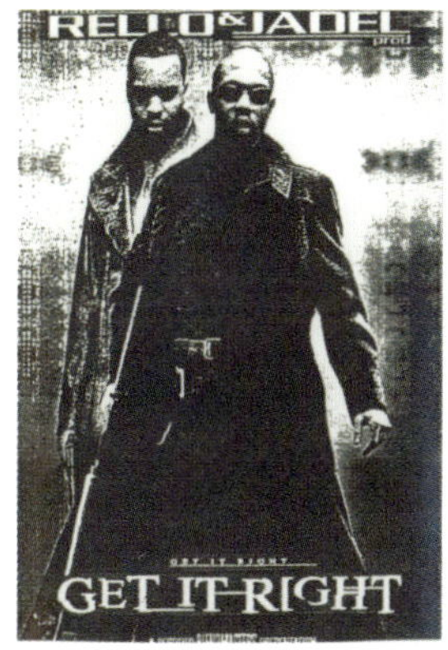
RELLO & JADEL
GET IT RIGHT

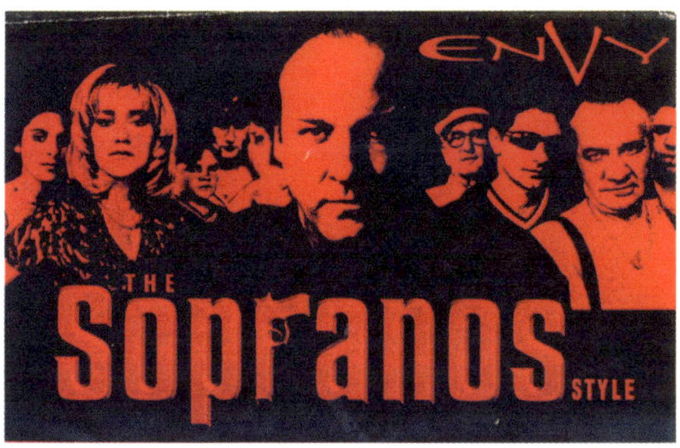
ENVY
THE
Sopranos
STYLE

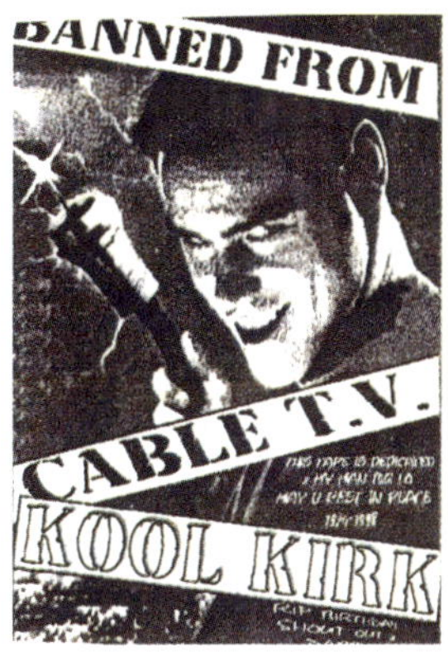
BANNED FROM
CABLE T.V.
KOOL KIRK

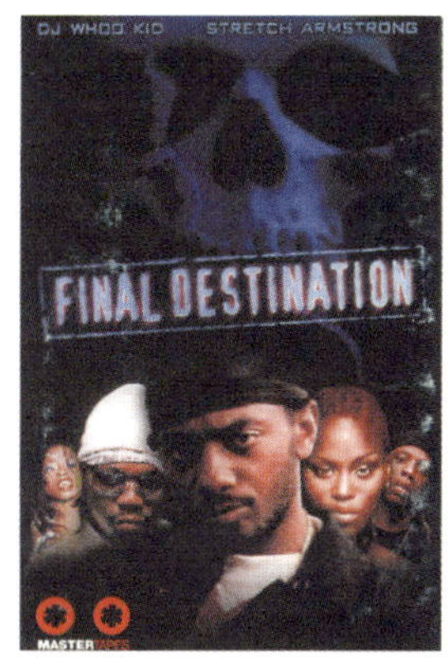
DJ WHOO KID
STRETCH ARMSTRONG
FINAL DESTINATION
MASTER

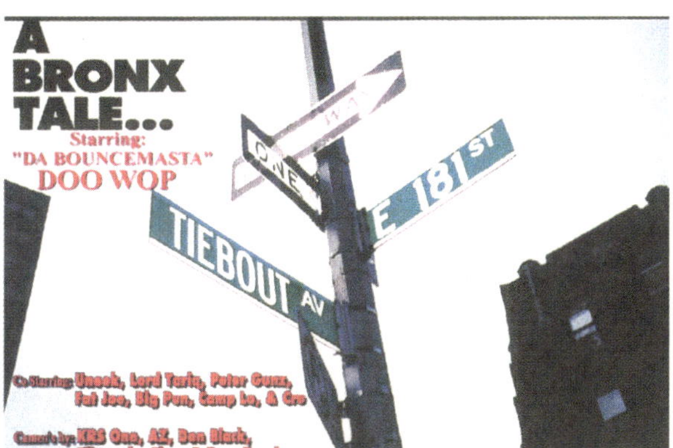
A
BRONX
TALE...
Starring:
"DA BOUNCEMASTA"
DOO WOP
ONE WAY
E 181 ST
TIEBOUT AV

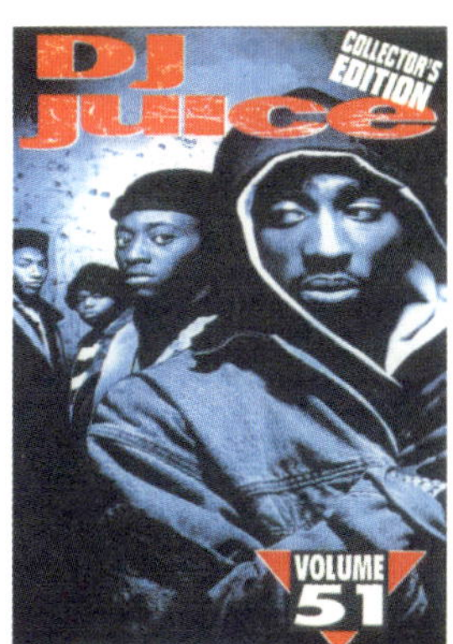
DJ
Juice
COLLECTOR'S EDITION
VOLUME
51
THE MOVIE SOUNDTRACK

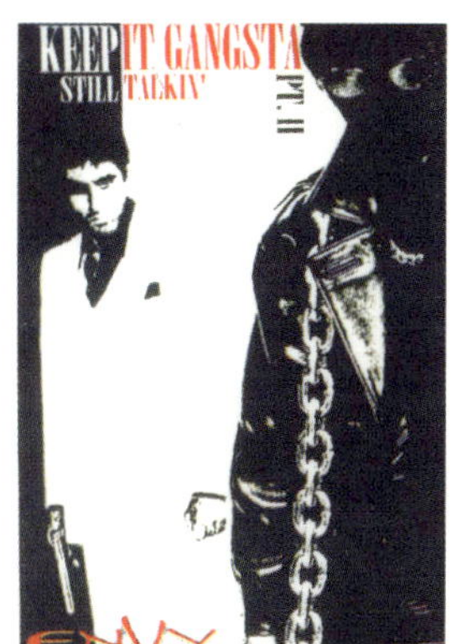
KEEP IT GANGSTA
STILL TALKIN'
PT. II
ENVY

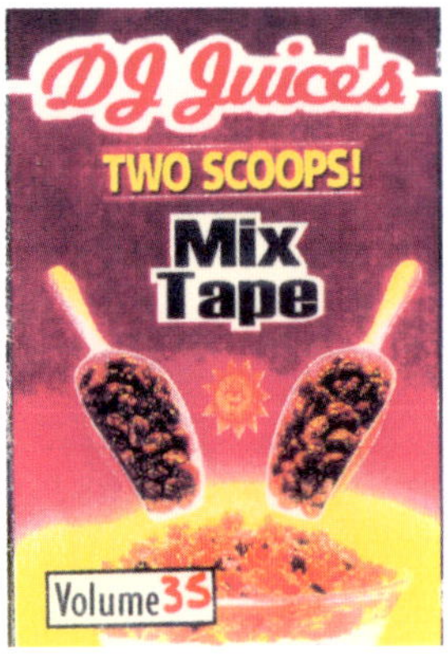
DJ Juice's
TWO SCOOPS!
Mix Tape
Volume 35

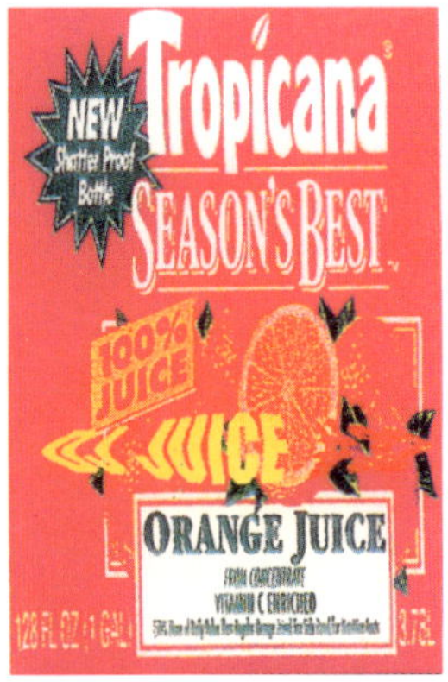
NEW Shatter Proof Bottle
Tropicana
SEASON'S BEST
100% JUICE
JUICE
ORANGE JUICE

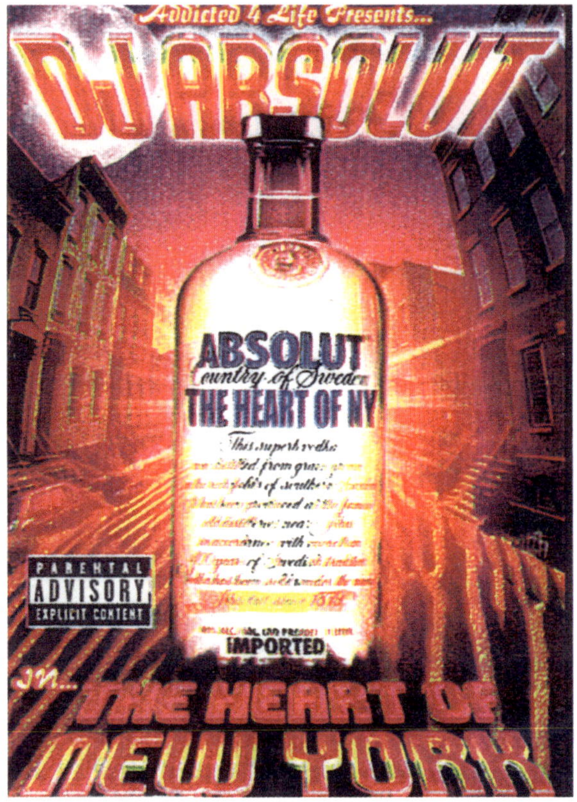
Addicted 4 Life Presents...
DJ ABSOLUT
ABSOLUT
Country of Sweden
THE HEART OF NY
PARENTAL ADVISORY
EXPLICIT CONTENT
IMPORTED
In... THE HEART OF NEW YORK

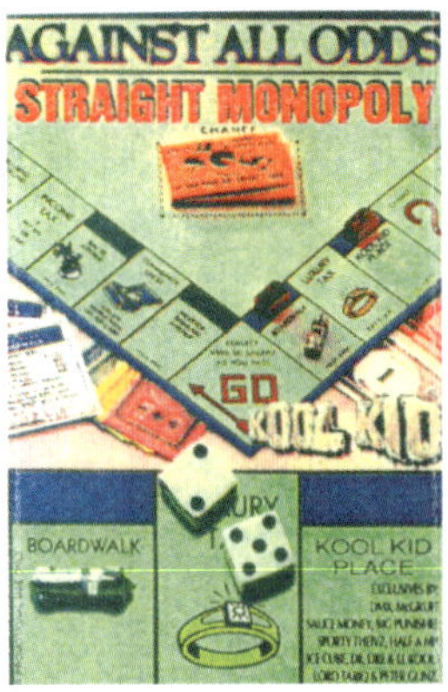
AGAINST ALL ODDS
STRAIGHT MONOPOLY
GO
KOOL KID
BOARDWALK
KOOL KID PLACE

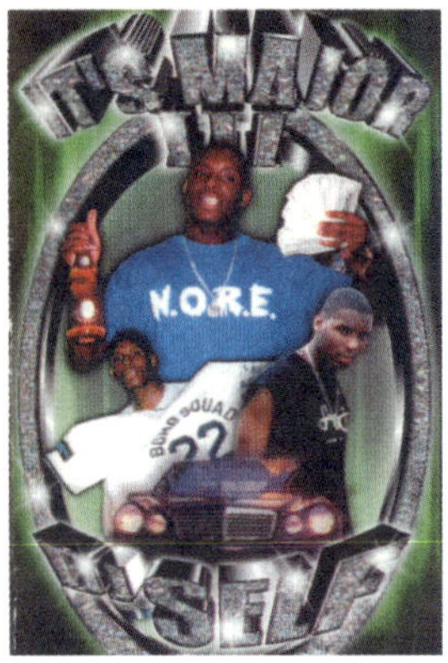
N.O.R.E.

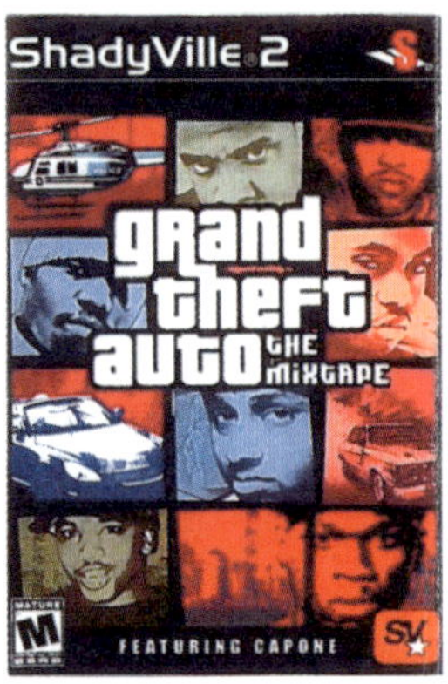
ShadyVille 2
grand theft auto the mixtape
FEATURING CAPONE

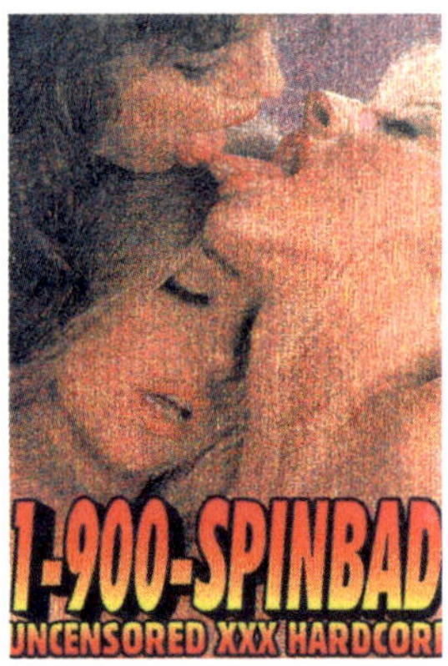
1-900-SPINBAD
UNCENSORED XXX HARDCOR

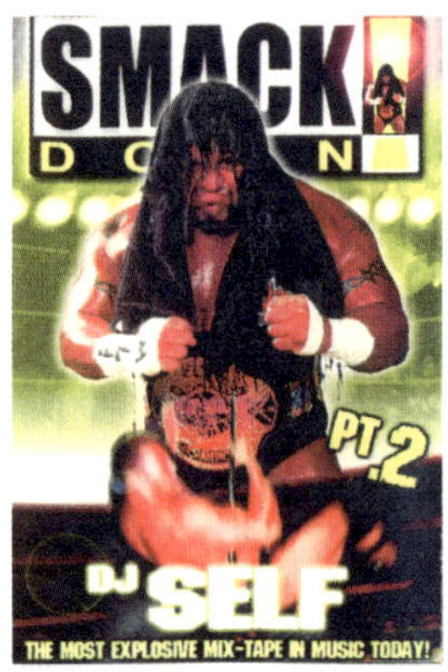
SMACK
PT.2
DJ SELF
THE MOST EXPLOSIVE MIX-TAPE IN MUSIC TODAY!

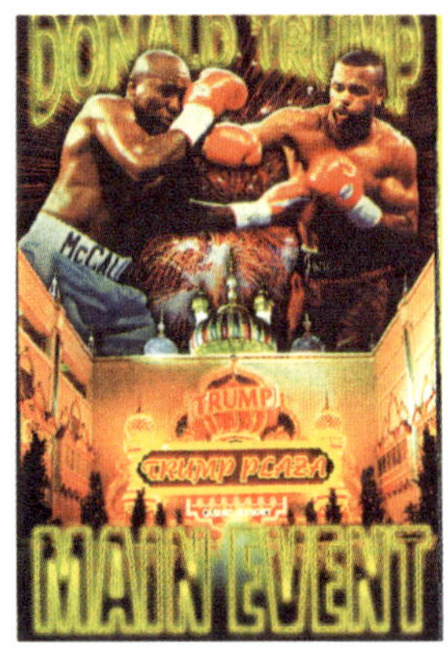
TRUMP
TRUMP PLAZA
MAIN EVENT

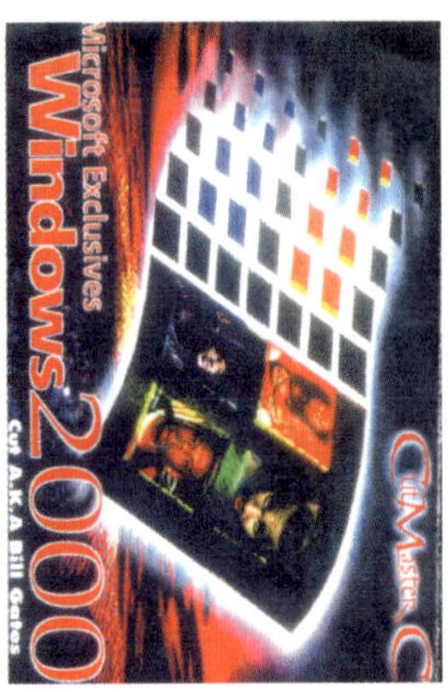
Microsoft Exclusives
Windows 2000

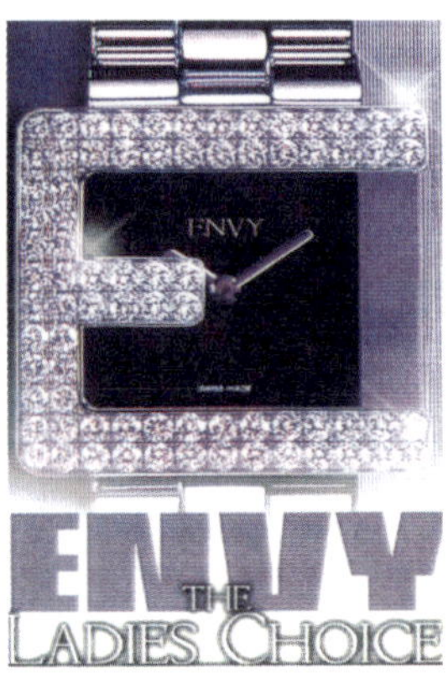
ENVY
ENVY
THE
LADIES CHOICE

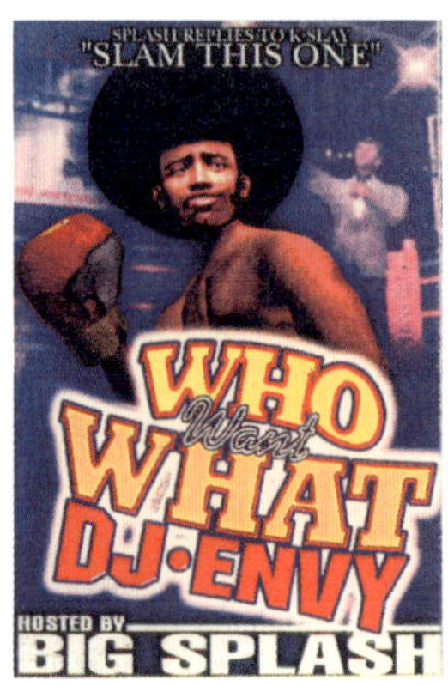
SPLASH REPLIES TO K-SLAY
"SLAM THIS ONE"
WHO Want WHAT
DJ-ENVY
HOSTED BY
BIG SPLASH

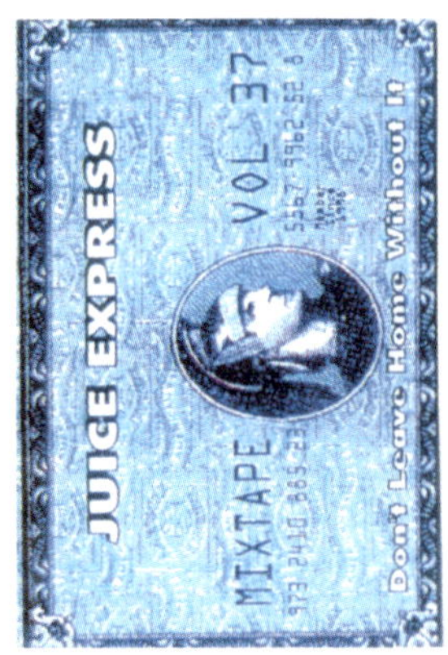
JUICE EXPRESS
MIXTAPE
VOL 37
Don't Leave Home Without It

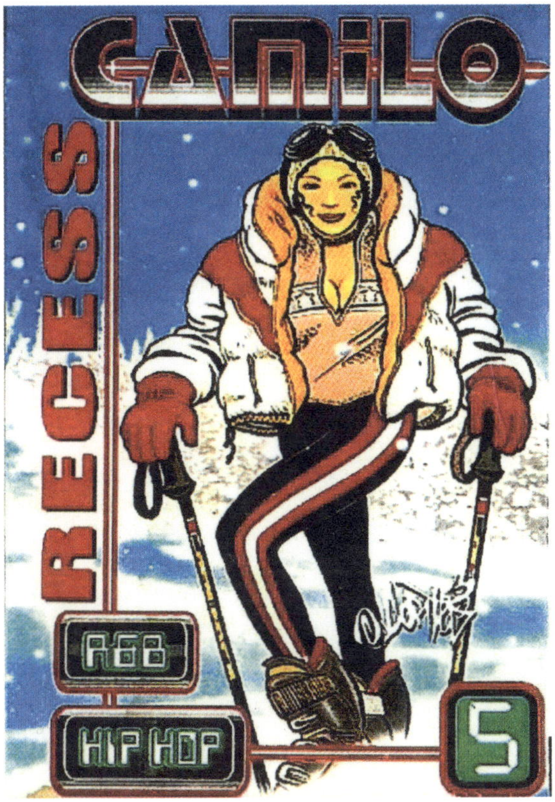
CAMILO
RECESS
R&B
HIP HOP
5

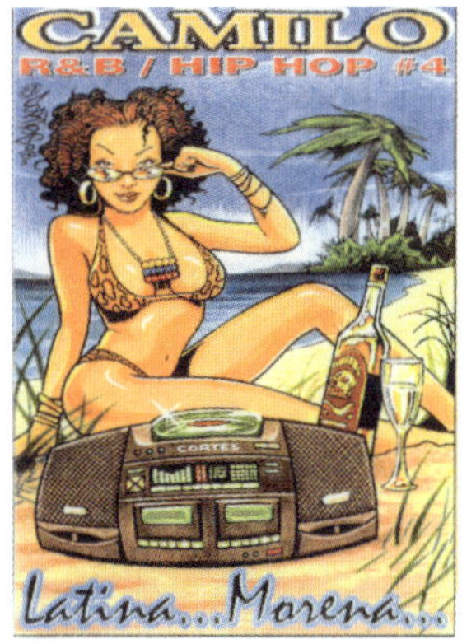
CAMILO
R&B / HIP HOP #4
Latina...Morena...

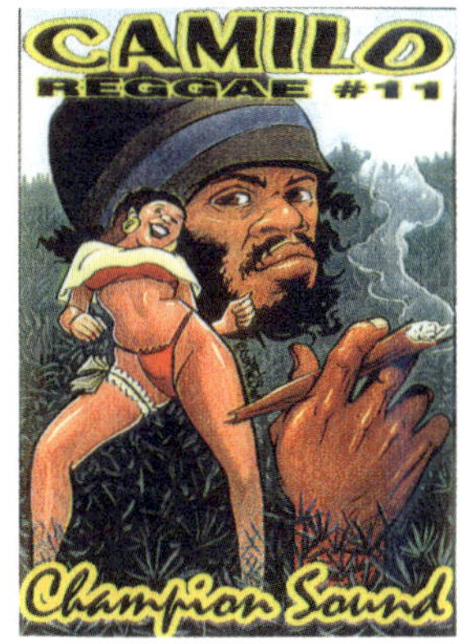
CAMILO
REGGAE #11
Champion Sound

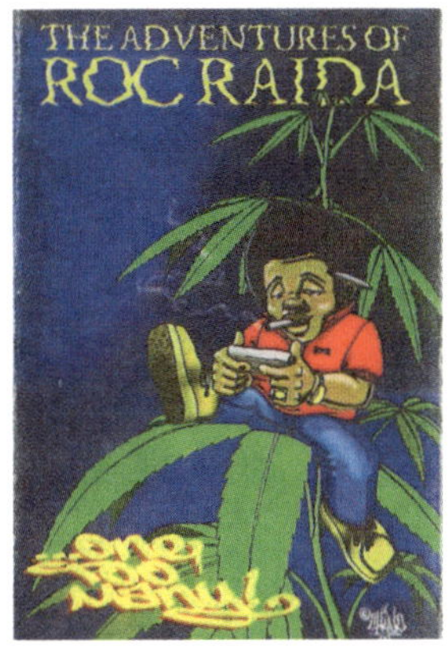
THE ADVENTURES OF
ROC RAIDA

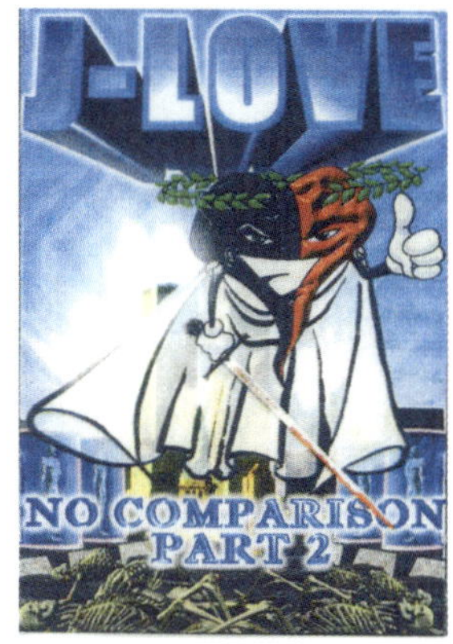
J-LOVE
NO COMPARISON
PART 2

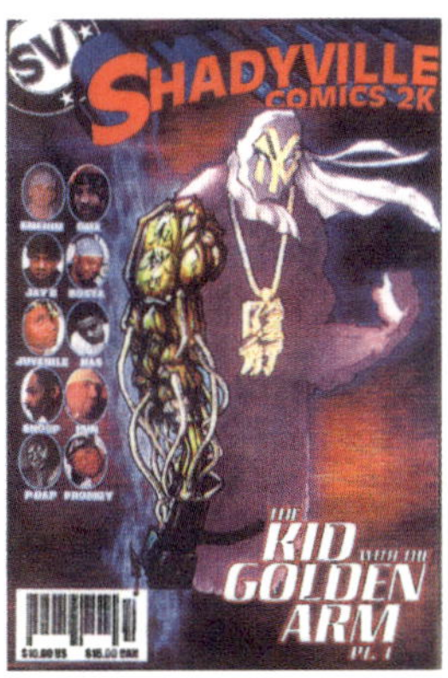
SV
SHADYVILLE
COMICS 2K
THE KID WITH THE GOLDEN ARM

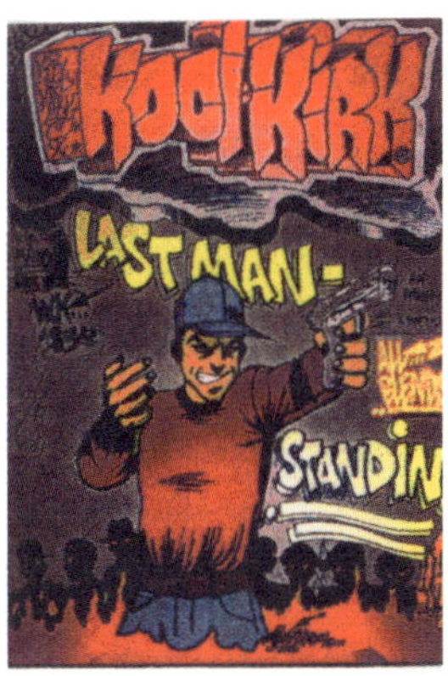
Kool Kirk
LAST MAN-
STANDIN

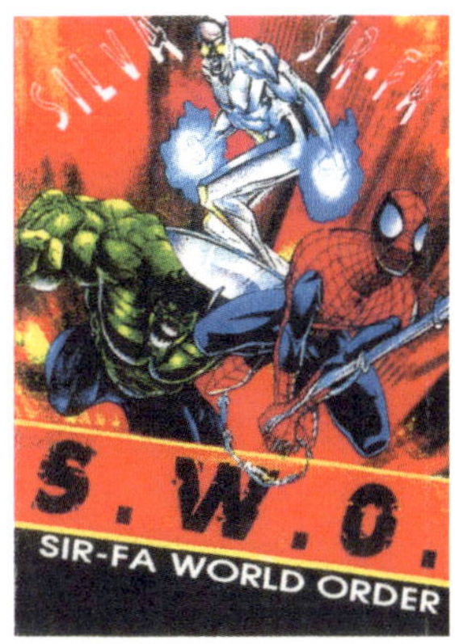
S.W.O.
SIR-FA WORLD ORDER

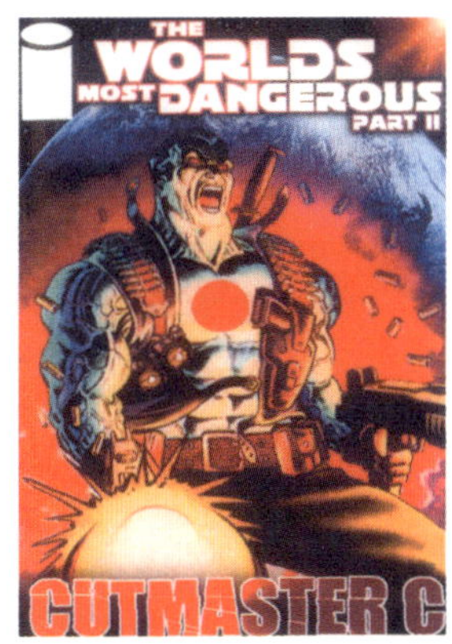
THE WORLDS MOST DANGEROUS PART II
CUTMASTER C

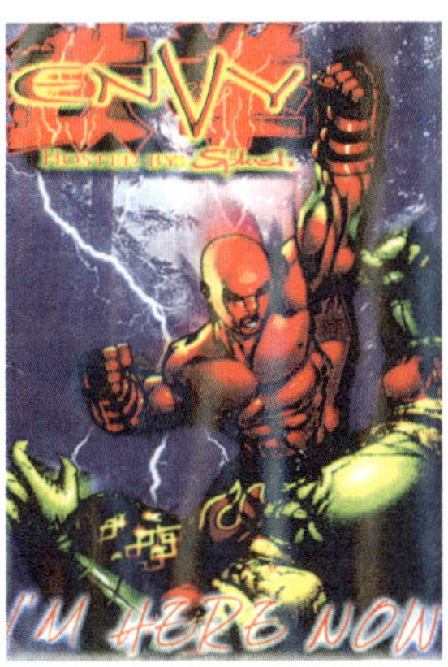
ENVY
I'M HERE NOW

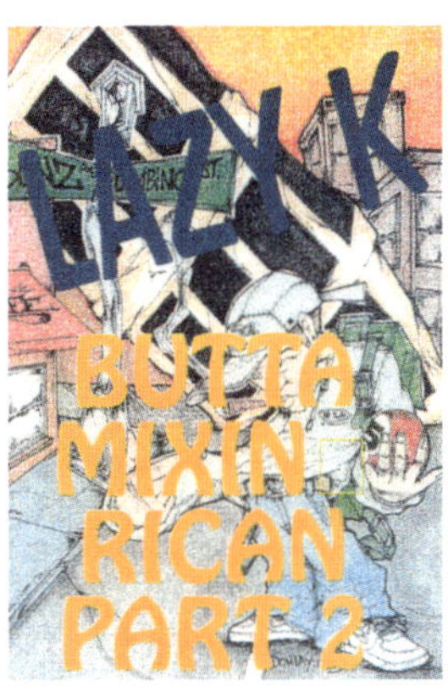
LAZY K
BUTTA MIXIN RICAN PART 2

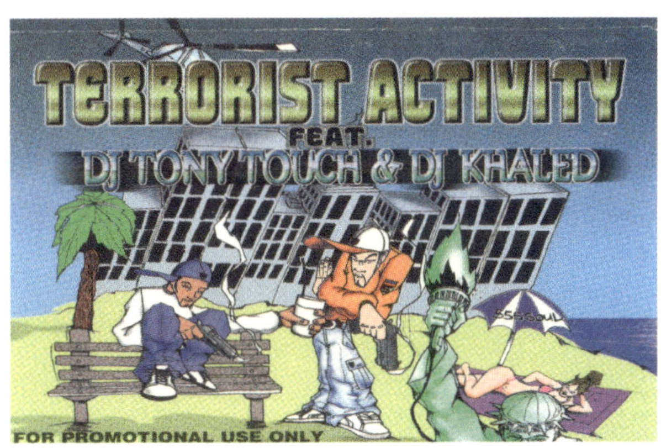
TERRORIST ACTIVITY
FEAT.
DJ TONY TOUCH & DJ KHALED
FOR PROMOTIONAL USE ONLY

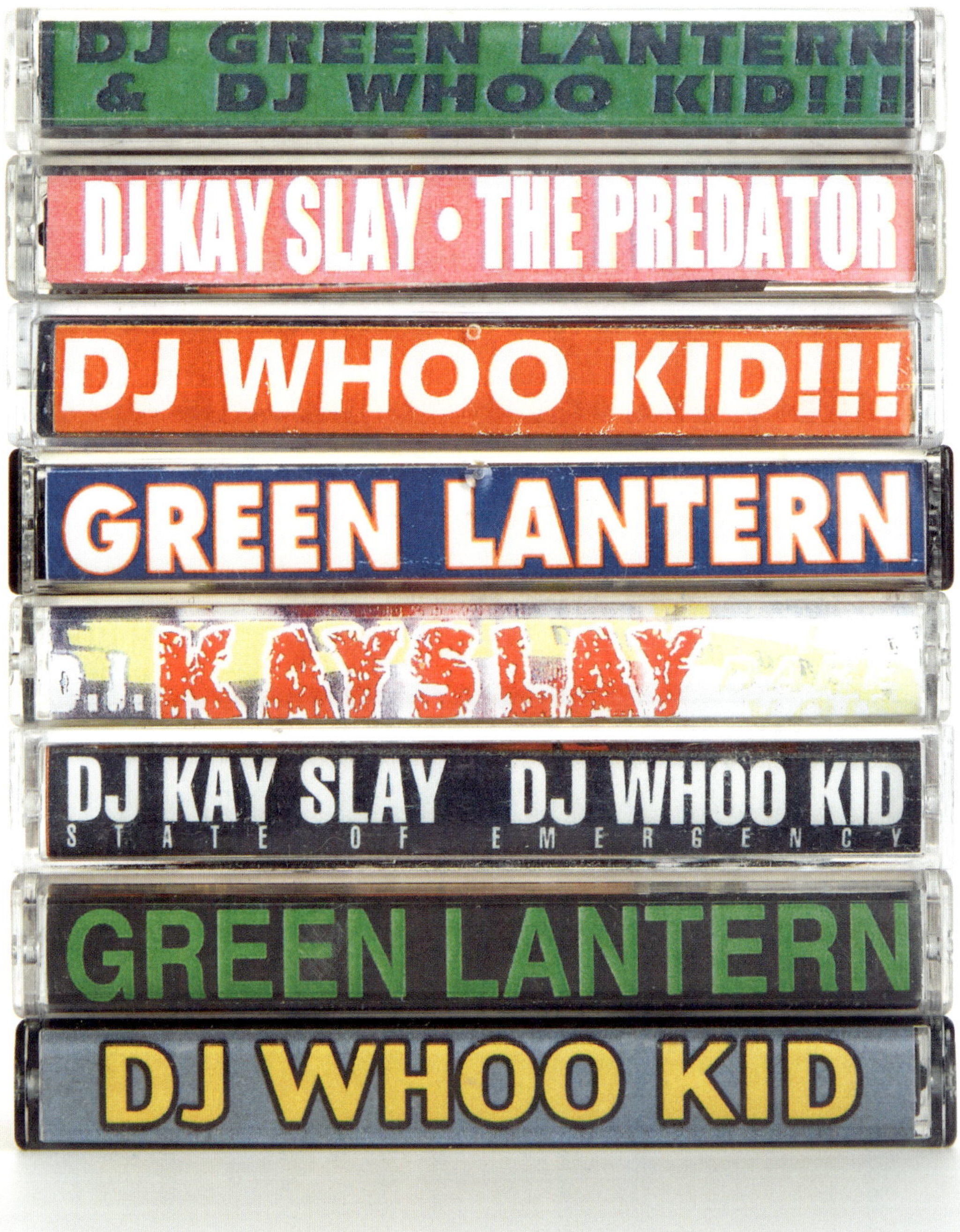
DJ GREEN LANTERN
& DJ WHOO KID!!!
DJ KAY SLAY • THE PREDATOR
DJ WHOO KID!!!
GREEN LANTERN
D.J. KAYSLAY
DJ KAY SLAY DJ WHOO KID
STATE OF EMERGENCY
GREEN LANTERN
DJ WHOO KID

THE TRENDSETTERS

As the turn of the century approached, a new class of mixtape DJs began to make their presence felt. Sure, guys like DJ Clue were still crushing the game, but this new DJ crop was finding ways to push the music and culture of mixtapes forward into the 2000s. Using their personalities, DJ skills, creativity, business sensibility, and industry relationships in progressive ways, the mixtape game was given more life thanks to THE TRENDSETTERS.

DJ KAY SLAY

Harlem's Finest: The Legendary Drama King Lives On

Seven months to the day before he passed away, DJ Kay Slay shared his mixtape memories exclusively for this book. Though Slay was not new to DJing in the late '90s and early 2000s—he had been DJing and writing graffiti since the '70s—it was during that time period when he became one of the top mixtape DJs in the game, reigning supreme with his multi-tape releases and exclusive interviews with the biggest names in the streets, including legendary Harlem hustlers Alpo and AZ. Plus, Kay Slay's tapes always featured the newest tracks and freestyles from hip hop's biggest artists—and they'd often host his tapes, too. In fact, Kay Slay was the first mixtape DJ to play the live version of Jay-Z premiering "Takeover" at Hot 97's Summer Jam and also Nas' clapback "Ether." It's no wonder he called himself the "Drama King."

Hip hop will never be the same without the gruffest mixtape DJ voice New York City has ever heard. RIP DJ Kay Slay.

FIRST MIXTAPE

Kay Slay: I was doing a lot of club events and built a heavy buzz, so the people in my neighborhood were telling me that I needed a mixtape to help push my brand further. At first, I wasn't really sure. But as I was paying attention and seeing brothers like Ron G, S&S, Starchild, Brucie B–a lot of them were doing their thing. Lovebug Starski, Rest in Peace. DJ Hollywood. And there was compensation coming through it too, so I decided to do a mixtape.

Shout out to Puerto Rican DJ Demo, that was the homie right there from my neighborhood. I did the mixtape with him and it took off through the borough. *Warning Part 1* was my first comeback in 1993. Then after that, I just proceeded with it.

DJ BEGINNINGS

I started in '76 as a rookie, trying to learn by '77. I was one of the nicest cats in my neighborhood. I was 12, I was young. I used to get compared to Jazzy Jay and Flash being as young as I was. But as time went on, we started putting cassettes inside our desks, making the 60 minute joints and passing them out in the neighborhood. No color tracklist–we used to write out the name of each break and put our name on it. That was the local thing to do back then so you could listen to your stuff. Everybody did it.

That was like the first generation, but back then they weren't even called mixtapes. It was leisure. Hip hop was just part of the culture, something that we did every day, whether we went out and did graffiti or we put on our t-shirts and went to breakdance against another crew in another project, or we brought equipment out in our project to MC, or we went to another block where somebody was jamming at, or we would study our lessons of Supreme Mathematics. That was just for the love of the culture, it had nothing to do with money.

A SECOND CHANCE

The second go-around was when I did a little bid, playing with the streets. My whole DJ stint was to take our minds off the fact that we were in the hood. We didn't have all that we wanted, but we made the best of what we had.

But then as you start getting older, all of that DJing for free and not making money shit wasn't enough. Niggas was starting to get pussy now. Chicks wanted you looking good. I had to step away from that and play with the street, and it came and bit me in the ass.

When I came back for the second go-around, I wanted to do it right. I was doing a lot of clubs, I used to run around with Frankie Cutlass from my block, hold him down, make sure he was straight. And he'd get me extra exclusive records and things like that. I had a lot of people help me out. As far as the mixtape game, DJ Demo was the person who kept telling me over and over, pressing me 'til I finally did it. And he was right.

PLAYER HATER ELIMINATORS AND STREET SWEEPERS SERIES

Dazon was a kid that I used to work with. He used to work in the Def Jam building. He was somebody that used to help me get a lot of exclusives and everything, and he wanted to DJ as well. Everybody back then had a little sidekick or whatever so I kind of put him under my wing, not in a disrespectful manner but rather to show him the ropes in that world. We called ourselves in the beginning, The Player Hater Eliminators. That was the first series we did.

After a while, he kind of phased out of the mixtape game and started moving around. I believe he was DJing for Murder, Inc. so I just started doing my own thing. Then it went to the Street Sweepers, that was the name of my entertainment. It started off with me naming the tapes that–you would see it on the top of the tape.

BUILDING THE BRAND

I ain't even gonna lie, I was getting a lot of exclusives. And if I'm gonna do something, I'm gonna go all the way hard with it. So I was just putting shit out. There was no game plan with this mixtape shit. Mixtape shit was a way of promoting for me, above all, to build a stronger name so I could make some money and take care of my family.

I didn't set out to be a mixtape king. I didn't set out to win awards. I ain't set out to get record deals or

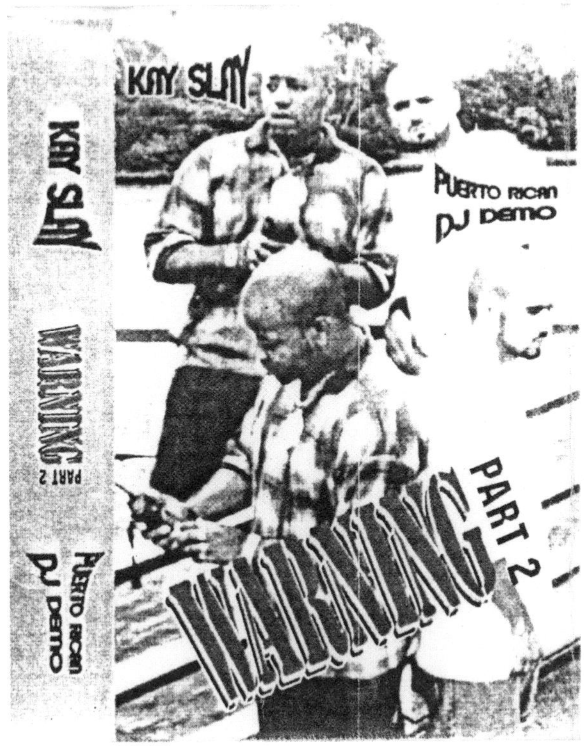

be on the radio. All that shit just happened. I guess that was just my destiny. This was something I could do to not wind up back in jail again. That's what it was to me.

I didn't wanna be fuckin' mixtape DJ or the mixtape king. To me, coming from the streets, that's some stupid shit. It took me a minute for me to even do it because Demo asked me on several occasions. There were even people in my crew telling me that shit was played out. All of this shit just happened. It was not a plan.

Chris Lighty sent Eric Nicks at me, saying that he wanted to sign me, this and that. When he explained it all to me, when I started seeing it was profitable. Before then, I would hear bad things about the industry, so I was never really too enthusiastic to be a part of it. I just wanted to continue to build my legacy and feed my family. The record deals showed me it was profitable.

DROPPING TAPES

I was making my mixtapes, of course, but I wasn't

going to every spot. I dealt with some of the main individual people that had names–Tape Kingz, Harlem Music Hut, shit like that. Other than that, I was into too much other shit. I had three motherfucking jobs, I used to hustle clothes. I was the "get money" dude. I couldn't cater to one thing.

Once I was being so consistent, people started reaching out to me. And then, I had record label guys that were getting exclusives, and they used to use the mixtape cats to see how their records were going to be perceived in the street before they were released.

It was just the consistency. They knew that I was constantly coming with music and people were starting to ask about me, so everybody started hitting me. It just organically kept bubbling up. It's hard to explain, but, you know, anything you do, if you do it to the death and you put a whole lot of hard work in it, people will recognize you. They're going to come to you.

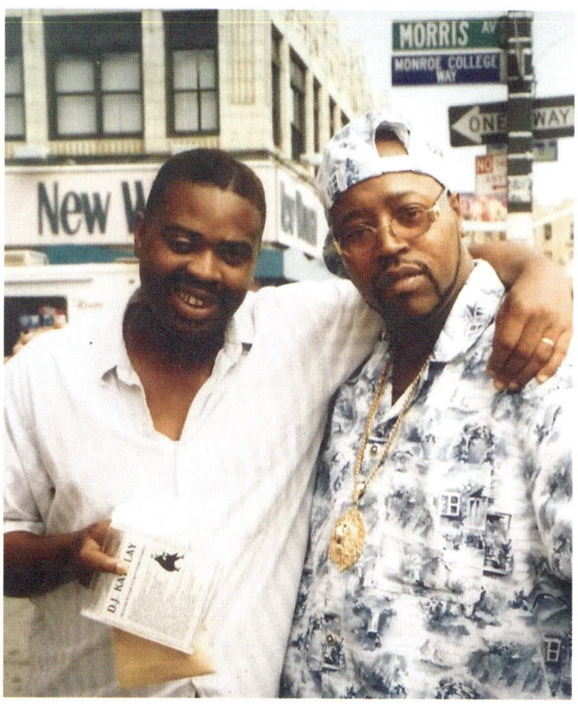

Kay Slay: I was making my rounds to drop some joints off on Fordham Road and saw Slick there. He didn't have the patch on. That's probably one of the only real pictures where you see him without the patch on his eye. I gave him my latest CD and asked him if we could take a picture and he was down. We took two of them actually.

TALKING ON TAPES

If your name's not on it, they're gonna take the credit for it and it's going to be like you just did the world a whole fucking favor. With these exclusives, we threw our tag on it so other DJs couldn't take our records. It was called stamping the record, not just talking on the record.

HARLEM HUSTLERS INTERVIEWED ON MIXTAPES

I'm always trying to find something different. I don't want to do what everybody else is doing. I have to give a big shout out to *F.E.D.S.* magazine because they were promoting their first issue with Alpo and them, and it was so big that I said to myself, "Man, if I can get the audio of him on my mixtape, it would kind of be like the audio to their magazine."

Fortunately, we lived in the same projects growing up. I reached out to Alpo's mother and asked if he would be willing to. He said, "Yeah, cool, send me your number." So that's how that happened. We did a separate conversation so the people could have a breakdown of certain things that he spoke about. They could hear him actually talking about it on the mixtape as opposed to having to read it.

The tape was hot. It went off the roof. But to me, it was just me doing what I do. I remember I had Larry Davis talking on one joint before. He wasn't on the cover, but he was first. I had a lot of brothers on the street on different joints, but that was just me trying to be different and give the audience something that nobody else was doing.

It was the first time they spoke. There were a lot of unanswered questions that people wanted to know about certain incidents. I had put that together. It was just entertainment. That's what the music industry is about, entertaining the people. Giving them what they want.

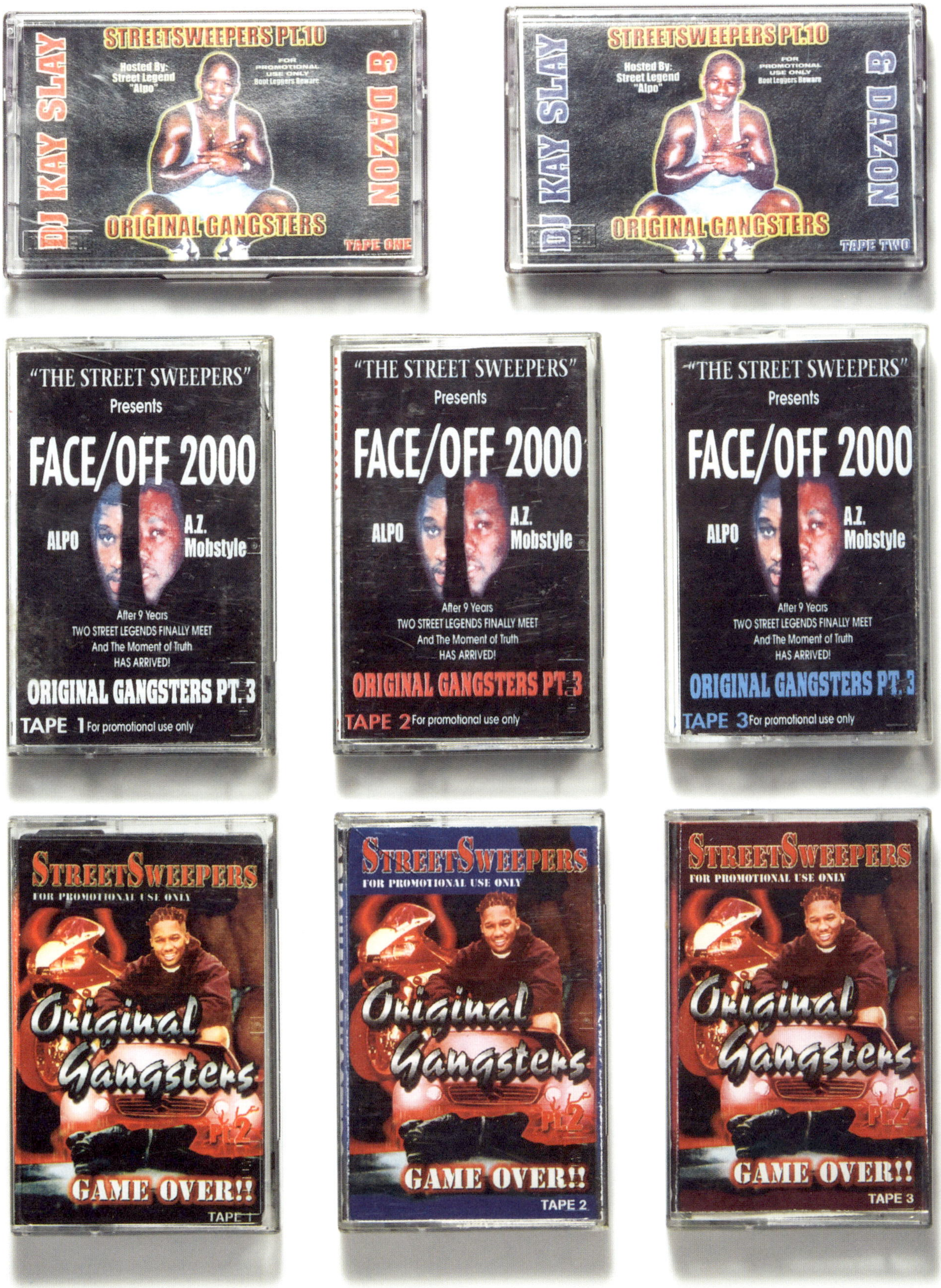

STREETSWEEPERS PT.10
Hosted By: Street Legend "Alpo"
FOR PROMOTIONAL USE ONLY Boot Leggers Beware
DJ KAY SLAY
DAZON B
ORIGINAL GANGSTERS
TAPE ONE
STREETSWEEPERS PT.10
Hosted By: Street Legend "Alpo"
FOR PROMOTIONAL USE ONLY Boot Leggers Beware
DJ KAY SLAY
DAZON B
ORIGINAL GANGSTERS
TAPE TWO
"THE STREET SWEEPERS" Presents
FACE/OFF 2000
ALPO
A.Z. Mobstyle
After 9 Years TWO STREET LEGENDS FINALLY MEET And The Moment of Truth HAS ARRIVED!
ORIGINAL GANGSTERS PT.3
TAPE 1 For promotional use only
"THE STREET SWEEPERS" Presents
FACE/OFF 2000
ALPO
A.Z. Mobstyle
After 9 Years TWO STREET LEGENDS FINALLY MEET And The Moment of Truth HAS ARRIVED!
ORIGINAL GANGSTERS PT.3
TAPE 2 For promotional use only
"THE STREET SWEEPERS" Presents
FACE/OFF 2000
ALPO
A.Z. Mobstyle
After 9 Years TWO STREET LEGENDS FINALLY MEET And The Moment of Truth HAS ARRIVED!
ORIGINAL GANGSTERS PT.3
TAPE 3 For promotional use only
STREETSWEEPERS
FOR PROMOTIONAL USE ONLY
Original Gangsters
PT.2
GAME OVER!!
TAPE 1
STREETSWEEPERS
FOR PROMOTIONAL USE ONLY
Original Gangsters
PT.2
GAME OVER!!
TAPE 2
STREETSWEEPERS
FOR PROMOTIONAL USE ONLY
Original Gangsters
PT.2
GAME OVER!!
TAPE 3

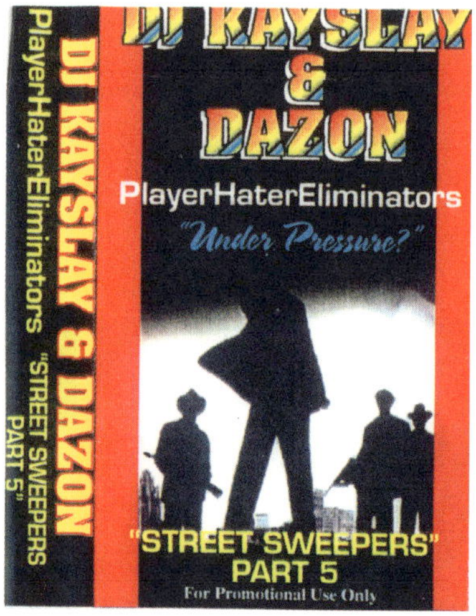
DJ KAYSLAY & DAZON
PlayerHaterEliminators "STREET SWEEPERS PART 5"
DJ KAYSLAY
&
DAZON
PlayerHaterEliminators
"Under Pressure?"
"STREET SWEEPERS"
PART 5
For Promotional Use Only
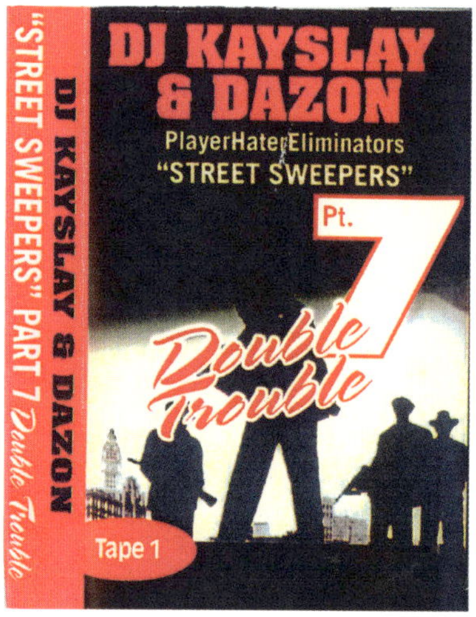
"STREET SWEEPERS" PART 7 Double Trouble
DJ KAYSLAY & DAZON
DJ KAYSLAY
& DAZON
PlayerHaterEliminators
"STREET SWEEPERS"
Pt.
7
Double Trouble
Tape 1
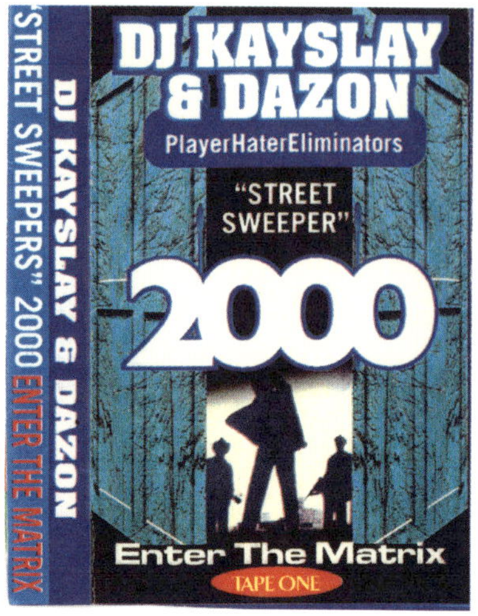
"STREET SWEEPERS" 2000 ENTER THE MATRIX
DJ KAYSLAY & DAZON
DJ KAYSLAY
& DAZON
PlayerHaterEliminators
"STREET
SWEEPER"
2000
Enter The Matrix
TAPE ONE
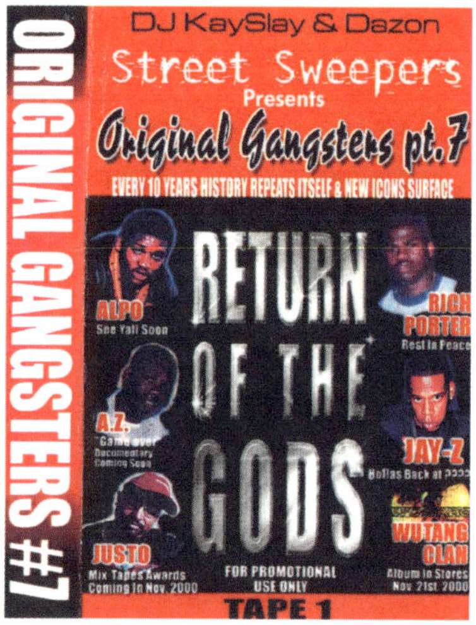
ORIGINAL GANGSTERS #7
DJ KaySlay & Dazon
Street Sweepers
Presents
Original Gangsters pt.7
EVERY 10 YEARS HISTORY REPEATS ITSELF & NEW ICONS SURFACE
RETURN OF THE GODS
ALPO
See Yall Soon
RICH PORTER
Rest In Peace
A.Z.
JAY-Z
WUTANG CLAN
JUSTO
Mix Tapes Awards
Coming In Nov. 2000
FOR PROMOTIONAL USE ONLY
TAPE 1
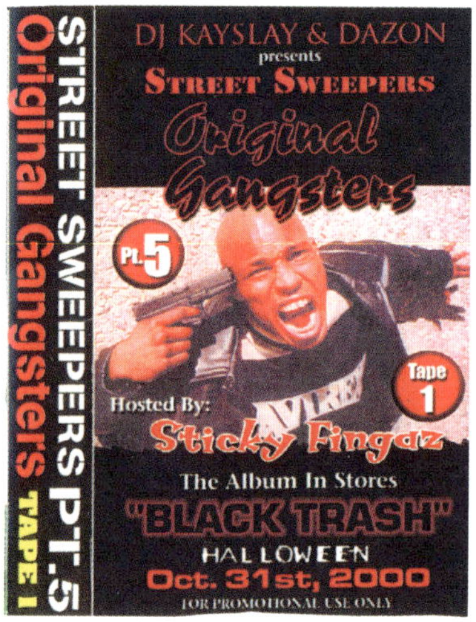
Original Gangsters
STREET SWEEPERS PT.5
TAPE 1
DJ KAYSLAY & DAZON
presents
STREET SWEEPERS
Original Gangsters
Pt.5
Tape 1
Hosted By:
Sticky Fingaz
The Album In Stores
"BLACK TRASH"
HALLOWEEN
Oct. 31st, 2000
FOR PROMOTIONAL USE ONLY
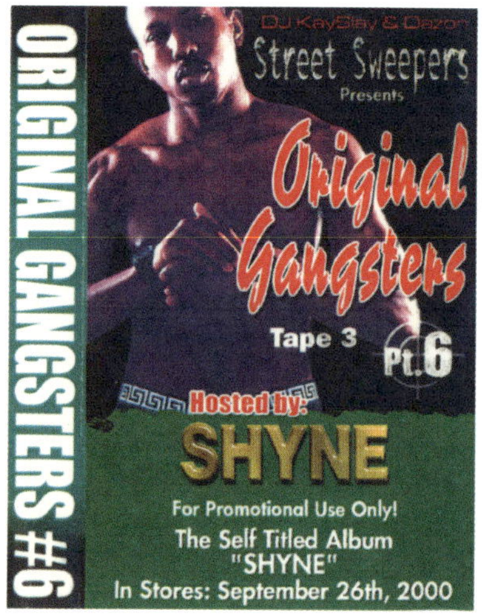
ORIGINAL GANGSTERS #6
DJ KaySlay & Dazon
Street Sweepers
Presents
Original Gangsters
Tape 3
Pt.6
Hosted by:
SHYNE
For Promotional Use Only!
The Self Titled Album
"SHYNE"
In Stores: September 26th, 2000
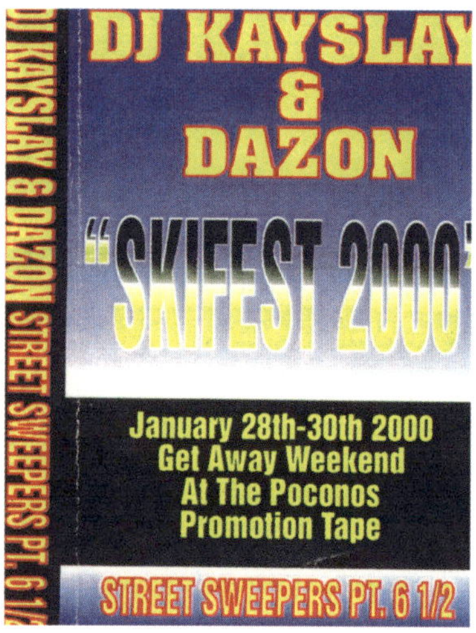
DJ KAYSLAY & DAZON STREET SWEEPERS PT. 6 1/2
DJ KAYSLAY
&
DAZON
"SKIFEST 2000"
January 28th-30th 2000
Get Away Weekend
At The Poconos
Promotion Tape
STREET SWEEPERS PT. 6 1/2
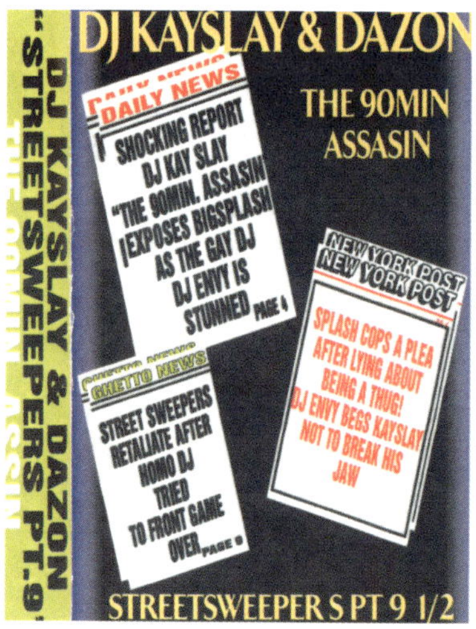
DJ KAYSLAY & DAZON
"STREETSWEEPERS PT.9"
DJ KAYSLAY & DAZON
DAILY NEWS
SHOCKING REPORT
DJ KAY SLAY
"THE 90MIN. ASSASIN
EXPOSES BIGSPLASH
AS THE GAY DJ
DJ ENVY IS
STUNNED
THE 90MIN
ASSASIN
NEW YORK POST
SPLASH COPS A PLEA
AFTER LYING ABOUT
BEING A THUG!
DJ ENVY BEGS KAYSLAY
NOT TO BREAK HIS
JAW
GHETTO NEWS
STREET SWEEPERS
RETALIATE AFTER
HOMO DJ
TRIED
TO FRONT GAME
OVER
STREETSWEEPER S PT 9 1/2
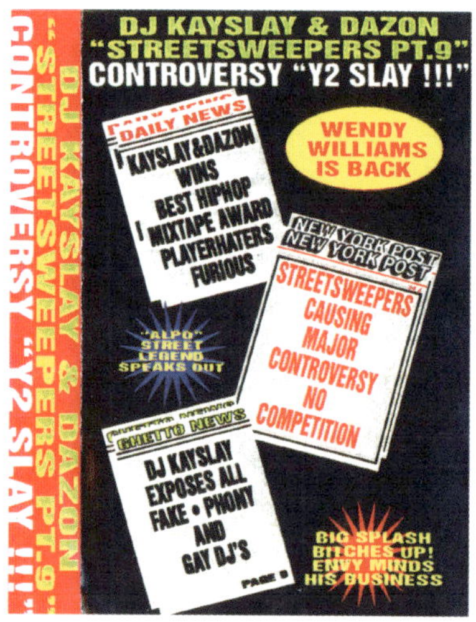
CONTROVERSY "Y2 SLAY !!!"
"STREETSWEEPERS PT.9"
DJ KAYSLAY & DAZON
DJ KAYSLAY & DAZON
"STREETSWEEPERS PT.9"
CONTROVERSY "Y2 SLAY !!!"
WENDY
WILLIAMS
IS BACK
DAILY NEWS
KAYSLAY&DAZON
WINS
BEST HIPHOP
MIXTAPE AWARD
PLAYERHATERS
FURIOUS
NEW YORK POST
STREETSWEEPERS
CAUSING
MAJOR
CONTROVERSY
NO
COMPETITION
"ALPO"
STREET
LEGEND
SPEAKS OUT
GHETTO NEWS
DJ KAYSLAY
EXPOSES ALL
FAKE • PHONY
AND
GAY DJ'S
BIG SPLASH
BITCHES UP!
ENVY MINDS
HIS BUSINESS

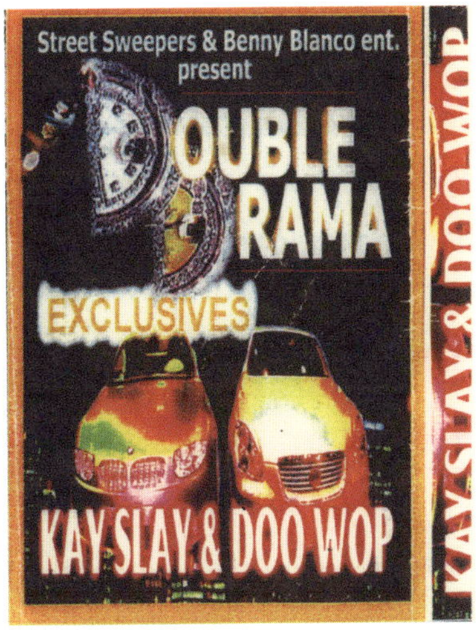
Street Sweepers & Benny Blanco ent.
present
DOUBLE DRAMA
EXCLUSIVES
KAY SLAY & DOO WOP
KAY SLAY & DOO WOP

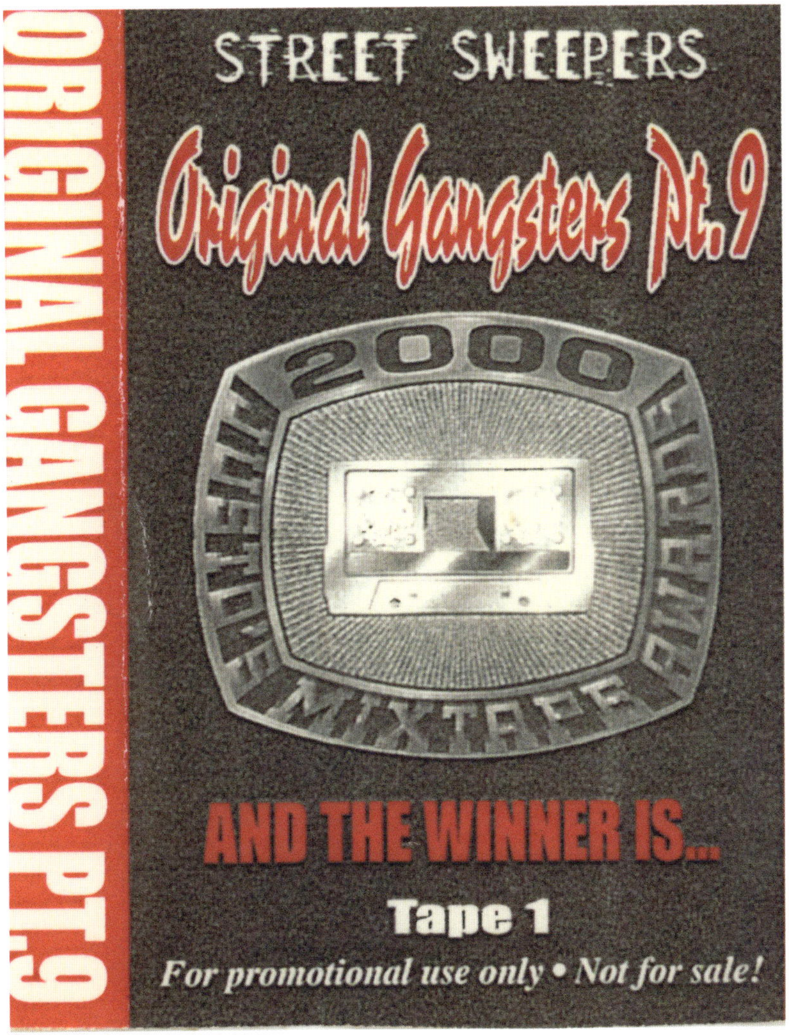
ORIGINAL GANGSTERS PT.9
STREET SWEEPERS
Original Gangsters Pt.9
2000
MIXTAPE
AND THE WINNER IS...
Tape 1
For promotional use only • Not for sale!

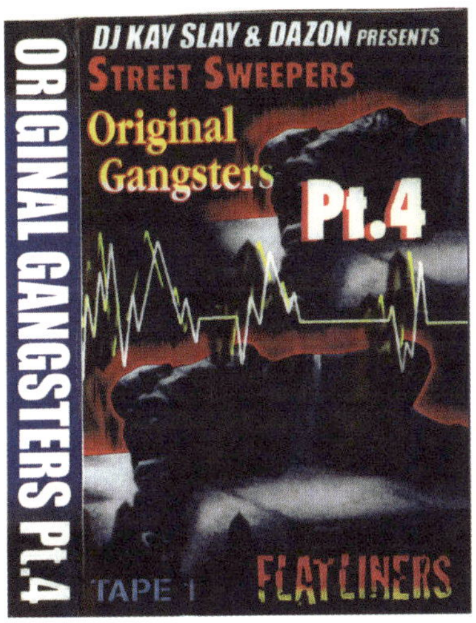
ORIGINAL GANGSTERS Pt.4
DJ KAY SLAY & DAZON PRESENTS
STREET SWEEPERS
Original Gangsters
Pt.4
TAPE 1
FLATLINERS

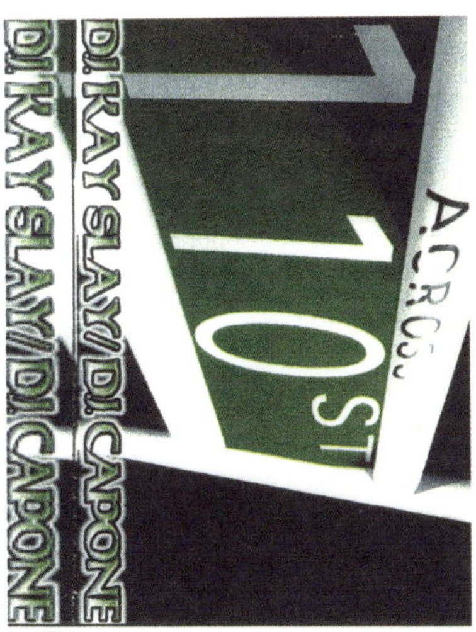
DJ KAY SLAY/DJ CAPONE
DJ KAY SLAY/DJ CAPONE
110 ST
A.C.R.O.S.

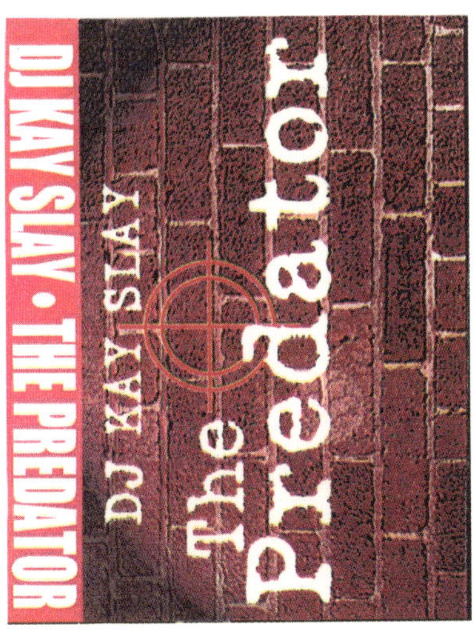
DJ KAY SLAY • THE PREDATOR
DJ KAY SLAY
The Predator

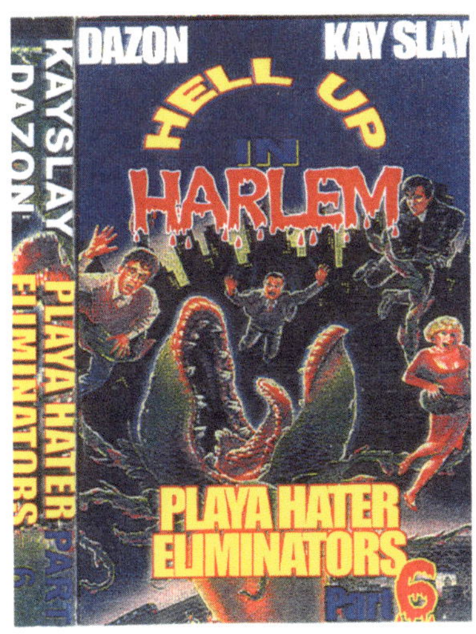
KAYSLAY
DAZON
PLAYA HATER ELIMINATORS
DAZON
KAY SLAY
HELL UP IN HARLEM
PLAYA HATER ELIMINATORS
Part 6

DJ GREEN LANTERN

The Invasion: Combining Skills, Exclusives, and Production Chops on Tapes

Never before had mixtape fans heard a combination of DJ skills, production skills, and exclusives on mixtapes like they had from DJ Green Lantern. Originally from Rochester, New York, Green Lantern made mixtape masterpieces dense with intricate intros, loads of unreleased music, freestyles, blends, and more, seamlessly stitched together to create a listening experience like no other. And each tape was wrapped with a clever concept, plus packaged with original cover artwork that aligned with his alias.

COMING UP IN ROCHESTER

Green Lantern: I got exposed to the tapes around '93, '94. That's when I started getting my hands on stuff. It kind of exploded around that time, in the mid-'90s. There were only a few stores in Rochester where you could get them. People would go to New York City and get them, then come back and make their copies. Or go buy copies.

I was going to the little mom-and-pop stores, copping the new Clue, Craig G, S&S. Then *95 Live* came out, and *50 MCs* came out, and they were making statements. Those were like albums.

PARTY TAPES

I was making beats and doing parties–this is a little past high school. I started making live recordings of the parties, and I would sell those. The parties were hectic, but not in a bad way. Like, really turnt up. So I started selling those at the mom-and-pop stores where they were selling real mixtapes. They were live recordings, and you could hear the crowd. That was my first experience with the tapes.

I wasn't going stupid hard with them. I just made a few of them, and they sold out. I didn't make a big deal about it. It was limited. I knew that it was just a party tape.

INSPIRATION

I was a fan of Dirty Harry and the creative guys that came from the blend tape era. Because at this point, in '96, '97, we were in full Clue era, and all the guys that came up after him and saw what he did wanted a piece of that. So now everybody's got exclusives. The front page of the mixtape game is now "exclusives." So I was like, "Alright, cool. But, let me try some other shit."

I wanna say it was Chill Will From The Eastside *Fruit Flava Vol. 6* and *7* that really inspired me. Me and my homies used to ride around listening to those like, "Wow, he's really getting it in." He was putting that work in with the acapellas, and mixing non-stop. So you know there was some 4-track action going on. It was exciting, and added some real substance to it–more than just, "Yo, here's a new song." Those types of tapes, the replay value was high. That was the angle I wanted to take.

FIRST MIXTAPE

My first tape ever was called *Green Adventures Volume 1*. And there never was a *Volume 2*. This was like, I wanna say '96, '97. There might have been a blend on there of Montell Jordan with something? I can't really remember. All I know is I got dissed.

There was a security guard who was a homie, and he didn't mean to diss me, but I took it as a diss and went back to the lab and got ferocious with it. He was like, "Yo, that tape was mad mellow, man." He thought he was giving me a compliment, and I was

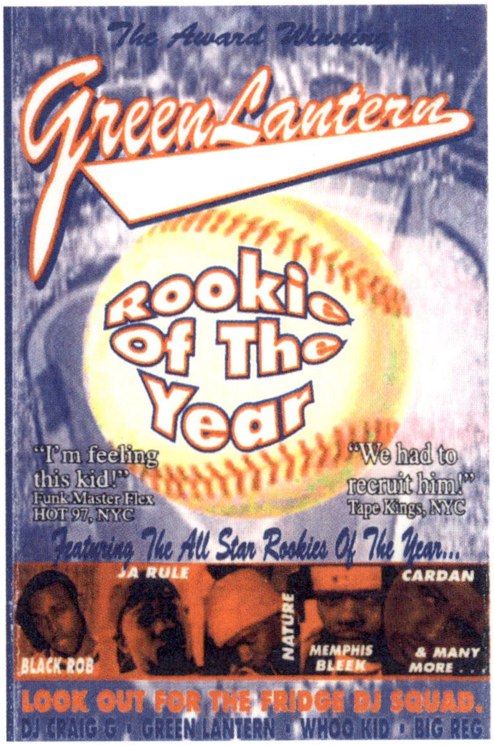

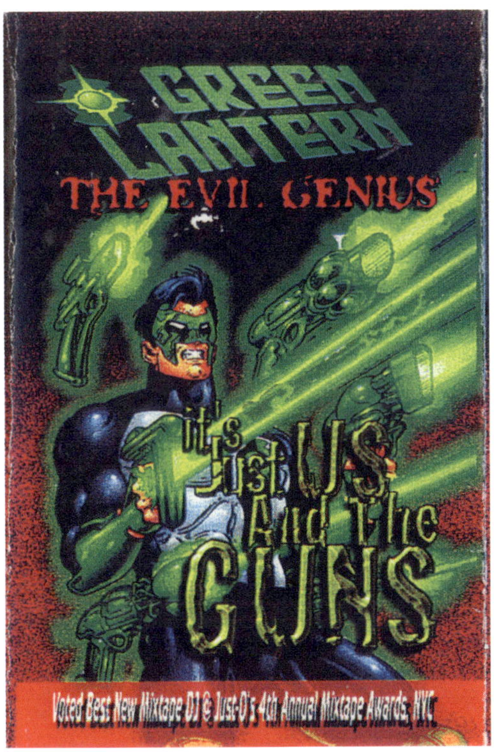

like, "Bruh, that ain't supposed to be mellow. That's supposed to be turnt up!" Like, "Huh? Mellow?" I did something wrong.

GETTING EXCLUSIVES

I went back to the lab, stirring the pot up a little more, taking it up a couple levels. I dug in and started really going crazy with the 4-track. And I was getting my hands on exclusives. I was living in Rochester, and in Toronto, which is like a two-and-a-half-hour drive, they would get these bootlegs at Play De Record, which is a legendary record store. Every Thursday, they would get these white labels. And for whatever reason, they would get exclusives.

I think the A&R dudes were selling it to them and they were pressing it up, and making a little money. Because these were exclusives that weren't on the tapes. I was keeping up with Clue and all the other dudes that were doing the exclusive shit, and they didn't have any of these songs. I'd be like, "Wow, this is a new Ma$e song. I'm going to make a tape now!" So that was a little goldmine. But the quality wasn't always good.

Upstate, baby. Blame the greed of whoever sold that shit–that's how I got it.

THE BIRTH OF THE EVIL GENIUS

I was still producing at this time. I had the Ensoniq ASR-X, which is like their version of the MPC. So I would take something that's low quality, and sample the whole song, because it had a lot of sample time in it. And I would put hi-hats on top of it, to mask the fact that there was a hiss, just to try and make it good quality.

I would do little tricks with songs that I would get that weren't on vinyl, that were on cassette or CD. This is before the CDJs came out. I would always want to be scratching a song, and manipulating a song somehow. So what I would do is sample a little piece of the song, like the top of the first verse, which is what a lot of DJs always bring back. I would bring that back in the sampler, just hitting it, and record that on one track in the 4-track. Then, I would find a song on vinyl that sounded sort of like the piece I was bringing in, to make it sound like I was scratching it in. But it was actually a whole other song I was scratching, and on a whole other track of the 4-track. That was the first step of me ever being an Evil Genius.

I made an instrumental out of the intro to Cam's "Horse & Carriage" that I had on a sampler tape. The beginning of it had a little piece of the beat, and I sampled it, chopped it up, remade it, and put it on a tape. Randomly, I got a call from Jacob York, who I didn't know and was one of the main guys at Cam's label. And he was like, "Yo, how did you get the instrumental to that?" And I was like, "I made it."

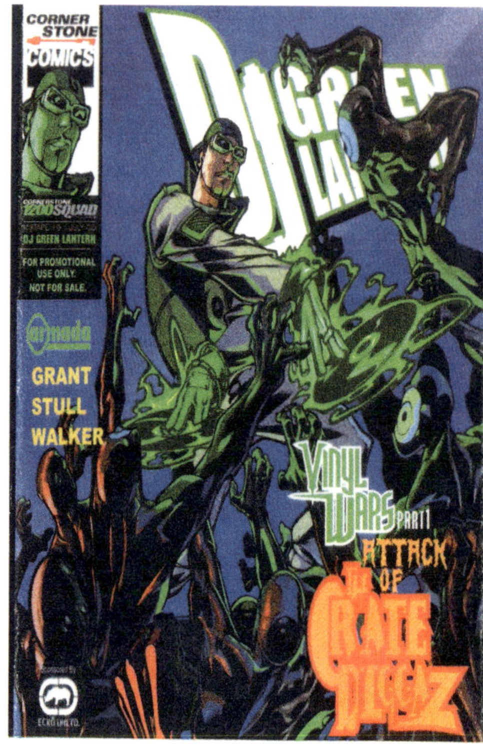

SKILLS VS. EXCLUSIVES

In those days, the consumers were cool with just hearing exclusives. But the DJs and the hip-hop heads were like, "Aw, man, you're just playing a song. That's a pause tape!" We were on the low hating, even though that's a brand new Biggie and I wanna hear that.

We'd say, "Oh, he ain't scratching on it," or, "He ain't doin' nothin'." Because we come from the era of, "Yo, did you hear what the fuck Ron G just did?!" So we were like, "That's what you're supposed to do. You're supposed to put in work." Not realizing that it was just another level of work.

I grew into realizing that getting exclusives was a whole other skill. But there definitely was a super divide in the community of DJs and hip-hop heads versus the guys who made the pause tapes. And the guys who made the pause tapes were like, "Fuck y'all, we're getting money. We're doing parties. Fuck you."

But now, I was getting exclusives, and I'm doing the cutting and scratching shit, making the songs talk to each other. It was hip-hop shit. Manipulating sounds, and turning them into a whole other thing.

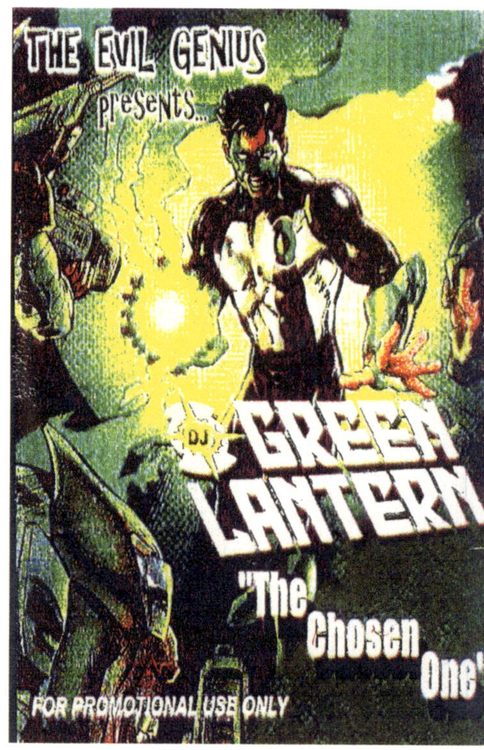

GREEN LANTERN INTROS

First tape out, the intros were important. I'm an intro guy. Intros were one of my calling cards. When you say my name to people, they may say "the beats," they may say "*The Champ is Here*," but some of them are going to be like, "Yo, that's the guy with the intros."

DJ Juice was killing the intros. Chill Will had his intros. The style of how Wop was doing the intros, it wasn't the same type of vibe, but it was a cut and paste that came from an era of guys like Dirty Harry, Double R, G-Bo The Pro who took audio and made it talk. That's really what it was to me, what it's always been is. "Let me just make this shit talk."

MAKING COPIES

There was this studio in Rochester–Dajhelon Studios–the famous studio that Jodeci rented out from like '92 to '93 to record *Diary of a Mad Band*. Timbaland used to live in that studio. And it had this cassette dubbing machine for people who had studio time there that wanted to get fifty copies of a cassette. One of my homeboys was an engineer there, so I had a pass to just kind of walk in there whenever.

I would go there late night and buy professional cassettes in bulk from this spot around the corner and spend all night dubbing tapes while they were in the next room making music. And I would walk out of there with 500 tapes dubbed. They would give you mass sheets of the stickers, and you would do that yourself. I was dubbing it, packing it, sending it, riding with it, everything. The grind.

GETTING TAPES IN STORES

By the time I got into the game in '98, you had a lot of stores. The infrastructure and foundation of the mixtape game had already been laid by the guys previous to that time. I walked into a damn near fully built industry. I'm thankful for that. I could have a conversation with somebody in my first year about a store list that was 200 stores long.

You're hearing Clue make the store people a little famous–"Shoutout to Youngstar on the Concourse." Then, fast forward, you're putting your own tapes out and now you're on the phone with Youngstar or you're on the phone with Phil from Harlem Music Hut talking about your shit–how much they potentially want to take. It felt like, "Yo, this shit is working, I'm getting in, I'm making my way in this space." It was a beautiful thing.

MOVING TO NYC

I moved way later than anyone thought I would've moved, in 2003. I ran through two trucks on the road, just putting miles on them. I had a kid up in Rochester, and a whole family and everything, so I was commuting way too much. It's six hours, and I'm doing that twice a week. The record label dudes that are still around from back then, like Pecas, they'll be like, "I remember him from when he used to drive from Rochester. That fool was crazy." I eventually ended up moving to Jersey City, which is right through the Holland Tunnel into lower Manhattan.

MIXTAPE MONEY

It was very lucrative if you were smart and knew how to do it, and kept the overhead low. I wish I did more. Even though it's years later, I don't really want to throw the whole number, because I still feel weird throwing those numbers out. That was our code. Don't talk about the numbers. But, it was nice. It was really nice. I bought a Cadillac truck off of two tapes.

Plus, people would literally book you in cities throughout VA, Hartford, that New England area, based on your damn tape. That shit was crazy.

COMIC BOOK COVERS

I was thinking, "How could I make some shit stand out?" I'm thinking about the people looking at the mixtape case. You walk into the store and you see all of these tapes–what cover is going to grab your eye and make you go, "What the hell is that?"

There were a couple local comic book stores in Rochester. I'd be in there going through stuff, like, "Oh this could actually work for a cover." All of those early Green Lantern comic book covers that I flipped, it was me finding the comic books that I wanted to use and sitting with a homie. I had a couple local guys that I would be like, "Okay, I want to use this, but I want this piece over here to say this, and I want to use this font." I knew exactly what I wanted, so we would just knock it out like that. I didn't know graphic design, but I just came with the assets and the direction. I produced it.

It was a little, "What is this, some kid shit? Some cartoon shit? " But by and large, it was a blessing.

I would do little tricks with songs that I would get that weren't on vinyl, that were on cassette or CD. This is before the CDJs came out. I would always want to be scratching a song, and manipulating a song somehow.

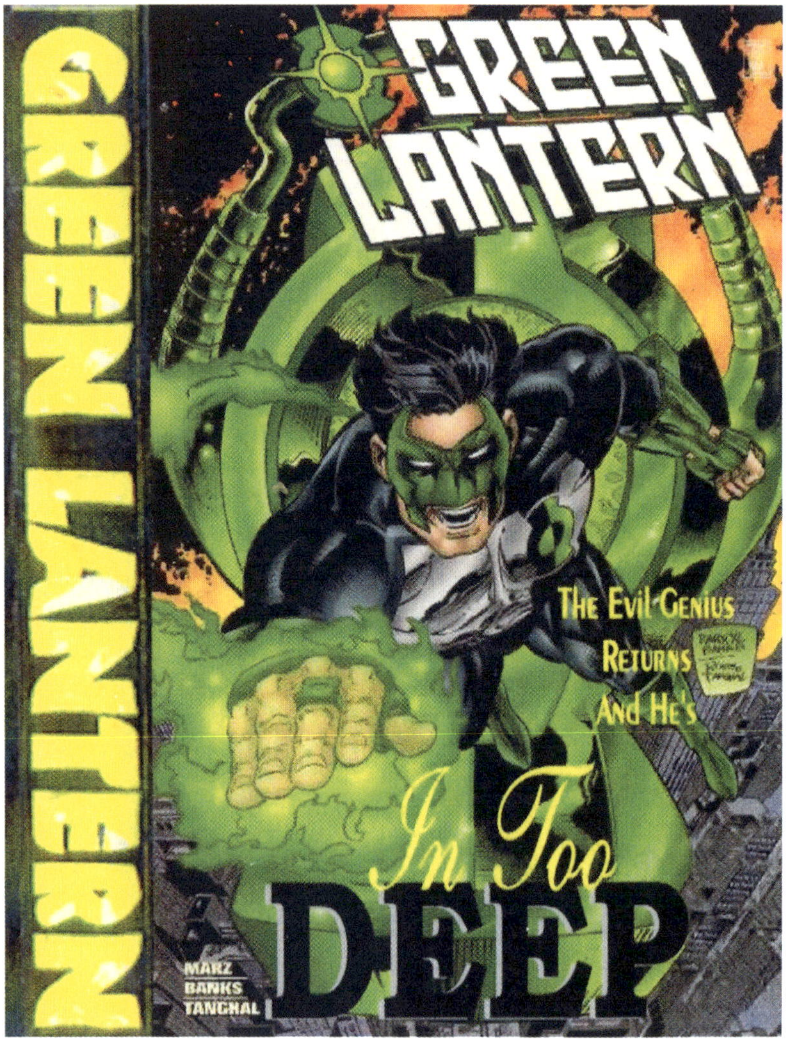
GREEN LANTERN
GREEN LANTERN
The Evil Genius
Returns
And He's
In Too
DEEP
MARZ
BANKS
TANGHAL

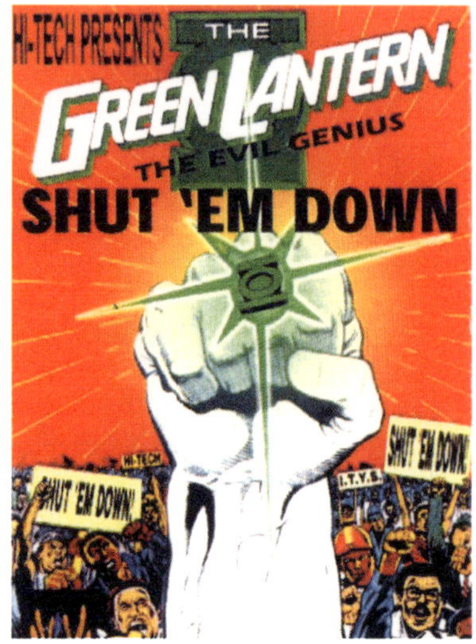
HI-TECH PRESENTS
THE
GREEN LANTERN
THE EVIL GENIUS
SHUT 'EM DOWN
SHUT 'EM DOWN
SHUT 'EM DOWN

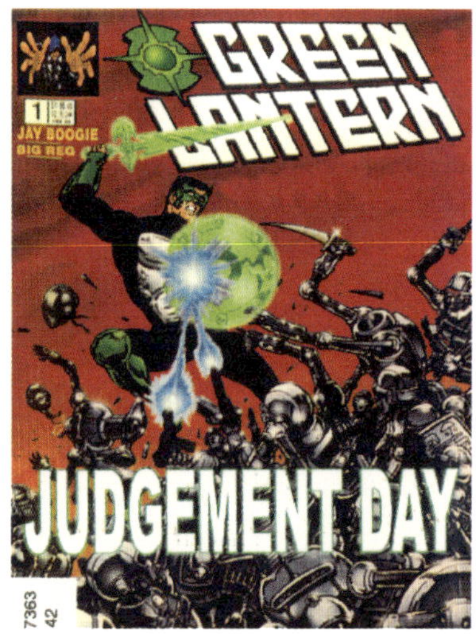
GREEN LANTERN
1
JAY BOOGIE
BIG REG
JUDGEMENT DAY

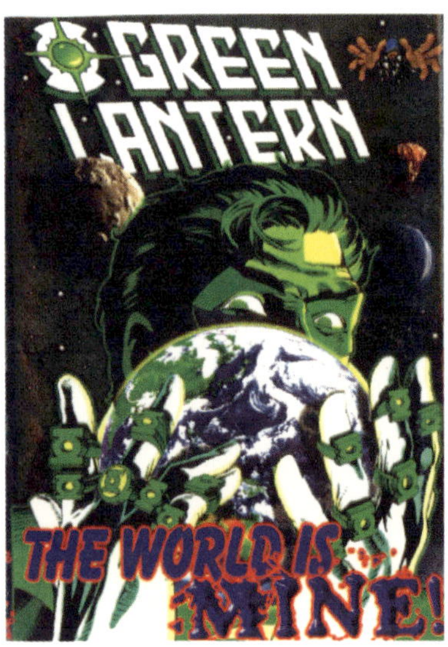
GREEN LANTERN
THE WORLD IS...
MINE!

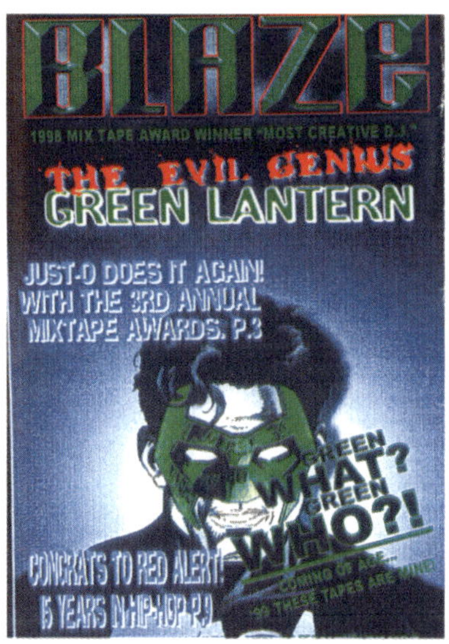
BLAZE
1998 MIX TAPE AWARD WINNER "MOST CREATIVE D.J."
THE EVIL GENIUS
GREEN LANTERN
JUST-0 DOES IT AGAIN!
WITH THE 3RD ANNUAL
MIXTAPE AWARDS. P.3
GREEN
WHAT?
GREEN
WHO?!
CONGRATS TO RED ALERT!
15 YEARS IN HIP-HOP P.9

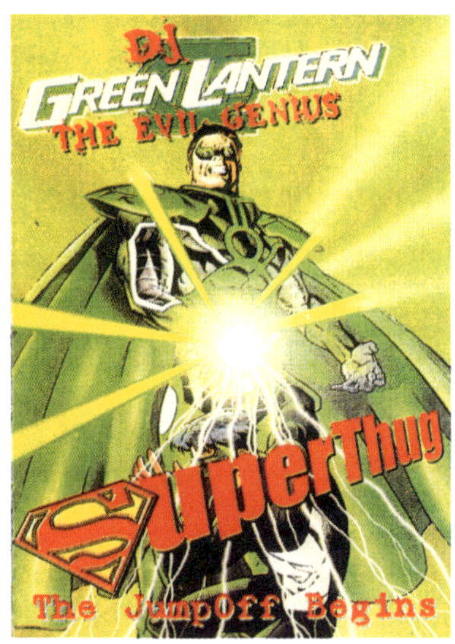
DJ
GREEN LANTERN
THE EVIL GENIUS
SuperThug
The JumpOff Begins

GREEN LANTERN'S TOP 5 CREATIVE TIPS FOR MAKING A MIXTAPE

1. COME UP WITH A THEME - Something that you can run with throughout your whole tape. For example, *Just Us And The Gunz*. I'm letting that shit float around the whole tape and it's interspersed with the music. Alive on Arrival, I'm over here making songs with people who come back from adversity. Come with a theme, map it out. Sometimes if you're in a creative space, make some shit, put some shit together. Take some acapellas, put it with some beats. Or just find songs that go with the concept that you thought of. Really make it consistent.

2. MANIPULATE THE MUSIC - The music that you want to use, you're going to have to manipulate that shit somehow if you want it to stand the test of time. Sometimes I want to hear the song, but really I want to hear what you did with it. I want that shit to have a little flare to it. I want you to have done something to the intro or made the shit do something to make me keep going back to it. Then add some details, some sprinkles to the music. And string it together properly.

3. DECIDE IF YOU WANT TO TALK OR NOT - You may want to talk, you may not want to talk. You might think that the consumer might not like that. That's a question you want to ask yourself as the DJ putting together your mix--talk or don't? That's up to you. But if you do, make sure you're saying something.

4. MAKE SURE YOUR COVER ART MATCHES THE MUSIC - What's this visual going to look like? Because this thing is going to be everywhere. Is it going to pop? Is it going to stand out? Is it gonna be laidback? Again, it's up to you. Just make sure that it's authentic to what the theme is and it goes with it. Sometimes people do something like, "I gotta use a bright color to stand out," but the mix was something about melancholy, sad songs. Don't do that. Make sure your shit fits.

5. BE CONFIDENT IN YOUR WORK - When you have all of those elements together, don't back down. Go hard. Put that shit together and stand on it, don't waiver on your choice. This shit is serious. Stand on what you played and stand on how you played it. Make it something you can play in fifteen years.

We come from the era of *Ultimate Breaks and Beats* with the space octopus on the cover–eye-catching shit.

DJ WHOO KID

New Energy: Going All Out to Get Ahead

Coming up in Queens, DJ Whoo Kid was there to witness his neighbors DJ Clue and DJ Envy blow up on the mixtape scene. And thanks to their mentorship, he was also able to carve out his own place in the game, loading his tapes with unheard tracks that were always complemented by his signature name drop and gunshot sound effects. Never afraid to take risks, Whoo Kid continued to push the boundaries, collaborating with fellow DJs to breathe new life into the mixtape game.

EARLY '90S

Whoo Kid: The first time I made a tape was at my boy's house. I used to hang with these Haitians that looked like they were Puerto Rican. DJ Cash–everyone thought he was my cousin because we went to the same college–he had turntables.

I couldn't afford turntables back then. They were like $1,000 or some bullshit each. I used to just practice and fuck around. He had all the records. And for me, it was like a hobby. I would to go to his house and do blend tapes. At that time, the Ron G tapes were out, Kid Capri had a mixtape. I was in college, so I was like 18 or 19. This is like '92.

Then, Dirty Harry came out, and he was a Queens DJ. I heard his tapes and I was like, "Holy shit." Meanwhile, I was living next door to Clue. Him and Envy both lived down the block, across from each other. So I was already influenced by what Clue was doing. But Clue was stealing music, and I didn't have any connections at that time.

I tried to emulate what Dirty Harry was doing, but he was doing, like, digital blending with his mixes, using like an early type of Pro Tools. He was ahead of his time. I was doing it the old school way, mixing like "The Way You Make Me Feel" with Rakim. I'd get an R&B acapella and mix it with a hip-hop joint that was new, like Das EFX or whatever. And blends were hot back then. If you did an ill blend, people would love it.

But I still wasn't a known DJ. I just did it because that's what I wanted to hear. I just loved the mixes. Dirty Harry, Ron G, Kid Capri, I used to look up to those dudes.

FIRST TAPE

The Afterparty was my first tape. Then professionally, when I started doing hip-hop mixtapes, I went heavy with *The Afterparty* series. I would come out with the hip-hop exclusives, and then if I wanted a little extra money because I was hot, I would come

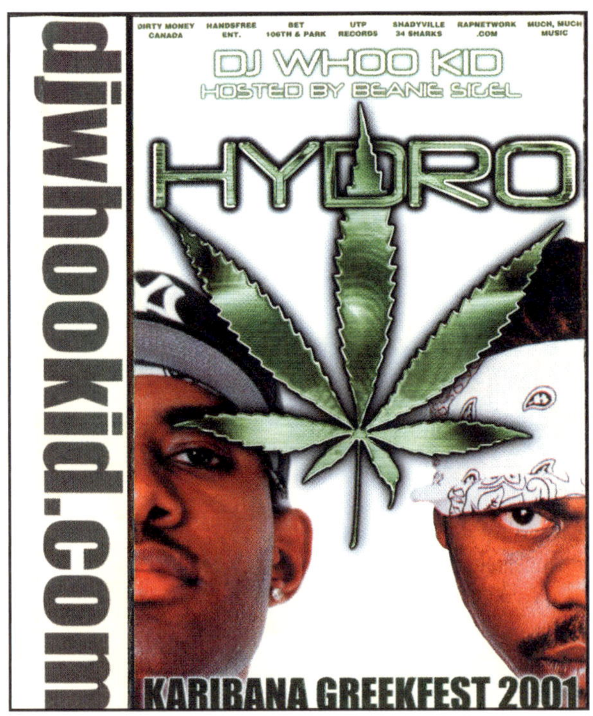

out with a blend joint. But back then, all I had was blends.

I made 300 copies and put them out on Jamaica Avenue, and was running around like I was famous. I used to have Clue's dubbing machine, but he was so famous that he never knew. The dubbing machines were like $3,000 at that time. When he would leave his parent's house, I'd go borrow the machine. I would copy all my tapes and give it back to him before he knew about it.

DJ CLUE INSPIRATION

We were all on the same block. I went to Queensborough Community College with him, and then he quit and took up DJing professionally. I stayed a little longer before I quit. I definitely got influenced by him. He had the Nissan Sentra, the box one, then went to like a BMW 320i. I was like, "This motherfucker got a Beemer, son! Fuck that shit, nigga! I'm gonna start doing tapes!"

GETTING EXCLUSIVES

After I did the blends for a good year and change, I linked up with Clue's camp. And Envy, who was like his underboss DJ, introduced me to how to get exclusives. So I would get in their whip, and go through to all the labels with them. We would go there and meet the A&Rs, and they'd give us DATs. Some A&Rs would give us unfinished stuff.

But the number one place where we used to get the music from was the rap magazines. They had to rate the albums, so labels had to send them advanced copies. And these guys that are rating the albums are making like $5 an hour, or they're interns. So we'd show up with $300 or $400, like, "Give us all the albums you got here," and they'd give you all of them. That's why labels started ink-marking or putting a drop saying "Property of Interscope" or whatever. So then the people who would rate them, that drop would be on their copy, and they could figure out who gave it out. For us, it was strictly some hustle shit.

Another way we would get songs was from mixers. They don't get paid either, and they're there mixing the shit until six, seven in the morning. They have all

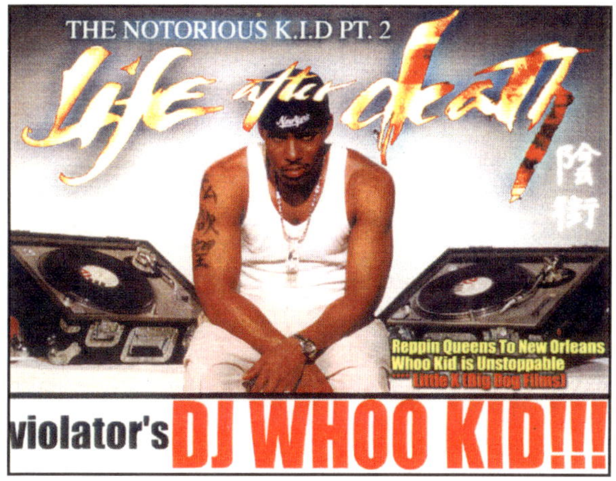

those recording DATs on the wall, and there's one DAT that records the whole session. So there would be different versions. That's why we had Biggie rapping Lil' Kim's verses on "Queen Bitch," talking about sucking dick and all this shit. So we'd save those for a month where we had no exclusives. Like, we know it's a reference track for Lil' Kim, but it sounds fucked up.

Labels didn't understand it. We didn't even understand it. We just saw it as a way to make money. If I have a Biggie exclusive, I'm outta here! But I used to look at DJ Clue like, "You're putting out all this new shit. You're down with Jay-Z and all these guys." It was too competitive. Every time I'd go to the store to sell my tapes, they'd be like, "Oh, we got Clue, we don't need your shit."

FREE WAX

I used to lie like crazy. I used to make believe I DJed in Asia and all this stupid shit. But I didn't even DJ in Queens. So I used to go to the old Def Jam building on Varick and be like, "Yo, I'm about to go to fucking Africa, I need some records." Because records were expensive back then. So I used to get free wax.

MIXTAPE HUSTLE

Clue was too big, so Envy was the only one I could get at. I knew Clue since we were kids, but I never asked him for a favor. And I hate when DJs come up to you and ask you for favors. Clue did it on his own, so it's like, "I don't got time for this shit." So when

Clue would drop, I would drop a week later and still make money.

We knew the African bootleggers, the Chinese bootleggers. There were Irish bootleggers. It got to a point where we were sending masters overseas. It was a really good hustle. Masters were the biggest thing, because people would pay $1,000 for a master, or $700 for a master, depending on what songs you had. It had to be worth it if you're going to steal somebody's record and hide.

That's why Whoo Kid made sense for me. I got my name from my mother taking a shit, and my father being like, "Whooo weee." But when I became a DJ it made sense because no one knew who the kid was that had the exclusive. And I never had my picture on the cover of my tapes. That's why they always thought I was Clue, like Clue had a secondary name.

COLLABORATING WITH STRETCH ARMSTRONG

Stretch Armstrong had the big radio show on Hot 97, so I abused his name in all my conversations. I was the king of using all my resources. I didn't have to lie anymore, so the lies at this point were minimal. "Yo, I produce Stretch Armstrong's show. We need this exclusive." Or I'd be like, "Stretch needs that song. He ain't playing your shit." Everybody wanted Stretch to debut their record, so it started off as me getting music for his show.

I'd be like to Stretch, "I'll get you this song, you blast it off Sunday, and I'll put it on my tape the following week." So for a while, I was getting exclusives off the strength of Stretch. He didn't have time to chase records and do all that street shit. So I was like, "Let me do that for you, and you let me be on the radio whenever you need me." So I made him look good because he had all the new shit, and then I could use the songs for my tapes. And he would let me be on the radio for like five minutes here and there, like, "Yo, Whoo Kid got me this new song." And he'd talk to me, and we'd laugh. That was my first introduction to the radio shit.

One day, I was like, "Why don't we do a tape?" And he was the king of having motherfuckers freestyle. So I was like, "Why don't we go through all those exclusive freestyles you have in the vaults, and put them out on tapes?" He had freestyles of Jay-Z doing ill shit. He had so much shit, we couldn't even go through his whole archives. We had mad Eminems, because Eminem was always on Stretch's show. So we did *Murda Mixtape 1, 2,* and *3*. Then we started getting people to come in and do exclusives.

COVER ART

Clue was our competitor. When Clue dropped, everyone just chilled, like, "Yo, we ain't dropping this week." So I had to go hard with the music, the hosting, and the covers. I had NOJO, who did everyone's cover at that time. But I used to pay NOJO extra to do ill shit. I used to do photo shoots.

Me and Stretch, we went to like a car crash dealership in Queens. We were like, "Yo, you got a Benz or something that's fucked up that we can sit in?" Dude was like, "You guys alright?" Just picture me walking into this car crash spot with this tall ass white dude, like an eight foot Jew. Then we had fatigues on, and wanted to look like CNN. Stretch saw the money and creativity with the music of course, but he saw that it was some funny, creative shit with the covers, too. He allowed me to make him do all this weird shit.

People thought we died when we did the fake crash cover. Imagine if we had Instagram or Twitter back then. I would've been killing it out there. There were rumors, like, "Yo, I heard Whoo Kid and Stretch Armstrong died in a car crash, and the cover's out." I was like, "Are these people stupid?" But it was like a comedic aspect to us putting out tapes together.

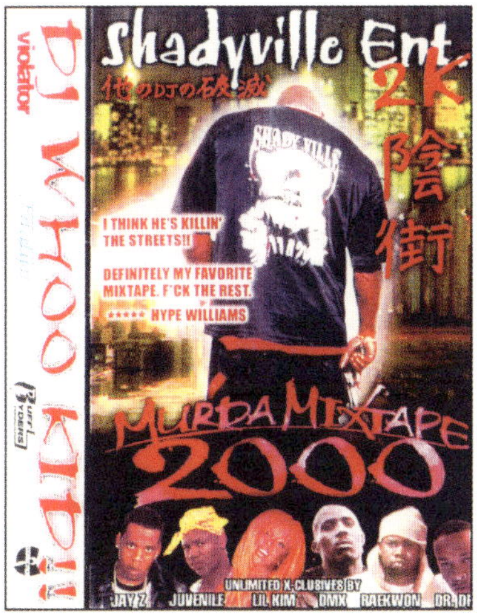
DJ WHOO KID!!
violator
Shadyville Ent.
2K
陰街
I THINK HE'S KILLIN' THE STREETS!!
DEFINITELY MY FAVORITE MIXTAPE. F*CK THE REST.
HYPE WILLIAMS
MURDA MIXTAPE
2000
UNLIMITED X-CLUSIVES BY
JAY Z
JUVENILE
LIL KIM
DMX
RAEKWON

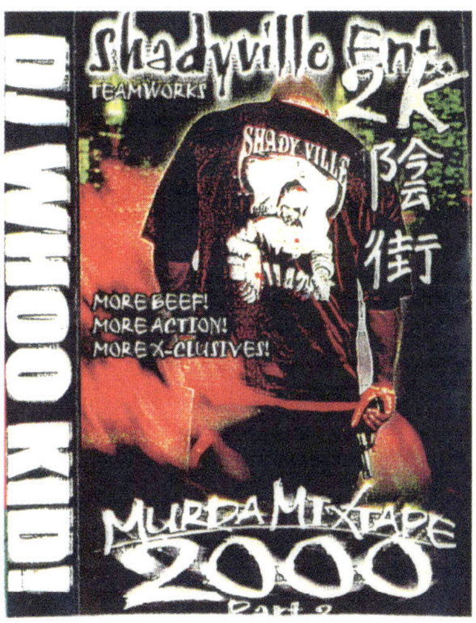
DJ WHOO KID!
Shadyville Ent.
TEAMWORKS
2K
陰街
MORE BEEF!
MORE ACTION!
MORE X-CLUSIVES!
MURDA MIXTAPE
2000

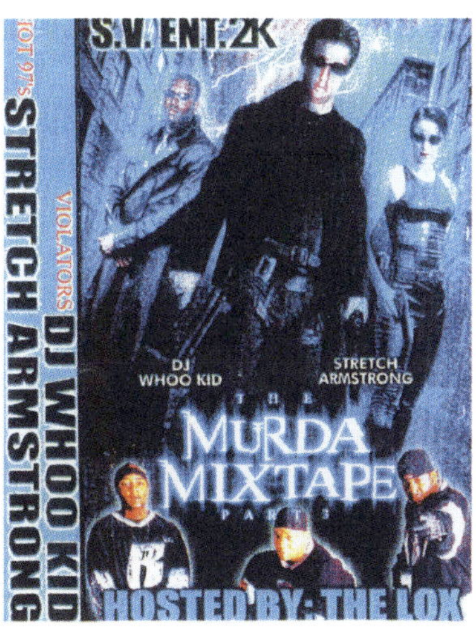
S.V. ENT. 2K
HOT 97'S STRETCH ARMSTRONG
VIOLATORS DJ WHOO KID
DJ WHOO KID
STRETCH ARMSTRONG
MURDA
MIXTAPE
HOSTED BY: THE LOX

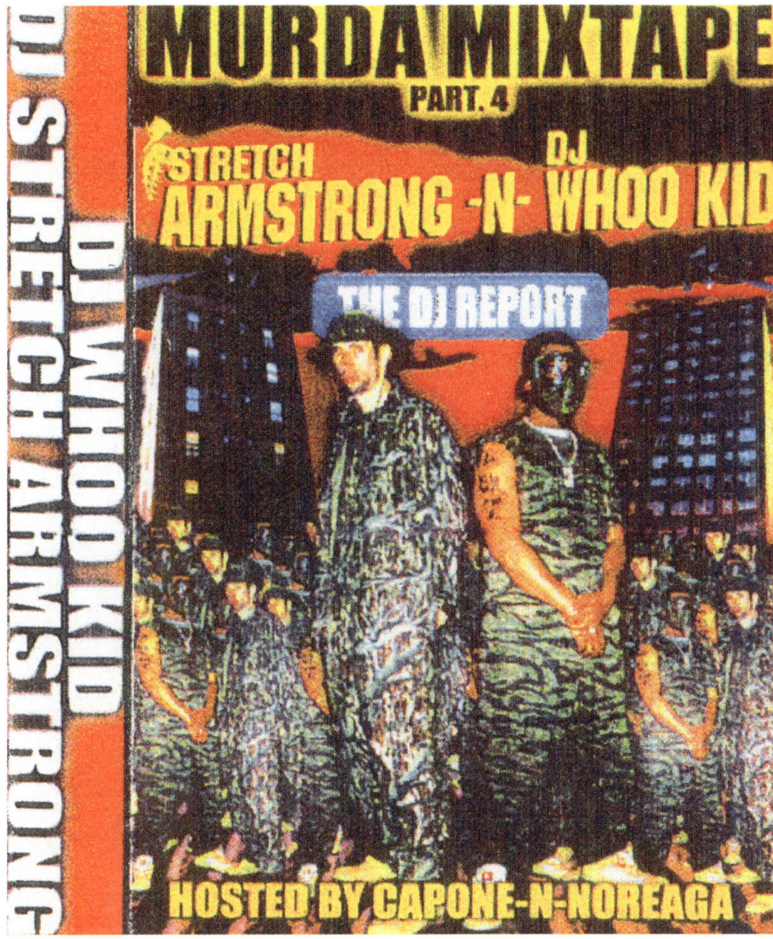
DJ WHOO KID
DJ STRETCH ARMSTRONG
MURDA MIXTAPE
PART. 4
STRETCH ARMSTRONG -N- DJ WHOO KID
THE DJ REPORT
HOSTED BY CAPONE-N-NOREAGA

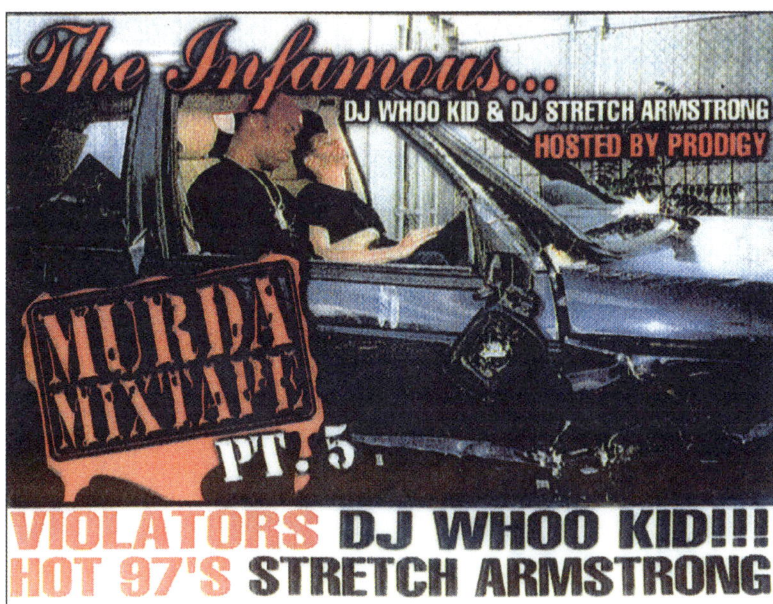
The Infamous...
DJ WHOO KID & DJ STRETCH ARMSTRONG
HOSTED BY PRODIGY
MURDA
MIXTAPE
PT. 5
VIOLATORS DJ WHOO KID!!!
HOT 97'S STRETCH ARMSTRONG

Whoo Kid: I played the original version of "Middle Finger U" on a tape. On the song, Sauce Money was killing Big Pun, because at the time I think Big Pun had beef with Jay-Z. His peoples supposedly hit Jay with a bottle in the club or some shit. But Jay never retaliated or did a record.

I think I got it from Envy and them, but they didn't want to play it because they knew Pun and the record I think was going at Pun. But I didn't know how real it was, because I wasn't out there like that. So I was like, "Give it to me, I'll play it."

The fucked up shit is, there were no ill head shots of Pun at that time. So when I went to do the cover, the only photo I had of Pun was him laying back on a chair looking crazy with his gut out. So he was kind of pissed about that, too. But the thing was, he didn't know who I was to catch me. So he finally got the number off the tape.

I did some free party with Flex in Queens. And Pun acted like he was gonna book me for somewhere in Harlem and pay me $1,000. It was Pun actually talking to me, but I didn't know. I thought the breathing was kind of weird, but I didn't know it was Pun. He was like, "Yeah, we got this show with Flex and Big Kap. You and Kap are gonna kill it. Where you wanna meet?" So I was like, "Holy shit," because I was getting like $150 to $300 to DJ at that time. So I said, "Don't call my manager. I'm gonna come out to the Apollo to meet you, and I'll DJ your show."

I called my boy who had a gun to come with me. And I had the Honda Accord with the lights that come up. I had a super-wack whip. So we're waiting for the guy to come meet me. I get out to use the payphone to call the number that called me, and I'm like, "Motherfucker, where the fuck you at?!" I thought it was a promoter, and I would yell at promoters. I had no respect for promoters. So I'm like, "Fuck you, nigga. You better hurry the fuck up! We've been waiting out here all day." So Pun was probably like, "Yo, who the fuck is this guy?!?! Let's get everybody!!"

Pun was doing the "Banned From TV" video that day. And this was before I was DJing for N.O.R.E. So Pun played the Sauce Money record off the tape at the video shoot, and had everybody from "Banned From TV" surrounding him listening to it. So he was like, "Yo, we're gonna get this nigga today. I wanna hurry up and finish this video so I can go get this nigga." N.O.R.E. was telling me they were all like, "I hope it ain't Clue. I think this might be Clue." So Pun finishes the "Banned From TV" video and goes to meet me at the Apollo.

I'm in the car, and I see a Benz. I'm like, "Oh shit, this guy's got the paper!" And my friends are in the car going crazy and shit. So I get out, and some Puerto Rican kid in the car is like, "Whooo Kiiiid," and does my shout. And I'm like, "Damn, Flex be hanging with Puerto Ricans?" So he's like, "Nah, follow me Uptown, and we'll do the business there." So I'm like, "Aiight, I'll follow you, kid," because it was an ill Benz. So I was like, "This guy means business."

I get there, and the road was like one of those project joints with the circle, where you can go left or right. So the way they mapped it out is they went to the right, and I had to park to the left. But there was a van in the middle. And the van in the middle had rims, and you could tell it had a big screen on the inside. So I was like, "Oh, Flex is here! I'm gonna go talk to Flex, God!" You know, because Flex had the car shit he was promoting. So I told my boys to chill, like, "I'm gonna get this money, then we'll go get some weed." So everybody's happy, because they just wanted some weed anyway. They just came for that.

I get out, and there's a Puerto Rican outside all happy, then another Puerto Rican sitting on the bench. And I'm like, "Flex got Puerto Ricans all over?" I wasn't even thinking about Pun or nothing until I went around the van. And the way they parked, the van blocked my friends from seeing me. So my friends are in the car chilling, bullshitting or whatever.

The door starts sliding, and I see this big shadow in the car. And I'm like, "Yo, I didn't know Flex was fucking fat like that. Is that Big Kap?" And once I saw Pun, the mixtape came into my head, and I was like, "Holy shit. I don't believe this shit."

Pun's like, "Come inside. Let me have a chat with you." And I'm like, "Hell no!" So I tried to back up, but I had to go far so my friends could see I was in trouble. And as I was backing up, my hands went down. And when my hands went down, Pun had an Uzi. I closed my eyes, and when I opened them, I was in the van. That's how fast they threw me in the van.

I'm like, "What the fuck! I'm gonna die for a fucking song!" I'm screaming, like, "Yo, are you serious!?" They had me on my knees, and his boys were yelling in Spanish, "Callate la boca," and all this crazy shit. So Pun is like, "Come here and sit next to me." But there was nowhere to sit, because he was taking up the whole shit.

I go to get up, and the tape with him on the cover falls out of my pocket. His boys are screaming in Spanish, and I'm like, "I'm gonna fucking die!"

Pun kicks his boy out, and he explained that the Latin Kings were laughing at him because of the tape. It was everywhere. It was at Beat Street, and all over the Bronx. It was not just about the picture on the cover, but because of the song. He was like, "You're making me look crazy out here because I didn't respond yet. The Latin Kings are laughing at me, like, 'Who is this Whoo Kid guy? Does he have no respect for you?'"

I'm like, "Do I look like a gangbanger or some shit?" And he's like, "I'm starting to figure that out right now. I'm gonna go to Roc-A-Fella and handle all this bullshit, like, tomorrow. And on the intro to your next tape, I want you to be like, 'Fuck Jay-Z, fuck Sauce Money.'" I was like, "Whatever, just let me outta here!"

That was my first reality check with anything that has to do with gangsterism in hip hop. Some people are fake, but some people are real.

I kept stealing shit after that because of that adrenaline rush. Once you get past a life-threatening situation, then you have no fear. All of a sudden I was DJing for CNN, even though N.O.R.E. was like, "I wanted to fuckin' kill you because you had mad shit of mine." Even Clue was like, "They want to kill me this year, but next year they want to hang with me." So you just gotta take risks. I had mad Jay-Z shit, mad Nas shit.

Once I bought my Benz, I quit my job working security at the airport. I was saving, living with my parents, but then I was like, "Fuck that job shit." You know, all a nigga need is a whip.

That was my first reality check with anything that has to do with gangsterism in hip hop. Some people are fake, but some people are real.

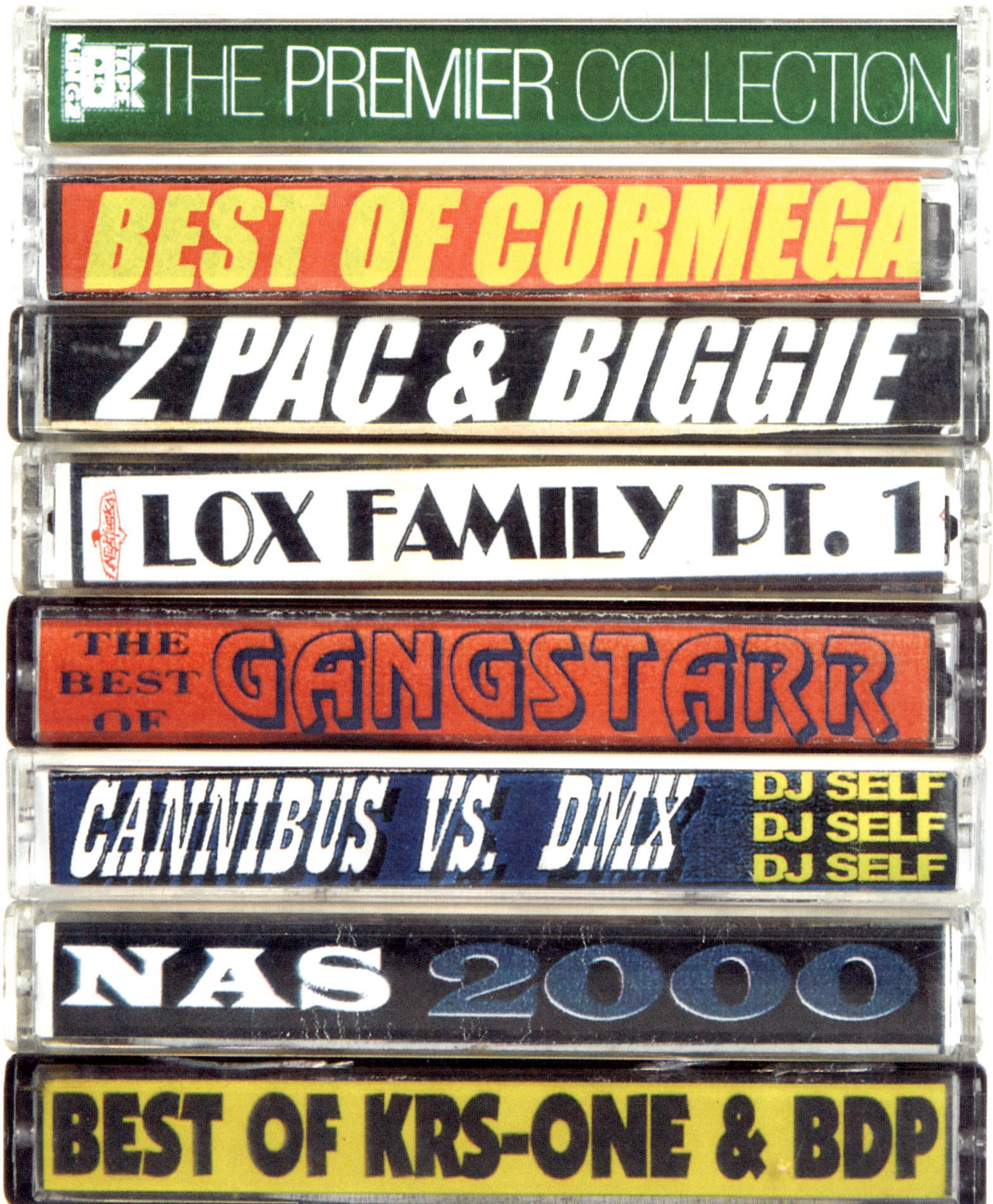
THE PREMIER COLLECTION
BEST OF CORMEGA
2 PAC & BIGGIE
LOX FAMILY PT. 1
THE BEST OF GANGSTARR
CANNIBUS VS. DMX
DJ SELF
DJ SELF
DJ SELF
NAS 2000
BEST OF KRS-ONE & BDP

THE BEST OFs

Though mixtapes began as a replication of the party experience featuring back-to-back songs by multiple artists, DJs knew they needed to innovate in order to separate themselves from their competitors. So as NYC-based artists began to bubble in the streets, a new trend in mixtape-making emerged. DJs started putting their own spin on the idea of a "greatest hits" compilation, making tapes chock-full of what they deemed to be a specific rapper or group or crew's illest cuts. These are THE BEST OFS.

DJ MISTER CEE

Best of the Best: Celebrating Artists on Mixtapes

Before Brooklyn DJ Mister Cee came out with *The Best of Biggie*, the idea of a hip-hop artist from New York having a greatest hits mixtape was unheard of—especially an MC who only had one album out. But in the years after Cee and Tape Kingz released it, "Best of" tapes became one of the most popular mixtape formats, with DJs gathering the illest singles, b-sides, deep cuts, and freestyles by one artist or group or crew and compiling them all on one tape. In that regard, Mister Cee created a whole genre of mixtapes.

MOTIVATION TO MAKE MIXTAPES

Mister Cee: In the '80s and early '90s, a lot of DJs wanted to DJ for a rapper or get connected with a rapper. Whereas I got to a point, being with Kane, where I wanted to branch out. There was no problem with me and Kane, but I just saw a vision for myself, standing and doing this thing alone as a DJ. That was the process for me. Now we call it "creating your brand," but back then it was just like, "I just need to get out there and let people see that I can DJ." So I remember doing that as a DJ early on. And, eventually in the early '90s, I started making mixtapes.

When I started doing mixtapes, it was really solely for me. It was to show people that I was beyond just being Big Daddy Kane's DJ. That I was a DJ for real.

120 MINUTE TAPES

One of the things that I was really proud of when I started doing the mixtapes was that I was the only DJ that made 120 minute cassette tapes. There was no other DJ that ever made a 120 minute cassette tape.

The only drawback with the 120 cassette is that it was easy to pop because it was a thinner cassette than a 90 or 60 minute cassette. Duplicating was the same, you just had to have the longer tape. And it was a pain in the ass for Tape Kingz to get 120 minute cassettes because everybody else did 90. But once we got into a rhythm of doing it, they were really excited.

RELATIONSHIP WITH TAPE KINGZ

My relationship with them was probably way more intimate than their relationship with any other DJ, because I was one of the first ones they dealt with. It was more than just us working together. We were dear friends.

The one thing I always loved about working with Steve and Iain is that if I had a vision or I had an idea, they never turned me down. They made sure that whatever I wanted to execute, it was executed 1000%.

I would not be DJ Mister Cee, as far as the brand, without Tape Kingz. They had the access to getting the mixtapes not only across America but around the world to Paris and to Japan. I'm eternally grateful to those guys.

"BEST OF" MIXTAPES

I was the absolute first DJ to ever do a "Best Of" mixtape, hands down. I did a Biggie, then I did Red and Meth second, then Mobb Deep, then Jay-Z.

My whole approach for doing all of the "Best Of" series was to display all the records that these artists did with other acts. It wasn't really about displaying the stuff they did on their own. And this is what made those tapes successful. After the Jay-Z tape, I just stopped doing the "Best of" tapes because then everybody was doing it.

My favorite one to listen back to is *Mobb Deep*. They're one of my favorite rap groups of all-time. There were like six unreleased songs on it and nobody had them. I can't even remember how I got them.

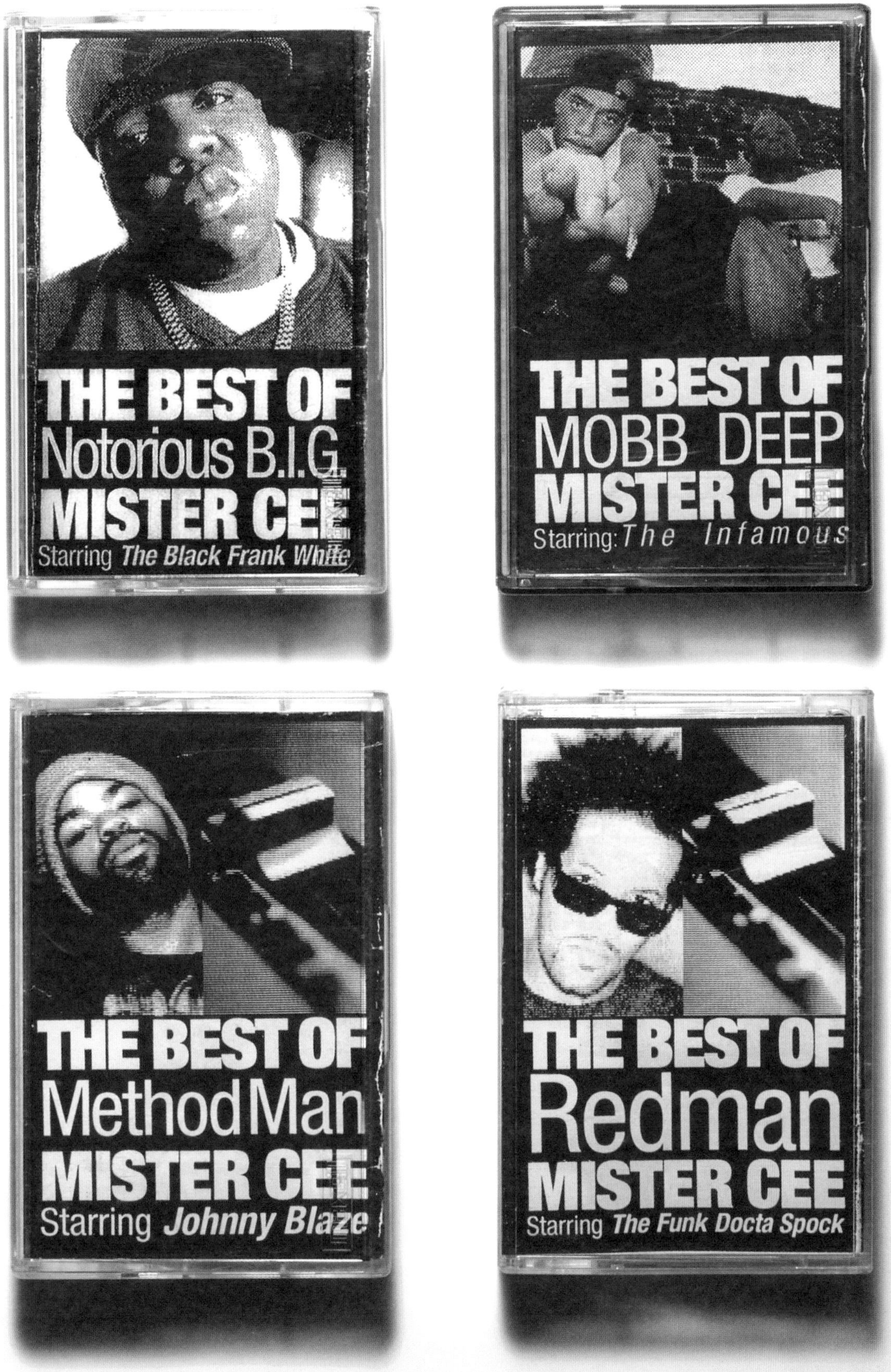
THE BEST OF
Notorious B.I.G.
MISTER CEE
Starring The Black Frank White
THE BEST OF
MOBB DEEP
MISTER CEE
Starring: The Infamous
THE BEST OF
Method Man
MISTER CEE
Starring Johnny Blaze
THE BEST OF
Redman
MISTER CEE
Starring The Funk Docta Spock

Mister Cee: I never even had a conversation with B.I.G. about doing *The Best of Biggie* tape. I just thought about doing it because he was on so many records at that time. When I put that tape out, it was really about me being so amazed with all the guest appearances that he did at that time, from "Real Love" with Mary J. Blige to "Buddy X" with Neneh Cherry. That really was my motivation for making the tape. It was just me being so proud of all the records he was on, and how rapidly big he had become as a rapper.

There were a lot of little nuggets on that *Best of Biggie* mixtape. It just showed all of the stuff that B.I.G. was associated with in such a short amount of time leading up to the *Ready to Die* album, because this is all the stuff he was on before *Ready to Die* came out. The stuff with Crustified Dibbs, the stuff with Red Hot Lover Tone, "All Men Are Dogs." It was just to display all the stuff that he was on with other artists.

RECORDING THE INTRO

We did that at my apartment in Bed-Stuy, Brooklyn. I used to live on Gates Avenue in Bed-Stuy, which was literally up the street from where B.I.G. lived. B.I.G. lived on St. James between Gates and Fulton. I lived on Gates between Franklin and Bedford, which was basically a three to five block walk from Biggie's house.

We did that with two turntables and a mic. That's all we used. One take, maybe two. When Biggie came to my place, we played a couple of instrumentals. Biggie picked the Casual beat, but I played him other songs that were out at that time.

THE BEST OF BIGGIE RECEPTION

When the tape came out, he hit me up and was like, "I need like 50 copies." So when he asked me for the copies of the mixtape, I knew that he was very proud of it.

But that mixtape is the defining moment. I wanted to become a name on my own, and *Best of Biggie* made me become that brand, like a ghetto household name. And it makes me tear up. I remember people telling me, "They're playing your mixtape at Freaknik, they're playing your mixtape in Virginia Beach." And I was just so proud of the success of that mixtape and the money that I made off of it. Hands down, I made more money off that *Best of Biggie* mixtape than any other mixtape I ever did.

PUFF DADDY'S SUPPORT

Arista Records sent me a cease and desist to stop putting the mixtape out, and this was early. It was only out a couple of weeks, maybe two or three weeks tops. And I was scared as shit because I didn't know what to do. I went to Iain and Steve at Tape Kingz and I was like, "Yo, they sent us a cease and desist. We're going to have to stop putting this mixtape out for a minute." So we stopped doing pressings of the mixtape maybe for like a week or two.

However, something just told me to call Puff about it. I said, "Yo, man, I got a letter from Arista, they don't want me to put this mixtape out." And Puff was like, "Fuck that, keep putting it out! Keep doing it, man. All this is doing is making Biggie hotter. Keep doing it!"

He was like, "I got you. I'll protect you. Don't worry about it. Just keep putting it out." So once Puff said we were good, I called Steve and Iain up or maybe went over to their house and I said, "Yo, we're back in business."

Iain McNee, Tape Kingz: That was by far and away the biggest seller. I remember meeting Cee outside on Sterling Place and it was a hot day. He calls and says, "I'm in a taxi downstairs." I go downstairs, he jumps out—he's about to go on tour with Big Daddy Kane. He says, "I'm gonna give you this now, you gotta get it out! Do it fast, fast, fast! I'm gonna be away for like 10 days." I was like, "Okay, fast, fast, fast—let's do it!"

I got the tape, back upstairs, duplicating the tapes, it's in Beat Street the same afternoon. Fantastic. Then when he comes back, he says, "How'd that tape do?" I said, "Incredible. You have no idea."

He was buzzing, it was just great. He got to feel it, because he was out of New York and he had no idea what was going on. But never did we ever have any demand like we had for that tape. The big three stores downtown Brooklyn—Jackpot, Beat Street, and Music Factory—were just relentless.

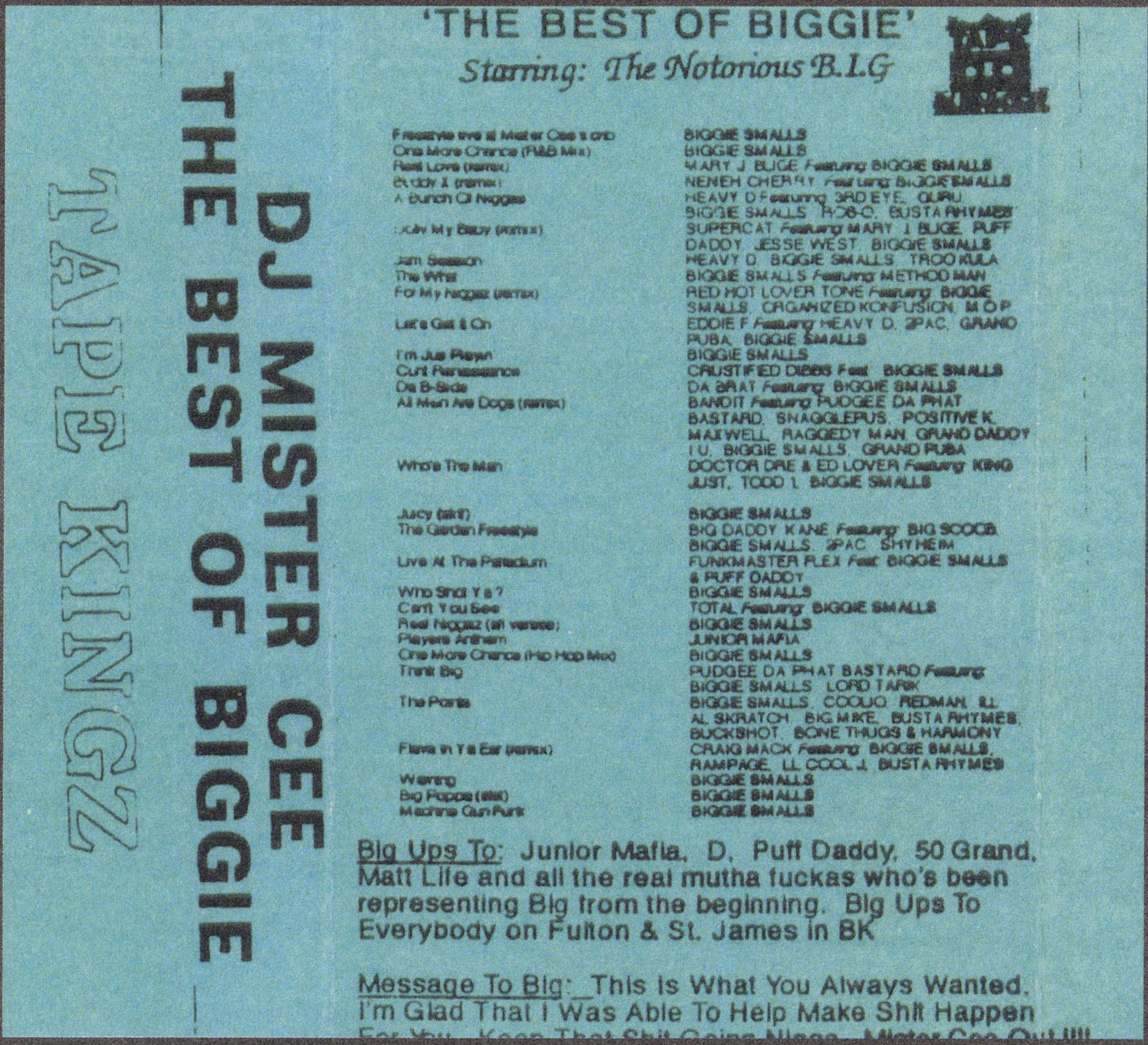
TAPE KINGZ
DJ MISTER CEE
THE BEST OF BIGGIE
'THE BEST OF BIGGIE'
Starring: The Notorious B.I.G
BIGGIE SMALLS
One More Chance (R&B Mix)
BIGGIE SMALLS
MARY J BLIGE Featuring BIGGIE SMALLS
NENEH CHERRY Featuring BIGGIE SMALLS
HEAVY D Featuring 3RD EYE, GURU
BIGGIE SMALLS, ROB-O, BUSTA RHYMES
SUPERCAT Featuring MARY J BLIGE, PUFF DADDY, JESSE WEST, BIGGIE SMALLS
Jam Session
HEAVY D, BIGGIE SMALLS, TROO KULA
BIGGIE SMALLS Featuring METHOD MAN
RED HOT LOVER TONE Featuring BIGGIE SMALLS, ORGANIZED KONFUSION, M O P
EDDIE F Featuring HEAVY D, 2PAC, GRAND PUBA, BIGGIE SMALLS
BIGGIE SMALLS
CRUSTIFIED DIBBS Feat. BIGGIE SMALLS
Da B-Side
DA BRAT Featuring BIGGIE SMALLS
BANDIT Featuring PUDGEE DA PHAT BASTARD, SNAGGLEPUS, POSITIVE K, MAXWELL, RAGGEDY MAN, GRAND DADDY I.U., BIGGIE SMALLS, GRAND PUBA
Who's The Man
DOCTOR DRE & ED LOVER Featuring KING JUST, TODD 1, BIGGIE SMALLS
BIGGIE SMALLS
The Garden Freestyle
BIG DADDY KANE Featuring BIG SCOOB, BIGGIE SMALLS, 2PAC, SHYHEIM
Live At The Palladium
FUNKMASTER FLEX Feat. BIGGIE SMALLS & PUFF DADDY
Who Shot Ya?
BIGGIE SMALLS
Can't You See
TOTAL Featuring BIGGIE SMALLS
BIGGIE SMALLS
Players Anthem
JUNIOR MAFIA
One More Chance (Hip Hop Mix)
BIGGIE SMALLS
PUDGEE DA PHAT BASTARD Featuring BIGGIE SMALLS, LORD TARIK
The Points
BIGGIE SMALLS, COOLIO, REDMAN, ILL AL SKRATCH, BIG MIKE, BUSTA RHYMES, BUCKSHOT, BONE THUGS & HARMONY
Flava in Ya Ear (remix)
CRAIG MACK Featuring BIGGIE SMALLS, RAMPAGE, LL COOL J, BUSTA RHYMES
Warning
BIGGIE SMALLS
BIGGIE SMALLS
BIGGIE SMALLS
Big Ups To: Junior Mafia, D, Puff Daddy, 50 Grand, Matt Life and all the real mutha fuckas who's been representing Big from the beginning. Big Ups To Everybody on Fulton & St. James in BK
Message To Big: This Is What You Always Wanted. I'm Glad That I Was Able To Help Make Shit Happen

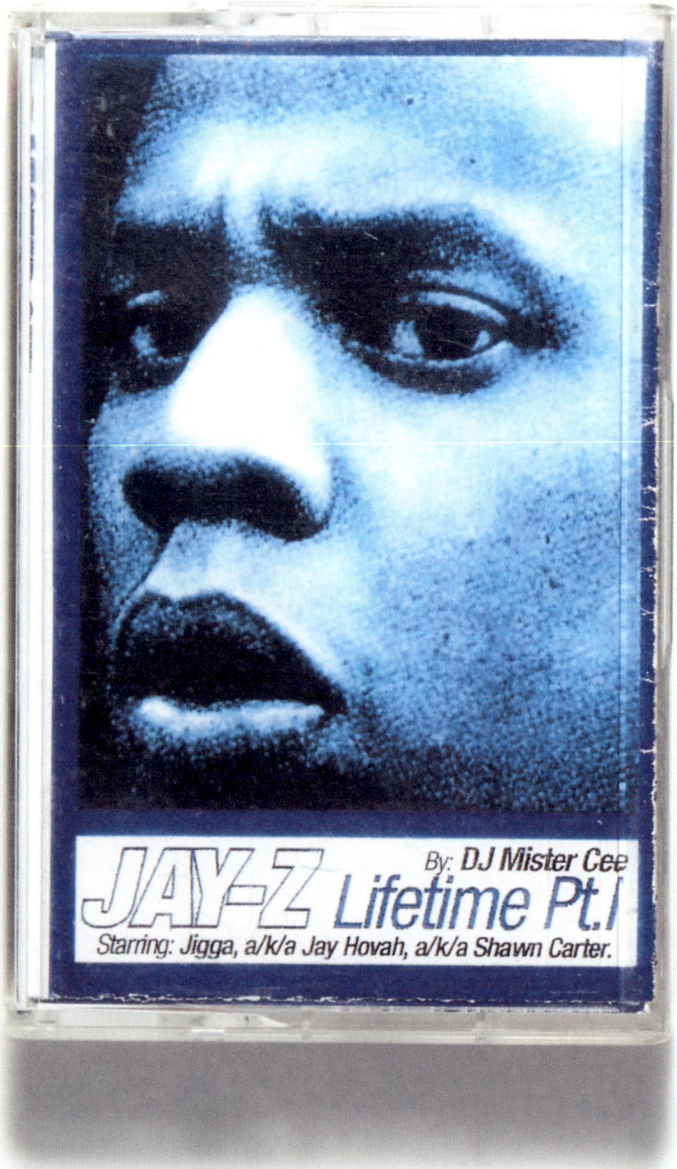
By: DJ Mister Cee
JAY-Z Lifetime Pt.I
Starring: Jigga, a/k/a Jay Hovah, a/k/a Shawn Carter.

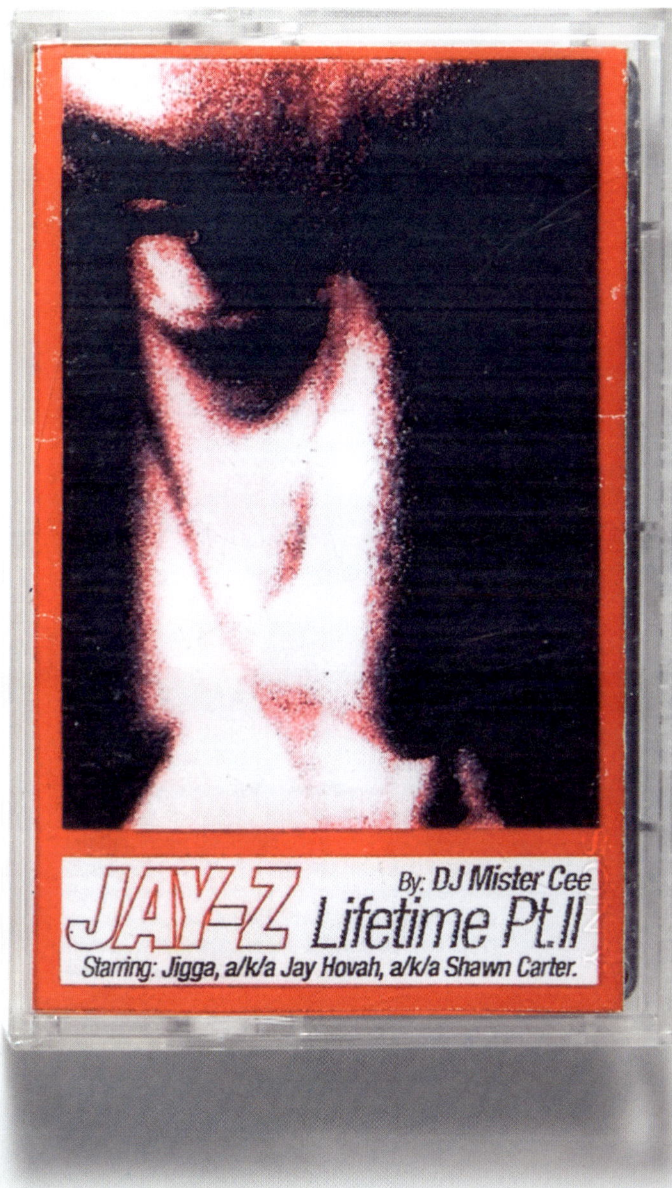
JAY-Z
By: DJ Mister Cee
Lifetime Pt.II
Starring: Jigga, a/k/a Jay Hovah, a/k/a Shawn Carter.

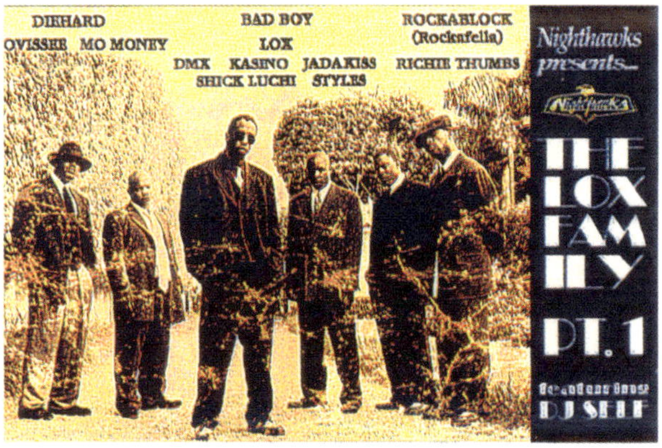
DIEHARD
OVISSHE MO MONEY
BAD BOY
LOX
DMX KASINO JADAKISS
SHICK LUCHI STYLES
ROCKABLOCK
(Rockafella)
RICHIE THUMBS
Nighthawks presents...
THE LOX FAMILY
PT.1
DJ SELF

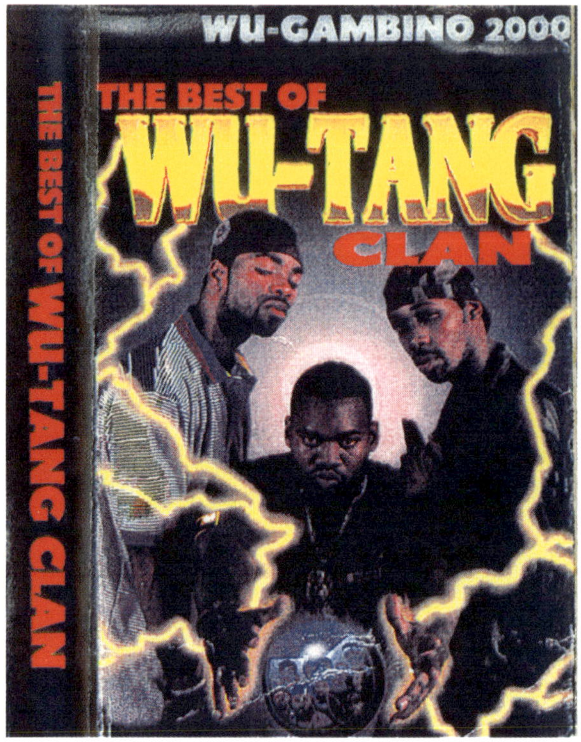
WU-GAMBINO 2000
THE BEST OF
WU-TANG
CLAN
THE BEST OF WU-TANG CLAN

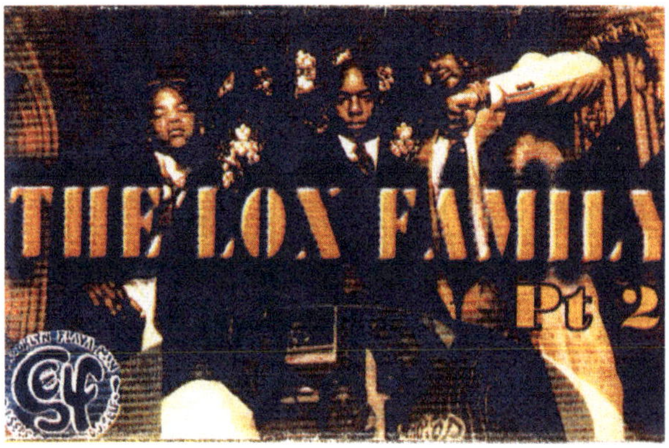
THE LOX FAMILY
Pt 2

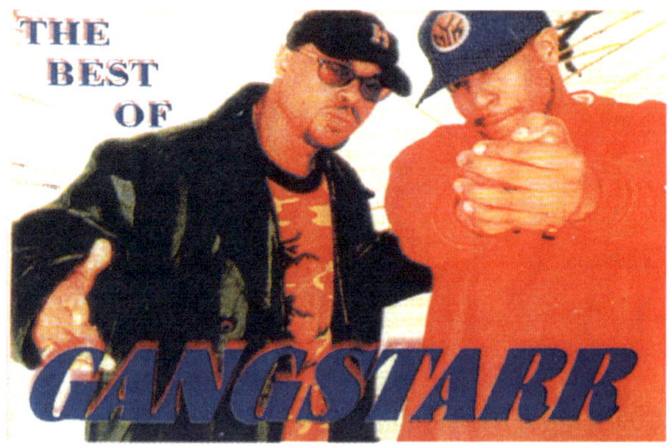
THE BEST OF
GANGSTARR

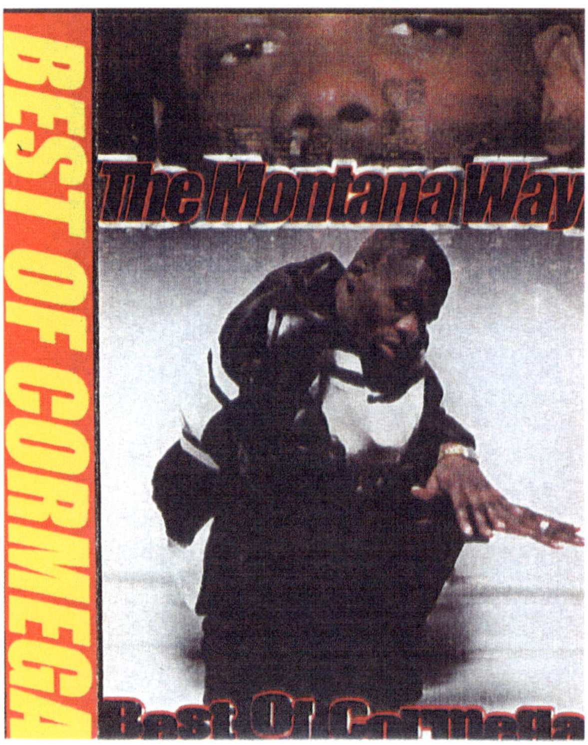
BEST OF CORMEGA
The Montana Way

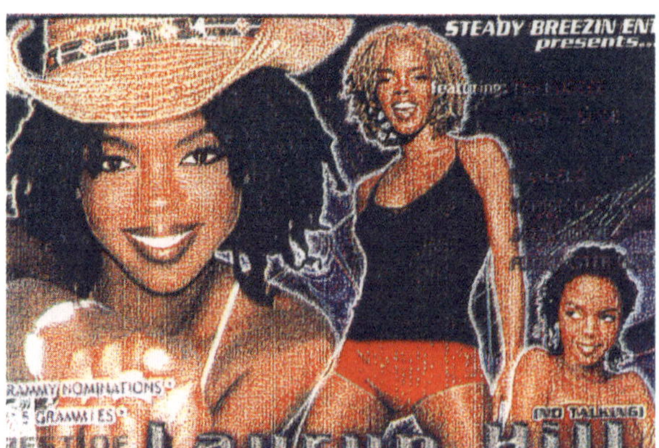
STEADY BREEZIN ENT
presents...
Laurun Hill

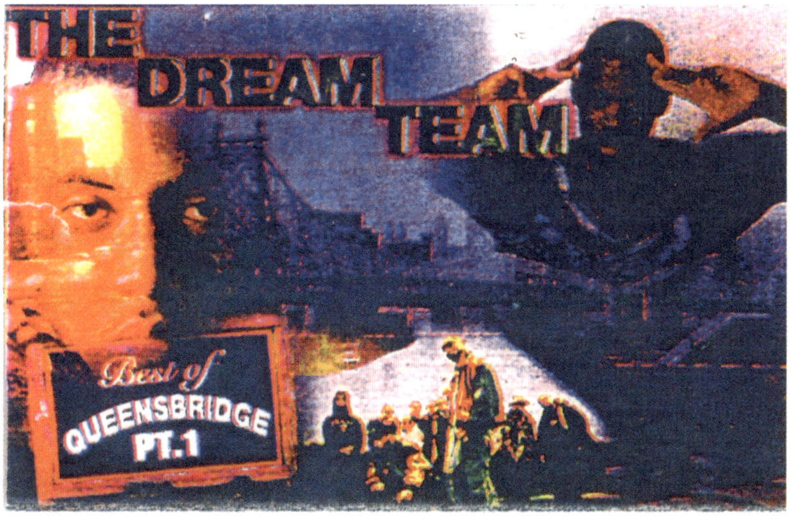
THE DREAM TEAM
Best of
QUEENSBRIDGE
PT.1

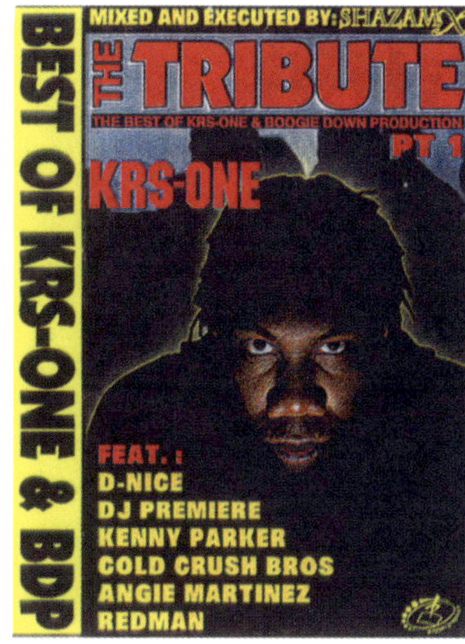
MIXED AND EXECUTED BY: SHAZAM X
THE TRIBUTE
THE BEST OF KRS-ONE & BOOGIE DOWN PRODUCTION
PT 1
KRS-ONE
BEST OF KRS-ONE & BDP
FEAT.:
D-NICE
DJ PREMIERE
KENNY PARKER
COLD CRUSH BROS
ANGIE MARTINEZ
REDMAN

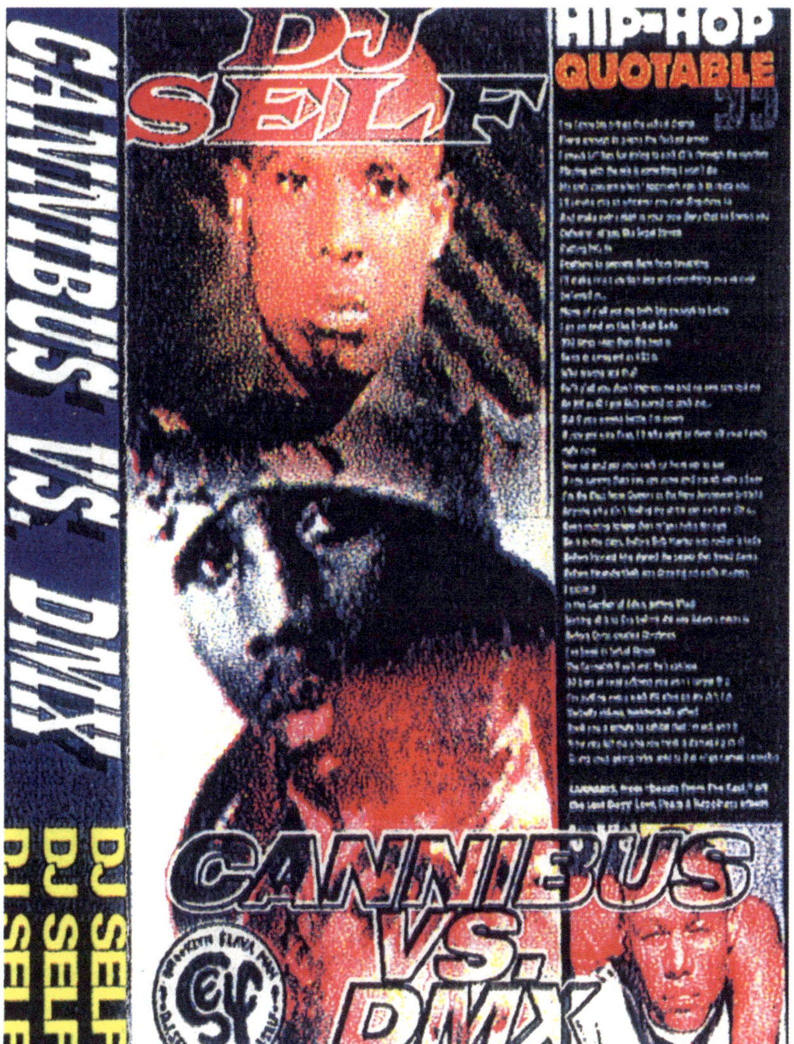
DJ SELF
HIP-HOP QUOTABLE
CANNIBUS VS. DMX!
DJ SELF
DJ SELF
DJ SELF
CANNIBUS VS. DMX

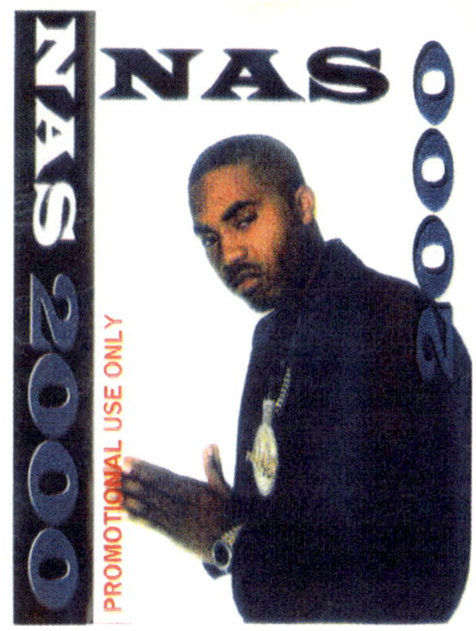
NAS
2000
NAS 2000
PROMOTIONAL USE ONLY
2000

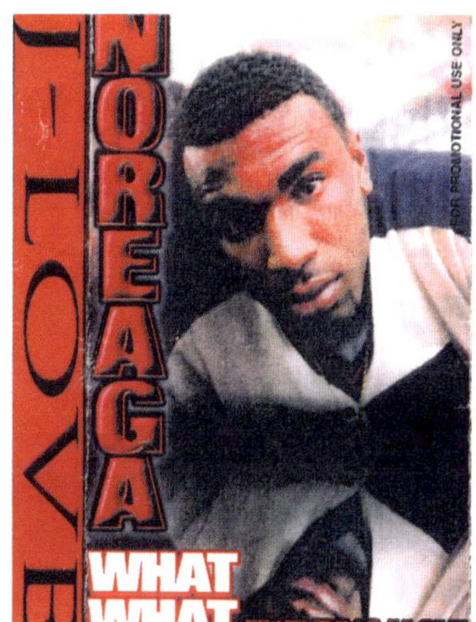
NOREAGA
J-LOVE
WHAT WHAT
FEATURING J-LOVE
FOR PROMOTIONAL USE ONLY

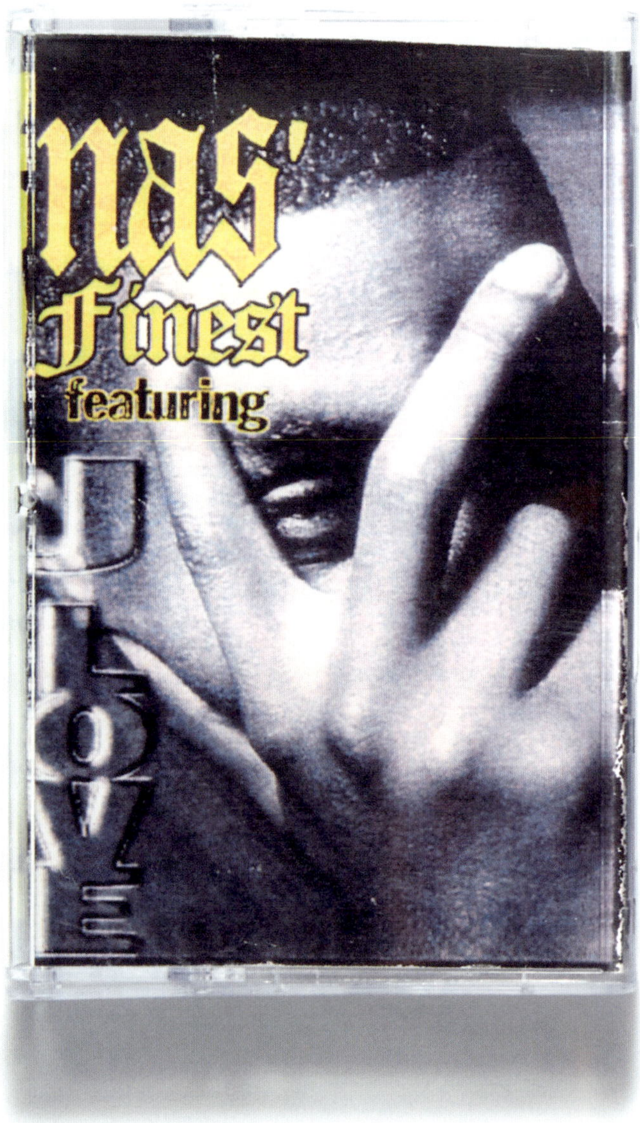
nas'
Finest
featuring
LOVE

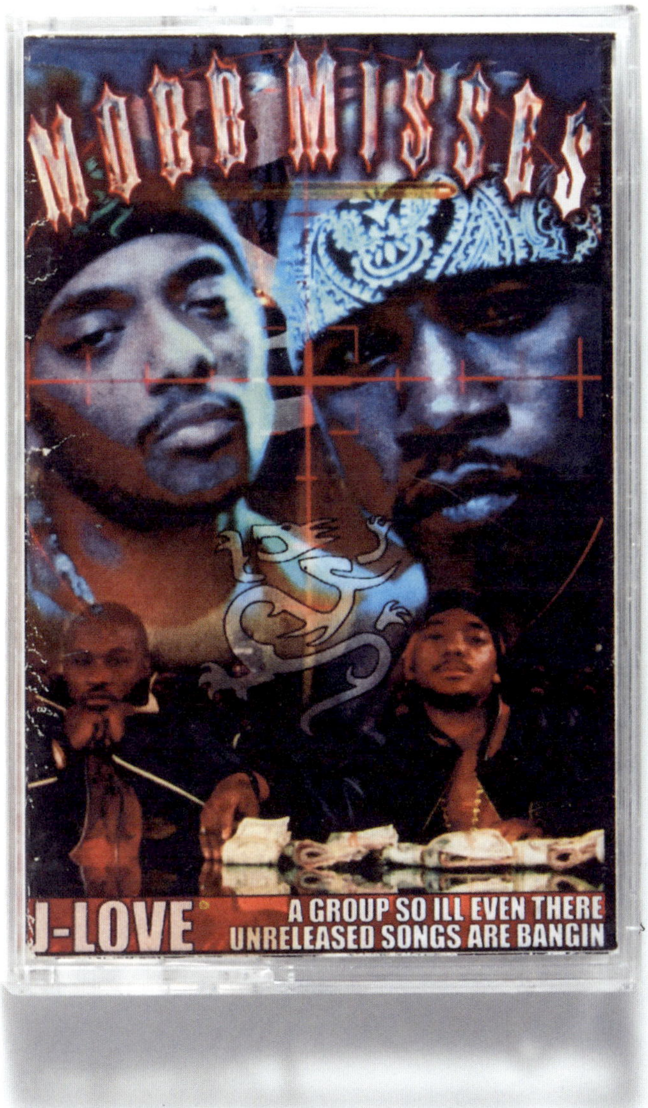
MOBB MISSES
J-LOVE
A GROUP SO ILL EVEN THERE
UNRELEASED SONGS ARE BANGIN

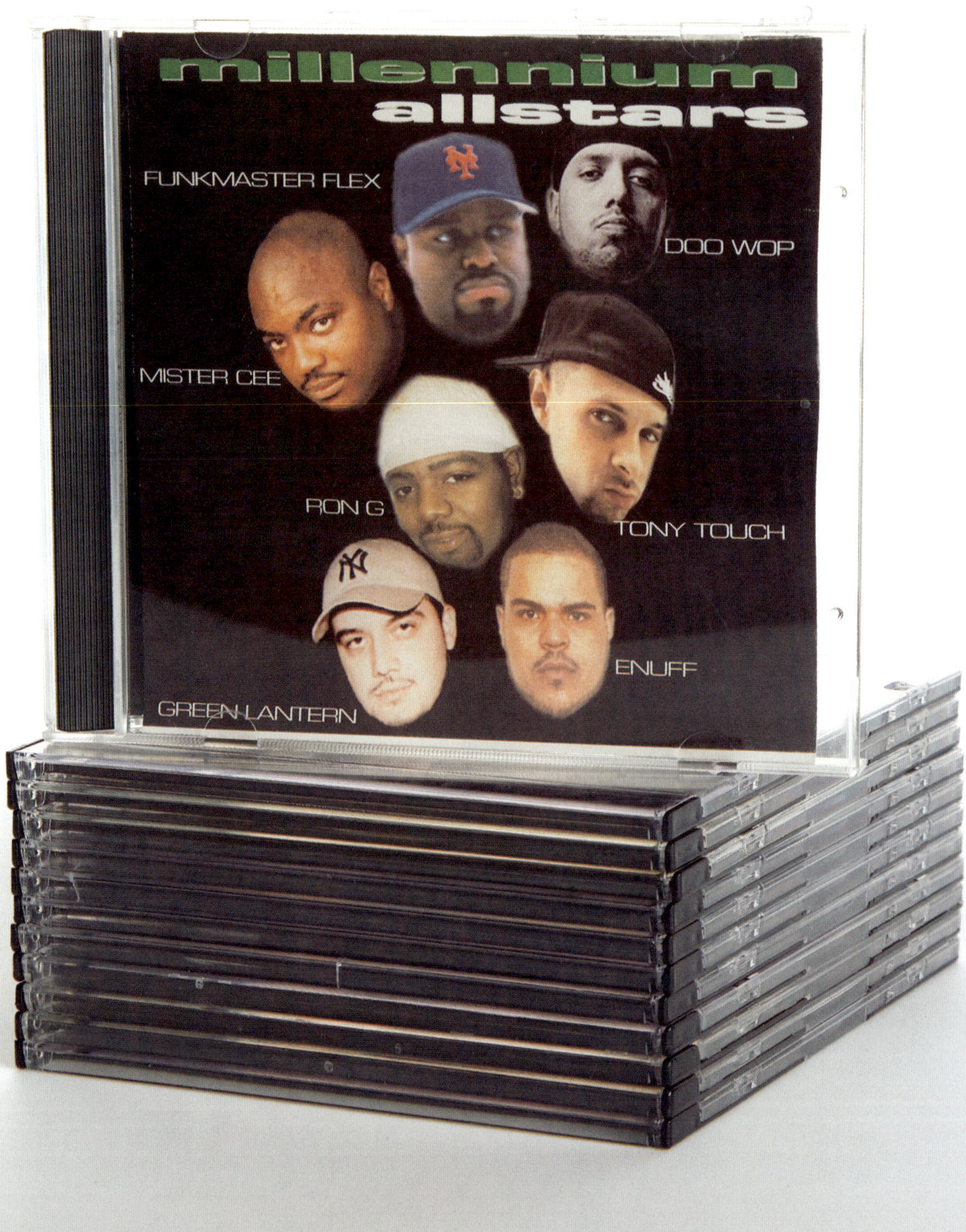
millennium
allstars
FUNKMASTER FLEX
DOO WOP
MISTER CEE
RON G
TONY TOUCH
ENUFF
GREEN LANTERN

THE SHIFT TO CDs

One of the biggest game-changers during the mixtape boom in NYC was the shift in formats from cassettes to compact discs. With CDs, DJs and stores could replicate mixtapes at a much faster and cheaper rate, plus it helped maintain quality with each generation of copy being made. It also changed the format, eliminating the need for a Side A and Side B, and extending the standard play time of a mixtape to 120 minutes. But with the change came some growing pains as it forced DJs and store owners to adapt to the challenges. And the ones who did benefited greatly from THE SHIFT TO CDs.

NEW FORMAT, NEW OPPORTUNITIES: ***Remembering how the evolution from tapes to CDs changed the game.***

Darryl McCray, House of Nubian: I was still making good money, but the cassette tapes flattened out and people started asking for CDs because that was the new thing. There were no longer cassette tapes in cars anymore. People were getting cars with CDs in them. So when the DJs finally got smart and started doing it, that's when it was big.

> **That CD had a great sound. There wasn't that cassette hiss anymore, you didn't have to fast-forward shit.**
>
> **-GREEN LANTERN**

Splash: The tapes were good for a while, and I think it was Clue that started transitioning to CDs. That's when we went and bought CD machines. In 2000, we had three 1 to 4 machines and they were like $2,000 a piece. I think we got them from Guitar Center or Sam Ash. We started doing that, and we had weekly trips to Beat Street Records. They would pay us every week, and then there was out-of-town money. We were living really well.

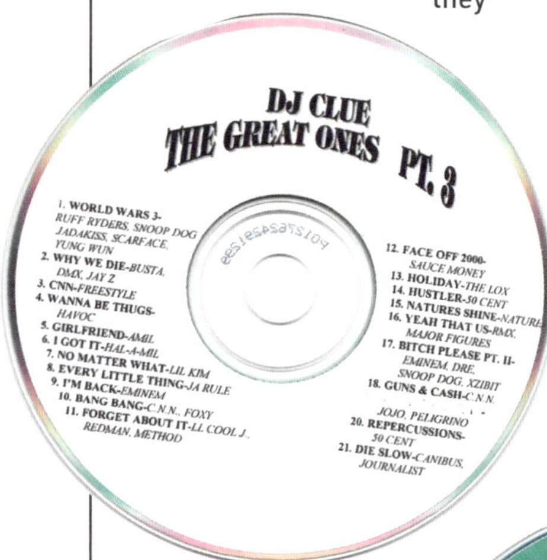

Green Lantern: I believe Clue was the first guy to really do it big. There might have been other guys, but he was definitely the biggest. He was already the biggest at that time.

Action Pac: You had no choice but to get CDs because the CD players were going to be the new wave. It was actually a good thing when it first started because you could sell tapes and CDs, a combination of the two.

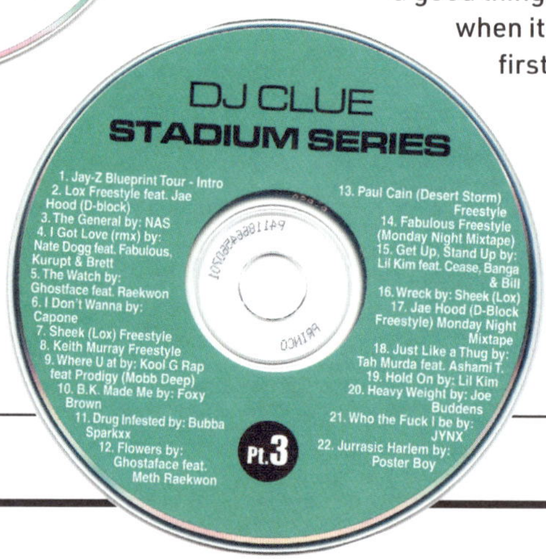

Tapes were good, but it cost a lot more to produce them. CDs became profitable when we were able to press them up ourselves. Then, more stores came about in the Bronx and all the boroughs. Then the clothing stores started selling them. Everybody was trying to generate any kind of money that was affiliated with hip hop. Dudes were selling the hats, the shirts, and the mixtapes. So the more stores, the more paper.

Green Lantern: When you look back and see what fucked it all up, it was the conversion of analog to digital. That CD had a great sound. There wasn't that cassette hiss anymore, you didn't have to fast-forward shit. There were certain blessings.

The profits were better out of the gate, but it quickly

went downhill. There were a few years where it was nice. A consumer can walk into a store and buy a cassette in '98 for $10. Here the CD comes in, and they can buy it for $15. It was a higher price point, so you got a bit more on the wholesale.

But what it ended up ultimately doing was leading to the destruction of the whole game. It was too easy to be bootlegged. There was never any problem when it was the cassette era and it was, "Don't get the bootleg from there, go get the official." Because the official sounded better. Not in the CD era. The bootleg sounded just as good because it's digital.

If you think about it, the introduction of the CD was the beginning of the end because as soon as that happened, the bootlegging came in crazy. My guys on Canal Street, I'm looking at you.

Ron G: When the CD circuit came out, I didn't have the equipment to do that, so I didn't really understand it. I would just do my normal, and the bootleggers would put it on CD. Then I would go to them and be like, "How'd you do this?" And they'd be like, "Ron G, my man Abraham, the best!" Then I started learning how to transform them over to CDs. But my first couple of mixtapes that were on CD weren't actually from me. They were from bootleggers.

Iain McNee, Tape Kingz: I definitely didn't like it. The whole culture shifted. I get it—people want to try new things, and it made duplication a lot easier. You could knock out a lot more CDs, but it took a lot more things away from the mixtape culture when it went to CDs, in my opinion. It suddenly became CDs and tapes of the same title. It was not fun having to do that.

The price also went down from $5 wholesale to selling them as low as $3. Also, when it became the mass duplication of CDs, so many DJs could just go to duplicate it and get 1,000 CDs done. And they didn't care if they sold them for $.50, they just wanted to get the product out. So around '97, everyone was a DJ, and the quality control just totally disappeared. Before that, it used to take real effort and time to make it work.

Once that effort and time weren't required anymore, that was the end of tapes and CDs really doing well in the store. Because too many people weren't familiar with the DJs. Now, there were so many of them. Lots of other stores, they wanted a piece of what was going on, which was fair enough—but there really wasn't that much of it to go around.

We survived by downsizing. Not having nowhere near the number of staff that we used to have. It was easier to duplicate, obviously it was quicker to get more stuff out. We were still getting orders from Japan. You could keep going with stuff like that.

And obviously we were still selling into New York as well. But the smaller stores really began to struggle and there were CODs coming back all the time. I get it—there was no profit on regular albums. The biggest profits were on CDs, but it was a real struggle to make a profit off them. Around '97, '98, '99—it was really tough. I guess we weathered it by just trying to come up with new projects.

I definitely didn't like it. The whole culture shifted. —IAIN MCNEE

LENNY S

The Takeover: Roc-A-Fella Puts on for Themselves

Lenny Santiago, best known as Lenny S, was a prominent Roc-A-Fella A&R who knew the importance of the mixtape. In fact, before he came to the Roc, he worked on Bad Boy's street team as they were pushing the groundbreaking Bad Boy mixtape series. Inspired by this and some of the challenges happening at the time at Roc-A-Fella, Lenny S took advantage of his in-house connections and teamed up with DJ Envy to start his own Roc-A-Fella mixtape series. This not only gave the label a chance to control their own mixtape narrative, but it allowed him to build his personal brand in the process.

THE IMPORTANCE OF LANDING EARLY JAY-Z MIXTAPE PLACEMENTS

Lenny S: At that time for us, it was monumental. Especially Clue–he was only going for the top notch. He was chasing down B.I.G. or Naughty By Nature, or whoever were the top people. Somebody like Jay, he wasn't B.I.G., he didn't have a hit record, he wasn't top of the charts, he wasn't any of that. He was just an ill, dope, self-contained, self-funded rapper from Brooklyn who hustled prior and got money.

Those Clue tapes spoke directly to the streets, so that was a big deal for us. You had the radio DJs at night doing their thing, but the mixtape lived 24 hours a day on every street corner. So that was important when those things got shuffled down to Baltimore, Philly, and North Carolina.

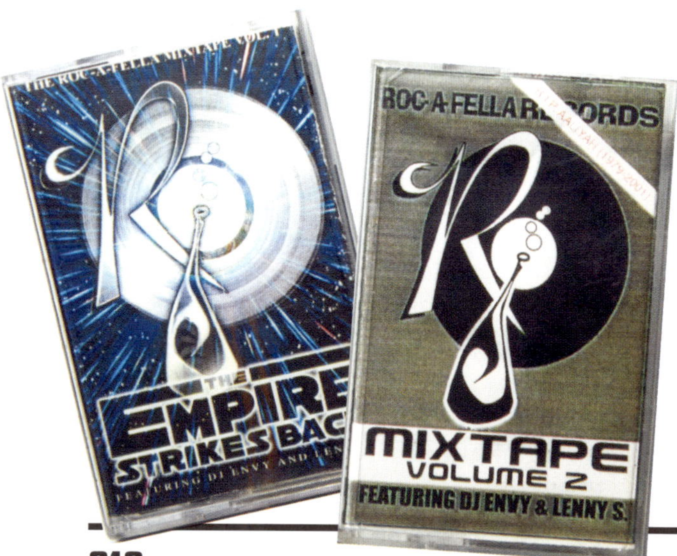

We depended on the mixtapes because they traveled around the country by getting bootlegged and copied, and by word of mouth. Mixtapes were how we discovered Nas introducing Nature, Clue introducing Fabolous–all those guys we found on mixtapes.

ROC-A-FELLA MIXTAPE SERIES

Somebody had a record of Jay's that they weren't supposed to have. Long story short, the guy got caught with the record. He had it outside the office and was playing it. Dame found out and was pissed, obviously, because we weren't supposed to let music leak. He was so pissed that the whole staff got docked because he was like, "One team, one family, one unit. One person gets in trouble, we all get in trouble."

Dame also gave us this crazy speech like, "Y'all better get your shit together because we could let people go for this. This is inexcusable. And if you guys were gone tomorrow, what the hell are you gonna do?" That's when I was like, "I gotta get something going on my own."

We wanted to do the Roc-A-Fella mixtape and get shit bubbling in the street. We wanted to control the narrative since it was our mixtape. DJs had their own mixtapes, but we didn't control that. We would just give them records and hope that they got on there.

I was instructed to go to Clue, because Clue was the hottest DJ at the time, or one of the hottest. Me knowing Clue, I just knew he was difficult. He just did things his own way. I wasn't going to be able to help control the narrative on the tape. I also wanted to put my name on it so I could start branding myself.

So I went to Jay-Z and I was like, "Yo, we gotta do this mixtape. Do you mind if we use Envy? Because Envy does all the distribution for Clue, so we'll open the same doors. I don't know if you're cool with it or Dame's cool with it."

Jay was like, "Okay, if Dame's cool with it, I'm cool with it." I went to Dame, same shit. "I spoke to Jay, I think we should go the DJ Envy route. Envy is new. He's hungry. He's hot. He's right under Clue. We'd have the distribution and we're good." Dame was like, "If Jay's cool with it, I'm cool with it." I did the mom/dad thing and kind of manipulated my way into letting them be okay with Envy. That way I guaranteed with Envy that my name would go on it beside his.

Envy was like, "Fuck yeah." Because at the time for Envy, that was the biggest opportunity of his career. He was doing his thing, but he was under Clue and he was still building. He didn't have anyone that embraced him to the value that Roc-A-Fella had to do a mixtape series. He was doing his own thing with Splash. So, boom, that's how the Roc-A-Fella mixtape *Empire Strikes Back Vol. 1* came about.

We were on fire. We started the mixtape off with Jay-Z's "You Don't Know," that was brand fucking new. Even today that record rings off. So imagine back then, first mixtape, first song, Jay vocals and ad-libs, talking on the mixtape. That was the birth of the Roc-A-Fella mixtape series.

MAKING A NAME

That's also when Lenny S was born. DJ Envy and Lenny S, that's how I got my name on there. And that's how I learned what self-branding was. I tried to make a name for myself, so that God forbid I wasn't at Roc anymore, I would have something to fall back on. So for me, that was the biggest thing of my career. The irony of it all is that Clue gave me the Lenny S name.

ARTIST ACCESS

What was really dope about making those tapes was we had people coming in and out of the studio the entire time. And for the most part, people doing mixtapes didn't have that access with artists. But me being in the studio when Cam came through, it was like, "Yo Cam, Jim, we need drops for the tape." Or, "We need a new song." Jim Jones, Cam, Beanie Sigel, Freeway, and all of those guys were going in the booth just doing studio quality shit-talking, ad-libs, and songs. I was with them all day, so it was easy for us to get something like "Flipside."

The mixtapes were ringing off. With the artists, it was almost like, "I want to be on it." It wasn't like, "Yo I got a mixtape, me and my man, help us out." They were meeting us halfway.

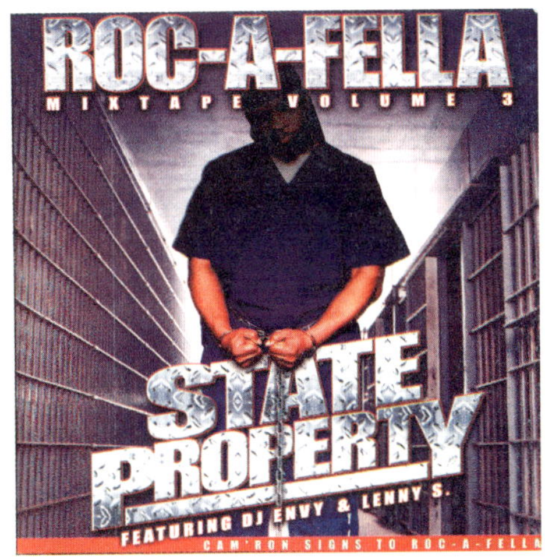

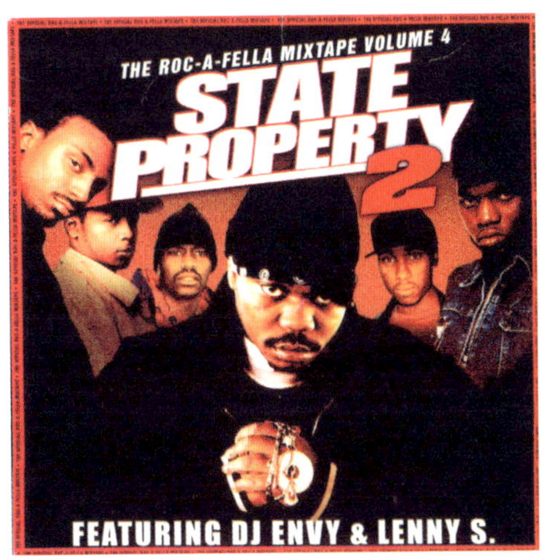

KYAMBO "HIP-HOP" JOSHUA

Diamonds Are Forever: Introducing Roc-A-Fella Music and Artists on Mixtapes

Roc-A-Fella Records understood the impact mixtapes made in the streets dating back to when they were first building a buzz for Jay-Z's debut album *Reasonable Doubt* in 1996. And thanks to guys like Kyambo "Hip-Hop" Joshua—Roc-A-Fella A&R and younger brother of label co-owner Kareem "Biggs" Burke—the label never lost sight of their importance. Whether it was getting major releases on the newest Clue tape or supporting the label's artists as they released their own tapes, Hip Hop was there to help the Roc dominate the mixtape game.

THREE PLATFORMS

Hip-Hop: The mixtape represented the streets. There were three things–the mixtapes, the clubs, and the radio. Those were the platforms that we made music for. We knew if we had one of those three things working, we needed to focus on the others.

Like "Dead Presidents" or some of those early records–we were thinking about mixtapes because we knew we could get there. It was accessible. We'd always have B-Sides for the mixtapes, like "Streets is Watching."

Same thing with the club–you could walk right up to a DJ and hand him a record. He might not play it right away, and you'd buy him a drink and toss him a couple of more dollars. Those things were penetrable and it would ease things when you took it to the radio.

When you took records to the radio that had been on mixtapes, the research was high and the call-out was high. It presented hip hop with a grassroots solution. There was a certain level of boundaries, but mixtapes gave us that local reach.

CLUE TAPES

I feel like Clue was the first one with that power, like being there meant something. I think that's when the boroughs got shattered. I knew Clue well, so I would always give him records. He would pass by my house to go drop his mixtapes off in Harlem. So I would go with him to Harlem Music Hut and other places.

I think he was the only person I dealt with on that level. The others were just guys I was a fan of. They didn't have that impact, because they were going to play it anyway. Flex might make a mixtape once in a blue, even Premier might make a mixtape. But they were coming from the other side, not the subculture. They were utilizing that format. Clue was the subculture at its peak.

I remember driving to Clue's crib to give him "Dead or Alive" and the mixtape was almost finished. His mother was cooking, and she was also making copies on the dining room table. Clue would also swing by the office. "Only a Customer" was one of the ones I gave Clue early. "People's Court," "Who U Wit," and a lot of Beanie Sigel was on the tapes. Like "100 Bars," and him and Bleek freestyles.

DIPLOMATS

Me and DukeDaGod went to the same school. And Jim Jones went to our school–we went to Julia Richman. Cam was one of my closest friends since we were 10 years old playing basketball.

When Cam came to Roc-A-Fella, they were still coming from Harlem with the same mentality of, "We gotta get it hot, we gotta make it pop." When they did the first mixtape, which I believe they did before G-Unit, everybody was mad from Roc-A-Fella because there were too many songs from the album on it.

RELATIONSHIP BETWEEN MIXTAPES AND ALBUMS

That was one of the biggest record label mistakes. I dealt with that a few times–seeing the mixtapes catch up to albums. When Cam and them did it, it took them a minute before there was separate original music that was just on a mixtape. Like when Juelz did his mixtape and then did his album, that was a whole different set of music to where you can throw some records off the album in there, maybe a single or some throwaways just to heat it up, but it was used as almost a completely separate tool.

THE S. CARTER COLLECTION

S. Carter came out in between the *The Blueprint 2* and *The Black Album*. He was doing it mainly as a marketing campaign for the shoes. He had a lot of rhymes at the time, and he needed a platform to get them out there.

MIXTAPE SUCCESS

During the time of the famous Hot 97 freestyle, I feel like everything we did hit the streets early and aggressively. If you think about it, all of Jay's albums got bootlegged. Anything that was happening for us was showing up on mixtapes. Even the performances at Summer Jam made the tapes. So of course they had "Supa Ugly," or the Jadakiss and Beans battle.

We were really trying not to get bootlegged, but when some of the early things we did started going further than we expected, it was good. All the mixtapes did better than expected–Dipset, Kanye. A lot of it came from feeling like we needed to do something, like hold some space. There was no proven track record that someone releasing a mixtape would boost their album sales.

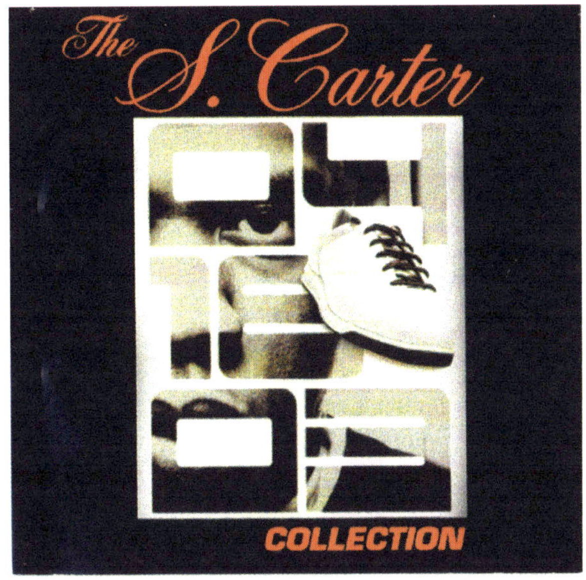

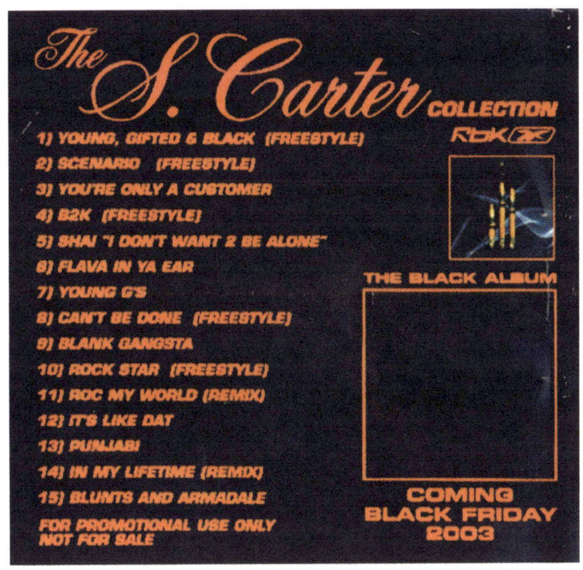

1. "CAN I LIVE" Premieres on DJ Clue Springtyme Stickup '96 - Being on the Clue tape and feeling that reaction, I feel like that was the song that really shifted Jay and put him in arguments alone. People heard "Ain't No Nigga" and "Dead Presidents" and they felt like it was dope, but I remember hearing that verse and feeling like it was creepy good, and saying that we should give them "Can I Live."

   We went to Virginia to perform, and people knew the record. The song really shifted a lot of things. That tape took us to other places, because at that time it was hard for your music to travel. That's when things turned real, because he started to figure out who his consumers were.

2. COSMIC KEV Best of Beanie Sigel - That was him having a "Best Of" before his album even came out. That worked in his favor so much, because everybody knew who he was off of those freestyles. I feel like it changed a lot for street rappers out of Philly because it was so raw.

3. DIPLOMATS VOLUME 1 - "Oh Boy," being that it was the first song, propelled the mixtape. "Oh Boy" was not a Cam record at first. It was a beat I had for a compilation. He was gonna put his verse on it, and then someone else was supposed to get on there. Once he did what he did, he started to claim ownership of the record and put Juelz on it. Dame might have not heard "Oh Boy" until it was on the radio. He took it to Flex, and Dame called an emergency meeting the next day. He was mad, and then found out Cam did it and he was like, "Alright, cool."

4. JAY-Z "I SHOT YA" Freestyle on Bad Boy Mixtape Vol. 3 - That was a verse I could play for people and be like, "Who's fucking with him." That was pre-"Can I Live." He went off on that one, and it was another moment that felt like a shift. I remember Jay going to Stretch to do it and coming back and playing it. I wasn't there when he did, and it was rare that I wasn't with him when he was rapping, but it was early so I wasn't there all the time yet.

   He usually tells me the rhymes first, but I had never had that one before. The "I Shot Ya" beat was his favorite beat. He probably has 10 verses off the "I Shot Ya" beat. He always rhymed on it on the radio. He also loved "Criminology." He always used to spit "Can't Knock the Hustle" over that beat. That's why I was so surprised when it came out so smooth on the original.

5. KANYE WEST Get Well Soon - I remember Kanye had one with songs he produced-*Behind the Beats*. That one surprised me, because there were songs on there that he also produced that were good. At that point, I might have been managing him, or was just about to. He had a bunch of Madd Rapper beats on there, and there were a few good records on

there that opened my eyes to him as an artist.

At that point, a mixtape made sense, because it was sort of like an industry thing. Something you would give out at the parties where he performed. It was more of a demo/EPK type of thing. We needed a tool to show who this guy was, and it worked because it was impressive. People started to get comfortable with him, because that's the first time you heard him as an artist.

When we started doing one, it was out of necessity. It didn't look like we were coming out on Roc-A-Fella or were on the schedule. So our plan was to do a video and a mixtape. The video was for "Through The Wire" and the mixtape was called *Get Well Soon*, because of the accident.

It was like, "How do we utilize this time and not let it go to waste?" We didn't think this mixtape was going to get him there, but we needed something to do and move the ball forward. Those two things really gave Kanye the credibility he needed as an artist. It worked like a charm breaking him in that market. It started to show up on the shelves of these regular places that sell mixtapes and the taste started to expand. Because at that time in the early 2000s, it was mostly street.

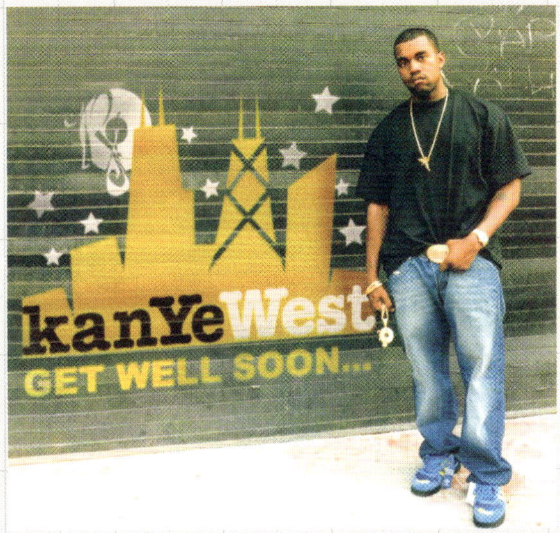

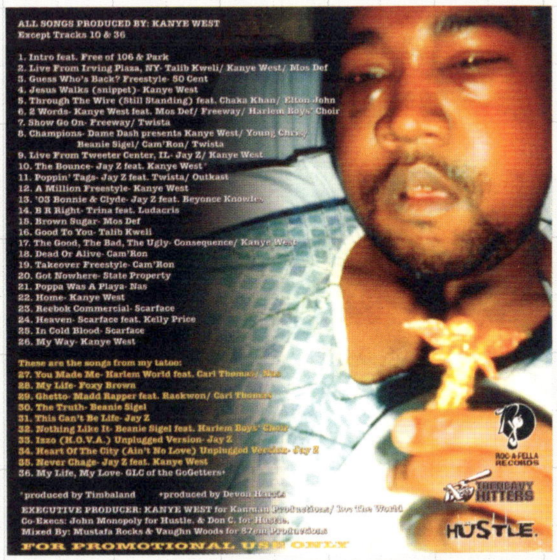

DJ KAY SLAY REMEMBERS THE DIPLOMAT MIXTAPE SERIES

DJ Kay Slay teamed up with his Harlem brethren The Diplomats for an unforgettable mixtape series jam-packed with exclusive songs and freestyles, helping to establish them as one of the most popular new rap crews in New York City.

Kay Slay: At that point, I was on fire on the streets, winning mixtape awards and so on and so forth. Cam'ron came to me and said he wanted to start a movement called Dipset—Harlem Diplomats. And he wanted me to be a part of it, and be the one to push the records and help filter the buzz on the streets. He said he was going to grab Juelz Santana, who was a part of a group called Draft Pick. And Jim Jones wasn't even rapping yet. He started rhyming once we put the movement together and everything. So, he came to me with this idea, and I agreed.

We just started bombing the streets with heat, on the radio killing them with the new records and everything. And then once he said he was ready to do the mixtape, all the songs were done. We went and put the mixtape together and man, some of the records that he had were so crazy. A lot of people don't even know that "Oh Boy" was just a short one-minute freestyle at first, it wasn't even a whole record. I remember hearing it and telling Cam that him and Juelz had to finish that. I told him it was outta here. I remember them finishing it and from there, we just had a nice movement going on. I helped them push the music and build the brand. It was a smart move, and I'm from Harlem as well so he came to me.

Cam'ron had the ideas, he had the records already. But what he would do, though, is ask me what I thought about the records. I can't take credit for anything else. He pretty much knew what he wanted, but he would play a snippet, a verse or hook, to see what the buzz was like.

At that point, I was at about three or four a month, so I'm doing my own shit at the same time. I'm giving them beats. There were plenty of beats that were on my tapes and everything that I gave to them that they spit on. Jim Jones, the first joint he rhymed on was a freestyle called "Motherless Child" with Juelz. So I was doing my thing at the same time they were.

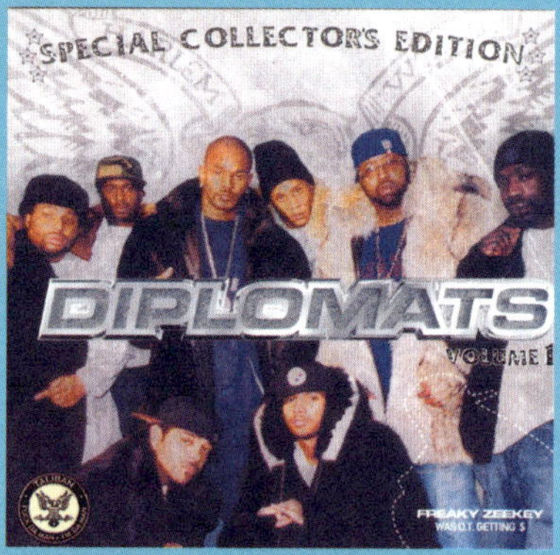

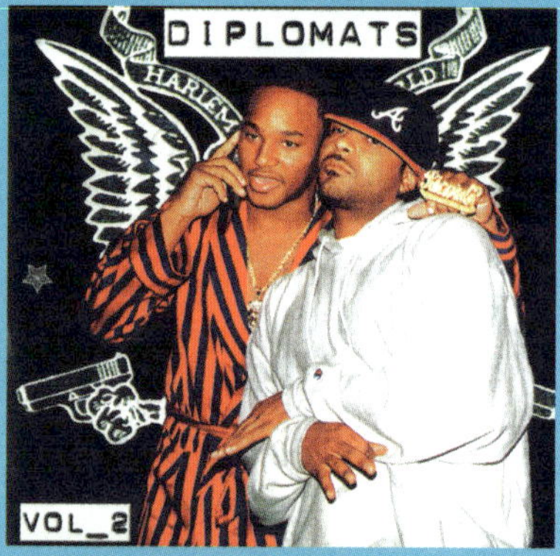

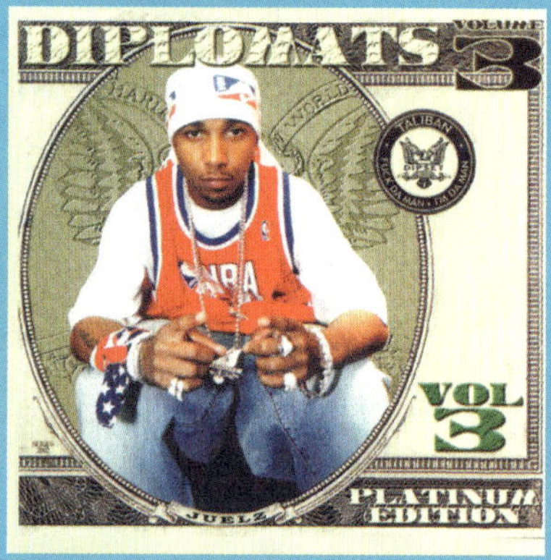

As more artists started having mixtape DJs host their tapes, the trend of artists hosting DJ's mixtapes grew more and more as well. And DJ Kay Slay was getting everyone in the game to sit-in as a guest host to provide commentary and drops throughout the tape, plus come through with exclusive freestyles and tracks. These were a few of his favorites, as remembered by the legend himself, Kay Slay:

1. EMINEM - That was big. He was really shining and doing his thing. Paul and them hit me up and told me he wanted to host my mixtape. He freestyled and let me put that on my first album.

2. 50 CENT - When he got out of the hospital, he got back on the road with a mixtape he hosted for me. The crazy exclusive on there was my own joint, "Problem Child." That was on my first album. That was the first joint he put out before "Wanksta" and all that, right after he had that situation where he got shot. He took the old LL beat "I Shot Ya" and did that joint.

3. CEELO GREEN - That did real good for me in the south. I caught a lot of love from Atlanta because he was also starting to do his thing, too.

4. SHYNE - That was a quadruple or triple *Original Gangsters*. It was right when Shyne was about to start trial for his mishap in the club.

5. N.O.R.E. - The joint N.O.R.E. hosted where I put "Ether" on it--Lord have mercy. That one there. Once they came to my crib with "Ether," I was forced to throw another tape out.

6. GHOSTFACE KILLAH - That's the God right there. He and I always gelled. He always had good energy, and that was somebody that I actually reached out to. There wasn't no real rocket science with that.

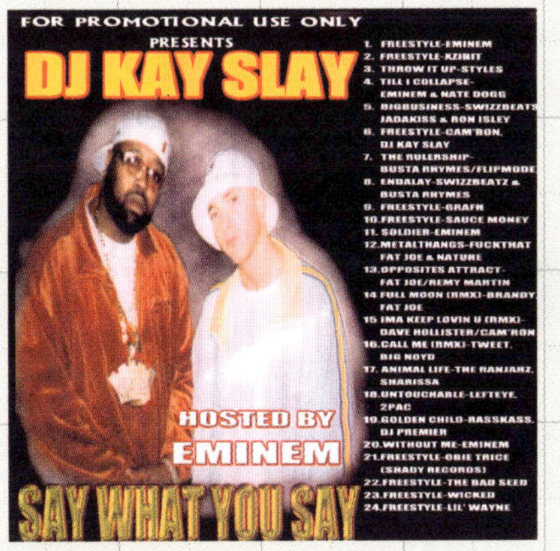

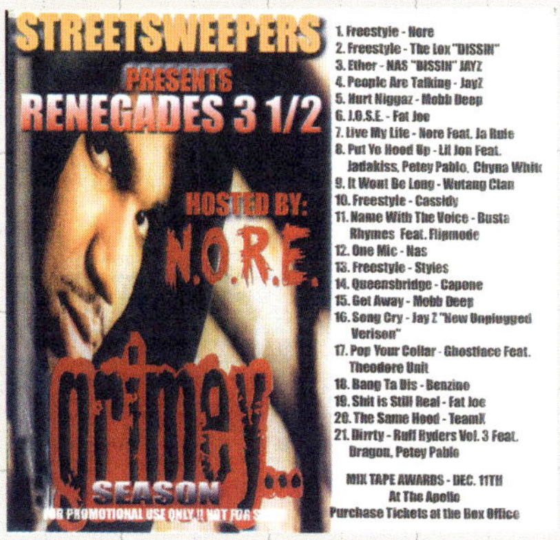

SHA MONEY XL

The Unit: 50 Cent and His Crew Release Their Own CD Mixtapes

50 Cent took hip hop by storm in the early 2000s, and much of that can be credited to his G-Unit mixtapes. There's no denying that the G-Unit mixtape series is among the most celebrated street releases of all-time, and Sha Money XL—who had been producing for fellow Queens artists like Cormega, Tragedy Khadafi, and Royal Flush—played a huge role in the success of those tapes, from the recording and production to the concepting and cover art.

MAKING CONNECTIONS

Sha Money XL: I was banging out beats, and interning at Def Jam. I was also on the street team for Nas' *It Was Written*, handing out the *It Was Written* books. Steve Stoute was from my neighborhood, so he let me be on the street team. Then, I got my first placement on a song by Cormega called "Angel Dust." Havoc was on the record with Prodigy in the studio. They got to know who I was, and I was on.

From interning at Def Jam, Jam Master Jay got me in his studio in Queens, and he's playing music. Onyx, Sweet Tee, Lost Boyz, and then he played 50. He saw me go crazy and he said, "You like that?" And I said, "Yo, this kid is dope, I wanna work with him." He wasn't yelling, he was just rapping like some different shit. This is the era where Nas had that smooth voice. He wasn't coming at you, so I was really into him. He saw my face, he went and got him, and that's how I met 50. Right through Jam Master Jay. From that moment, it changed the course for all of us.

POWER OF THE DOLLAR/GUESS WHO'S BACK?

I did the title track for *Power of the Dollar*. A small version with like five records came out, but it wasn't a whole album. *Power of the Dollar* was what the album was supposed to be with Trackmasters. He got shot, and at that moment, they didn't want to deal with him anymore.

He got dropped, and I knew all the records. I'm sitting here telling them, "What we need to do is take the best records off of the album that didn't come out, and put it out. I knew this dude Bob Perry because I had my indie label, so I would press vinyl and Bob would sell it. So I took the best records from *Power of the Dollar*, the new records that he was coming to my house to do, "50 Bars of Pleasure," "Follow Me Gangster," and those type of joints, and then put it on the *Guess Who's Back?* mixtape. That was his first thing. Then *50 Cent is the Future* came a month after that.

50 CENT IS THE FUTURE

A lot of the records–"50 Bars," "Many Men," "High All the Time," even on the album, *Get Rich or Die Tryin'*, I recorded those vocals on ADATs. I only had one ADAT, my boy Kyle had the other, so I used to have to borrow ADATs and do all this back and forth shit. That was wack.

So when I went to Guitar Center, they were like, "Yo, there's this new thing, Pro Tools." You could buy it for like $1,000. I just made a deal, I had bought my first crib, I was 24 years old. I made like $50,000, so I was feeling like I had money at the time. So I was like, "Yo, you serious?" So I bought it, but he was like, "You need a computer too." And I was like, "Fuck!" I didn't know. I was a self-taught engineer. Dude was literally on the phone with me teaching me how to record.

The way Pro Tools worked and what I was realizing was, you could take different pieces, you just had to blend it right and make it sound good. The song comes on, "You should be here," then Raphael Saadiq's part comes on–I had to do all of that. From instrumentals, no instrumental, him rapping over

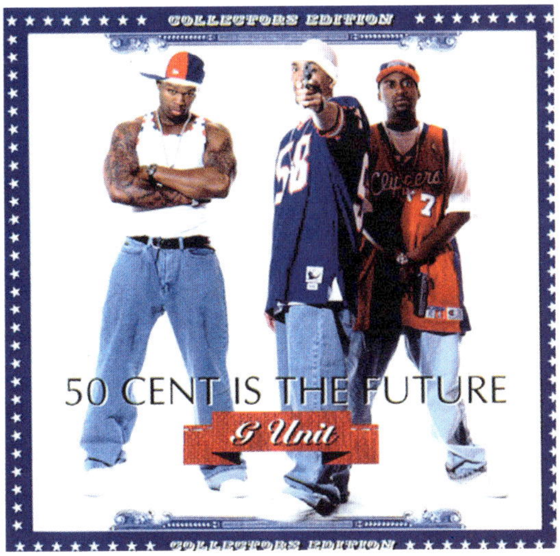
COLLECTORS EDITION
50 CENT IS THE FUTURE
G Unit
COLLECTORS EDITION

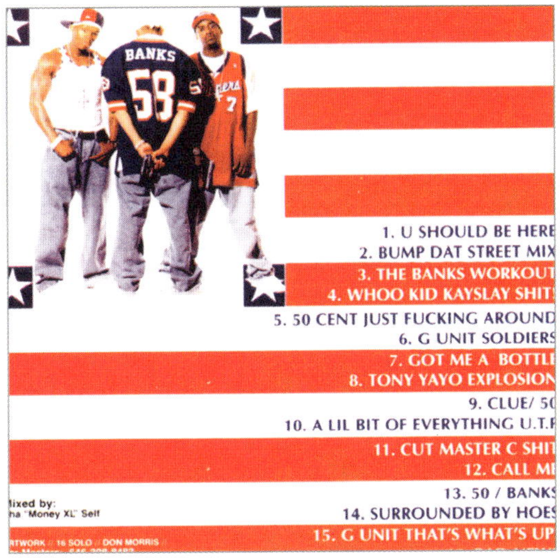
BANKS
1. U SHOULD BE HERE
2. BUMP DAT STREET MIX
3. THE BANKS WORKOUT
4. WHOO KID KAYSLAY SHIT!
5. 50 CENT JUST FUCKING AROUND
6. G UNIT SOLDIERS
7. GOT ME A BOTTLE
8. TONY YAYO EXPLOSION
9. CLUE/ 50
10. A LIL BIT OF EVERYTHING U.T.P
11. CUT MASTER C SHIT
12. CALL ME
13. 50 / BANKS
14. SURROUNDED BY HOES
15. G UNIT THAT'S WHAT'S UP
Mixed by:
Sha "Money XL" Self

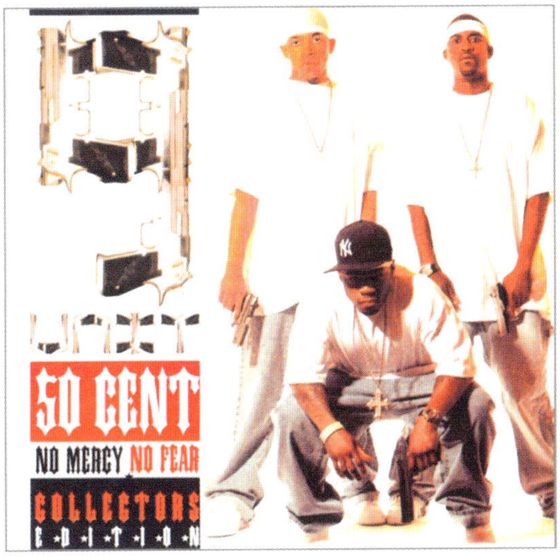
50 CENT
NO MERCY NO FEAR
COLLECTORS
E·D·I·T·I·O·N

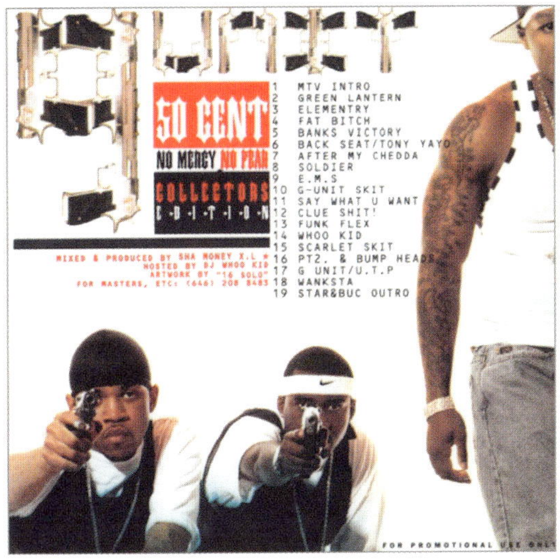
50 CENT
NO MERCY NO FEAR
COLLECTORS
E·D·I·T·I·O·N
1 MTV INTRO
2 GREEN LANTERN
3 ELEMENTRY
4 FAT BITCH
5 BANKS VICTORY
6 BACK SEAT/TONY YAYO
7 AFTER MY CHEDDA
8 SOLDIER
9 E.M.S
10 G-UNIT SKIT
11 SAY WHAT U WANT
12 CLUE SHIT!
13 FUNK FLEX
14 WHOO KID
15 SCARLET SKIT
16 PT2. & BUMP HEADS
17 G UNIT/U.T.P
18 WANKSTA
19 STAR&BUC OUTRO
MIXED & PRODUCED BY SHA MONEY X.L.
HOSTED BY DJ WHOO KID
ARTWORK BY "16 SOLO"
FOR MASTERS, ETC: (646) 208 8483
FOR PROMOTIONAL USE ONLY

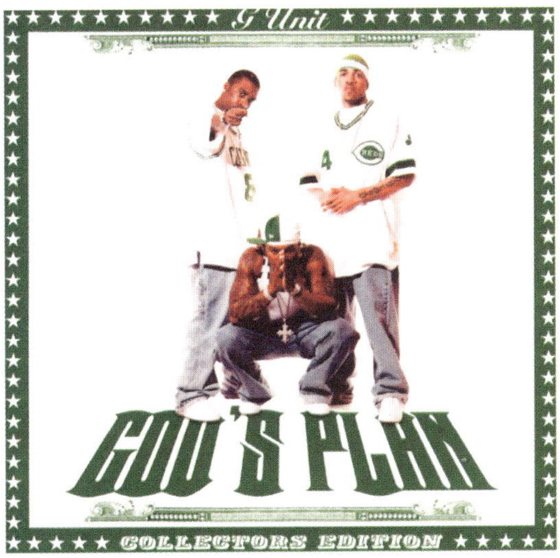
G Unit
GOD'S PLAN
COLLECTORS EDITION

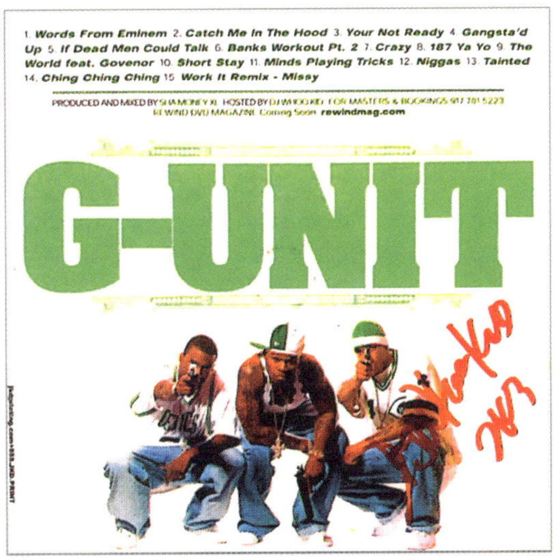
1. Words From Eminem 2. Catch Me In The Hood 3. Your Not Ready 4. Gangsta'd Up 5. If Dead Men Could Talk 6. Banks Workout Pt. 2 7. Crazy 8. 187 Ya Yo 9. The World feat. Govenor 10. Short Stay 11. Minds Playing Tricks 12. Niggas 13. Tainted 14. Ching Ching Ching 15 Work It Remix - Missy
rewindmag.com
G-UNIT

the fucking vocals. If you listen to it, the vocals are still in there.

We started doing a bunch of freestyles. He's doing a freestyle for Kay Slay, freestyle for Enuff, one for Clue, one for Flex and Whoo Kid. Banks is doing his shit, Yayo. "Bad News," we did that for my boy who put out this anti-backpack mixtape. I was like, "Yo, we should take all of these songs and freestyles and put them together and put them on one thing, and put it in the streets." And he was with it.

SHA MONEY XL'S TOP 5 G-UNIT FREESTYLES

1. "BANKS VICTORY" (No Mercy, No Fear)
2. "SOLDIER" (No Mercy, No Fear)
3. "BANKS WORKOUT PT. 2" (God's Plan)
4. "U SHOULD BE HERE" (50 Cent is the Future)
5. "CUTMASTER C SHIT" (50 Cent is the Future)

The freestyles were out, but you only heard it if you were following that DJ. Mix show wasn't there yet, so nobody was going to the radio to hear it. If you listened to the Cutmaster C mixtape, that's the only time you heard that. I was like, "They all need to hear this shit. Yo, I'm telling you man, that Cutmaster C shit–classic." Eminem loved that shit. This is the shit that got us signed.

RECORDING

50 would be at my house every day, and this dude worked. He'd come to my house at 10, 11 a.m. and work until about 10 p.m.. The dude was laying a few records every day. He's like, "Give me this, give me that instrumental." That's why all these Sickamore and J. Armz instrumental mixtapes mattered. We would grab those, get the instrumental, do the songs, and mix it with the original songs. That became the street album. That shifted the game. That was the last moment where the DJ mattered. It was about who the artist was.

COVER ART

The photoshoot was with my boy Don Morris, he used to be an *XXL*, *Source* photographer. I called him and he was like, "Come to my studio," and we did it. Then I did the artwork. I was like, "Yo Fif, what's going to be the artwork?" And he was like, "Write G-Unit in script." That's it. He brought his homies, Tony Yayo and Banks, and we made some classics. Shit is fucking classic.

NO MERCY, NO FEAR

There's a few new songs where he's introducing you to new talent–"Banks Victory" is Biggie Smalls "Victory." "After My Chedda" is LL Cool J, "Bump Heads," that's Mobb Deep. You got Funk Flex, you got Whoo Kid. And then you have this new song called "Wanksta." That ends up being on the *8 Mile* soundtrack, but guess what? It's on a mixtape first and it explodes.

This was a two track mix–I played the bass on it. 50, I don't know where he got the beat from, but he came with that beat and then I was like, "It sounds hollow, it needs a little bass on it." So that was my first time doing a co-production on something.

This mixtape went out, and I've never seen a response like, "This is the single." I didn't even think "Wanksta" was the single. Mix shows had a lot to do with that. Because I know DJ Enuff and everyone that had a radio hour where they could play whatever they wanted, they played "Wanksta." That shit was going crazy in New York.

GOD'S PLAN

We dropped almost three mixtapes that year. *God's Plan* and probably one more. He wasn't playing because he wanted to drop them before the album. Dre was like, "You aren't going to drop them when the album comes out." I even think he dropped a mixtape like two months after the album came out, and they were pissed about that.

We were still recording everything in my crib. It was my first crib I bought when I was 24 in Westbury, a suburb like 15 to 20 minutes out of Queens. I had a basement studio. We were just smoking, chilling, working every day. I want to go buy that crib back, that shit is like a museum now to me.

DJ WHOO KID REMEMBERS *50 CENT IS THE FUTURE*

After making his own noise across the five boroughs, DJ Whoo Kid would eventually link up with fellow Queens natives 50 Cent and G-Unit to release one of the most influential mixtape series of all-time.

DJ Whoo Kid: I left the exclusives game, because it's hard to have ten rappers with a new song and every one of them be hot. So I switched it to one-artist tapes. 50 Cent was the first one who woke me up with that.

I knew 50 musically, and he knew I was playing his music, but I didn't know him personally. I used to see him on my block, on 111th. 50 got shot the fuck up, and he didn't trust nobody. So 50 told Sha Money XL, who's my blood cousin, "Why don't you get your cousin to host the mixtape?"

The first time I got to meet Fif, Banks looked like he was gonna rob me. Yayo didn't want to talk to me. They were street thugs, and they didn't trust nobody. They just tried to kill their boss, so they were on some not-trusting shit. There were guns everywhere, and vests. I was like, "What am I getting involved in?"

I didn't even take the music with me. I just did the drops and everything right there in Sha Money's basement, and I left. Then Sha Money was like, "I'm gonna put it together, and you put it out there." And Fif was like, "After this shit comes out, we're out. We're gonna go on tour. So whoever you're with, fuck 'em."

We did 300 shows off the strength of *50 Cent Is the Future.* People knew the raps from beginning to end. I couldn't believe it. Freestyles. And it was like I just got thrown in the car while they were robbing the bank. I was a passenger, and they were like, "Motherfucker, play the songs." They did freestyles for me, but I didn't have any creative input until maybe like the third one.

ROB MARKMAN REMEMBERS HEARING *50 CENT IS THE FUTURE* FOR THE FIRST TIME

Rob Markman is a seasoned hip-hop journalist who grew up during the golden era of mixtapes in New York City. With experience writing and creating content for outlets like XXL, MTV, and Genius, Rob's voice has become one the most credible and respected in the industry—and mixtapes like the G-Unit series played a huge role in his hip-hop upbringing.

Rob Markman: I remember when my boy Timm Hotep brought me a copy of *50 Cent is the Future*—you could just feel the shift that was about to take place. Growing up in New York, mixtapes were always prevalent, they just continued to evolve over time.

When I was a kid, blend tapes were big, or just dope mixes. The first tape I ever bought was an S&S tape. Then DJ Clue really made exclusives and freestyles important. He wasn't the first, but he represented a shift. Then when 50 started his mixtape run, it was another shift. From the first track, "U Should Be Here," you could just feel the energy, how him and Banks took the Raphael Saadiq song and just rapped and sang over it. Yayo doing the drops. Just sitting in the car listening to that tape for the first time, it was a moment for sure.

Mixtapes overall were just inspirational. It was motivation, and it proved that hip-hop culture can exist outside of these labels and major companies. Hip hop started in the streets, and the music spread across New York City—and the world—with mixtapes.

***The Champ Is Here* mixtape was a chance for Jadakiss to flex his self-proclaimed "Top 5 Dead Or Alive" status with the help of DJ Green Lantern and Connecticut's exclusives kingpin Big Mike. It represented a new trend in artists releasing their own tapes to promote upcoming label drops, and featured unreleased songs from Jada's forthcoming sophomore album, new freestyles over current and classic beats, Green Lantern-concocted blends, and guest spots by his D-Block brothers Styles P, Sheek Louch, and Jae Hood—resulting in one of the greatest solo artist mixtape releases of all-time.**

Jadakiss: I had to do a mixtape for the second album, before it was about to come out. Green actually thought of the name. He sampled "The Champ is Here" from the *Ali* movie. That's Will Smith saying that.

Whenever you're in mixtape mode where you're rhyming on other people's beats, you can just say whatever you feel. That's the good thing about mixtapes. You ain't worried about radio, you ain't worried about who cares. I wish I could get in mixtape mode when I'm making albums, but it's hard due to the politics of it. But if you could, it would be beautiful, because you don't give a fuck.

All the beats you ever hear me use when they're somebody else's, they're beats that I really liked when I first heard it, or those are songs I liked as a fan that I probably played with their words on it.

Green Lantern: That's definitely one of the Holy Grails, a top five in my catalog. That was slated to just be him and Big Mike. Mike was competing with Kay Slay for that "new shit" lane, and Jada was rocking with him.

Jada said to me, "Yo, you take mad time with your shit. Your shit is stupid." So I was like, "Let's do something." And he was like, "Well, I got this tape coming out with Big Mike. You wanna hop on it?" And I was already cool with Mike, so we just ended up doing it together.

He already had the ideas of some specific instrumentals he wanted to rap over, some old shit. So I took those, and I took acapellas, started scratching shit in, and did my little frosting-on-top-of-the-cake. It would've been a great ass tape even without me, but it probably would've just been in and out. Song starts, song stops, and that's the tape.

I'll never forget this shit. We were in the studio, and Big Mike was in there, and he was like, "Yo Green. I have never taken this long in my life to do a fucking tape, you are killing me right now." I was like, "Welcome to my world, bro!"

But it's worth it. This is how I made my career. The details. When you listen back to it, that gives it the replay value. That's what I built my whole career off of. I'm gonna go above and beyond to give the listener an experience.

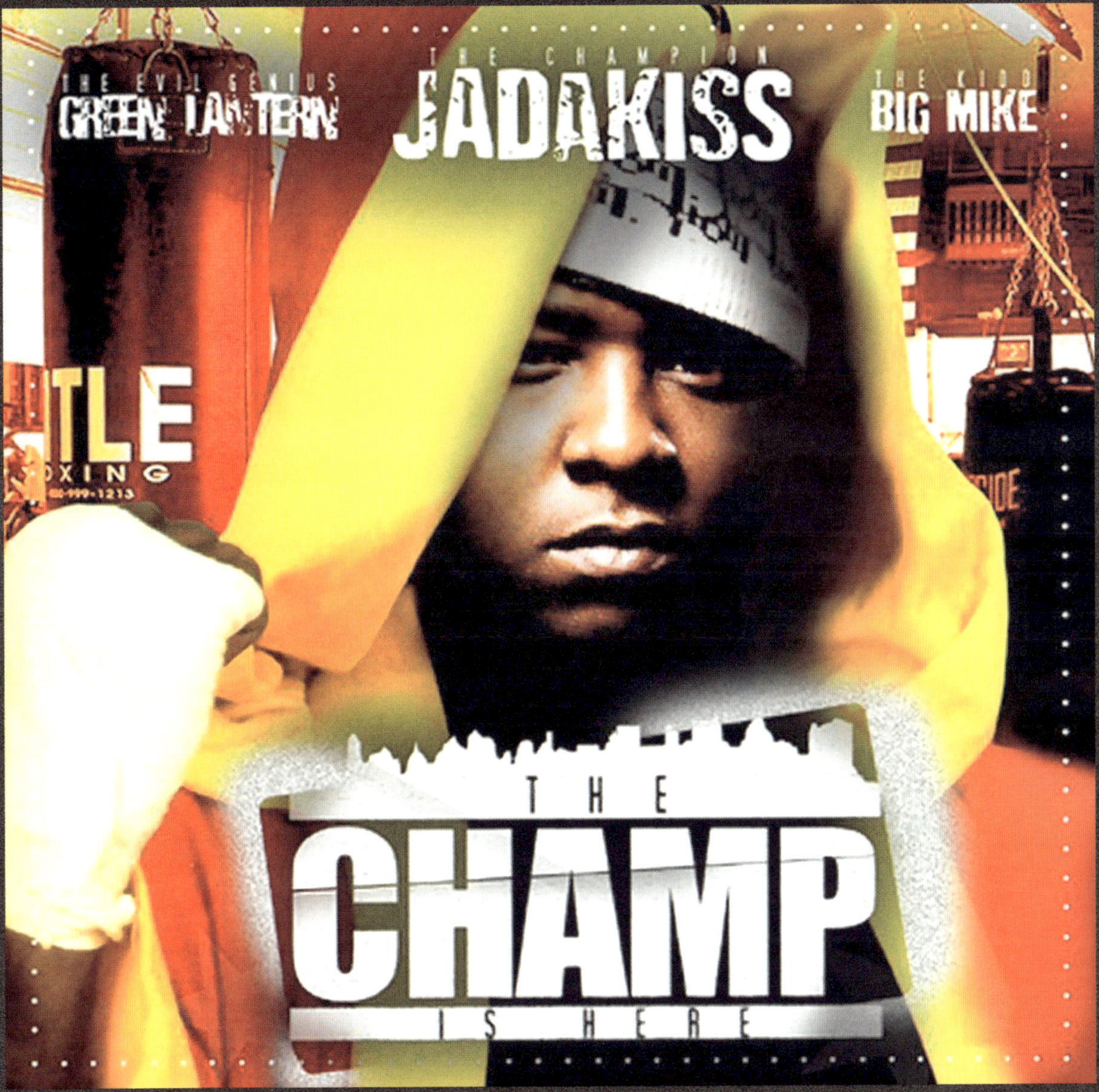
THE EVIL GENIUS
GREEN LANTERN
THE CHAMPION
JADAKISS
THE KIDD
BIG MIKE
THE
CHAMP
IS HERE

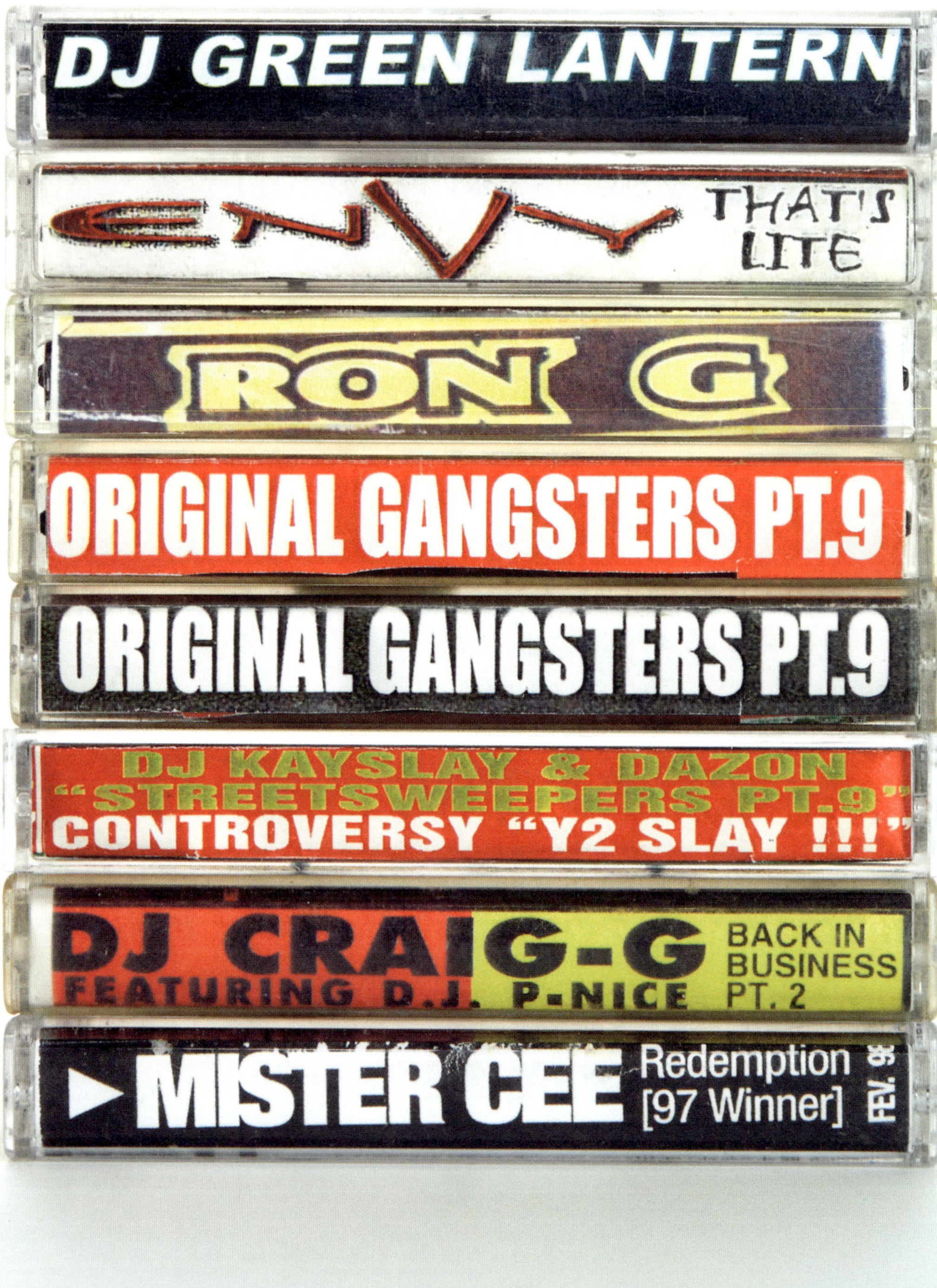
DJ GREEN LANTERN
ENVY
THAT'S LITE
RON G
ORIGINAL GANGSTERS PT.9
ORIGINAL GANGSTERS PT.9
DJ KAYSLAY & DAZON
"STREETSWEEPERS PT.9"
CONTROVERSY "Y2 SLAY !!!"
DJ CRAIG-G
FEATURING D.J. P-NICE
BACK IN BUSINESS PT. 2
MISTER CEE
Redemption
[97 Winner]
FEV. 9

THE MIXTAPE AWARDS

As Mixtape DJs in New York City were helping to push hip-hop culture forward in the '90s, one record promoter in the music industry—Justo Faison—decided to create an annual Mixtape Awards as a way to celebrate the achievements, success, and contributions of mixtape DJs across the five boroughs and beyond. In 1995, the first Mixtape Awards was held, where Justo handed out awards in multiple categories to the best mixtape DJs in the city.

Sadly, Justo was killed in a car accident in 2005 in Richmond, Virginia. But his legacy lives on through the memories of his friends and peers, who fondly remember everything he did for mixtape DJs throughout his career, and the pride he instilled in all of them with THE MIXTAPE AWARDS.

REMEMBERING JUSTO'S MIXTAPE AWARDS

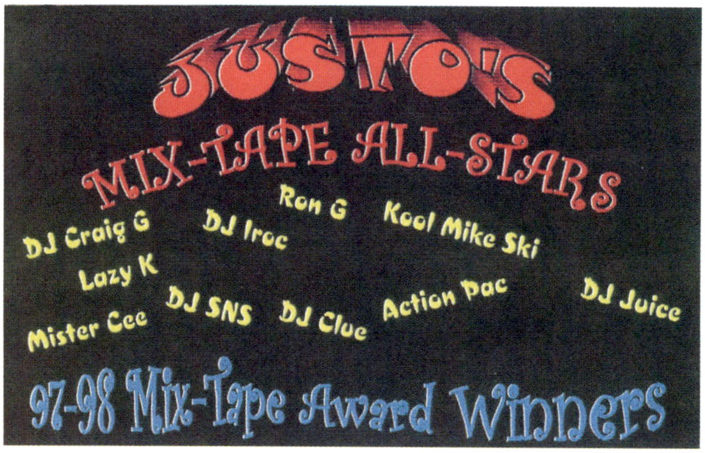

WHO WAS JUSTO?

Green Lantern: His real name was Orpheus and that's how he got the nickname Justo, because people would try to pronounce the name and he'd be like, "It's just O, okay! It's just O."

Bobbito: That was my man, fuck industry shit. He used to do a radio show from Cayuga Community College, and I was at Def Jam from '89 to '93. I forgot what year he graduated, but I would send him records.

Justo was from New York and into hip hop, so we hit it off. And he played ball, so then it was like, "We got too much in common." He was just a beautiful dude. So we developed a rapport, even though Cayuga Community College wasn't on my Top 10 stations to service. And we started playing ball together when he came back to the city.

Green Lantern: Justo was such a great individual. He was the champion of the mixtapes DJs. Once the groundwork was laid and the shit got big, he was the one that said, "Y'all are moving the future."

He did promotions for Epic Records and other labels like that, so he was always in contact with street DJs, radio DJs, mixtape DJs. He was like, "You guys are relegated to the streets—we need a damn Mixtape Awards for these guys." And he did that shit. He organized it and put it together and had awards. Real fucking physical awards.

Bobbito: When he started the Mixtape Awards, I remember him calling me with the idea like, "Would you support this?" I was like, "That's brilliant bro."

PURPOSE AND PASSION

G-Bo: Justo was kind. He was somebody who was really at the forefront of recognizing these mixtape DJs. He wanted to do something special for us—he wanted to do an award show. He put himself at the center, which was kinda dope.

Nobody had thought to create relationships with all these mixtape DJs. He became a focal point, a liaison between all the DJs. And he wanted to recognize this culture that was unfolding. So he created this award thing, and it just took on a life of its own.

Green Lantern: Justo was the guy who validated us in an industry that wanted to shut us down. He turned them around and said, "No you dummies, they need an award because they're promoting your fucking artist—idiot." He put us on a pedestal and let us be able to say, "Nine-Time Mixtape Award Winner," "Official Justo Mixtape Award Winner." That means something.

Doo Wop: It made us feel like we were getting to the next level. We were already moving up slowly in our careers, but I thought, "Wow, they're actually going to present us with awards. It's going to be official. They're going to have one at the Apollo Theater." He did so much for the mixtape game in that sense. Just put us on a freaking pedestal like, "These guys deserve more than what they're getting right now."

Bobbito: We were all part of this ecosystem that was really trying to uphold and be a vanguard for hip hop, but at the same time raise the bar and the proper digestion of what was real. When Justo did the Mixtape Awards, he did exactly that.

G-Bo: It added a different dimension to the mixtape culture. Not only are we selling tapes at stores and people are enjoying them, but now there's an award show? This is crazy. So, it was a nice recognition of the culture and how it was expanding and growing. Justo was a great guy to foster the culture and push it forward.

Cipha Sounds: Mixtapes were evolving with Green Lantern and guys like Spinbad and Dirty Harry, where they started incorporating the 4-track mixes, blends and stuff. Not just turntables, but actually producing. Justo recognized all of that, and that it was something that needed to be celebrated.

Kay Slay: The fact that he did it on his own, money out his own pocket and even cared enough to do it. The DJ is the backbone of the culture. So for Justo to kick, punch, and scratch these different labels and sponsors to do this Awards every year—it was a blessing to have somebody like that man.

THE EVENT

Tytanic: One of the reputations of the Mixtape Awards was that it was unorganized. But that's the genuineness of what the Mixtape Awards was. It was hood. It was our awards show. If it was organized, it wouldn't have felt right.

Mixtapes are street albums, period. It had to be grungy. The artists used to come there and battle other artists. It was street, so how could you have it organized? Justo wasn't worried about that.

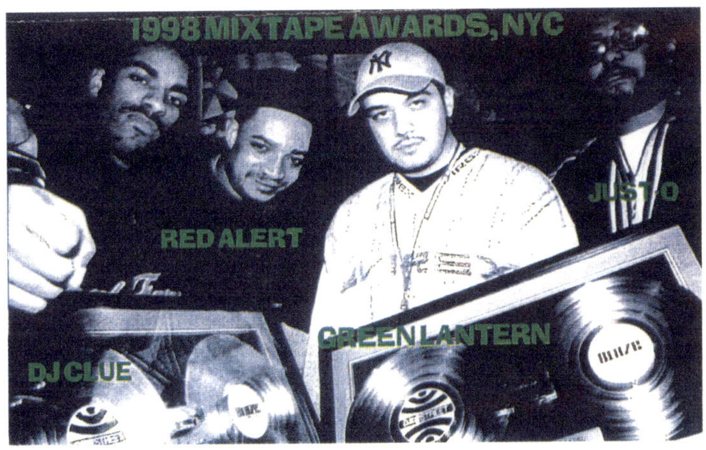

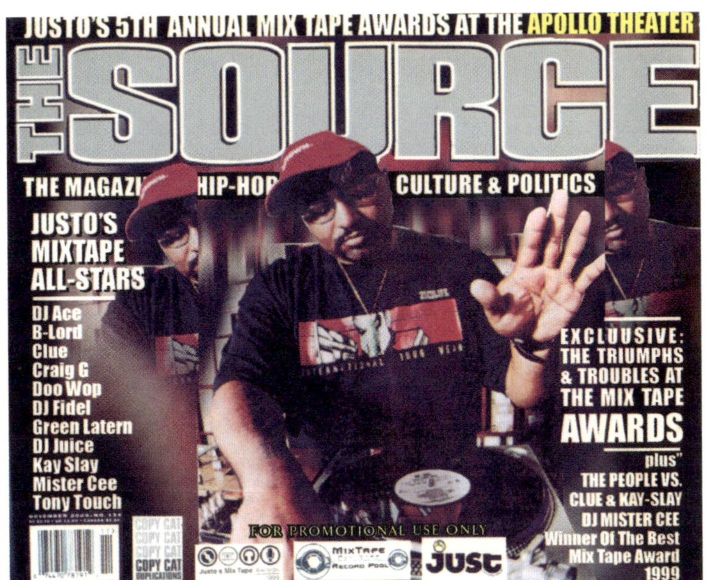

Green Lantern: It was just amazing to be in that spot with everybody.

Mister Cee: It was raw. It was real. It was unorganized, but I think that's what made it great. Everybody was just being honest with how they felt.

Kay Slay: I feel like that was like the DJ Grammys, right?

Green Lantern: That was the Oscars and the Grammys and the BET Awards and All-Star rolled up into one. Sometimes it was a little dicey, sometimes it was a little dangerous, but that's what the mixtape game was! You had to be outside.

S&S: It was dope for the cause, but a lot of DJs made it chaotic. The fact is that some DJs put themselves in the grave. Why would you start trouble with Kay Slay knowing he's going to be there? You know he's going to come smack the shit out of you, but you keep causing problems with Kay Slay on tapes. And then he sees you in person—you think he's the type of person that's not going to say anything? I used to laugh at it—"These guys are crazy."

Kay Slay: I got the top award, and an incident happened and I got pissed off and shut the whole awards show down. Hammerstein Ballroom got nasty backstage.

Doo Wop: The Apollo was the dopest one to me. Everybody showed up to the Apollo. There were some that I couldn't even go to—I might have been booked. And some that I went to and I didn't see a lot of the big dogs there. I didn't see Ron G or something. But that one, everybody was there. It was like the red carpet.

Green Lantern: One year it was at Speed. And it was so uncomfortably packed in that bitch that I left. It was so crazy. As I'm leaving, I'm walking down the street to get to the car and I run into Whoo Kid who's walking to the spot. He's got 35, 40 dudes with him, because it's like that. I'm looking at him laughing, like, "Bro, y'all gonna be really uncomfortable down there, dog. There's no room for none of y'all done there!" That's how poppin' it was.

Doo Wop: I remember meeting DJ Envy for the first time at the Apollo. For some reason me and Queens DJs never got along. There's no backstory to that, I don't know what it was. I never really took a liking to them and I think the feeling was mutual. He was so humble and cool that it changed my whole perception about him, and about these Queens guys. I was like, "Ah man, what's going on here? Let me focus and stop thinking about the bullshit."

THE WINNERS

Tytanic: Justo had a committee of people. It wasn't that organized, but we all came to the table. It was emails, phone calls, and all of that. It was the relationships. Red Alert was on the committee. A lot of people, not just DJs, but execs at labels, people who were heads of promotion teams that he knew. He had to wean out the favoritism of some of the people that would bring up a DJ like, "That's my man." That was a conscious thing he had to go through.

G-Bo: We won an award, but Double R and I did not go. Speaking for myself, I was so paranoid that I was like, "This mixtape award shit—nah, they ain't getting me, yo." Because obviously we were very mindful of the fact that this was illegal activity and you could see how easily somebody would get caught under the auspices of, "This is an award show, come get your flowers." I wasn't falling for it, but it ended up being a legit award show.

Doo Wop: I got three I believe one year. I got the Most

Creative, and me and Tony Touch won an award for the Best Duo. It was huge. I left it at my mom's crib. It looks real nice in the living room, so it's over there.

The Most Creative meant the most to me because it was when I put all that work in for *95 Live*. Part One came out at the end of November or beginning of December in '95—I literally remember starting that shit in August. There was a lot of thought put into that tape, so winning that award really meant something.

Green Lantern: I think I got my first award the second year—I missed the first year. By the time that second year came around I had put out some joints and I got nominated, but I didn't think I was going to win. This was for Most Creative, I think it was '98 or something.

Cipha Sounds: I did a mixtape album for Rawkus called *Soundbombing III* and I got Best Commercial Mixtape—Mr. Choc and Cipha Sounds.

Kay Slay: The biggest one for me was 1999, the first time I won. I didn't know Justo, I just knew of him. I bumped into him somewhere on 125th, and he asked me to come to the Mixtape Awards. I went by myself that night.

So I'm in there talking, having a few drinks. And I hear them say, "Best Mixtape DJ of the Year, DJ Kay Slay." I went up on stage and he told me, "That's why I wanted you to come." I was so excited, I couldn't believe it. Clue was reigning supreme back then. So for me to win over him was just like, "Okay, I'm here now. This is real life. Shit is real."

Green Lantern: I was happy that I was nominated, and I was pleasantly surprised that I won. It was a battery in my back that just kept me pushing even longer. Like, "Wow, I really did that?!" It really turned the light on for a lot of people. They were like, "Oh word? We've heard of this dude, but he fucking won. There are a couple guys in that lane and we're saying their names all the time—and we gotta start saying this guy's name now too."

Mister Cee: I did Sunday nights at Speed from 2000 to 2006. If I remember correctly, I won Best Club DJ three years in a row. That was a proud moment for me, to be recognized as a club DJ back then when Justo was doing the Mixtape Awards. I got a plaque from Justo—and another time, I got a ring. I can find these awards very handy in my house. These things aren't tucked away, because they mean so much to me.

Tytanic: He gave out these rings. I was like, "Wow, you're just giving that away?" That's when I didn't know the actual price of the ring. I didn't find out until later that the people who made the Super Bowl ring also made the Justo ring. That was Justo's game—to understand all these gimmicks and create promotion.

REMEMBRANCE

Green Lantern: I just want to say thank you to Justo. Thank you for believing in the DJs. Thank you for elevating the DJs. May God be pleased with your soul. May He bless your family, your son—thank you, Just.

S&S: That's my brother, RIP Justo.

Bobbito: May he rest in peace.

One of the reputations of the Mixtape Awards was that it was unorganized. But that's the genuineness of what the Mixtape Awards was. It was hood. It was our awards show. If it was organized, it wouldn't have felt right. —TYTANIC

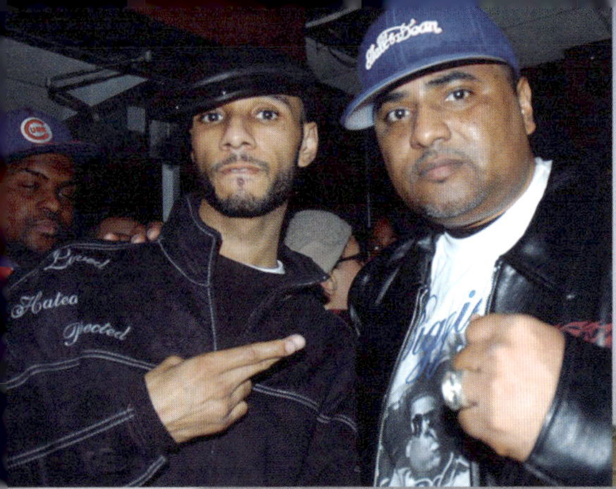

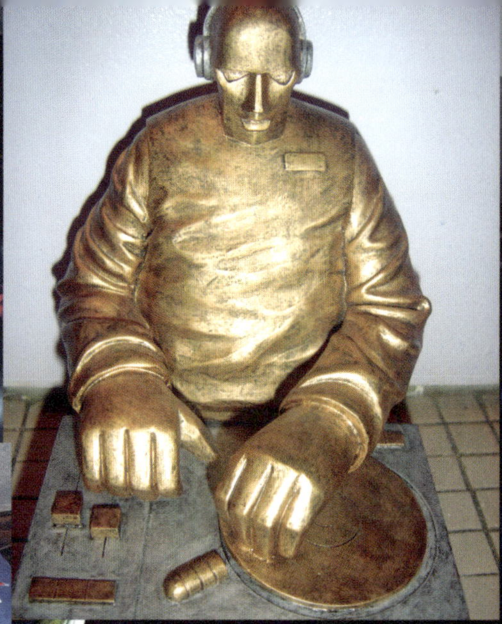

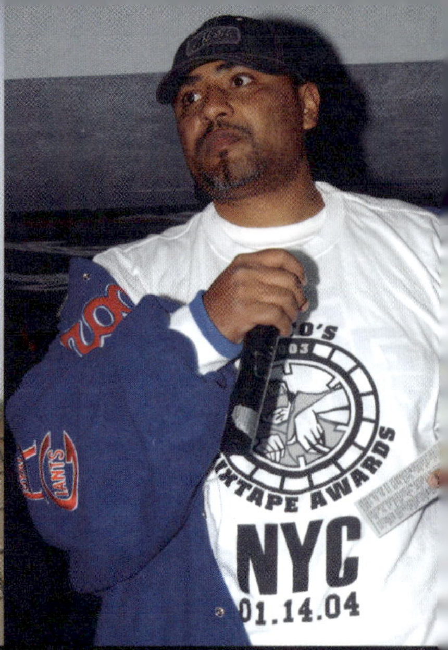
MIXTAPE AWARDS
NYC
01.14.04

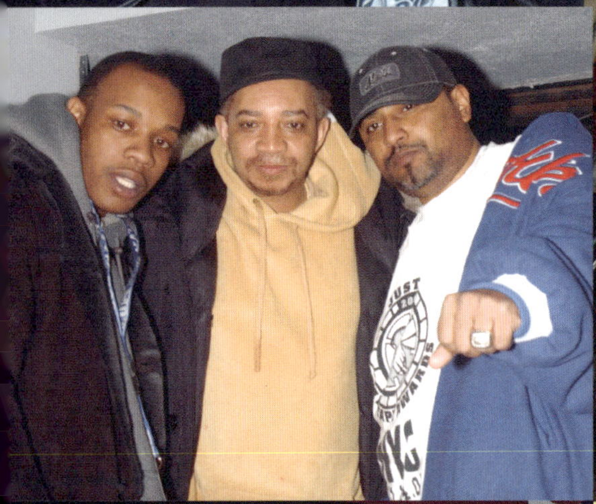

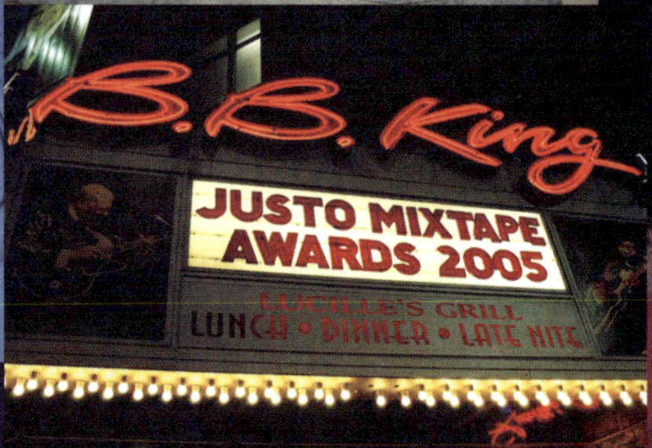
B.B. King
JUSTO MIXTAPE
AWARDS 2005
LUCILLE'S GRILL
LUNCH • DINNER • LATE NITE

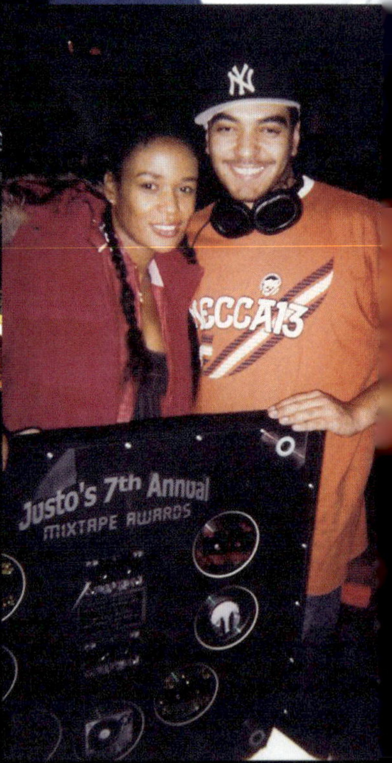
Justo's 7th Annual
MIXTAPE AWARDS

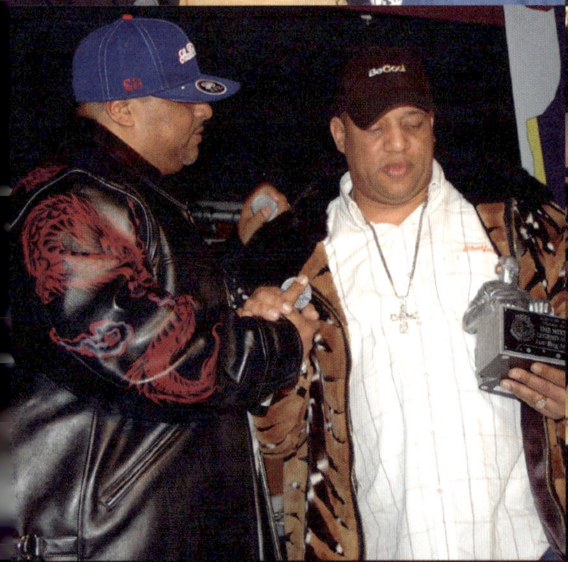

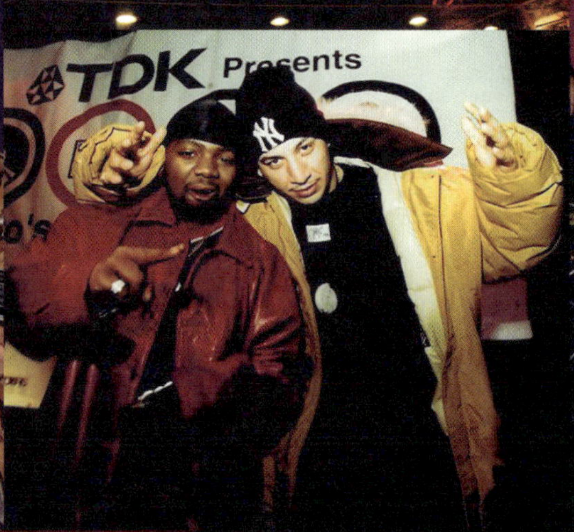
TDK Presents

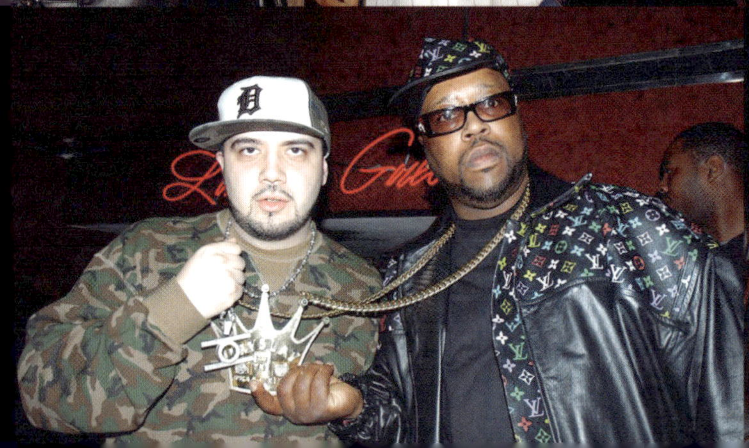

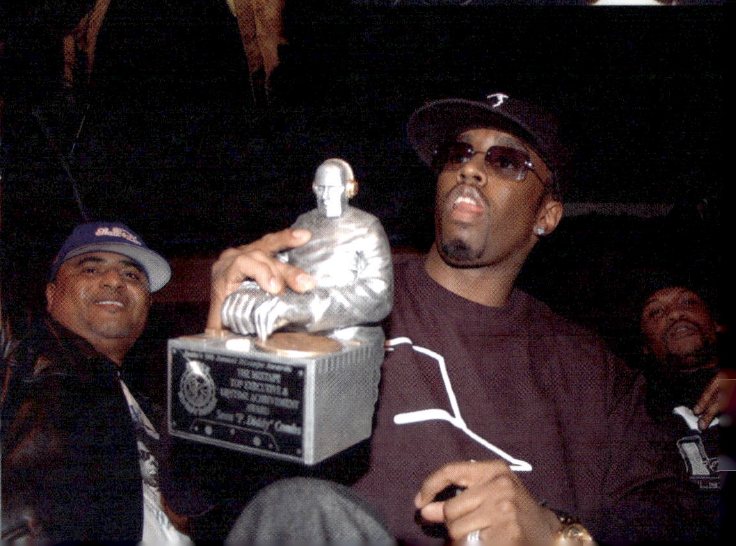

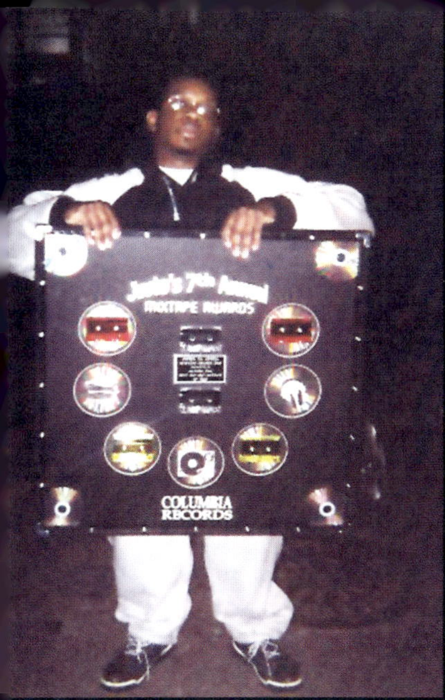
Justo's 7th Annual
MIXTAPE AWARDS
COLUMBIA RECORDS

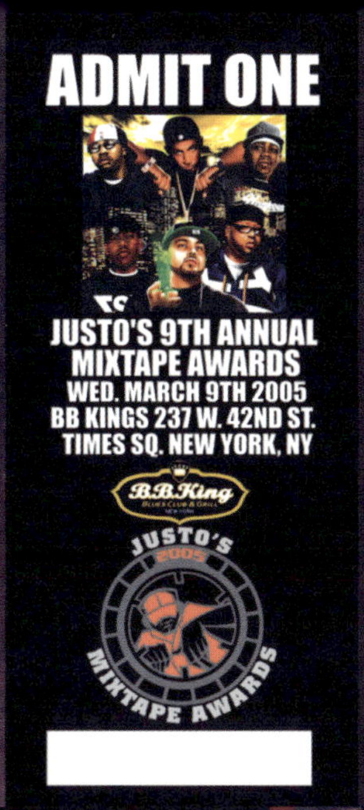
ADMIT ONE
JUSTO'S 9TH ANNUAL
MIXTAPE AWARDS
WED. MARCH 9TH 2005
BB KINGS 237 W. 42ND ST.
TIMES SQ. NEW YORK, NY
B.B.King
JUSTO'S
2005
MIXTAPE AWARDS

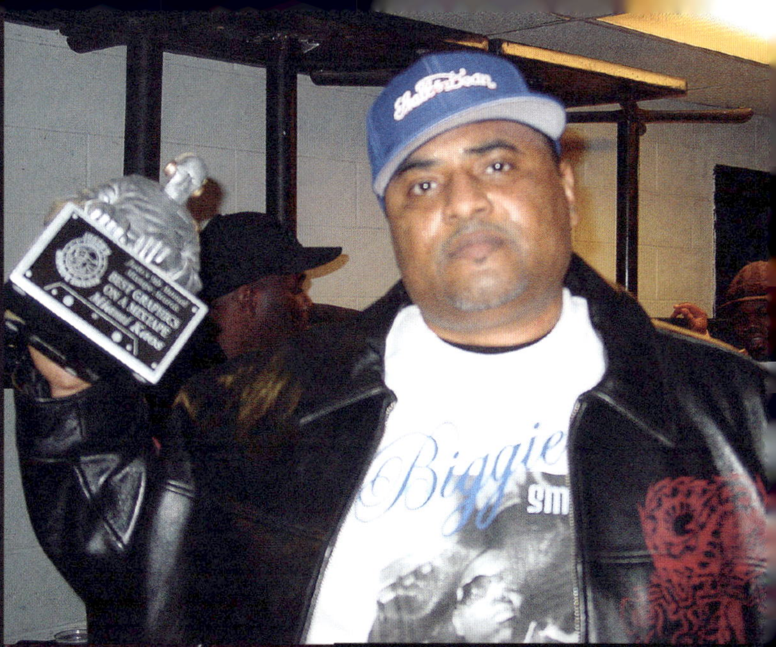

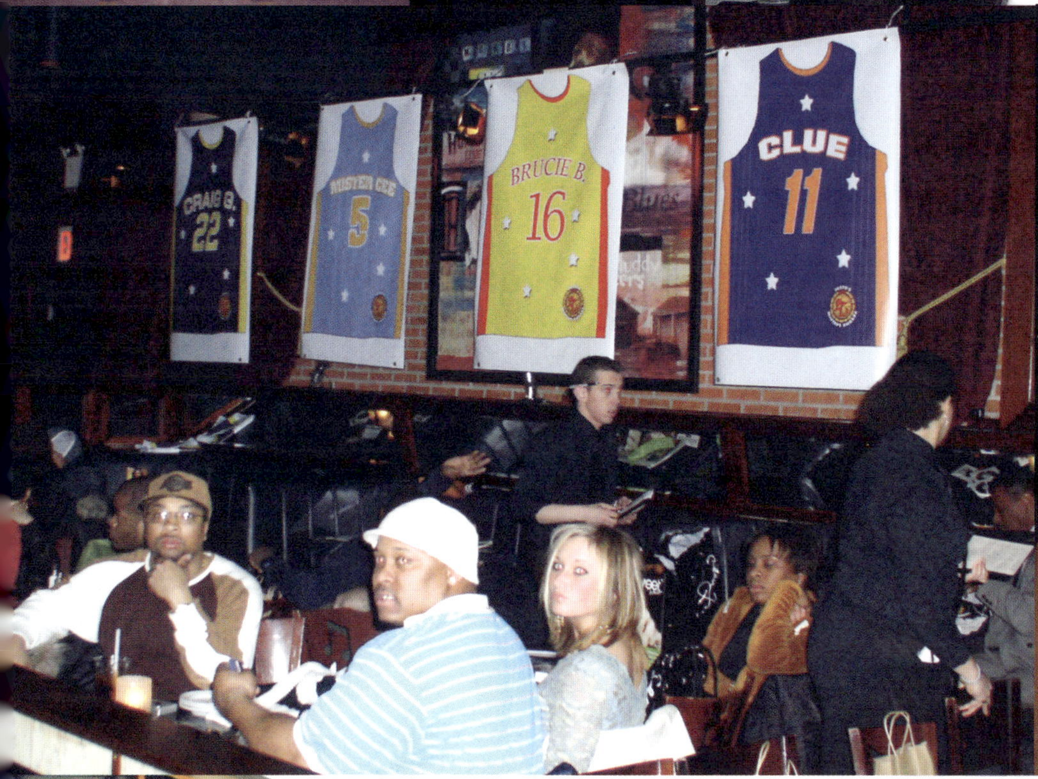
CRAIG G.
22
MISTER CEE
5
BRUCIE B.
16
CLUE
11

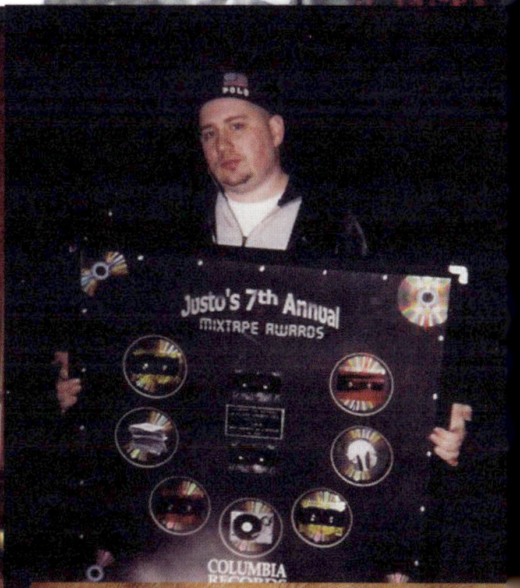
Justo's 7th Annual
MIXTAPE AWARDS
COLUMBIA RECORDS

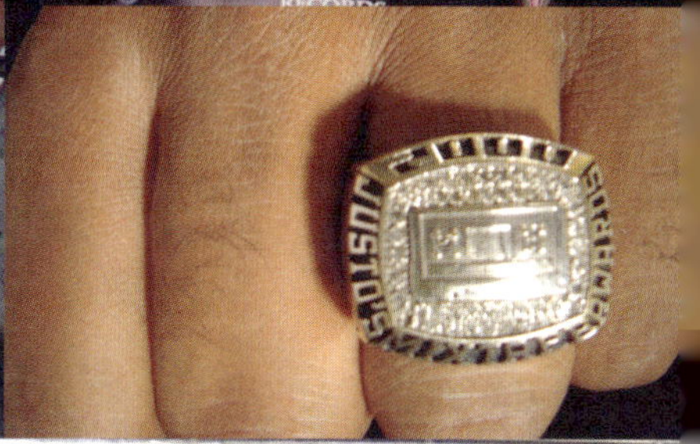

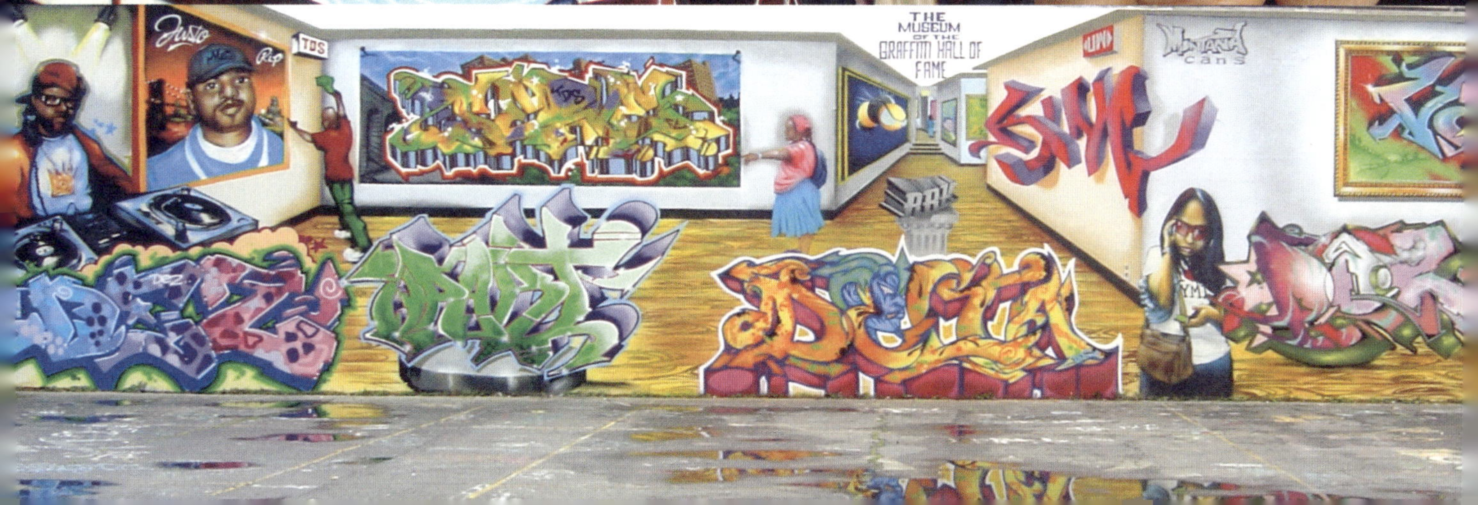
THE MUSEUM OF THE GRAFFITI HALL OF FAME

ACKNOWLEDGMENTS

Fat shout to all the DJs who inspired us to make this book, and the people who helped bring it to life.

The Creators: Absolut, Action Pac, Arson, A.Vee, Awesome Two, Big Mike, Biz Markie (RIP), Bobbito, Brucie B, Buckwild, Camillo, Capone, Cipha Sounds, Clark Kent, Chill Will FTE, Chubby Chub, Chuck Chillout, Clue, Craig G, Cutmaster C, Dazon, Demo, Dexterity, Dirty Harry, Doggtime, Doo Wop, Dream Team, Eclipse, E-Kim, E Bros, Enuff, Envy, Evil Dee, EZ Elpee, Fashion, Famous, Funkmaster Flex, G-Bo The Pro, Grandmaster Flash, Grandmaster Vic, Green Lantern, Hollywood, J. Armz, J-Love, Jazzy Joyce, Juice, Kay Slay (RIP), Kid Capri, Kool Kid, Kool Kirk, Kool Mike Ski, Kurupt, LA Luv, Lazy K, Lord Finese, LS One, Lovebug Starski (RIP), Marley Marl, Max Glazer, Mista Rello & Jadel, Mister Cee, Most Crew, P-Nice, Pete Rock, PF Cuttin, Premier, Rated R, Red Alert, Double R, Rhythm, Riz, Rob Swift, Roc Raida (RIP) Ron G, S&S, Selecta Bam Bam, Self, Showtime, Shazam X, Sickamore, Silva Sir-fa, Spinbad (RIP), Starchild (RIP), Stretch Armstrong, Technician, Ted Smooth, Three, Tony Touch, Triple C, and Whoo Kid

The Collaborators: Andy Cruz, Jason Sifre, Michael Krumtinger, Muktaru Jalloh, and Sam Hadelman

The Contributors: Anthony aka G (G Spot Clothing), Bahr Brown, Big Chew, Casey Westfall, DIMEZ, DJ ROZ, DJ SNS, DJ Step One, Eric Johnson, eskay (NahRight), Geno Sims, Genovese, Grime & Lime, Iain McNee, KamTV, Mixtape Classics, Pat Jones, Pete Nice, Phil Orama, Rock, Sommer McCoy (The Mixtape Museum), Splash, Tapemasta, Tim Burton, Tytanic, and Zvi Edelman

All interviews were edited for brevity and clarity.

All or portions of the interviews with Ron G, DJ S&S, DJ Craig G, DJ Ron G, DJ Doo Wop, DJ Tony Touch, DJ Green Lantern, DJ Whoo Kid, DJ Drama, and Cormega were originally conducted by Daniel Isenberg and published on NahRight.com.

Interviews with Fat Joe and Jadakiss were originally conducted by Daniel Isenberg and published on Complex.com.

First published in the United States of America in 2023 by
Rizzoli International Publications, Inc.
300 Park Avenue South
New York, NY 10010
www.rizzoliusa.com

Foreword: Fab 5 Freddy

Publisher: Charles Miers
Associate Publisher: Jessica Fuller
Associate Editor: Elise Johnson
Design: Diane Shaw
Production Manager: Colin Hough-Trapp
Proofreader: Sarah Stump

Printed in China

2023 2024 2025 2026 2027 /
10 9 8 7 6 5 4 3 2 1

ISBN: 978-0-8478-7224-4
Library of Congress Control Number: 2023936775

Visit us online:
Facebook.com/RizzoliNewYork
Twitter: @Rizzoli_Books
Instagram.com/RizzoliBooks
Youtube.com/user/RizzoliNY
Issuu.com/Rizzoli

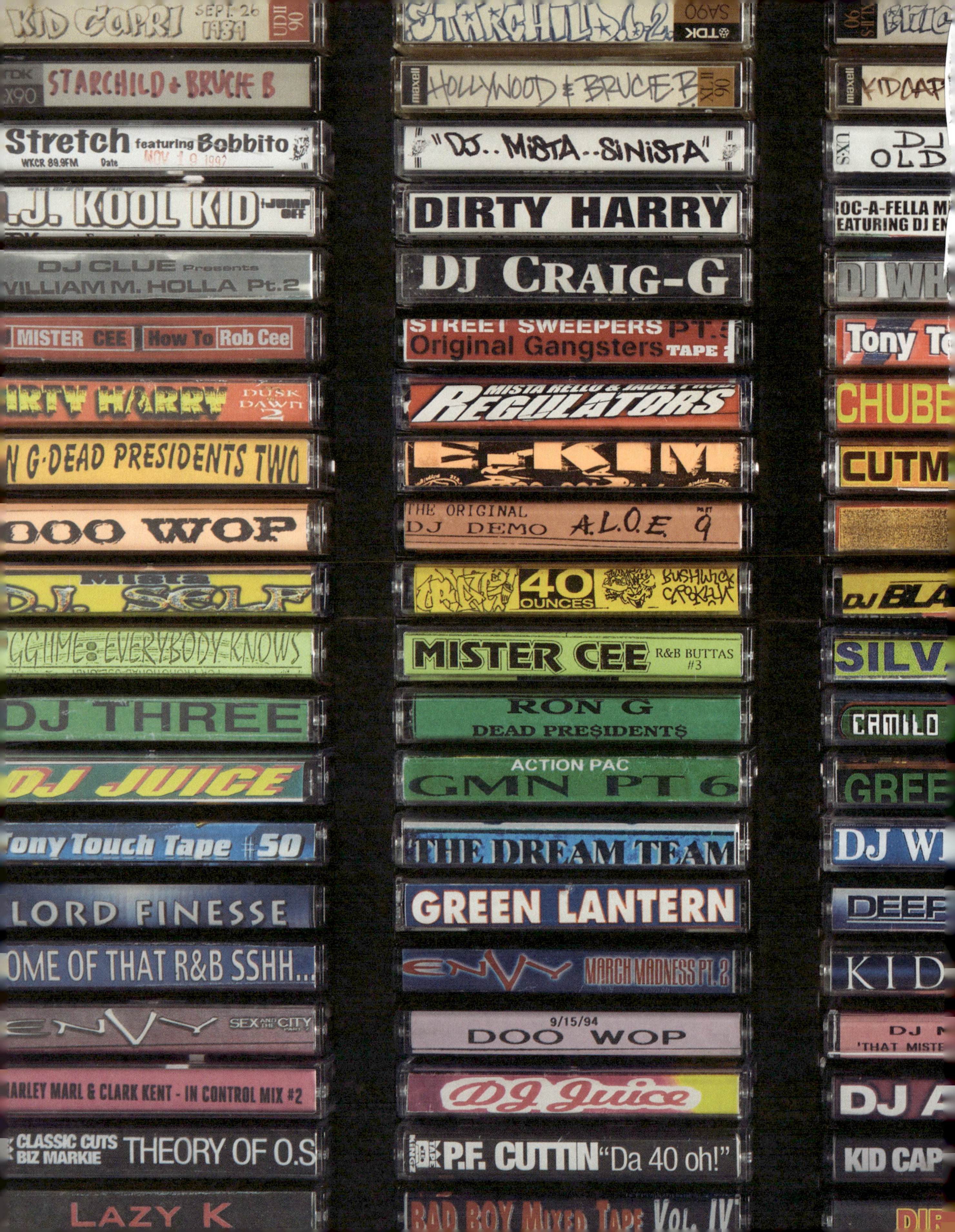
KID CAPRI
STARCHILD + BRUCE B
Stretch featuring Bobbito
WKCR 89.9FM
KOOL KID
DJ CLUE Presents
MISTER CEE
How To Rob Cee
DEAD PRESIDENTS TWO
DOO WOP
Mista
EVERYBODY KNOWS
DJ THREE
DJ JUICE
Touch Tape #50
LORD FINESSE
OF THAT R&B SSHH...
SEX AND THE CITY
CLARK KENT - IN CONTROL MIX #2
CLASSIC CUTS
BIZ MARKIE
THEORY OF O.S
LAZY K
TDK
maxell
HOLLYWOOD & BRUCIE B
"DJ.. MISTA.. SINISTA"
DIRTY HARRY
DJ CRAIG-G
STREET SWEEPERS
Original Gangsters
REGULATORS
THE ORIGINAL
DJ DEMO A.L.O.E. PART 9
40 OUNCES
MISTER CEE R&B BUTTAS #3
RON G
DEAD PRE$IDENT$
ACTION PAC
GMN PT 6
THE DREAM TEAM
GREEN LANTERN
ENVY MARCH MADNESS PT. 2
9/15/94
DOO WOP
DJ Juice
P.F. CUTTIN "Da 40 oh!"
BAD BOY MIXED TAPE VOL. IV
CAMILO
Tony
KID